The Forties
in America

The
Forties
in America

Volume II
Godfrey, Arthur—"Rosie the
Riveter"

Editor
Thomas Tandy Lewis
St. Cloud State University

SALEM PRESS
Pasadena, California
Hackensack, New Jersey

Editor in Chief: Dawn P. Dawson

Editorial Director: Christina J. Moose   *Research Supervisor:* Jeffry Jensen
Project and Development Editor: R. Kent Rasmussen   *Photo Editor:* Cynthia Breslin Beres
Manuscript Editors: Tim Tiernan, A. J. Sobczak,   *Indexer:* R. Kent Rasmussen
Christopher Rager, Rebecca Kuzins   *Production Editor:* Joyce I. Buchea
Acquisitions Editor: Mark Rehn   *Graphics and Design:* James Hutson
Editorial Assistant: Brett Weisberg   *Layout:* Mary Overell

Title page photo: *Photographers, sailors, and others crowd the upper decks of the USS* Missouri *seeking firsthand views of the signing of Japan's formal surrender in Tokyo Bay on September 2, 1945.* (National Archives)

Cover images: (pictured clockwise, from top left): Hiroshima atom bomb blast, 1945 (The Granger Collection, New York); Joe DiMaggio, 1947 (Time & Life Pictures/Getty Images); Betty Grable, pin up girl, 1942 (The Granger Collection, New York); U.S. bombers formation, 1942 (The Granger Collection, New York)

Library of Congress Cataloging-in-Publication Data

The forties in America / editor, Thomas Tandy Lewis.
    p. cm.
Includes bibliographical references and index.
ISBN 978-1-58765-659-0 (set : alk. paper) — ISBN 978-1-58765-660-6 (vol. 1 : alk. paper) —
ISBN 978-1-58765-661-3 (vol. 2 : alk. paper) — ISBN 978-1-58765-662-0 (vol. 3 : alk. paper)
  1. United States—Civilization—1945—Encyclopedias. 2. United States—Civilization—1918-1945—
Encyclopedias. 3. Canada—Civilization—1945—Encyclopedias. 4. United States—History—
1933-1945—Encyclopedias. 5. United States—History—1945-1953—Encyclopedias.
6. Canada—History—1945—Encyclopedias. 7. Canada—History—1914-1945—Encyclopedias.
8. Nineteen forties—Encyclopedias. I. Lewis, Thomas T. (Thomas Tandy)
  E169.12.F676 2011
  973.91—dc22
                                                                                    2010028115

■ Table of Contents

■ Complete List of Contents

Volume I

Volume II

Contents xxix

Volume III

The Forties in America

■ Godfrey, Arthur

Identification American radio and television
  personality
Born August 31, 1903; New York, New York
Died March 16, 1983; New York, New York

*Although it could be argued that Godfrey basically did not
"do" anything, his personal tastes and opinions influenced
large numbers of people. He was possibly the first-ever variety show host to become hugely popular, and as a major force
in radio and television, he inspired many performers who
succeeded him.*

The 1940's saw Arthur Godfrey rise to become a
great media star. Although his smoothly drawling
baritone voice (that some mistakenly assumed was
southern in inflection) had been heard on the radio
since the early 1930's, Godfrey became nationally
known in April, 1945, for his broadcast of President
Franklin D. Roosevelt's funeral procession. Soon,
the Columbia Broadcasting System (CBS) gave him
his own Monday-Friday morning radio show, *Arthur
Godfrey Time*, which featured his monologues, interviews with media stars, and music. He gradually
amassed an audience of millions to whom he dispensed his inimitable brand of folksy humor and dis-
armingly delivered, but strong, opinions. In late
1948, the self-styled "Old Redhead" moved into television, where he quickly became an influential figure during the early days of that medium.

Especially popular on both radio and television
was the *Arthur Godfrey's Talent Scouts* program, on
which were discovered many a talented newcomer
and little-known professional. His equally popular
Arthur Godfrey and His Friends television variety show
began airing in 1949. The cast, which included singers Julius La Rosa, the Chordettes quartet, and
Frank Parker, soon became well known.

On the surface, Godfrey's own talents were minimal. His singing, occasional film acting, and ukulele
plucking were at best mediocre, but his laid-back
persona was perfect for radio. His real talent lay in
getting people to take action. For example, his longtime affection for the Hawaiian Islands almost sin-
gle-handedly boosted tourism to that territory,
which at the time was rarely visited. His constant re-
ferral to the joys of piloting his own plane apparently

encouraged many to try the same thing. He was said
to have boosted aviation more than any man since
Charles Lindbergh.

Godfrey's ability to both make fun of, and successfully peddle, his sponsors' products eventually
earned him a million dollars a year. Although the
president of CBS, William Paley, supposedly disliked
Godfrey, he was an undeniable—and apparently un-
touchable—asset to the network. His shows were less
expensive to produce than comparable programs,
thereby earning greater profits for the network.

Although Godfrey lived a wealthy and privileged
life, most of his audience naïvely supposed him to be
just like the person they heard and saw on the air. His
impulsive and arrogant on-air firing of the popular
young singer Julius La Rosa in 1953 was perhaps a
turning point in audience perceptions of him. By
the late 1950's, his popularity had waned considerably, though he remained on the radio until the
early 1970's.

Impact Godfrey was much more than just an on-air
personality. He could make (and break) careers,
and his popularity contributed greatly to sales of his
sponsors' products. In the tradition of such commentators as Will Rogers, he had the ability to talk to
audience members as if were speaking directly to
each of them. He was a taste-maker and, as such, had
the power to influence huge numbers of listeners
and viewers. Some have speculated that he was the
model for the unflatteringly portrayed lead character in Al Morgan's hard-hitting novel *The Great Man*
(1955), a look at media personalities. For some time,
Godfrey seemed to be omnipresent, with two con-
current weekly television shows and a radio program
for CBS.

Roy Liebman

Further Reading

Godfrey, Arthur. *Stories I Like to Tell.* New York: Simon
  & Schuster, 1952.
Morgan, Al. *The Great Man.* New York: Dutton, 1955.
Singer, Arthur J. *Arthur Godfrey: The Adventures of an
  American Broadcaster.* Jefferson, N.C.: McFarland,
  2000.

See also Benny, Jack; Berle, Milton; Radio in the
United States; Television.

■ Golf

The success of several stars, both men and women, increased the popularity of golf among fans and encouraged people to take up the sport. The game extended its reach into different economic classes, from being a sport played primarily by the rich, and it became a popular form of recreation, with war veterans finding it a good form of rehabilitation.

With champions such as Ben Hogan, Byron Nelson, and Mildred "Babe" Didrikson Zaharias, golf survived and flourished during the 1940's. Prior to the 1940's, golf was played primarily by the rich. Because of the Great Depression, many American golfers who could no longer afford their country club memberships turned to public courses that survived the economic downturn; more members of other economic classes also became interested in the game. In 1941, for example, nearly 2.5 million people played on more than five thousand American golf courses.

Following the attack on Pearl Harbor in 1941, tournament play was suspended from 1942 to 1945. Both the United States Golf Association (USGA) and the Professional Golf Association (PGA) became active in the sale of war bonds and organizing charity golf matches for military hospitals. Actors Bob Hope and Bing Crosby were among many public figures who raised money through golf tournaments for the Red Cross and other philanthropic groups.

After the war ended in 1945, veterans, including those who suffered disabling injuries, returned to or took up the sport as part of their therapy. As the popularity of golf expanded, the game changed in its scope and rules.

Among golf's major events during the 1940's were the founding in 1943 of the Women's Professional Golf Association (WPGA) and initiation of the Women's Open Championship in 1946. A golf match was first televised in 1947. In the same year, the first resort golf course opened in Myrtle Beach, South Carolina. Also in that year, Babe Didrikson Zaharias achieved an unsurpassed level of professional recognition when she added the British Ladies Amateur Golf Championship title to her long list of wins; she was the first American woman to win that British title. She later signed with Wilson Sporting Goods to act as her sponsor. Despite a disparity in prize money among men and women, women's professional golf continued to develop through the efforts of Zaharias and other accomplished women with the founding of the Ladies Professional Golf Association (LPGA) in 1949. Sportswriters started the Golf Writers Association, and *Golf World*, a news weekly on golf and golfers, began publication in 1947.

After the war, African American golfers mounted a failed effort to integrate the PGA by filing a lawsuit to force integration in January, 1948. African American women golfers similarly attempted to join the UGA as part of a larger aim to join the USGA and then the LPGA. In 1946, blind golfers Charley Boswell and Clinton Russell competed against each other. Russell would later aid in the formation of the United States Blind Golfers Association.

Surviving the War During the war, players experienced a shortage of golf balls because industrial resources were shifted to the war effort. Golf courses found novel ways to keep golf balls in supply, including aggressive efforts at ball retrieval from ponds. The USGA made a significant rule change in 1942 regarding the distance a ball should travel. The Initial Velocity Test set 250 feet per second as the average distance the ball should travel when in flight. Wilson Sporting Goods, a major producer of golf equipment, expanded with the purchase of champion Walter Hagen's golf club company. Irons, clubs that are used for shorter shots, were redesigned, and the club face of the iron was weighted to create a smoother swing path. The 1940's did not see many changes in golf instruction, though Percy Boomer's *On Learning Golf* (1946) continued the discussion begun during the 1930's on the physiology of the golf swing.

Major Players Byron Nelson was among those drafted, then disqualified from active service. He, Sam Snead, and Ben Hogan were the major forces in golf between 1938 and 1947. Nelson retired from the professional circuit in August, 1946, in the wake of eighteen victories the year before. His game was extremely accurate and consistent; he was said to resemble a playing machine. In 1940, Nelson won the PGA Championship; in 1942, the Masters Tournament; and in 1945, the PGA Championship. Ben Hogan, another star of the decade, turned professional in 1931 at the age of nineteen and won four tournaments in 1940. In 1942, he won six times and then joined the Army Air Corps, returning to golf in 1945. He won the PGA Championship in 1946, along with twelve other matches. After seven more victories in 1947, Hogan won the U.S. Open in 1948, and after surviving a car accident that nearly killed him in early 1949, Hogan made the Ryder Cup Team and went to England for the competition but could not play. He continued a successful career, and in 1953, he won five of the six tournaments he entered, including the first three major championships of the year.

On the women's circuit, Patty Berg, who served in the Marine Corps Reserve, was named woman athlete of the year by the Associated Press (1943). She became a professional player in 1940, which allowed her, with the sponsorship of Wilson Sporting Goods, to travel and teach golf as well as play in promotional exhibitions for the equipment company. She won the Women's Western Open in 1941, as well as in 1943, after recovering from injuries sustained in an auto accident, and again in 1947. In 1946, she won the U.S. Open Championship, and in 1947 and 1948, she amassed a total of eight titles.

Babe Zaharias, a phenomenal golfer, was the highest earning woman player between 1948 and 1951. During the war, Zaharias performed in many exhibitions that popularized golf. Between 1946 and 1947, she achieved seventeen wins, followed in 1948 by the U.S. Women's Open. She continued to win regularly and also made golf instructional films until her early death from cancer in 1956. Other prominent golfers of the decade included Craig Wood, Jimmy Demaret, and Betty Jameson, who won the 1947 U.S. Women's Open Championship.

Impact The American public became more interested in golf during the war years, perhaps because many of the athletes who would have played on college and professional sports teams had been drafted and were serving overseas. Golf tended to be played by older athletes, more of whom were exempt from the draft, and it was more of a participant sport for adults than most college and professional sports. The achievements of the stars of the era also helped build enduring popularity for the sport.

Beverly Schneller

Further Reading

Dodson, James. *Ben Hogan: An American Life.* New York: Doubleday, 2004. While applauding Hogan

Two of the top male golfers of the 1940's, Byron Nelson (left) and Ben Hogan preparing for the Masters Tournament at Augusta, Georgia, in April, 1946. (AP/Wide World Photos)

and his accomplishments, this biography does not shy away from discussing his personality and its darker aspects, including his obsessive side and self-doubts. Good source for both professional accomplishments and personal life.

Kirsch, George B. *Golf in America.* Urbana: University of Illinois Press, 2009. Good social history of the game, tracking growth of the game and its popularity. Includes biographical stories of major players and their rivalries, but not heavy on statistics.

Peper, George, ed., with Robin McMillan and James A. Frank. *Golf in America: The First One Hundred Years.* New York: Harry N. Abrams, 1988. Discusses all aspects of the game, including its history and appeal, major stars of each decade, courses, and equipment, even providing a bit of instruction in the game. Written principally by editors at *Golf* magazine. Almost five hundred illustrations.

Wind, Herbert Warren. *The Story of American Golf: Its Champions and Championships.* New York: Farrar, Straus, 1948. Relates the story of golf, up to the mid-1940's. The book has been updated several times, but this edition provides more focus on the 1940's.

See also Crosby, Bing; Hogan, Ben; Hope, Bob; Sports in Canada; Sports in the United States; Tennis; Zaharias, Babe Didrikson.

■ The Good War: An Oral History of World War II

Identification Collection of more than 120 interviews with veterans and other persons involved in World War II

Editor Studs Terkel (1912-2008)

Date Published in 1984

The Good War *is historian Studs Terkel's attempt to capture the memories and the impact of World War II. In this epic account of World War II, the author expanded his oral history approach to a global scale, producing a history that won him both critical acclaim and the Pulitzer Prize.*

In *The Good War,* Studs Terkel used an approach similar to that of his earlier classic, *Hard Times: An Oral History of the Great Depression* (1970), seeking to produce a history of the era by interviewing scores of Americans and others who had served either in the war itself or on the home front. The volume is divided into four sections, or books. The first section includes individual memories of the attack on Pearl Harbor; recollections of subsequent fighting in the Pacific, Europe, and Africa; thoughts of women who identified with "Rosie the Riveter"; and memories of ordinary soldiers. As one example of the memories presented in this section, Dempsy Travis, recalling the Jim Crow aspects of the war, describes it as "the turning point of my life." The second section includes interviews with individuals of high rank, both military and civilian; people who bombed others or who were bombed; people who grew up in Europe and Asia as well as the United States; memories of D Day; and an interview with one of the Andrews Sis-

ters. In this section, Lean Wood, a Londoner visiting New York, remembers the bombing of London and the deaths of young children who had "cardboard coffins."

The third section focuses more on the economic effects of the war and includes interviews with government policy makers as well as journalists. John Kenneth Galbraith, who was put in charge of organizing price controls, describes the necessity of implementing rationing during the war. The last section of the book focuses on the final months of the war and its aftermath, including the atomic bombings of Hiroshima and Nagasaki, the war crimes trials at Nuremberg, and the onset of the Cold War. Hajimi Kito, a survivor of Hiroshima, states, "What I remember most are the screams for water." One of the strengths of the book is that it captures the voices of a vast array of individuals of all classes and many nationalities whose stories rivet readers and draw them into the chaos of a world war.

Impact *The Good War* appeals to a broad audience: to the historian seeking a personalized history of the war, to the individual who experienced the war itself, and to more recent generations who have no memory of the war years. Although Terkel's approach records the experiences of individuals, it offers a larger panorama of the war and its effect on the world.

Yvonne Johnson

Further Reading

Ambrose, Stephen. *The Victors: Eisenhower and His Boys: The Men of World War II.* New York: Simon & Schuster, 1999.

Gilbert, Martin. *The Second World War: A Complete History.* New York: Henry Holt, 2004.

Ryan, Cornelius. *The Longest Day: The Classic Epic of D-Day.* New York: Simon & Schuster, 1994.

Weinberg, Gerhard L. *A World at Arms: A Global History of World War II.* New York: Cambridge University Press, 2005.

See also Casualties of World War II; Films about World War II; Historiography; *Studies in Social Psychology in World War II;* Wartime industries; Wartime propaganda in the United States; Wartime rationing; World War II; World War II mobilization.

■ **Goodman, Benny**

Identification Big band leader and clarinetist
Born May 30, 1909; Chicago, Illinois
Died June 13, 1986; New York, New York

Benny Goodman was nicknamed the "King of Swing" because of his mass appeal and virtuosic clarinet playing. His success can be attributed to his technical mastery of the clarinet. His fame during the 1930's and 1940's contributed to the international popularity of swing, especially among young white audiences.

Benny Goodman, who was reared by Russian-Jewish immigrant parents, began his musical training at a local Chicago synagogue. He was greatly influenced by 1920's New Orleans jazz, which was known for virtuosic clarinetists. Goodman organized his own twelve-piece swing band in 1934, and it gained national exposure through radio broadcasts on the Columbia Broadcasting System (CBS) until 1940. It is arguable that Goodman's career peaked in 1940 after several notable events, including his 1937 Paramount Theater concert and his 1938 Carnegie Hall concert. Goodman was famous for his clean image, smooth sound, and utilization of the clarinet's high register.

Goodman's career significantly shifted during the 1940's. First, his jazz orchestra had a different sound as the result of new band members and the addition of vocalists. New music arrangements were influenced by contemporaries such as Duke Ellington, rather than older models such as Fletcher Henderson. The second shift was Goodman's departure from jazz. He took classical clarinet lessons and commissioned several compositions by renowned composers, including a clarinet concerto by Aaron Copland in 1947. He also embraced Broadway and appeared in the musical *Seven Lively Arts* in 1944. His third career shift was his experimentation with the "bop" musical style. He organized a bop ensemble in 1947, but this new group was unpopular and disbanded in 1949. The story of his rise to fame was portrayed in the 1955 film *The Benny Goodman Story.*

Impact Benny Goodman's jazz orchestra played a large part in the popularity of swing among white audiences during the 1930's and 1940's. His most famous pieces include "Clarinet a la King," "Stompin' at the Savoy," and "Sing Sing Sing." Throughout his

Benny Goodman. (Library of Congress)

career, Goodman emphasized his ability to exploit the capabilities of his instrument. One of the few American musicians to be accepted by both classical and popular audiences, Goodman is remembered as a great performer, an influential big band leader, and the "King of Swing."

Elizabeth Whittenburg Ozment

Further Reading

Firestone, Ross. *Swing, Swing, Swing: The Life and Times of Benny Goodman.* New York: W. W. Norton, 1993.
Shuller, Gunther. *The Swing Era: The Development of Jazz, 1930-1945.* New York: Oxford University Press, 1991.
Wilson, John S. "Benny Goodman, King of Swing, Is Dead." *New York Times,* June 14, 1986, p. A1.

See also Dance; Dorsey, Tommy; Ellington, Duke; Miller, Glenn; Music: Classical; Music: Jazz; Music: Popular; Radio in the United States.

■ Grable, Betty

Identification   Stage actor and film star
Born   December 18, 1916; St. Louis, Missouri
Died   July 2, 1973; Santa Monica, California

During the 1940's, the American beauty Betty Grable became a cultural icon. Her beautiful legs and wholesome personality created an image offering diversion from the events of World War II.

While appearing in a 1939 Broadway show, Betty Grable garnered the attention of Twentieth Century-Fox Film Corporation. In 1940, her roles in that studio's *Down Argentine Way* and *Tin Pan Alley* led her to stardom; these films were followed by more than a decade of Technicolor musicals. The petite, blue-eyed blonde Grable was known as a hardworking and personable actor with great appeal. One particularly attractive full-length photograph of Grable, dressed in a white bathing suit and high heels and looking back over her right shoulder, was sent to millions of servicemen. Her image became a familiar sight in barracks and on warplanes, and it was even used for map training.

Impact   Throughout the 1940's, Grable was a smashing box-office success for Twentieth Century-Fox. Still-life photos and dozens of musical films, as well as radio and personal appearances, led Grable to become, by the end of the 1940's, the highest-paid female star in Hollywood, earning more than $300,000 a year. She had such value as a star that her legs were insured for $1 million with Lloyds of London. She also was the first, and the best-known, pinup girl for American troops. Grable's success and "girl next door" image inspired many other women. The energetic Grable was a compelling image and top star from 1941 until the early 1950's; she made her last film, *How to Be Very, Very Popular*, in 1955.

Cynthia J. W. Svoboda

Further Reading

McGee, Tom. *Betty Grable: The Girl with the Million Dollar Legs.* New York: Vestal Press, 1995.

Schiach, Don. *Movie Stars.* Southwater, London: Anness, 2005.

Warren, Doug. *Betty Grable: The Reluctant Movie Queen.* New York: St. Martin's Press, 1974.

See also   Film in Canada; Films about World War II; Hayworth, Rita; Lombard, Carole; Pinup girls; Rogers, Ginger; War bonds; Women's roles and rights in the United States.

■ Graham, Billy

Identification   American preacher and evangelist
Born   November 7, 1918; near Charlotte, North Carolina

During the 1940's, Graham preached on the radio, traveled widely to conduct evangelistic campaigns, and held a college presidency, all of which elevated him to national standing as one of the leading figures of American Protestantism.

A religious conversion in 1934 at a revival meeting and attendance at Bob Jones College and Florida Bible Institute set the stage for Billy Graham's entry to Wheaton College, a prestigious fundamentalist institution, in 1940. There Graham met Ruth Bell, the daughter of missionaries to China; they married in 1943. Already an ordained Baptist preacher, Graham attracted the notice of mentors who admired his earnestness, sincerity, and energy. Graham relinquished the pulpit of his small church to join Youth for Christ after its leaders heard him on the radio. This dynamic evangelistic organization offered Graham his first big platform—a "Chicagoland Youth for Christ" rally of several thousand people at which he preached and offered an evangelistic invitation. He traveled widely, including trips to the British Isles, and formed a lifelong association with Cliff Barrows, his song leader.

In 1947, Graham accepted the presidency of Northwestern Baptist Bible College in Minneapolis, Minnesota, from retiring president William Bell Riley. A largely absentee president who served until 1952, Graham had others tend to administrative matters. One of Graham's hallmarks was the lack of scandal associated with his ministries. This and Graham's anticommunist, moralistic message attracted media magnate William Randolph Hearst, who had followed Graham's work with Youth for Christ, giving it widespread, favorable publicity. Hearst directed the editors of his newspapers to promote Graham's evangelistic campaign in Los Angeles in 1949; this encouraged attendance at the "canvas cathedral" and helped elevate Graham to national status.

Impact   Graham became famous as a radio evangelist and later televangelist, promoting his brand of fundamentalist religion for more than fifty years, into the twenty-first century. He reached live audiences totaling more than 200 million people, in most of the countries of the world. His patriotic messages, good looks, and charm endeared him to many in the United States.

Mark C. Herman

Further Reading

Bruns, Roger. *Billy Graham: A Biography*. Westport, Conn.: Greenwood Press, 2004.

Graham, Billy. *Just as I Am: The Autobiography of Billy Graham*. San Francisco: HarperSanFrancisco, 1997.

Lowe, Janet, comp. *Billy Graham Speaks: Insight from the World's Greatest Preacher*. New York: John Wiley & Sons, 1999.

Pollock, John. *Billy Graham: The Authorized Biography*. New York: McGraw-Hill, 1966.

_____. *To All the Nations: The Billy Graham Story*. San Francisco: Harper & Row, 1985.

See also   Anticommunism; Chaplains in World War II; Religion in Canada; Religion in the United States; Theology and theologians.

Evangelist Billy Graham preaching to ten thousand people in a tent in Los Angeles in November, 1949. (AP/Wide World Photos)

■ *The Grapes of Wrath*

Identification   Film about Dust Bowl refugees seeking farm work in California
Director   John Ford (1895-1973)
Date   Released on March 15, 1940

This film was one of the first and most memorable to make a strong statement on a serious social issue in the United States.

The year 1940 was a good time in which to make John Steinbeck's *The Grapes of Wrath* (1939) into a film. A timely exposition of economic conditions during the previous decade's Great Depression, the book had been a best seller the year it came out and would win the author a Pulitzer Prize for 1940. *The Grapes of Wrath* is the story of the Joads, an impoverished Dust Bowl family who are forced off their family farm in Oklahoma and join the great "Okie" migration to California, lured by advertisements promising high-paying jobs picking fruit.

The masterful director John Ford's genuine sympathy for the film's Joad family truly resonates here. Each scene of the film offers a moving depiction of the hardships the family must endure. By 1940, camera and lighting techniques were sufficiently advanced for cinematographer Gregg Toland to produce a stark black-and-white film that often resembles a documentary. Almost perfect casting was achieved by reliance on the black-and-white photographs of migrant farm workers that had been taken by Dorothea Lange for the Farm Security Administration.

On its release, the film proved very popular among audiences, who rallied to the story's American themes of hard work and perseverance. As protagonist Tom Joad, Henry Fonda delivered one of his most memorable performances in *The Grapes of Wrath*, and it helped start him on an acting career in which he would eventually achieve legendary status during the 1940's. However, it was Jane Darwell, who as a determined yet sensitive Ma Joad, who won the Academy Award in 1940 for best supporting actress. John Ford also received an Oscar for best director, for creating this truly outstanding American classic film.

Impact   John Steinbeck's novel *The Grapes of Wrath* was the quintessential American novel of the Great Depression, and its film adaptation enjoys a similar reputation. Because of the power of its story, its strong cast, masterful direction, and stunning cinematography, the film has come to be recognized as one of the great American classic films. More important and more immediately, it helped ensure that full and permanent public attention was focused on the plight of displaced, unemployed farm workers in the United States.

Patricia E. Sweeney

Further Reading

Bloom, Harold, ed. *John Steinbeck's "The Grapes of Wrath."* Philadelphia: Chelsea House, 2005.

Eyman, Scott. *Print the Legend: The Life and Times of John Ford.* New York: Simon & Schuster, 1999.

Sennett, Ted. *Great Hollywood Movies.* New York: Harry N. Abrams, 1983.

Steinbeck, John. *"The Grapes of Wrath": Text and Criticism.* Edited by Peter Lisca. New York: Penguin Books, 1977.

See also   Academy Awards; Agriculture in the United States; Film in the United States; Ford, John; New Deal programs; Unemployment in the United States.

■ Gray, Pete

Identification   American professional baseball player
Born   March 6, 1915; Nanticoke, Pennsylvania
Died   June 30, 2002; Nanticoke, Pennsylvania

Gray's ability to play professional baseball despite having only one arm gave hope to thousands of disabled World War II veterans returning home.

After having his right arm amputated at the elbow in a farming accident at the age of six, Pete Gray might well have given up his dream of playing professional baseball. Instead, his accident only fired his ambition. Originally a right-handed batter, he learned how to hit from the left side and developed into a line-drive hitter, superb bunter, and speedy runner. In the outfield, Gray developed a lightning-fast fielding method. He wore a glove with almost no padding. After catching the ball, he would stick the glove under the stump of his right arm, grab the ball with his left hand, and throw it infield.

In 1944, Gray hit .333, stole sixty-three bases, and was voted most valuable player in the minor league's Southern Association. The St. Louis Browns of the American League purchased Gray's contract for the 1945 season. Despite his heroic efforts, however, Gray simply could not compete. His line drives became hard outs; his bunts were fielded by expectant fielders. He hit only .218 for the Browns, and he struggled against a perception that he was just being exploited for publicity purposes. That was his only season in professional baseball.

Impact   Gray was an inspiration to combat amputees, but he also suffered verbal abuse from teammates because of his handicap. Two years after Gray's professional debut, another athlete came along who also overcame discrimination in the major leagues: Jackie Robinson.

Russell Roberts

Further Reading

Kashatus, William C. *One-Armed Wonder: Pete Gray, Wartime Baseball, and the American Dream.* Jefferson City, N.C.: McFarland, 1995.

Lee, Bill, with Jim Prime. *Baseball Eccentrics: The Most Entertaining, Outrageous, and Unforgettable Characters in the Game.* Chicago: Triumph Books, 2006.

Mead, William B. *Even the Browns.* Chicago: Contemporary Books, 1978.

See also   All-American Girls Professional Baseball League; Baseball; Gehrig, Lou; Negro Leagues; Robinson, Jackie; Sports in the United States; World War II.

■ Great Blizzard of 1949

The Event   Several severe winter storms affecting the Great Plains and Rocky Mountains
Date   Winter of 1948-1949
Places   Mainly Nebraska, South Dakota, Minnesota, Colorado, and Wyoming

The storms were so severe that the Army, Air Force, National Guard, and Red Cross coordinated a six-thousand-person workforce in a special rescue effort dubbed Operation Snowbound. Temperatures at times reached –50 degrees Fahrenheit, and it felt even colder due to strong winds. More than one hundred people died in the storms, most of them stranded in their homes or on the road.

The fall of 1948 was notable for unusual warmth and outstanding harvests of several crops, including soybeans, wheat, and corn. Beginning on November 18, however, a blizzard roared into Nebraska from the Rockies carrying with it heavy snow, sleet, and winds as strong as seventy miles per hour. This storm buried northeastern Nebraska in as much as two feet of snow, snapping telephone poles and impeding train travel.

Another storm hit the area at the end of 1948, and yet another on January 2, 1949, a three-day event that paralyzed western, central, and northern Nebraska, as well as areas to the north, west, and northeast, with wind-driven snow and winds up to sixty miles per hour. As coal and fuel oil supplies ran out, some stranded farmers burned their furniture to keep warm. Small aircraft dropped food to many families. Yet another storm followed much the same track at the end of January. The weather pattern continued into March, when North Platte, Nebraska, was buried in twenty inches of snow. At one location in Antelope County, Nebraska, drifts of thirty feet did not melt until early June.

Impact   The Great Blizzard of 1949 was one of the worst natural disasters in Nebraska history. While nearly a quarter million people were stranded because of the storms, rescue personnel helped clear more than 100,000 miles of road and airdrop food to families and feed to 4 million cattle and sheep.

Bruce E. Johansen

Further Reading
Bradford, Marlene, and Robert S. Carmichael, eds. *Natural Disasters.* 3 vols. Pasadena, Calif.: Salem Press, 2001.

Rosado, Maria. *Blizzards! and Ice Storms.* New York: Simon Spotlight, 1999.

See also   Armistice Day blizzard; Natural disasters; Texas City disaster.

■ Great Books Foundation

Identification   Nonprofit organization, established by scholars at the University of Chicago and the *Encyclopedia Britannica*, dedicated to popular intellectual self-improvement through support of reading and discussion of the *Great Books of the Western World* (1952)
Date   Established in 1947

During the early 1940's, University of Chicago president Robert Hutchins and philosopher Mortimer Adler encouraged a movement among the local public for studying the Great Books. The popularity of the movement prompted establishment of the Great Books Foundation, which aided the organization of reading and discussion clubs and published sets of the Great Books, marketed through the Encyclopedia Britannica.

Among the innovations Robert Maynard Hutchins and Mortimer Adler established at the University of Chicago was an emphasis on general, or liberal, education, especially through debate of the great ideas in Western culture as expressed in classical works of thought. William Benton, a business executive and later a U.S. senator, was enthused by their ideas. In 1941, he bought the *Encyclopedia Britannica* from the Sears, Roebuck and Company and in 1943 transferred the publishing concern to Chicago. Principally, Hutchins and especially Adler reviewed titles for inclusion in a collection of Great Books and elaborated an index to the essential ideas contained in them.

Impact   Comprising a fifty-four-volume set, the Great Books of the Western World appeared in 1952. Tens of thousands of Great Books clubs appeared over the next two decades. However, criticism of the movement arose over its middlebrow character and the bias of the collection toward Western culture and white, male authors. The movement withered during the 1970's, but the foundation and respect for liberal education continued.

Edward A. Riedinger

Further Reading

Adler, Mortimer Jerome. *How to Read a Book: The Art of Getting a Liberal Education.* New York: Simon & Schuster, 1940.

Beam, Alex. *A Great Idea at the Time: The Rise, Fall, and Curious Afterlife of the Great Books.* New York: PublicAffairs, 2008.

See also   Book publishing; Education in the United States; Literature in Canada; Literature in the United States; *Reader's Digest.*

■ *The Great Dictator*

Identification   Film spoofing Adolf Hitler and appealing for democracy and universal brotherhood

Director and producer   Charles Chaplin (1889-1977)

Date   Opened on October 15, 1940

Chaplin's The Great Dictator *lampoons Adolf Hitler, his Nazi officials, and Benito Mussolini, sometimes with wonderfully comedic touches. In an abrupt shift near the film's end, Chaplin steps out of character to deliver an impassioned speech in his own voice, decrying hatred and greed, as well as looking toward creation of a decent and tolerant world.*

Charles Chaplin held Jews in high esteem, and he was savagely criticized by commentators in Germany, where his films were banned. He began filming *The Great Dictator* just days after Hitler invaded Poland in September, 1939, beginning World War II in Europe. The film provides a sympathetic view of a Jewish community in fictional Tomania—a country much like Germany—beset by oppressive government policies and thuggish storm troopers.

Chaplin has two roles in the film, first as the Jewish ghetto's barber. The story line hinges on the barber's remarkable resemblance to the dictator of Tomania, Adenoid Hynkel (modeled on Hitler)—the other role played by Chaplin. Hynkel's mock ballet, danced with a globe floating in the air like a balloon representing his intent to dominate the world, is one of the film's iconic scenes. Hynkel's chief underlings are Herring (Hermann Göring) and Garbitsch (Joseph Goebbels); his chief rival is Napaloni (Mussolini, played by Jack Oakie) of Bacteria (Italy).

The farcical interaction of Hynkel and Napaloni gets a great deal of screen time. Eventually, Hynkel orders the ghetto crushed and Osterlich (Austria) invaded. When the victorious troops turn to their leader for a triumphal harangue, Hynkel's look-alike, the Jewish barber now in military uniform, steps forward. He begins to speak, and it is clearly Chaplin himself now doing the talking. War is condemned, not praised, and the speaker offers a vision of human goodness and peaceful cooperation.

Impact   Some critics found *The Great Dictator* flawed, and American isolationists considered it provocative. Nevertheless, the film was a popular and financial success, and it was nominated for five Academy Awards. It was also popular with the British and was a morale booster in Great Britain at a time when Hitler's bombers were pounding London. After the war

Actor/director Charles Chaplin (center) as Adenoid Hynkel, the dictator of Tomania, entertaining Napaloni (Jack Oakie), the visiting dictator of Bacteria, as his aide Garbitsch (Henry Daniell) looks on. Chaplin also played a gentle Jewish barber who happens to look exactly like Hynkel. (Getty Images)

ended, Chaplin said that had he known the full monstrosity of Hitler, he would not have made the film.

Richard Gruber

Further Reading

Chaplin, Charles. *My Autobiography.* New York: Simon & Schuster, 1964.

Kamin, Dan. *The Comedy of Charlie Chaplin.* Lanham, Md.: Scarecrow Press, 2008.

Robinson, David. *Chaplin: His Life and Art.* 2d ed. New York: McGraw-Hill, 2001.

See also Academy Awards; *Casablanca*; Film in the United States; Films about World War II; Hitler, Adolf; *They Were Expendable*; Wartime propaganda in the United States; *Yankee Doodle Dandy.*

■ "Great Escape" from Stalag Luft III

The Event Mass escape of Allied prisoners from a German prisoner-of-war camp

Date March 25, 1944

Place Sagan, Poland (now Zagan, Poland)

The escape of Allied prisoners of war (POWs) from Sagan was World War II's largest mass escape, but the subsequent execution of fifty of the recaptured escapees inhibited further attempts at such large-scale breakout attempts. The American military also came to realize that air crews needed training in the skills of evasion, escape, and resistance to interrogation—skills that would be vital in later American wars.

At the time when the United States entered World War II, its servicemen had received no training in evasion or resisting interrogation, and the American armed services had little history of escapes from enemy captors. In contrast, the British saw escape attempts as a legitimate way to undermine enemy morale and divert enemy resources and personnel away from the front, with a side benefit of the possibility of escape bolstering prisoners' morale. This attitude was strengthened by MI9, a department of British military intelligence created to aid European resistance organizations and to facilitate the escape attempts of allied POWs. In response, Germany built a number of "escape-proof" prisoner camps. One was Stalag Luft III, which was located near the town of Sagan in Poland. ("Stalag" is the abbreviation for *Stamlager*, or prisoner camp and "Luft" is an abbreviation of Luftwaffe, the name of the German air force.)

Throughout 1943 and 1944, increasing numbers of American air crews were shot down during the strategic bombing offensive. Many of these crew members soon embraced the British enthusiasm for escape. In Stalag Luft III, escapes were overseen by the "X Organization," which sanctioned escape attempts and coordinated prisoners' labor to provide the infrastructure necessary for successful escapes. X Organization was headed by Squadron Leader Roger Bushell, a South African. X Organization was a cosmopolitan group that included Americans, Britons, Canadians, Czechs, Norwegians, and members of other nationalities. More than eight hundred POWs directly supported escapes through tunneling, constructing improvised tools, shadowing German guards, and creating forged documents and civilian-looking clothing. Although X Organization was originally British, many Americans soon filled pivotal roles. Lieutenant Colonel Albert P. Clark became "Big S," the head of security, and Major David Jones, a veteran of Doolittle's Raid on Japan who was later shot down over North Africa, became a leader of the tunnelers.

Bushell aimed to obstruct Germany's war effort through a mass escape and the inevitable disorder that efforts to recapture the escapees would generate. On March 25, 1944, seventy-six men escaped through a tunnel. Americans were not among these escapees because a few weeks earlier, they had been transferred to one of Stalag Luft III's compounds other than the one with the tunnel. Ultimately, all but three POWs were recaptured, but the disruption of Germany's home front was so public and widespread that an incensed Adolf Hitler ordered that all recaptured escapees be executed; eventually, fifty were executed. As a consequence, both POWs and MI9 refused to plan mass escape attempts for the remainder of the war.

Impact Although Americans were not among the executed, they learned much about prisoner organization and escape technologies while working within X Organization, and they communicated this knowledge to prisoners in other camps. Although Americans at home were generally unaware of the fifty executions, the postwar furor over mistreatment of POWs and minorities such as Jews hardened American resolve to fight against dictatorships. During the late 1940's, this distrust took the form of Cold War antipathy toward the Soviets. The release of the film *The Great Escape* in 1963 reaffirmed these lessons for later generations of Americans.

Kevin B. Reid

Further Reading

Brickhill, Paul. *The Great Escape.* London: Faber & Faber, 1951.

Carroll, Tim. *The Great Escapers: The Full Story of the Second World War's Most Remarkable Mass Escape.* Edinburgh: Mainstream, 2004.

Clark, Albert P. *Thirty-three Months as a POW in Stalag Luft III.* Golden, Colo.: Fulcrum, 2004.

Durand, Arthur A. *Stalag Luft III: The Secret Story.* Baton Rouge: Louisiana State University Press, 1988.

See also Air Force, U.S.; Films about World War II; Geneva Conventions; Hitler, Adolf; Prisoners of war, North American; Strategic bombing; War crimes and atrocities.

■ Great Marianas Turkey Shoot

The Event American naval victory over a Japanese fleet
Also known as Battle of the Philippine Sea
Date June 19-20, 1944
Place Philippine Sea, west of the Mariana Islands

In the largest aircraft carrier battle in history, the U.S. Navy destroyed almost five hundred Japanese aircraft in the air, on the ground, and on carriers, as well as three carriers. These irreplaceable losses allowed the United States to capture the Marianas, Iwo Jima, and the Philippines without significant air opposition.

To stop American advances in the Pacific, the Japanese decided to retake the offensive by attacking the naval units supporting the American landing at Saipan in the Marianas Islands that began on June 14, 1944. American submarines discovered the approaching Japanese force of nine carriers and alerted Admiral Raymond Spruance. Fearful of a trap, Spruance's fifteen carriers approached the Japanese

cautiously. On June 19, Admiral Jiraburo Ozawa ordered a series of raids, but American radar, superior airplanes (particularly the Grumman Hellcats), and inexperienced Japanese pilots led to a decisive victory. It was so easy that one American pilot exclaimed it was "like an old-time turkey shoot!" Japanese attacks on June 20 also failed.

Meanwhile, American submarines sank two large carriers, and aircraft destroyed another. Of 430 Japanese planes launched on both days, only 35 survived. Aircraft from the Japanese base at Guam also were eliminated. Although the U.S. Navy lost 123 planes, only seventy-six fliers were killed and no ships were sunk.

Impact After their crushing defeat, the Japanese unrealistically depended on their army to stop the American advance in the Pacific. The capture of the Marianas gave the United States runways for long-range bombers to devastate the Japanese home islands.

M. Philip Lucas

Further Reading

Hastings, Max. *Retribution: The Battle for Japan, 1944-45.* New York: Alfred A. Knopf, 2008.

Tillman, Barrett. *Clash of the Carriers: The True Story of the Marianas Turkey Shoot of World War II.* New York: New American Library, 2005.

Marines firing a mountain gun captured from the Japanese on Saipan. (National Archives)

Y'Blood, William T. *Red Sun Setting: The Battle of the Philippine Sea.* Annapolis, Md.: Naval Institute Press, 1981.

See also Aircraft carriers; Bombers; Hiroshima and Nagasaki bombings; Iwo Jima, Battle of; Navy, U.S.; Philippines; Radar; Submarine warfare; World War II.

■ "Greatest Generation"

Definition Term popularized by newscaster Tom Brokaw's 1998 book *The Greatest Generation* to describe the generation of Americans who led their country through World War II

Referring to a particular generation as the "Greatest Generation" both attempts to measure the social impact of a specific generation and establishes a benchmark by which to compare the social impact of preceding and succeeding generations. Although difficult to measure quantifiably, it does provide some basis for comparison and discussion.

World War II was considered "The Good War," and the American contribution to victory was comprehensive and decisive. Across battlefronts in all military theaters, American forces led major invasions and claimed decisive victories. On the home front, women entered factories to manufacture war material. Citizens of all social strata participated in the Allied effort, whether by purchasing war bonds, salvaging scrap aluminum, or engaging in many other war-related efforts.

Applying the term "greatest" to any generation is problematic as a measure of social impact. Its use sets up a competitive comparison. Was not the founding generation of George Washington, Benjamin Franklin, Thomas Jefferson, and John Adams the greatest? Or perhaps the Civil War generation? It is an interesting debate but one that is difficult to quantify, and for that reason must be entered into with caution.

Impact After World War II, social roles, such as the acceptance of women in the workforce and racial integration, began to shift. In addition, affluence was on the rise, and a social cohesion existed among many of that generation, setting standards for civic engagement that have not yet been matched.

Steve Neiheisel

Further Reading
Brokaw, Tom. *The Greatest Generation.* New York: Random House, 1998.
_____. *The Greatest Generation Speaks: Letters and Reflections.* New York: Random House, 1999.
Greene, Bob. *Duty.* New York: William Morrow, 2000.

See also Casualties of World War II; Films about World War II; *Studies in Social Psychology in World War II*; World War II; World War II mobilization.

■ *Greer* incident

The Event First incident in which a U.S. warship engaged a German submarine, shortly before American entry into World War II.
Date September 4, 1941
Place En route to Iceland

The incident helped President Franklin D. Roosevelt adopt measures to ensure the delivery of Lend-Lease supplies to Great Britain, but in doing so the United States became involved in an undeclared naval war with Germany in late 1941.

The USS *Greer,* an American destroyer, was en route to Iceland with mail and supplies for a small Marine garrison posted there when it received reports from a British pilot of a German U-boat spotted ten miles ahead. The *Greer* tracked the German submarine for over three hours, notifying British aircraft overhead of its location. When British pilots tried to sink it by using depth charges, the German U-boat fired a torpedo at the *Greer.* The *Greer* retaliated with several depth charges. Two hours later, the two warships again exchanged fire before the *Greer* proceeded to Iceland.

President Franklin D. Roosevelt told the American public that a German submarine had fired on the *Greer* in a deliberate attempt to sink it. He described the attack as an act of piracy, part of a Nazi attempt to eliminate freedom of the seas and dominate the Western Hemisphere. He then announced the extension of U.S. naval escort service for merchant ships of any flag as far as Iceland. He also issued a "shoot on sight" order against German and Italian vessels operating within the American security zone in the Atlantic.

Despite favorable public reaction to the president's speech, isolationists accused Roosevelt of trying to maneuver an unwilling country into war. They noted several discrepancies in the president's version of the incident: He had failed to disclose that the *Greer* was a U.S. warship, that it had prompted the attack by tracking the German submarine, and that it had not been hit by German torpedoes. The isolationists could not stop Roosevelt from extending U.S. naval escorts of Lend-Lease supplies to Great Britain, but the president, seeing that Adolf Hitler had not been baited into a shooting war in the Atlantic, and recalling the opposition of isolationists in the recent vote to renew the Selective Service Act of 1940, did not ask Congress for a declaration of war.

Impact In his attempt to use the incident to justify taking the United States into a full-blown war, Roosevelt misled the public by suggesting that Germany posed a direct threat to American security and had to be defeated by military intervention in the war. Consequently, he left himself open to charges of deceit.

Dean Fafoutis

Further Reading

Langer, William L., and S. Everett Gleason. *The Undeclared War, 1940-1941.* New York: Harper & Brothers, 1953.

Morison, Samuel Eliot. *The Battle of the Atlantic, September 1939-May 1943.* Boston: Little, Brown, 1947.

See also Atlantic, Battle of the; Isolationism; Lend-Lease; Navy, U.S.; Roosevelt, Franklin D.; Submarine warfare.

■ Gross national product of Canada

Definition Canada's national total of consumption outlays, private investment inside the country, and expenditures of governments for both goods and services, minus imported goods and services

Canada's economy grew significantly throughout the 1940's, led by government spending during World War II and by a combination of government programs and postwar consumer spending in the latter half of the decade. Canada emerged from the 1940's as a major economy by global standards.

Canada's gross national product (GNP) grew at unprecedented rates during World War II, had a small dip in growth immediately following the war, and began a period of robust and steady growth in 1947. Measured in 1971 dollars, Canada's real GNP went from $17.8 billion (Canadian dollars) in 1939 to $27.5 billion in 1942, with more modest growth to $31.4 billion in 1949. Nominal GNP—that is, gross national product in current dollars—went from $5.6 billion in 1939 to $16.8 billion in 1949. This threefold increase indicates the enormous inflationary pressures occurring during and immediately after World War II.

Wartime Production During World War II, Canada's federal government, led by Prime Minister William Lyon Mackenzie King, adopted drastic economic policies under the War Measures Act. As a result, government grew enormously, going from 46,000 civil servants in 1939 to 116,000 in 1945. Government spending as a percentage of GNP increased even more dramatically, going from 11 percent of GNP in 1939 to 45 percent in 1943. Much of this spending was on defense, and many industries thus created continued to be profitable after the war.

Furthermore, the Canadian government provided Great Britain with approximately $4 billion in direct aid and loan forgiveness during and immediately after the war—the largest aid package ever given from one country to another at that time. Most of this money was spent in Canada on the war effort, so it stimulated the Canadian economy in Keynesian fashion. In fact, real consumption per head went from $731 in 1939 to $992 in 1945. Unemployment, which had increased drastically during the Great Depression, decreased to 4.4 percent by 1941 with the ramp up of the war effort.

GNP experienced double-digit real growth in the first three years of the war, and 1943 and 1944 saw steady growth at 4 percent per year. GNP dipped slightly immediately following the war, decreasing by 2.2 percent in 1945 and 2.7 percent in 1946.

Postwar Prosperity The Canadian government had learned important lessons after the Great Depression that followed World War I. Key players in keeping Canada's GNP on a positive trend after World War II included Prime Minister King, with his Ph.D. in economics; Deputy Minister of Finance Clifford Clark, a committed Keynesian; C. D. Howe,

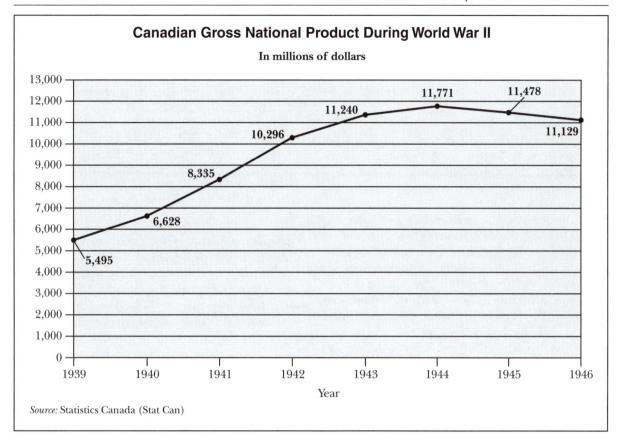

Canadian Gross National Product During World War II

In millions of dollars

Source: Statistics Canada (Stat Can)

who headed the newly created Department of Reconstruction; and Leonard Marsh, whose 1943 Marsh Report was seen as overly optimistic in its goals of universal employment and welfare in Canada but which set the stage for many of the social programs introduced during the 1940's.

The Liberal government took several steps toward minimizing postwar economic downturn. At war's end, much-heightened wartime taxes were quickly reduced. In 1944, family allowances, colloquially called "baby bonuses," were sent directly to mothers, who tended to spend them immediately on their children's needs, thus stimulating the economy. Because the struggles of veterans after World War I had had a negative impact on both social welfare and on GNP, the newly founded Department of Veterans Affairs provided numerous programs to help veterans transition into the workforce.

The years following the war saw modest increases in real growth of GNP, with an average of 3.5 percent growth in 1947, 1948, and 1949. This growth resulted from aggressive government measures as well

as from Canadians' eagerness to purchase goods and services unavailable during wartime and from Europe's demand for Canadian products during its reconstruction.

Impact Canadian censuses from 1921 to 1941 defined about two-thirds of Canadians as living below the poverty line, while the census of 1951 found only one-third to be poor; this remarkable shift highlights the impact of Canada's move to a welfare state as well as its significant GNP growth throughout the 1940's.

The 1940's marked two significant shifts in the percentage of GNP associated with the major sectors of Canada's economy. Agriculture began a downward shift at the end of the 1940's that would lead to significant decreases of this sector during the 1950's. Manufacturing, which accounted for, on average, 22.8 percent of gross domestic product at factor cost by industry from 1926 to 1939, jumped to an average of 28.8 percent during the 1940's—approximately where it would stay throughout the 1950's. The steady growth of overall GNP in the last years of the 1940's, which many attribute to the Keynesian model followed during the decade, was also to continue for the decades to follow.

Pamela Bedore

Further Reading

Bothwell, Robert. *The Penguin History of Canada.* Toronto: Penguin Canada, 2006. Provides useful information about broad trends in the Canadian economy during the war years and immediately thereafter.

Bothwell, Robert, Ian Drummond, and John English. *Canada Since 1945: Power, Politics, and Provincialism.* Rev. ed. Toronto: University of Toronto Press, 1989. Provides political perspectives on economic decisions made in the postwar years.

Churchill, Gordon. *National Accounts Income and Expenditure, 1926-1956.* Ottawa: Queen's Printer, 1962. Invaluable resource provides prose accounts of trends in GNP and other economic factors as well as detailed numerical data of all key economic indicators in Canada over a three-decade period.

Finkel, Alvin. *Social Policy and Practice in Canada: A History.* Waterloo, Ont.: Wilfrid Laurier University Press, 2006. Explores economic practices during the 1940's within the context of social and political pressures in the useful chapter "Paradise Postponed, 1939-50: World War II and Its Aftermath."

Gillespie, W. Irwin. *Tax, Borrow, and Spend: Financing Federal Spending in Canada, 1867-1990.* Ottawa: Carlton University Press, 1991. Chapters on financing war and postwar debt reduction provide excellent economic overviews. Appendixes provide data for nominal and real GNP and related economic factors.

Statistics Canada. *National Income and Expenditure Accounts: Annual Estimates, 1926-1986.* Ottawa: Canadian Government Publishing Centre, 1988. Bilingual publication provides brief prose notes and detailed tables of all economic indicators in Canada over a six-decade period.

See also Agriculture in Canada; Business and the economy in Canada; Credit and debt; Housing in Canada; Income and wages; International trade; Keynesian economics; King, William Lyon Mackenzie; Unemployment in Canada.

■ Gross national product of the United States

Definition Economic indicator that measures the value, at market prices, of the total national output of goods and services produced during a year

In 1940, concepts and measurements of gross national product were in their early stages. The measures showed the interaction among total spending for output, incomes received by the various segments of the economy, output, and prices.

Gross national product (GNP) measures the value of the nation's production. Products are included only as they reach their final buyer. Each product is valued at its market price. "Nominal" GNP has two dimensions, the quantity of output and the price level. Presumably the public's economic welfare increases as the quantity of production rises, as measured by "real" GNP adjusted to remove the effects of price increases. Pioneering statistical work involving GNP was done in the privately run National Bureau of Economic Research directed by Simon Kuznets. His landmark study, *National Income and Its Composition, 1919-1938*, appeared in 1941. By that time, his work had moved into the U.S. Department of Commerce.

Between 1940 and 1942, the nominal GNP of the United States increased by 50 percent; however, half of this increase merely reflected price increases. After price controls were firmly in place, price increases between 1942 and 1945 were not nearly so large. Peak wartime production yielded a quantity of output in 1945 that was 50 percent above that of 1940. The rise in output was aided by putting the unemployed back to work and by drawing many women into the wage-labor force.

Wartime Spending GNP is the sum of expenditures to buy current output by households (consumption), by business firms purchasing physical capital goods (investment), and by government. Government spending enters GNP when government agencies buy goods and services, including their payrolls. The early 1940's witnessed a rise in government purchases to finance American involvement in World War II. By 1945 the government was spending more than five times as much as it had in 1940. With the end of the war that year, government spending was cut back severely. During the war, business investment (to buy capital goods such as machinery and buildings) fell below $10 billion by 1945. Then it jumped to levels much above those of the Depression years. Most surprising, American households were able to achieve a major rise in their consumption levels during the war, even after adjusting for inflation. Family incomes rose greatly as formerly unemployed persons went back to work or into military service and many women entered the labor force.

As Keynesian economics became popular during the 1940's, American economists came to view nominal GNP as a measure of the aggregate demand for goods and services. The experience of the 1940's indicated that vigorous expansion of aggregate demand could reduce the unemployment rate and greatly increase total output. However, many economists feared that after wartime spending was cut back, private investment spending would not be sufficient to offset saving, and the national economy might again lapse into a depression. Such fears motivated adoption of the Employment Act of 1946. The Council of Economic Advisers established by this law, focussed continuing attention on the behavior of GNP. As GNP data became available, economists developed statistical techniques—known as econometrics—in attempts to forecast postwar levels of consumption, investment, and saving. These forecasts were generally pessimistic, but they were also wrong. Private investment surged to take up the slack created when government spending was cut after 1945. Public policy continued to give attention to GNP and to techniques of "demand management," notably monetary policy (conducted by the Federal Reserve) and fiscal policy (changes in government spending and tax rates).

Money and Velocity   GNP can also be expressed as the quantity of money (M) multiplied by its velocity (V), with V representing the average number of times each dollar is spent to buy currently produced goods and services in a year. The velocity of money is inversely related to the proportion of income that people choose to hold in the form of money. For example, a velocity approximating 1.5 reflects desired money holdings equal to two-thirds of GNP. That level was surprisingly stable across 1940, 1945, and 1949. Thus the increase in nominal GNP across those years was proportional to the increase in the money supply. Most of the increase in M resulted from expansion of bank credit as banks bought secu-

rities issued by the Treasury to finance government deficits.

GNP as the Sum of Income Components   The elements of GNP were defined and measured in such a way that all the money spent to buy current output would become income for someone—households, businesses, or government. The bulk of the increase in GNP expenditures over the 1940's flowed to workers and to owners of business. Employee compensation (including fringe benefits) rose from $52 billion to $142 billion, and business income increased from $23 to $66 billion.

As economists refined Keynesian analysis during the 1940's, an increasingly important concern was the relationship between saving and investment. Saving potentially withdrew money from the expenditure flow, while investment spending put it back. So long as saving financed investment, there would be no problem of maintaining the flow of expenditure. However, if saving potentially exceeded investment, more money would be taken out of the flow than put back, and the flow itself would decline, reducing output and employment.

Personal saving increased greatly during the war, rising to one-fifth of disposable income by 1945. However, this trend reflected abnormal wartime conditions reflected in the fact that automobiles and other durables were unavailable to buy. Many households feared there would be a postwar depression and built up their holdings of cash and savings bonds in self-defense. The war's end brought new

---

Nominal and Real Gross National Product (GNP)

In billions of dollars

Year	Nominal GNP	Real GNP	Price index in 1929 prices (1929 = 100)
1940	101	121	83
1942	159	155	103
1945	214	181	118
1949	258	171	151

Source: U.S. Bureau of the Census. *Historical Statistics of the United States, Colonial Times to 1957.* Washington, D.C.: Government Printing Office, 1960, p. 139.

products pouring on the market. It became clear that prices were not going to fall back to earlier levels, but would rise a lot. Millions of recently released veterans wanted to marry, have children, and buy homes. Consumer spending, which had dropped to only 80 percent of disposable income by 1945, rebounded to 95 percent by 1949.

Impact The development of gross national product accounting greatly aided the government in assessing the tendency for higher government spending to raise household incomes and consumption spending. The surging aggregate demand measured by GNP stimulated rapid growth in output and employment but also generated upward pressure on prices. By 1949, government was expected to use monetary and fiscal policies to help manage aggregate demand to achieve full employment.

Paul B. Trescott

Further Reading

Carson, Carol S. "The History of the United States National Income and Product Accounts." *Review of Income and Wealth* 21, no. 2 (June, 1975): 153-181, Clear and simple description of the meaning and interpretation of income data, as well as the statistical techniques used to compile them.

Carter, Susan, et al., eds. *Historical Statistics of the United States: Earliest Times to the Present.* New York, Cambridge University Press, 2006. Comprehensive reference source on economic statistics. Includes a very readable overview of national income accounting by Richard Sutch. Most data on gross national product are in this chapter, but more can be found in other chapters.

Hughes, Jonathan, and Louis P. Cain. *American Economic History.* 4th ed. New York: HarperCollins, 1994. Chapters 26 and 28 of this volume provide a concise assessment of the 1940's centered around gross national product and its components.

Samuelson, Paul, and William D. Nordhaus. *Economics.* 19th ed. New York: McGraw-Hill, 2010. First published in 1948, Samuelson's now-classic work was the first major college textbook to cover gross national product, with an extensive layout of its components and a Keynesian analytical structure to explain aggregate demand, output, and employment.

Trescott, Paul B. *Money, Banking and Economic Welfare,* New York: McGraw-Hill, 1960. Chapter 17 of this book presents a macroeconomic view of the 1940's, centered around GNP and its components.

Wilson, Richard L., ed. *Historical Encyclopedia of American Business.* 3 vols. Pasadena, Calif.: Salem Press, 2009. Comprehensive reference work on American business history that contains substantial essays on almost every conceivable aspect of U.S. economic history.

See also Business and the economy in the United States; Credit and debt; Fair Deal; Housing in the United States; Income and wages; Inflation; Keynesian economics; Social sciences; Unemployment in the United States.

■ Groves, Leslie Richard

Identification Head of the project that developed the first atomic bomb

Born August 17, 1896; Albany, New York

Died July 13, 1970; Washington, D.C.

As the head of the Manhattan Project, Groves played a key role in the research and development that led to the creation of the first atomic bombs, which were used to hasten the end of World War II in the Pacific theater of the war.

As the son of a U.S. Army chaplain, Leslie Richard Groves seemed destined to a career in the military service. After briefly attending the University of Washington and the Massachusetts Institute of Technology, he entered the U.S. Military Academy at West Point. He received his commission as a second lieutenant in the Army Corps of Engineers in 1918 after graduating fourth in his class.

Over the next twenty years, Groves worked for the Army Corps of Engineers on numerous assignments throughout the United States and Nicaragua and saw service during World War I. Through all his work he gained the reputation of being highly energetic, forceful, and effective, but he was also regarded as abrasive and ruthless. In 1931, he was attached to the Office of the Chief of Engineers in Washington, D.C. Three years later, he was promoted to captain. In 1939, he was assigned to the general staff in Washington. The following year, he was promoted to major and temporary colonel in 1940 and was responsible for overseeing the construction of the Pentagon building.

On September 17, 1942, Groves was selected to

head the Manhattan Project, also known as the Manhattan Engineering District, which was created to develop nuclear weapons. Groves oversaw the construction of many of the factories built to produce highly enriched uranium and plutonium, and he helped select the sites and personnel for the facilities at Los Alamos, New Mexico; Oak Ridge, Tennessee; and Pasco, Washington, that would develop and test the first atomic bombs. Building these facilities required making contracts with many firms, such as du Pont, Union Carbide, and Eastman Kodak. Groves selected J. Robert Oppenheimer, a theoretical physicist, to direct the laboratory research at Los Alamos. Funded with a $2 billion budget (measured in 1945 dollars) and employing almost 175,000 people, the Manhattan Project developed a nuclear-fission bomb, which was successfully tested at Alamogordo, New Mexico, on July 16, 1945.

As the bomb was being developed, Groves also oversaw the production of several dozen B-29 aircraft that were specially designed to carry five-ton bombs. Groves also organized the 509th Composite Group of the Army Air Force, which would deliver the bombs, and oversaw the establishment of special training bases for the planes' crews on Tinian, an island located near Guam in the Pacific Ocean, and at Wendover, Utah. All these many operations were conducted in almost total secrecy, which was never breached under Groves's leadership.

For his role in the planning of the atomic-bomb attacks on the Japanese cities of Hiroshima and Nagasaki in August, 1945, Groves was awarded the Distinguished Service Medal in 1945 and promoted to permanent brigadier general.

Postwar Career   After the dropping of the bombs on Japan brought about the end of World War II, Groves continued as head of the Manhattan Project. In this capacity, he was responsible for a massive U.S. stockpiling of nuclear weapons until the end of 1946, when his project was placed under the direction of the new Atomic Energy Commission. In 1948, Groves retired from the U.S. Army and returned to civilian life. However, he remained active as vice president in charge of research at the Remington Rand Corporation until his final retirement in 1961. At Remington Rand, he was responsible for the development of the UNIVAC computer.

After retiring, Groves wrote several books, gave many speeches, and presented General Douglas MacArthur with the Sylvanus Thayer Award at West Point in 1962. Groves died from heart disease on July 13, 1970, and was buried at Arlington National Cemetery, where his wife was buried with him. Along the Columbia River the Leslie Groves Park is a memorial to him, which is appropriately located less than five miles from the site of the former Hanford Nuclear Reservation near Pasco, Washington.

Jean L. Kuhler

Further Reading

Hales, Peter B. *Atomic Spaces: Living on the Manhattan Project.* Urbana: University of Illinois Press, 1997.

Kelly, Cynthia C. *Remembering the Manhattan Project: Perspectives on the Making of the Atomic Bomb and Its Legacy.* Hackensack, N.J.: World Scientific, 2004.

Norris, Robert S. *Racing for the Bomb: General Leslie R. Groves, the Manhattan Project's Indispensable Man.* South Royalton, Vt.: Steerforth Press, 2002.

Rhodes, Richard. *The Making of the Atomic Bomb.* New York: Simon & Schuster, 1986.

Stoff, Michael B., Jonathan F. Fanton, and R. Hal Williams, eds. *The Manhattan Project: A Documentary Introduction to the Atomic Age.* Philadelphia: Temple University Press, 1991.

See also   Atomic bomb; *Enola Gay*; Fermi, Enrico; Hanford Nuclear Reservation; *Hiroshima*; Hiroshima and Nagasaki bombings; Manhattan Project; Nuclear reactors; Oppenheimer, J. Robert.

■ Guadalcanal, Battle of

The Event   First significant U.S. offensive against Japan during World War II
Date   August 7, 1942-February 7, 1943
Place   Southern Solomon Islands

The U.S. invasion of Guadalcanal and nearby islands stopped the Japanese advance toward Australia and New Zealand, dealt the Japanese army a crushing defeat, leaving the Japanese military primarily on the defensive for the rest of the war.

After inflicting severe losses on the Japanese navy at the battles of Coral Sea and Midway, the Allies decided to launch their first significant offensive in the Pacific theater by seizing a Japanese airfield on Guadalcanal as well as attacking naval facilities on nearby islands. U.S. Marines landed on the islands, which

Battle of Guadalcanal, 1942-1943

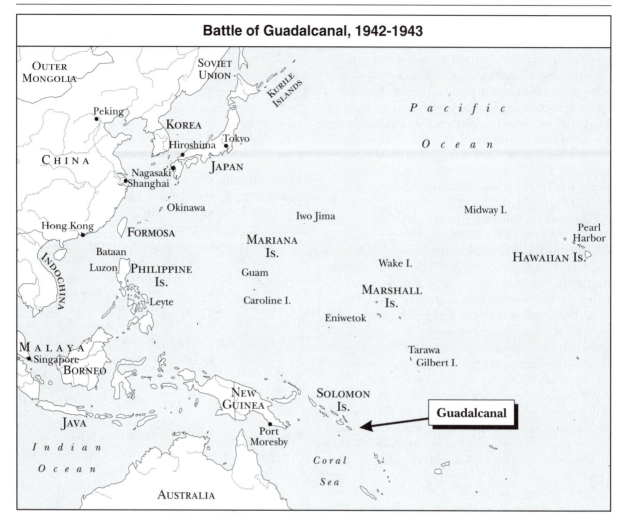

lie to the northeast of Australia, on August 7, seized the airfield that day, and conquered the neighboring islands in the next few days. The American invasion triggered an immediate countermove by the Japanese, who landed additional troops on Guadalcanal determined to retake the newly named Henderson airfield. A Japanese ground attempt to retake the airfield on August 21 was crushed, but the sinking of four U.S. naval cruisers during the Battle of Savo Island forced the U.S. Navy to withdraw temporarily, stranding the Marines on Guadalcanal and allowing the Japanese to land more soldiers on the island.

From August through October, the Japanese attempted to create a numerical advantage in troops by transporting soldiers from their New Britain base in Rabaul through a chain of islands—the "slot"—southeast to Guadalcanal. The Americans tried to interdict them and strengthen their own position. The clash of navies resulted in three major, though indecisive, battles, at the Eastern Solomons, Cape Esperance, and Santa Cruz Islands. The Marines, despite frequent nighttime Japanese air and naval bombardments that they called the "Tokyo Express," held on defensively, and they decisively defeated major Japanese assaults in September (the Battle of "Bloody Ridge") and October (the Battle for Henderson Field).

By November, the tide of the campaign turned. Three naval battles in November—Guadalcanal I, Guadalcanal II, and Tassafaronga—led to significant ship losses for both sides, leading the waters off the northeast coast of Guadalcanal to become known as "Ironbottom Sound." Tactically, the naval contests amounted to a draw; strategically, Japanese troop transport losses stemmed the flow of soldiers to the island and forced the Japanese to switch to a defensive role. A Marine offensive that began on November 1 was augmented by Army units who had landed on the island in October. By December, the Japanese had decided to fight a delaying action and remove their forces from Guadalcanal. Japanese strongpoints called "galloping horse," "sea horse," and Gifu were conquered by mid-January, and Japan's headquarters at Kokumbon was taken on January 23. The Japanese successfully withdrew between 10,000 and 13,000 troops from Cape Esperance in early February, ending the campaign.

American losses were high and not fully released to the public until years later: approximately 7,000 men (1,600 dead), more than 600 aircraft, and 30 ships. Two of the five aircraft carriers and seven of the ten heavy and light cruisers sunk during World War II were lost during the Guadalcanal campaign. Japanese losses were higher: approximately 25,000 men (battle and disease), nearly 700 planes, and an estimated 30 ships.

Impact The battle for Guadalcanal was the single longest American campaign during the war and was one of the turning points in the Pacific war theater, along with the Battle of Midway. Strategically, the American victory forced the Japanese to abandon hope of further conquests in the South Pacific; for the remainder of the war, Japan emphasized primarily a defensive posture. Psychologically, Guadalcanal provided a huge morale boost for Americans on the home front and was a stunning blow to Japanese war aspirations.

Paul J. Chara, Jr.

Further Reading

Hammel, Eric. *Guadalcanal: The U.S. Marines in World War II: A Pictorial Tribute.* Osceola, Wis.: Zenith Press, 2007.

Jersey, Stanley Coleman. *Hell's Islands: The Untold Story of Guadalcanal.* College Station: Texas A&M University Press, 2008.

Tregaskis, Richard. *Guadalcanal Diary.* New York: Modern Library, 2000.

See also Aircraft carriers; Army, U.S.; Casualties of World War II; *History of the United States Naval Operations in World War II*; Landing craft, amphibious; Marines, U.S.; Navy, U.S.; World War II.

■ Guthrie, Woody

Identification   American composer and folk singer
Born   July 14, 1912; Okemah, Oklahoma
Died   October 3, 1967; Queens, New York

Widely known as the composer of "This Land Is Your Land," Guthrie focused his attention on the less fortunate of American society throughout the 1940's. In so doing, he painted an elaborate picture not only of the diversity of the American landscape—particularly the vast Southwest—but also of the imbalances in its social structures.

Much of Woody Guthrie's association with the American Southwest influence predates the 1940's. However, his earlier life in Oklahoma, Texas, and California formed a solid foundation that flowed from his creative mind into the 1940's and beyond. In February, 1940, he made the geographical transition to the urban environment of New York City. There he built a number of personal connections with other singers and musicians, such as Pete Seeger, Huddie "Leadbelly" Ledbetter, and Alan Lomax—all of whom recorded some of his earlier folk songs and other compositions within a month of his arrival in New York.

Guthrie's move to New York occasioned his transition from a provincial songster emerging from the 1930's Dust Bowl experience to a more stylish and polished spokesperson for left-wing socialist values. By this time, his experiences had already included riding the rails as a hobo, radio appearances, and writing a weekly column, "Woody Sez," for the communist newspaper, *The Daily Worker.* In New York, he began appearing regularly on a popular radio program, *Back Where I Come From.*

In 1941, twenty-six songs Guthrie wrote for Washington State's Bonneville Power Administration were used to help promote sale of state bonds to finance the big hydroelectric dam project so it could bring cheap electricity to poverty-stricken rural towns. During the same year, he also traveled around the United States with Pete Seeger and others in a group called the Almanac Singers. Their goal was to encourage the formation of labor unions that would fight injustices in the capitalist system.

Guthrie's autobiography, *Bound for Glory,* which he published in 1943, recalls events in his life, from his early childhood through the beginning of World War II, when he joined the merchant marine. His

Woody Guthrie performing on radio in March, 1943. (AP/Wide World Photos)

major musical works of the 1940's include such albums as *Dust Bowl Ballads, Deep Sea Chanteys and Whaling Ballads*, and *Sod-Buster Ballads*. He also recorded more than one hundred individual songs with Moses Asch, the founder of Folkway Records. Among the best known of these are "Pastures of Plenty," "This Land Is Your Land," "Sinking of the Reuben James," "Worried Man Blues," "Roll on Columbia," "So Long, It's Been Good to Know You," and "Go Tell Aunty Rhody." Many of these were his original compositions; others were traditional folk songs sung with his own special flavorings.

Impact Guthrie was one of the most influential American cultural figures of the twentieth century. He established the modern genre of the traveling folk poet while defending himself and his work from a variety of would-be censors.

Dennis E. Ferguson

Further Reading

Buchstein, Fred. "Woody Guthrie." In *Popular Musicians*, edited by Steve Hochman. Pasadena, Calif.: Salem Press, 1999.

Guthrie, Woody. *Bound for Glory*. Introduction by Joe Klein. New York: Penguin Classics, 2004.

Klein, Joe. *Woody Guthrie: A Life*. New York: Delta, 1999.

See also Anticommunism; Communist Party USA; New Deal programs; Seeger, Pete; Williams, Hank.

H

■ Hairstyles

Definition   Cuts and arrangements of hair, many of which reflected sentiments and practical needs of World War II

Women's hairstyles during the 1940's were curled, feminine, and dressed, though as the decade progressed hairstyles grew simpler and practical due to war shortages. Headscarves, turbans, and snoods were popular options for women who covered their hair in the workplace for safety, vanity, and other reasons.

During the 1940's, women took cues from Hollywood as to how to style their hair. Hair was parted on the side, mimicking Veronica Lake's peek-a-boo style of long hair with curled ends. Vivien Leigh's nineteenth century snood in *Gone with the Wind* (1939) inspired women to contain the length of their hair in a fashionable net. Upswept styles like the pompadour and chignon were fashionable yet practical for keeping hair out of the way. The pompadour's smooth crown allowed hat wearing, though hats fell somewhat out of fashion by the end of the decade. The omelette was parted at the back and styled in a criss-cross to produce a folded effect. The victory roll, introduced after the war, was named for the *V* shape made between the rolls on each side of the head. "Rats," or pads, were used underneath the hair to give it form, shape, and stability in this ornate style. The bubble cut was inspired by Ingrid Bergman's hair in *For Whom the Bell Tolls* (1943).

As women entered industrial workplaces to meet the war's need for labor, they used turbans, headscarves, and snoods to prevent long hair from falling into machinery and tangling, which could result in serious injury. Bangs were waved and modeled after Betty Grable's style. Women often covered their hair to hide oiliness resulting from lack of shampoo. In factories, women tied scarves over rollers and pin curls so that a complex curled style would be formed by evening. Visits to salons were rare, and most hairstyling was done at home, including bleaching using peroxide. Women were resourceful and used rags as curlers to attain sausage ringlet styles. As styling products grew scarce, a concoction of sugar and water was used with pipe cleaners to set curls.

During the early 1940's, film star Veronica Lake made famous the peek-a-boo look—long hair that often covered one of her eyes. She later admitted that she always regarded that style as foolish and was consequently glad to make a government film in 1943 in which she demonstrated the danger of wearing long hair near machinery. (AP/Wide World Photos)

African American women straightened their hair to dress it according to fashions depicted in white fashion magazines but also drew inspiration from actors such as Lena Horne and Dorothy Dandridge. Popular hairstyling tools included straightening irons, steel curling irons, crimping irons, marcel irons, and electric permanent wave machines. Chemical hair relaxers were developed and advertised just after the war. The brushed-straight style was popular, and products such as Satin Tress hair relaxer helped maintain "sleek cap" hairstyles.

The war and its deprivations had little effect on men's hairstyles. The most common style was traditional, with short sides and back, and was based on Army regulations stipulating that hair at the back not touch the collar. Men kept their hair longer on top and usually parted their hair on the side, keeping it swept across the head and in place with pomade or brilliantine. Civilian males adopted crew cut, butch, and flattop styles. Many African American men wore their hair "conked," straightening it chemically with a hair relaxer. Once conked, the hair was styled in a pompadour or quaff, or slicked back against the head. Conks took effort to maintain, and men wore do-rags at night to keep sweat from taking hair back to its natural state.

Impact   Hairstyles of the decade were elaborate but modified by wartime, with too much frippery considered unpatriotic. By 1945, hairstyles were longer again, with a trend toward upswept styles and topknots. The decade saw a variety of styles, so that women could choose ones most flattering to them as individuals.

Rebecca Tolley-Stokes

Further Reading

Turudich, Daniela. *1940's Hairstyles*. Long Beach, Calif.: Streamline Press, 2001.

Walker, Susannah. *Style and Status: Selling Beauty to African-American Women, 1920-1971*. Lexington: University Press of Kentucky, 2007.

See also   Fads; Fashions and clothing; Film in the United States; *For Whom the Bell Tolls*; Grable, Betty; Horne, Lena; "Rosie the Riveter"; Wartime industries; Women in the U.S. military; Women's roles and rights in the United States.

■ Hale telescope

Identification   200-inch telescope erected at Palomar Observatory
Date   Dedicated on June 3, 1948
Place   San Diego County, California

For nearly three decades after its construction, the Hale telescope was the largest telescope in the world. It remained one of the world's five largest telescopes until early in the twenty-first century, when several larger telescopes were built. It remains a major research facility.

The idea for a 200-inch (5-meter) telescope originated with George Ellery Hale as early as 1928. Hale secured a grant from the Rockefeller Foundation to build a new observatory. The site for the telescope, on Palomar Mountain in northern San Diego County, California, was selected in 1935. The telescope's mirror used Pyrex glass with a waffled back to reduce weight. Upon completion, the mirror blank was shipped across the country from New York's Corning Glass Works to a mirror laboratory in Pasadena, California, where it was to be ground into the proper shape for use in the new telescope. Long before it was finished, however, the nation was plunged into World War II. Work on the mirror stopped and did not resume until 1945. In 1947, the mirror was moved to the Palomar Observatory, where it was installed in the telescope. The telescope was named for its creator, who had died in 1938. Operations at the observatory began in 1948, nearly two decades after the telescope was conceived.

Impact   As the world's largest telescope, the Hale telescope was a source of pride for American scientists. It was also seen by many as an important symbol for the peaceful uses of science following the weapons developed during World War II. The telescope remained the largest effective telescope in the world until 1993, when it was surpassed in size and resolving power by the Keck 1 telescope in Hawaii.

Raymond D. Benge, Jr.

Further Reading

Florence, Ronald. *The Perfect Machine: Building the Palomar Telescope*. New York: HarperCollins, 1994.

Mason, Todd, and Robin Mason. "Palomar's Big Eye." *Sky and Telescope* (December, 2008): 36-41.

Osterbrock, Donald E. *Pauper and Prince: Ritchey,*

Hale, and Big American Telescopes. Tucson: University of Arizona Press, 1993.

See also   Astronomy; Inventions; Science and technology; Wartime industries.

■ Hallaren, Mary A.

Identification   American military leader
Born   May 4, 1907; Lowell, Massachusetts
Died   February 13, 2005; McLean, Virginia

Hallaren was the first woman commissioned an officer in the regular U.S. Army. Her leadership of the Women's Army Corps expanded opportunities for women in the armed forces during and after World War II, and she worked to convert the corps from auxiliary status to permanent status as part of the regular Army.

Mary Agnes Hallaren's desire to serve her country as her brothers were doing led her to join the Women's Army Auxiliary Corps (WAAC) in 1942. In August of that year, she was selected to be in the first class at the WAAC Officer Candidate School at Fort Des Moines, Iowa. Hallaren's first assignment was to be assistant WAAC commandant at the second WAAC Training Center in Daytona Beach, Florida. In July, 1943, her battalion was sent to Europe, the first WAAC battalion to serve in the European theater of operations in World War II. She served as the WAAC staff director attached to the U.S. Eighth and Ninth Air Forces.

From June, 1945, to June, 1946, Hallaren was the WAAC staff director in Europe. She was selected by General Dwight D. Eisenhower to oversee the transition of the WAAC to the Women's Army Corps (WAC). In May, 1947, she was promoted to colonel, becoming the first woman commissioned in the regular Army. She served as the WAC director from December, 1948, through May, 1953. As WAC director, she worked with Congress to enact the Women's Armed Services Integration Act of 1948, making the WAC a permanent part of the military.

Impact   Hallaren was a leader in expanding the opportunities for women in the U.S. military. She remained humble about her effect on the lives of women, explaining to interviewers that she was only being a good citizen serving her country.

John David Rausch, Jr.

Further Reading

Brokaw, Tom. *The Greatest Generation.* New York: Random House, 1998.

Nathan, Amy. *Count on Us: American Women in the Military.* Washington, D.C.: National Geographic Society, 2004.

Witt, Linda. *"A Defense Weapon Known to Be a Value": Servicewomen of the Korean War Era.* Hanover, N.H.: University Press of New England, 2005.

See also   Army, U.S.; Eisenhower, Dwight D.; Women in the U.S. military; Women's roles and rights in the United States; World War II mobilization.

■ Halsey, William F. "Bull"

Identification   American naval admiral
Born   October 30, 1882; Elizabeth, New Jersey
Died   August 16, 1959; Fisher's Island, New York

One of the most colorful figures of the Pacific theater in World War II, Halsey helped restore the morale of American forces after the devastating attack on Pearl Harbor.

Barrel-chested and craggy-faced, Admiral William F. Halsey had an aggressive personality that earned him the nickname "Bull," although friends always called him "Bill." He was trained on destroyers but saw the growing importance of naval aviation and learned to fly so that he would be able to command an aircraft carrier. As the 1940's opened, he saw that the war would soon involve the United States.

When Japan struck a blow against the United States with its December 7, 1941, attack on Pearl Harbor, Halsey swore to strike back. Within hours after putting to port at the damaged Pearl Harbor, his task force was under way once again, heading out to strike the Japanese-held Marshall Islands. Over the next several months, Halsey commanded a number of such missions, working himself to exhaustion and thus unable to command at the Battle of Midway in June, 1942.

After recuperating in the United States, Halsey returned to duty for the battle for Guadalcanal, which began in August, 1942, and he helped revitalize the demoralized fighting forces. His performance at the Battle of Leyte Gulf, October 23-26, 1944, came under heavy criticism, largely because of his ill-considered chase after a group of nearly worthless ships that left another U.S. task force without cover at a key point in the battle. Leading task forces into two separate typhoons added to his growing reputation as a heedless and impetuous officer. Military command considered putting him at a desk job, where he could not make such dangerous decisions, but the effect of his removal upon fleet morale was deemed to be more destructive. He remained in place through the Japanese surrender. At that time, his flagship was the USS *Missouri*, on which the surrender was signed at Tokyo Bay.

Impact   Although Halsey was no great strategist, his determination to go straight at the enemy made him valuable to the U.S. Navy in the first months after Pearl Harbor, when American morale was low. In a series of daring raids on various Japanese outposts, he showed his forces that they could fight back and that the Japanese were not invincible, no matter how successful they had been in the initial strike at Pearl Harbor. As the war progressed, he was progressively eclipsed by the cooler-headed Raymond Spruance, but his contribution was still sufficiently significant that Chester Nimitz chose him as one of the men to

stand behind him while he signed the surrender documents on behalf of U.S. forces.

Leigh Husband Kimmel

Further Reading

Drury, Bob, and Tom Clavin. *Halsey's Typhoon: The True Story of a Fighting Admiral, an Epic Storm, and an Untold Rescue.* New York: Atlantic Monthly Press, 2007.

Potter, E. B. *Bull Halsey.* Annapolis, Md.: Naval Institute Press, 1985.

Sears, David. *The Last Epic Naval Battle: Voices from Leyte Gulf.* New York: NAL Caliber, 2005.

See also   Guadalcanal, Battle of; Japan, occupation of; Navy, U.S.; Nimitz, Chester W.

William F. Halsey. (Library of Congress)

■ Hanford Nuclear Reservation

Identification   First plutonium production facility
Also known as   Hanford Engineer Works
Date   Established in March, 1943
Place   By the Columbia River, near Pasco, Washington

The plutonium used in the first atomic bomb test and in the Nagasaki atomic bomb was produced, separated, and refined at the Hanford Nuclear Reservation.

Because of size and safety constraints at other sites involved with the Manhattan Project (the code name for the project to develop an atomic bomb), a new site was found for the plutonium production facility. For safety and security reasons, an isolated area on the Columbia River in Washington State was chosen. Within two years, the site went from an almost empty area to a working facility. The pace of building the plant was phenomenal. Within thirty months, 554 buildings for the plant as well as housing and other buildings for the tens of thousands of workers were built.

As well as the buildings, new technology had to be developed. Plutonium had been produced only a few years before, and its properties were mostly unknown. The equipment to produce the plutonium, separate it, and refine it had to be developed as it was built.

Hanford was successful. On February 3, 1945, the first shipment of plutonium was sent from Hanford to Los Alamos, New Mexico, another site of the

Manhattan Project. Soon, a new shipment was made every five days. The first test atomic bomb, Trinity, and the Nagasaki bomb, Fat Man, were plutonium bombs. The Nagasaki bomb was dropped on August 9, 1945; six days later, Japan offered unconditional surrender.

After World War II ended, Hanford still produced weapons-grade plutonium for the "Cold War" armament. The facility was expanded but operated at a less frantic pace. Two plutonium bombs were exploded at the Bikini Atoll as a demonstration of atomic power.

Although the facility had always been more closely monitored for radiation than other industrial facilities, no one really knew the effects of long-term exposure or the effects on the environment. There was concern for the workers. A manual of procedures was produced with the idea of reducing the amount of radiation exposure. Because little was known of the long-term effects, radioactive materials were not intentionally released into the environment. The waste materials were stored in the hope that radiation levels could be reduced to safe levels at a later time.

Impact The Hanford Nuclear Reservation was an important part of the Manhattan Project, whose purpose was to build an atomic weapon. This was achieved, at a cost of $1.8 to $2.2 billion. The Hanford Nuclear Reservation was an expensive part of that total. Knowledge acquired while building the Hanford facility has been extremely useful in many areas of science. Building a nuclear reactor that would continuously produce energy, separating the radioactive materials, using remote-control devices, and building remote-control devices are just a few of the areas in which knowledge was pushed forward by building and operating the Hanford facility. The effects of radiation on equipment, on people, and on

Nuclear waste storage facility under construction at the Hanford Nuclear Reservation in 1944. (U.S. Department of Energy)

the environment are valuable pieces of knowledge also contributed by the Hanford facility. There is some concern that these lessons were learned at a high cost of contaminating the environment.

C. Alton Hassell

Further Reading

Dalton, Russell J., et al. *Critical Masses: Citizens, Nuclear Weapons Production, and Environmental Destruction in the United States and Russia.* Cambridge, Mass.: MIT Press, 1999.

Energy Research and Development Administration. Richland Operations Office. *Hanford, Yesterday, Today, and Tomorrow.* Hanford, Wash.: U.S. Energy Research and Development Administration. Richland Operations Office, 1975.

Raven, Peter H, Linda R Berg, and David M. Hassenzahl. *Environment.* Hoboken, N.J.: John Wiley & Sons, 2008.

See also Atomic bomb; *Enola Gay*; Groves, Leslie Richard; Hiroshima and Nagasaki bombings; Nuclear reactors; Oppenheimer, J. Robert; Plutonium discovery.

■ Harlem Globetrotters

Identification Traveling African American basketball team combining athletic skills with comedic showmanship

At a time when African American players were banned from many sports leagues, including the National Basketball Association, the Harlem Globetrotters simultaneously entertained audiences with comedic routines and proved that their athletic prowess equaled that of white players, thus paving the way for future acceptance into those leagues.

Founded by Abe Saperstein in 1926 in Chicago, the Harlem Globetrotters slowly built a reputation over the next decade as entertaining yet skilled athletes. They originally played serious basketball, but because they usually led opponents by many points, they eventually began clowning around, inventing wild antics that audiences welcomed enthusiastically. In 1940, the Globetrotters soared to new heights when they won their first World Basketball Championship title. Later that year, they lost narrowly to a college all-star team, helping to secure their reputation.

In 1946, the National Basketball Association (NBA) was formed, but it included no African American players. In 1948, the all-black Globetrotters narrowly defeated the NBA's all-white Minneapolis Lakers in a historic match. The Globetrotters continued to sell out arenas across the country, developing signature comedy routines but always displaying impressive athleticism.

Impact The Harlem Globetrotters greatly helped promote the acceptance of African American athletes in the United States. During the late 1940's, the Globetrotters often played NBA teams in exhibition games, providing increased exposure to both parties. During the 1950's, the team was featured in films and television shows, which helped ensure that their popularity would endure for decades to come.

Amy Sisson

Further Reading

Christgau, John. *Tricksters in the Madhouse: Lakers vs. Globetrotters, 1948.* Lincoln: University of Nebraska Press, 2004.

Green, Ben. *Spinning the Globe: The Rise, Fall, and Return to Greatness of the Harlem Globetrotters.* New York: Amistad/HarperCollins, 2005.

See also African Americans; Basketball; Sports in the United States.

■ Hayworth, Rita

Identification American film star
Born October 17, 1918; Brooklyn, New York
Died May 14, 1987; New York, New York

A popular female star during the 1940's, Hayworth set the standard as a feminine sex symbol for a generation of Americans.

Born Margarita Carmen Cansino, Rita Hayworth was the daughter of Eduardo Casino, a vaudeville performer, and Volga Hayworth, a Ziegfeld Follies showgirl. In 1937, she legally changed her name to Rita Hayworth and signed a multiyear contract with Columbia Pictures Corporation. In 1939, she earned her first leading role, in the film *Only Angels Have Wings*. By the early 1940's, she had starred in numerous box-office successes, including the musicals *You'll Never Get Rich* (1941), *My Gal Sal* (1942), *You Were Never Lovelier* (1942), and *Cover Girl* (1944).

In 1941, *Life* magazine published a seductive photograph of Hayworth wearing black lace. The photograph of the five foot, six inch beauty—relatively tall for her time—not only became a favorite pinup for American servicemen during World War II but also catapulted Hayworth to superstardom. She became even more popular after she starred in the film *Gilda* (1946), in which she performed a seductive striptease. Hayworth ended the decade with the films *Down to Earth* (1947), *The Lady from Shanghai* (1948), and *The Loves of Carmen* (1948).

Impact During the 1940's, Hayworth's sensuality on screen and in photographs defined what constituted a glamorous movie star and sex symbol. Hayworth continues to be considered one of the most talented and sexiest movie stars in American cinematic history.

Bernadette Zbicki Heiney

Further Reading

Leaming, Barbara. *If This Was Happiness: A Biography of Rita Hayworth.* New York: Viking Press, 1989.

McLean, Adrienne L. *Being Rita Hayworth: Labor,*

Identity and Hollywood Stardom. New Brunswick, N.J.: Rutgers University Press, 2004.

See also Film in the United States; Garland, Judy; Grable, Betty; *Life*; Lombard, Carole; Pinup girls; Welles, Orson.

■ Health care

Despite the casualties generated by combat, World War II stimulated improvement in health care for people inducted into the military. The 1940's accelerated such important developments as antibiotic medications and employer-provided medical-expense insurance. Infant and maternal mortality was significantly reduced, and life expectancy increased in both the United States and Canada

World War II produced major short-run and long-run effects on health and medical care. About 16 million Americans served in the military during the war. Ten million American men were inducted through the military draft. Deaths in combat numbered about 292,000, and an additional 114,000 died from noncombat causes. The number who sustained nonfatal wounds was about 671,000.

For those neither killed nor wounded, military service brought strongly positive influences on health and medical care. Military service provided exercise and abundant nutrition, as well as cost-free access to medical personnel, including dentists. Total military medical admissions were estimated at about 23.4 million. On average, then, each service person experienced between one and two medical admissions. Military people received numerous vaccinations and inoculations. After their discharge, veterans had access to the extensive medical and hospital facilities of the Veterans Administration (VA). Although theoretically restricted to service-connected problems and to low-income veterans, these restrictions were not rigorously enforced. In 1940, VA expenditures on medical, hospital and domiciliary care totaled only $78 million. By 1949, the total was about $700 million.

The war also stimulated government research into treatment of many types of injuries and illnesses. In the summer of 1941, President Franklin D. Roosevelt established the Office of Scientific Research and Development (OSRD), with a component on medical research. This agency made major contributions to the development of penicillin and antimalarial drugs. By 1947 national expenditures on medical research were estimated at $87 million, The National Institute of Health, which had been created in 1930, accounted for $8 million of this expenditure.

Each potential draftee was subjected to a careful physical and psychological examination. Data for American men age eighteen through thirty-seven who were examined between October, 1940, and May, 1944, provide a good reflection of national health. Of the 16 million men examined, 5 million were rejected outright, 1.5 million were inducted and rehabilitated in the service, and another 1.5 million men were subsequently discharged for mental and physical defects not resulting from military conditions.

Life Expectancy and Mortality The decade of the 1940's brought forth a major improvement in life ex-

Life Expectancy at Birth, United States, 1940-1949

Year	All	White Men	White Women	Black and Other Ethnic Minority Men	Black and Other Ethnic Minority Women
1940	62.9	62.1	66.6	51.5	54.9
1945	65.9	64.4	69.5	56.1	59.6
1949	68.0	66.2	71.9	58.9	62.7
Percentage change, 1940-1949	+8.1	+6.6	+8.0	+14.4	+14.2

Source: U.S. Bureau of the Census. *Historical Statistics of the United States, Colonial Times to 1970, Bicentennial Edition, Part 2.* Washington, D.C.: U.S. Government Printing Office, 1975, p. 55.

Sign at a South Pacific Marine base encouraging the use of insecticides to combat insect-borne malaria. (AP/Wide World Photos)

pectancy at birth for Americans. From a life expectancy at birth of about 63 years in 1940, the figure rose to 68 years by 1949, for the entire population. The proportional improvement was much greater for African Americans and members of other ethnic minorities. However, even this improvement only slightly reduced the large disparity in life expectancy between white and nonwhite Americans that had existed in 1940. Aside from the major improvements in health care during the decade, life expectancy improved because of the return of prosperity and full employment to North America. People, in general were better fed, better housed, and better clothed than they had been during the 1930's. Moreover, they were also better able to afford doctor visits. Meanwhile, however, the public remained concerned about diseases such as syphilis and poliomyelitis. In 1949, there were 30,000 polio victims in North America.

Much of the improvement in life expectancy in the United States involved child-bearing. In Canada, life expectancy at birth showed very similar levels

and improvements. Between the census years of 1941 and 1951, life expectancy for male Canadians increased from 63.0 to 66.3 years, and that for female Canadians from 66.3 to 70.8 years. As in the United States, sharp decreases in infant mortality were a large contributor. Infant deaths from communicable diseases declined from 449 per 100,000 life births in 1941-1945 to 143 in 1951-1955. Infant deaths from diarrhea dropped from 625 to 211, from respiratory disease from 780 to 522, and from birth defects from 1092 to 865 over the same period.

In the United States, life expectancy improved for older people as well. This was true for ages 60 and 70, for whites and nonwhites, and for males and females. Canadian data for 1941 show life expectancies at age 60 about one year higher than those for white Americans, with similar improvements over the ensuing decade.

Costs of Health Care Expenditures in the United States for health services and supplies increased from $3.9 billion in 1940 to $10.8 billion in 1949. Part of this increase reflected inflation—the price index of medical goods and services increased by 43 percent. However, when adjusted to remove inflation, the total real output of medical goods and services approximately doubled. Health expenditures were about 4 percent of gross national product in 1940 and rose to 4.5 percent by 1949. This increase occurred despite the fact that the number of medical schools remained virtually unchanged, as did the number of physicians per capita.

The great postwar boom in higher education showed up in a great rise in applications to medical schools between 1939-1940 and 1949-1950. However, the increase in admissions to the schools was much smaller, as the number of schools able to take student increased only slightly. Meanwhile, legal barriers to licensing immigrant physicians were reduced. By 1950-1951, a total of 29,000 residency and internship positions were offered to newly trained doctors. About 2,000 of these positions were filled by foreign medical graduates; however, more than 7,000 positions were not filled at all.

In Canada, expenditures for hospitals, physicians and dentists rose from $172 million in 1940 to $407 million in 1949. Over that period, the consumer price index increased from 38.2 to 58.0. Adjusted to remove inflation, the real quantity of medical goods and services rose from $450 million in 1971 prices to $702 million, an increase of 56 percent. Over the decade, the number of physicians in Canada increased in step with population growth, but Canada had significantly fewer physicians per capita than the United States. In the United States, the ratio was about one physician for every 750 people; in Canada it was about one for every 970 people. The number of hospital beds in the United States increased more rapidly than the population (17 percent vs. 13 percent). Expansion was aided by the Hill-Burton Act of 1946, which began sustained federal financial aid for hospital construction and modernization. In Canada the 19 percent rise in the number of hospital beds slightly outpaced the 18 percent rise in population.

Technological Advances The decade saw important improvements in medicines. Sulfa drugs were introduced during the late 1930's but gained wide acceptance in treating military medical needs. The sulfa drugs, which originated in the German dye industry, worked by weakening the metabolism of harmful bacteria. Sulfa drugs were used against streptococcus infections, pneumonia, gonorrhea, meningitis, and many other diseases.

Sulfa was soon followed by modern antibiotics—bacterial agents that attacked harmful bacteria. The treatment of infections was greatly improved with the introduction of penicillin, which after having been used extensively for military personnel in 1943 soon became available for general use. Streptomycin was discovered in 1943 and used effectively against tuberculosis. Chlormycetin, which was found to be effective against typhus and typhoid fever, was first identified in soil samples. Parke, Davis produced it for general use in 1949.

The U.S. Atomic Energy Commission assisted in the development of nuclear medicine. Radiation as a part of cancer treatment was initiated in 1949. Many beneficial discoveries involved hormones and steroids. In 1949, localities began to promote the use of sodium fluoride to reduce tooth decay. Fluoridation of public water supplies became a highly controversial issue. Ultimately, however, the benefits went far beyond dental conditions when it was discovered that heart problems were closely related to dental problems.

Introduction of the insecticide DDT brought the incidence of malaria down from 59 cases per 100,000 population in 1940 to 3 cases in 1949. During the war, the federal government established the Office of Malaria Control in War Areas, headquartered in Atlanta, Georgia. In 1946, this agency was renamed the Communicable Disease Center and in 1970 it became the Centers for Disease Control. The numerous distressing effects of allergies were greatly reduced when antihistamines were developed. Benedryl, developed in 1946, was the first of many such drugstore remedies.

Monitoring of drug safety and drug advertising was extended by federal legislation in 1938. The Food, Drug, and Cosmetic Act required the Food and Drug Administration (FDA) to determine the safety of new drugs; it also extended FDA regulation to medical devices and cosmetics. The Wheeler-Lea Act of the same year gave the Federal Trade Commission authority to prevent false and misleading advertising.

World War II stimulated the development of new techniques for treating and storing blood plasma, paving the way for the expanding importance of blood donation. Birth control technology still relied mainly on condoms for men, but the female diaphragm was coming into use by 1950.

Health Insurance Very limited forms of medical expense insurance were provided by workmen's compensation. By 1940, each state had such a program,

Private Medical Expense Insurance in the United States, 1940-1949

Number of persons enrolled, in millions

Type	1940	1945	1949
Hospitalization	12.0	32.7	66.0
Blue Cross	6.0	18.9	33.4
Surgical	5.0	13.2	41.1
Blue Shield	0.4	2.5	11.9
Medical	3.0	4.7	16.9

Source: U.S. Bureau of the Census. *Historical Statistics of the United States: From Colonial Times to 1957.* Washington, D.C.: U.S. Government Printing Office, 1960, p. 677.

Note: Many persons were covered by more than one type of policy.

but their details varied widely. Similar programs were in place in Canada. Compensation was available for death or injury occurring in connection with one's job. Cash benefits were paid to disabled workers or to survivors. Typically, medical expenses of injured workers were paid. In most states, "workmen's comp" was arranged by individual employers with insurance companies. A few states managed their own funds. Total compensation payments in the United States in 1940 were $259 million, rising to $580 million by 1949. Payments specifically for medical expenses rose from $95 million in 1940 to $185 million in 1949. In 1940. about 25 million workers were covered, rising to 36 million by 1949.

Presidents Franklin D. Roosevelt and Harry S. Truman urged the U.S. Congress to adopt a federal program of medical-expense insurance, but none was adopted until the coming of Medicare during the 1960's. Instead, private medical insurance spread rapidly. The main focus was on insurance contracted by employers, who bore most of the premium cost. Employer-provided insurance provided a channel for evading wartime wage controls (which did not cover fringe benefits). Employer-paid premiums could be tax-deductible as business expenses but did not constitute taxable income for the workers.

Medical benefits began to be an element in collective bargaining by labor unions, which were gaining membership rapidly during the 1940's. By 1950, collective-bargaining agreements were committing employers to pay about one third of premiums for workers. In 1949, after a series of strikes, the United Mine Workers union, for example, created a health and welfare fund with substantial responsibility for medical benefits.

Blue Cross and Blue Shield were confederations of nonprofit benefit plans affiliated with organizations of medical professionals. Blue Cross, which had originated in 1937, covered hospitalization expenses, and Blue Shield offered surgical coverage. They provided programs for individual households and also for employee groups.

By 1950, about half of all employees in the United States were covered by some form of medical insurance. Medical costs had not yet begun their rapid relative increase. Between 1940 and 1949, while consumer prices in general rose by 70 percent, prices of medical goods and services rose only 43 percent. Hospital expenses per patient ranged around five dollars per day during the mid-1940's. rising to eight dollars by 1950. Consequently, medical insurance premiums were relatively low. Individual insurance coverage for hospitalization might be as low as one dollar per month, and surgical coverage between two and three dollars per month. As late as 1949, the total payout under health insurance policies was $767 million. This represented about 10 percent of personal health care expenses.

In Canada, the number of persons enrolled in nonprofit medical insurance plans skyrocketed during the 1940's. From only 25,000 in 1940, the number rose to 888,000 in 1949 and continued to escalate.

Impact Many factors contributed to substantial improvement in health indicators for the United States and Canada during the 1940's. Despite casualties, military service improved medical care for most who served, and wartime conditions generated many improvements which passed into civilian use. In 1940, typical physicians—most of whom were men—carried on their practices in individual offices, many with nurses to assist them. They were accustomed to making house calls. Medications were simple. A family typically relied on the drugstore for over-the-counter remedies such as iodine or hydrogen peroxide for cuts, Alka-Seltzer for indigestion, and aspirin for pain. By 1949, innovation in medications had brought great improvement in controls of illness and infection, with attendant increases in expenses for prescription drugs.

Wartime experience had opened many eyes to the potential benefits of group practice among physicians, spurred by improvements in equipment and surgical techniques. The American Medical Association succeeded in preventing a significant increase in the number of medical schools and medical students in the United States. Consequently, it remained difficult for women and members of racial minorities to become doctors. Meanwhile, a steadily increasing proportion of newly trained doctors were becoming specialists.

Many economists were critical of the spread of employer-financed health insurance, arguing that its exemption from taxation created discrimination against people lacking such insurance. They subsequently argued that such insurance set in motion a powerful upsurge of spending on medical care, originating in the fact that individual patients typically did not bear significant out-of-pocket costs for individual treatments or purchases. This upsurge paved the way for the great rise in medical costs that would come in later decades.

Paul B. Trescott

Further Reading

Armstrong, Pat, et al. *Universal Health Care: What the United States Can Learn from the Canadian Experience.* New York: New Press, 1999. Study tracing the emergence of Canada's health care system after 1947.

Bordley, James, III, and A. McGehee Harvey. *Two Centuries of American Medicine.* Philadelphia: Saunders, 1976. Comprehensive survey, dealing with medical science, medical practices, medical education, and medical policies in U.S. history, from independence through the first three quarters of the twentieth century.

McIntosh, Tom, et al., eds. *Governance and Health Care in Canada.* Toronto: University of Toronto, 2003. Not only covers issues pertinent to health care in the twenty-first century but also traces the historical evolution of the system.

Park, Buhm Soon. "The Development of the Intramural Research Program at the National Institutes of Health After World War II." *Perspectives in Biology and Medicine* 46 (2003): 383-402. Brief account of the rise of medical research sponsored by the federal government.

Shryock, Richard H. *American Medical Research, Past and Present.* New York: Commonwealth Fund, 1947. Captures the acceleration of medical research associated with World War II.

Somers, Herman M., and Anne R. Somers. *Doctors, Patients, and Health Insurance.* Washington: Brookings Institution, 1961. Excellent descriptions of the medical situation during the 1940's and 1950's, with emphasis on the evolution of medical-expense insurance.

Starr, Paul. *The Social Transformation of American Medicine.* New York: Basic Books, 1982. Emphasizes government policies toward financing medical services, particularly the role of the American Medical Association and other organized groups.

See also Antibiotics; Cancer; Casualties of World War II; DNA discovery; Fluoridation; Lobotomy; Medicine; Psychiatry and psychology; Sexually transmitted diseases.

■ Helicopters

Definition Innovative type of vertical-takeoff aircraft that became more widespread and functional during the 1940's

These recently invented aircraft, which could take off and land vertically within small spaces, greatly facilitated military maneuvers and rescue efforts during the 1940's, and they also caught the public imagination.

Helicopters fly with what are, in effect, rotating wings—huge horizontal propellers that give them the ability to hover in one place and go straight up and down. The idea of vertically flying aircraft goes back at least as far as 400 B.C.E., when the ancient Chinese invented tops. During the late fifteenth century, the Italian artist and inventor Leonardo da Vinci sketched a hypothetical flying machine very similar in appearance to a modern helicopter. Other European inventors built flying models during the eighteenth and nineteenth centuries. The great American inventor Thomas A. Edison patented plans for a full-scale helicopter-like device in 1910, but he never actually constructed such an aircraft.

Between 1907 and 1920, primitive helicopters actually lifted human beings off the ground for short periods, but these machines were unstable and difficult to control. No human-piloted helicopter achieved true flight until the early 1920's. By the end of that decade, inventors in France, Russia, Italy, Denmark, Austria, Spain, and the United States all had flown some version of a functional helicopter, but they were not able to do much more than make short hops flying slowly. Major advances in the development of a practical helicopter occurred in the mid-1930's when some of the chief problems of stability and power were resolved. The most successful designs were developed in the late 1930's and early 1940's in the United States, as the beginning of World War II in 1939 stopped helicopter work in Europe.

Military Uses The U.S. military became interested in helicopters during the 1930's and began funding efforts to advance the technology. Igor Sikorsky, a Russian immigrant with his own aircraft company, began production of the R-4 model helicopter for the U.S. Army by 1941. His company was the first to produce large quantities of helicopters and the only one in the world producing a significant volume of military helicopters during World War II. By 1943, several hundred of Sikorsky's R-5 models were being used in the Pacific theater of the war. These helicopters were small but powerful enough to perform rescue missions and deliver supplies. The helicopters could stop and start faster than a car and traveled at air speeds of up to eighty miles per hour.

The military also used Bell Aircraft Corporation helicopters designed by Arthur Young. In 1942, the Bell-30 model could fly faster than seventy miles per hour and was used for scouting for submarines, rescue missions, and supply delivery. Frank Piasecki designed and built helicopters used by the U.S. Navy in 1947. Sikorsky, Young, Piasecki, and Stanley Hiller, Jr. had the only four companies in the world that manufactured helicopters in large numbers before 1950.

Civilian Use   Helicopter rescues made the news in both war and peace. The first rescue of a civilian by a

Army Sikorsky R-5 helicopter demonstrating its lifting strength by rising with seventeen men, plus its pilot, in early 1946. (AP/Wide World Photos)

helicopter occurred in April, 1944, in New York. In January, 1944, a helicopter was used to deliver blood plasma to badly injured people in New York when airplanes were grounded by snow, wind, and clouds, and cars, and boats were too slow to deliver the blood in time. Before helicopters became available, rescues in remote areas had to have surfaces big enough for airplanes to land and take off.

The companies of Young, Piasecki, and Hiller also produced commercial helicopters. Their designers truly believed that there would be a large civilian market for helicopters after the war. Some people predicted that thousands of people would commute by helicopter, thereby easing urban automobile congestion. In 1946, the Bell Model 47 was the first American helicopter certified for sale to the public. In California, New York, and Chicago, heliports were built to help realize the dream of personal-use helicopters.

Despite a great deal of publicity and public fascination with helicopter travel, large-scale individual ownership of helicopters never materialized, due mainly to the high cost of helicopters. Instead, helicopters were used for rescue and police work, as well as for hauling equipment, mail delivery, wilderness surveying and transportation, firefighting, fertilizing and insect control for crops, power-line patrols, film photography, charter work, aerial photography, sightseeing, and traffic and live news reports. In 1948, political campaigning was added to the list of helicopter tasks, when future president Lyndon B. Johnson was flown by helicopter to small Texas towns while he ran for reelection to Congress. His numerous visits to rural Texas are credited with helping him win reelection.

Impact   Helicopters had limited use in World War II because they were not ready for heavy use until near the end of the war, and because they were small, with limited power. Continuous improvements during the 1940's resulted in more powerful aircraft. With the beginning of the Korean War in 1950, the military had further use for helicopters with greater range and carrying capacities. The helicopters were used to bring reinforcements and ammunition to battle areas and to rescue the wounded, as well as perform battlefield surveillance. During the Vietnam War in the 1960's, helicopters were used heavily to transport troops, provide air assaults, and perform large-scale evacuations.

Civilian uses also expanded. During the late 1970's and early 1980's, helicopters were used to bring equipment for oil exploration to remote areas and off-shore rigs. Medical helicopters became more prominent in the mid-1980's and news helicopters were widespread by the 1990's. Large helicopters are even able to pull ocean freighters. Ground and sea rescues by helicopters became more common. In the aftermath of Hurricane Katrina in 2005, two hundred helicopters were used to rescue more than 35,000 people from flooding.

Virginia L. Salmon

Further Reading

Chiles, James R. *The God Machine: From Boomerangs to Black Hawks: The Story of the Helicopter.* New York: Bantam, 2007. Excellent overview of the people, events, and developments involved in helicopter history. Includes pictures, extensive bibliography, index, and appendixes.

Genat, Robert. *Choppers: Thunder in the Sky.* New York: MetroBooks, 1998. Well-written and accessible illustrated history of helicopters.

Hunt, William E. *'Heelicopter': Pioneering with Igor Sikorsky.* Shrewsbury, England: Airlift Publishing, 1998. Personal account of Sikorsky's work from 1908 to 1945. Includes sketches, photographs, and index.

Jackson, Robert. *Helicopters: Military, Civilian, and Rescue Rotorcraft.* San Diego: Thunder Bay Press, 2005. Covering the history and development of 120 different kinds of helicopters. Includes pictures and diagrams.

Spenser, Jay P. *Whirlybirds: A History of the U.S. Helicopter Pioneers.* Seattle: University of Washington Press, 1998. Focuses on the life and work of four men credited in the 1940's with solving the technology problems. Heavily illustrated, with notes, index, and appendices.

See also Air Force, U.S.; Aircraft design and development; Army, U.S.; *History of the United States Naval Operations in World War II*; Inventions; Navy, U.S.; Science and technology; Wartime technological advances.

■ Hillman, Sidney

Identification Lithuanian-born American labor leader
Born March 23, 1887; Zagare, Lithuania
Died July 10, 1946; Point Lookout, New York

Though largely forgotten in recent years, during his lifetime Hillman was the rare labor leader who enjoyed a public regard equal to that of many captains of industry. As president of the Amalgamated Clothing Workers of America and one of the founders of the Congress of Industrial Organizations, he helped to elevate thousands of workers to middle-class prosperity and to bring the American labor movement more fully into the fold of mainstream American politics.

Sidney Hillman, long regarded as one of America's greatest labor leaders, began as a skilled cutter at the Chicago clothing firm Hart, Schaffner, and Marx in 1907. He first rose to prominence during the 1910 clothing workers' strikes, and in 1914 he was chosen as the first president of the Amalgamated Clothing Workers of America (ACWA), a new union that had broken away from the United Garment Workers over its attempt to dominate the urban immigrant workers who were rapidly becoming its majority. Under Hillman's leadership, the ACWA grew and moved from an "outlaw" status as a union outside the American Federation of Labor to mainstream respectability. During the 1930's, Hillman became one of the founders of the rival Congress of Industrial Organizations.

Impact In 1943, Hillman founded the CIO-PAC, a political action committee that was intended to support all prolabor candidates, but ended up focusing on reelecting President Franklin D. Roosevelt in 1944. Throughout World War II, Hillman gained enough clout in the Roosevelt administration to be appointed head of the National War Labor Board, as well as head of the labor section of the Office of Production Management. He also served on three other presidential commissions, and as he came into closer contact with the powers that were increasingly governing the American labor movement, Hillman sometimes walked a difficult tightrope between representing labor's interest to the government and gaining labor's cooperation with wartime policies. After the war ended, Hillman sought to advance the public role of the American labor movement as a delegate to the World Federation of Trade Unions in 1945. His early death from a heart attack in 1946 was mourned by the general public. The loss of Hillman's leadership was just one factor in the increased political vulnerability of the American labor movement by the late 1940's.

Susan Roth Breitzer

Further Reading

Fraser, Steven. *Labor Will Rule: Sidney Hillman and the Rise of American Labor.* New York: Free Press, 1991.

Pastorello, Karen. *A Power Among Them: Bessie Abramowitz Hillman and the Making of the Amalgamated Clothing Workers of America.* Urbana: University of Illinois Press, 2008.

See also American Federation of Labor; Business and the economy in the United States; Congress of Industrial Organizations; Economic wartime regulations; Roosevelt, Franklin D.; Unionism; Wartime industries; World War II mobilization.

■ *Hiroshima*

Identification Partly fictionalized account of six survivors of the atomic bomb dropped on Hiroshima

Author John Hersey (1914-1993)

Date Published in 1946

Although not the first account to inform Americans of human suffering caused by the atomic bomb dropped on Hiroshima, Japan, this novel was the first to cause readers to identify on a personal level with victims.

Hiroshima is the account of six people—five Japanese and one German—who survived the dropping of the first atomic bomb on the Japanese city of Hiroshima on the morning of August 6, 1945. Originally comprising four parts, the narrative follows the lives of the six people from the moment the bomb explodes to a period several months later. Using a panoramic technique evocative of cinematic methods, the original narrative moves back and forth among these survivors, who represent a broad cross-section of Hiroshima's inhabitants.

In 1985, Hersey added a fifth section, "The Aftermath," for an edition commemorating the fortieth anniversary of the bomb to summarize what became of the six survivors. These include a Japanese minis-

John Hersey working as a war correspondent in 1944. (AP/Wide World Photos)

ter who had many American friends countering suspicion of his loyalty by working tirelessly to help other victims. After his radiation sickness subsided, he toured the United States to raise money for a church and a World Peace Center. A widow who freed herself and her children from her collapsed house suffered from radiation sickness and became destitute. A severely wounded doctor later opened a clinic where he treated and befriended many American occupation personnel. The German priest, Father Wilhelm Kleinsorge, suffered from the strain of being a foreigner and was rescued by a Japanese woman, an act that moved him to tears. A doctor who worked for days with only one hour of sleep learned the importance of compassion. A severely wounded worker lost her family; her fiancé broke their engagement when she became a *hibakusha,* one with radiation sickness. As a nun, she helped the elderly die peacefully.

Impact As an article in *The New Yorker,* "Hiroshima" was given most of the space in the magazine. Read on radio, it was also a complementary selection for the Book-of-the-Month Club membership. Many people believe the book awakened a dread of, and guilt about, nuclear warfare. The book has remained in print continuously since its first publication.

Victoria Price

Further Reading

Bataille, Georges. "Concerning the Accounts Given by the Residents of Hiroshima." In *Trauma: Explorations in Memory*, edited by Cathy Caruth. Baltimore: Johns Hopkins University Press, 1995.

Sanders, David. *John Hersey Revisited.* New York: Twayne, 1991.

Sharp, Patrick B. "From Yellow Peril to Japanese Wasteland: John Hersey's *Hiroshima.*" *Twentieth Century Literature* 46, no. 4 (2000): 434-452.

See also   Atomic bomb; Book publishing; Hiroshima and Nagasaki bombings; Japan, occupation of; Unconditional surrender policy; World War II.

■ Hiroshima and Nagasaki bombings

The Event   U.S. dropping of atomic bombs on Japanese cities
Date   August 6 and 9, 1945
Place   Hiroshima and Nagasaki, Japan

Toward the end of World War II, U.S. military planes dropped atomic bombs on two Japanese cities with human and environmental consequences of unprecedented proportions. Within a week of the second bombing, Japan surrendered, thereby ending World War II in the Pacific and signaling the start of an age of nuclear weaponry. The American decision to use the bomb has become controversial, but at the time, it seemed necessary.

On August 6, 1945, a lone American B-29 bomber flew over the Japanese city of Hiroshima and dropped an atomic bomb. Three days later, another B-29 dropped a second atomic bomb on another Japanese city, Nagasaki. More than sixty-five years later, these two events remained the only instances in history when atomic bombs were used by one nation against another, and they helped end World War II.

By August, the Allied forces in World War II included the United States, Great Britain, and the So-

viet Union, which had decisively defeated Nazi Germany and turned their full attention on the Pacific theater of the war. Earlier, even though U.S. forces had had to divide their attention between the Pacific and Europe, they had secured victories in virtually every island battle in which they had been engaged—beginning with Guadalcanal in 1942 and ending with Okinawa in June, 1945. Every battle had been difficult, with the Japanese doing everything possible to defend their surrounding islands.

Allied Plans for Invading Japan   Although U.S. forces had won their battle with the Japanese on Okinawa, they also incurred fifty thousand casualties—one of the highest casualty rates they had endured. The Japanese had twice as many casualties but remained determined to fight. They realized that the United States planned to use Okinawa as a staging point from which to launch its invasion of the Japanese home islands, which lay only 340 miles to the north.

The Allies had every reason to believe that the Japanese would defend their home islands with vigor at least equal to that they had displayed on Okinawa and other islands. At the Potsdam Conference in the summer of 1945, U.S. president Harry S. Truman, along with British prime minister Clement Attlee and Soviet premier Joseph Stalin, had issued the Potsdam Ultimatum, demanding that the Japanese surrender or face an all-out Allied invasion. The Japanese refused the offer, however, and on July 31, Japanese emperor Hirohito stated that Japan must be defended at all costs. Part of his concern stemmed from the refusal of the Allies to allow the Japanese to keep him on his imperial throne in the event of Japan's surrender.

The American invasion of Japan was set to begin on September 1, 1945, but a way to avoid invading Japan and incurring extremely high casualty rates presented itself. Throughout the war, American scientists had been developing an atomic bomb. In July, 1945, they finally perfected and tested one. In the face of Japan's refusal to surrender, President Truman advised Secretary of War Henry L. Stimson to use the bomb. The U.S. Army had already selected several prospective targets for the bomb, concentrating on urban centers where the bomb could do the most damage. The selected cities were large enough so that if a bomb were not dropped in the ideal spot, it would still destroy most of the city. Meanwhile, the prospective cities—which included Kyoto, Yoko-hama, and Hiroshima, were deliberately left un-touched by ordinary bombing raids, so that the true destructive power of the atomic bomb could be ef-fectively measured. Kyoto was regarded as having the greatest strategic importance, but Stimson re-fused to allow it to be a target because he had honey-mooned there several decades earlier and loved the city.

Hiroshima ultimately became the first bombing target because its weather conditions were good for a bomb attack and because its location near moun-tains might magnify a bomb's damage. The city also had some military and industrial significance, so its loss would damage the Japanese war effort. The bombing mission was not slated until August 6, due to persistent cloud cover over the target. Colonel Paul Tibbets, of the 509th Composite Group based on Tinian Island, was selected to pilot the plane, which was named *Enola Gay* after Tibbets's mother.

Mushroom cloud rising from the atomic bomb dropped on Naga-saki on August 9, 1945. (National Archives)

Dropping the Bomb On August 6, the morning of the bombing, Japanese radar detected a small num-ber of planes flying toward the Japanese home is-lands. However, Japanese officers judged that the danger of a bombing raid was so slight, given the small number of planes that were approaching, that it was not worth the cost of fuel to intercept them. Approximately one hour later, at 8:15 A.M. local time, the *Enola Gay* released its bomb; a uranium-fueled "gun-type" bomb nicknamed "Little Boy," over Hiroshima. Although it missed its selected tar-get, a major bridge, it was still extremely destructive.

The bomb's blast—equivalent to thirteen kilo-tons of trinitrotoluene (TNT)—destroyed approxi-mately 4.7 square miles of the city. The Japanese later determined that nearly 69 percent of Hiro-shima's buildings were completely destroyed, and another 6-7 percent were badly damaged. Between 70,000 and 80,000 people—about 30 percent of Hi-roshima's population—died almost instantly, and an equal number were badly injured. Many of the in-jured died later. By the end of the year, the number of deaths from burns and radiation poisoning from the bomb was estimated at between 90,000 and 140,000 people.

The Nagasaki Bomb Despite the obvious devasta-tion left by the Hiroshima bomb, Emperor Hirohito still refused to make an unconditional surrender. The Japanese were willing to surrender only on the conditions that they could maintain their emperor, that there would be no occupation force, and that their own government would be responsible for the punishment of war criminals. The Allies would not agree to any of these terms. In response to Japan's re-fusal to surrender, President Truman ordered the dropping of a second atomic bomb.

On August 9, Major Charles Sweeney, piloting an-other B-29 called *Bockscar*, dropped another atomic bomb, this time on Nagasaki, a major Japanese port. The second bomb, a plutonium device nicknamed "Fat Man," was initially intended for Kokura, but the crew could not deploy the device there because cloud cover prevented them from seeing the target.

"Fat Man" fell on Nagasaki at 11:01 A.M. The bomb missed its target by nearly three kilometers. It landed directly between two major factories but ex-ploded in a valley, whose surrounding hills shielded much of the city from the blast. Although this bomb had the destructive force of twenty-one kilotons of

TNT, it killed only between forty and seventy thousand people—far fewer than the Hiroshima blast. It also destroyed most buildings within a mile radius of its epicenter and caused major damage within a two-mile radius.

Even after the second bomb had been dropped, the Japanese still refused to surrender, prompting the United States to consider using a third bomb, which was expected to be ready for delivery by the middle of August. However, at the moment the United States was dropping its second bomb on August 9, its Soviet allies were declaring war on Japan and preparing for an invasion. By August 12, the Japanese emperor, seeing no way for his nation to resist these combined assaults, finally decided to surrender. He announced his intentions on August 15, thereby bringing World War II to its conclusion.

Postwar Controversy Although the Allies were initially relieved that the atomic bombs had helped bring the war to a satisfactory end, this relief eventually gave way to controversy over why the U.S. government had decided to use the bomb in the first place. Scholars have debated for decades whether the Japanese would have surrendered soon even if Hiroshima and Nagasaki had not been bombed. Some scholars cite the fact that the Japanese were running out of the resources they needed to continue waging war and claim that the Japanese would have had to surrender by the end of 1945, even without the bomb. They postulate that the true reason for the American decision to use atomic weapons was to intimidate their increasingly estranged ally, the Soviet Union.

A second contingent argues that while the Hiroshima bomb may have been a military necessity required in order to expedite a Japanese surrender, the second bombing in Nagasaki was unnecessary and morally objectionable. After all, the Japanese

did not fully understand what had happened in Hiroshima until nearly a full day after the attack and were only beginning to understand the ramifications of the atomic bomb when the second bomb hit. These scholars, while not having a moral objection to the bomb as a concept, have objections to the overuse of such deadly weapons.

Still other scholars have argued that using a second bomb made it impossible for the Japanese government to try explaining away Hiroshima's destruction as a natural disaster or some kind of fluke. Indeed, in the aftermath of the Nagasaki bombing, even Japanese hard-liners who had wanted to continue the war after the first bombing now wanted to end it, citing the apparently unlimited American capability to wage war.

"The Most Terrible Thing Ever Discovered"

On July 25, 1945, U.S. president Harry S. Truman wrote in his diary about his decision to drop atomic bombs on Japan.

We have discovered the most terrible bomb in the history of the world. It may be the fire destruction prophesied in the Euphrates Valley Era, after Noah and his fabulous Ark.

Anyway we "think" we have found the way to cause a disintegration of the atom. An experiment in the New Mexican desert was startling—to put it mildly. Thirteen pounds of the explosive caused the complete disintegration of a steel tower 60 feet high, created a crater 6 feet deep and 1,200 feet in diameter, knocked over a steel tower 1/2 mile away and knocked men down 10,000 yards away. The explosion was visible for more than 200 miles and audible for 40 miles and more.

This weapon is to be used against Japan between now and August 10th. I have told the Sec. of War, Mr. [Henry L.] Stimson, to use it so that military objectives and soldiers and sailors are the target and not women and children. Even if the Japs [*sic*] are savages, ruthless, merciless and fanatic, we as the leader of the world for the common welfare cannot drop that terrible bomb on the old Capitol or the new.

He and I are in accord. The target will be a purely military one and we will issue a warning statement asking the Japs to surrender and save lives. I'm sure they will not do that, but we will have given them the chance. It is certainly a good thing for the world that Hitler's crowd or Stalin's did not discover this atomic bomb. It seems to be the most terrible thing ever discovered, but it can be made the most useful.

Impact Eliminating the Allied need to invade Japan saved countless American and Japanese lives. Estimates for American casualties alone stemming from such an invasion ranged from 100,000 to 1.6 million, according to reports created by the Joint Chiefs of Staff in April, 1945. Japanese casualties would have also been high. By all indications, the Japanese were still adhering to the traditional Bushido code, the so-called "way of the warrior" which forbade surrender and encouraged fighting to the death whenever possible. The government had trained civilians to defend themselves with objects such as bamboo spears, and there was even the possibility of civilians strapping bombs on their bodies and throwing themselves at Allied vehicles and tanks. The Japanese had extended their draft to include young teenagers and women, adding 28 million additional soldiers to their army. Given this information, the U.S. government believed it had no choice but to deploy the bomb.

Sara K. Eskridge

Further Reading

Bird, Kai, and Lawrence Lifschultz, eds. *Hiroshima's Shadow*. Stony Creek, Conn.: Pamphleteer's Press, 1998. Exploration of the moral and ethical aspects of the American decision to drop atomic bombs on Japan.

Hersey, John. *Hiroshima*. New York: Alfred A. Knopf, 2002. Originally published in 1946, this classic work adds a chapter written nearly forty years after the original and recounts the author's search for the six original survivors of Hiroshima whose stories were documented in the first edition of the book.

Hogan, Michael J., ed. *Hiroshima in History and Memory*. New York: Cambridge University Press, 1999. Work of memory and remembrance focusing on how Hiroshima and Nagasaki have remained poignant symbols in the national consciousnesses of both Japan and the United States.

Ishikawa, Eisei, and David L. Swain, trans. *Hiroshima and Nagasaki*. New York: Basic Books, 1981. Prepared by a committee of Japanese commissioned by the two cities to report on the physical, medical, and social effects of the bombings. Extensive bibliography, photographs, maps, charts, and tables.

Kurzman, Dan. *Day of the Bomb: Countdown to Hiroshima*. New York: McGraw-Hill, 1986. Highly readable work with citations from personal interviews, unpublished documents, and papers. Extensive bibliography.

Walker, J. Samuel. *Prompt and Utter Destruction: Truman and the Use of Atomic Bombs Against Japan*. Rev. ed. Chapel Hill: University of North Carolina Press, 2004. Analysis of Truman's decision to drop the atomic bombs. Especially suitable for general readers and students.

_____. "Recent Literature on Truman's Atomic Bomb Decision: A Search for Middle Ground." *Diplomatic History* 29, no. 2 (April, 2005). Revisionist examination of Truman's decision to use nuclear weapons against Japan.

See also Atomic bomb; Bombers; Doolittle bombing raid; Hanford Nuclear Reservation; *Hiroshima*; Japan, occupation of; Manhattan Project; Strategic bombing; Unconditional surrender policy.

■ Hiss, Alger

Identification U.S. diplomat and lawyer
Born November 11, 1904; Baltimore, Maryland
Died November 15, 1996; New York, New York

In 1948, Hiss was accused of being a communist spy, but he fervently denied the charges and aggressively declared his innocence until his death. Hiss was found guilty on two counts of perjury and sentenced to five years in prison.

Alger Hiss graduated from Johns Hopkins University in 1926, where he excelled both academically and socially. In 1929, he graduated from Harvard Law School, where he became acquainted with U.S. Supreme Court justice Felix Frankfurter, who recommended Hiss as a private law clerk to fellow justice Oliver Wendell Holmes.

Finding instant success as a lawyer and government employee, Hiss played major roles in creating the United Nations and serving as a member of the American delegation at Yalta in 1945. In 1947, he became president of the Carnegie Endowment for International Peace.

After World War II, the Second Red Scare exacerbated fears that communists were infiltrating government agencies. In this turbulent climate, Whittaker Chambers, writer and former Communist Party member, met with the Federal Bureau of Investigation (FBI). He accused Hiss of being a communist, but the FBI did not take direct action until gathering further evidence. Later, during a meeting with the FBI, Hiss denied being a communist.

Chambers appeared before the House Committee on Un-American Activities (HUAC) hearings in 1948 and reiterated his accusation against Hiss. Appearing before HUAC, Hiss declared that he was not a communist and did not know Chambers. At a subsequent meeting, Hiss admitted knowing Chambers by a different name. Chambers later testified that Hiss had supplied him with secret government documents, including the "Pumpkin Papers," documents Chambers had hidden in a pumpkin patch, which Chambers subsequently produced. Charges against Hiss now escalated from being a communist to being a spy. Although Hiss declared the documents fraudulent, a grand jury indicted him for perjury in December, 1948.

In May, 1949, Hiss's trial commenced. The prosecution produced a typewriter owned by Hiss and on which government documents had been copied. The defense acknowledged that Hiss had owned the typewriter and disposed of it and that others had copied the documents. Several prominent character witnesses testified on Hiss's behalf. The trial resulted in a hung jury, but a second trial commenced in November.

During this trial, the prosecution presented additional evidence. Because the three-year statute of limitations on espionage had expired, the jury could only find Hiss guilty of two counts of perjury. Hiss received a five-year prison sentence but only served forty-four months.

Hiss adamantly proclaimed his innocence until his death. He produced documents he obtained through the Freedom of Information Act (enacted in 1966) and requested documents from Russian officials. Although these papers were initially favorable to Hiss, Soviet documents such as the Venona files (declassified in 1995) weakened his case.

Impact   Cold War attitudes and Red Scare hysteria in postwar America dramatically influenced the conviction of Hiss in an era that witnessed attacks on political and civil rights. A division still exists between those who support and those who reject Hiss's claims of innocence.

Sharon K. Wilson and Raymond Wilson

Further Reading
Weinstein, Allen. *Perjury: The Hiss-Chambers Case.* New York: Alfred A. Knopf, 1978.

Alger Hiss testifying before the House Committee on Un-American Activities in August, 1948. (AP/Wide World Photos)

White, G. Edward. *Alger Hiss's Looking-Glass Wars: The Covert Life of a Soviet Spy.* New York: Oxford University Press, 2004.

See also   Anticommunism; Cold War; Federal Bureau of Investigation; House Committee on Un-American Activities; United Nations; Wartime espionage in North America; Yalta Conference.

■ Historiography

Definition   Studies of the events and thoughts of the 1940's, interpreted and reinterpreted from various perspectives, in an attempt to find themes, support theories, and discover what "really" happened

The decade of the 1940's is one of the most commonly discussed periods in American history. The amount of material written about World War II and the Cold War is daunting and includes a number of different interpretations of the war's impact on the United States. Many books use these

events as a way to make broader statements about American history.

The decade of the 1940's was defined by two significant historical events: World War II and the emergence of the Cold War. Whereas World War II—at least from the American perspective—was contained entirely within the decade, the Cold War lasted into the 1980's and profoundly impacted international relations for nearly fifty years. World War II in many ways laid the foundations for the development and evolution of the Cold War, and both events have been discussed by professional historians and popular writers for generations.

World War II   Histories of World War II typically focus either on the home front or on the war itself. Most early histories of the war tended to emphasize the diplomatic or military aspects of America's involvement, without much consideration of the social or economic impact. Apart from personal memoirs by prominent figures of the time, one of the most visible topics for texts written during and shortly after the war was the attack on Pearl Harbor. Significant battles also were often the subjects of early works. Over time, however, more authors began describing the war's impact on domestic society. Broad social transformations received more attention, as did more limited topics.

Studies of the changes the war caused in gender and race relations, regional histories, and genre-specific treatments emerged during the 1970's and 1980's to broaden the field. During the 1980's and 1990's, the major change in World War II scholarship was the emergence of revisionist history. Although generally a minority of works can be classified as revisionist, the approach had a significant impact on the field and was also a source for broader debates on the nature of historical (and academic) objectivity.

World War II has long been seen as the last—and perhaps one of the only—wars that was justifiable. Because the United States and the rest of the Allied powers were fighting against the racist, fascist Nazi and Italian systems as well as the Japanese Empire, which had engaged in a sneak attack on Pearl Harbor, nearly all histories of the war take as a central feature the "rightness" of the Allied cause. Even revisionist histories, discussed later, rarely take issue with the appropriateness or necessity of waging war in such an instance.

The War and the Home Front   On one hand, the war has been described as a watershed event in the development of American society during the twentieth century. *War and Society: The United States, 1941-1945* (1972) by Richard Polenberg and *Home Front U.S.A.: America During World War II* (1986) by Allan M. Winkler both discuss the war's impact on daily life. Each work makes the case that Pearl Harbor and the war itself signified a dramatic shift into the modern world. Other authors, including John Morton Blum in *V Was for Victory: Politics and American Culture During World War II* (1976), disagree with the idea of the war as a watershed event and instead point to the continuities in American society that lasted throughout the war. Arguing that the complexities and vicissitudes of a world at war made the 1940's a period of profound inner turmoil, Willaim Graebner's book *The Age of Doubt: American Thought and Culture in the 1940s* (1990) takes a completely different view of the United States during the war years. Graebner suggests that the cultural and intellectual trends of the 1940's were rooted in anxiety and uncertainty caused in large part by the war itself.

World War II also furthered the rapid and profound growth of the American state begun during the New Deal. This process has been traced by Bartholomew H. Sparrow in *From the Outside In: World War II and the American State* (1996). Sparrow describes how involvement in economic planning, labor relations, and veterans' affairs contributed to an enlarged federal government during the postwar years.

Oral Histories, Memoirs, and Biographies   Oral histories can be a useful source for researchers and can give the depth of personal accounts to coverage of an event, such as the war. In addition to Studs Terkel's landmark collection of oral histories *The Good War: An Oral History of World War II* (2007), other texts compile reminiscences about the war's impact on the home front. *The Homefront: America During World War II* (1984) by Mark Jonathan Harris, Franklin Mitchell, and Steven Schechter, and Roy Hoopes's *Americans Remember the Home Front: An Oral Narrative* (1977) both give readers a sense of everyday citizens' reactions to the war. Along these lines, wartime memoirs are also useful, though their numbers are daunting. Among the best of these are E. B. Sledge's *With the Old Breed at Peleliu and Okinawa* (2007), *Unsung Valor: A GI's Story of World War II* by

A. Cleveland Harrison (2000), and *Visions from a Fox-hole: A Rifleman in Patton's Ghost Corps* (2003) by William A. Foley, Jr. Each describes the experiences of an individual soldier during the war.

Not surprisingly, there are a number of biographies about the major political and military figures of the war. Most notable among these are biographies of President Franklin D. Roosevelt. Although many works on Roosevelt are multivolume texts or at the very least cover his entire presidency, several focus on Roosevelt as a wartime leader. James MacGregor Burns's *Roosevelt, the Soldier of Freedom: 1940-1945* (2006) is among the best of these. The second volume of Burns's Roosevelt biography traces Roosevelt's burden of balancing America's isolationist tendencies with his understanding of the demands of a world at war. It also deals with the government's efforts at war mobilization and Roosevelt's skillful diplomacy in maintaining the fragile coalition of Allied nations. *Commander in Chief: Franklin Delano Roosevelt, His Lieutenants, and Their War* (2004) by Eric Larrabee argues that Roosevelt was the most active commander in chief in American history. Larrabee's at times blunt, generally even-handed book weaves biographies of all the significant American generals and military minds during the war into a narrative that places Roosevelt at the heart, portraying the president as the mastermind of U.S. strategy and the military establishment as the implementers of his grand plan.

America at War   The complexity of America's involvement in World War II resulted in many books describing the major theaters of operation as well as specific battles. Suggesting that Roosevelt's policies toward Imperial Japan almost goaded Japan into attacking Pearl Harbor, Gordon Prange's *At Dawn We Slept: The Untold Story of Pearl Harbor* (1981) is one of the definitive treatments of the event that brought the United States into the war. *Eagle Against the Sun: The American War with Japan* (1985) by Ronald Spector describes the major battles of the Pacific theater while also including the contributions of often-marginalized groups such as women and African Americans. Richard Frank's *Downfall: The End of the Imperial Japanese Empire* (1999) describes the final months of the war in the Pacific and puts into context the chaotic and divisive relations between the United States and the Japanese empire.

The development of the U.S.'s military and politi-cal role as the dominant force in the Allied war against Adolf Hitler's Germany is traced in *An Army At Dawn: The War in North Africa, 1942-1943* (2002) by Rick Atkinson. Atkinson argues that the U.S. Army evolved during the African campaign into a modern and effective war machine. Moreover, the defeat in North Africa (along with Japan's loss at Midway and the Soviet victory at Stalingrad) permanently destroyed the Axis powers' initiative.

Revisionist Histories   Revisionism is a historiographical approach that emphasizes a reinterpretation of existing facts and analyses. It is intended to present alternative viewpoints or contradictory interpretations of widely held assumptions. Overly patriotic or ethnocentric descriptions of World War II have been targeted repeatedly by historians. One of the earliest of these was written by Charles A. Beard in 1948. His book *President Roosevelt and the Coming of the War, 1941: A Study in Appearances and Realities* argues that restrictive American policies toward Japan in part led to the attack at Pearl Harbor. Moreover, Beard suggests that Roosevelt knew in advance of Japan's intentions but misled the American public in an effort to draw the United States into the war.

World War II has often been portrayed as "The Good War." Recent histories, however, have begun to take some exception to this representation. Two books in particular trace this more revisionist interpretation of the war. Paul Fussell's *Wartime: Understanding and Behavior in the Second World War* (1989) and *The Best War Ever: America and World War II* (1994) by Michael C. C. Adams are both critical of certain aspects of the idea of the Good War and puncture common myths about the reality of the war versus popular representations, the nobility of American soldiers, and the organization and preparedness of the military. Even in these cases, though, the tendency is to counter the positive or at times sentimentalist approach of authors such as Stephen Ambrose who often portray American soldiers as chivalrous and fully capable warriors. Adams and Fussell, by contrast, point out that often Americans were undertrained, poorly equipped, or just as liable to engage in questionable behaviors as their "evil" opponents. Rarely do even the most revisionist histories reject the assumption that the war was justifiable, however.

One fascinating revisionist text, John Dower's *War Without Mercy: Race and Power in the Pacific War*

(1986), expands on this suggestion and argues that racial attitudes on both sides of the Pacific evolved over the course of the war. Moreover, Dower sees these racist assumptions as having contributed to the extreme brutality of the Pacific war when compared to the war in Europe. Again, Dower's book helps to move the field beyond stereotypes and mythologies that are common in many treatments of the war.

The Cold War The uneasy wartime alliance between the United States and the Soviet Union became strained even before the surrender of Germany in May, 1945. Although the United States was willing to overlook the Soviet Union's occupation of much of Eastern Europe during the drive to Germany, shortly after the war the Soviets refused to abandon their control of regions of Poland and eastern Germany in particular. Tensions rose between the two remaining superpowers. Events such as the Berlin airlift were early examples of an American policy known as containment. Containment, the use of military, diplomatic, or economic pressure to prevent the Soviet Union from expanding its influence or control to additional areas of the world, was a concept largely attributed to American diplomat George Kennan. Kennan outlined his early ideas in *American Diplomacy, 1900-1950* (1951) and then in refined form, with the help of hindsight, in *American Diplomacy* (1984). His belief that Soviet communism required expansion to remain viable—and the corollary that the system, prohibited from such expansion, would necessarily collapse—caused American political and military strategists to define U.S.-Soviet relations in terms of containment for the next several decades.

Historian John Lewis Gaddis stands at the center of academic work on the origins of the Cold War. His book *Strategies of Containment: A Critical Appraisal of Postwar American National Security Policy* (1982) traces the evolution of American emphasis on containment as a foreign relations paradigm from the end of World War II through the 1980's. Gaddis believes that containment, though not clearly defined, guided Roosevelt's and Harry S. Truman's treatment of Joseph Stalin throughout the war. Although Gaddis has written several major works on the subject, his other crucial book, *The United States and the Origins of the Cold War, 1941-1947* (1972; revised, 2000) works hard to place the Cold War in the context of World War II international relations.

Because newly ascendant President Truman was the first to deal with the postwar realities of the Cold War, Melvyn Leffler traces Truman's role in creating the postwar world in *A Preponderance of Power: National Security, the Truman Administration, and the Cold War* (1992). Leffler argues that the Truman administration developed American policy specifically to enhance American interests in the postwar world. According to Leffler, few top American officials worried about a "hot war" between the United States and the Soviet Union. Rather, the guiding principle of American policy was the protection of friendly European and Asian governments as a counterweight to Soviet power.

Impact Few events in American history have been subject to such ongoing scrutiny as have World War II and the Cold War. Authors have struggled to evaluate the two events' roles in defining the American experience during the second half of the twentieth century, alternately choosing to support or criticize long-standing interpretations of social, political, economic, and military developments.

Shawn Selby

Further Reading

Burns, James MacGregor. *Roosevelt: The Soldier of Freedom, 1940-1945.* New York: Harcourt Brace Jovanovich, 1970. This second volume of Burns's two-part Roosevelt biography adeptly analyzes Roosevelt's political leadership and his approach toward critical foreign policy issues through the final years of his presidency.

Gaddis, John Lewis. *Strategies of Containment: A Critical Appraisal of American National Security Policy During the Cold War.* New York: Oxford University Press, 2005. This book has become a standard scholarly study of Cold War policy from the end of World War II to the aftermath of the fall of communism in Europe.

_____. *Surprise, Security, and the American Experience.* Cambridge, Mass.: Harvard University Press, 2004. Compelling account of the behind-the-scenes machinations of the Truman administration to thwart communist expansionism following World War II.

Graebner, William. *The Age of Doubt: American Thought and Culture in the 1940's.* Boston: Twayne, 1991. Thorough and perceptive analysis of all the cultural elements of American life during the

1940's that helped create and define the decade's thought and culture.

Lee, Loyd E., ed. *World War II in Asia and the Pacific and the War's Aftermath, with General Themes: A Handbook of Literature and Research.* Westport, Conn.: Greenwood Press, 1998. Companion to the book on the European and North African theaters of the war that Lee published a year earlier, this volume contains comprehensive overviews of almost every major aspect of the Pacific theater—culture, the arts, science and technology, international relations, and the postwar world. Supporting materials include excellent bibliographies

_____. *World War II in Europe, Africa, and the Americas with General Sources: A Handbook of Literature and Research.* Westport, Conn.: Greenwood Press, 1997. Comprehensive survey of the historiography of the European and North African theaters of World War II, with the full scope of its companion volume on the Pacific theater of the war.

Winkler, Allan M. *Home Front U.S.A.: America During World War II.* Wheeling, Ill.: Harlan Davidson, 2000. Exhaustive study that details the main contributions to the American war effort undertaken on the home front.

See also   Book publishing; Cold War; Education in the United States; Films about World War II; *History of the United States Naval Operations in World War II; President Roosevelt and the Coming of the War;* Roosevelt, Franklin D.; *Studies in Social Psychology in World War II;* Truman, Harry S.; Truman Doctrine; World War II.

■ History of the United States Naval Operations in World War II

Identification   Officially sponsored naval history
Author   Samuel Eliot Morison (1887-1976)
Date   Published in 1947-1962

Morison's multivolume history is thorough, informative, and sufficiently entertaining that he later put out a one-volume popular abridgement. His work is a model of official history worthy of emulation by later historians.

Morison provides careful, detailed coverage of United States naval operations throughout World War II, including the undeclared war against Germany in late 1941. This includes landings in both

theaters (with brief coverage of land operations), the various submarine campaigns, and all the naval actions in the Pacific—not only major ones, such as the carrier battles and the many night actions in the Solomons, but obscure ones such as the Komandorski Islands. He briefly discusses the earlier naval disarmament treaties and strategic plans. He readily expresses his own opinions of operations and other issues—defending President Franklin D. Roosevelt's undeclared war against Adolf Hitler because of the latter's treatment of neutrals, but also arguing that Admiral Husband Kimmel and General Walter Short deserved another chance after Pearl Harbor.

Morison sought to be extremely fair in these assessments, readily admitting embarrassments such as the 1943 Battle of the Pips (which led to the greater embarrassment of attacking Kiska in the Aleutian Islands without realizing that the Japanese had already evacuated it). For both sides, he praises some operational decisions and criticizes others. This often displeased his targets; Admiral William Halsey was livid about the discussion of Leyte Gulf, arguing that Morison failed to differentiate adequately between the information available at the time and what was known in hindsight.

Impact   Morison's history is remarkably accurate and objective for a government-sponsored publication. Although dated in some aspects, it has remained a useful source and a model for future historians.

Timothy Lane

Further Reading

Dunnigan, James, and Albert A. Nofi. *The Pacific War Encyclopedia.* New York: Checkmark Books, 1998.

Morison, Samuel E. *History of the United States Naval Operations in World War II.* 15 vols. Reprint. Urbana: University of Illinois Press, 2002.

_____. *The Two-Ocean War: A Short History of the United States Navy in the Second World War.* 1963. Reprint. Annapolis, Md.: U.S. Naval Institute Press, 2007.

Potter, E. B. *Bull Halsey.* Annapolis, Md.: Naval Institute Press, 1985.

See also   Aircraft carriers; Atlantic, Battle of the; Guadalcanal, Battle of; Halsey, William F. "Bull"; Historiography; Iwo Jima, Battle of; Midway, Battle of; Navy, U.S.; Nimitz, Chester W.; Okinawa, Battle of; Pearl Harbor attack; Submarine warfare.

■ Hitchcock, Alfred

Identification   British film and television director
Born   August 13, 1899; Leytonstone (now in London), England
Died   April 29, 1980; Bel Air, California

Hitchcock spent the 1940's perfecting the formula at which he had labored for over a decade in England: the expansion of the commercial, artistic, and emotional vistas of the thriller genre by combining romantic and political intrigue, often simultaneously, in plots that promised, and usually delivered, maximum suspense.

By the time Alfred Hitchcock directed his first film in 1926, he had already worked as a director's assistant and as an employee of Henley's, a London-based electronics firm that sent him to art school, where he developed a keen visual sense, and that published a magazine for which he wrote short stories combining suspense and black humor. In retrospect, they read like embryonic future Hitchcock film scripts. He was also an inveterate, and precociously critical, theatergoer. So it was that he was especially well prepared to direct. That his first ten efforts were silent films required him to learn to tell a story visually. That his most successful early film was *The Lodger* (1927), based on a novel about Jack the Ripper, foreshadowed the subject matter that would soon make him famous.

Hitchcock spent the 1930's making seminal "talkie" thrillers such as *The Thirty-nine Steps* (1935), *Secret Agent* (1936), and *The Lady Vanishes* (1938) for British production companies (and incorporating his signature habit of making cameo appearances in his films). His rapidly growing clout enabled him to direct first-rank talent (John Gielgud, Peter Lorre, Charles Laughton) and attracted the attention of Hollywood, to which he relocated in 1939. The winning of the Academy Award for best picture by his American debut, an eponymous adaptation of Daphne du Maurier's novel *Rebecca*, starring Laurence Olivier and Joan Fontaine, confirmed the compatibility of the Hitchcock-Hollywood pairing.

The twelve feature films that Hitchcock directed during the 1940's starred the likes of Ingrid Bergman, Cary Grant, James Stewart, and Gregory Peck and found him experimenting with a variety of subject matter including comedy (*Mr. and Mrs. Smith*, 1941) and romance (*Under Capricorn*, 1949). However, the films that have proved most enduring were grounded in the international tension resulting from World War II or the high-risk unraveling of a murder mystery. Hitchcock's favorite among the latter was *Shadow of a Doubt*, a 1943 film starring Teresa Wright and Joseph Cotten that also doubled as a loss-of-innocence story. While international conflict and murder would continue to play a large role in the next three decades of Hitchcock's work, never again would he attempt to convey a character's coming of age.

Impact   Hitchcock's main contribution to the making of films was the potential of indirection to heighten suspense and humor. His favorite device was the "MacGuffin" (a term he coined in 1939), an apparently inconsequential plot element that actually serves as a reason for the coming

Director Alfred Hitchcock (center) with British actor Michael Wilding and Swedish actor Ingrid Bergman in 1948. (AP/Wide World Photos)

together of two unlikely characters and as a distraction from their gradually developing relationship (a relationship that would often prove to have been his film's true reason for being). He also circumvented the stringent censorship of the era by resorting to a suggestive implicitness that respected the intelligence of his audience by taking for granted their ability to make intelligent inferences regarding moral depravity and its manifold manifestations. These techniques would also characterize the thirty-minute episodes of *Alfred Hitchcock Presents*, the television series for which he served as a dryly sardonic master of ceremonies (and occasional director) during its decade-long run (1955-1965) and that inspired other suspense-driven series devoted to the macabre such as *One Step Beyond* and *The Twilight Zone*.

Arsenio Orteza

Further Reading

DeRosa, Steven. *Writing with Hitchcock: The Collaboration of Alfred Hitchcock and John Michael Hayes.* New York: Faber & Faber, 2003.

McGilligan, Patrick. *Alfred Hitchcock: A Life in Darkness and in Light.* New York: Regan Books, 2003.

Truffaut, François. *Hitchcock.* New York: Simon & Schuster, 1967.

See also   Academy Awards; Davis, Bette; Film in the United States; Film noir; *The Great Dictator*; Lombard, Carole.

German chancellor Adolf Hitler (right) with Italian premier Benito Mussolini during their May, 1942, meeting in Salzburg, Austria. (AP/Wide World Photos)

■ Hitler, Adolf

Identification   Chancellor of Germany, 1933-1945
Born   April 20, 1889; April 20, 1889; Braunau am Inn, Austro-Hungarian Empire (now in Austria)
Died   April 30, 1945; Berlin, Germany

Adolf Hitler's meteoric rise to power in Germany during the 1930's and his ambition to make Germany the most powerful nation in Europe ignited the international conflict that developed into World War II.

From a decorated army corporal in World War I, Adolf Hitler recreated himself into a Napoleonic force that within a five-year period brought Germany from a defeated and chaotic nation to one that mirrored the Roman Empire. Combining magnetic rhetoric with a willingness to take risks, Hitler used his leadership of the Nazi Party as a stepping-stone to the chancellorship of Germany. From there, with strong support from the German population, as well the industrial and military bases, he assumed dictatorial powers and soon set out to rearm Germany and create a new German empire.

Between 1938 and 1940, Austria, Czechoslovakia, Poland, Belgium, Holland, France, Norway, Denmark—all fell before Hitler, leaving Great Britain alone to face Hitler and a German army willing to follow his bidding. The fact that Hitler sprang up so quickly and was able to resurrect completely a disorganized nation suffering from the reparations and restrictions demanded of it by the treaty that ended World War I was a shock to a Europe that had yet to recover from World War I. Few people had read Hitler's book *Mein Kampf* (1925-1926; English translation, 1939), which laid out his military ambitions for Germany.

American and Canadian Perspectives Before Hitler began his aggressive military campaigns, many Americans and Canadians saw him as a kind of caricature rather than as a legitimate political leader. During the 1930's, Americans tended to be more interested in ending the Great Depression than they were in events in Europe. Canada, however, was a member of the British Commonwealth and was thus drawn into European affairs earlier, and it became involved in World War II before the United States, although its largest military role would not come until the Normandy invasion in 1944. With a relatively small population made up primarily of people of British and French descent, Canada's views of Hitler tended to coincide with those held by the British, who regarded Hitler as a dictator whose military successes and potential made him a world threat.

In contrast to Canada, the United States was a nation with more than 130 million people, of whom some 30 million were of German ancestry. Like many immigrant groups who settled in America, the Germans, particularly the most recent arrivals, organized clubs and associations that enabled them to keep alive their Old World traditions. One of the largest and best organized of these was the German American Bund. It had numerous branches, some of which went so far as to identify not only with Germany, but also with Hitler himself. Although the Bund's membership in the United States probably never numbered more than 20,000—and may have had as few as 6,000 members—it nevertheless played a significant role in how Hitler was viewed in America. Wherever the Bund was active, it stirred up anti-German sentiments. Meanwhile, however, the vast majority of German Americans strove to prove their loyalty to America. Indeed, many fought against Germany during World War II.

Impact Hitler's invasion of the Soviet Union in June, 1941, and American entry into the war at the end of the year were the first steps toward the end of Hitler's reign. In 1945, Hitler's career would end in suicide and cremation amid the rubble of Berlin as Allied armies closed in on his capital.

Wilton Eckley

Further Reading

Evans, Richard J. *The Coming of the Third Reich.* New York: Penguin Books, 2004.

_____. *The Third Reich in Power.* New York: Penguin Books, 2006.

Hughes, Matthew, and Chris Mann. *Inside Hitler's Germany,* New York: MJF Books, 2000.

Kershaw, Ian. *The Hitler Myth: Image and Reality in the Third Reich.* New York: Oxford University Press, 1987.

See also German American Bund; Germany, occupation of; Isolationism; Jews in Canada; Jews in the United States; World War II.

■ Hobbies

Hobbies provided outlets for Americans in civilian and military life, and hobby participation flourished to an unprecedented degree during the 1940's. Wartime conditions led to the curtailing of some popular activities, but aeromodeling rose to the level of a nearly national pastime. The drafting of young men into the armed forces had the effect of changing the age-group norms for some traditional hobbies.

Even as America was turning its attention to national defense, hobbies continued to flourish and grow in popularity during the early 1940's. Stand-alone hobby stores, which had begun appearing in major cities during the 1930's, remained viable, while hobby sections in department, hardware, and dime stores increased in number. For example, one Seattle department store, Bon Marche, devoted first-floor space to its hobby section in 1941. Previously, relegation of hobby departments to upper floors was typical.

Some hobbies were brought to a near standstill by the war, however, as was the case with home photography. After having established a firm foothold in American households during the 1930's, the hobby became nearly impossible to pursue because necessary supplies were reserved largely for military use. Another extremely popular hobby of the late 1930's, competitions of gasoline-powered miniature racecars, faced a similar situation. The metal-bodied racers were made from materials, including aluminum and rubber, needed by the military. The racers also utilized small engines made with precision tooling. Companies capable of their manufacture soon found themselves engaged instead in production useful to the war effort.

Rationing had some positive effects in daily life. A do-it-yourself mind-set was encouraged in American households as a means of working around shortages of various goods and services. It resulted in increased interest in such activities as crocheting of current-fashion hats and bags, and it encouraged some to return to traditional hobbies such as leathercraft, quilting, and woodworking. Millions also became de facto horticultural hobbyists through the cultivation of victory gardens.

In line with the encouragement of adults to follow "victory" pursuits, children were provided with an increasing number of hobby and craft kits and sets to offset the sharply decreased number of available toys. The Build Your Own U.S. Defenses kit of 1941 was an early example of craft sets that would become typical during the next few years. This kit educated children about defense plans, and Pan American Paint Sets informed children about the Good Neighbor Policy. Both were produced by a major manufacturer, Brooklyn's Standard Toycraft Products.

The building of miniature railroad layouts by both youth and adults continued unabated into the war years. The option of building miniatures from scratch compensated for the lessened availability of ready-to-use train sets for sale. Even the do-it-yourself hobby suffered from decreasing availability of parts. As early as 1941, hobby shops reported problems in obtaining steel parts for use with all models, including trains, boats, and planes.

Aeromodeling The kit-building of miniature versions of various vehicles of transportation, especially boats and airplanes, had grown steadily in the previous decade. Especially popular was the building and flying of motorized aircraft, sometimes in competitive situations. Although model aircraft were made of simpler materials than were gas-powered racing cars or electric train sets, airplane modelers likewise found themselves faced with problems of materials rationing, with the most affected material being balsa wood. Somewhat suitable replacements, such as pine and basswood, were introduced, although they, too, eventually were subject to military needs. All the same, the hobby not only survived but grew in popularity throughout the years of the war, in both the United States and Canada. It did so in part because model companies were quick to release kits based on the new military aircraft being put into action. The hobby also was being perceived as helpful to the overall war effort. "Aeromodeling," the more official-sounding name adopted by 1942, taught

hobbyists the rudiments of aeronautical design, the theory of flight, and meteorology. Because the activity appealed to people ranging from their teen years through all ranges of adulthood, some hobbyists found aviation-related work in the military.

The hobby was promoted with an industry-produced film showing all phases of model building, shown by civic groups and schools, and with demonstrations, modeling competitions, and flying events. Reflecting the growth of model-making into a mainstream activity, the first National Trade Show of the Model Industry Association was held in July, 1941, in Chicago in conjunction with the National Model Airplane Championships. The hobby's popularity was further boosted by official recognition from the U.S. Office of Education and the Civil Aeronautics Administration, which extended their aviation-education efforts to secondary schools for the first time. Classes began to be taught in the fall of 1942, often tied into extracurricular model-plane activities. These preflight aviation courses, together with the spread of such model-aircraft recreational sites as Modelhaven Airport in Baltimore, greatly encouraged the hobby. Hollywood assisted as well, with films including cameo scenes such as one showing young actor Jackie Cooper holding a model airplane. Interest in model gliders was also mounting by 1942, thanks to widespread interest in the experimental gliders being developed by the U.S. Army and Marines.

By 1943, most manufacturers in the model industry were producing tools or parts for war purposes. Many, however, managed to cater simultaneously to hobbyist needs. Philadelphia's Megow, one of the largest model airplane manufacturers, was engaged in war work by early 1943 but maintained its position as an industry leader in that year and the ones following. The fact that the government continued to see the hobby as beneficial to the nation helped ensure its continued ability to produce models. Also helpful was a statement by the Office of Price Administration declaring that gas-rationing policies would allow model-plane builders the fuel they needed for flying.

By 1943 and 1944, aeromodeling was being rivaled by plane-spotting, which was pursued by military personnel as well as the general public. By using silhouette models of military aircraft, people practiced identifying friendly and enemy fighters and bombers. The Air Scouts were groups within the Boy

Scouts of America whose activities included the development of plane-spotting skills. The economic impact of this activity, which attracted all age groups, was significant, with model-industry companies including Strombeck-Becker of Moline, Illinois; Joe Ott Manufacturing of Chicago; and Sil-O-Models of Cincinnati manufacturing the silhouette models and distributing them nationally.

Similarly stimulated by the war was the enjoyment of target games of many kinds. Dartboard manufacturers produced a variety of colorful and sometimes topical targets for home use in response to this upsurge of interest. Archery, likewise embraced as a hobby sport, ranked among the activities most rapidly increasing in popularity during the decade.

Traditional Hobbies Two traditional hobbies, philately (stamp collecting) and numismatics (coin collecting), were boosted by developments during World War II. Although some hobby shop owners saw stamp and coin collecting as an entry-level activity for younger children, and not a hobby that greatly interested older children, more experienced collectors found their field energized by the introduction of wartime coin issues of historic interest. Collectors were particularly interested in the wartime issues of other countries, especially China, where war and unrest raised the likelihood of uncommon and rare items entering circulation.

In numismatics, interest in older coins was intensified both by coin-metal changes during the war and by changes in design. The 1943 U.S. steel and zinc pennies, the shortage of dimes brought about by the hoarding of silver speculators, and the use of silver in wartime Jefferson nickels, due to inadequate nickel supplies, all contributed to heightened public interest in coinage. Responding to the popular call for having a coin honoring the late President Franklin D. Roosevelt, the U.S. Mint issued a redesigned dime in his honor in 1946. The design change stimulated collector interest in both the new coin and its predecessor.

Traditional hobbies virtually unaffected by the war years included ones based in natural history, archaeology, mineralogy, and astronomy. One event of the decade that stimulated a high degree of interest in astronomy was the eclipse of the sun on July 9, 1945.

The Postwar Years Although some people lost interest in their victory gardens at the end of the war, many found that gardening remained interesting and enjoyable. Technological developments aided their efforts, particularly the quick-freezing process that took the United States by storm in 1945, making it much easier to store homegrown produce.

Some decline in aeromodeling occurred with the end of the war, although not immediately. In September, 1946, for example, fifteen thousand people attended the Third Annual Model Plane Contest in Golden Gate Park, San Francisco.

Photography fairly quickly returned to the civilian sphere, with new developments in color photography bringing even more interest to the hobby. Cameras, which were absent from most catalogs and stores through the 1945-1946 season, become more widely available in 1946 and 1947. Similarly, home filmmaking returned to the realm of possibility. War-

President Franklin D. Roosevelt's deep interest in stamp collecting helped to popularize the hobby during the 1940's. (Getty Images)

time technological developments also boosted phonograph record collecting, with the introduction of more durable records to the civilian sphere in 1945.

Large numbers of servicemen with technical training returned to civilian life, boosting the popularity of various power tools for hobbyists and do-it-yourselfers. Home woodworking became more popular, and metal-machining equipment and even small-scale plastic-molding machines were manufactured and sold for the home hobbyist market. Radio hobbyists also found their field expanding with the introduction of new technology.

The changes that were sweeping American society inclined many adults, particularly in older age brackets, to engage in nostalgic pursuits, including the collecting of antiques and old toys. The manufacturing of nostalgic reproductions would become a profitable endeavor as a result.

Among young hobbyists, a minor fad of "knotting and braiding" swept the United States in 1946. Introduced through Boy Scouting and summer camps, the hobby required yards of colorful plastic lace or cord, swivel hooks, and cardboard tubes for making woven bracelets and other items.

Impact The war years changed the nature of hobbies in America. In some cases, hobbyists were forced to cease or change their activities because of material shortages. In other cases, hobbies changed because of the rapid advances made in technology during the war. Among traditional hobbies, many were altered by the cultural transformation forced upon America by having its youth thrust into military service. The average age of enthusiasts pursuing some hobbies, such as model building, fell as a consequence. Some of these hobbies never entirely reacquired their status as activities of interest to young adults and adults.

Mark Rich

Further Reading

Blom, Philipp. *To Have and to Hold: An Intimate History of Collectors and Collecting.* New York: Penguin Books, 2003. A far-ranging and engaging study of collecting that covers influences and trends in the collecting hobbies, with subjects ranging from the 1940's and 1950's back to previous centuries.

Dilworth, Leah, ed. *Acts of Possession: Collecting in America.* New Brunswick, N.J.: Rutgers University Press, 2003. Provides historical perspective on the development of American collecting hobbies.

Lingeman, Richard R. *Don't You Know There's a War On? The American Home Front, 1941-1945.* New York: Nation Books, 2003. Depicts America's domestic, social, and cultural life during the first half of the 1940's, while also addressing work, business, and housing issues. Particularly relevant is chapter 8, "Pleasures, Pastimes, Fads and Follies."

Matthews, Jack. *Toys Go to War: World War II Military Toys, Games, Puzzles and Books.* Missoula, Mont.: Pictorial Histories Publications, 1995. A useful look at the pastimes pursued by children of the 1940's.

Sickels, Robert. *The 1940's.* Westport, Conn.: Greenwood Press, 2004. This volume in the American Popular Culture Through History series surveys changes in popular interests through the decade due to the shift from rural to urban lifestyles as well as the effects of World War II.

See also Astronomy; Coinage; Fads; Fashions and clothing; Photography; Polaroid instant cameras; Postage stamps; Radio in the United States; Sports in Canada; Sports in the United States; Wartime rationing.

■ Hobbs Act

The Law Federal legislation making it a federal crime to obstruct or delay commerce through robbery or extortion

Date Enacted July 3, 1946

Also known as Anti-Racketeering Act

The Hobbs Act is an extension of the 1934 Anti-Racketeering Act, which prohibited specific acts of violence and threats of violence, specifically excluding lawful labor activities. The Hobbs Act was perceived by some as antilabor because it placed restraints on the 1934 law's exemptions for some labor activities.

The Hobbs Act was an effort against organized crime, specifically robbery, extortion, labor racketeering, and the obstruction of commerce. The law's sanctions include fines not more than $10,000 and up to twenty years of incarceration. The law defines robbery as unlawfully taking another's property by force, violence, or threatened violence. Extortion is obtaining property with consent that is induced by violence or threats of violence. Commerce refers to activity within the United States, its territories, and other jurisdictions of control.

The act was sponsored by Alabama representative Sam Hobbs and was designed to address improper union activities such as work-related extortion and even minor interference with commerce. At the time the law was passed, prosecutors were concerned about mobsters extorting truckers. The law gave prosecutors a powerful tool, in that any violence or threat of violence that affects commerce could bring the Hobbs Act into relevance. As long as commerce is affected, the act does not require that prosecutors establish exactly which party involved in an offense committed specific acts of violence.

Reportedly, what fueled Hobbs's ire in advocating for the law was the U.S. Supreme Court decision *United States v. Local 807* (1942), which excluded racketeering-like behavior if undertaken by a union, as opposed to a crime syndicate. The Supreme Court had affirmed the idea that a New York City union could exact a fee from truckers to enter the city. The fee was not for any services by the union, and to many, including Hobbs, its collection appeared to be racketeering. For the Supreme Court, the circumstances constituted a real labor dispute where conspirators had attempted to negatively impact the employment of city workers. The union's behavior was deemed in the interest of workers and not for the individual gain of union leaders, as prosecutors had argued.

Impact The Hobbs Act has remained in effect into the twenty-first century, with most alleged violations investigated by the Federal Bureau of Investigation and the U.S. Department of Labor. The subsequent Racketeer Influenced and Corrupt Organizations Act (RICO) of 1970 is a more advanced prosecutorial tool. The Hobbs Act is still used, however, to prosecute corruption and violence by individuals who are not members of crime syndicates or unions, but whose crimes have impacted commerce.

Camille Gibson

Further Reading

Lane, Charles. "An Unlikely Law Bolsters Sniper Case Prosecution." *The Washington Post*, October 31, 2002, p. A13.

Lindgren, James. "The Elusive Distinction Between Bribery and Extortion: From the Common Law to the Hobbs Act." *UCLA Law Review* 35 (1988): 815.

See also American Federation of Labor; Business and the economy in the United States; Fair Employment Practices Commission; Federal Bureau of Investigation; Organized crime; Unemployment in the United States; Unionism.

Hockey. *See* **Ice hockey**

■ Hogan, Ben

Identification Golfer
Born August 13, 1912; Dublin, Texas
Died July 25, 1997; Fort Worth, Texas

Hogan was one of the greatest golfers of all time and is recognized by many as the greatest of his era. During his illustrious career, he won sixty-four Professional Golfers' Association (PGA) events, nine major championships, four U.S. Open titles, and the career Grand Slam.

After becoming a professional golfer in 1929, Ben Hogan did not win a PGA Tour event until 1938. In 1940, he won four PGA events, was the PGA money leader, and received the Harry Vardon Trophy for lowest scoring average. He was the PGA money leader again in 1941 and 1942. After serving a stint in the U.S. Army Air Forces, Hogan was the top PGA money winner in 1946, when he won the PGA Championship and twelve other PGA events.

In 1948, Hogan became the first golfer to win three major PGA events in the same year. He won the Western Open, the National Open, and the U.S. Open. After winning two events in early 1949, Hogan was severely injured in an automobile accident, and doctors thought he would never walk again. Due to his dedication, courage, and tenacity, Hogan taught himself to walk and golf again. He won the U.S. Open in 1950. During the 1940's, Hogan garnered fifty-two PGA Tour wins.

Impact Hogan is credited with ushering in the modern era of golf. He made a significant impact on the correct way to swing a golf club and on ball-striking ability. His legendary, relentless practice sessions, his intense drive for perfection, and his determination and perseverance became the standard for other professional golfers.

Alvin K. Benson

Further Reading

Bertrand, Tom, with Printer Bowler. *The Secret of Hogan's Swing*. Hoboken, N.J.: John Wiley & Sons, 2006.

Dodson, James. *Ben Hogan: An American Life*. New York: Doubleday, 2004.

See also   Golf; Recreation; Sports in Canada; Sports in the United States; Zaharias, Babe Didrikson.

■ Holiday, Billie

Identification   American jazz singer
Born   April 7, 1915; Philadelphia, Pennsylvania
Died   July 17, 1959; New York, New York

Holiday was one of the premier jazz vocalists of the 1940's, performing widely across the United States. The high point of Holiday's career was from the late 1930's through the 1940's, a time documented especially by her recordings from 1936 to 1944.

Discovered in 1933 by talent scout John Hammond, Billie Holiday quickly made a name for herself in jazz circles. After early recordings with Benny Goodman (1933) and Teddy Wilson (1935), she sang with Count Basie (1937) and Artie Shaw (1938). Particularly noteworthy were her collaborations with tenor saxophonist Lester Young. In 1939, she began an engagement at New York's Café Society that further contributed to her popular success. Holiday's hit songs included "God Bless the Child" and "Lover Man." In 1948, she sang to a sold-out Carnegie Hall. Sadly, physical and legal problems related to drug addiction began to hamper her career during the late 1940's and eventually led to her early death in 1959.

Acknowledging the influence of Bessie Smith and Louis Armstrong, Holiday crafted an intensely personal and beautiful vocal style. Her singing was characterized by her unique vocal timbre; her spectacular sense of phrasing, rhythm, and pitch; and her expressive, supple, and often melancholic sound. Her signature tunes included "Body and Soul," "Lady Sings the Blues," and "Strange Fruit."

Impact   Holiday is generally considered one of the greatest vocalists in jazz history and had significant influence on later singers. Her honors include the film *Lady Sings the Blues* (1972; starring Diana Ross), the U2 tribute song "Angel of Harlem" (1988), and induction into the Rock and Roll Hall of Fame (2000).

Mark A. Peters

Further Reading

Holiday, Billie, and William Dufty. *Lady Sings the Blues.* 1956. Reprint. New York: Broadway Books, 2006.

Nicholson, Stuart. *Billie Holiday.* Boston: Northeastern University Press, 1995.

See also   African Americans; Ellington, Duke; Goodman, Benny; Horne, Lena; Music: Jazz; Music: Popular; Parker, Charlie.

Billie Holiday singing at New York City's Carnegie Hall in March, 1948. (Redferns/Getty Images)

■ Hollywood blacklisting

The Event Informal banning of individuals from employment in the motion-picture industry based on alleged political beliefs or associations

Date Began in 1947

Many individuals' lives and livelihoods were damaged or destroyed by their appearance on the list and the lack of work they suffered as a result.

The Hollywood blacklist was a semiformal list of American entertainers who were barred from employment because of their real or suspected links to the Communist Party. In November, 1947, ten writers, directors, and actors (the so-called Hollywood Ten) refused to testify before the House Committee on Un-American Activities (HCUA). As a result, studio executives began compiling a list of individuals who either had ties to the American Communist Party or were less than enthusiastic in their dealings with congressional investigations into communist activities in the entertainment industry.

Shortly after the Hollywood Ten were cited for

contempt of Congress for their refusal to comply with HCUA subpoenas, forty-eight studio executives met at the Waldorf-Astoria hotel in New York City. The result of the meeting was the "Waldorf Statement," released to the public on December 3, 1947, in which the executives announced the firing of the Hollywood Ten, whose actions were deemed to have harmed the motion-picture industry and who were therefore no longer employable. The Waldorf Statement also declared the industry's support for the congressional hearings, rejected the employment of anyone known to be a communist or a member of any radical organization, and assured that Hollywood had never included any subversive or un-American content in its motion pictures.

Although the statement included assurances that the executives and the industry as a whole would work to protect the freedoms of innocent men and women, many found themselves on the blacklist based on nothing more than hearsay or innuendo. Over time, the list came to be used as much as a tool for private retribution and vengeance as as a method of screening potentially subversive influences.

In some instances, the unions or guilds that were intended to support the rights of workers in the industry were supportive of the lists. The Screen Actors Guild (SAG) and the Screen Writers Guild (SWG) both actively supported the blacklisting of men such as screenwriters Dalton Trumbo and Ring Lardner, Jr., and actors Richard Attenborough, Charles Chaplin, and Kim Hunter. In some cases, unions required loyalty oaths from members, while in the SWG, writers' names were omitted from the credits. Though the list most famously included prominent screenwriters, directors, and performers, there were blacklistees who had been employed in less visible roles throughout the entertainment industry. Gaffers, grips, and continuity checkers were also prevented from working because of their real or perceived ties to the Communist Party or even because of

---

"Are You a Member of the Communist Party?"

Screenwriter John Howard Lawson was made to testify before HUAC on October 29, 1947. His interrogation by a member of the committee typified that of many in Hollywood who refused to "name names" and cooperate with the committee.

Interrogator: "Are you a member of the Communist Party or have you ever been a member of the Communist Party?"

John Howard Lawson: "It's unfortunate and tragic that I have to teach this committee the basic principles of Americanism."

Interrogator: "That's not the question. That's not the question. The question is—have you ever been a member of the Communist Party?"

Lawson: "I am framing my answer in the only way in which any American citizen can frame . . . absolutely invades his privacy . . ."

Interrogator: "Then you deny it? You refuse to answer that question, is that correct?"

Lawson: "I have told you that I will offer my beliefs, my affiliations and everything else to the American public and they will know where I stand as they do from what I have written."

Interrogator: "Stand away from the stand. Stand away from the stand. Officers, take this man away from the stand."

their support of various liberal or humanitarian causes that some associated with communism.

The list expanded through the 1950's to include as many as three hundred people. In 1960, director Otto Preminger announced that his release *Exodus* had been written by Trumbo. The same year, Kirk Douglas, the star and an executive producer of *Spartacus*, demanded that Trumbo's name appear in the credits. The executives at Universal Pictures acquiesced, and the blacklist was effectively ended.

Impact Dozens, perhaps hundreds, of men and women were prohibited from working in films or television because of the blacklist. Though it was never a formal or official document and its existence was often denied, the list damaged or ended the careers of many entertainers and industry workers.

Shawn Selby

Further Reading

Ceplair, Larry, and Steven Englund. *The Inquisition in Hollywood: Politics in the Film Community, 1930-1960.* Urbana: University of Illinois Press, 2003.

Dick, Bernard F. *Radical Innocence: A Critical Study of the Hollywood Ten.* Lexington: University Press of Kentucky, 1989.

See also Anticommunism; Civil rights and liberties; Communist Party USA; Film in the United States; Hoover, J. Edgar; House Committee on Un-American Activities; Seeger, Pete.

■ Home appliances

Fueled by a housing boom and a rising standard of living, sales of home appliances, which had already increased during World War II, grew dramatically during the late 1940's. Increased availability and use of home appliances transformed the American household and symbolized the prosperity and modernity of the postwar era in the United States and Canada.

A critical component of the postwar economic boom in North America was a dramatic increase in the sale of durable goods, the most popular of which were automobiles and home appliances. In the years immediately following World War II, consumer spending on sales of washing machines, refrigerators, electric ranges, and water heaters as well as small appliances such as toasters, vacuum cleaners, and electric mixers increased by approximately 60 percent in the United States, and the amount of money that American households spent on home appliances and household furnishings increased by approximately 240 percent. This boom in home appliance purchases permeated every region of North America and every level of socioeconomic status, introducing to many consumers goods that had previously not been available, affordable, or practical.

Supply and Demand During the 1920's and 1930's, a variety of home appliances, large and small, were introduced to the North American public. The availability of refrigerators, toasters, electric ranges, and other devices previously unavailable to consumers, combined with installment-plan financing that allowed middle-class consumers to purchase these items, appeared to mark the beginning of an economic and societal transformation in which labor-saving devices would improve quality of life in the United States and Canada. The effects of the Great Depression, however, squelched the demand for consumer goods and devastated the appliance industry. Demand for home appliances rebounded modestly as the continent emerged from the Depression during the late 1930's and as government stimulus programs, most notably rural electrification projects in the United States, encouraged appliance purchases by rendering them available and practical to a growing number of households.

The entry of Canada and the United States into World War II in 1939 and 1941, respectively, and the resultant retooling of factories for the war effort severely decreased the production of consumer goods, producing a shortage of the supply of home appliances. Meanwhile, demand continued to increase in both countries as wartime production increased civilian employment opportunities, raised household incomes, and attracted women to the workforce in unprecedented numbers. Consumers with more disposable income and less time to maintain their households rushed to purchase home appliances when and where they were available. By the early 1940's, however, inventories of home appliances had dwindled, and the diversion of industrial production to the war effort had brought the manufacture of new appliances to a virtual halt. Still, demand for home appliances persisted; a market survey conducted in 1944 revealed that appliances were the most-desired items among American consumers.

Postwar advertisement enticing housewives with a diverse array of specialized kitchen appliances. (Getty Images)

The Postwar Boom The transition from a wartime to a consumer economy released the pent-up demand for home appliances that had been developing since the outset of the Great Depression and revived the advance in appliance technology that had characterized the pre-Depression years.

This demand for home appliances paralleled and was driven by a general demand for consumer goods as well as an acute shortage of housing, which produced a boom in the construction of new homes. By the late 1940's, millions of Americans whose lives had been disrupted by years of war and depression had acquired sufficient financial means to pursue deferred dreams of owning their own homes and starting families. In response to this demand, real estate developers constructed residential subdivisions on the outskirts of major cities, offering affordable homes of modern, uniform construction. Assistance from government programs such as the G.I. Bill and

the Federal Housing Administration (FHA) in the United States provided additional aid and incentives to consumers seeking to become homeowners. These new homes were built to accommodate the latest in modern appliances, such as electric ranges, water heaters, automatic dishwashers, and family-size refrigerators.

The late 1940's saw a collective effort from a number of business and governmental industries to promote the purchase and use of home appliances. The appliance industry in the United States successfully lobbied the FHA to include the cost of household appliances in the mortgage loans that the administration guaranteed, and appliance manufacturers often struck deals with developers to install their appliances in new homes. The electric power industry conducted advertising and lobbying campaigns to promote air conditioning, washing machines, and other large appliances. The real estate and banking professions also actively lobbied federal, state, and local governments to bolster the appliance industry and promote appliance purchases. Advertising for home appliances abounded in newspapers, in magazines, on the radio, and on the fledgling medium of television during the late 1940's.

As the market for home appliances continued to grow during the late 1940's, advances in technology and design made a wider variety of appliances available to consumers. Appliances in a variety of sizes, shapes, colors, and configurations made it possible for consumers to customize the decor of kitchens to fit individual utilitarian and aesthetic demands. In addition, new types of appliances would enter the marketplace. In 1947, the Raytheon Corporation introduced the Radarange, the first microwave oven. Although initially impractical for home use, the microwave oven would eventually become a staple of modern American life.

Socioeconomic Implications The boom in home appliances was but one of many factors transforming North American society during the 1940's, yet the influence of home appliance use upon the economy and culture of the postwar United States and 1940's Canada was dramatic and enduring. By increasing the efficiency of the home kitchen, appliances markedly reduced the amount of time required to prepare meals and manage other household tasks. As a result, many American women experienced an increase in time available to manage growing families as well as to pursue interests outside the confines of the home. Home appliances increased the cleanliness and efficiency of the American household, leading to changes in societal standards for hygiene and personal appearance. Appliances also exerted an influence upon residential design, as the opulent Victorian homes and cozy bungalows of the early twentieth century gave way to ranch-style homes with kitchens designed for maximum efficiency and the accommodation of modern appliances. The marketing of consumer goods processed and packaged for use with modern appliances, such as "TV dinners," also began in the waning years of the 1940's.

Impact The impact of the home appliance boom of the 1940's upon the United States and Canada was rapid and pervasive. By the mid-1950's, many households in which modern conveniences were uncommon prior to World War II benefited from the efficiency, safety, and cleanliness that accompanied the use of electrical appliances. The wide availability of these appliances contributed to an increased sense of social and economic equality, as most consumers regardless of socioeconomic status had access to many types of electrical appliances. Home appliances also became symbols of Western economic prosperity and were touted as evidence of the superiority of capitalism over communism. In addition, the societal effects brought about by the mass consumption of home appliances fueled a number of social trends and movements, including feminism and reactions against the social conformity and conspicuous consumption that accompanied the growing role of material goods in the lives of North Americans.

The ubiquitous presence of home appliances in modern society and the variety of designs available to consumers also influenced popular fashion and art in North America. Many artists—most notably Andy Warhol—drew inspiration from home appliance design and advertising from the 1940's, and appliances from this decade became coveted items for collectors and models for designers of appliances in "retro" styles popular during the 1990's and early twenty-first century.

Michael H. Burchett

Further Reading

Cohen, Lizabeth. *Consumer's Republic: The Politics of Mass Consumption in Postwar America.* New York: Alfred A. Knopf, 2003. History of consumerism in twentieth century United States; includes analysis of home appliance consumption during and after World War II.

Cross, Gary. *An All-Consuming Century.* New York: Columbia University Press, 2002. Discusses purchases of appliances during the 1940's in the context of postwar consumer culture.

Hurley, Andrew. *Diners, Bowling Alleys, and Trailer Parks: Chasing the American Dream in the Postwar Consumer Culture.* New York: Basic Books, 2002. Places demand for and purchases of home appliances in context of class consciousness and working-class consumer culture in 1940's America.

May, Elaine Tyler. "The Commodity Gap: Consumerism and the Modern Home." In *Consumer Society in American History: A Reader,* edited by Lawrence B. Glickman. Ithaca, N.Y.: Cornell University Press, 1999. Discusses how the economic and social impact of the Great Depression and World War II affected demand for home appliances and other consumer goods in the 1940's.

Pursell, Carroll. *Technology in Postwar America: A History.* New York: Columbia University Press, 2007. Overview of technological advances during the postwar era. Contains some details of appliances introduced to the consumer market during the mid- and late 1940's.

See also Advertising in the United States; Business and the economy in Canada; Credit and debt; Home furnishings; Housing in the United States; Microwave ovens; Telephone technology and service; Television; Women's roles and rights in Canada; Women's roles and rights in the United States.

■ Home furnishings

Definition The furniture, appliances, lighting, and accessories that decorate domestic interiors and help make them more livable and comfortable

Wartime shortages of labor and materials and postwar restrictions led to a need for affordable, simple, and durable home products. New modern designs blending art with function resulted from a unique collaboration among designers, retailers, and manufacturers. As military technology and materials became adapted for civilian use, high-quality furnishings became mass-produced, with new shapes and materials.

During the 1940's, wartime rationing and scarcity led to new values of economy, austerity, and efficiency. New technology and materials developed for the military became available for consumer products. Traditional classical and ornate designs remained in use, but trends moved toward a modern, simplified aesthetic in which new materials such as aluminum, stainless steel, chrome, and plastics such as Lucite (a synthetic polymer of methyl methacrylate sometimes referred to as PMMA) and Bakelite were being combined in home products. Nylon, which was invented in 1939 and used in American parachutes during the war, was introduced into use in upholstery fabric.

To satisfy postwar consumerism, designers created home products that were of high quality, but affordable and mass-produced. The standard furniture of earlier decades was heavy, with glossy finishes, shiny fabrics, or complex hardware. Modern designs were streamlined, light pieces that often were sculptural or modular.

The 1940's color palette was limited, often using pastels and neutrals rather than the multicolored schemes of earlier decades. Wallpaper and fabrics used beige and muted pinks, blues, and greens. Pink was a favorite bathroom tile color. Garnet red was a favorite linoleum floor color. Motifs from Asian, African, North American Indian, and other cultures also were popular.

Home Decor, Appliances, and Accessories Common home styles of the 1940's were ranch and Cape Cod models. After the war, suburban Levittown-style communities of low-priced, mass-produced houses sprang up. The average home was not spacious but had modern, functional bathrooms and many affordable appliances and electronics.

The 1940's kitchen was relatively small, frequently less than 250 square feet. Wartime restrictions and rationing resulted in designs that used available, affordable materials. Linoleum, because it was inexpensive and easy to install, was a popular finish. Kitchen counters usually were linoleum or tile, with stainless steel trim. Floors were linoleum, usually in a two-toned geometric design. Cabinets often were white, and yellow was a favorite color for walls, ceilings, and accent pieces. Blues, greens, and combinations of red and white also were popular in kitchens. A favorite style of kitchen table had a white porcelain enamel top that was stain resistant and easy to clean, with steel legs in bright chrome plate.

Kitchens emphasized functionality and were full of time-saving products and appliances. Many modern conveniences were especially suited to the lifestyles of working women during the war, as many women took jobs outside the home traditionally held by men but now open to women because of labor shortages. Both gas and electric stoves had been in use for decades, offering a choice. The Kalamazoo gas range cost about $199, whereas a Frigidaire electric cooker range with a forty-inch cabinet and a stainless porcelain top cost about $179. Also useful in the kitchen were mixers, such as the versatile Sunbeam Mixmaster, which multitasked as a mixer, juicer, or grinder. Another essential kitchen appliance was the modern electric refrigerator. By 1944, 85 percent of American kitchens had a refrigerator. The automatic ice maker appeared later, in 1952.

By the mid-1930's, the radio had become a common part of household furniture. The radio was a major source of entertainment and news, and it often was combined with a phonograph into one unit or into a cabinet designed with an amplifier and speakers.

Although television was introduced at the 1939 World's Fair, further production was discontinued during World War II. In 1945, there were only five thousand television sets in American homes. After the war, television broadcasting stations proliferated, reaching ninety-eight television stations by 1949. In 1946, Radio Corporation of America (RCA) released its instantly successful RCA 630TS, a tabletop television with a ten-inch screen. In 1948, General Electric marketed its Model 805, which was a ten-inch set with a Bakelite case. By the end of the decade, there were one million television sets in the United States. The first home theater or entertainment center had appeared by 1949. Admiral's Three-Foot Home Theatre included a triple-play phonograph, an FM/AM Dynamagic radio, and a 12.5-inch television picture tube. A similar console was Motorola's combination television, FM/AM radio, and phonograph.

Chair designed by Charles and Ray Eames for the International Competition for Low-Cost Furniture Design in 1948. (©Robert Levin/CORBIS)

Other popular home furnishings and appliances included vacuum cleaners, rotary phones, portable electric heaters, and automatic washing machines. Gas and electric clothes dryers were sold by companies such as Hamilton Manufacturing and General Electric, but fewer than 10 percent of households had dryers because of their high cost.

New Designs, Technology, and Materials Under the leadership of Eliot Noyes, director of the new Department of Industrial Design, the Museum of Modern Art (MOMA) in 1940 held a unique competition called Organic Design in Home Furnishings. A collaboration between MOMA and various department stores, this competition aimed to discover designers who could create beautiful and functional lighting, furniture, and fabrics. Noyes believed that a new design approach was necessary to match new ways of living. The team of Eero Saarinen, a Finnish American, and Charles Eames won in two out of the nine categories. They had created futuristic molded plywood chairs and modular cabinets. The method of molding laminated wood to construct the form-fitting shell chairs was in harmony with processes of mass production. The cabinet storage pieces represented the modern movement toward interchangeability, simplicity, and amorphism.

One of the most influential and original designers in the postwar years was George Nelson, who cowrote the best-seller *Tomorrow's House: How to Plan Your Post-War Home Now* (1945). A gifted design theorist, he proposed that the new materials and processes developed for military use be adapted for civilian products. For example, he thought that the process of molding a laminate of plastic and fabric to make ammunition boxes could be used to create inexpensive household storage cabinets. In 1945, Nelson and Henry Wright developed the revolutionary concept of storage wall systems.

In 1946, Nelson became director of design for the Herman Miller Furniture Company, for which he created the Basic Storage Components system that same year. In 1949, he designed a complete line of storage components that filled the need for home storage space and space dividers. In 1948, he designed such classic icons of modern design as the Tripod Clock (1947), Night Clock (1948), and "ball" or "atomic" wall clock (1949).

Nelson also recruited the couple Charles and Ray Eames to work for Herman Miller in 1946. Prewar industrial technology was not advanced enough to economically manufacture the futuristic chairs that won the 1940 MOMA competition. The Eameses, however, continued to experiment with molded laminated wood. In 1946, they introduced their modern LCW lounge chair, folding wood screen with canvas hinges, and coffee table, all made from molded plywood. These could be mass-produced at low cost. In 1999, *Time* magazine named the Eames molded plywood LWC chair the "chair of the century." In 1948, Herman Miller bought the exclusive distribution and marketing rights to the Eames molded plywood products.

In 1948, using molding techniques developed during the war and their new method of making a bent, welded wire base, the Eameses created the first industrially manufactured one-piece plastic chairs, the molded plastic armchair and side chair. That year the Eameses also designed La Chaise for MOMA's International Competition for Low-Cost Furniture Design. Inspired by Gaston Lachaise's 1927 sculpture *Reclining Nude*, the organically shaped La Chaise became a design icon. The new technology for molding fiberglass enabled them to create the two free-form shells in this work of art. Other entries at this competition included Scandinavian knockdown (KD) furniture, which could be packed flat in cartons and later assembled by the consumer.

One of the co-designers of the 1940 winning chairs, Eero Saarinen, created the womb chair and ottoman in 1948 for Knoll Furniture Company. Constructed with foam over a molded, reinforced fiberglass shell and upholstered, it was a comfortable chair in which a person could curl up.

Another innovative designer was sculptor Isamu Noguchi, who in 1945 started designing his Akari lamps, or light sculptures. Consisting of handmade paper on a bamboo frame, the Akari lamp suggests weightlessness. Noguchi eventually designed more than 150 different shapes. In 1948, Noguchi blended sculptural form and function in his famous three-legged table, with a free-form glass top on a curved, solid wood base.

In 1946, Earl Silas Tupper developed Tupperware, airtight plastic containers for storing food and liquids. They were made of a a new lightweight flexible plastic called polyethylene. Brownie Wise conceived of the Tupperware party, a successful direct marketing strategy.

Impact Technological developments of the 1940's had significant impact even into the twenty-first century. By 1960, there were almost 160 million television sets in the United States, and since then television has become a central part of the home, often in a separate home theater. During the 1940's, the drying mechanism for dishwashers was patented and the first electric-powered dishwashers were sold. After smaller models were introduced during the 1950's, sales increased dramatically. Another significant 1940's invention was the microwave oven, patented in 1940. In 1947, Raytheon Company used its radar technology to build the first commercial microwave, the Radarange, which weighed almost eight hundred pounds and was more than six feet tall. Not long after a compact, countertop oven became available in 1967, the microwave became commonplace in homes.

Wartime scarcity and scientific research into new materials led to numerous home furnishing products that are still popular in the twenty-first century. Some design innovations remained popular, with items designed by Saarinen and Noguchi still sold in the twenty-first century. Tupperware helped legitimize plastics, and the company's home parties became accepted as a new business model. In 2009,

Tupperware was sold in more than one hundred countries through almost two million consultants.

Alice Myers

Further Reading

Abercrombie, Stanley. *A Century of Interior Design, 1900-2000: A Timetable of the Design, the Designers, the Products, and the Profession.* New York: Rizzoli, 2003. This beautifully illustrated history describes each year's design, cultural, and technological milestones, including a furniture and furnishings section. Index.

_____. *George Nelson: The Design of Modern Design.* Cambridge, Mass.: The MIT Press, 1994. Based on interviews, Nelson's personal papers, corporate archives, and published materials, this is the definitive biography about this influential modernist designer. Illustrated, with bibliography and index.

Albrecht, Donald. *The Work of Charles and Ray Eames: A Legacy of Invention.* New York: Harry N. Abrams, 2005. Published in conjunction with an international Eames exhibition by the Library of Congress, this is a beautifully illustrated collection of essays about the husband-and-wife team whose work from the 1940's into the 1970's revolutionized twentieth century furniture, building, and interior design. Bibliography, index, and filmography.

Bony, Anne. *Furniture and Interiors of the 1940s.* Paris: Flammarion, 2003. A well-researched study of European and American interior design in this transitional period. Beautiful illustrations on every page. Bibliography and index.

Fiell, Charlotte, and Peter Fiell. *Decorative Arts, 1930s and 1940s.* London: Taschen, 2000. Source book about design trends and styles in furniture, interiors, glassware, lighting, ceramics, architecture, metalware, and textiles. Illustrated, with index.

Mossman, Susan T. I. *Fantastic Plastic: Product Design + Consumer Culture.* London: Black Dog, 2008. This comprehensive history of plastic considers both the technological and aesthetic qualities of plastic, including a section on plastics form and design during the 1940's. Illustrated, with bibliography.

Swedberg, Robert W., and Harriett Swedberg. *Furniture of the Depression Era: Furniture and Accessories of the 1920s, 1930s, and 1940s.* Paducah, Ky.: Collector Books, 1987. This is a detailed, illustrated guide to this era's home furnishings, including their development and manufacturers. Bibliography and index.

See also   Architecture; Art movements; Art of This Century; Fashions and clothing; Home appliances; Housing in the United States; Inventions; Levittown; Microwave ovens.

■ Homosexuality and gay rights

During the 1940's, homosexuality as a subject within American society was discussed chiefly within the fields of literature and science, The manpower demands of World War II forced the military to shift its policy on homosexuals from penal treatment to mandatory discharge.

During the decade of World War II, homosexuality was a nearly invisible topic in North America, continuing a status accorded to it during the 1930's. The degree to which American culture defined the subject out of existence can be seen in the *Reader's Guide to Periodical Literature* a ubiquitous basic reference work that was in every public library. The publication had no heading for homosexuality until 1947, and the 1947 heading merely directed readers to look under "Sex Perversion."

The scientific literature available in book form was a mixture of English translations of works by German sexologists and a continuation of a clinical approach that treated homoerotic behavior as a neurosis. It could also be found in reprints of works by writers such as Edward Carpenter from earlier in the century who had favored a more balanced social place for the "invert." Physician George Henry's massive anthology *Sex Variants: A Study of Homosexual Patterns* which appeared in 1941 with a second edition in 1948 is perhaps the best assessment of the state of medical and clinical thinking about homosexual behavior during the decade. Virtually all other works appeared shortly before or after World War II, with the last three years of the decade showing the most activity in the journals of medicine and psychology. The manpower requirements of all branches of the United States military together with efforts at reform led by military psychiatrists also caused the replacement in 1941 of the prior policy of segregation and imprisonment for persons charged with committing homosexual acts with mandatory discharges.

In August, 1944, an essay by San Francisco poet Robert Duncan titled "The Homosexual in Society" appeared in the journal *Politics*. Duncan both admitted that he was a homosexual and attacked the idea held by many homosexuals at that time that their difference made them better than heterosexuals. He opposed the persecutions and distortions to which homosexuals were subjected and emphasized the humanity of both gay and straight people. Three years later, in June, 1947, *Vice Versa*, the first American periodical published for lesbians, made its appearance in Los Angeles. However, it lasted only nine months.

The work discussing homosexuality that occasioned the greatest public uproar and debate during the 1940's was Alfred Kinsey's 1948 book, *Sexual Behavior in the Human Male*. Kinsey's work was controversial for both its frank discussions of topics that had previously been considered taboo and the breadth of claims it made based on a large sample of the population. Among Kinsey's assertions was the startling conclusion that fully 10 percent of the American male population had engaged in homosexual behavior at some time in their lives. Kinsey's findings challenged the long-held belief that homosexuals constituted only a tiny portion of the general public—a picture based on case studies from various branches of psychology and clinical psychiatry.

Impact The 1940's saw a discernible shift in American attitudes toward homosexuality, and the subject was beginning to lose its unmentionable status to become more frequently presented as an acceptable topic of scientific investigation and personal testimony. The mass mobilizations occasioned by wartime demands for industry and the military also served to bring together gay women and men who had never before met others who were drawn to their own sex. This phenomenon promoted formation of an incipient sense of gay community that would start to coalesce with the formation of the first homophile organizations in the following decade. For the general public, however, homosexuals continued to be viewed as threats to American society and values.

Robert Ridinger

Further Reading

Aldrich, Robert, and Garry Wotherspoon. *Who's Who in Contemporary Gay and Lesbian History: From World War II to the Present Day*. New York: Routledge, 2001.

Berube, Alan. *Coming Out Under Fire : Gays and Lesbians in World War II*. New York: Free Press, 1990.

D'Emilio, John. *Sexual Politics, Sexual Communities: The Making of a Homosexual Minority in the United States 1940-1970*. Chicago: University of Chicago Press, 1983.

Marcus, Eric. *Making Gay History: The Half Century Fight for Lesbian and Gay Equal Rights*. New York: Perennial, 2002.

See also Censorship in the United States; Civil rights and liberties; Hoover, J. Edgar; Psychiatry and psychology; Stein, Gertrude; *A Streetcar Named Desire*.

■ Hoover, J. Edgar

Identification First director of the Federal Bureau of Investigation

Born January 1, 1895; Washington, D.C.

Died May 2, 1972; Washington, D.C.

J. Edgar Hoover's aggressive direction of the Federal Bureau of Investigation during the 1940's created an operational structure and engendered public support for the investigations during the 1950's, spearheaded by Senator Joseph McCarthy of Wisconsin, of U.S. citizens with suspected communist sympathies.

Hoover's tenure as the director of the Federal Bureau of Investigation (FBI) has been the subject of much criticism as well as praise. In some ways, Hoover's work at the FBI is as enigmatic as Hoover's life itself, and many of the organization's activities during his long period of leadership remain shrouded in unanswered questions and controversy. What is clear, however, is that the decade of the 1940's was an exemplar of some of the FBI's most controversial activities, especially regarding the Pearl Harbor attack in December, 1941, and the FBI's surveillance of journalists, academics, and other well-known national personalities.

Pearl Harbor Why the attack on December 7, 1941, seemed to take U.S. leaders by surprise has been a subject of ongoing debate. Hoover's role stems from information the FBI received several months prior to the attack concerning the activities of Dušan Popov, a Yugoslav lawyer turned double agent, a spy who worked for both the British and the German intelligence agencies. In 1941, the Germans sent him to the United States with a mission to establish a spy network. Significantly, they gave him a questionnaire that was encoded with a relatively new "microdot" technology. The questions, which could be read only using a microscope, included a section concerning logistical information about the defense system of Pearl Harbor. When FBI agents interrogated Popov upon his arrival in New York, he showed them the questionnaire and discussed its contents.

Hoover, in a letter sent to Edwin W. Watson, a White House presidential secretary, included a small part of the questionnaire, without the items relating to Pearl Harbor. This letter emphasized the microdot technology. He forwarded copies of it to officials in other U.S. military and naval intelligence agencies, but the full version of Popov's questionnaire was kept on file at the FBI. The ineffective interagency communication in this instance may have helped to ensure the surprise of the ultimate attack; it also is reminiscent of claims regarding communication failures between the FBI and the Central Intelligence Agency (CIA) in the months preceding the terrorist attacks on the United States of September 11, 2001. Historians cite it as supporting a culture of "one-upmanship" that influenced Hoover's decision making during this decade. He apparently was more concerned with impressing the president with the FBI's ability to access German technology in secretive communications than with relaying the catastrophic implications of the questionnaire items themselves. The reluctance to share information with the other intelligence agencies reflects the rivalry that existed between them at the time, to the ultimate detriment of U.S. national security interests.

FBI Surveillance Activities Much of the FBI's activity regarding the investigation of journalists, academics, and other prominent Americans suspected of having communist ties were fueled by Hoover himself. The investigations were part of a broader spectrum of activities culminating in the McCarthyism that gripped the country during the 1950's. Hoover interpreted President Franklin D. Roosevelt's authorization for the FBI to handle investigations of aliens engaged in subversive activities as a license to establish a list of foreigners and U.S. citizens who could be arrested during any national emergency.

Roosevelt was concerned about fascist and communist threats to national security and in 1940 allowed the FBI to use electronic surveillance methods despite of the U.S. Supreme Court's 1937 *Nardone v. United States* decision prohibiting this. The FBI targeted the American Newspaper Guild, an organization of journalists whose members were suspected of communist ties. The FBI sent its field offices a list of more than one hundred such journalists in October, 1941. In subsequent years, it undertook electronic surveillance of personnel in different guild offices and at the Guild's 1944 convention. The consequences for reporters were devastating, especially when they refused to answer questions when brought before governmental investigative committees. They were often fired from their posts, effectively ending their professional careers. A simi-

FBI director J. Edgar Hoover (left) watching a heavyweight title match between Joe Louis and Jersey Joe Walcott at New York City's Yankee Stadium on June 25, 1948. Seated next to him are banking official H. C. Flannigan and actor Adolph Menjou. (Louis retained his title with an eleventh-round knockout.) (AP/Wide World Photos)

lar fate awaited academics who were accused during the 1940's of having communist ties. In one celebrated case, however, the board of trustees of Sarah Lawrence College would not fire a member of its anthropology faculty, Irving Goldman. When questioned by the Senate Judiciary Committee Investigating the Subversive Influence in the Education Profession, he refused to implicate academic colleagues allegedly engaged in communist-related activities.

Impact Hoover has been revered as a dedicated public servant, but aspects of his public and private lives remain mired in controversy. The FBI's loose conception of civil liberties, including its practices during the 1940's, might be seen as an early prototype for the type of governmental investigative authority authorized by the USA Patriot Act of 2001, a controversial law that drew criticism because it could be interpreted as allowing for infringements of civil liberties.

In the highly conservative era in which Hoover functioned, his unmarried status helped to feed rumors about his private life and even his sexual identity. His vigorous reactions to such insinuations, as well as his aggressive management of the agency, paved the way for the realization by some citizens that a public official's private life, whatever it may be, is often a matter that can and should remain private, as long as it does not affect work performance. The difficulties Hoover faced in this area may have motivated later FBI directors, notably Louis Freeh, to introduce the American public in a prominent way to their wives and families (in Freeh's case, this included six sons). They often highlighted the extent of the time they devoted to their families, in spite of the intense professional demands of the position. Regardless of the various charges and insinuations against him, Hoover retains his legendary status as the agency's first and longest-term director, instrumental in helping the FBI attain and retain its status as one of the world's most effective and efficient investigative agencies.

Eric W. Metchik

Further Reading

Alwood, Edward. "Watching the Watchdogs: FBI Spying on Journalists in the 1940's." *J&MC Quar-* terly 84, no. 1 (2007): 137-150. Well-referenced account of FBI surveillance of newspaper activists with suspected communist ties.

Fox, John F., Jr. "Unique unto Itself: The Records of the Federal Bureau of Investigation 1908 to 1945." *Journal of Government Information* 30 (2004): 470-481. A balanced perspective on FBI record keeping during this period, emphasizing efficiency and data centralization goals, in contrast to more popularized and sensationalistic accounts of witch-hunting and character assassination.

Gentry, Curt. *J. Edgar Hoover: The Man and the Secrets.* New York: Norton, 1991. Unflattering political biography based on more than three hundred interviews and on thousands of pages of previously classified documents. Argues that Hoover used illegal methods to build the image of an invincible FBI and that he used his power to influence many high-level government officials, including Supreme Court justices and U.S. presidents.

Morris, Charles E. "Pink Herring and the Fourth Persona: J. Edgar Hoover's Sex Crime Panic." *Quarterly Journal of Speech* 88, no. 2 (2002): 228-244. Theoretical analysis of Hoover's sexual identity in the light of the cultural norms of the mid-twentieth century.

Price, David H. "Standing Up for Academic Freedom." *Anthropology Today* 20, no. 4 (2004): 16-21. A case study of the FBI's investigation of Sarah Lawrence College anthropologist Irving Goldman, with an emphasis on the FBI's contacts within academia and the role of academic freedom in this process.

Vizzard, William J. "The FBI, a Hundred-Year Retrospective." *Public Administration Review* 68, no. 6 (2008): 1079-1086. Broad overview of the FBI's structure and functioning since its founding. Includes laudatory and critical literature written by FBI personnel and external scholars.

See also Anticommunism; Central Intelligence Agency; Civil rights and liberties; Cold War; Communist Party USA; Federal Bureau of Investigation; Hollywood blacklisting; House Committee on Un-American Activities; Roosevelt, Franklin D.; Supreme Court, U.S.; Wartime espionage in North America.

■ Hoover Commission

Identification Body that provided recommendations for reform of the executive branch of the federal government

Also known as Commission on Organization of the Executive Branch of the Government

Date Established on September 29, 1947

The Hoover Commission, named for its chairman, former president Herbert Hoover, was a late 1940's study of the executive branch of the U.S. government. Congress created the bipartisan task force at the behest of President Harry S. Truman, who believed in an activist government, but one with minimal waste and bureaucracy.

The objective of the Hoover Commission was to study how the executive branch could be more efficient and effective in its operations, including how to improve the financial reporting system. Although named for its chairman, and manned by distinguished government leaders such as former postmaster general James Farley and former ambassador Joseph P. Kennedy, Sr., much of the study was conducted by task forces headed by notable certified public accountants, namely T. Coleman Andrews, Paul Grady, and Arthur Carter. A large staff supported the commission's work.

In early 1949, the commission forwarded nineteen separate reports to Congress, which included 273 recommendations. By the mid-1950's, 116 of the recommendations had been fully implemented and another 80 had been partially implemented.

Impact When implemented, the recommendations of the Hoover Commission resulted in more efficient and effective operations in the executive branch. Moreover, the success of the Hoover Commission spawned similar studies, often called "little Hoover commissions," in some of the states wherein the efficiency and effectiveness of state government was evaluated. A second Hoover Commission was created at the federal level in 1953 by President Dwight D. Eisenhower; it finished its work in 1955.

Dale L. Flesher

Further Reading

Gervasi, Frank. *Big Government: The Meaning and Purpose of the Hoover Commission Report.* New York: Whittlesey House, 1949.

Hoover, Herbert C. *The Hoover Commission Report on Organization of the Executive Branch of the Government.* New York: McGraw-Hill, 1949.

See also Executive orders; Presidential powers; Presidential Succession Act of 1947; Roosevelt, Franklin D.; Truman, Harry S.

■ Hope, Bob

Identification English-born American comedian and film actor

Born May 29, 1903; Eltham, England

Died July 27, 2003; Toluca Lake, Los Angeles, California

A noted comedian who appeared on stage and in radio, television, and film, Hope was also known for his overseas tours entertaining military personnel during the 1940's and throughout his long career.

The fifth of seven sons, Bob Hope immigrated to the United States from England with his family when he was only five years old. While he was in high school, he decided that he wanted to go into acting and soon discovered he had a talent for comedy. During the 1920's, he danced, sang, and performed comedy routines in vaudeville shows. During the early 1930's, he started working in radio. After appearing in the Broadway show *Ballyhoo of 1932*, Hope met the singer Bing Crosby, and the two became good friends. In 1933, he met Dolores Reade, whom he soon married.

During the mid-1930's, Hope began making short films, increased his radio appearances, and worked in Broadway shows. During the late 1930's, he began appearing in feature films, many of which were cheaply made "B movies." A turning point in his career came when he signed with Pepsodent toothpaste to produce what would be a highly rated radio show that aired from 1938 to 1952. In that show, Hope usually opened with a humorous monologue, followed by a funny routine with his regular cast, some kind of interaction with a guest star, and, finally, a song. In 1947, he began appearing on television, on which he had continued success until 1992. His most popular programs were his Christmas specials.

Meanwhile, Paramount Pictures finally cast Hope in a major film in 1939's *The Cat and the Canary.* He then went on to make twenty major films during the

1940's. The most popular of his 1940's features were the "Road" films he made with Bing Crosby and Dorothy Lamour, such as *Road to Singapore* (1940). These light comedies paired Hope and Crosby as travelers bumbling their way through exotic adventures, usually while competing for the romantic attention of Lamour. The three leads often ignored their scripts and ad-libbed many of their lines. Lamour later said that she gave up trying to memorize her lines because Hope and Crosby never followed their own lines. By the early 1940's, Hope was famous and people flocked to his movies and personal appearances. He made twenty-six additional movies after the 1940's.

Such was Hope's popularity by 1940, that he was invited to host the Academy Awards ceremonies eighteen times between 1940 and 1978. He received no acting-award nomination but was given several lifetime achievement awards. Meanwhile, he began to broadcast radio programs from military bases in 1941. Hope and his regular troupe spent much of their time during World War II working with United Service Organizations (USO) to give free performances to American military personnel stationed throughout the world. He routinely played before jam-packed and enthusiastic audiences, and sometimes performed in the midst of enemy attacks in which his troupe narrowly escaped harm. While they were in Sicily in 1943, for example, German forces dropped bombs within two blocks of the hotel in which Hope and his crew were staying. Hope continued his performances for the military until the early 1990's.

Impact Already a star by 1940, Bob Hope saw his career take off during the 1940's, went on to enjoy one of the longest show business careers in entertainment history, and became an admired comedian through his work in radio, television, movies, and personal appearances, and for his charitable work.

Robert Cullers

Actor Bob Hope talking to American service personnel during a mid-1943 USO tour of England. At the upper right is singer Frances Langford. (AP/Wide World Photos)

Further Reading

Faith, William Robert. *Bob Hope: A Life in Comedy.* New York: Putnam, 2003.

Hope, Bob, and Pete Martin. *Have Tux, Will Travel: Bob Hope's Own Story.* New York: Simon & Schuster, 2003.

McCaffrey, Donald W. *The Road to Comedy: The Films of Bob Hope.* Westport, Conn.: Praeger, 2005.

Quirk, Lawrence. *Bob Hope: The Road Well Traveled.* New York: Applause Books, 2000.

See also Academy Awards; Broadway musicals; Crosby, Bing; Film in the United States; United Service Organizations; World War II.

■ Hopper, Edward

Identification American realist painter
Born July 22, 1882; Nyack, New York
Died May 15, 1967; New York, New York

Hopper's realism contributed to American painting a stern integrity of the mundane that is consistent with existentialist authenticity and the aura of film noir.

Edward Hopper studied painting at the New York School of Art between 1901 and 1906. Among his teachers were Robert Henri and John Sloan, who were part of the realist Ashcan School. In Europe, chiefly France, Hopper studied the Impressionists, sharing their preoccupation with the painting of light but retaining his penchant for realism. After 1910, he supported himself by commercial illustrations and etchings, one of which, *Night Shadows* (1921), anticipated the dramatic chiaroscuro of film noir. In 1924, he married the artist Josephine Nivison, whom he had known in his art student days; she became the exclusive model for his female figures.

The Hoppers settled in New York's Greenwich Village and, after Edward achieved financial success with oil paintings, purchased a summer home in South Truro, Massachusetts, in 1934. Edward's success began with *Early Sunday Morning* (1930), a study of morning sunlight and shadow on a red-brick building: The scene is bleak, but the ugly building projects a pristine solidity that accepts the transient, varying glow of early sunlight. An earlier painting, *Sunday* (1926), presents equivalent bleakness: a bald man sitting on a wooden boardwalk before closed wooden shops. The man appears to be unhappy or bored; but a cigar held firmly in his mouth and the strong fold of his arms contribute to a mien of pensive strength, and an urgent sunlight yields its color to the structures.

During the 1940's, Hopper concentrated on light (sunlight, twilight, artificial light), solidity in the bleak simplicity of older structures, and individuals whose self-possession belies their solitary status (they may be alone or ineffectively communicative, but they are not lonely). The harsh artificial light of his masterwork, *Nighthawks* (1942), amplifies the inscrutable attitudes of customers in a diner; and the garish bulb-light of *Summer Evening* (1947) eerily illumines a shorts-and-halter-clad young woman "holding out for matrimony" (according to Mrs. Hopper) and her boyfriend with his unconvincing demurral. All of Hopper's individuals are real human beings, whose minds and feelings, Hopper insisted, could not be reduced to the conceits of abstract expressionism, the contemporary movement that he eschewed.

Impact Hopper's main subjects were summer, the inchoate clarity of light, tradition, lighthouses, the solitariness of uncertainty, and the unapologetic dignity of plainness. His paintings, as established Americana, have been imitated in popular art, reproduced on book jackets and in movies (for

example, *Pennies from Heaven*, 1981), and incorporated with literature (for example, Lyons and Weinberg's *Edward Hopper and the American Imagination*, 1995).

Roy Arthur Swanson

Further Reading

Levin, Gail. *Edward Hopper: An Intimate Biography.* Rev. ed. New York: Rizzoli, 2006.
Souter, Gerry. *Edward Hopper: Light and Dark.* New York: Parkstone Press International, 2007.
Strand, Mark. *Hopper.* Rev. ed. New York: Alfred K. Knopf, 2001.

See also   Art movements; Art of This Century; Film noir; Literature in the United States.

■ Horne, Lena

Identification   Singer and film star
Born   June 30, 1917; Brooklyn, New York
Died   May 9, 2010; New York, New York

During World War II, Horne rose to prominence as a groundbreaking African American film star with a seven-year Metro-Goldwyn-Mayer contract. Although prejudice within Hollywood limited Horne's access to complex film roles, her refusal to play stereotypical characters challenged the film industry's racist representations of black women on the silver screen.

Under the mentorship of Walter Francis White, executive secretary of the National Association for the Advancement of Colored People (NAACP), Lena Horne signed a historic Metro-Goldwyn-Mayer (MGM) contract and launched her Hollywood career by singing in *Panama Hattie* (1942). The year 1943 was pivotal for her. *Life, Newsweek,* and *Time* featured articles introducing Horne, lauding her Savoy-Plaza performances and publicizing her burgeoning film career. Also in 1943, MGM and Twentieth Century-Fox produced two all-black musicals starring Horne: *Cabin in the Sky* and *Stormy Weather,* respectively. However, when Horne appeared in other MGM films showcasing primarily white casts, she was given singing roles but none with speaking parts. Her brief singing appearances, unimportant to plot development, allowed editors to cut her scenes for southern release.

Throughout World War II, Horne, a favorite

pinup girl among black G.I.'s, traveled America entertaining soldiers in segregated training camps. In 1947, Horne married Lennie Hayton, a Jewish composer, hiding her interracial marriage from fans until 1950. That same year, as a consequence of her civil rights activism, the anticommunist tract *Red Channels* listed her as a communist sympathizer; she was blacklisted as a result.

Impact Horne, the beautiful black chanteuse entertaining white characters in Hollywood films, was considered a new type of black female entertainer. She is still remembered for refusing to play the maid and mammy roles popular among white audiences of the 1940's.

Megan E. Williams

Further Reading

Bogle, Donald. *Bright Boulevards, Bold Dreams: The Story of Black Hollywood.* New York: One World/Ballantine Books, 2005.

_____. *Brown Sugar: Over One Hundred Years of America's Black Female Superstars.* New York: Continuum, 2007.

Buckley, Gail Lumet. *The Hornes: An American Family.* New York: Applause Books, 1986.

See also African Americans; Holiday, Billie; Hollywood blacklisting; Music: Popular; National Association for the Advancement of Colored People; Pinup girls; *Stormy Weather*; White, Walter F.

■ Horney, Karen

Identification Neo-Freudian psychoanalyst and theorist
Born September 16, 1885; Hamburg, Germany
Died December, 4, 1952; New York, New York

Horney was a follower of Sigmund Freud but later diverged from him. Particularly notable were her different views of women's psychology and her focus on culture.

Born Karen Danielsen, Horney taught at the New York Psychoanalytic Institute until 1941. She led the way to the founding of the Association for the Advancement of Psychoanalysis, was the founding dean of the American Institute for Psychoanalysis (1941-1952), and was founding editor of the *American Journal of Psychoanalysis* (1941-1952). She helped lay the groundwork for the Karen Horney Clinic, which was

established in 1955. Horney opposed Freud's ideas that penis envy, rejection of femininity, and wanting to be men were central in women's psychology. She also stressed the importance of culture in shaping women's psychology and neurosis. Her best-known book, *The Neurotic Personality of Our Time* (1937), was popular with the general public but made enemies for her among psychoanalysts. She was dropped from the New York Psychoanalytic Society in 1941 and excluded from the American Psychoanalytic Association. She found herself unable to publish her work in mainstream professional journals.

Impact Horney made significant contributions not only to psychoanalysis but also to the fields of humanism, self-psychology, and the psychology of women. Her analysis of neurosis and her revisions of Freud's theory of personality remain influential. The Karen Horney Clinic in New York continued to operate into the twenty-first century.

Ski Hunter

Further Reading

Paris, B. J. *Karen Horney: Gentle Rebel of Psychoanalysis.* New York: Dial Press, 1978.

Quinn, S. *A Mind of Her Own: The Life of Karen Horney.* New York: Summit Books, 1987.

Westcott, M. *The Feminist Legacy of Karen Horney.* New Haven, Conn.: Yale University Press, 1987.

See also Censorship in the United States; Education in the United States; Medicine; Philosophy and philosophers; Science and technology.

■ Horse racing

Definition The industry of breeding, marketing, and racing horses

The sport underwent changes to make it more fair, more reputable, and more popular with the public, and it saw four Triple Crown winners during the 1940's.

As the 1940's began, thoroughbred racing was a dynamic sport with racetracks throughout the country and a large contingent of fans. The large crowds at the racetracks were composed of both horse enthusiasts who appreciated the ability of the horses and individuals who were there to bet on the horses. The pari-mutuel system of legalized wagering had been introduced in the United States at Arlington Park

(Chicago) in 1933 and had contributed to an increase in attendance at the racetracks.

With the beginning of World War II, thoroughbred horse racing suffered greatly, with reduced attendance and decreases in the number of events. Just as the crowds were composed of two disparate groups, so the sport itself was, and remains, divided into two different classes: everyday races and prestigious stake races. The war effort severely disrupted daily racing at tracks throughout the country; however, the major races, in particular the Triple Crown races (the Kentucky Derby, the Preakness Stakes, and the Belmont Stakes), were not interrupted.

Four horses—Whirlaway (1941), Count Fleet (1943), Assault (1946), and Citation (1948)—won the Triple Crown, giving the 1940's more Triple Crown winners than any other decade. Both Whirlaway and Citation were owned by Calumet Farms, which dominated the sport during the 1940's, and were ridden by Eddie Arcaro, the only jockey to win two Triple Crowns. Each of these champions had unique characteristics. Whirlaway's speed and eccentricity made him special to the sport. Count Fleet was undefeated as a three-year-old and won the Belmont Stakes by a margin of twenty-five lengths. Citation was the first horse to win a million dollars and is still cited by some as the greatest racehorse that ever lived. Assault succeeded in the sport although he had suffered a crippling injury as a yearling and walked with a limp.

The practice of tattooing identifications onto horses was initiated during the 1940's. The sport had been plagued by disreputable individuals who won large sums of money by racing and betting on "ringers," horses that were raced with fictitious names and false papers so as to hide their identities as fast horses or to masquerade as slower horses. Early attempts at tattooing horses under the upper lip were not successful because the procedure caused considerable pain to the animals. In 1947, a method was de-

> ### Triple Crown Winners in Horse Racing
>
> *As of 2010, only eleven horses had won the Triple Crown. Four of the horses that have accomplished the feat did so in the 1940's, more than in any other decade. The Triple Crown of horse racing consists of the Kentucky Derby, the Belmont Stakes, and the Preakness.*
>
> | | | |
> |---|---|---|
> | Sir Barton (1919) | **Whirlaway** (1941) | Secretariat (1973) |
> | Gallant Fox (1930) | **Count Fleet** (1943) | Seattle Slew (1977) |
> | Omaha (1935) | **Assault** (1946) | Affirmed (1978) |
> | War Admiral (1937) | **Citation** (1948) | |

veloped that eliminated the pain; since that year, all racing thoroughbreds are required to be tattooed and are checked before each race. The Thoroughbred Racing Association was created in 1942, and in 1946, the Thoroughbred Racing Protection Bureau was established as a means to further protect the integrity of the sport.

Impact During the 1940's, the establishment of the Thoroughbred Racing Association, the implementation of horse identification by tattoos, and more stringent regulation of the industry improved the management and the image of the sport. The four exceptional horses that won the Triple Crown during the 1940's contributed immensely to the popularity of the sport and to creating traditions associated with it.

Shawncey Webb

Further Reading

Drager, Marvin. *The Most Glorious Crown: The Story of America's Triple Crown Thoroughbreds from Sir Barton to Affirmed.* Chicago: Triumph Books, 2005.

Georgeff, Phil. *Citation: In a Class by Himself.* Lanham, Md.: Taylor Trade, 2003.

Simon, Mary, and Mark Simon. *Racing Through the Century: The Story of Thoroughbred Racing in America.* Irvine, Calif.: Bow-Tie Press, 2002.

See also Arcaro, Eddie; Gambling; *National Velvet*; Recreation; Sports in Canada; Sports in the United States.

■ House Committee on Un-American Activities

Identification   Specially appointed congressional investigating committee

Also known as   House Un-American Activities Committee (HUAC); House Committee Investigating Un-American Activities

Date   Established in 1938; dissolved in 1975

This committee was assigned the responsibility of investigating possible cases of subversion, whether by individuals or by organizations, that might endanger the security of the United States. The main targets of its hearings were suspected communists.

During the mid-1930's, opposition to President Franklin D. Roosevelt's New Deal legislation prepared the way for a move to appoint a committee to investigate subvention of the security of the United States. A key figure behind this move was Texas Democratic congressman Martin Dies, Jr., who was elected to the House of Representatives in 1930. During the height of the Depression, Dies blamed part of the country's economic woes on the high numbers of immigrants to the United States, many of them poor, who he said often brought with them nondemocratic ideologies.

Given the rising wave of communism in Russia and the success of the Nazis in Germany, Dies argued the need for a special congressional committee to investigate presumed perpetrators of anti-American plots and spreaders of anti-American propaganda. He introduced a bill for a short-term (seven months, extendable by congressional vote) House Committee on Un-American Activities (commonly labeled HUAC). When the legislation passed on June 7, 1938, Dies became HUAC's chair, a post he would hold for almost eight years. He seemed determined to use the committee to undermine New Deal legislation for its "leftist-leaning" content. He included as targets union leader Harry Bridges and the Congress of Industrial Organizations (CIO), which he and his supporters viewed as sympathetic to communist influences. In 1938, Dies received the *Washington Post*'s Americanism award for his patriotic service.

The clouds of World War II, and especially the 1939 Molotov-von Ribbentrop Treaty, enabled supporters of HUAC to applaud Dies's inclusion of Adolf Hitler alongside Joseph Stalin as a champion of "double dealing" that menaced the future of the world. By the time the United States entered the war in 1941, the Nazi-Stalinist pact had collapsed, making the Soviet Union an appropriate military ally. Nevertheless, during the war HUAC continued to stress the dangers of communism as equal to, if not more significant than, those of fascism and Nazism.

After 1945, when HUAC became a permanent (standing) congressional committee, fear quickly mounted concerning the spread of communism not only abroad but also within the United States. A series of apparent advances made by communist regimes both by the Soviet Union, which spread its "protection" over Eastern Europe, and by China exacerbated fears in the West generally, and in the United States in particular. Alarming events abroad included a year-long Soviet blockade of Berlin beginning in 1948 and the testing of Russia's first atom bomb in August, 1949. In Asia, there was the takeover of the Chinese government by communists (followed by the onset of the Korean War about a year later).

HUAC Investigations of Entertainment   Such grave international situations notwithstanding, HUAC had begun to emphasize mainly domestic security issues. Some seven years after Dies had raised the issue of communist "inspiration" in the Hollywood film industry, the committee called a number of actors, producers, and directors to testify concerning allegations of possible communist influences in their work. When some—who became known as the "Hollywood Ten"—invoked the Fifth Amendment to avoid answering questions about communist associations, a blacklist was initiated that eventually would include more than three hundred names. The list included not only actors (perhaps the most famous being Charles Chaplin, who chose to leave the United States to continue his career abroad), but also screenwriters and playwrights, the German immigrant Bertolt Brecht among them, as well as directors and a handful of radio commentators. In the latter sphere, HUAC was encouraged to some degree by a campaign of denunciation by the well-known columnist and gossip figure Walter Winchell.

The strongly anticommunist testimony of Russian-born writer Ayn Rand as early as 1947 is often cited as representative of "cooperative" informants who came before the committee. Rand's testimony was particularly critical of representations of Soviet life in the work of the Hollywood producer Louis B. Mayer (cofounder of Metro-Goldwyn-Mayer), particularly the film *Song of Russia*, done in 1944. She felt that the film falsely depicted a generally contented population in a country of "slavery and horror."

Anticommunist sentiments and fears spread beyond the blacklisted individuals who were unable to find employment. Film studio and filmmakers avoided actions that could put them under HUAC's scrutiny, and many studios actually chose by the end of the 1940's and the early 1950's to produce clearly anticommunist films to prove their patriotic commitment. Films such as *Guilty of Treason* (1950), directed by Felix Feist, and *Big Jim McLain* (1952), starring John Wayne and John Arness as HUAC investigators, soon came to represent a patriotic backlash to "suspicious" productions under investigation by HUAC. Not only Hollywood personalities but also musicians, writers, and academic figures faced denunciation in front of HUAC from the mid-1940's and into the height of what came to be known as the "Red Scare," associated with the investigations of Senator Joseph McCarthy of Wisconsin, who was not a member of HUAC, which was a committee of the House of Representatives. Those under investigation included composer and conductor Leonard Bernstein, writer Langston Hughes, playwright Lillian Hellman, author Dashiell Hammett, and chemist and Nobel laureate Linus Pauling.

The Alger Hiss Case Although considerable attention would develop around HUAC's questioning of well-known figures in the artistic and literary worlds, one early case in particular—involving accusations of communist involvement by the former State Department official Alger Hiss—created political shock waves that would attract historians' attention long after the first HUAC hearings on this case were held in 1948. Hiss's principal accuser before the committee was writer and editor Whittaker Chambers, a disillusioned former communist who had provided vital wartime information to the U.S. government concerning Soviet double agents. On August 17, 1948, Chambers charged that Hiss had collaborated with the communist underground, of which Chambers himself had been a part. This set off a series of claims and counterclaims that led to Hiss's condemnation for perjury in 1950. Chambers's own autobiographical account, published as

Witness in 1952, went beyond the particulars of the Hiss case to focus on communist infiltration of a variety of key U.S. public and private institutions. By 1950, HUAC seemed eager to uncover evidence that the Hiss case was not an isolated one. Although nothing as spectacular as Whittaker Chambers's confrontation with Hiss would attract public attention, the committee would hear a large number of witnesses whose testimony harmed the careers of government employees in a number of departments at all levels.

HUAC's decline came gradually, despite condemnation of its methods by major figures including former president Harry S. Truman. As long as the Cold War posed a menace to American security, the committee's eagerness to investigate leftist extremists found support among politicians and at least a portion of the general public. Hearings during the Vietnam War era had an aura different from those of the 1940's and 1950's, with the hearings sometimes

Author Ayn Rand testifying before the House Committee on Un-American Activities in 1947. (Time & Life Pictures/Getty Images)

marked by denunciation of the committee by those called before it. HUAC was abolished in 1975, with its functions tranferred to the House Judiciary Committee.

Impact   Controversy concerning HUAC's activities occurred throughout its operation and decades beyond. Criticism from many fronts varied, ranging from regrets over its reflection of exaggerated fears of communist influence inside the United States to open condemnation of what some considered to be the committee's encroachments on the basic freedoms of thought and expression guaranteed by the Constitution of the United States.

Byron Cannon

Further Reading

Chambers, Whittaker. *Witness.* New York: Random House, 1952. An autobiographical account by a former communist who testified against former State Department official Alger Hiss before HUAC.

Goodman, Walter. *The Committee.* New York: Farrar, Straus and Giroux, 1968. A popular and complete history of HUAC's activities through most of the years of its operation.

Heale, M. J. *McCarthy's Americans: Red Scare in State and Nation, 1935-1965.* Athens: University of Georgia Press, 1998. An ambitious and well-researched study of McCarthyism.

Jacoby, Susan. *Alger Hiss and the Battle for History.* New Haven, Conn.: Yale University Press, 2009. A scholarly study of the Alger Hiss case and HUAC.

Klingaman, William. *Encyclopedia of the McCarthy Era.* New York: Facts On File, 1996. A complete compilation not only of issues and personalities connected with McCarthy's "one man campaign" itself but also of the entire atmosphere that prevailed in the heyday of HUAC's activities.

Swan, Patrick A., ed. *Alger Hiss, Whittaker Chambers, and the Schism in the American Soul.* Wilmington, Del.: ISI Books, 2003. Among the best recent historical surveys of the Hiss testimony before HUAC and its wider ramifications.

See also   Censorship in the United States; Civil rights and liberties; Communist Party USA; Films about World War II; Hiss, Alger; Hollywood blacklisting; Rand, Ayn; Socialist Workers Party; Unionism; Wartime espionage in North America.

■ Housing in Canada

After going through a decade during which the national housing situation had been constrained by a shortage of financing for construction, Canada faced new housing challenges during the early 1940's under the changing conditions brought by its entry into World War II, as a pressing issue became the need to provide housing for the increased number of employees in wartime industries. As the demand for housing grew throughout the decade, the Dominion government played an increasing role in making financing available.

In 1941, Canada's federal government created Wartime Housing, Ltd., to produce housing for people needed by the demands of wartime production. Within two years, 11,434 units of new housing were constructed under this program. In 1944, the rate of new building was accelerated by enactment of the National Housing Act. This legislation authorized local lending entities, chiefly banks, to lend up to 80 percent of the costs of construction of houses. Such loans were then rediscounted by the Dominion government, with the costs to be shared 75 percent by the Dominion and 25 percent by the provinces.

In 1948 another new entity, the Central Mortgage and Housing Corporation, absorbed Wartime Housing, Ltd., which, after the war, had continued to build housing for veterans. The corporation was authorized both to construct housing and to own and rent such housing as it was constructed. Cooperatives and other entities that wanted to sponsor low-rent housing were authorized to borrow up to 90 percent of the costs.

The Dominion government continued to build housing for the families of members of the military services. Canada's housing sector really took off, after the end of World War II, driven by the substantial population growth of the postwar era. In 1945 alone, 41,785 new housing units were built. This number jumped to 60,575 units in 1946, to 72,346 in 1947, to 76,097 in 1948 and to 80,000 in 1949.

The government guarantees of the mortgages financing these suburban developments continued to assist the local financing, notably the banks, that initially put up the money. Canada, however, continued to restrict most of its government support of housing financing to 80 percent of the cost, requiring new homeowners to finance the other 20 percent. Special loans were available to farmers, but that need was much reduced thanks to agricultural mechanization. During the prosperous postwar years, however, Canada's population largely became rehoused, mostly in single-family dwellings constructed of wood that the country had in large quantities, especially in the forests of British Columbia.

Impact By the end of the 1940's, Canada had largely reversed the housing deficit that had existed before the outbreak of World War II. A large number of these new housing units were in suburbs surrounding Canada's major cities and closely resembled new suburban housing being built in the United States.

Nancy M. Gordon

Further Reading

Fallick, Arthur L., and H. Peter Oberlander. *Housing a Nation: The Evolution of Canadian Housing Policy.* Ottawa: Canadian Mortgage and Housing Corporation, 1992.

A National Affordable Housing Strategy. Ottawa: Federation of Canadian Municipalities, 2000.

See also Architecture; Business and the economy in Canada; Demographics of Canada; Gross national product of Canada; Home furnishings; Housing in the United States; Urbanization in Canada.

■ Housing in the United States

The 1940's saw the beginning of mass-produced housing and changes in styles and sizes of housing, as well as changes in how and where the typical American family lived, with these changes sparked in part by the end of World War II and the return of millions of servicemen and -women.

In 1940, the existing housing stock was relatively primitive and small compared to that of the twenty-first century. Only about 54 percent of American houses had complete plumbing—running water, private bath, and flush toilet. Almost one-fourth had no electric power. Economists estimated that most American homes in 1940 had one thousand square feet of living space or less. In contrast, in 1998, new single-family homes on average had more than two thousand square feet of living space.

The years after 1940 also witnessed a dramatic change in the nature of American folk housing, those dwellings designed to provide basic shelter with little regard for changing stylistic fashions. Early twentieth century homes were generally small, unadorned houses. Beginning in the late 1940's, newly constructed minimalist dwellings took the form of prefabricated factory-built houses, beginning with the Quonset huts of World War II and later including other forms of mass-produced housing.

Most domestic building stopped between 1941 and 1945 as the United States prepared for and fought in World War II. When construction resumed in 1946, housing designs based on historical precedents were largely abandoned in favor of modern styles that had only begun to flourish in the prewar years.

New Housing Styles The earliest of the modern styles, the minimal traditional style, was a simplified form based on the previously dominant Tudor styles of the 1920's and 1930's. Like Tudor houses, those in the minimal traditionalist style generally had a dominant front gable and massive chimney, but the steep Tudor roof pitch was lower and the facade simplified by omitting most of the detailing. These houses first became popular in the late 1930's and were the dominant style of the postwar 1940's and early 1950's.

During the 1930's, a compromise style developed that retained the traditional main part of the house, but without the decorative detailing. Eaves and rake were close, rather than overhanging as in the coming ranch style. These houses were built in great numbers in the years immediately preceding and following World War II. They commonly dominated large tract-housing developments. They were built of stone, wood, brick, or a mixture of these materials. Although most were relatively small, one-story houses, some two-story houses were built in this style.

The ranch-style house originated with several California architects during the 1930's. It gained in popularity during the 1940's to become the dominant style throughout the United States during the 1950's and 1960's. "Rambling" ranch houses were made possible by the country's increasing use of the automobile. Streetcar suburbs of the late nineteenth and early twentieth centuries used relatively compact house forms on small lots because land in and near cities was relatively expensive. People needed to live near their jobs, however, because they depended on streetcars and other forms of public

Newly built postwar housing tract in Westchester, near Los Angeles International Airport. Homes selling there for about $12,000 in 1949 were valued at $600,000 to $800,000 in 2010. (Time & Life Pictures/Getty Images)

transportation that didn't extend far outside cities. As more people used automobiles, however, they could drive from further outlying areas, where they could afford land to build larger houses. This trend began in the immediate postwar years and accelerated in the 1950's and 1960's. The rambling form of the ranch house emphasized the increased use of space by maximizing the front width with an attached garage, side-by-side with the house.

Postwar Housing Shortages Because of the war and the Great Depression preceding it, very few new homes had been built since 1929, resulting in a severe housing shortage as soldiers returned home. New housing starts had fallen from about 1 million a year to fewer than 100,000. The birthrate had increased sharply, however, reaching 22 per 1,000 in 1943, the highest it had been in twenty years. Couples who now had children wanted houses of their own, or larger houses. During the war, it was reported that some 50,000 people were living in Army Quonset huts. The federal government quickly passed legislation banning nonessential construction so that all materials and labor could be focused on the immediate need to supply new housing.

A report to the U.S. House of Representatives in

1946 warned that housing shortages represented a national emergency. It stated that existing facilities were inadequate to provide the needed housing accommodations for the large number of veterans returning to civilian life. Based on past performance, it seemed unlikely that the private housing industry would be able to meet the challenge, especially given the economy's difficult return to normalcy after the war.

Two men in the construction business stand out in meeting the postwar challenge of providing housing: Carl Strandlund, who developed the Lustron style of home, and William Levitt, the driving force behind "Levittown" communities. About 2,500-3,000 of the porcelain-enameled, prefabricated Lustron houses were produced at a plant in Columbus, Ohio, beginning in 1948. The plant shut down as a result of bankruptcy and foreclosure in 1953. The first Levittown, on Long Island, New York, was built between 1947 and 1951 as a planned community of mass-produced houses designed to be built economically. The houses proved popular beyond expectations, so that the original plan for about 2,000 houses was expanded by several times, with more than 17,000 houses built in Levittown and the surrounding area. Similar communities were built in other states, and the ideas of efficiency in housing construction took root throughout the construction industry.

Levittowns The story of the Levittowns is instructive. In 1941, with a plan borrowing mass-production techniques popularized by Henry Ford in the automobile industry, the firm of Levitt and Sons, headed by Abraham Levitt and his sons William and Alfred, won a government contract to build 2,350 war workers' homes in Norfolk, Virginia. They suffered some disastrous weeks when everything seemed to go wrong, and they were unable to make a profit; they blamed the financial difficulties on high worker wages and difficulties in staying on schedule. They analyzed the construction process, breaking it down to some basic components. They figured out there were twenty-seven separate steps in building a house, so they planned to train twenty-seven separate teams—each team specializing in one step. This solution enabled them to speed up the entire process and eliminated the need to pay union wages because they could train unskilled workers. The firm applied these lessons and ideas in building the first Levittown and several subsequent planned communities.

Within the first Levittown, a bungalow designed for a young family, with four and one-half rooms including two bedrooms and one bath, rented to a veteran for $65 a month. That rent was relatively affordable: Right after the war, autoworkers made about $60 a week, and workers in other manufacturing sectors typically made about 80 percent of that. Each house came with radiant heating, a General Electric range, a refrigerator, and venetian blinds. The grounds were landscaped and featured concrete roads. Levittown was zoned as a park district, and one swimming pool was planned per thousand

houses. The community also featured three shopping centers, five schools built by the county on public contract, and six churches.

The first 1,500 veterans who rented for a year were given the option to buy a house. If the house was not purchased, the Levitt firm would agree to rent it for only one more year. The veteran homebuyers were backed by G.I. loans that required no cash down payment. The monthly carrying charges on G.I. loans were less than the rent paid, making home ownership difficult to resist. As Paul Goldberger of *The New York Times* noted years later, "Levittown houses were social creations more than architectural ones." He noted that they changed the detached single-family house from a distant dream to a real possibility for thousands of middle-class American families.

Lustron Homes Constructed entirely of steel, the modest ranch-style houses were Strandlund's answer to the severe housing shortage after World War II. Prefabricated of porcelain-enameled steel compo-

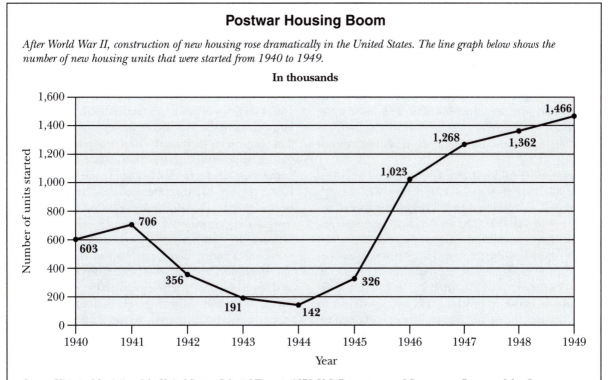

Postwar Housing Boom

After World War II, construction of new housing rose dramatically in the United States. The line graph below shows the number of new housing units that were started from 1940 to 1949.

In thousands

Number of units started (Year): 603 (1940), 706 (1941), 356 (1942), 191 (1943), 142 (1944), 326 (1945), 1,023 (1946), 1,268 (1947), 1,362 (1948), 1,466 (1949)

Source: Historical Statistics of the United States: Colonial Times to 1970. U.S. Department of Commerce, Bureau of the Census, 1975, p. 392.

nents, the houses could be mass-produced. They were marketed through an automobile-style dealer system to individual consumers, who would then erect the houses on site. The various houses offered for sale were about one thousand square feet. They all featured an exterior sheathing made of two-foot steel panels. The entire structure consisted of steel framing, interior and exterior walls, roof trusses, and even roof "tiles" made of enameled steel.

The business model failed. Even with new loans, the company was unable to produce the promised one hundred houses a day. Back orders accumulated, and buyers faced long delivery delays. The first Lustron home came off the assembly line in March, 1948. The factory turned out only twenty-six a day, with fifty needed to break even. Whatever the ultimate reason for the Lustron company's failure, the claims of durability and ease of maintenance of the steel houses have proved true. The majority of the Lustron houses remained standing into the twenty-first century, many with their original siding and roof as well as many inside features such as built-in cabinets.

The Government's Role in Housing The government influenced the housing market in other ways. Most of the changes were considered beneficial to the housing industry and to Americans generally, even those who had not served in the armed forces. Not all the legislation, however, can be considered as unqualified positive contributions. The most notable example of a policy decision later deemed regrettable was the internment of Japanese Americans.

President Franklin D. Roosevelt signed Executive Order 9066 on February 19, 1942. This order, though not related to housing directly, began the forced internment of 120,000 U.S. residents of Japanese ancestry, 77,000 of them American citizens. Its intent was to remove these people from coastal areas because of the perceived threat that they were enemy agents or saboteurs. Early in 1942, Italian and German aliens living in coastal areas were ordered to move, but by June of that year the order had been rescinded, and there was no major relocation for those groups. Italian and German immigrants were detained and questioned closely; following that, they retained all their rights. That was not true for Japanese Americans.

Japanese families were told to prepare whatever personal possessions they could carry and to vacate their homes on short notice. Tom Brokaw, in his book *The Greatest Generation* (1998), described the experience of one family that was relocated to one of several internment camps set up by the federal government. The relocation centers were not fully ready by the time the first people were forced to leaves their homes, and this family was taken to the Tulare County fairgrounds in central California. The family was housed in a converted horse stable, with the entire family sharing one stall. Fifteen thousand people were housed there for up to three months, then loaded onto a train with the blinds drawn. They were not told their destination and found themselves in the middle of the Arizona desert. In 1988, Congress passed an act calling for an official apology and reparations of twenty thousand dollars to each of the survivors of the internment camps. In signing the congressional action, President Ronald Reagan admitted that the United States had committed a "grave wrong."

In other housing-related governmental activity, on May 8, 1945, the Supreme Court declared unconstitutional any restrictive covenants regarding segregation. Such covenants, directed largely against African Americans, stipulated that a member of a particular racial or ethnic group could not buy a home within a particular area. Various "gentlemen's agreements" still existed, however, continuing cultural patterns that fostered the existence of segregated sections of many communities. In many of the large cities of the North, the area segregated as African American assumed the characteristics of a ghetto: inadequate municipal services, little police protection, and crowded housing, often at prices inflated relative to other areas of the city. Although it became illegal to enforce segregation by municipal ordinances, restrictive covenants were written into housing deeds, whereby all but Caucasians were shut out. Segregation, taking various forms in the North and the South, and in urban and rural areas, continued and by some measures actually increased between 1940 and 1950 through gentlemen's agreements between property owners and real estate agents.

The G.I. Bill On August 15, 1945, Japan surrendered, marking the end of World War II. Eight million servicemen and -women returned to civilian life in the United States, creating a severe housing shortage. Owning a home has always been central to the American Dream, and the G.I. Bill (the Servicemen's Readjustment Act of 1944) helped millions of young people to realize it, simultaneously revolutionizing the construction industry and housing development patterns across the United States. Prior to the G.I. Bill, many people who had desired to own a home had instead rented an apartment because that was all that was both available and affordable. Apartment occupancy meant not only a lack of housing space but also a lack of independence and security.

President Roosevelt signed the G.I. Bill into law on June 22, 1944. The Veterans Administration (VA) was responsible for carrying out the law's key provisions regarding education and job training; loan guarantees for homes, farms, or businesses; and unemployment pay. From 1944 to 1952, the VA backed nearly 2.4 million home loans for World War II veterans. Any veteran who had been honorably discharged could apply for a loan to buy a house. The government guaranteed the lending bank repayment of 50 percent of the loan, up to $2,000, and many homes could be purchased for less than $4,000. A loan could be used to purchase undeveloped residential property or construct a dwelling on unimproved property owned by the veteran.

Other Legislation　In 1945, in his first postwar message to Congress, President Harry S. Truman included an extension of the War Powers and Stabilization Act. Among other things, this meant that the government would provide federal aid for housing that made possible one million new homes a year. In 1948, Truman called for action on a program that would strengthen rent controls and further promote housing construction. In 1949, he issued an executive order authorizing twenty million dollars for low-rent housing in twenty-seven states, the District of Columbia, and Puerto Rico. He also issued an executive order to the Federal Housing Administration (FHA), which insures some home loans, to deny financial assistance to new housing projects with racial or religious restrictions.

In May, 1946, the Veterans' Emergency Housing Act implemented the Veterans' Emergency Housing Program, which called for significant government involvement in housing production, particularly in controlling critical materials, allocating factories that had been used for military purposes during the war, and providing loans through the Reconstruction Finance Corporation. Not everyone welcomed government intervention, particularly private housing developers, who challenged the existence of a housing crisis and saw the act as a threat to the private sector. The government set the ambitious goal of having 250,000 prefabricated houses erected in 1946 and 600,000 in 1947.

The Housing Act of 1949 provided federal financing for slum clearance programs associated with urban renewal projects in American cities in its Title I, allowed the FHA to insure mortgages in Title II, extended federal money to build more than 800,000 public housing units in Title III, and permitted the FHA to provide financing for rural home owners. In his state of the union address announcing the Fair Deal, President Truman observed that five million families lived in "slums and firetraps," with three million families sharing their homes with others. The Housing Act of 1949 was intended to redress those problems.

Impact　Laws and regulations from the 1940's related to housing shaped the future development of housing and housing policy. Most notably, segregation became illegal and the government took a larger part in promoting home ownership through insuring home loans. The decade saw the beginning of trends toward a greater proportion of stand-alone single-family dwellings and the creation of suburbs.

Jo Ann Collins

Further Reading

Brokaw, Tom. *The Greatest Generation*, New York: Random House, 1998. Nostaglic look back at the generation that carried America through World War II.

Mason, Joseph B. *History of Housing in the U.S., 1930-1980*. Houston, Tex.: Gulf, 1982. History of housing, housing policy, and domestic architecture from 1930 to 1980.

Mitchell, J. Paul. *Federal Housing Policy and Program: Past and Present*. New Brunswick, N.J.: Rutgers University Press, 1985. Examination of the political philosophy of postwar housing policies.

Squires, Gregory D., ed. *Urban Sprawl: Causes, Consequences and Policy Considerations*. Washington, D.C.: Urban Institute Press, 2002. Excellent collection of twelve articles on the legacy of suburbanization and its largely negative impacts.

Weiss, Marc. *The Rise of Community Builders: The Amer-*

ican Real Estate Industry and Urban Land Planning. New York: Columbia University Press, 1987. Useful history of tract housing and the landmark changes in American housing that unfolded during the 1940's and 1950's.

Wright, Gwendolyn. *Building the Dream: A Social History of Housing in America.* Cambridge, Mass.: MIT Press, 1983. An important work on the rich diversity of American architecture and housing from the colonial era through 1980.

See also   Architecture; Business and the economy in the United States; Credit and debt; Home appliances; Home furnishings; Housing in Canada; White House renovations; Wright, Frank Lloyd.

■ *Howdy Doody Show*

Identification   Children's television program
Date   Aired from 1947 to 1960

Originally broadcast on NBC radio, the Howdy Doody Show *became a pioneer television program that entertained children and provided a new medium for merchandizing and advertising.*

The *Howdy Doody Show* was one of the first television programs to prominently feature audience participation. At the beginning of every show, host Buffalo Bob Smith would ask his child audience, which sat in the Peanut Gallery bleachers, "Say kids, what time is it?" The children would shout, "It's Howdy Doody time!"

The Western-themed *Howdy Doody Show* took place in the fictional world of Doodyville. Smith supplied voices for Howdy Doody, a red-haired, freckled-face marionette in cowboy clothes. Other puppet characters included Phineas T. Bluster, Doodyville's mayor and Howdy's nemesis, and the Flub-a-Dub, a combination of eight animals. Among the notable human figures were Clarabell the Clown, who communicated by honking a horn and squirting a seltzer bottle; Princess Summerfall Winterspring, originally a marionette; and Chief Thunderthud, a foil to Clarabell.

Each show contained songs and skits, edu-

cational messages, moral lessons, and active participation from the children in attendance. Approximately 2,500 episodes were aired between 1947 and 1960. On the final show, a silent Clarabell finally spoke: "Good-bye, kids."

Impact   The *Howdy Doody Show* created American cultural icons, served as a model for other children's programs, and dramatically increased merchandising for toys, clothing, and lunch boxes for children.

Sharon K. Wilson and Raymond Wilson

Further Reading

Davis, Stephen. *Say Kids! What Time Is It?* Boston: Little, Brown, 1987.

Smith, Buffalo Bob, and Donna McCrohan. *Howdy and Me.* New York: Plume, 1990.

See also   Advertising in the United States; *Kukla, Fran, and Ollie;* Radio in the United States; Television.

Bob Smith with Howdy Doody sitting on his shoulders around 1948. (Getty Images)

■ Hughes, Howard

Identification American industrialist and owner
of RKO Pictures
Born December 24, 1905; Houston, Texas
Died April 5, 1976; in an airplane over southern
Texas

*Hughes's innovations and philanthropic endeavors
changed the way Americans worked and lived during the
1940's. His contributions to and involvement in aerospace
engineering, entertainment, and politics had a major influence on on the country's aviation, medical, and filmmaking industries.*

Howard Robard Hughes, Jr., was a man ahead of his
time. When he took over struggling Radio-Keith-
Orpheum (RKO) in 1948, he became the only individual to have sole control of a major Hollywood studio. As RKO's producer, director, writer, and editor,
filmmaking at the studio declined while problems
increased. Due to impending lawsuits from minority
shareholders accusing him of financial misconduct
and complaints from female actors about not honoring their contracts, Hughes later sold RKO theaters
as part of a settlement. The sale allowed him to refocus on aircraft manufacturing.

By the early 1940's, Hughes had become the new
owner of Transcontinental and Western Air (TWA),
a company he lost and regained ownership of three
times amid scandal. Transcontinental and Western
Air soon expanded to become Trans World Airlines.
Under Hughes's leadership, and despite looming legal and financial troubles, TWA became the second
American airline to fly overseas.

Hughes's continuous contributions to aviation attracted national and worldwide attention. In 1947,
the U.S. government contracted one of his inventions for use in World War II. The H-4 Hercules was
supposed to transport troops and equipment across
the Atlantic Ocean in lieu of sea transports that
were susceptible to the threat of German boats, but
his flying boat was not completed until just after
World War II had ended. It flew only once. At that
time, the 190-ton H-4 Hercules was the largest aircraft ever built and the largest made from wood. By
then, Hughes had founded several companies, including Hughes Aerospace Group, which specialized in manufacturing, developing, and acquiring
aircraft.

Impact Although Hughes was a controversial philanthropist who lived in seclusion and secrecy for
most of his life, he was one of the most influential
men during the mid-twentieth century. His countless acquisitions and numerous business dealings
made him one of the world's richest people. By the
end of the 1940's, the entrepreneur, pilot, and aircraft engineer had become a one of the world's first
billionaires.

Hughes's legacy continues through his enduring contributions to medicine and aviation. The
Howard Hughes Medical Institute (HHMI), established in 1953, is now one of the largest nonprofit organizations for biological and medical research in
the United States. In addition, his early work with
aircraft and his involvement in now-defunct TWA
significantly helped advance the American airline
industry.

Ramonica R. Jones

Further Reading
Phelan, James. *Howard Hughes: The Hidden Years.*
New York: Random House, 1976.
Tinnin, David B. *Just About Everybody Vs. Howard
Hughes.* Garden City, N.Y.: Doubleday, 1973.

See also Aircraft design and development; Film in
the United States; Ford Motor Company; General
Motors; Hughes, Howard; Inventions; Trans World
Airlines.

■ Hull, Cordell

Identification U.S. secretary of state, 1933-1944,
and winner of the Nobel Peace Prize in 1945
Born October 2, 1871; near Byrdstown, Overton
(now Pickett) County, Tennessee
Died July 23, 1955; Bethesda, Maryland

*Hull served as U.S. secretary of state through much of the
Great Depression and most of World War II. He believed
that the economics of free trade and reciprocity would establish harmonious international relations and ensure peace.*

A lawyer, circuit judge, and congressman (1907-
1921, 1923-1931) and senator (1931-1933) from
Tennessee, Cordell Hull politically represented the
farming interests of his constituents. After resigning
his Senate seat to serve as secretary of state (1933-
1944) under President Franklin D. Roosevelt, he

lobbied for low tariffs and reciprocal trade agreements.

Lower Tariffs   Throughout the 1940's, Hull continued policies he had launched during the 1930's. He had attended the London Economic Conference and well represented America's solutions for combating the Great Depression. Hull attended a pan-American meeting in Montevideo, Uruguay, the Seventh International Conference of American States, where he was supported by Argentina's foreign minister Carlos Saavedra Lamas, who desired a peace resolution that Hull encouraged. Hull secured Lamas's support for lower trade tariffs between nations of the Western Hemisphere. This partnership spawned a declaration stating that the United States would not intervene in the internal affairs of Latin American nations, thereby establishing the basis of Roosevelt's Good Neighbor Policy. This later proved crucial to hemispheric security, with most Latin American states declaring war against the Axis Powers after the attack on Pearl Harbor in December, 1941.

Hull had pushed for the Reciprocal Trade Agreements Act passed by Congress in 1934 that established the "most favored nation" policy written into future treaties, including the General Agreement on Tariffs and Trade. Hull promoted free trade and reciprocal trade agreements throughout Asia to combat Japan's ambitions and aggressions, and he hoped to extend the Good Neighbor Policy across the Pacific. He attended the Inter-American Conference for the Maintenance of Peace in Buenos Aires, Argentina, in 1936, and attended a pan-American meeting in Peru in 1938, producing additional endorsement of the Good Neighbor policy and hemispheric solidarity with the Declaration of Lima. In 1939, in an attempt to ensure peace for the Western Hemisphere, Hull proposed a hemispheric "neutrality zone" into which no belligerent warships could sail. In 1940, he stepped up negotiations for reciprocity, especially with Japan, China, and Pacific nations, believing that prosperous trade relations and neighborly economic policies could stave off war and dampen aggressors' ambitions. Seeking economic opportunities in China as well as an alliance, Hull supported Chinese Nationalist leader Chiang Kai-shek with political recognition and military supplies to counter Japanese threats of direct invasion of northern China from Manchuria. Hull distinguished himself at the Pan-American Conference in Havana in 1940. Hull, ever the optimist about the curative powers of free trade in establishing international harmony, continued to negotiate with Japan right up to the attack on Pearl Harbor.

U.S. secretary of state Cordell Hull (center) with Japanese ambassador Kichisaburo Nomura (left) and diplomat Saburo Kurusu preparing for diplomatic talks in Washington, D.C., only a few days before Japan launched its December 7, 1941, attack on Pearl Harbor. (Time & Life Pictures/Getty Images)

Wartime   During World War II, Hull coordinated details and policies of the State Department with war urgencies and was in contact with the president on a daily basis. The State Department's operations intersected with those of other U.S. departments and decisions such as the freezing of Japanese assets, internal security measures following Pearl Harbor, the de-colonization of European empires, as when France's Vichy government emerged in 1940 following German occupation, and issues involving war refugees. Hull exercised decisive leadership throughout the war and replaced personnel to harmonize his department, including Assistant Secretary of State Sumner Welles, whom he replaced in 1943 with Edward Stettinius, Jr., who would succeed him as secretary of state. He won support of other major countries for the plan to form the United Nations at a conference held in Moscow in October, 1943. (The name came from Roosevelt's use of "United Nations" for the nations fighting the Axis.) Hull spoke before Congress about postwar security arrangements and was lauded for his efforts in securing Moscow's endorsement for the United Nations. Hull worked behind the scenes to ensure that formation of the United Nations would not become a campaign issue in 1944; he convinced both presidential candidates to lend their support.

As the war neared its end, Hull sought to strengthen world postwar harmony through the establishment of the United Nations and spoke extensively in its support via national radio. Hull was the natural spokesman at the formative gathering of nations endorsing the United Nations at the Dumbarton Oaks Conference near Washington, D.C., in August, 1944. Hull's forcefulness and prestige, in addition to President Roosevelt's tremendous international respect and popularity, helped secure the placement of the United Nations' headquarters in the United States.

Hull retired from the State Department in November, 1944, due to ill health caused by tuberculosis. The United States was on the verge of victory in World War II, and Hull felt compelled to withdraw when victory was in sight. He became senior delegate to the United Nations conference in San Francisco, where the U.N. Charter was finalized and signed. For these efforts toward ensuring future peace, Hull won the Nobel Peace Prize in 1945. He wrote *The Memoirs of Cordell Hull* (1948), an account of his life as a public servant and promoter of world peace both through the United Nations and through his early efforts to create world prosperity through reciprocity and reciprocal trade agreements. He died after suffering a stroke and is buried in the National Cathedral in Washington, D.C.

Impact   As secretary of state, Hull rallied diplomatic forces and support for President Roosevelt's New Deal domestic agenda and for American strategic military efforts overseas during World War II. He hoped to regenerate prosperity for the world through trade negotiations and economic agreements. For Hull, peace was a by-product of world prosperity, and he strove to protect both through the establishment of the United Nations.

Barbara Bennett Peterson

Further Reading

Butler, Michael A. *Cautious Visionary: Cordell Hull and Trade Reform.* Kent, Ohio: Kent State University Press, 1998. Explains U.S. trade policies from 1933 to 1937, in which Hull played a major role.

Gellman, Irwin F. *Secret Affairs: FDR, Cordell Hull, and Sumner Wells.* New York: Enigma Books, 2003. Discusses intricate relations within the State Department from 1933 to 1944.

Hinton, Harold. *Cordell Hull: A Biography.* Garden City, N.Y.: Hinton Press, 2008. An authoritative and laudatory biography, originally published in 1942.

Hull, Cordell. *The Memoirs of Cordell Hull.* 2 vols. New York: Macmillan, 1948. Reprint. Irvine, Calif.: Reprint Services Corp., 1993. Hull candidly recounts his career in public service.

Pratt, Julius. *Cordell Hull, 1933-1944.* Vols. 12 and 13 of *The American Secretaries of State and Their Diplomacy,* edited by Robert Ferrell. New York: Cooper Square, 1964. Well-researched study of Hull's years as secretary of state.

See also   Acheson, Dean; Bretton Woods Conference; Byrnes, James; Convention on the Prevention and Punishment of the Crime of Genocide; Decolonization of European empires; Foreign policy of the United States; France and the United States; General Agreement on Tariffs and Trade; Geneva Conventions; Inter-American Treaty of Reciprocal Assistance; Marshall, George C.

■ *The Human Comedy*

Identification   Novel written in the form of loosely connected stories about a boy growing up during World War II

Author   William Saroyan (1908-1981)

Date   First published in 1943

The Human Comedy *was a best-selling novel that typified the move toward positivism in popular entertainment during the most challenging phases of World War II.*

The Human Comedy began as a 1943 film script by Armenian American author William Saroyan. Saroyan wrote the story for Metro-Goldwyn-Mayer (MGM), but he was fired because of creative differences. He quickly turned the script into a series of interrelated nostalgic and pensive stories that follow Homer Macauley, a fourteen-year-old boy growing up fatherless during World War II. Homer's older brother Marcus is a soldier destined to never return, so the young boy matures to become the man of the family, taking an evening job with the local telegraph office. In one of the novel's more poignant scenes, Homer has to inform a family that a son has been killed. Homer's siblings include a four-year-old brother named Ulysses, and some of the more powerful passages in the novel are told from his point of view.

The script and novel were created to offset the constant negative news from the war in Europe, and as such they were extremely popular. *The Human Comedy*, nonetheless, transcends simple Americana, as it alludes to Homer's epic poem, *The Odyssey*, through various character names and traits, the journey motif, place names, and relationships. For example, Homer's hometown is Ithaca, and he is in love with a young girl named Helen. Historian Steven Mintz describes *The Human Comedy* as a coming-of-age story in which the boys "gradually escape the fantasy world of childhood and become aware of the imperfections, sorrows, and tragedies of the adult world." The 1943 film, completed without Saroyan, won the Academy Award for best story and was adapted for television in 1959, and later for Broadway in 1984. Told from the point of view of the deceased father and through Marcus's stories, the film starred Mickey Rooney and Donna Reed.

Impact   Although Saroyan has lost some stature as an author, *The Human Comedy* is the paramount example of his ability to write for both high and popular culture. The original screenplay garnered an Oscar for the author, while the novel is studied in academia as an example of writing that affirms American optimism and humanistic values.

Anthony J. Fonseca

Further Reading

Floan, Howard R. *William Saroyan*. Twayne's United States Authors Series, 100. New York: Twayne, 1966.

Leggett, John. *A Daring Young Man: A Biography of William Saroyan*. New York: Alfred A. Knopf, 2002.

Stevens, Janice. *William Saroyan: Places in Time*. Fresno, Calif.: Craven Street Books, 2008.

See also   *The Best Years of Our Lives*; Film in the United States; Literature in the United States; *The Naked and the Dead*; *Studies in Social Psychology in World War II*; World War II.

■ Ice hockey

By the 1940's, amateur and professional hockey in North America had been organized for nearly a half century, and the game was increasing both in number of participants and in its commercial appeal. The National Hockey League (NHL), with amateur hockey following suit, undertook several changes during the 1940's that made ice hockey more exciting for both players and spectators.

During the war years of the early 1940's, professional ice hockey experienced a shortage of players. Physically fit men between the ages of eighteen and forty-five were drafted into the U.S. and Canadian armies. During the war years, the NHL sent as many as ninety players to the war and subsequently shrank from ten teams down to six. Many of these enlisted players competed for their countries' military teams, which are considered amateur, thus boosting the level of the amateur ranks. In 1942, the RCAF (Royal Canadian Air Force) Flyers won the Allan Cup, given to the champion senior amateur men's team in Canada.

After the war, professional and amateur ice hockey stabilized in the number of participants. The NHL was a solid six-team league: the Montreal Canadiens, Toronto Maple Leafs, Boston Bruins, New York Rangers, Chicago Black Hawks, and Detroit Red Wings. The Toronto Maple Leafs were the dominant team of the 1940's, winning the Stanley Cup (for the league championship) in 1942, 1945, and 1947-1949. The Montreal Canadiens and Detroit Red Wings were also top-notch teams. The Chicago Black Hawks often finished at the bottom of the league, and this prompted the

league to request other teams to send the Black Hawks any players they could spare. The Boston Bruins and New York Rangers started the 1940's strongly but then struggled, typically ending up near the bottom of the six-team league.

One NHL hockey legend was created in 1941, the year after the New York Rangers won the Stanley Cup. The Rangers, after paying off the mortgage on their home arena at Madison Square Garden, burned the mortgage certificate in the sacred Stanley Cup. This was said to start a curse that kept the Rangers from winning the Stanley Cup again until 1994.

Rule Changes   Professional ice hockey made some changes during the 1940's to develop the game. Whatever the NHL did, amateur hockey across North America tended to follow its lead. The NHL changed a rule to allow a forward pass across the blue line, which was not allowed prior to 1943. Play-

Detroit Red Wings goalie Johnny Bowers making a difficult save against the Boston Bruins in a 1941 NHL game. (AP/Wide World Photos)

Hart Memorial Trophy Winners, 1940-1949

Year	Player	Team
1940	Ebbie Goodfellow	Detroit Red Wings
1941	Bill Cowley	Boston Bruins
1942	Tommy Anderson	Brooklyn Americans
1943	Bill Cowley	Boston Bruins
1944	Babe Pratt	Toronto Maple Leafs
1945	Elmer Lach	Montreal Canadiens
1946	Max Bentley	Chicago Blackhawks
1947	Maurice "Rocket" Richard	Montreal Canadiens
1948	Buddy O'Connor	New York Rangers
1949	Sid Abel	Detroit Red Wings

Note: The Hart Memorial Trophy is synonymous with the most valuable player award.

ers now could pass from their defensive zone across the blue line, up to the newly created center red line. Prior to the red line being added, players had to skate the puck across the blue line, even if their team had a penalty. This rule revolutionized ice hockey, changing it from a puck-handling sport to a faster-paced passing game. Because of the lack of players during the war years, overtime in the regular season stopped in 1942 and was not brought back for forty-one years.

To capitalize on the more exciting version of ice hockey, the NHL in 1949 increased the number of games each team played, from forty-eight games to seventy. In 1949, the president of the NHL, Clarence Campbell, declared that he did not favor televising games because that would keep fans from coming to see games live, but they continued to be telecast. Within a few years, the NHL was broadcasting hockey in Canada nationwide, and it became a fixture of Canadian households.

The NHL also made changes to players' standard equipment and to arenas during the 1940's. Maple Leaf Gardens, home of the Toronto Maple Leafs, installed herculite glass above the boards in 1947, the first arena in the world to do this. All players used simple leather gloves until a Detroit goalie in 1948 introduced the trapper and blocker, a rectangular piece of leather on one hand and a glove similar to a baseball catcher's on the other. Players' equipment

incorporated plastic inside the equipment for the first time during the late 1940's. For the start of the 1949 season, the NHL painted the ice surface white so the puck would be more visible to fans.

Rising Stars Although many potential star players were in the military during the early 1940's, one player did emerge as a superstar. Maurice "Rocket" Richard, a French Canadian who played for the Montreal Canadiens, had a fiery personality and intense playing style. He was rejected from military service because he had brittle bones. During the 1944-1945 season, Richard scored fifty goals in fifty games, a feat that would not be matched for thirty-six years. He also scored five goals in one playoff game in 1944, a record that had not been matched as late as 2010. Future star Gordie Howe began his NHL career in 1946 at the age of eighteen.

Impact Professional and amateur ice hockey evolved into a fast-paced game with heavy body contact. This created many rivalries among players and teams. The game changed rules and adapted its arenas and players' equipment, all of which made the game more exciting and added to its commerical appeal. The changes in professional and amateur ice hockey during the 1940's propelled ice hockey into the modern era.

Timothy Sawicki

Further Reading

Askin, Mark, and Malcolm G. Kelly. *The Complete Idiot's Guide to the History of Hockey.* Toronto: Pearson Education Canada, 2000. A quick overview of the game's history.

Houston, William. *Pride and Glory: 100 Years of the Stanley Cup.* Whitby, Ont.: McGraw-Hill Ryerson, 1992. A history of winners of the professional championship.

McKinley, Michael. *Hockey: A People's History.* Toronto: Canadian Broadcasting Corporation, 2006. Chronicles the game from its beginning, including the teams, rules, and equipment. Boxed features highlight individuals and oddities of the game.

Pincus, Arthur, with David Rosner, Len Hochberg, and Chris Malcolm. *The Official Illustrated NHL*

History: The Story of the Coolest Game. Chicago: Triumph Books, 2001. Authoritative and comprehensive look at the game, filled with statistics and other information. Numerous historical and contemporary photographs.

See also   Baseball; Basketball; Football; Richard, Maurice; Sports in Canada; Sports in the United States.

■ Ickes, Harold

Identification   U.S. secretary of the interior, 1933-1946
Born   March 15, 1874; Frankstown Township, Pennsylvania
Died   February 3, 1952; Washington, D.C.

During World War II, Ickes was a major force in mobilizing oil resources for the war effort, expanding the nation's wilderness areas, and defending minority rights.

In 1933, Democratic president Franklin D. Roosevelt selected Harold Ickes, a progressive Republican lawyer from Chicago, to be his secretary of the interior. Ickes, an avowed curmudgeon, became a major voice against appeasement and a harsh critic of Nazi Germany and Imperial Japan long before World War II broke out. By 1940, the issues of the war were overshadowing those of the Great Depression.

During the war, Ickes headed the Petroleum Administration for War and was a major force behind the construction of the "Big Inch" and "Little Big Inch" pipelines, which by war's end were bringing 390,000 barrels of oil per day from the Southwest to the East Coast. He was also responsible for the establishment of the Jackson Hole National Monument in 1943. Though a vocal critic of Japanese internment during the war, in 1944 Ickes was given responsibility for the many thousands of Japanese Americans held in relocation centers throughout the country.

Ickes remained as secretary of the interior after Roosevelt's death in 1945, but his troubled relationship with President Harry S. Truman led to his resignation in February, 1946. He died in 1952.

Impact   Ickes was among the earliest to advocate a firm response to the totalitarian threat in Europe and a key figure in many domestic events of the war

years. Never an easy person to work with, he was one of the last of the New Deal liberals.

Eugene Larson

Further Reading
Ickes, Harold L. *The Secret Diary of Harold L. Ickes.* Vol. 3, *The Lowering Clouds, 1939-1941.* New York: Simon & Schuster, 1955.
Kennedy, David M. *Freedom from Fear: The American People in Depression and War, 1929-1945.* New York: Oxford University Press, 1999.
Watkins, T. H. *Righteous Pilgrim: The Life and Times of Harold L. Ickes, 1874-1952.* New York: Henry Holt, 1990.

See also   Elections in the United States: 1940; Jackson Hole National Monument; Japanese American internment; National parks; Natural resources; Roosevelt, Franklin D.

■ Illinois ex rel. McCollum v. Board of Education

The Case   U.S. Supreme Court decision on religious instruction in public schools
Date   Decided on March 8, 1948

This decision invalidated a state released-time program to facilitate religious instruction during the school day, on school property, and articulated a robust theory of the separation of church and state.

The city of Champaign, Illinois, released public school students in grades four though nine from class to attend religious instruction once a week. Clergy and lay members of participating faiths were permitted to offer religious instruction during the school day, using classrooms in the public school building.

The parent of a child in the Champaign schools brought suit challenging the program under the First Amendment to the U.S. Constitution. The state argued that the clause "Congress shall make no law respecting an establishment of religion" only prohibited discrimination in favor of one sect over another, and did not prohibit aid to all religions equally. Arguably, the program failed under the state's proposed understanding of the First Amendment since only mainstream Protestants, Roman Catholics, and Jews were offered instruction. However, the Court, through Justice Hugo L. Black, held the program unconstitutional due to the use of tax-supported public school facilities to hold religious classes and the close cooperation between school officials and religious organizations in administering the program.

Impact   The decision held that a state may not aid religion over secularism, or vice versa. *Zorach v. Clauson*, in 1952, would uphold religious instruction off school property, even during the compulsory school day, because it did not involve the use of public facilities or funds.

John C. Hughes

Further Reading

Hall, Kermit L., *The Oxford Companion to the Supreme Court of the United States.* New York: Oxford University Press, 1992.

Pfeffer, Leo. *Church, State, and Freedom.* Boston: Beacon Press, 1967.

See also   Civil rights and liberties; Education in the United States; *Everson v. Board of Education of Ewing Township*; Religion in the United States; Supreme Court, U.S.

■ Immigration Act of 1943

The Law   Federal law that repealed the Chinese Exclusion Acts, which since 1882 had prevented Chinese nationals from immigrating to the United States and seeking naturalization

Also known as   Chinese Exclusion Repeal Act; Magnuson Act

Date   Signed into law on December 17, 1943

The act was passed at a time when the United States needed to promote goodwill with China, an ally during World War II. Its passage represented the first step toward liberalizing the immigration of Filipino and Asian Indians in 1946, and it led to passage of broader immigration acts in the years that followed.

The Chinese Exclusion Act of 1882 had made it virtually impossible for Chinese citizens to immigrate to the United States legally and to seek U.S. citizenship. Many Chinese nationals or their offspring then lived in the United States, mostly workers who arrived during California's gold rush and who subsequently stayed to work in helping to build the trans-

continental railroad system. The exclusion act and subsequent similar acts imposed staunch prohibitions on Chinese immigration and forbade any Asians from attaining U.S. citizenship.

During the 1940's, the United States was drawn into World War II by the Japanese attack on Pearl Harbor on December 7, 1941. Many Americans were isolationists, and the Pearl Harbor attack aroused anti-Asian sentiments in many moderate Americans who distrusted all Asians because of the Japanese attack.

In 1943, because China had become a valued supporter of the United States against the Japanese aggressors, President Franklin D. Roosevelt urged Congress to repeal the Chinese Exclusion Act of 1882 and similar exclusionary acts aimed specifically at the Chinese. Roosevelt sent a special message to Congress calling for the repeal of the exclusionary acts then in effect. On December 17, 1943, Congress voted in favor of the repeal and the president signed the act into law.

The Terms of the Repeal   A consummate politician, Roosevelt realized that the United States could garner the goodwill of China by repealing its former repressive immigration acts aimed specifically at the Chinese. Following his advice, Congress modeled the act of repeal on provisions set by the Immigration Act of 1924. This earlier act limited immigration from any country to 2 percent of the number of people from that country who were residents of the United States in 1890 or earlier—certainly a substantial restriction.

In the case at hand, the annual Chinese immigration to the United States under the terms of this policy would number 105, such a paltry number that even the xenophobes and isolationists in Congress could not strongly object to the passage of the bill, particularly when the president had made a compelling case for rewarding China in this way for its wartime support that was still desired and needed.

The legislation Roosevelt hoped to see Congress pass was formally proposed by Warren G. Magnuson, a respected member of Congress from Washington, a state that had a considerable Chinese population. The bill permitted Chinese nationals already living in the United States to become naturalized citizens. The passage of this bill marked the first time since the Naturalization Act of 1790 that Asians could be naturalized.

Impact The immediate impact of this legislation was a strengthening of the bond between the United States and China, a desirable outcome that President Roosevelt had foreseen and strongly supported. Because this bill opened the door to Asian immigration, however slightly, immigration regulations pertaining to people from the Philippines and India were enacted in 1946 and permitted Filipinos and Asian Indians to immigrate to the United States in small numbers and to seek naturalization.

All these changes in immigration regulations for Asians resulted in the passage of the Immigration and Nationality Act of 1952, based upon an ethnic quota system. The Immigration and Nationality Act of 1965 completely did away with a quota system based on national origins.

R. Baird Shuman

Further Reading

Aarim-Heriot, Najia. *Chinese Immigrants, African Americans, and Racial Anxiety in the United States, 1848-1882*. Urbana: University of Illinois Press, 2003. An interesting comparative overview of early Chinese immigration to the United States during the gold rush and in the years following it.

Chan, Sucheng, ed. *Chinese American Transnationalism: The Flow of People, Resources, and Ideas Between China and America During the Exclusionary Period*. Philadelphia: Temple University Press, 2006. A penetrating account of the interactions between the American and Chinese communities during a period when American discrimination against Asians was rife.

_____. *Entry Denied: Exclusion and the Chinese Community in America, 1882-1943*. Philadelphia: Temple University Press, 1991. Among the best accounts of the legislation and events that led up to the repeal of the Chinese Exclusion Act of 1882. Strongly recommended.

Daniels, Roger. *Coming to America: A History of Immigration and Ethnicity in American Life*. 2d ed. New York: HarperCollins, 2002. A comprehensive look at the lives of Asian immigrants to the United States and their struggle to attain the right to remain there.

_____. *Guarding the Golden Door: American Immigration and Immigration Policy Since 1882*. New York: Hill & Wang, 2003. Well-written and accessible account of the various acts that Congress has passed regarding Asian immigration.

Gyory, Andrew. *Closing the Gate: Race, Politics, and the Chinese Exclusion Act*. Chapel Hill: University of North Carolina Press, 1998. Although Gyory does not discuss the Immigration Act of 1943 specifically, the background information that he provides will help readers to understand the necessity of such an act.

Koehn, Peter H., and Xiao-huang Yin, eds. *The Expanding Roles of Chinese Americans in U.S.-Chinese Relations*. Armonk, N.Y.: M. E. Sharpe, 2002. A close look at the growing relations between the United States and China and the effect that the repeal of the Chinese Exclusion Acts had upon these relations.

See also Asian Americans; China and North America; Foreign policy of the United States; Immigration to the United States; Isolationism; National Security Act of 1947.

■ Immigration to Canada

By the end of the 1940's, the Canadian government became pressured to accept large numbers of European immigrants to meet the labor needs of Canada's growing economy. However, many European lives might have been saved had the state not shut its doors to immigration during World War II. The Canadian government also repealed its exclusionary immigration acts directed at visible minorities after 1947, yet continued to deny people of color immigration to Canada.

Canadian immigration policy during the 1940's was shaped by two factors. In the first half of the decade, the outbreak of World War II virtually halted any immigration to Canada. In the period after the war, the Canadian government slowly began to open its doors to immigrants, especially after 1947. Nevertheless, postwar immigration during the late 1940's consisted primarily of immigrants from Europe.

Immigration During World War II, 1940-1945 During World War II, the Canadian government drastically reduced immigration, which already had been minimal as a result of the Depression and large-scale unemployment. Fewer than one thousand European refugees managed to enter Canada during the war. Even after the Holocaust and Nazi persecutions became widely known, the anti-Semitic and xenophobic sentiments that permeated Canadian public opinion shaped the government's immigration policy, which continued to deny the admission of Jewish and non-Jewish refugees.

The criteria for immigration to Canada throughout the 1940's continued to reflect the traditional prejudices of the Canadian public and Canadian officials, with "preferred" and "desirable" immigrants being British, American, and Western European, and "nonpreferred" and "undesirable" immigrants being Eastern and southern European. Canadian anti-Semitism, racism, and xenophobia permeated immigration policy, under which various groups of people continued to be denied immigration through exclusionary legislation such as the Chinese Exclusion Act, the Gentlemen's Agreement (excluding immigrants from Japan), and the Continuous Journey Stipulation (denying immigrants from India). Jewish immigration was severely restricted. Canadian state officials discouraged African Americans from crossing the border into Canada. Japanese Canadians were seen as a threat to Canada after Pearl Harbor; similar to their treatment in the United States, they were labeled "enemy aliens," stripped of their property and personal effects, and placed in internment camps in British Columbia.

Immigration in the Postwar Period, 1946-1949 In the immediate postwar era of the late 1940's, many Christian and Jewish Europeans sought immigration to Canada to start new lives. Many of these applicants were refugees or "displaced persons" who had been in concentration or labor camps, had their homes and livelihoods destroyed by the war, or were fleeing political, religious, racial, and social oppression.

Despite growing labor demands from the business sector, the Canadian government was reluctant to open the country's doors to new immigrants in 1946. Although the Canadian public remained opposed to immigration, business leaders were able to convince the government to admit more immigrants, but the government proceeded cautiously. In 1946, the government focused its attention on allowing the foreign dependents of members of the Canadian armed forces, namely the wives, children, and fiancées of Canadian military personnel.

By 1947, the Canadian government began to explore a slightly expanded immigration policy that was focused on expanding Canada's economy both domestically and internationally. The government recognized that it was necessary to recruit workers of all skill levels—skilled, unskilled, and semiskilled. The Canadian government also realized that it should participate in solving the problem of vast numbers of displaced persons. New immigration regulations, however, echoed prewar Canadian immigration policy, with preference given to British, American, and Western European immigrants, along with Eastern Europeans suited to specified farming, mining, or forestry jobs. These new regulations kept to a minimum Jewish refugees, the vast majority of whom were Holocaust survivors.

An Order in Council was passed in early 1947 that stated five categories of immigrants who would be permitted entry. The first category allowed the immigration of sponsored immediate relatives of Canadians who were in a position to accept full responsibility for the care of their immigrant relatives. Other categories included farmers with sufficient means to establish and run their own farms, immigrants with relatives in Canada willing to accept responsibility for the applicant and establish the applicant on a farm, and immigrants with guaranteed employment as farmworkers. The last category specified immigrants with work experience in mining or forestry who had guaranteed employment in one of these industries. These categories essentially denied Jewish refugees admission to Canada, given that Jews had little or no experience in farming and rural work because historically they had been banned from the practice of farming in Europe. Furthermore, in the aftermath of the Holocaust, few Canadian Jews had living first-degree relatives in Europe.

In 1947, the Worker's Project was established to admit immigrants from Europe who could fulfill the needs of Canadian business. The relevant Order in Council granted permission for 2,136 tailors, 500 furriers, 3,000 domestics, and 260 dressmakers. Immigrants were selected by Canadian immigration labor teams in Europe. The Canadian Jewish community had assumed that this program would enable European Jewish refugees to immigrate to Canada, but once the project was approved in Parliament, the government stipulated that only half of the workers could be Jewish and that their immediately family members, including spouses and children, would be counted in the quota. The government demanded that for every Jew brought over under this project, a non-Jew must also be recruited. Because the professions of tailor and furrier typically had been Jewish occupations, it was difficult to find non-Jews for recruitment under this program. Non-Jewish European refugees also had other Canadian immigration schemes open to them, including one concerning farming, forestry, and mining.

Under the War Orphans' Project, established in 1947, the government gave permission for one thousand Jewish orphans to come to Canada, provided that they were under the age of 18 years, both parents were dead, and Jewish child care agencies across Canada would accept complete responsibility for their care.

A revised Family Reunification Plan was estab-

lished in 1948 that broadened the parameters defining people eligible for sponsorship by Canadian relatives. European immigrants who could now be sponsored by their Canadian relatives included spouses, parents, children and siblings with their spouses and unmarried children, orphan nephews and nieces under the age of twenty-one, and fiancés. In many cases, however, the European relatives of Canadian Jews had died in concentration camps. Those European Jews who had come to Canada under the Worker's Project were not in a financial position to assume the economic responsibility for their sponsored family members. In these cases, Jewish social services assumed social and financial responsibility for these Jewish refugees. The number of Euro-

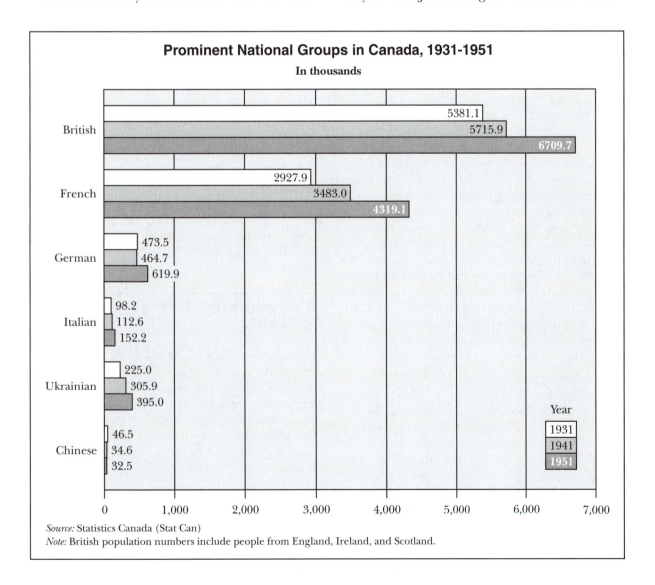

Prominent National Groups in Canada, 1931-1951

In thousands

British: 5381.1 (1931), 5715.9 (1941), 6709.7 (1951)
French: 2927.9 (1931), 3483.0 (1941), 4319.1 (1951)
German: 473.5 (1931), 464.7 (1941), 619.9 (1951)
Italian: 98.2 (1931), 112.6 (1941), 152.2 (1951)
Ukrainian: 225.0 (1931), 305.9 (1941), 395.0 (1951)
Chinese: 46.5 (1931), 34.6 (1941), 32.5 (1951)

Year: 1931, 1941, 1951

Source: Statistics Canada (Stat Can)
Note: British population numbers include people from England, Ireland, and Scotland.

pean Jews admitted to Canada in the period from 1946 to 1949 was negligible in comparison to the steady stream of white, Christian, European immigrants, some of whom were Nazi war criminals. Immigration officials also rejected prospective immigrants perceived as communist sympathizers on the basis of "national security interests."

In 1947, the Canadian government repealed the Chinese Exclusion Act and the Continuous Journey Act, the latter as a concession to British Commonwealth solidarity. That same year, the Canadian government released Japanese Canadians from internment. Although the exclusionary legislation barring immigration of people of color was removed, immigration of non-Europeans was negligible throughout all of the 1940's.

Impact Canada's immigration policy throughout the 1940's was based first and foremost on the criteria of race and ethnicity. Had the country not had such a restrictive policy during and prior to World War II, many thousands of European lives might have been saved. Even in the postwar 1940's, immigrant selection remained exclusive, indirectly limiting the number of European Jewish refugees and unofficially denying the entrance of people of color.

Throughout the late 1940's, the Canadian government found itself pressured by business leaders to admit more immigrants to meet the growing demand for labor in the booming Canadian economy. The need for labor would fuel immigration policy changes during the 1950's that would facilitate the unrestricted admission of European immigrants who previously had been considered "undesirable," including Jewish and non-Jewish refugees from Europe, as well as southern and Eastern Europeans. Non-European immigrants continued to be denied immigration to Canada.

Kelly Amanda Train

Further Reading

Hawkins, Freda. *Canada and Immigration: Public Policy and Public Concern.* Kingston, Ont.: McGill-Queen's University Press, 1988. Explores Canadian immigration policy and how it has been implemented in the post-World War II era.

Jakubowski, Lisa Marie. *Immigration and the Legalization of Racism.* Halifax, N.S.: Fernwood, 1997. Jakubowski analyzes how Canadian immigration policy was aimed at building a white, British settler nation until the early 1960's.

Kelley, Ninette, and Michael J. Trebilcock. *The Making of the Mosaic: A History of Canadian Immigration Policy.* Toronto: University of Toronto Press, 1998. A detailed examination of Canadian immigration policy, exclusionary acts, and discriminatory practices aimed at various immigrant groups from pre-Confederation to the 1990's.

Knowles, Valerie. *Strangers at Our Gates: Canadian Immigration and Immigration Policy, 1540-2006.* Toronto: Dundurn Press, 2007. Critically examines Canadian immigration policy and how it was shaped by social, economic, and political factors.

Satzewich, Vic, and Nikolaos Liodakis. *"Race" and Ethnicity in Canada: A Critical Introduction.* Toronto: Oxford University Press, 2007. Explores how Canadian immigration policy and Canadian nation-building have been shaped through the notions of race and ethnicity, and in relationship to the international political economy.

Walker, Barrington, ed. *The History of Immigration and Racism in Canada: Essential Readings.* Toronto: Canadian Scholars' Press, 2008. This collection of scholarly works discusses the role of race and ethnicity in Canadian immigration policy.

See also Canadian Citizenship Act of 1946; Canadian minority communities; Immigration to the United States; Israel, creation of; Jews in Canada; Jews in the United States; King, William Lyon Mackenzie; Racial discrimination; Refugees in North America.

■ Immigration to the United States

The admission of Jewish refugees from Europe, the limited admission of Chinese and other Asian immigrants after decades of exclusion, and the recruitment of guest workers from Mexico to address wartime agricultural labor shortages shaped U.S. immigration policy during the 1940's. Each of these elements engendered varying degrees of controversy, and each had long-term effects on American immigration policy.

Immigration to the United States fell sharply with the passage of the Immigration Act of 1924 (Johnson-Reed Act) and the National Origins Act of 1927. Largely ignored during the 1930's, immigration policy resurfaced as an issue in the United States during the 1940's as the result of three international issues—World War II, the Holocaust, and the early Cold War. During the late 1930's, most Americans, suffering from the effects of the Great Depression, saw little reason to oppose the immigration restrictions that had been imposed during the 1920's. Economic hard times and the scarcity of jobs meant that employers had little interest in importing labor from abroad, and most Americans, viewing immigration as a social issue, believed that the decline in new immigration helped speed the Americanization of previous immigrants and their children.

The rise of Nazi Germany and its known persecution of Jews, political minorities, and other "undesirables," however, as well as the rise of fascist regimes in Italy and Spain, raised concerns about the fate of refugees from those countries. Initially, there was little interest in admitting refugees because of a widespread belief that to do so would only encourage further persecution in their home countries, as well as expulsion. By the war's end, however, both widespread knowledge of the truth of Germany's so-called final solution (the extermination of Jews) and the widespread problem of war refugees sparked efforts to at least temporarily relax immigration restrictions, while emphasizing repatriation for most European refugees and immigration to Palestine for Jewish refugees. After the United States entered the war, embraced China as an ally against Japan, and experienced an agricultural labor shortage resulting from widespread conscription, the country dealt with new issues that would result in the immigration of more non-white immigrants than ever previously.

The early Cold War also had a lasting impact on American immigration policy, based on the combination of concern for refugees, including from communist regimes, and concern for keeping "subversives" and potential spies from entering the United States. Although these events and concerns would not immediately end the race- and ethnicity-based restrictions of the 1920's, they forced a reconsideration and reshaping of American immigration policy that culminated in the 1965 immigration reforms that ended racial exclusion and created new categories of priorities for the admission of immigrants to the United States.

Immigration Policy and the Holocaust The Nazi Holocaust began during the 1930's, but its impact on American immigration lasted well beyond World War II. Although the persecution of Jews in Germany had been a feature of German life and government since Adolf Hitler's seizure of power in 1933, the November 9-10, 1938, attack on German Jews and their homes, businesses, and institutions, commonly known as *Kristallnacht* (the night of broken glass), brought to the world's attention the seriousness of the Nazi regime's anti-Jewish intentions. American enthusiasm remained limited, however, for accepting the growing number of Jewish refugees. The Department of State made it difficult to fill even the limited immigration quotas for Germany, by strictly applying the test of whether a refugee was likely to become a public charge and emphasizing caution against unwittingly admitting spies. In 1940, the Smith Act, which criminalized antigovernment activity and required the registra-

U.S. immigration officials and Coast Guard officers boarding a liner arriving from Europe to inspect passengers' passports in 1949. (AP/Wide World Photos)

Immigration to the United States by Country, 1940-1949

Year	Total from all countries	Great Britain	Germany	Italy	China	Canada	Mexico
1940	70,756	6,158	21,520	5,302	643	11,078	2,313
1941	51,776	7,714	4,028	450	1,003	11,473	2,824
1942	28,781	907	2,150	103	179	10,599	2,378
1943	23,725	974	248	49	65	9,761	4,172
1944	28,551	1,321	238	120	50	10,143	6,598
1945	38,119	3,029	172	213	71	11,530	6,702
1946	108,721	33,552	2,598	2,636	252	21,344	7,146
1947	147,292	23,788	13,900	13,866	3,191	24,342	7,558
1948	170,570	26,403	19,368	16,075	7,203	25,485	8,384
1949	188,317	21,149	55,284	11,695	3,415	25,156	8,083

Source: Historical Statistics of the United States: Colonial Times to 1970. U.S. Department of Commerce, Bureau of the Census, 1975. Based on U.S. Immigration and Naturalization Service, unpublished data.

tion of all adult noncitizens, further stigmatized immigrants.

The outbreak of war and the breaking of diplomatic relations with Germany made any prewar arrangements for the admission of refugees difficult to carry out. Two barriers to greater action were a reluctance to accord any group of refugees special treatment, even though Jews alone were being targeted for death, and an unwillingness to risk letting rescue efforts take away from the war effort, even as Germany willingly sacrificed its own war effort toward the destruction of European Jewry. The divided and largely powerless American Jewish community had limited influence on the actions of the Franklin D. Roosevelt administration, and many organizations were reluctant to push the issue too hard.

For much of the early war years, the Department of State and Congress resisted proposals to admit more refugees, arguing that to do so would merely encourage Nazi Germany's persecutions, and many other nations followed the American example. The British-sponsored 1943 Bermuda Conference on Refugees attempted to find other solutions to the Jewish refugee problem, but it was severely limited in its permissible actions and had almost no Jewish participation. Its only concrete recommendation was the transport of twenty-one thousand refugees

from Spain to North Africa, an effort that was subsequently blocked by U.S. secretary of state Cordell Hull, who also continued to oppose relaxing immigration quotas or even granting visitor's visas to Jewish refugees. News of the conference's limited actions, at a time when Jews were being killed at an accelerating pace and when the inmates of the Warsaw ghetto were fighting a month-long pitched battle against deportation to concentration camps, sparked Jewish and even some congressional outrage and demands for more serious rescue efforts.

It was not until later in the war, however, when victory over Nazi Germany seemed relatively assured, that Roosevelt took any significant action. Even then, it was only as the result of the efforts of Secretary of the Treasury Henry Morgenthau and his subordinates Randolph Paul and John Pehle to wrest control of the refugee issue from the State Department, after the latter had spent eight months delaying the mere approval of funds to assist Jewish refugees in Romania and France. After Morgenthau received evidence of the delay, as well as the State Department's effort to withhold information, Morgenthau authorized Paul, Pehle, and Josiah DuBois to author a damning documentation of the State Department's actions and inactions, originally titled "Report to the Secretary on the Acquiescence of This Government in the Murder of the Jews." On

January 16, 1944, Morgenthau presented to Roosevelt an abridged version of the document with the less provocative title of *Personal Report to the President*. Six days later, Roosevelt issued Executive Order 9417, creating an independent War Refugees Board, with Pehle appointed as acting executive director. The War Refugee Board's many rescue efforts included the opening of a refugee camp near Lake Oswego in upstate New York. Although the effort proved to be too little, too late, it did show the potential for the rescue the U.S. government might have accomplished had a concerted effort been mounted earlier. In the end, most of the Jewish refugees who received safe passage to the United States were well-off and well connected, many with some kind of organizational sponsorship.

Other Wartime Immigration Issues The U.S. government proved to be restrictive against refugees, but immigration policy and legislation were not uniformly about keeping people out. Many of the immigration policy decisions made by the U.S. government during World War II relaxed and even eliminated long-established racial restrictions on immigration. For example, since 1882, the Chinese Exclusion Act had banned Chinese immigration to the United States and excluded Chinese immigrants from U.S. citizenship. When China became a key U.S. ally during World War II, however, this discriminatory policy became much harder to justify, and on December 17, 1943, Congress passed the Magnuson Immigration Act, also known as the Chinese Exclusion Repeal Act, which allowed legal Chinese immigration and made it possible for Chinese immigrants in the United States to apply for citizenship. Although the act allowed only a severely limited quota of new Chinese immigrants per year, it was a significant break from the racially based ban on Chinese immigration. In 1946, Asian Indians were permitted to immigrate and become citizens under the same conditions.

By contrast, following the Japanese attack on Pearl Harbor, Japanese immigrants (who were still barred from citizenship) and their American-born descendants were targeted by the federal government as potential spies and agents of espionage. Roosevelt's Executive Order 9066 forcibly removed people of Japanese descent from West Coast communities and forced them into internment camps in the Western interior. The camps were ordered

closed following the Supreme Court case *Ex parte Endo* (1944). The plaintiff's case was based on her status as an American citizen, and it only tangentially addressed the issue of discrimination against Japanese immigrants.

During the 1940's, American immigration policy and the underlying racial issues also were affected by wartime labor shortages. Although Mexican immigration was not limited under the national origins quota restrictions of the 1920's, in practice the southern border of the United States was strictly guarded for much of the interwar years. When the United States entered World War II, however, the draft created a severe shortage of agricultural labor, which led to the 1942 creation, in cooperation with Mexico, of the Emergency Farm Labor Supply program, commonly known as the bracero program.

The bracero program (the name is derived from the Spanish word *brazo*, meaning "arm") was intended as a wartime guest worker program but ended up lasting into the 1960's. The thousands of Mexicans who migrated to the United States through the bracero program both affirmed relatively open American borders and created new problems for the Mexican American community in the Southwest. Mexican Americans had long been subject to Anglo-American discrimination and prejudice. Many were descendants of people who had suddenly become residents of the United States when Mexico ceded large amounts of territory to end the Mexican-American War in 1848, and many were deliberate immigrants or descendants of immigrants. For much of their history, many of them had pursued and encouraged assimilation, pressing for equal treatment on the basis of their "whiteness" through organizations such as the League of United Latin American Citizens (LULAC, established in 1929). Many Mexican Americans opposed the bracero program and the liberalized Mexican migration it allowed, as a threat to their own status, but paradoxically they defended those Mexican migrants who already were in the United States.

During the war years, anti-Mexican incidents such as the zoot-suit riots prompted a number of Mexican Americans toward greater solidarity with new immigrants and led to the creation of progressive organizations such as the Congress of Spanish-Speaking Peoples that challenged the assimilationist stance of LULAC. Mexican American union activists became increasingly vocal in support of the rights of alien Mexican workers as well as Mexican American workers. Both U.S. citizens and Mexicans working and living in the United States contributed to the postwar rise of the Mexican American civil rights movement.

Impact The biggest challenges to prewar immigration policies and the racial and ethnic assumptions behind them came in the postwar years. The revelation of the reality behind Hitler's so-called final solution and the reality of eight million European refugees, known as displaced persons, sparked unprecedented efforts toward immigration reform during the immediate postwar years. Although most refugees eventually were repatriated and many European Jewish survivors responded to encouragement to migrate to Palestine, the arrival of the Cold War created additional refugees as well as the political necessity of the United States to accept at least some refugees, even against congressional and popular opposition.

The Displaced Persons Act of 1948, which President Harry S. Truman signed with reluctance because of its discriminatory features, authorized the admission and transportation to the United States of 205,000 displaced persons, as well as 17,000 orphans, mostly from Eastern Europe. Rather than waiving immigration quotas, the act continued to limit Jewish immigration and merely reshuffled the numbers by allowing higher levels of current immigration that were traded against the quotas of future years. Despite these limitations, the Displaced Persons Act for the first time allowed refugee status to override racial and ethnic restrictions, a policy that was continued with the admission of Chinese political refugees following the 1949 Chinese Revolution, which in turn more firmly brought an end to the Chinese Exclusion Act.

The 1950 McCarran-Walter Act did not end the national origins quota system, but it allowed for considerations such as needed skills even while it reemphasized maintaining restrictions against potential "subversives" and reshaped quotas to prevent non-white nationals of Britain's colonies from taking advantage of Britain's substantial quota. Even with these limitations, however, the combination of the post-World War II immigration legislation and the growing political power of ethnic Americans led to the end of the national origins quotas with the Immigration and Nationality Act of 1965 (Hart-Celler Act).

Susan Roth Breitzer

Further Reading

Graham, Otis L. *Unguarded Gates: A History of America's Immigration Crisis.* Lanham, Md.: Rowman & Littlefield, 2004. History of the changing politics of American immigration restriction and reform.

Gutiérez, David G. *Walls and Mirrors: Mexican Americans, Mexican Immigrants, and the Politics of Ethnicity.* Berkeley: University of California Press, 1995. A history of Mexican American ambivalence regarding Mexican immigration that reflected conflicting ideas about assimilation to Anglo-American society.

Morse, Arthur D. *While Six Million Died: A Chronicle of American Apathy.* New York: Random House, 1968. One of the first histories of the Holocaust to focus on the inaction and silence of the United States and the rest of the world.

Newton, Verne W., ed. *FDR and the Holocaust.* New York: St. Martin's Press, 1996. The published proceedings on the controversial issue of President Roosevelt's actions and inactions during the Holocaust.

Wyman, David. *The Abandonment of the Jews: America and the Holocaust, 1941-1945.* New York: Pantheon Books, 1984. A searing indictment of the inaction and apparent indifference on the part of the U.S. government during the Holocaust.

Zolberg, Aristide. *A Nation by Design: Immigration Policy in the Fashioning of America.* New York: Russell Sage Foundation, 2006. A history of the varying roles of politics and government policy in the shaping of American immigration.

See also Asian Americans; Bracero program; China and North America; Demographics of the United States; Foreign policy of the United States; Immigration Act of 1943; Jews in the United States; Latin America; Latinos; Mexico; Refugees in North America; Smith Act.

■ Income and wages

Definition   Wages, including salaries, represent compensation to hired labor, paid in money paid to hired labor; other types of income include property income and government transfer payments

During the 1940's, rapid increases in the aggregate demand for goods and services raised demand for real output and consequently for labor. Average annual earnings rose about 40 percent during the war and maintained that level afterward.

In 1940, the American economy was expanding rapidly but was still far from full employment (which is different from zero percent unemployment because a smoothly running economy will have some people unemployed as the economy adjusts to various changes). Real gross national product (the dollar amount of production divided by a measure of the average level of prices) had finally exceeded the 1929 level, but there were still eight million workers unemployed, representing 15 percent of the labor force.

Incomes in 1940   Personal income in 1940 was about $78 billion. About two-thirds of this figure was in the form of wages and salaries. Another one-sixth went to owners of unincorporated businesses, including farmers, professionals such as doctors and lawyers, shopkeepers, and repairpeople. Most of this also was labor income. The $12 billion of property income (rents, interest, and dividends) was far below the $18 billion of 1929. Transfer payments from government, made to individuals but not in exchange for their labor, were relatively small. Benefit payments were just beginning for Social Security— only $35 million was paid in 1940. Personal taxes were also low. Most families did not pay federal income tax, and the Social Security tax on individual wage earners was only 1 percent.

Annual earnings in the different sectors fell into three broad groups. High pay ($1,700+) was generated by finance, transport, and communications, reflecting high levels of skill and education. Intermediate pay ($1,300+) was found in manufacturing, mining, construction, trade, and government. Extremely low pay was observed in services, especially in agriculture. In addition to their wages, many farmworkers received some room and board

as well, and its value is not reflected in income figures.

Wages in 1940 were affected by two important developments from the 1930's. The Fair Labor Standards Act of 1938 set the federal minimum wage at $0.40 an hour, and its requirement to pay time and a half for hours in excess of forty per week went into effect in 1940. Under the influence of the Wagner Act of 1935, membership in labor unions was expanding rapidly, and unions attempted to use the combined bargaining power of workers to raise wages. These two developments undoubtedly raised wage incomes for some workers, but increases in wages may have impeded the reduction in unemployment.

Developments During the 1940's   Powerful forces affected the American labor market during the 1940's. Aggregate demand, as measured by gross national product (GNP) in current prices, was already rising rapidly by 1940, and defense spending drove it up more strongly beginning in 1941. Between 1940 and 1945, nominal GNP more than doubled, going from $100 billion to $212 billion. The end of the war brought a slight drawback in 1946, but the surge was renewed quickly as taxes were cut and wartime controls on wages and prices were removed. By 1948, GNP reached $258 billion, then remained at about that level during the recession of 1949. U.S. Census estimates showed a huge increase in employment, from 45 million workers in 1940 to 58 million in 1949. The number working in agriculture, where productivity and pay were relatively low, dropped from 8.4 million in 1940 to 6.9 million in 1950.

Another powerful force was the military draft, which removed a large number of young men from the civilian labor force. By 1945, about 12 million people were in military service. The draft reduced unemployment, contributed to labor shortages, and encouraged more women to work in defense industries. Labor unions were able to expand their membership from about nine million in 1940 to fifteen million in 1945.

Increased demand for labor and a reduced labor supply combined to send wages strongly upward. Annual average earnings rose from about $1,300 in 1940 to $2,200 in 1945, easily outrunning inflation, so that real earnings (adjusted to remove price increases) rose about 40 percent. The apparent rise in

U.S. Personal Income and Related Items, 1941 and 1949

Type	1941 Total in billions of dollars	1941 Percentage of total	1949 Total in billions of dollars	1949 Percentage of total
Employee compensation	49.8	63.6	134.6	65.2
Proprietors' incomes	13.0	16.6	35.3	17.1
Interest, dividends, rent	12.3	15.7	24.1	11.7
Transfer payments, net	3.1	4.2	12.4	6.0
Total personal income	78.2	100.0	206.4	100.0
Less personal taxes	2.6	4.0	19.0	9.0
Total disposable personal income	75.6	—	187.4	—

Source: U.S. Bureau of the Census. *Historical Statistics of the United States, Colonial Times to 1970, Bicentennial Edition, Part 2.* Washington, D.C.: Government Printing Office, 1975, pp. 241-242.

Notes: Proprietors' incomes indicates income of unincorporated businesses and farms. Transfer payments, net indicates net of contributions for social insurance.

real wages may be misleading. Some products (for example, automobiles) either were unavailable or were available in lower quantities than people wanted to buy, so that their prices, and therefore average prices, were not pushed up. Money wages, or nominal wages, continued to rise after the war, reaching $2,800 by 1949, but continued inflation kept apparent real wages essentially unchanged between 1945 and 1949. The effective increase in real wages during the war likely is exaggerated by the data; if so, then the effective increase after 1945 is larger than shown by the data.

During the war, wage controls were imposed as part of the federal government's price-control system. The Stabilization Act of October, 1942, authorized wage controls as well as price controls. The National War Labor Board became the principal agency regulating wage increases. Although manufacturing wage rates rose by 14 percent between October, 1942, and August, 1945, the increase was much less than the 17 percent rise from January, 1941, to October, 1942.

Wage controls began to erode immediately after the war ended. A series of wage disputes and work stoppages affected the petroleum refining, automobile, steel, meatpacking, and farm machinery industries, among others, in the fall and winter of 1945-1946. When President Harry S. Truman vetoed a bill to extend the stabilization acts in June, 1946, the control system essentially collapsed. Between August, 1945, and November, 1946, manufacturing wage rates rose 19 percent, while consumer prices rose 18 percent. The end of controls was appropriate, allowing private market forces free rein as the economy underwent a massive shift away from war-related production. Some ten million people were released from military service in 1945-1946, prompting fears of a major depression and widespread unemployment, but these fears were not realized.

A long-term result of wage controls, combined with high wartime income tax rates, was the expansion of employer-financed fringe benefits, such as insurance and retirement programs. These fringe benefits provided ways employers could reward workers without violating wage controls or incurring tax liabilities.

Labor market conditions were turbulent during the late 1940's, as prices continued to move upward. Union membership continued to grow, and labor disputes were frequent and disruptive. A response was the adoption of the Taft-Hartley Act in 1947. As noted above, money wages continued to rise, but they only kept pace with rising prices. In 1948, the inflationary pressure from rapidly rising aggregate demand slacked off, and the economy entered a recession in 1949. Unemployment rose to 3.6 million in 1949, but even this was only about 6 percent of the civilian labor force.

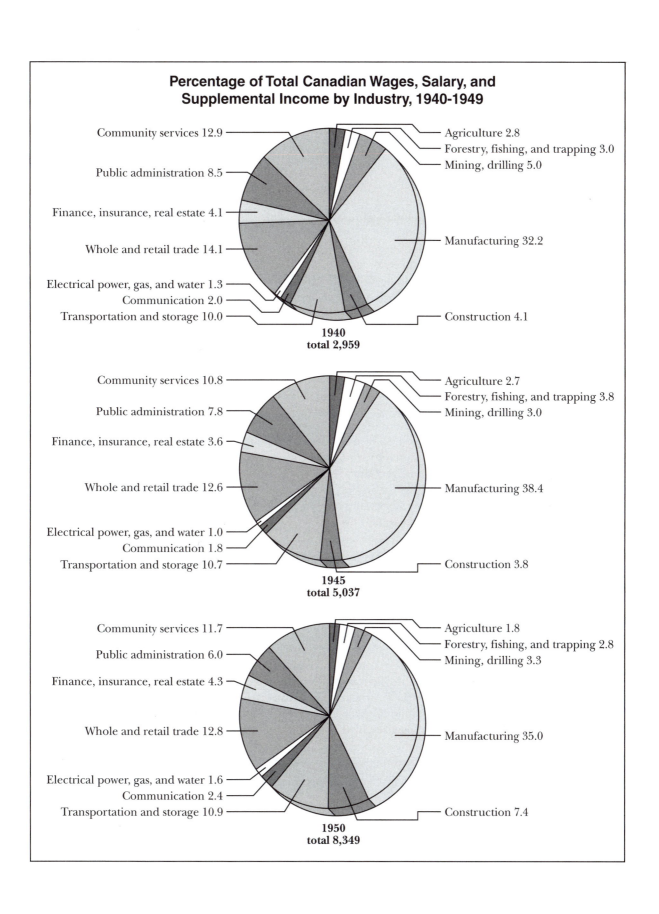

Percentage of Total Canadian Wages, Salary, and Supplemental Income by Industry, 1940-1949

1940
total 2,959

Community services 12.9
Public administration 8.5
Finance, insurance, real estate 4.1
Whole and retail trade 14.1
Electrical power, gas, and water 1.3
Communication 2.0
Transportation and storage 10.0
Agriculture 2.8
Forestry, fishing, and trapping 3.0
Mining, drilling 5.0
Manufacturing 32.2
Construction 4.1

1945
total 5,037

Community services 10.8
Public administration 7.8
Finance, insurance, real estate 3.6
Whole and retail trade 12.6
Electrical power, gas, and water 1.0
Communication 1.8
Transportation and storage 10.7
Agriculture 2.7
Forestry, fishing, and trapping 3.8
Mining, drilling 3.0
Manufacturing 38.4
Construction 3.8

1950
total 8,349

Community services 11.7
Public administration 6.0
Finance, insurance, real estate 4.3
Whole and retail trade 12.8
Electrical power, gas, and water 1.6
Communication 2.4
Transportation and storage 10.9
Agriculture 1.8
Forestry, fishing, and trapping 2.8
Mining, drilling 3.3
Manufacturing 35.0
Construction 7.4

Incomes and Wages in 1949   Despite the recession, the American economy in 1949 was vastly improved from that of 1940. With the end of the war in 1945, pent-up demand was released for automobiles, houses, home furnishings, appliances, and other items that were not available during the war or were not affordable with temporarily low incomes. In addition, young people married and bore children in record numbers, adding to the demand for products and services. The G.I. Bill enabled millions of veterans to attend college and raise their marketable skills. Even in 1949, the economy was still a full-employment economy, with more and better jobs. Personal income, which had been $78 billion in 1940, reached $207 billion in 1949. Over the same period, however, consumer prices had risen by 70 percent, and the population was 13 percent larger. Adjusting for these changes indicates that real personal income per capita rose by 38 percent from 1940 to 1949. The federal minimum wage was increased from $0.40 to $0.75 an hour in 1949.

The table on page 512 shows components of personal income for 1949. In comparison with 1940, the proportions of the three private components did not change much. Both personal tax rates and transfer payments were moving upward, however, in the start of a long trend. In 1939, only 3.9 million families paid personal income tax. By 1943, this had risen to 40 million families, then fell slightly to 36 million in 1949. In 1943, the government began to withhold income tax from people's pay. By 1949, more than 1 million families were receiving Social Security benefits. About 2 million unemployed workers were receiving unemployment compensation, and benefits totaled about $1.7 billion, helping to relieve the recession of 1949.

Wage and salary incomes showed differences in race, gender, and age. In 1939, white workers received more than double the annual pay of African Americans and other ethnic minorities. Female workers received less than two-thirds as much as males. Many factors contributed to these differences. Among these, four are worth noting. Men and women tended to hold different kinds of jobs and in different sectors. Ethnic minorities were heavily concentrated in agriculture. Large differences in skill and education existed among different groups of workers. Finally, discrimination affected all of these variables. By 1950, the pay difference between white males and other male workers had fallen substantially, but women's pay relative to white men's slipped slightly.

In 1941, the top one-fifth of families received nearly half of the total of personal income, and the top 5 percent received nearly one-fourth. By 1950, the distribution had shifted strongly toward equalization. The lower three quintiles all increased their shares substantially, largely at the expense of the top fifth. The share of the top 5 percent declined by about 3 percentage points.

Two major contributors to the equalization were the large increase in employment of the formerly unemployed and the shift of workers out of farming and into higher-paid industrial work. Furthermore, between 1940 and 1950, the percentage of women in the labor force increased from 25 to 31 percent. This meant higher money incomes for households but fewer unpaid household services.

The equalization of incomes was reflected in the reduction of poverty across the 1940's. According to Oscar Ornati, about 32 percent of the population was in poverty in 1941. By 1944, only 15 percent of people were poor. The proportion rose again after the war's end, reaching 28 percent in 1950.

Impact   Although the war brought pain and suffering to many Americans, it was the centerpiece of a decade in which prosperity and full employment returned. The war completed recovery from the Great Depression. Aggregate demand grew vigorously throughout most of the decade. Benefits were widely shared, and poverty was reduced.

Paul B. Trescott

Further Reading

Chandler, Lester V., and Donald H. Wallace. *Economic Mobilization and Stabilization.* New York: Henry Holt, 1951. Extensive discussion of wartime wage controls and their relationship to price controls.

Kersten, Andrew. *Labor's Home Front: The American Federation of Labor During World War II.* New York: New York University Press, 2006. Gives detailed attention to issues such as race, gender, and work safety.

Lebergott, Stanley. *Manpower in Economic Growth: The American Record Since 1800.* New York: McGraw-Hill, 1964. The historical development of wages is integrated with all elements of labor supply and demand. Numerous examples.

Lichtenstein, Nelson. *Labor's War at Home: The CIO in World War II.* New York: Cambridge University Press, 1982. Discusses the role and development of the Congress of Industrial Organizations, a federation of labor unions. Good summary chapters on both prewar and postwar periods.

Robertson, Ross M. *History of the American Economy.* 2d ed. New York: Harcourt, Brace & World, 1964. Chapter 23 of this readable college text places labor developments of the 1940's in a long-run perspective.

Wilson, Richard L., ed. *Historical Encyclopedia of American Business.* 3 vols. Pasadena, Calif.: Salem Press, 2009. Comprehensive reference work on American business history that contains substantial essays on almost every conceivable aspect of U.S. economic history.

See also   American Federation of Labor; Business and the economy in the United States; Congress of Industrial Organizations; Gross national product of Canada; Gross national product of the United States; Inflation; Labor strikes; National War Labor Board; Smith-Connally Act.

■ Indian Claims Commission

Identification   Federal agency concerned with Native American legal suits

Date   August 13, 1946-September 30, 1978

The Indian Claims Commission was a three-person panel authorized to hear and resolve Native Americans' suits against the federal government, involving issues including treaty violations, inadequate payment for land, and mismanagement of tribal funds, among others.

Before 1946, Native American tribes and bands generally had no right to sue the U.S. government, for two reasons. First, Native American possession of land was not recognized as a compensable property right under the Fifth Amendment. Second, the doctrine of sovereignty immunity prohibits suits against the government without its permission. During the 1930's, efforts to persuade Congress to authorize tribal suits were unsuccessful, but the contributions of Native American soldiers in World War II increased public sympathy for such legislation.

In voting to create the Indian Claims Commission (ICC), members of Congress were motivated by a variety of considerations. Many liberals felt a strong sense of guilt concerning the government's historical treatment of Native Americans. Others, in the light of Cold War propaganda, believed it was important to improve the country's treatment of minority groups. In addition, some conservative members hoped to settle long-standing claims as a necessary step toward terminating the federal government's trust relationship with the tribes.

The act creating the ICC passed on August 13, 1946, authorized settlement of claims by an appointed commission rather than the federal courts in order to provide national uniformity and to emphasize fairness over legal technicalities. The commission was given broad authority to provide monetary compensation, but it had no power to return any land. In calculating the size of awards, the commission did not pay interest, and it reduced payments by "gratuitous offsets" in recognition of past governmental services that had been provided. By accepting a monetary settlement, the aggrieved tribe abdicated all rights to raise the claim in the future. Native American plaintiffs were required to assume the burden of proof and to pay attorney fees as well as the costs for historical research.

Lawyers in the U.S. Department of Justice were given the job of defending the government's position in each claim, and because of the large amounts of money often involved, they typically conducted a vigorous defense. Many of the cases involved complex legal issues, and the available historical evidence was often weak. Settlements, therefore, tended to require long periods of time—sometimes twenty or more years.

The statute creating the ICC required the tribes to register their claims within five years, and the vast majority of the 176 recognized tribes filed at least one claim prior to the deadline. About two-thirds of the claims were land claims, and most of the others dealt with mismanagement of trust funds or natural resources. Although the ICC was expected to operate for only ten years, Congress extended its life several times. By the time it was adjourned in 1978, the ICC had rendered verdicts in 546 cases, with awards of $818,172,606 in judgments. The awards ranged from a few thousand dollars to $31 million. Records of the completed hearings filled more than forty large volumes.

About 170 cases remained unsettled when Congress adjourned the ICC through Public Law 94-465.

These cases were transferred to the U.S. Court of Claims on September 30, 1978, for adjudication.

Impact Scholars disagree about whether the work of the ICC was an adequate attempt to redress historical injustices. The awards provided many Native Americans with needed funds, even though almost all recipients considered the amounts to be insufficient. Because payments were distributed to individuals rather than to tribal governments, the awards had limited effects on tribes' long-term financial stability. From the experience of filing claims, many Native Americans learned the potential benefits of seeking legal redress. The commission hearings, moreover, required historical and anthropological research that later would be useful in suits against state and local governments. From the Native American perspective, one negative consequence of the ICC was its encouragement of movement in the direction of terminating the government's trust relationship with the tribes.

Thomas Tandy Lewis

Further Reading

Lieden, Michael, and Jake Page. *Wild Justice: People of Geronimo v. the United States.* Norman: University of Oklahoma Press, 1997.

Lurie, Nancy O. "The Indian Claims Commission." *Annals of the American Academy of Political and Social Science* 436 (1978): 97-110.

Rosenthal, Harvey. *Their Day in Court: A History of the Indian Claims Commission.* New York: Garland, 1990.

Washburn, Wilcomb. *Red Man's Land/White Man's Law.* New York: Charles Scribner's Sons, 1971.

See also Civil rights and liberties; Fair Deal; Native Americans; Racial discrimination.

■ Inflation

During the decade, the general level of prices rose by about 70 percent. Rising prices in turn led to imposition of comprehensive controls of wages and prices. Although the inflation injured some persons, including those on fixed incomes, the attendant increases in output, employment, and wages benefited the great majority of Americans.

Inflation followed the tempo set by the aggregate demand for goods and services, as measured by gross national product (GNP). GNP began rising rapidly in 1940-1941 as European countries responded to the war in Europe by buying more American goods, and as the U.S. government began preparing for war. The process accelerated after U.S. entry into war in December, 1941. In 1942, nominal GNP was more than 50 percent higher than in 1940. By 1945, nominal GNP was double its 1940 level. The driving force was the rapid increase in federal government expenditures, many of them war-related, largely financed by borrowing in ways that produced a rapid increase in the money supply.

Wartime Developments Federal government military expenditures increased from $2 billion in 1940 to $81 billion in 1945. These expenditures raised people's incomes, leading to expansion of consumer spending. Despite massive increases in tax rates and tax receipts, the federal government needed to borrow half of the money it spent. The government issued large amounts of new bonds and other interest-bearing debt claims. Between 1940 and 1945, the Federal Reserve added $22 billion of government securities to its holdings. Buying these caused an increase in the amount of currency in circulation and in the reserves held by commercial banks. The additional reserves enabled the banks to buy $74 billion of bonds for themselves. In the process, they created a large amount of new deposits. By 1945, the public's money supply was 2.5 times what it had been in 1940.

At the beginning of the 1940's, interest rates were at abnormally low levels. The Federal Reserve committed itself to buy government securities at prices that would maintain those low interest rates. Long-term bonds paid 2.5 percent or less, and short-term bills yielded only 0.375 percent.

An anti-inflation policy innovation by the Federal Reserve was the imposition of direct controls over consumer credit, beginning in 1941. The program set minimum down payments and maximum loan maturities for various kinds of consumer purchases. The shutdown in production of automobiles eliminated a major outlet for consumer credit.

Tax policy was used as a deliberate anti-inflation measure. The spread of Keynesian economics had established the principle that taxes should not be used solely to raise revenue for government, but also to reduce the spendable incomes of households and business to keep aggregate demand in check when inflation was perceived as a problem. Personal taxes, which were 3 percent of personal income in 1940, rose to 12 percent by 1945.

Controls on Inflation   The inflationary potential of monetary growth and rising aggregate demand was held in check by two main forces. First, the American economy entered the decade of the 1940's with a large amount of unemployment and unused productive capacity. The unemployment rate dropped from 15 percent in 1940 to 1 percent in 1944. Total output rose by nearly 60 percent over the same period. Much of this output went into military uses, but household incomes and consumption also rose.

The second factor holding inflation in check was price controls. After consumer prices rose by 1 percent per month in 1941, Congress passed the Emergency Price Control Act in January, 1942. In April, 1942, comprehensive controls were imposed on prices, and soon afterward, wages also were controlled.

Price controls slowed the actual inflation rate, and it became evident that people did not expect inflation to be serious. The prevailing attitude was that the American economy was in danger of falling back into depression once the war came to an end. High wartime prices thus appeared to be a temporary condition, likely to be reversed when the war ended. Consequently, many people were eager to build up their holdings of cash and savings bonds, even though these paid little or no interest. The result was a decline in the velocity of money (how many times the average dollar changes hands in a year, a measure studied by economists). Because of this desire to save, the government was able to meet its substantial borrowing needs without causing significant increases in interest rates.

As a result of higher output, price controls, and the absence of inflationary expectations for the future, the annual inflation rate slowed dramatically, from 10.7 percent in 1942 to 6.1 percent in 1943, then to 1.7 percent in 1944

and 2.3 percent in 1945, the last war year. Despite wage controls, workers benefited from the wartime conditions. As a result of full employment and overtime pay, real average annual earnings (actual earnings with the higher average price level factored out) per employed worker rose about 40 percent from 1940 to 1945. Fringe benefits such as medical insurance and retirement funds were created by employers to evade wage controls and high rates of personal income tax. These became a permanent feature of the economic landscape.

Postwar Conditions   When the war ended in mid-1945, federal spending fell drastically. Between mid-1945 and mid-1946, nine million persons were released from military service. The much-feared postwar depression did not materialize. Instead, private spending surged upward to take the place of reduced government spending.

Although aggregate demand was relatively level, around $210 billion a year across 1944-1946, the inflation rate rebounded. Wage and price controls were phased out over 1946. Many products that had been unavailable during the war, such as automobiles, went back into production. Construction of new housing boomed, after more than a decade of

New York City butcher shop closed down in July, 1948, because of the owner's self-professed shame about constantly raising his prices. (AP/Wide World Photos)

low output that created housing shortages. By 1948, consumer prices were about one-third above 1945 levels. The renewed inflationary upsurge reflected the delayed release of all the liquid assets people had been accumulating as savings. The money supply did not rise much in 1946-1948, but its velocity increased. In 1946, the average dollar was spent 1.7 times; by 1948, the rate had risen to 2.2.

As federal spending declined, federal tax rates were cut in 1945, but rates remained far above prewar levels. In 1946-1948, personal taxes averaged 10.6 percent of personal income. President Harry S. Truman vetoed two tax-cut bills in 1947. Retaining high tax rates actually was appropriate if inflationary pressure was a problem. In 1948, Congress passed a tax cut over the president's veto. The timing was fortunate, as the economy was moving into a recession. By 1949, personal taxes took only 9 percent of personal income.

Between 1945 and 1948, the average price level increased by about 40 percent. Some of this could be viewed as a delayed response to wartime expansion of money and spending. From 1945 to 1948, average annual earnings of full-time employees increased from $2,190 to $2,786, a gain of 27 percent, meaning that wages did not keep pace with prices. This comparison is misleading, however, for two main reasons. First, more and better products were available by 1948, meaning that consumers had better choices available for their spending, and a given product likely was better in some ways than the same product in previous years. That meant that consumers often were getting more for their money. Second, a significant proportion of the labor force had moved out of military service into the free labor market. That addition to the labor market held wages down, but at higher levels than people typically earned in the military.

The postwar inflation was accompanied by extreme turbulence in the labor market, as workers struggled to achieve wage increases higher than the inflation rate. Between 1945 and 1949, however, the increase in wages did not outrun the inflation rate. During the war, labor unions succeeded in expanding their membership substantially, and they sought to continue this trend through the militant pursuit of benefit increases. Work stoppages were numerous and disruptive in the winter of 1945-1946. One response was the passage in 1947 of the Taft-Hartley Act, which imposed limits on union power.

In 1948, President Truman called a special session of Congress to deal with the inflation. Only minor measures resulted—authority to restore controls over consumer credit and increase bank reserve requirements. The economic recession that began in 1948, however, effectively ended the postwar inflation. Consumer prices actually fell slightly from 1948 to 1949.

Impact Between 1940 and 1949, consumer prices increased by 70 percent. Over the same period, average annual earnings per full-time worker rose 119 percent, and the total flow of labor income (including fringe benefits) rose 171 percent. The inflation was simply one dimension of the great expansion of aggregate demand that moved the economy out of the Great Depression and into a new world of relatively full employment. A lasting effect of the wage controls of the era is that many jobs continue to have fringe benefit and retirement packages attached to them.

The inflation of the 1940's was quite atypical compared with earlier and subsequent inflation experiences. First, the increase in prices was much smaller, proportionately, than the increase in the money supply. Second, the actual inflation experience did not generate expectations of further inflation to come.

The 1940's created the impression that wage and price controls could be made effective rather easily, and that rapid growth in money would tend to lower interest rates. These conditions did not hold up in subsequent inflation experiences.

Paul B. Trescott

Further Reading

Chandler, Lester V. *Inflation in the United States, 1940-1948.* New York: Harper, 1951. Depicts the inflation as a response to the rise in aggregate demand generated by monetary and fiscal policies.

Chandler, Lester V., and Donald H. Wallace. *Economic Mobilization and Stabilization.* New York: Henry Holt, 1951. Extensive depiction of the inflation problem attending World War II and the apparatus of wage and price controls.

Fishback, Price, et al. *Government and the American Economy: A New History.* Chicago: University of Chicago Press, 2007. Most relevant is chapter 14, by Robert Higgs, on the effects of the two world wars on the economy.

Schmukler, Nathan, and Edward Marcus, eds. *Infla-

tion Through the Ages: Economic, Social, Psychological, and Historical Aspects. New York: Brooklyn College Press, 1983. Numerous essays deal with American experience, particularly in parts 2, 7, and 8.

Trescott, Paul B. *Money, Banking, and Economic Welfare.* New York: McGraw-Hill, 1960. Chapter 17 deals extensively with the causes and consequences of the inflation of the 1940's.

See also   Business and the economy in the United States; Credit and debt; Economic wartime regulations; Emergency Price Control Act of 1942; Gross national product of the United States; Income and wages; Keynesian economics; Labor strikes; Unemployment in the United States; War debt.

■ Inter-American Treaty of Reciprocal Assistance

The Treaty   Collective security pact, signed by the United States, twenty Latin American nations, and Canada in 1947, to provide for a common defense against foreign aggression and settle inter-American disputes peacefully

Also known as   Rio Treaty; Rio Pact

Date   Adopted on September 2, 1947

The Rio Treaty enshrined the Monroe Doctrine into international law, placing the Western Hemisphere under American military protection at a particularly perilous moment, when the U.S. government believed that the Americas were threatened by the Soviet Union at the start of the Cold War.

The Monroe Doctrine, promulgated in 1823, declared the Western Hemisphere to be off-limits to further European colonization and also reserved for the United States the right to keep foreign powers out of the Americas. Since that date, the U.S. government had sought to formalize this proclamation in a written treaty, much to the chagrin of the Latin American countries.

Hemispheric Cooperation   The experience of World War II, with the declaration of war against the Axis powers by all Latin American countries except Uruguay, as well as Latin American military assistance in both the Atlantic and Pacific theaters, afforded the United States the opportunity to sign a collective security pact with its Latin American neighbors,

plus Canada, on the principle that an attack against one was an aggression against all. Contrary to the spirit of the Monroe Doctrine, however, unilateral U.S. protection over the hemisphere was to be replaced with multilateral military cooperation. The fear of many Latin American countries that the United States would use such an agreement to interfere in their internal affairs was assuaged by the promise by the administration of Harry S. Truman (1945-1953) that no signatory nation would be compelled to utilize military force against its will.

The Inter-American Treaty of Reciprocal Assistance, ratified in Rio de Janeiro, Brazil, in 1947, and hence popularly known as the Rio Treaty or the Rio Pact, was a legacy of World War II, but with the souring of relations between the United States and the Soviet Union, a wartime ally, it soon evolved into a weapon for the American government to wield in the emerging Cold War between the two victorious superpowers. The growth of communist parties in Latin America during the 1940's, particularly in Cuba and Brazil, was deemed extremely dangerous by the U.S. Department of State, and it strengthened Washington's resolve to stop the spread of communism inside the hemisphere.

Provisions of the Treaty   Negotiations for the treaty began in 1945, and its principle clauses were first outlined at the Inter-American Conference of War and Peace in Mexico City that year. The conference in Rio de Janeiro in 1947 declared that provisions of the treaty were in keeping with the purposes and principles of the United Nations (U.N.), formed in 1945, but also established an Inter-American Peace System to prevent and repel foreign aggression against any and all nations in the Western Hemisphere. The mere threat of an attack, and not simply aggressive action, was sufficient to trigger a response from all member states, whereas disputes between the American nations had to be resolved peacefully. In keeping with the anticommunist spirit of the Cold War, the Rio Treaty preamble declared that the pact was dedicated not solely to mutual defense but also to upholding democratic ideals and the fulfillment of peace—a jab at the Soviet Union and its communist allies in Latin America.

Although the treaty required a two-thirds majority vote and the approval of the United Nations before collective action against aggression could be undertaken, two clauses in the treaty made it clear

Highlights from the Inter-American Treaty of Reciprocal Assistance

Article 1

The High Contracting Parties formally condemn war and undertake in their international relations not to resort to the threat or the use of force in any manner inconsistent with the provisions of the Charter of the United Nations or of this treaty.

Article 2

As a consequence of the principle set forth in the preceding article, the high contracting parties undertake to submit every controversy which may arise between them to methods of peaceful settlement and to endeavor to settle any such controversy among themselves by means of the proce-

dures in force in the Inter-American System before referring it to the General Assembly or the Security Council of the United Nations.

Article 3

The High Contracting Parties agree that an armed attack by any state against an American state shall be considered as an attack against all the American states and, consequently, each one of the said Contracting Parties undertakes to assist in meeting the attack in the exercise of the inherent right of individual or collective self-defense recognized by Article 51 of the Charter of the United Nations.

---

that the United States reserved for itself the right to command hemispheric defense. First, a single member might take measures against the threat or use of force, and afterwards submit justification to the other signatories. Second, for the sake of self-defense, a member nation could take military action without prior approval by the United Nations. In practice, because the United States saw local communist parties and other radicals as pawns of the Soviets, the Rio Treaty provided the underpinning for closer cooperation between U.S. and Latin American armed forces in combating internal subversion and ridding the region of regimes designated as insufficiently anticommunist, such as that of President Juan Perón of Argentina.

Impact During the late 1940's, the United States had the military strength and diplomatic clout to bend the Rio Treaty to suit its purposes in pursuing the Cold War against the Soviet Union in Latin America. What was supposed to be a pact for mutual military collaboration, philosophically repudiating the Monroe Doctrine, in fact wound up reinforcing that unilateral declaration, detested by many Latin American nations. Ironically, the agreement bolstered the political clout of anti-American politicians from Cuba to Argentina, and no Latin American nation that became independent after 1947 signed the Rio Treaty.

Julio César Pino

Further Reading

Atkins, G. Pope. *Encyclopedia of the Inter-American System.* Westport, Conn.: Greenwood Press, 1997. Exhaustive reference work on all aspects of U.S.-Latin American diplomatic relations from the era of Latin American independence to the end of the Cold War.

Brewer, Stewart, with foreword by Michael LaRosa. *Borders and Bridges: A History of U.S.-Latin American Relations.* Westport, Conn.: Praeger Security International, 2006. Perceptive history of how the United States has employed the concept of hemispheric security and the purported threat of foreign aggression to impinge on Latin American sovereignty.

Connell-Smith, Gordon. *The Inter-American System.* New York: Oxford University Press, 1966. Based on both primary sources and interviews with diplomats, this seminal work explores the failure to create a viable system of collaboration between the United States and Latin America, with discussion of the Rio Treaty.

García-Amador, F. V., ed. *The Inter-American System: Treaties, Conventions and Other Documents.* New York: Oceana, 1983. A collection of primary documents on inter-American relations. Places the Rio Treaty in historical context.

Smith, Peter H. *Talons of the Eagle: Dynamics of U.S.-Latin American Relations.* New York: Oxford University Press, 2000. Explores the history of U.S.-

Latin American relations, including the forging of military alliances such as the Rio Treaty, by examining the ideological motives of United States foreign policy.

See also　Acheson, Dean; Department of Defense, U.S.; Foreign policy of the United States; Hull, Cordell; Latin America; Mexico; Organization of American States; Truman Doctrine.

■ International Business Machines Corporation

Definition　Manufacturer of information-handling machines

Date　Founded in 1896 as the Tabulating Machine Company

International Business Machines became one of the leading computer and information-processing companies during the 1940's and played a significant role in World War II, not only through the work done by its modified calculating machines and research facilities but also by expanding its product line to include ordnance devices, such as bombsights and engine parts.

Herman Hollerith founded the Tabulating Machine Company in 1896, in Broome County, New York. Thomas J. Watson, Sr., joined the company as general manager in 1914. In 1924, the company adopted the name International Business Machines (IBM), taken from its Canadian and South American subsidiary. The company grew even during the Depression years, so that by the beginning of the 1940's it was famous around the world. Watson believed that world peace was possible through world trade, and in the years leading up to World War II he attempted to convert Adolf Hitler to that idea. IBM continued its growth during the 1940's, going from revenues of $45 million and 12,656 employees in 1940 to annual revenues of $183 million with more than twice as many employees in 1949.

New Products　IBM introduced many new machines and innovations during the 1940's that improved information handling practices. Some of its 1941 electric typewriters featured proportional spacing of characters, with characters of different widths assigned different amounts of horizontal space on the typewritten line, creating a more attractive page and using less paper for a given amount of printed matter. They also included better ribbon design. These improvements resulted in typewritten work that looked as though it had been typeset and printed. In 1943, IBM produced an experimental machine, the Vacuum Tube Multiplier, by adapting vacuum tubes from the radio industry for primitive computers. This prototype vacuum tube calculator was the first machine to use electronics in executing math and significantly enhanced the speed of information processing over machines using electrical relays.

The company became involved in various charitable programs during the 1940's. One program supported widows and orphans of war-stricken IBM employees. During the early 1940's, IBM was a leader in employing and training disabled people throughout the United States, resulting in an invitation for IBM to join the President's Committee for Employment of the Handicapped. Watson also took care of his employees during the 1940's with several safety innovations and benefit plans that provided health care, hospitalization, total and permanent disability income, and pensions.

The Prewar Years　IBM played a major role in supporting the United States and its allies during World War II, but many in the U.S. military establishment were already making use of IBM's technology before the United States became involved in the war. Wallace Eckert, who joined the U.S. Naval Observatory as its head astronomer and director in 1940 and was director of the Thomas J. Watson Astronomical Computing Bureau at Columbia University, used IBM machines to produce almanacs that became vital for air and sea navigation during World War II. If the United States was to become involved in the war, Eckert knew he needed to improve upon the accuracy, readability, and timely production of the original almanac, known as the Air Almanac, which was printed by using hand-set, movable type, resulting in multiple errors.

To improve upon accuracy and clarity of the almanacs, Eckert wanted to develop a computer-driven typesetter in which computing machines would output tables of numbers that could be input into composing typewriters. In 1941, he developed specifications for a card-driven composing typewriter to be built by IBM. It took IBM until 1945 to deliver the first machine, which connected an IBM electronic typewriter to an IBM keypunch machine. None of the U.S. or Allied forces that relied on Eckert's air and nautical almanacs, produced with IBM machines, ever reported any errors.

The War Years   In 1944, after six years of collaborative design work with Harvard University, IBM launched its first large-scale calculating computer, known as the Mark I, which could automatically execute addition, multiplication, and division problems in seconds. IBM opened its first pure science research facility in 1945, known as the Watson Scientific Computing Laboratory. The U.S. government made use of both the Mark I and the IBM research facilities throughout World War II.

The U.S. Army Signal Corps used IBM 405s as input/output devices that were linked to relay computers to decode German and Japanese messages.

General George S. Patton and the Third Army enhanced mechanization by using IBM Mobile Machines Records and punched-card machines. Radiotype, an IBM product that allowed messages to be sent and received using short-wave radios and the messages to be typed out automatically on IBM typewriters, was an important communication device during the war.

IBM also switched its facilities to producing war-related products. Among these were the M1 carbine rifle, the Browning Automatic Rifle, aircraft cannon, anti-aircraft gun directors, and the Norden bombsight.

Impact   By 1945 and 1946, IBM was producing accounting machines with multiple line listings, vacuum tube multipliers that were part of its super-calculator program, and wireless translator systems

Navy technician adjusting IBM's Automatic Sequence Controlled Calculator in 1944. (AP/Wide World Photos)

that enabled people to move about while receiving a message. Other postwar IBM products that helped it gain a monopoly in the computing and information-handling industries included digital calculating machines that were able to modify a stored computer program, mass-produced electronic calculating punches with replaceable parts, and card-programmed electronic calculators designed for use in large centers. These products all were part of the eventual development of modern computers.

Carol A. Rolf

Further Reading

Bashe, Charles J., Lyle R. Johnson, John H. Palmer, and Emerson W. Pugh. *IBM's Early Computers.* Cambridge, Mass.: MIT Press, 1985. Provides a historical perspective focused on engineering, technology, and the people who shaped IBM.

Maney, Kevin. *The Maverick and His Machine: Thomas Watson, Sr., and the Making of IBM.* Indianapolis: John Wiley & Sons, 2004. Provides a history of how Watson turned a disorganized tabulating and computing company into a respected global technology corporation.

Pugh, Emerson W. *Building IBM: Shaping an Industry and Its Technology.* Cambridge, Mass.: MIT Press, 1995. Explains IBM's history and its near monopoly of the computer industry after 1945.

Pugh, Emerson W., Lyle R. Johnson, and John H. Palmer. *IBM's 360 and Early 370 Systems.* Cambridge, Mass.: MIT Press, 1991. Discusses IBM's development of successive postwar computer systems.

See also Binary automatic computer; Business and the economy in Canada; Business and the economy in the United States; Computers; ENIAC; Radar; Transistors; Wartime industries.

■ International Court of Justice

Identification Principal judicial organ of the United Nations
Also known as ICJ; World Court
Date Established in 1945; began operations in 1946
Place Peace Palace in the Hague, Netherlands

The International Court of Justice adjudicates legal disputes submitted by nation-states. It also offers legal opinions to U.N. organs and agencies. Through these contentious cases and advisory opinions, the court plays a major role in the development of international law and the peaceful settlement of disputes.

The International Court of Justice (ICJ) was established in 1945 to replace the Permanent Court of International Justice, the judicial organ of the defunct League of Nations. The ICJ Statute, part of the U.N. Charter, establishes the court's organization, jurisdiction, and procedures. In article 38, it identifies four sources of law on which the court may rely and which have become widely accepted as the sources of international law: international conventions, customary international law, general principles of law recognized by civilized nations, and writings of legal scholars.

Though not bound by precedent as are common law courts, the ICJ may take its own rulings into consideration in deciding cases. The court's opinions, binding only on parties to the case, typically become persuasive sources of international law. A nation-state may not be taken before the ICJ against its will, which may be expressed by prior acceptance of the compulsory jurisdiction of the court, by an agreement with another nation-state to submit a particular dispute for adjudication, or in a dispute-resolution provision in a treaty. The fifteen judges represent diverse geographical areas and all major legal systems; a party that does not already have a judge on the court may nominate an ad hoc judge.

The ICJ decided one contentious case during the 1940's—the Corfu Channel Case of 1949. However, it turned out to be one of the most important and most cited cases in international law. The case was submitted to the ICJ by Great Britain and Albania at the suggestion of the U.N. Security Council, after forty-four mariners died when two British warships struck mines in Albanian waters. The ICJ awarded Britain two million U.S. dollars in damages after finding Albania responsible because the mines could not have been laid without its knowledge. It also held that Britain was within its rights to traverse these Albanian territorial waters because the channel was a strait used for international navigation between two parts of the high seas, making it available in international law for innocent passage by vessels of any country. The ICJ also held that when Britain subsequently swept the channel for further mines, it violated Albanian sovereignty and international law.

The ICJ handed down two advisory opinions during the 1940's: Conditions of Admission of a State to Membership in the United Nations (1948) and Reparation for Injuries Suffered in the Service of the United Nations (1949). In the former case, the court, in response to a query from the U.N. General Assembly, interpreted the U.N. Charter in a way that encouraged the admission of states to the United Nations and allowed fewer barriers to admission. The latter case recognized that international organizations such as the United Nations could, like states, have rights and duties and be subjects of international law.

Impact The ICJ has been instrumental in the development of international law. The Reparation Case helped pave the way for nongovernmental organizations, national liberation movements, and individuals to participate in the international legal system, reshaping the landscape of international law. The Corfu Channel Case was the first of many instances where the ICJ helped resolve a dispute that might otherwise have developed into international military conflict.

William V. Dunlap

International Court of Justice, The Hague

Further Reading

Lowe, Vaughn, and Malgosia Fitzmaurice, eds. *Fifty Years of the International Court of Justice: Essays in Honour of Sir Robert Jennings.* New York: Cambridge University Press, 2007.

Oellers-Frahm, Karin. "International Court of Justice." In *Encyclopedia of Public International Law,* edited by Rudolf Bernhardt. New York: Elsevier, 1995.

See also Convention on the Prevention and Punishment of the Crime of Genocide; International League for the Rights of Man; Supreme Court, U.S.; Truman proclamations; United Nations.

■ International League for the Rights of Man

Identification International nongovernmental human rights organization

Also known as International League for Human Rights

Date Established in 1942

The International League for the Rights of Man is one of the oldest continuing human rights organizations.

In January, 1941, President Franklin D. Roosevelt gave his "Four Freedoms" speech, highlighting freedom of speech, freedom of religion, freedom from want, and freedom from fear as rights common to all people. This speech brought to U.S. consciousness the need to defend human rights.

In 1942, Roger Nash Baldwin, a leader of the American Civil Liberties Union, along with Henri Laugier of France and other European refugees, formed the International League for the Rights of Man. Stated purposes of the league were to raise awareness of human rights issues and to defend those persecuted for defending these rights. The league was granted consultative status with the United Nations Economic and Social Council in 1946, giving it the right to testify before that body about human rights abuses. On December 10, 1948, the United Nations ratified the Universal Declaration of Human Rights, with the United States as one of the signatories. The league embraced this document and used it to build the platform for the organization.

Impact   The organization became known as the International League for Human Rights in 1976. In addition to advocating for human rights, the organization is consulted by the United Nations, the Council of Europe, and the International Labour Organization. The league has a strong history of leading the United States in the human rights movement.

Tessa Li Powell

Further Reading

Korey, W. *NGOs and the Universal Declaration of Human Rights: A Curious Grapevine.* New York: St. Martin's Press, 1998.

Martens, K. "Professionalised Representation of Human Rights NGOs to the United Nations." *International Journal of Human Rights* 10, no. 1 (2006): 19-30.

See also   Civil rights and liberties; "Four Freedoms" speech; International Court of Justice; United Nations; Universal Declaration of Human Rights; Women's roles and rights in Canada; Women's roles and rights in the United States.

"Four Freedoms"

U.S. president Franklin D. Roosevelt presented his "Four Freedoms" speech to Congress in January, 1941, a speech that helped to inspire the formation of the International League for the Rights of Man in 1942:

In the future days, which we seek to make secure, we look forward to a world founded upon four essential human freedoms.

The first is freedom of speech and expression—everywhere in the world.

The second is freedom of every person to worship God in his own way—everywhere in the world.

The third is freedom from want—which, translated into world terms, means economic understandings which will secure to every nation a healthy peacetime life for its inhabitants—everywhere in the world.

The fourth is freedom from fear—which, translated into world terms, means a world-wide reduction of armaments to such a point and in such a thorough fashion that no nation will be in a position to commit an act of physical aggression against any neighbor—anywhere in the world.

That is no vision of a distant millennium. It is a definite basis for a kind of world attainable in our own time and generation. That kind of world is the very antithesis of the so-called new order of tyranny which the dictators seek to create with the crash of a bomb.

To that new order we oppose the greater conception—the moral order. A good society is able to face schemes of world domination and foreign revolutions alike without fear.

Since the beginning of our American history, we have been engaged in change—in a perpetual peaceful revolution—a revolution which goes on steadily, quietly adjusting itself to changing conditions—without the concentration camp or the quick-lime in the ditch. The world order which we seek is the cooperation of free countries, working together in a friendly, civilized society.

This nation has placed its destiny in the hands and heads and hearts of its millions of free men and women; and its faith in freedom under the guidance of God. Freedom means the supremacy of human rights everywhere. Our support goes to those who struggle to gain those rights or keep them. Our strength is our unity of purpose.

To that high concept there can be no end save victory.

■ International trade

By 1940, the American economy was rapidly emerging from the Great Depression. Imports and exports were both expanding rapidly as aggregate demand increased at home and abroad. During World War II, international trade carried the abundant output of the United States and Canada to support Allied economies and war efforts worldwide. After the war, American leadership helped to create the United Nations and to reconstruct the world economy.

In 1940, total expenditures for goods and services in North America were rising rapidly, following the misfortunes of the Great Depression. The demand for imports rose as well. In Europe, the outbreak of war in 1939 added to the ongoing expansion of aggregate demand, much of which found its way to buy from the United States and Canada. For the United States, imports and exports were a relatively minor part of the national economy. U.S. exports in "normal" years, such as 1940 and 1949, amounted to only about 6 percent of gross national product (GNP), while imports were slightly under 4 percent. Canada's total output was only about 6 percent that of the United States. However, international trade played a much larger role in its economy. Canada's exports account for 25 to 30 percent of its GNP, and imports were slightly smaller.

The war brought growth to both imports and exports. Some strategic imports were cut off by Japanese conquests in the Pacific theater of the war—most notably natural rubber. Fortunately, domestic production of synthetic rubber filled the gap. The volume of U.S. exports ballooned in response to demand from the areas of war—by 1944, exports accounted for 10 percent of American GNP. Export sales slackened a little when the war ended, but hit another peak in 1947 at 9 percent of GNP. The U.S. government financed much of the huge U.S. export surplus by loans and foreign aid.

Government Policies During the 1930's, the pattern of world international trade was seriously distorted by trade restrictions, exchange rate irregularities, and a great general decline of production. World War II created new abnormalities in international trade, as the major combatants struggled to make use of the world's resources. The United States became a leader in working toward greater liberalization of world trade, beginning with the adoption

of the Reciprocal Trade Agreements Act in 1934. This led in turn to steady effort to reduce trade barriers. Canada meanwhile maintained relatively high tariffs through the 1940's. Indeed, they were sufficiently high that some American manufacturers established branch plants in Canada to avoid the tax.

As a member of the British Empire, Canada entered the European war immediately in 1939. While technically neutral until December of 1941, when Japan attacked Pearl Harbor, the United States also strongly supported the Allied side. In March, 1941, the U.S. Congress adopted the Lend-Lease Act. This authorized the government to provide supplies on credit to any country whose defense the president deemed vital to the defense of the United States.

During the war, both Canada and the United States showed an enormous expansion of exports, which peaked in 1944, the last full year of war. By war's end in 1945, the United States had supplied about $50 billion of goods under Lend-Lease. In December, 1945, $25 billion of the indebtedness associated with the program was forgiven.

The United States and Great Britain played major roles in the Bretton Woods Conference in 1944. From this meeting evolved the establishment of the International Bank for Reconstruction and Development—which would become better known as the World Bank—and the International Monetary Fund (IMF) The World Bank provided long-term loans for fixed capital projects, initially targeted at recovery from war destruction. Its first loan, of $250 million, went to France in May, 1947, for reconstruction. The IMF created a formal regime of fixed foreign-exchange rates. This was backed by a facility for short-term credit to assist countries to withstand an international payments crisis without resort to devaluation of their currency.

In 1945 Congress extended the reciprocal trade agreements program, broadening the president's authority to reduce tariffs. In 1948, another renewal was voted. However, this included a provisions requiring the Tariff Commission to designate "peril points" below which tariff rates could not be reduced without harm to domestic producers. Between 1934 and 1947, American tariff rates had been reduced by about one fourth from their initial high levels.

The United States provided major support for European economic recovery in other ways. The capital of the U.S. Export-Import Bank was increased by three billion dollars. The Anglo-American Financial

Agreement in 1946 provided a loan of $3.8 billion to Britain. By 1947 the threat of spreading communism was evident. Congress responded by adopting the European Recovery Program—better known as the Marshall Plan. This program provided donated supplies worth more than $12 billion in 1948-1951. The United States maintained armies of occupation in defeated Germany and Japan and steered both countries toward policies which emphasized free markets and unrestricted international trade. Both Germany and Japan emerged as export powerhouses in subsequent decades.

The United States and Canada also provided substantial support for the United Nations Relief and Rehabilitation Administration and for the General Agreement on Tariffs and Trade (GATT, organized in 1947). GATT was an extension of the U.S. Reciprocal Trade Agreements program. Originally, twenty-three countries participated; by 1963 that number had grown to fifty. Periodic meetings of GATT nations (most noncommunist countries) became forums for multilateral swapping of trade concessions. The same principles were involved in the formation in 1958 of the European Economic Community, initiated by the Marshall Plan, and leading ultimately to the European Union. President Harry S. Truman's inaugural address of January, 1949, advocated a program ("point four") of foreign aid to promote growth in less-developed countries. Ultimately foreign aid became a staple of policy, but with little success.

For all this, there was much talk of "dollar shortage," bemoaning the difficulty of other countries in buying as much from America as they wished. The United States recorded a cumulative excess of exports over imports of $32 billion over the years 1946-1949. Nevertheless, the leadership of the United States helped move toward a system of world trade and finance conducive to free markets and rapid economic growth. A glaring exception was U.S. agricultural policy, where price supports for domestic products were accompanied by restrictions on imports.

By far the largest share of Canada's exports went to Great Britain and the United States. The proportion going south of the border remained remarkably stable around 37 percent. However, the British share was significantly lower by 1945 than it had been in 1940.

Postwar Trade International trade came more nearly into line with underlying patterns of resources and demand in the postwar period. The impact of the Marshall Plan and other programs is evident in the large spike of exports in 1947, extending to all major categories. However, the decade of the 1940's witnessed the shift by the United States from being a net exporter of petroleum to a net importer. In 1940, oil imports were only 3 percent as large as U.S. oil production. By 1949, with the flood of cheap and abundant Persian Gulf supplies, oil imports were 8 percent—and headed steadily higher. Can-

U.S. Trade with Canada, 1941-1949

Year	U.S. exports to Canada		U.S. imports from Canada	
	In billions of U.S. dollars	Percentage of total U.S. exports	In billions of U.S. dollars	Percentage of total U.S. imports
1941-1945 average	1.3	13	0.9	26
1946	1.4	14	0.9	18
1947	2.1	15	1.1	19
1948	1.9	15	1.6	23
1949	1.9	16	1.6	24

Source: U.S. Bureau of the Census. *Statistical Abstract of the United States, 1951.* Washington, D.C: U.S. Department of Commerce, 1952, p. 846.

Note: Totals include imports and exports of goods only.

U.S. and Canadian Imports and Exports

U.S. numbers are in billions of U.S. dollars; Canadian numbers are in billions of Canadian dollars

Year	U.S. Imports	U.S. Exports	Canadian Imports	Canadian Exports
1940	3.6	5.4	1.6	1.8
1941	4.5	6.9	2.0	2.5
1942	5.4	11.8	2.3	2.4
1943	8.1	19.1	2.9	3.4
1944	9.0	21.4	3.6	3.6
1945	10.2	16.3	2.9	3.6
1946	7.0	14.8	2.9	3.2
1947	8.2	19.8	3.6	3.6
1948	10.3	16.9	3.6	4.1
1949	9.6	15.8	3.9	4.0

Sources: U.S. Bureau of the Census. *Historical Statistics of the United States, Colonial Times to 1970, Bicentennial Edition, Part 2.* Washington, D.C.: Government Printing Office, 1975, p. 864. *Historical Statistics of Canada.* Toronto: Macmillan Company of Canada, 1965, p.131.

Note: The U.S. dollar was worth $1.11 Canadian in 1940-1945, $1.06 Canadian in 1946, $1 Canadian in 1947-1948, and $1.03 Canadian in 1949.

ada did not export a significant amount of petroleum until the 1950's.

In 1940, the export markets for U.S. products were still burdened by import restrictions imposed by other countries in response to the Great Depression. In contrast, in 1946, major parts of Europe and Asia were desperately short of domestic production as a result of war and were eager for U.S. products. Postwar relief programs often provided funding for such purchases. American agriculture was producing at record levels and farmers were grateful for the apparently unlimited international markets. Farm products of all types furnished $3.8 billion of U.S. exports by 1949, 30 percent of total exports. Government programs financed 60 percent of these agricultural exports. However, the United States imported large quantities of such food products as sugar, coffee, and tropical fruits.

The listings of major Canadian exports during the late 1940's were dominated by agricultural products and raw materials—wheat and wheat flour,

barley, wood products, and crude or semi-fabricated aluminum, nickel, copper, and zinc. Canada's production of wheat and rye was three times domestic consumption. However, fully manufactured products by 1950 constituted 41 percent of Canadian exports, down from an abnormal 52 percent in 1946. The share of Canadian exports going to the United States remained stable around 38 percent in 1946-1947, then leaped to 50 percent in 1948-1949. This made Canada's macroeconomy extremely sensitive to aggregate-demand conditions in the United States. The mild American recession of 1949 brought a mild dip in Canada's exports, but their gross national product continued to rise vigorously.

With thousands of miles of frontier between the two countries, and with the major Canadian cities located close to the border, it is not surprising that trade between the two countries was a major part of each country's total trade. Exports to Canada constituted 14-16 percent of total U.S. exports. And imports from Canada were an impressive 19-24 percent of total U.S. imports.

Impact The economic muscle of the United States and Canada provided a crucial contribution toward Allied victory in World War II. Their exports directly supplied military resources—tanks, aircraft, weapons and ammunition—and economic support, notably foodstuffs. Wartime cooperation set the stage for ambitions and high-minded efforts to create international institutions for peace and prosperity. The shattered economies of Germany and Japan were restored to productivity. Shipments of machinery from North America helped this restoration. The economic reconstruction of the European economy enabled those countries to produce more and export more. In the process, the condition of "dollar shortage" began to reverse.

Paul B. Trescott

Further reading

Carter, Susan, et al., eds. *Historical Statistics of the United States: Earliest Times to the Present.* New York: Cambridge University Press, 2006. Comprehensive reference source on economic statistics, with considerable data on trade.

Caves, Richard E., and Richard H. Holton. *The Canadian Economy, Prospect and Retrospect.* Cambridge:

Harvard University Press, 1959. Chapter 13 of this comprehensive study is directed to Canada's international trade.

Condliffe, J. B. *The Commerce of Nations.* New York: Norton, 1950. Encyclopedic history of the international economy; devotes three chapters and 150 pages to postwar conditions and all the policy innovations.

Kindleberger, Charles P. *The Dollar Shortage.* New York: John Wiley & Sons, 1950. Examines United States trade and payments during the late 1940's, exploring policies to assist the rest of the world in buying more American stuff. A chapter each on U.S. imports and exports.

Snider, Delbert. *Introduction to International Economics.* Homewood, Ill.: Richard D. Irwin, 1954. This well-written college textbook draws extensively on the data and developments of the 1940's.

Thorp, Willard L. *Trade, Aid, or What?* Baltimore: Johns Hopkins Press, 1954. Extensive consideration of foreign-exchange markets and controls; valuable assessment of U.S. import restrictions.

Vatter, Harold G. *The U.S. Economy in World War II.* New York: Columbia University Press, 1985. The international aspects are interwoven into a comprehensive view of the war and its consequences.

Wilson, Richard L., ed. *Historical Encyclopedia of American Business.* 3 vols. Pasadena, Calif.: Salem Press, 2009. Comprehensive reference work on American business history that contains substantial essays on almost every conceivable aspect of U.S. economic history, including foreign trade.

See also Agriculture in Canada; Agriculture in the United States; Bretton Woods Conference; Business and the economy in Canada; Business and the economy in the United States; Canada and Great Britain; General Agreement on Tariffs and Trade; Lend-Lease; Marshall Plan; World War II.

■ Inventions

From the atomic bomb to the Slinky, and from color television to the plastic Frisbee, the inventions of the 1940's had major impacts on American life for the years and decades that followed. Few periods in American history can compare to this war-torn decade for inventiveness and technological advancement.

Largely because of the war effort, the decade of the 1940's was a particularly prolific period of technological advance. Well-known inventions of the decade include the atomic bomb, the transistor, and the jeep; fewer people would guess that products such as the microwave oven, color television, and electronic digital computer also were invented in that decade.

Inventions of War The most significant weapons development in the history of humankind was the invention of the atomic bomb. During the early days of World War II, many in the scientific community strongly suspected that the Nazis were investigating the possibility of a nuclear chain reaction. Acting on his own concerns and the urging of other concerned scientists, Albert Einstein wrote a letter to President Franklin D. Roosevelt in 1939 suggesting that the United States look into the possible use of nuclear weapons. The president's first response was to form a lightly funded committee to research the use of uranium, but one month after the Japanese surprise attack on Pearl Harbor in December, 1941, he approved the construction of an atom bomb. After spending $2 billion (approximately $25 billion at 2010 values) and employing more than 125,000 people, the project resulted in the first successful detonation of an atomic bomb, in a remote area of New Mexico on July 16, 1945. That blast ushered in the nuclear age and changed the world's military and political landscape forever. On August 6, 1945, the atom bomb was dropped on Hiroshima, Japan, where an estimated 140,000 people were killed. Three days later, another bomb fell on Nagasaki, Japan, killing another 80,000.

On October 3, 1942, after decades of trial and error, a group of German scientists under the leadership of Wernher von Braun successfully launched the world's first ballistic missile. This missile, the A-4 rocket, also was the first rocket to reach the edge of space. The launch originated in Peenemünde, Germany, and reached an altitude of sixty miles. In 1943, German chancellor Adolf Hitler declared it a "vengeance weapon," and the rocket was renamed the V-2. It was first fired on Western Europe in September, 1944, and it was used repeatedly on Britain for the duration of the war.

A less formidable but no less useful war machine was developed in 1940. After the U.S. Army sent specifications for a general-purpose vehicle to more

than one hundred manufacturers, several proto-
types were developed. The Willys Truck Company's
prototype eventually won the contract. Willys's prototype was built using a Bantam Car Company design, and the "jeep" was born. General Dwight D. Eisenhower later stated that World War II could not
have been won without it.

Transistors and Computers An invention that rivals the atomic bomb for lasting significance is the
transistor, a tiny replacement for the bulky and fragile vacuum tubes used as amplifiers, detectors, and
switches in electronic circuits. Thanks to the work of
Bell Laboratories scientists Walter Brattain, John
Bardeen, William Shockley, and others, the transistor made solid-state electronics a reality during the
decade, and the space age and information age possible.

The first model was a point-contact transistor developed by Brattain and Bardeen near the end of
1947. Compared to later transistors, it was huge, almost half an inch thick, whereas millions of modern transistors fit on a single computer chip. In
1948, Shockley conceived the idea of the junction
transistor, but it was not built until early in the next
decade.

Opinions differ regarding the invention of the

electronic computer. The IBM Automatic Sequence
Controlled Calculator, named the Mark I, as developed at Harvard University in 1942 and is often cited
as the first, but by 1940 John Vincent Atanasoff and
Clifford Berry at Iowa State College (now Iowa State
University) had already developed the ABC special-
purpose computer to solve systems of linear equa-
tions. John Mauchly of the Moore School of Electrical Engineering at the University of Pennsylvania
viewed the Atanasoff-Berry computer in 1940, two
years before submitting his proposal for a vacuum-
tube, digital computer. In May, 1943, following
Mauchly's proposal, work began on the Electronic
Numerical Integrator and Computer, the ENIAC.
The ENIAC, funded by the Army, was successfully
demonstrated in February, 1946, and is considered
by many to be the most important of the early electronic computers.

In 1944, John von Neumann, a well-known math-
ematician, presented his idea for an Electronic Dis-
crete Variable Automatic Computer, the EDVAC, in
which memory would be used to store both data,
as was common, as well as programming, the storage
of which was an innovation. Known as the von
Neumann architecture, this idea was first implemented in Great Britain in 1949, when Maurice
Wilkes at Cambridge University built the Electronic
Delay Storage Automatic Calcula-
tor, EDSAC. Some consider this
stored-program computer the first
modern computer.

Medical Inventions and Advances
In May, 1940, a team of scientists brought together by Howard
Florey injected mice with a lethal dose of streptococci bacteria.
They then treated half of the mice
with penicillin, which was discovered in 1928 by Alexander Fleming but had not been widely
tested, purified, or successfully
mass-produced. The treated mice
recovered, and the others died. In
1941, Florey successfully treated
with penicillin a patient who had
an infection from a thorn scratch.
The man had already lost one eye,
and his eyes, face, and scalp were
badly swollen. The patient im-

Thirty-ton ENIAC computer at the University of Pennsylvania in 1946. (AP/Wide
World Photos)

proved, but when Florey ran out of penicillin, he died. Florey later sought help in production of penicillin in the United States, where ensuing work by the U.S. Department of Agriculture and others led to large-scale production of the drug, though not with the mass-production efficiency of later methods. It was used on Allied soldiers before the war was over.

In 1943, a Dutch physician, Willem Kolff, built the first kidney dialysis machine. During the Nazi occupation of the Netherlands, Kolff carried on his work with limited resources and under considerable personal danger. Using a washing machine, metal cans, and even sausage skins, he built a machine and began treating patients. It was not until 1945 that he had his first success, however, when dialysis brought a sixty-seven-year-old woman out of a uremic coma.

Selman A. Waksman, chairman of the War Committee on Bacteriology, studied soil organisms for possible use against infectious diseases. During the 1940's, Waksman and his team of graduate students and postdoctoral fellows discovered ten antibiotics, including actinomycin (1940), streptomycin (1944), and neomycin (1949). Streptomycin was the first successful antibiotic treatment for tuberculosis, a drug sorely needed at the time.

In 1947, while studying a soil sample from near Caracas, Venezuela, a research group at Parke-Davis and Company in Detroit, Michigan, discovered the drug chloromycetin, a metabolic product of *Streptomyces venezuelae* found in the soil. Chloromycetin was the first broad-spectrum antibiotic. It is toxic and is used primarily to treat life-threatening infections such as meningitis and typhoid fever.

Other Inventions   The first color television was built in 1940. Peter Goldmark led a team at CBS Laboratories to produce a working color television set, based on a 1928 design by John Baird. However, it was not until 1951 that the first color sets were available to consumers.

The first artificial nuclear reactor was brought to criticality in December, 1942. A team of scientists at the University of Chicago led by Enrico Fermi built the reactor from wood and graphite blocks. Fermi and Leó Szilárd, a physicist credited with first conceiving of a nuclear chain reaction, applied for a patent on the reactor in 1944. Because of wartime se-

crecy, the patent was not awarded until a decade later.

Another invention related to study of the atom was the atomic clock, the first of which was built in 1949 by the U.S. National Bureau of Standards (now the National Institute of Standards and Technology). The clock was built using atomic beam magnetic resonance, developed a decade earlier by Isidor Rabi. This first atomic clock used ammonia molecules as a vibration source; the clock measured time by counting atomic vibrations.

The microwave oven was invented in 1946. Percy Spencer with the Raytheon Corporation was performing tests on a new vacuum tube for radar systems when he noticed that a nearby chocolate bar had melted. After experiments with other items, including popcorn and an exploding egg, he built a metal cabinet that effectively contained and focused the microwave power, and the microwave oven was born.

The first synchrocyclotron was built in 1946 at the University of California at Berkeley. The cyclotron, invented a decade earlier, could not accelerate protons to the desired energy because of their relativistic increase in mass at high speeds. The frequency of a synchrocyclotron's electric field is adjusted to compensate for the changes in the particles' mass as they approach the speed of light, increasing the attainable energies more than tenfold.

Cloud seeding to produce precipitation was first practiced in November, 1946, when General Electric chemist Vincent Joseph Schaefer seeded clouds in New England's Berkshire Mountains with dry ice. In that same month, Bernard Vonnegut, a colleague of Schaefer and brother of the novelist Kurt Vonnegut, noted that the distance between molecules in the crystalline lattice of silver iodide was the same as ice. Because of this, Vonnegut pursued the use of silver iodide as a cloud-seeding medium. Both methods were adopted for use in cloud seeding.

Polaroid photography was invented in 1947 and patented in 1948. Edwin Land's postwar research on quick-developing film led to the unveiling in 1947 of the Polaroid Land Camera, which produced a fully developed print in sixty seconds. Land's Polaroid Corporation sold the first instant camera in November, 1948.

The long-playing record was invented in 1948. Peter Goldmark of CBS Laboratories, who already had worked on color television, reduced the speed of the

78-rpm record to $33\frac{1}{3}$ rpms and increased the number of grooves to 300 per inch. The results were higher quality, longer-lasting playback. It was put on the market in June, 1948, but several years passed before it became a success. It became the standard of the recording industry and remained so for long-playing records until the development of the compact disc.

The remarkable decade produced a wide array of other inventions, possibly of lesser importance on a grand scale but certainly recognizable in everyday life. These include M&M candy in 1940, Velcro in 1941, the Slinky toy and Silly Putty in 1943, Tupperware in 1946, and the modern plastic Frisbee in 1948.

Impact The incredible impact of the coincidental development of the atomic bomb and the ballistic missile rivals the impact of the coincidental development of solid-state electronics and the electronic computer. The availability of information and the power of computation afforded humankind by solid-state computers have produced advances in science, technology, and daily life comparable to the discovery of fire and the invention of the wheel. Nuclear weapons and ballistic missiles had mixed effects. It is likely that their existence kept the world from another war during the 1950's, but their continued existence threatens the very survival of humankind. Other inventions of the 1940's, though not of such obvious importance to human civilization, have enormous impacts on people's daily lives. The average American on a daily basis uses a microwave oven and spends hours watching color television.

Wayne Shirey

Further Reading

Braun, Ernest, and Stuart MacDonald. *Revolution in Miniature.* 2d ed. Cambridge, Mass.: Cambridge University Press, 1982. Excellent account of the fascinating history of the development of transistors.

Goldmark, Peter C., and Lee Edson. *Maverick Inventor: My Turbulent Years at CBS.* New York: Saturday Review Press, 1973. Autobiography of the key inventor of television at CBS. Three of its chapters detail the development of color television.

Hoddeson, Lillian, and Vicki Daitch, *True Genius: The Life and Science of John Bardeen.* Washington, D.C.: Joseph Henry Press, 2002. Biography of a scientist who played a key role in the development of the transistor.

Riordan, Michael, and Lillian Hoddeson. *Crystal Fire: The Invention of the Transistor and the Birth of the Information Age.* New York: Norton, 1998. Account of the scientific and industrial developments behind the invention of the transistor and its subsequent applications in computing and other information-based technologies.

Webb, Richard C. *Tele-visionaries: The People Behind the Invention of Television.* Hoboken, N.J.: J. Wiley & Sons, 2005. Details both the technical details of television's invention and the creation of broadcasting networks to capitalize on the new medium.

Wensberg, Peter C. *Land's Polaroid.* Boston: Houghton Mifflin, 1987. Well-written account of Polaroid's growth from a small private company to a giant corporation. Contains photographs of Land with some of his inventions.

See also Atomic bomb; Computers; ENIAC; Kidney dialysis; Microwave ovens; Nuclear reactors; Polaroid instant cameras; Rocketry; Transistors.

■ Iran

During World War II, Iran's geography and oil resources made Iran a center of conflict between Nazi Germany and the Allies and after the war between the Soviet Union and the United States.

Modern Iran entered the decade of the 1940's under the leadership of Reza Shah Pahlavi, the Iranian general who prevented Soviet forces from taking over the nation in 1920, overthrew the Qajar Dynasty in 1921, and proclaimed himself shah of Iran in 1925. Iran's acceptance of financial and military assistance from Nazi Germany contributed to Reza Shah's abdication under pressure from the Soviet Union and Great Britain in 1941. Iran's historic location along the crossroads of the Middle East and the rest of Asia and its vast oil resources made the nation too important in the Allied struggle against Adolf Hitler. Mohammed Reza Pahlavi, the son and heir of Reza Shah, found his ability to lead Iran limited by Soviet influence in the northern half of the country and British influence in the southern portion.

From 1941 until 1946, Iran was virtually an occupied state. In 1943, President Franklin D. Roosevelt briefly visited Iran's capital, Tehran, for a meeting with Winston Churchill and Joseph Stalin. While Iran was not a conference participant, Roosevelt offered Iran tanks and fighter planes in exchange for Iran becoming the conduit of weaponry for the Soviet Union to fight Nazi Germany. From 1946 to 1953, Iran's new shah worked to reassert his power by reinvigorating the monarchy with a sense of nationalism. With a rebuilt and reequipped army, Mohammed Reza Pahlavi forced the withdrawal of Soviet troops in the Azerbaijani region in northern Iran. The shah's newly won popularity enabled him to recentralize the government, become the national advocate of social reform, and the champion of the youthful radical intelligentsia. By the end of the decade, disillusionment with the shah's policies and the financial extravagance of the imperial family led to a failed 1949 assassination attempt. The shah's late 1949 visit to President Harry S. Truman in search of economic and military aid was a failure because Iran's internal affairs were unstable and the United States had yet to develop a coherent communist containment policy for the Middle East.

Impact Iran's border with the Soviet Union became an essential listening post for the West, particularly for the United States during the Cold War. The development of Iran's oil wealth by British and American oil companies would ultimately force the United States to intervene in Iranian affairs in the next decade.

William A. Paquette

Further Reading

Ansari, Ali M. *Modern Iran Since 1921: The Pahlavis and After.* New York: Pearson Education, 2003.

Azimi, Fakhreddin. *Iran: The Crisis of Democracy, 1941-1953.* London: I.B. Tauris, 1989.

Pahlavi, Mohammed Reza. *Mission for My Country.* London: Hutchinson, 1960.

See also China and North America; Roosevelt, Franklin D.; Tehran Conference; Truman, Harry S.; Turkey; World War II.

■ "Iron Curtain" speech

The Event Speech delivered by former British prime minister Winston Churchill that popularized the term "Iron Curtain" to describe the division between Western nations and the territories in Eastern Europe coming under Soviet domination

Also known as "Sinews of Peace" speech

Date March 5, 1946

Place Fulton, Missouri

Churchill sought to strengthen Anglo-American ties to provide greater cooperation to face what he perceived as a growing Soviet threat to international peace and stability. Because President Harry S. Truman was present and introduced Churchill, the speech appeared to reflect U.S. policy. The speech is widely regarded as an important landmark in the history of the Cold War.

Winston Churchill, who had been defeated by Clement Attlee in the 1945 British general election, was on a Florida vacation after he was invited with the blessings of Harry S. Truman to speak at a small Presbyterian school, Westminster College, in Fulton, Missouri. Churchill visited Washington, D.C., several times to discuss the contents of the speech with Truman. While traveling by train to Missouri, Churchill made final adjustments to the speech and distributed copies to Truman, his advisers, and the media. Although Truman would subsequently claim not to have known of the contents in advance, he read the speech prior to its delivery. Entitled "The Sinews of Peace," the lengthy speech was warmly received by the audience and Truman, who was on the

---

Extract from Churchill's Speech

From Stettin in the Baltic to Trieste in the Adriatic, an iron curtain has descended across the Continent. Behind that line lie all the capitals of the ancient states of Central and Eastern Europe. Warsaw, Berlin, Prague, Vienna, Budapest, Belgrade, Bucharest, and Sofia . . . lie in what I must call the Soviet sphere and all are subject in one form or another, not only to Soviet influence but to a very high and increasing measure of control from Moscow.

platform. Churchill called for Anglo-American solidarity in the face of the Iron Curtain that divided Europe.

Impact In contrast to the warm reception inside the auditorium, the reaction in the media and among political commentators was negative. Soviet leader Joseph Stalin compared Churchill to Adolf Hitler by saying that both sought to unleash war based on racial theory. The term "Iron Curtain" became fixed in popular usage, and the Cold War grew "hotter" in the ensuing years.

Mark C. Herman

Further Reading

Harbutt, Fraser J. *The Iron Curtain: Churchill, America, and the Origins of the Cold War.* New York: Oxford University Press, 1986.

Muller, James W., ed. *Churchill's "Iron Curtain" Speech Fifty Years Later.* Columbia: University of Missouri Press, 1999.

See also Anticommunism; Berlin blockade and airlift; Churchill, Winston; Cold War; Foreign policy of the United States; Truman, Harry S.; Truman Doctrine.

■ Isolationism

Definition Within the context of American politics, isolationism traditionally refers to a belief that the nation should neither establish politics alliances with foreign powers nor intervene in foreign, especially European, wars

Isolationist sentiment and ideas were primary determinants of American foreign policy up to the moment of the Japanese attack on Pearl Harbor in December, 1941. Isolationism was a stumbling block for President Franklin D. Roosevelt's attempts to arm Great Britain, France, and China in their struggles against German and Japanese aggression. Isolationism's demise after Pearl Harbor and its inability to reassert itself successfully after World War II was a decisive turning point in American relations with the rest of the world.

Isolationism was implanted in the American psyche long before the twentieth century. It was rooted in the nation's founding as providing a new and innocent society, far from the evils and oppressions from Europe. In his farewell address in 1789, President George Washington called for as little political connection as possible with Europe. Later, president Thomas Jefferson spoke of honest friendship with all nations, entangling alliances with none.

During the twentieth century, American entry into World War I departed from isolationist sentiment. When the war was over, however, the nation returned to its previous isolationism when the U.S. Senate refused to ratify the Versailles Treaty of 1919. During the 1930's, when Nazi Germany was menacing its European neighbors and Japan was invading China, many Americans feared that their own country would be drawn into war. Between 1935 and 1939, the U.S. Congress passed a series of Neutrality Acts to prevent direct American involvement, against the wishes of President Roosevelt, who sought discretionary powers to arm the victims of aggression.

As 1940 began, war had already broken out in Europe and was continuing in China. American voices urged the U.S. government to aid Britain and other victims of aggression, but isolationism was still a strong impulse. In September, 1940, the isolationist America First Committee (AFC) was founded at Yale University. The organization quickly became a powerful opponent to U.S. entry into World War II. At its height, its membership totaled 800,000, including many prominent citizens. Leaders of the AFC argued that the nation should concentrate on building its own impregnable defenses and that American democracy could only be preserved by avoiding military intervention.

During the spring of 1941, however, national policy made a decisive break from war neutrality when Congress passed the Lend-Lease Act, which broke the isolationist spell by authorizing loans without repayment provisions for the sale of war materiel. Then, on December 7, the Japanese attack on Pearl Harbor dealt a fatal blow to American isolationism. A few days later, the AFC disbanded.

After the war, the forces of isolationism failed to reassert themselves with any effect. The nation accepted American membership in the United Nations in 1945, and events catapulted the United States to world leadership. The first crisis of the new Cold War with the Soviet Union, the Soviet blockade of Berlin, came in 1948. In 1949, a military alliance, the North Atlantic Treaty Organization, formally "entangled" the United States with Europe. In June, 1950, the United States embarked on another foreign war, this time in Korea.

Impact   Thanks to American involvement in World War II during the 1940's, isolationism never acted as a governing force in American foreign policy in the postwar period. On the contrary, the United States entered into a multitude of military alliances around the world. On a number of occasions, the nation militarily intervened abroad, most notably in the Korean and Vietnam wars and later in Iraq and Afghanistan. Opposition to the Vietnam War during the 1960's, however, led to a marked increase in anti-interventionism.

After the end of the Cold War in 1992, some observers perceived an America longing for withdrawal from foreign military involvement. However, the terrorist attacks of September 11, 2001, launched from abroad, ended this possibility at least for the time being.

Charles F. Bahmueller

Further Reading

Foster, H. Schuyler. *Activism Replaces Isolationism: U.S. Public Attitudes, 1940-1975*. Washington, D.C.: Foxhall Press, 1983.

Holbo, Peter Sothe. *Isolationism and Interventionism, 1932-1941*. Skokie, Ill.: Rand McNally, 1969.

See also   America First Committee; "Arsenal of Democracy" speech; Berlin blockade and airlift; Cold War; Foreign policy of the United States; Lend-Lease; McCormick, Robert R.; North Atlantic Treaty Organization; World War II.

Young Israelis in Tel Aviv celebrating the proclamation of the new state of Israel on May 14, 1948. (AFP/Getty Images)

■ Israel, creation of

The Event   Establishment of the state of Israel
Date   May 14, 1948

When the United States extended diplomatic recognition to the state of Israel on May 14, 1948, President Harry S. Truman did so despite strong objections raised by a U.S. Department of State attuned more to Arab than Jewish sensibilities. Truman acted from deeply held personal beliefs, but he also did so in response to an organized campaign by majorities of state legislatures, state governors, and members of Congress, along with millions of Americans who urged him to do so.

Beliefs central to President Harry S. Truman guided him to support the creation of a state by the Jewish people in Palestine. Beyond pro-Jewish sympathies that he developed through lifelong friendships with individual Jews such as his former business partner Eddie Jacobson, Truman studied closely the Christian Old Testament. Firm guidance from the Scriptures appeared in speeches he delivered as a senator, in which he cited biblical passages linking the Jewish people to Palestine such as 1 Deuteronomy 8. He told friends that the explicitly Zionist Psalm 137 was his favorite psalm in the Bible.

As a senator from Missouri from 1935 until 1944, Truman had often acted to assist individual European Jewish refugees in finding sanctuary in the United States. With voice and vote, he joined congressional majorities in resolutions deploring both Nazi anti-Semitism and British backsliding from their earlier promises to support creation of a national home for the Jews in Palestine. Thus, when World War II ended and Britain announced its intention soon to cede its authority over Palestine to the United Nations, leading American advocates for Jewish interests, such as Rabbi Abba Hillel Silver, looked to President Truman for support. By 1947, polls showed that by a margin of two to one, Ameri-

Israel, 1947-1948

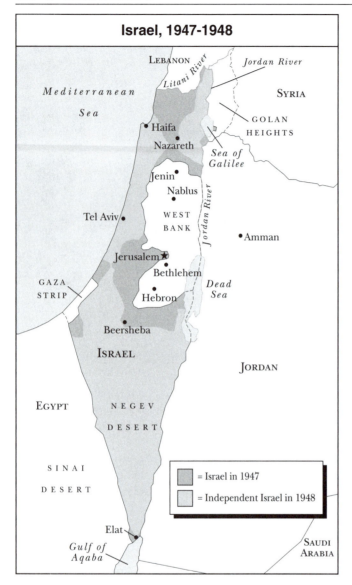

= Israel in 1947

= Independent Israel in 1948

president openly declared his support for creation of a viable Jewish state in Palestine in a 1947 message to American Jews issued on the eve of the holiest day in Judaism, Yom Kippur. Following Truman's explicit instructions, on November 29, 1947, the U.S. delegation to the U.N. General Assembly joined a majority of thirty-three countries voting in favor of Resolution 181, partitioning Palestine into these two states. Thirteen countries, including all Arab members of the United Nations, opposed partition (and ten abstained).

Opposition to partition by all Arab U.N. members had likely consequences that troubled Central Intelligence Agency (CIA) analysts, Secretary of State George C. Marshall, and Secretary of Defense James Forrestal. To placate his cabinet, Truman announced an arms embargo on the entire region in December, 1947. Meanwhile, Truman relied on White House counselor Clark Clifford to try to persuade reluctant cabinet officials to concur with the president's preferences. Ultimately, the Truman-Marshall relationship was damaged beyond repair over the issue after Truman penned the May 14, 1948, note announcing that the United States recognized Israel. It was released just hours after the Zionist provisional government, including Wisconsin-raised U.S. citizen Golda Meir, declared independence at Tel Aviv Museum.

That same day, Egyptian jets strafed Tel Aviv. Diplomatic acts, whether in New York or Washington, could not secure the creation of Israel. Violence between Arabs and Jews had erupted shortly after the 1947 U.N. partition vote, and clashes continued as besieged British forces prepared to leave by the planned date in May, 1948. Denied requests for official U.S. funds with which to help build an army, Zionist activist Meir returned to North America to raise more than $50 million in private contributions. Substantial numbers of American and Canadian Jews contributed, but major donors also included many non-Jews, especially in Hollywood, including singer Frank Sinatra.

Impact Outright war greeted Israel within hours of its declaration of independence, as the national ar-

can public opinion favored the Zionist project to achieve a state in Palestine for both the Jewish victims of Nazi oppression and other Jews.

Support and Opposition An early and key supporter of the United Nations, the Truman administration backed Jewish ambitions by both words and deeds. In May, 1947, the United States voted to authorize creation of a United Nations Special Commission on Palestine to investigate the situation, and Truman endorsed the September, 1947, recommendation of that commission that two states be established in Palestine: one Jewish and one Arab. The

mies of Jordan, Egypt, Syria, Lebanon, and Iraq invaded. Moral encouragement followed formal U.S. recognition, but the U.S. government did not extend military aid to Israel for more than a decade. Primarily, the new state was secured by Israeli military efforts using arms purchased from Czechoslovakia. Some 4,000 World War II veterans from allied armies, chiefly Americans, did travel to Palestine to fight alongside the new Israeli Defense Forces. These seasoned volunteers arrived as the 30,000-member irregular Jewish militias of pre-independence days swiftly were transformed into a disciplined army of more than 65,000 by July, 1948. The participation of these Americans, and later immigration of American Jews to Israel, reinforced the misimpression in the Arab world that the United States had a central role in the creation of Israel. This perception gained some substance when, as the tide of battle turned in favor of the new Jewish state, U.S. diplomat Ralph Bunche guided United Nations mediation efforts to secure a cease-fire between Israel and its neighboring Arab states. For these efforts, he was awarded the 1950 Nobel Peace Prize, but the Arab state in Palestine envisioned in the partition plan did not come into existence over the next sixty years.

Gordon L. Bowen

Further Reading

Cohen, Hillel. *Army of Shadows: Palestinian Collaboration with Zionism, 1917-1948*. Berkeley: University of California Press, 2008. Uses declassified and other rare documents to illuminate pre-independence relations between Arabs and Jews in Palestine.

Laqueur, Walter, and Barry Rubin, eds. *The Israel-Arab Reader: A Documentary History of the Middle East Conflict*. 7th ed. New York: Penguin, 2008. Thorough collection of original documents from American, British, Israeli, and Arab governmental, political, and cultural sources.

McCullough, David. *Truman*. New York: Simon & Schuster, 1992. Definitive biography of this key decision maker and his thinking. Richly describes his decades of friendly relations with individual American Jews and his testier encounters with Jewish organizations.

Morris, Benny. *1948: A History of the First Arab-Israeli War*. New Haven, Conn.: Yale University Press, 2008. Examines British, Jewish, and Arab actions as it depicts the course of the political and military conflict of 1947-1949.

Oren, Michael B. *Power, Faith, and Fantasy: America in the Middle East, 1776 to the Present*. New York: W. W. Norton, 2007. Places U.S. official approaches toward the founding of Israel within longer historic patterns in U.S. regional Middle Eastern policy, as well as within a social milieu of plentiful non-Jewish support for Zionism, especially among some American Protestants. Demonstrates State Department identification with both oil interests and Arab perspectives as it details Zionists' campaigns to influence U.S. presidents, the U.S. Congress, and U.S. foreign policy.

See also   Bunche, Ralph; Clifford, Clark; Einstein, Albert; Foreign policy of the United States; Jews in Canada; Jews in the United States; Marshall, George C.; Nobel Prizes; Truman, Harry S.

■ Italian campaign

The Event   Allied military offensive against Axis forces in Italy during World War II
Date   July 10, 1943-May 2, 1945
Places   Sicily and Italy

The Italian campaign saw the most drawn-out and bloody fighting of World War II in Western Europe. The Allied invasion of Italy was intended to strike the Axis Powers at a vulnerable point and divert German troops from other fronts. Allied forces then became embroiled in a grueling struggle for control of the Italian peninsula.

The defeat of Axis forces in North Africa in 1943 spurred the Western Allies to assess their strategy. American military planners regarded the campaign in the Mediterranean as a sideshow and were anxious to build up forces in Britain for the cross-channel invasion of France. The British wanted to follow up success in the Mediterranean, moving against what Prime Minister Winston Churchill called the "soft underbelly" of Europe. The Allies ultimately agreed on an invasion of France in 1944. In the meantime, operations would continue in the Mediterranean.

Sicilian Prelude   Allied planners decided to strike at Sicily. The island was garrisoned by unreliable Italian troops and two refitting German divisions. Overall command of the invasion of Sicily was given to American general Dwight D. Eisenhower. Operational command went to British general Harold Alexander.

The Allied landings in Sicily began on July 10, 1943. The seven-division landing force was larger than that which would land at Normandy. British general Bernard Montgomery's Eighth Army landed near Syracuse and began driving north toward Messina. American general George S. Patton's Seventh Army was landed on the south coast and protected Montgomery's left flank. Italian opposition was weak, but the Germans fought back fiercely. Montgomery was held up by German defenses around Mount Etna. Patton took advantage of weaker opposition to drive north to Palermo, and then east to Messina, arriving shortly before Montgomery's advance guard on August 17.

The Allies conquered Sicily, but the Germans successfully evacuated all their forces across the Straits of Messina. Though militarily incomplete, victory in Sicily had important consequences. The Italian dictator Benito Mussolini was overthrown in a coup supported by King Victor Emmanuel III. Marshal Pietro Badoglio became the new head of the Italian government and began negotiating surrender with the Allies. The Germans responded to Mussolini's fall by moving more troops into Italy. On September 12, German commandos rescued Mussolini from imprisonment.

War in Italy　Success in Sicily persuaded the Allies to attack the Italian mainland. Montgomery's Eighth Army crossed to the toe of Italy on September 3 and began a slow advance to the north. On September 9, American general Mark Clark's Fifth Army went ashore at the Gulf of Salerno, south of Naples. The German field marshal Albert Kesselring believed that the Allies could be held south of Rome, and counterattacked at Salerno with the limited forces that he had available. The Fifth Army was hard pressed, and only the firepower provided by waves of bombers and naval gunfire saved the beachhead. The Eighth Army finally linked up with the Fifth Army on September 16, forcing a German retreat. Kesselring's forces fell back slowly, skillfully making the most of defensive positions sited in the Apennine Mountains, which run like a spine up central Italy. The advance north proved painfully slow and costly, as the Allied troops battled their way through the mountains. By January 1, 1944, the Allied offensive had stalled in front of Kesselring's for-

Allied Invasion of Italy, September, 1943

tified Gustav Line, almost one hundred miles south of Rome.

By this time, Eisenhower and Montgomery had transferred to Britain to plan the Normandy invasion. General Alexander commanded the Allied forces in Italy. When frontal assaults on the Gustav Line failed, Alexander tried an end run. On January 22, he boldly landed the U.S. VI Corps behind the Gustav Line at Anzio, thirty-three miles south of Rome. Alexander hoped that this force would rapidly strike at the German lines of communication. General Clark ordered the commander at Anzio to consolidate his beachhead before advancing. This gave Kesselring time to concentrate forces to meet this threat. Within a week, the VI Corps was besieged and fighting for its survival. The Germans stationed at the Gustav Line did not budge. Alexander was forced to hammer away at the German defenses. Much of the fighting centered on the ancient monastery of Monte Cassino, which became a bitter symbol to the attacking Allied troops. The Allies did not pierce the Gustav Line until May, with Monte Cassino falling on the 18th of that month.

The Allies now had a chance to destroy the retreating Germans. The American troops at Anzio launched an attack that threatened to cut the German escape route. Clark, anxious to liberate Rome, ordered these forces to change the direction of their attack. Clark entered Rome on June 4, but the Germans escaped, and settled into the Gothic Line, 150 miles to the north. Italy was now a secondary theater, and Alexander lost seven divisions, which were sent to invade southern France. Alexander wanted to continue the offensive into northern Italy and then press through the Alps into Austria. Allied forces penetrated the Gothic Line in September. The Germans continued to resist fiercely, taking advantage of the rugged terrain. Alexander called off offensive operations in December, with his troops still south of Bologna.

The Allied armies, now under the command of General Clark, attacked again in April, 1945, making the most of an advantage in numbers and equipment. The Germans were overwhelmed. Cut off while retreating, the German forces surrendered unconditionally on May 2.

Impact The Italian campaign cost both sides more than 300,000 casualties, and it remains controversial. Some historians believe that the campaign used up German troops needed elsewhere. Others argue that the occupation of Sicily and southern Italy alone would have compelled the Germans to retain large forces near the Alps, and that the costly and destructive Italian campaign was unnecessary.

Daniel P. Murphy

Further Reading

Atkinson, Rick. *Day of Battle: The War in Sicily and Italy.* New York: Henry Holt, 2007. Superbly written narrative by a Pulitzer Prize-winning historian.

Botjer, George. *Sideshow War: The Italian Campaign, 1943-1945.* College Station: Texas A&M Press, 1996. Scholarly and balanced account of the campaign.

Graham, Dominick, and Shelford Bidwell. *Tug of War: The Battle for Italy, 1943-1945.* Barnsley, England: Pen and Sword, 2004. Reprint of a respected study, paying special attention to Allied generalship.

Lamb, Richard. *War in Italy, 1943-1945: A Brutal Story.* New York: Da Capo Press, 1996. Reprint of a highly regarded history that highlights Italian suffering during the war.

See also Army, U.S.; Bradley, Omar N.; Casablanca Conference; Churchill, Winston; Eisenhower, Dwight D.; Marshall, George C.; North African campaign; Patton, George S.; Roosevelt, Franklin D.; World War II.

■ *It's a Wonderful Life*

Identification Film about how one ordinary person's life touches others
Director Frank Capra (1897-1991)
Date Released on December 20, 1946

Initially overshadowed by a film about American soldiers returning from World War II, director Frank Capra's home-front tale about an uncelebrated but influential common man gained steady popularity to become an enduring Christmas classic. The film reinforces the idea of the positive power of friendship, integrity, self-sacrifice, and acts of compassion among ordinary people.

Only moderately successful in movie theaters during the postwar period, *It's a Wonderful Life* was later popularized via annual Christmas showings on television. Adapted from Philip Van Doren Stern's short story "The Greatest Gift" (1943), the film traces the personal history and kindnesses of George Bailey (played by James Stewart), a promising young man poised for travel and a big-city architecture career. George settles for small-town life, puny earnings, and thwarted dreams to save his father's modest building and loan—and its working-class customers—from Mr. Potter (Lionel Barrymore), Bedford Falls's property-grubbing money mogul. Suicidal on Christmas Eve over a business-breaking financial shortfall, George is rescued by his guardian angel, Clarence Odbody (Henry Travers), who enables the despondent mortal to view how poorly his family and community would have fared if George had never lived. By the time George appreciates his humble life and returns to wife, Mary (Donna Reed), and family, grateful townspeople are pooling their money to prevent his ruin.

Impact   Eclipsed in 1946 by interest in the postwar film *The Best Years of Our Lives,* and initially branded as saccharine by some critics, *It's a Wonderful Life* was rediscovered in subsequent decades by viewers taken with George Bailey's everyman struggle with light and darkness.

Wendy Alison Lamb

Further Reading

Basinger, Jean. *The "It's a Wonderful Life" Book.* New York: Alfred A. Knopf, 1986.

Dixon, Wheeler Winston, ed. *American Cinema of the 1940's: Themes and Variations.* New Brunswick, N.J.: Rutgers University Press, 2006.

See also   *The Best Years of Our Lives;* Capra, Frank; Film in the United States; *The Human Comedy; Miracle on 34th Street.*

■ Iwo Jima, Battle of

The Event   Battle for and seizure of the Japanese island of Iwo Jima by the United States during World War II

Date   February 19-March 26, 1945

Place   Iwo Jima, Ogasawara Islands, Pacific Ocean

The Battle of Iwo Jima was the first American attack on the Japanese home islands. By winning this battle, the United States acquired an emergency landing and refueling site for Boeing B-29 Superfortresses and escort airplanes at the midpoint between Tokyo and the Mariana Islands, which include Guam, Saipan, and Tinian.

Iwo Jima, also known formally as Iōtō (a different pronunciation of the same Japanese characters for the island's name), means "sulfur island" in Japanese. As the name indicates, this small island, whose entire area is about one-third the size of Manhattan, has heavy deposits of sulfur, and sulfur mining was a major occupation on the island prior to World War II. Despite the severe living environment, Iwo Jima was strategically important for Japan because of its landscape and location. The relatively flat landscape was suitable for building runways: The island had two airfields, and a third was under construction at the time of the battle. Located 660 nautical miles south of Tokyo and 700 nautical miles north of Guam, Iwo Jima provided an air base for Japanese fighter planes to attack American aircraft coming from the Mariana Islands to the main islands of Japan. Warning from the radar station on Iwo Jima allowed several additional hours for Japanese air defenses to prepare for coming attacks.

The seizure of Iwo Jima was geographically crucial for the United States, as it would provide a base for escort fighters to support long-range bombers, the B-29 Superfortresses, on missions to Japan. In October, 1944, Admiral Chester W. Nimitz ordered Lieutenant General Holland Smith to undertake the invasion of Iwo Jima, known as Operation Detachment. On February 19, 1945, the first wave of Marines landed on the beach of Iwo Jima after a bombardment by the U.S. Navy. On February 23, the Marines reached the summit of Mount Suribachi, the 545-foot volcanic mountain at the south end of the island, and an American flag was raised by five Marines and one Navy corpsman. A photograph of this event by Joe Rosenthal, *Raising the Flag on Iwo Jima,* was used as a symbol of the seventh war-bond campaign and won the 1945 Pulitzer Prize in news photography.

Although the United States estimated completion of the mission in five days, it lasted more than a month because of a unique strategy undertaken by Lieutenant General Tadamichi Kuribayashi, who was in charge of the defense of Iwo Jima. Unlike typical Japanese strategy to defend against landings of opponents on the beach, Kuribayashi ordered more than ten miles of tunnels to be built throughout the island, connecting more than 1,500 underground

Joe Rosenthal's Pulitzer Prize-winning photograph of Marines raising an American flag at Iwo Jima. (National Archives)

bunkers. Some of the Japanese heavy artillery was hidden, not visible from the sea. Although the network of tunnels was never fully completed, it still worked effectively: American soldiers had to fight against "invisible" enemies who hid underground.

Impact   The Battle of Iwo Jima was one of the most brutal ones for both the United States and Japan. American troops suffered nearly 20,000 wounded, more than 6,000 killed in action, and thousands of victims of battle fatigue. Approximately 20,000 Japanese died during the battle, and only a few hundred survived as prisoners. Clint Eastwood's film *Flags of Our Fathers* (2006) portrays the lives of six men who raised the flag at Mount Suribachi, and the same director's *Letters from Iwo Jima* (2006) portrays the battle from the viewpoint of Japanese soldiers. Iwo Jima

was occupied by the United States until June, 1968, when the island was returned to Japan.

Fusako Hamao

Further Reading

Bradley, James, with Ron Powers. *Flags of Our Fathers.* New York: Bantam Books, 2006.

Burrell, Robert S. *The Ghosts of Iwo Jima.* College Station: Texas A&M Press, 2006.

Ross, Bill D. *Iwo Jima: Legacy of Valor.* New York: Random House, 1986.

See also   Casualties of World War II; Films about World War II; Great Marianas Turkey Shoot; *History of the United States Naval Operations in World War II*; Landing craft, amphibious; Marines, U.S.; Pyle, Ernie; Strategic bombing; War bonds; War heroes; World War II.

J

■ Jackson, Mahalia

Identification   American gospel singer
Born   October 26, 1911; New Orleans, Louisiana
Died   January 27, 1972; Evergreen Park, Illinois
(near Chicago)

Jackson was an inspirational gospel singer who touched the hearts of many people through her spirit-filled singing and religious passion. After launching her recording career in 1946, her unique singing style captivated listeners and made her the most influential gospel singer of her era.

At an early age, Mahalia Jackson became committed to singing gospel music, which she believed could heal the soul. She spent hours listening to popular blues singers, trying to capture their nuances and tone quantity and eventually molded her own voice into a powerful and distinct timbre filled with religious passion. She used this gift to uplift people. Her unique vocal techniques fascinated audiences, as her full-throated singing, bent pitches, and high soprano tones helped many people forget their troubles. Mahalia's emotional singing made audiences cheer, cry, and sometimes even faint.

During the Depression years, World War II, and the civil rights era, people flocked to churches for spiritual healing. Jackson sang for congregations and public engagements. Her expressive voice moved leaders such as the Reverend Martin Luther King, Jr., and President John F. Kennedy.

During the 1940's, Jackson became one of the leading African American gospel singers. She began her recording career in October, 1946. Her initial recordings sold poorly, but in September, 1947, she first made gospel music history with her recording of "Move On Up a Little Higher," which would sell more than one million records. This success secured her bookings on weekly radio shows and moved her career forward.

Impact   During the 1940's, Mahalia Jackson launched an influential recording career that included a contract with Columbia Records and popu-

Photograph of Mahalia Jackson made by Carl Van Vechten in 1962. (Library of Congress)

larity that transcended racial lines. She was one of several important African American performers to bring gospel music into the mainstream of the U.S. recording industry. As the first gospel singer to broadcast pure sanctified gospel music, she earned the title Queen of Gospel Song.

Monica T. Tripp-Roberson

Further Reading

Goreau, Laurraine. *Just Mahalia, Baby: The Mahalia Jackson Story.* Gretna, La.: Pelican, 1984.
Gourse, Leslie. *Mahalia Jackson: Queen of Gospel Song.* New York: Franklin Watts, 1996.

Jackson, Mahalia, with Evan McLeod Wylie. *Movin' On Up.* New York: Avon Books, 1969.

Orgill, Roxane. *Mahalia: A Life in Gospel Music.* Cambridge, Mass.: Candlewick Press, 2002.

See also   African Americans; American Negro Exposition; Dorsey, Tommy; Music: Jazz; Music: Popular; Women's roles and rights in the United States.

■ Jackson, Shirley

Identification   American author of the 1948 short story "The Lottery"

Born   December 14, 1916; San Francisco, California

Died   August 8, 1965; North Bennington, Vermont

Jackson's short story "The Lottery" caused a sensation by emphasizing the ease with which otherwise ordinary people can be led to commit heinous acts.

For a readership coming to terms with the effects of Nazism and the atomic bombings of Hiroshima and Nagasaki, and dealing with xenophobia and the rising tensions over civil rights, Shirley Jackson's "The Lottery" defined the capacity for brutality as central to each individual but particularly alluring to unthinking mobs. The story, in which a small town conducts an annual murder of a member of its citizenry, underscores the dangers that arise when prejudices and ritualized activities are left unexamined by an apathetic public. Thus, it inspired heated debate about the ways in which dominant cultures disenfranchise individuals based on their race, ethnicity, class, and gender. Its 1948 publication in *The New Yorker* inspired more letters than any story the magazine had published to date, and it remains Jackson's most anthologized work.

Impact   A successful novelist, dramatist, lecturer, autobiographer, and short-story writer, Jackson is often recognized for her complex psychological portraits and influence on the female Gothic genre. However, she remains best known for "The Lottery" and its poignant depiction of the dangers of mob mentality.
Priscilla Glanville

Further Reading

Hattenhauer, Darryl. *Shirley Jackson's American Gothic.* Albany: State University of New York Press, 2003.

Murphy, Bernice M., ed. *Shirley Jackson: Essays on the Literary Legacy.* Jefferson, N.C.: McFarland, 2005.

Oppenheimer, Judy. *Private Demons: The Life of Shirley Jackson.* New York: Putnam, 1988.

See also   Civil rights and liberties; Literature in the United States; Lynching and hate crime; Racial discrimination; Women's roles and rights in the United States; World War II.

■ Jackson Hole National Monument

Identification   New national monument
Date   Established on March 15, 1943
Place   Jackson Hole, Wyoming

The creation of Jackson Hole National Monument served to protect a valley of exceptional natural beauty from commercial development.

Jackson Hole is the scenic valley bordering the east side of the dramatic Teton Range. Through the years, attempts were made to add this region to Grand Teton National Park. Established in 1929, the park itself included only the Teton Range and six adjacent lakes. However, many local residents and ranchers were against enlarging the park.

Philanthropist John D. Rockefeller, Jr., visited the area during the 1920's, and had become concerned about its protection. He eventually purchased 35,000 acres in the region, planning to give this land to the federal government to expand Grand Teton National Park. For years, legal actions blocked his efforts. Finally, at the urging of Secretary of the Interior Harold Ickes, and using powers granted him by the Antiquities Act of 1906, President Franklin D. Roosevelt accepted the gift for the park service and declared the valley Jackson Hole National Monument on March 15, 1943. Legal challenges were finally resolved by the end of the decade.

Impact   Although a coalition of landowners attempted to block the monument's creation, Roosevelt was successful. Congress passed a bill abolishing the monument, but the president vetoed it. On September 14, 1950, President Harry S. Truman signed a bill that merged most of Jackson Hole National Monument with Grand Teton National Park.
Russell N. Carney

Further Reading

Butcher, Devereux. *Exploring Our National Parks and Monuments.* Boulder, Colo.: Roberts Rinehart, 1995.

Harmsen, Debbie, and Michael Nalepa, eds. *The Complete Guide to the National Parks of the West.* New York: Fodor's Travel Publications, 2007.

Tilden, Freeman. *The National Parks.* 3d ed. New York: Alfred A. Knopf, 1986.

See also Congress, U.S.; Ickes, Harold; Mount Rushmore National Memorial; National parks; Roosevelt, Franklin D.; Truman, Harry S.

■ Japan, occupation of

The Event U.S. military occupation of Japan as part of the country's restructuring after World War II

Dates September 2, 1945-April 28, 1952

After Japan surrendered to end World War II, U.S. occupation officials began working successfully to demilitarize and democratize Japan to prevent a postwar revival of imperialism. However, the "reverse course" in U.S. policy soon began to transform Japan into an anticommunist bastion, halting further reforms and building a security alliance.

The United States declared victory over Japan in World War II on V-J Day, August 15, 1945, following Japan's unconditional surrender. On September 2, 1945, the date of Japan's formal surrender, General Douglas MacArthur, as Supreme Commander of the Allied Powers (SCAP), took control over Japan, but the U.S. government had decided upon basic policies beforehand. SCAP also worked through existing parliamentary institutions and the bureaucracy. General Order Number One assigned the task of demobilizing the Japanese armed forces to the Japanese themselves, a task they completed in two months. MacArthur and his staff, however, would not let the Japanese decide the nature and scope of subsequent reform. When Japanese leaders prepared a draft providing for modest revisions in the Meiji Constitution, U.S. officials instantly rejected it and formulated a new document. Effective in May, 1947, the American-written constitution swept away all vestiges of elitism, militarism, and authoritarianism. Trials punished war criminals, and 200,000 military, government, and business leaders who had supported the war were purged.

Areas of Reform Five areas of reform brought fundamental and permanent changes in Japan's economic, political, and social systems. First, in October, 1946, SCAP forced the Diet to approve a sweeping land redistribution plan that sought to replace large landowners with yeoman farmers who were expected to be the bulwark of democracy. Under provisions of the reform, 2.3 million landowners had to sell their land to the government at greatly undervalued prices. By 1950, about 4.75 million tenants had bought roughly five million acres of land at low prices and on generous credit terms. A huge demand for food and raw materials in postwar Japan resulted in rising prices that spurred production and rural prosperity. The emergence of an independent, prosperous, and conservative farmer class in postwar Japan achieved a key U.S. occupation goal.

A second thrust of democratic reform promoted labor unions. The Trade Union Law of December, 1945, made strikes legal and mandated joint collective bargaining. Two years later, another law set minimum standards for working hours, safety provisions, and accident compensation. By 1948, 6.5 million workers, constituting about half the workforce, belonged to labor unions. Labor leaders acted with increasing assertiveness to control occupation policies, leading to a growing pattern of violence and acts of sabotage when U.S. officials would not cooperate. In 1948, SCAP, in partnership with Japanese leaders, took strong steps to limit labor's power, achieving passage of a new law aimed at restraining the unions and implementing a new purge of communist leaders.

Third, the United States wanted to eliminate the *zaibatsu*, believing that these large conglomerates in banking, shipping, international trade, and heavy industry had been partners with the military in waging war. SCAP implemented reforms requiring the sale of *zaibatsu* stock and dissolution of holding companies, expecting that a more equitable division of wealth and economic power would foster democratization. SCAP froze the assets of *zaibatsu* families and purged family members and top executives from management with prohibitions against resuming work with the same firms. Fears of economic stagnation and growing complaints about "socialist schemes" caused SCAP to abandon plans to break up remaining monopolistic firms.

Education was the fourth area of reform, focusing on encouraging individualism and creating a truly egalitarian society. SCAP abolished educational practices aimed at molding students into willing servants of the state, especially the teaching of morals that indoctrinated youths to embrace extreme nationalism. Many teachers were purged after SCAP investigated prewar activities. Militarist propaganda and references to the Shinto system of spiritualism were absent from new textbooks, which were designed to foster an acceptance of democracy and civil rights. Students also were freed from prewar channels of vocational, normal, technical, or university training.

Finally, a new constitution assigned sovereignty to the people, while the emperor became the "symbol" of the state. Citizens at least twenty years of age had the right to vote for members of a bicameral legislature, or Diet, without regard to sex, income, or social status. Primary power was in the lower house, which controlled the budget, ratified treaties, and could veto bills the upper house passed. It elected a prime minister, who named cabinet members. The cabinet chose and voters confirmed judges on a supreme court that had the power to determine the constitutionality of laws and name justices on lower courts. Thirty-one articles guaranteed "fundamental human rights," among them respect as individuals, freedom of thought, education, and sexual equality.

Returning Power to the Japanese The Japanese elections of 1947 and political reshuffling among the major parties led to the Japan Socialist Party obtaining a plurality, allowing it to form a cabinet. It lasted less than a year, however, and former prime minister Yoshida Shigeru of the more conservative Liberal Party returned to that post, which he held until 1955.

Some of MacArthur's reforms were rescinded under guidance from the U.S. Department of State as early as 1948, and MacArthur himself turned power over to the newly formed Japanese government in 1949. MacArthur remained in Japan until April 11, 1951, when President Harry S. Truman replaced him as SCAP leader with Army general Matthew Ridgway. The San Francisco Peace Treaty, signed by forty-one nations on September 8, 1951, called for

U.S. general Douglas MacArthur and Japanese emperor Hirohito on September 27, 1945. To dramatize the reduction of the emperor's once exalted status, MacArthur used his authority as supreme administrator of Japan to insist that the emperor come to him at the American embassy. Moreover, he received the emperor in a nondress uniform, further diminishing the emperor's prestige. (AP/Wide World Photos)

the end of the Allied occupation, and it came into force on April 28, 1952.

Some reforms did not survive after the U.S. occupation ended in May, 1952, but the new Japanese constitution escaped major alterations. Those on the Left and the Right acknowledged the benefits of Article 9, outlawing war, despite their disagreement on how to interpret it. Some of SCAP's reforms slowed economic recovery. Widespread destitution forced the United States to send more than $2 billion in food, fuel, and medicine to prevent mass starvation and disease. Economic stabilization came in 1949 with termination of war reparations payments and the Dodge Plan. Japan's recovery soon turned into prosperity, also partly as a result of the Korean War.

Impact Early assessments viewed the U.S. occupation of Japan as positive, benevolent, and enlightened, promoting the emergence of a democratic society. Later historians would criticize the American integration of Japan into a Cold War strategy that aimed to defeat the goals of Asian revolutionary nationalist movements. U.S. policy toward Japan turned toward a focus on containing communism and maintaining a security alliance. Cold War partnership between the United States and Japan became concrete in 1951 with the San Francisco Peace Treaty and the U.S.-Japan Security Treaty.

James I. Matray

Further Reading

Borden, William S. *The Pacific Alliance: United States Foreign Economic Policy and Japanese Trade Recovery, 1947-1955.* Madison: University of Wisconsin Press, 1984. Shows how economics dictated U.S. security policy toward Japan after 1945, stressing the importance of Southeast Asia becoming a market for Japan's exports and a source for its raw materials.

Dower, John W. *Embracing Defeat: Japan in the Wake of World War II.* New York: W. W. Norton, 1999. Portrays American policy as ambiguous, arrogant, and bungling, and provides graphic and moving descriptions of life in Japan between the end of the war and the improvement of economic conditions beginning in 1949.

Finn, Richard B. *Winners in Peace: MacArthur, Yoshida, and Postwar Japan.* Berkeley: University of California Press, 1992. De-emphasizing security concerns behind U.S. policy, Finn stresses Japanese cooperation with the Americans in a benevolent venture to create a self-sufficient and stable Japan.

Schonberger, Howard B. *Aftermath of War: Americans and the Remaking of Japan, 1945-1952.* Kent, Ohio: Kent State University Press, 1989. Demonstrates that rather than General Douglas MacArthur determining occupation policies in Japan, an array of Americans with conflicting views and representing different segments of U.S. society and government jointly formed those policies.

See also Cold War; Freezing of Japanese assets; Germany, occupation of; Hiroshima and Nagasaki bombings; Japanese American internment; Japanese Canadian internment; MacArthur, Douglas; Potsdam Conference; Unconditional surrender policy.

■ Japanese American internment

The Event Involuntary assignment of about 120,000 Japanese Americans and other persons of Japanese descent to internment camps during World War II

Dates March, 1942-March, 1946

Following the Japanese bombing of Pearl Harbor in 1941, Americans reacted with fear and hostility toward those of Japanese descent living in the United States. Official government apologies and reparations for the great economic, social, and personal hardship suffered by the internees were decades in coming.

During World War II, acting in what was later declared by Congress to be a time of "racial prejudice" and "wartime hysteria," the U.S. government interned 120,000 of its own citizens and legal immigrants of Japanese descent. On short notice, people were forced to sell, give away, or abandon their belongings, including their cars, houses, farms, and businesses. Internment camps operated from 1942 to 1946. Shortly after the war ended, the government offered minimal reimbursement to the internees for their property losses and no apology for the injustices involved in the internees' experiences. It was not until four decades later that Congress officially apologized for these governmental abuses and made reparations of $20,000 to each surviving internee.

Pearl Harbor and Japanese Americans World War II began in Europe in September, 1939, when Germany invaded Poland. Germany was later joined by Italy and Japan, which together were the primary Axis Powers. On December 7, 1941, Japanese forces bombed the U.S. naval base at Pearl Harbor, Hawaii, sinking 21 ships and destroying 188 aircraft. Casualties numbered about 2,400 Americans, mostly sailors. At that time, Hawaii was a U.S. territory (it became a state in 1959). In response to the attack, the United States declared war and aligned itself with the Allied powers, which included Great Britain and the Soviet Union.

Immediately after the attack on Pearl Harbor, suspicions began to focus on Japanese immigrants who lived in Hawaii and on the West Coast. Japanese people had begun to immigrate to the United States during the late nineteenth century. Immigrants themselves were known as the first generation, or

Issei. The early immigrants remained "aliens" because even those Japanese who had immigrated legally were prohibited from becoming citizens through naturalization. Their children, however, were U.S. citizens by reason of their birth in the United States; they were known as the second generation, or Nisei. Third-generation Japanese Americans are known as Sansei. By 1940, according to U.S. Census data, there were almost 127,000 Japanese immigrants and their descendants living in the United States and another 158,000 living in the Territory of Hawaii. They thus constituted only 0.02 percent of the overall U.S. population and about 2 percent of California's population. The Issei and Nisei faced a great deal of prejudice, but as a group they managed to overcome such challenges to become an economically successful people, often owning businesses, farms, and houses.

In the days following the attack on Pearl Harbor, arrests began of Japanese "aliens" who were thought to be a threat. The arrestees were primarily Issei men, many of them leaders within the Japanese American community. By mid-February, 1942, more than 3,000 men from the West Coast and Hawaii were in custody. In those early days of U.S. participation in the war, the Treasury Department also froze the bank accounts of all the Issei. All borders also were closed to anyone of Japanese ancestry. As the weeks passed, however, some Americans were not content with these measures. Some politicians, some military officials, and some in the media argued that more action was necessary. Questions of loyalty were raised, and arguments were made, fueled by prejudice and fear, that both Issei and Nisei would join the fight against the United States by engaging in acts of espionage and sabotage.

Roosevelt's Internment Order

On February 19, 1942, U.S. president Franklin D. Roosevelt ordered the internment of all Japanese Americans living on the Pacific Coast. The majority of the internees were U.S. citizens.

Whereas the successful prosecution of the war requires every possible protection against espionage and against sabotage to national-defense material, national-defense premises, and national-defense utilities . . . ;

Now, therefore, by virtue of the authority vested in me as President of the United States, and Commander in Chief of the Army and Navy, I hereby authorize and direct the Secretary of War, and the Military Commanders whom he may from time to time designate, whenever he or any designated Commander deems such action necessary or desirable, to prescribe military areas in such places and of such extent as he or the appropriate Military Commander may determine, from which any or all persons may be excluded, and with respect to which, the right of any person to enter, remain in, or leave shall be subject to whatever restrictions the Secretary of War or the appropriate Military Commander may impose in his discretion. The Secretary of War is hereby authorized to provide for residents of any such area who are excluded therefrom, such transportation, food, shelter, and other accommodations as may be necessary, in the judgment of the Secretary of War or the said Military Commander, and until other arrangements are made, to accomplish the purpose of this order. The designation of military areas in any region or locality shall supersede designations of prohibited and restricted areas by the Attorney General under the Proclamations of December 7 and 8, 1941, and shall supersede the responsibility and authority of the Attorney General under the said Proclamations in respect of such prohibited and restricted areas.

Military Areas and "Enemy Aliens"   President Franklin D. Roosevelt responded to this public clamor by issuing Executive Order 9066 on February 19, 1942. That order authorized the secretary of war and his military commanders to declare portions of the United States as military areas "from which any or all persons may be excluded." The next day, Secretary of War Henry L. Stimson authorized Lieutenant General John L. DeWitt to implement the order within the Western Defense Command. Via Public Proclamation No. 1, DeWitt designated the states of Washington, Oregon, California, and Arizona as military areas.

Japanese American Internment, Western United States

- = WCCA Assembly Center
- ▲ = WRA Relocation Center
- ✕ = WRA Isolation Center
- = Pacific coast exclusion area

Territory of Hawaii; no mass internment occurred there. Several factors likely contributed to this. With one-third of Hawaii's population of Japanese descent, racism was not the driving factor it was on the mainland. Furthermore, those of Japanese ancestry were critical to Hawaii's workforce and economy. Finally, the islands were already under martial law, imposed shortly after the attack on Pearl Harbor and continuing until 1944.

On the mainland, after the establishment of the military areas but before internment began to be implemented, DeWitt encouraged "enemy aliens" residing in the military area to move "to the interior." Few people of Japanese descent evacuated voluntarily. With little guidance, few resources, and a lack of housing and work opportunities, relocation was not an obvious choice. It was made even more unattractive by the "greetings" offered by some of the potential new communities, where it was not uncommon to see signs mounted on businesses asserting "No Japs Wanted Here." It became clear that mass voluntary relocation away from the coast and into the interior of the country was not tenable.

Internment Camps Beginning in March, 1942, the process of interning Issei and Nisei moved forward rapidly. DeWitt issued a series of Civilian Exclusion Orders in the spring and summer of 1942, commanding "all persons of Japanese ancestry" to report to be evacuated. The orders typically provided one week's notice. This proved not nearly enough time for anyone to pack up his or her life and satisfactorily arrange financial affairs. Those to be interned stored what they could (and after the war reported that pilfering was common) and attempted to sell the rest. It was without a doubt a buyer's market, and most personal belongings, vehicles, houses, businesses, and farms were sold for a small fraction of their worth. Internees were allowed to bring little

The coastal regions of the first three of those states were declared prohibited areas, meaning that "enemy aliens" could be excluded. A curfew was also imposed between 8:00 P.M. and 6:00 A.M. "Enemy aliens" were defined as all persons of Japanese descent, as well as German and Italian aliens. Although it is not as well known or as well documented, many people of German and Italian ancestry living in the United States also suffered legal discrimination and hardship during the war. They carried enemy alien identification cards and were subjected to the curfew and to travel restrictions for several months in 1942. Thousands, especially those who were well educated and community leaders, were deemed dangerous to American security and were also incarcerated.

It is also of interest to note that although those interned were not all of Japanese descent, not all persons of Japanese descent were interned. The notable exceptions were Issei and Nisei living in the

with them: bedding, extra clothing, and what personal effects they could carry.

The first stops for internees were Assembly Centers. These were hastily converted from other uses, such as fairgrounds and horse racetracks. Internees reported living in stalls that until the previous week had housed horses. In general, the accommodations were barely fit, if that, for human use. The Assembly Centers operated for about six months, as the War Relocation Authority (a civilian agency established by Roosevelt in March, 1942) hastily built ten camps in isolated areas, including Manzanar and Tule Lake in California and Heart Mountain in Wyoming. The government's name for these camps was "Relocation Centers, but the term by which they are most commonly known is "internment camps."

Conditions for Internees   Eventually, some 120,000 persons of Japanese ancestry were interned in these camps. The majority—two-thirds of them—were American-born citizens. They would spend up to four years imprisoned. Barbed wire and armed guards surrounded barracks made with relatively flimsy materials. The housing lacked plumbing or cooking facilities, and some of the camps were in hot, dry, and dusty locations. There was little privacy: both showers and latrines were open. Poor sanitation and inadequate food and medical care were common. The camps nevertheless became like small towns, and internees tried to use their time productively: Children went to school, and adults worked at camp jobs.

In February, 1943, the government reversed its prohibition against Japanese Americans serving in the armed forces. Three thousand Nisei from Hawaii were joined by eight hundred from the mainland (released from internment camps after taking a confusing and controversial loyalty oath). That group became the 100th Battalion, 442d Infantry, a mostly segregated unit with a few white officers. Its distinguished service is reflected in the honors it accrued: The unit became the most highly decorated of its size and duration during World War II.

The legality of the internment mechanism remained in question. President Roosevelt, with support and encouragement from Congress, had set the internment process in motion. When the legislative branch of the government weighed in, along with U.S. Supreme Court decisions, it was to affirm the constitutionality of both the curfew and the exclusion of citizens from their own homes. The Court declared that the curtailment of rights was a valid exercise of war powers by the president and Congress. It held, with little analysis, that such orders did not violate the Fourteenth Amendment's equal protection clause, with *Hirabayashi v. United States* (1943) validating curfews and *Korematsu v. United States* (1944) ruling that the exclusion order was constitutional.

Postwar Readjustments   On August 15, 1945, President Harry S. Truman announced the end of World War II. The last American internment camp closed in March, 1946. With the citizen exclusion orders lifted, Issei and Nisei were allowed to return to their previous homes, although there was often little awaiting them. Ultimately, only about half returned to the West Coast. In a tragic footnote, more than

Japanese American internees lining up at a Southern California assembly center in April, 1942, awaiting transportation to the inland camps in which most of them would live through the duration of the war. (National Archives)

5,000 Japanese Americans renounced their citizenship under a 1944 law. Almost all of the renunciations occurred at the Tule Lake camp and apparently resulted from misinformation and a fear that families would be separated after the war, with the Issei being sent back to Japan. Ultimately, only about 1,000 expatriated to Japan. The rest remained in the United States, and some years later most of them had their American citizenship restored through the work of a dedicated San Francisco attorney.

Impact   The nation was slow to acknowledge its wrongdoing. In 1948, Congress passed the Evacuation Claims Act and settled property claims for losses resulting from internment. It is estimated that at most ten cents on the dollar was paid for each claim. In 1952, the Japanese American Citizens League successfully lobbied Congress to grant the Issei's right to American citizenship. After these small concessions, decades of silence ensued. The American government preferred to forget this grim chapter in its history, and for many years the Issei and Nisei joined this silence. They coped with their losses and their shame by renewing their dedication to educate their children well and to once again achieve economic success in American society. The collective desire to let the past be past was expressed in the statement *shikata ga nai*, which can be tranlated as "nothing can be done" or "it cannot be helped."

It was the Sansei, the children of the Nisei, who took action. Through their efforts, Executive Order 9066 was officially rescinded in the nation's bicentennial year, on February 19, 1976. A federal court vacated Fred Korematsu's earlier criminal conviction; he was later awarded the Presidential Medal of Freedom. Further, a Commission on the Wartime Relocation and Internment of Civilians was established and heard the testimony of 750 witnesses, many of them internees. Based on the commission's findings, Congress enacted the Civil Liberties Act of 1988, which declared that a "grave injustice" had been done and acknowledged that the internment was motivated largely by "racial prejudice, wartime hysteria, and a failure of political leadership." Congress apologized, and on November 21, 1989, President George H. W. Bush signed an appropriations bill authorizing payments of $20,000 in reparations to each of the surviving internees, who were estimated to number 60,000.

Kimberlee Candela

Further Reading

Daniels, Roger. *Prisoners Without Trial: Japanese Americans in World War II*. Rev. ed. New York: Hill & Wang, 2004. Concise and readable account by a leading scholar in this field.

Gordon, Linda, and Gary Y. Okihiro, eds. *Impounded: Dorothea Lange and the Censored Images of Japanese American Internment*. New York: W. W. Norton, 2006. These famously censored vivid pictures combine with a scholarly narrative of the internment.

Houston, Jeanne Wakatsuki, and James D. Houston. *Farewell to Manzanar: A True Story of Japanese American Experience During and After the World War II Internment*. Carmel, Calif.: Hampton-Brown, 2002. Assigned to generations of high school students, this book, originally published in 1973, provides a compelling account of the Manzanar camp through the eyes of a little girl.

Inada, Lawson Fusao, ed. *Only What We Could Carry: The Japanese American Internment Experience*. Berkeley, Calif.: Heyday Books, 2000. Striking collection of first-person accounts, poetry, fiction, and art. Publicly funded as part of California's reparation activities.

Weglyn, Michi Nishiura. *Years of Infamy: The Untold Story of America's Concentration Camps*. Seattle: University of Washington Press, 1996. Thorough and well-documented look at the camps.

See also   Civil rights and liberties; Freezing of Japanese assets; Japan, occupation of; Japanese Canadian internment; *Korematsu v. United States*; Pearl Harbor attack; Racial discrimination; Roosevelt, Franklin D.; Stimson, Henry L.; Supreme Court, U.S.; World War II.

■ Japanese Canadian internment

The Event   Compulsory resettlement based on ethnicity during World War II

Dates   January 2, 1942, to January 24, 1947

Places   British Columbia and other Canadian provinces

The government of Canada resettled more than 22,000 persons of Japanese ancestry into internment camps, even though none of the internees had ever been found guilty of a disloyal act.

Persons of Japanese ancestry began to settle in the coastal regions of British Columbia late in the nineteenth century, and by 1942 their numbers had grown to 22,096, including 16,532 Canadian citizens and 5,564 Japanese nationals. The majority were fishermen or market gardeners, while a few owned small service businesses. Although they were hardworking and law-abiding people, a large percentage of the white Canadians in the region harbored anti-Asian prejudices. There were numerous attempts to reduce the number of fishing licenses issued to Asians, and anyone who retained Japanese citizenship, even those born in Canada, were denied the vote.

Shortly after Canada declared war against Japan following the attack on Pearl Harbor on December 7, 1941, numerous politicians, journalists, and business leaders in British Columbia warned of possible espionage and called for the internment of the Japanese minority. Several companies, including the Canadian Pacific Railway, fired all employees of Japanese ancestry. The Royal Canadian Mounted Police arrested thirty-eight Japanese suspected as potential subversives. Japanese fishermen were confined to port, and 1,200 of their fishing boats were impounded. General Kenneth Stuart, chief of the General Staff, expressed the opinion that no further measures were necessary to protect national security, but public opinion demanded otherwise.

On January 14, 1942, the Canadian government utilized its powers under the War Measures Act to order that all Japanese nationals between eighteen and forty-five years be evacuated and settled in a variety of working camps located at least one hundred miles west of the Pacific coast. Further yielding to public opinion, the federal government on February 27 announced the mass evacuation of all "persons of Japanese racial origin." During the next seven months, a new federal agency settled more than 21,000 evacuees in a variety of "relocation camps," located in isolated regions British Columbia, Alberta, Manitoba, and western Ontario. Takeo Nakano remembered that most of his fellow internees were nonpolitical, but he also referred to rebellious *gambariya* who supported Japan's cause and harassed those who cooperated with Canadian authorities.

Conditions in the camps were generally poor. Canada spent only about one-third of the per capita amount that the United States spent on its Japanese American evacuees. Unlike prisoners of war held in custody, Japanese internees were required to pay for their living expenses. Beginning in 1943, the "Custodian of Aliens" began to hold auctions for their possessions, including their farmlands and houses. Officially, those living in the camps were not legally interned and could leave with permission, but until late in the war they were not allowed to work or attend school outside the camps. Finally, in late 1944, some 7,000 were permitted to leave the camps in order to work in eastern Canada. A small number of Japanese Canadians of military age agreed to serve in the army as interpreters and in signal/intelligence units.

In early 1945, the federal government required the Japanese evacuees to choose between resettlement east of the Rocky Mountains and repatriation to Japan. Initially, almost 11,000 chose to go to Japan, but more than two-thirds of them later changed their minds. About 4,000 eventually left voluntarily for Japan. Some of the internees challenged the constitutionality of the evacuation order, but the Canadian Supreme Court upheld the government's policy by a 3-2 vote in 1946. The evacuation was finally repealed on January 24, 1947. By then, some 20,000 Japanese lived in Canada, with about one-third of them residing in British Columbia.

Impact   After the war's end, a large percentage of Canadians believed that the evacuation policy had been a mistake, and the government in 1947 appointed a Royal Commission, chaired by Justice Henry Bird, to consider compensation for confiscated property. In 1950, the commission awarded $1.3 million for actual loss of property, but without any funding for loss of earnings or disruption of education. During the 1980's, the National Association of Japanese Canadians began a campaign for additional compensation and for recognition that the general internment had been unnecessary and unjust. In 1988, Prime Minister Brian Mulroney made a long-awaited apology on behalf of the Canadian government, and he announced a compensation package that included $21,000 for each of the 13,000 surviving internees.

Thomas Tandy Lewis

Further Reading

Adachi, Ken. *The Enemy That Never Was: A History of the Japanese Canadians.* Toronto: McClelland and Stewart, 1991.

Broadfoot, Barry. *Years of Sorrow, Years of Shame: The Story of the Japanese Canadians in World War II.* Toronto: Doubleday Canada, 1997.

Nakano, Takeo Ujo. *Within the Barbed Wire Fence: A Japanese Man's Account of His Internment in Canada.* Seattle: University of Washington Press, 1981.

Sunahara, Ann. *The Politics of Racism: the Uprooting of Japanese Canadians During the Second World War.* Toronto: Lorimer, 2004.

See also   Canadian participation in World War II; Demographics of Canada; Immigration to Canada; Japanese American internment; King, William Lyon Mackenzie; Racial discrimination; Wartime propaganda in Canada.

■ Jefferson Memorial

Identification   Presidential memorial
Date   Dedicated on April 13, 1943
Place   Washington, D.C.

The dedication of the Jefferson Memorial served as a rallying point for patriotism and national purpose during World War II. President Franklin D. Roosevelt's address at the dedication ceremony made clear connections between the ideals of Thomas Jefferson and the war currently taking place.

The Jefferson Memorial was dedicated by President Franklin D. Roosevelt on April 13, 1943, the two hundredth anniversary of Thomas Jefferson's birth. Construction had begun in December of 1938. Since the dedication of the memorial took place during the midst of World War II, extensive security was in place for the event. Members of the Secret Service as well as military and local police lined the route taken by the president to the dedication site. In his dedication address, the president referred to the memorial as "a shrine of freedom" and made frequent references to the war currently being waged to preserve freedom. The large, nineteen-foot statue of Jefferson by sculptor Rudulph Evans, planned for the interior of the memorial, was originally cast in plaster and painted with bronze-colored paint. The final bronze version was not put in place until 1947, two years after the war ended.

Impact   President Roosevelt used the dedication of the Jefferson Memorial in 1943 to promote the war-

time ideals of struggle and self-sacrifice in the pursuit and preservation of freedom. The memorial continues to symbolize these values and remains an important part of the Washington landscape, along with the memorials to George Washington, Abraham Lincoln, and Roosevelt himself.

Scott Wright

Further Reading

Goode, James M. *Washington Sculpture: A Cultural History of Outdoor Sculpture in the Nation's Capital.* Baltimore, Md.: Johns Hopkins University Press, 2008.

Shalett, Sidney. "Roosevelt, Hailing Jefferson, Looks to Gain in Liberty." *The New York Times*, April 14, 1943, pp. 1, 16.

See also   Architecture; Mount Rushmore National Memorial; National parks; Pentagon building; Roosevelt, Franklin D.

■ Jet engines

Definition   Engines that combine compressed air and fuel to ignite and blast rearward, causing the jet-propelled vehicle to thrust forward

Originally developed to make military airplanes more effective in war, jet engines eventually revolutionized world travel. The "jet age" brought greatly reducing travel time to the masses.

Although Wilbur and Orville Wright's first powered flight on December 17, 1903, is one of the great milestones in aviation history, the creation of the jet engine is arguably of equal importance. World War II is often thought of as the catalyst for the idea of the jet engine, but the concept actually had been developed centuries before. The war served more as the motivation to revisit and perfect the concept. The gas turbine engine, commonly known as the jet engine, was theorized as far back as the late eigthteenth century in Europe, and models were built at the beginning of the twentieth century. Romanian inventor Henri Coand exhibited his Coand-1910 aircraft, a hybrid of jet and piston technology, at the Second International Aeronautical Exhibition in Paris in 1910. Doubts about the practicality of the use of jet engines in aircraft caused delays in jet engine design, and the piston engine remained the

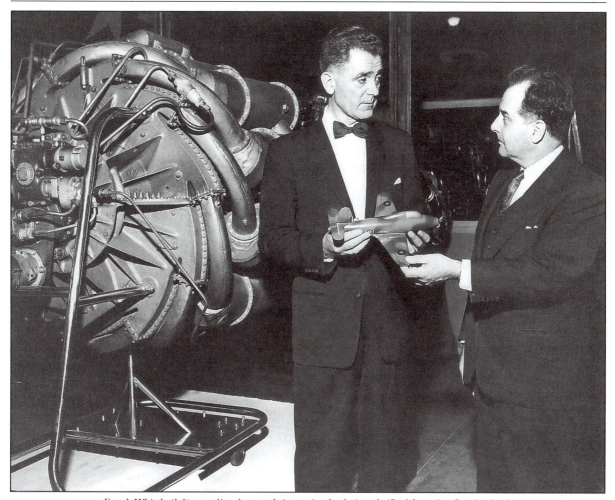

Frank Whittle (left) standing by a turbojet engine he designed. (Smithsonian Institution)

only form of propulsion for aircraft up through the late 1920's.

Perhaps no person is more identified with the jet engine's history than British engineer and pilot Frank Whittle. Between 1928 and 1937, Whittle worked on a variety of compressors for jet engines before settling on the centrifugal compressor, a prototype of which he completed in 1937. A number of historians and Whittle himself blame the British government's lack of interest in his device for the Germans (rather than the British) being the first to develop a jet-propelled airplane. German scientists led by Hans van Ohain also worked on jet engine technology and manufactured the first turbine jet plane, the Heinkel He 178 prototype, which Erich Warsitz piloted on a test flight on August 27, 1939.

Jets in World War II and Beyond   Adolf Hitler ordered a hold on all long-term military development projects in order to focus on what he saw as more pertinent issues. This directive significantly slowed development of the first German fighter jet, the Messerschmitt Me 262, which was not developed until 1942. The German military did not use the Me 262 in action until the summer of 1944, when it was employed both as a fighter jet and as a bomber. Initially, the airplane was not effective because of difficulties in taking off and landing, as well as a limited range. German jet fighters eventually began to have success, but by then the war was already a lost cause for the Axis countries, which were being bombed heavily by the Allied Powers. By the end of World War II, nearly all of the participating militaries had jet-propelled fighters in their air forces. The jet airplane had become a global phenomenon.

Following World War II, the remaining world powers competed for supremacy in the air, with the United States and the Soviets using jet aircraft in covert missions. By the early 1950's, the jet airplane had become the military's aircraft of choice. The new jet airplanes and their increased speed, however, created a number of complexities not realized in the slower piston-engine airplanes. These difficulties would become more highly publicized with the creation of the first commercial jet airliners.

The first commercial jet airliner was the de Havilland Comet. The first Comet aircraft flew in Europe in 1949, but it was not until 1952 that paying passengers flew on a Comet aircraft. The Comet initially was a success but later was plagued by a series of disasters. Investigators learned that metal fatigue associated with the rivets on the aircraft was the primary cause of the disasters. Meanwhile, commercial airlines had expanded their operations and international travel, with Pan American World Airways (Pan Am) becoming the initial leader.

Impact Jet engines transformed the aviation industry and made air travel the most popular form of long-distance travel worldwide. The speed of jet aircraft shortened travel times, and the reduced noise of jet engines allowed for more comfortable travel. Although jet aircraft were plagued by a series of catastrophes during their early years, these setbacks led to higher standards for airlines, including maintenance, employee training, and aircraft quality.

Brion Sever

Further Reading

Golley, John. *Genesis: Frank Whittle and the Invention of the Jet Engine.* Wiltshire, England: Crowood Press, 1997. Discusses Frank Whittle's invention of the first turbojet engine in 1937. Also examines the impact of Whittle's invention on American jets.

Gunston, Bill. *The Development of Jet and Turbine Aero Engines.* Sparkford, England: Haynes, 2006. Gunston follows the histories of engines used in jets, rockets, and helicopters, describing the differences among the engines. He traces the evolution of each engine to its present forms.

Kay, Anthony. *German Jet Engine and Gas Turbine Development, 1930-1945.* Wiltshire, England: The Crowood Press, 2002. A comprehensive examination of the attempts in Germany to invent a jet-propelled aircraft, focusing on the experiments that led to Germany's first jet aircraft.

Nahum, Andrew. *Frank Whittle: Invention of the Jet.* Lanham, Md.: Totem Books, 2006. Examines the race among the United States, Britain, and Germany to develop the jet engine and criticizes literature that suggests that the British government did not provide sufficient resources to Whittle's pursuit. Follows Whittle's early ideas about jet propulsion through his business ventures trying to develop and exploit them.

See also Aircraft design and development; Inventions; Wartime technological advances; World War II.

■ Jews in Canada

In the light of World War II, Canadian anti-Semitism, and the Holocaust, a majority of Canadian Jews, including the mainstream Jewish political body of the Canadian Jewish Congress, with the exception of the Jewish communists, held widespread support for Zionism and the creation of the state of Israel, which occurred in 1948.

By the 1940's, the Canadian Jewish community totaled 168,585 and was made up almost entirely of Ashkenazi Jews from Western and Eastern Europe. Nonetheless, the community was anything but homogenous. Differences ranged from new immigrants to several-generation Canadians; upper-middle-class professionals to poor, unskilled workers; religious adherents to secular persons; and conservatives to left-wing and communist political radicals, all of whom were from diverse ethnic and national backgrounds. The vast majority of Canadian Jews lived in cities across Canada from Halifax to Vancouver, with Montreal, Toronto, and Winnipeg being the three largest Jewish communities in Canada. Only small numbers of Jews lived in rural Western Canada.

For most of the 1940's, anti-Semitism permeated mainstream Canadian society, from state policies to the individual prejudice of Canadian policy makers, state officials, and the general public. For example, Canadian immigration policy severely restricted Jewish immigration to Canada until the late 1940's. The Canadian Jewish Congress spent the years during and after the war lobbying the Canadian government to allow Jewish refugees from Europe. Nonetheless, state officials and policy makers were well aware of widespread anti-Semitic public opinion in Canada and strongly opposed Jewish immigration. Jews were barred membership to clubs and organizations, denied professional employment in certain institutions, and refused admission to universities.

For many Canadian Jews, although not all, participating in the defeat of Nazi Germany abroad as part of the Canadian Forces went hand-in-hand with fighting anti-Semitism at home. Many Canadian Jews across the political spectrum, from those in the Canadian Jewish Congress to the secular communist Jewish left, supported Canada's involvement in fighting Nazi Germany and enlisted in the army themselves. Many Canadian Jews were concerned for their family members still living in Europe. This concern heightened as reports of Jewish deportation to the Nazi death camps in Europe and the "final solution" began to surface after the spring of 1942. The Canadian Jewish Congress encouraged Jews to enlist. Still, there were others who did not join the Canadian Forces, possibly because Eastern European Jewish families feared that participation in the Canadian military would mirror their own families' experiences of conscription in the armies of Eastern Europe, where Jews were subject to severe persecution.

Impact In the aftermath of World War II and the Holocaust, Canadian anti-Semitism and the Canadian government's severe restrictions on Jewish immigration to Canada remained significant concerns for Canadian Jews. The Canadian Jewish Congress was acknowledged as the official voice of the community, fighting anti-Semitism and lobbying the Canadian government for the admission of Jewish refugees from Europe.

Canadian Jewry, with the exception of some non-Zionists and anti-Zionists in the community, became engaged in the struggle for the establishment of a Jewish state in Palestine as a place of Jewish refuge, especially after the spring of 1942, when news of the mass genocide of Jews reached North America. The Canadian Jewish Congress lobbied Canadian prime minister William Lyon Mackenzie King to pressure

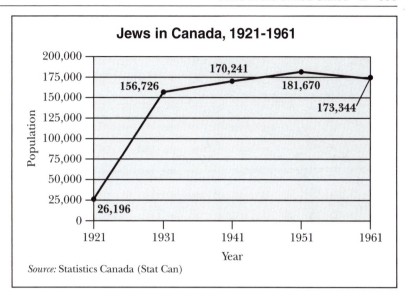

Jews in Canada, 1921-1961

Source: Statistics Canada (Stat Can)

the British government to allow Jewish immigration to Palestine and obtained the Canadian government's official recognition of the State of Israel in 1948.

Kelly Amanda Train

Further Reading

Abella, Irving. *A Coat of Many Colors: Two Centuries of Jewish Life in Canada.* Toronto: Key Porter Books, 1999.

Tulchinsky, Gerald. *Canada's Jews: A People's Journey.* Toronto: University of Toronto Press, 2008.

Vigod, Bernard L. *The Jews in Canada.* Saint John, N.B.: Canadian Historical Association, 1984.

See also Canadian minority communities; Canadian participation in World War II; Immigration to Canada; Israel, creation of; Jews in the United States; Racial discrimination; Refugees in North America; Religion in Canada.

■ Jews in the United States

After World War II, large numbers of Jewish refugees arrived in the United States from Europe. These immigrants, added to the existing population resulting from earlier immigration of Eastern European Jews fleeing persecution during the late 1880's, created the largest national Jewish population in the world.

Jewish refugees arriving in Palestine in early 1948, waving an Israeli flag before the state of Israel was declared. (Time & Life Pictures/Getty Images)

Most Jews of the time were insecure and defensive, and they often chose to keep a low profile rather than attract attention to themselves that they feared would be negative. African American civil rights activists Bayard Rustin and A. Philip Randolph threatened a march on Washington in 1941, and such pressure caused President Franklin D. Roosevelt to sign Executive Order 8802, which prohibited discrimination on the basis of race or religion in the national defense industries and government. It also created the Fair Employment Practices Commission (FEPC) to enforce the executive order.

When conservatives tried to abolish the FEPC, Jewish groups became involved with the National Council for a Permanent FEPC, created by A. Philip Randolph in 1943. This coalition marked the beginning of what came to be known as the Civil Rights movement in the United States. Among others, Rabbi Stephen S. Wise, a leader of the American Jewish Congress and the National Association for the Advancement of Colored People (NAACP), understood that the struggle for human rights benefited all minorities, including Jews. Addressing the problems of employment discrimination, Jewish leaders established the National Community Relations Advisory Council, which was incorporated in 1944.

During the 1940's, world Jewry suffered the devastating tragedy of the Holocaust, in which more than six million Jews were slaughtered. Jews also celebrated the establishment of Israel as a Jewish state in 1948. These events had profound effects on American Jews during the 1940's, especially after 1941, when the true extent of the genocide perpetuated against the Jews in Europe became known. Even in the light of the tragedy of the Holocaust, the tight immigration quotas of the United States were not increased. Some experts claim that about 200,000 Jews could have been rescued during World War II if it had not been for bureaucratic obstacles to immigration reform, largely coming from the State Department. During the Holocaust, fewer than than 30,000 Jews a year reached the United States, and some were turned away because of immigration policies.

Important Legislation During the 1940's, institutional discrimination against Jews in education, housing, and employment was widely practiced.

The Late 1940's Harry S. Truman, president of the United States from 1945 to 1953, favored a liberal immigration policy, but Congress did not act in response. On December 22, 1945, Truman issued an executive order called the Truman Directive, which required that existing immigration quotas be designated for displaced persons. The Truman Directive allowed more than 16,000 Jewish people to enter the United States from December, 1945, through 1947, along with about 6,000 other displaced persons. Immigration quotas, however, had not been increased, but instead redesignated for displaced persons. The

American Jewish community lobbied Congress vigorously, and under great pressure, Congress in 1948 passed legislation to admit 400,000 displaced persons. About 20 percent of those who came were Jewish.

The creation of the state of Israel in 1948 gave American Jews, and Jews worldwide, cause for celebration. The rise of the Nazis during the late 1930's and 1940's had caused the influx of a quarter of a million Jews into Palestine. In November, 1947, the newly created United Nations approved the U.N. Partition Plan, which would divide the territory into two states, one Arab and one Jewish. The Jewish community accepted the plan, but the Arab League and the Arab Higher Committee rejected it. Civil war broke out, but on May 14, 1948, the Jewish Agency proclaimed independence and named the country Israel. Without the generous financial support of American Jews, the state of Israel would not have been founded so quickly. Like other Americans, many Jews had prospered during the economic boom of the 1940's, which allowed them to give generously to the young state. The United Jewish Appeal held a fund-raising drive in 1948 that was without parallel: American Jews donated more than $200 million to Israel.

Impact   Both the Holocaust and the establishment of Israel have been focal points in the history of American Jewish life since the 1940's. A steady stream of academic books about the Holocaust has been published by both Jewish and non-Jewish political scientists, sociologists, psychiatrists, and historians. Prominent fiction writers and poets also often use the Holocaust as a theme or background in their works. Memorial institutions, museum displays, religious services, and public performances continue to remind the American public of this unique historical event.

After the end of the war, the establishment of the state of Israel, so closely tied to the Holocaust, was supported by 97 percent of American Jews. Although they approved of Jewish immigration to the new state, they felt little obligation to move to Israel. American Jews have supported Israel financially and politically, but they continue to identify with Jewish organizations within the United States as well as, or in addition to, Israel. The U.S. government usually has supported Israel in its international relations.

Sheila Golburgh Johnson

Further Reading

Harap, Lewis. *Creative Awakening: The Jewish Presence in Twentieth-Century American Literature, 1900-1940s.* New York: Greenwood Press, 1987. Chapter 4, "The Jews of War: The 1940's," discusses how war shaped the consciousness of American Jews.

Hertzberg, Arthur. *The Jews in America.* New York: Simon & Schuster, 1989. Particularly strong on social and political trends. The author is one of the most prominent Jewish leaders of the twentieth century.

Howe, Irving, with Kenneth Libo. *World of Our Fathers.* New York: Harcourt Brace Jovanovich, 1976. Section 4 of the book, "Dispersion," provides a broad and interesting discussion of how the major events of the 1940's were reflected in art and intellectual Jewish culture.

Mamet, David. *The Wicked Son: Anti-Semitism, Self-Hatred, and the Jews.* New York: Schocken, 2006. The famed American playwright addresses Jewish self-hatred.

Morawska, Ewa. *Insecure Prosperity: Small-Town Jews in Industrial America, 1890-1940.* Princeton, N.J.: Princeton University Press, 1996. Documents a Jewish community in Johnstown, Pennsylvania. The story is surprisingly different from many accounts of Jewish immigrants to metropolitan areas, where they tended to assimilate. In the small Johnstown, they instead maintained a tightly knit group.

See also   Convention on the Prevention and Punishment of the Crime of Genocide; Demographics of the United States; Hitler, Adolf; Immigration Act of 1943; Immigration to the United States; Israel, creation of; Religion in the United States.

■ Jim Crow laws

Definition   Discriminatory laws limiting the civil rights of African Americans' and their access to resources

Laws that restricted African American civil rights and liberties at the state and local levels allowed southern whites legally to practice racial discrimination and segregation throughout the 1940's.

The 1940's saw the beginnings in many areas of resistance to Jim Crow policies, most prominent in the

Deep South, that restricted the rights of African Americans. Segregation of public schools, other public places, and public transportation was sanctioned by many states and localities. The armed forces had been racially segregated, and many veterans returning from World War II agitated for change. In 1944, Corporal Rupert Timmingham, an African American soldier, lamented the fact that an African American soldier could not enter a restaurant in the South, but former German prisoners of war could do so.

Numerous boycotts and demonstrations against segregation were instrumental in the continued efforts of political activism against Jim Crow policies. Pittsburgh and other cities saw demonstrations against unfair employment practices. The United States Supreme Court, in *Irene Morgan v. Commonwealth of Virginia* (1946), ruled segregation in interstate transportation to be unconstitutional, and in 1948, in *Shelley v. Kraemer*, it ruled against some forms of private discrimination, saying that "restrictive covenants" that barred sale of homes to African Americans, or Jews or Asians, were unconstitutional.

Jim Crow was challenged in many arenas. In sports, Jackie Robinson integrated baseball in 1947. Also in 1947, the Journey of Reconciliation tested the *Morgan* ruling, as sixteen men from the Congress of Racial Equality, eight white and eight black, rode together in buses through several southern states, breaking state laws against segregated travel on public transport. Some of the riders were arrested and subjected to physical attacks. The ride drew publicity, but convictions against the riders stood. The two-week ride was a model for the Freedom Rides of the 1960's.

Impact The 1940's was a time of increased social activism in the fight against discrimination and segregation that Jim Crow laws enforced. Many of the demonstrations and boycotts were successful in both changing practices and garnering support for the downfall of Jim Crow, but such practices and laws continued.

Judy Porter

Further Reading

Barnes, Catherine A. *Journey from Jim Crow: The Desegregation of Southern Transit.* New York: Columbia University Press, 1983.
Dailey, J., G. E. Gilmore, and B. Simon, eds. *Jumpin' Jim Crow: Southern Politics from Civil War to Civil Rights.* Princeton, N.J.: Princeton University Press, 2000.
Litwack, L. F. *Trouble in Mind: Black Southerners in the Age of Jim Crow.* New York: Alfred A. Knopf, 1998.
Rasmussen, R. Kent. *Farewell to Jim Crow: The Rise and Fall of Segregation in America.* New York: Facts On File, 1997.
Woodward, C. Vann, and William S. McFeely. *The Strange Career of Jim Crow.* New York: Oxford University Press, 2001.

See also African Americans; Civil rights and liberties; Congress, U.S.; Congress of Racial Equality; Desegregation of the U.S. military; National Association for the Advancement of Colored People; Negro Leagues; Racial discrimination; *Shelley v. Kraemer*.

■ Jitterbug

Definition Flamboyant two-step swing dance

As the defining dance craze of the war years, the jitterbug, with its near-acrobatic improvisational feel, represented a singular cultural expression in that it defied America's traditional racial and economic boundaries, bringing together black people and white people, rich and poor. With the exportation of the dance to continental Europe by millions of American troops, the jitterbug in turn became a significant element of the American postwar international cultural signature.

The jitterbug, with its free-hip swings and bold twirls, its spinning gyrations and improvised footwork, had its roots in the defiantly unconventional dance moves of the early jazz years, specifically the swing dances such as the Lindy Hop and jive that developed in the high-voltage environment of the speakeasy. Jitterbug dancers abandoned conventional step patterns of more traditional ballroom dancing; couples moved to the syncopated beat of the band. The term "jitterbug" itself evolved during the 1930's, a reference to the "jitters," the convulsive movements of an alcoholic during delirium tremens. According to popular legend, Cab Calloway, the bandleader and scat singer whose 1935 recording "Call of the Jitterbug" introduced the term to a national audience, said the dancers on the floor looked like crazy bugs.

The dance itself required a high degree of athleticism and creative ad-libbing (it was largely a dance for the young and fit): The dancers engaged fluid hand gestures, sweeping arm gyrations, deep shoulder dips, carefree hip swings, and even exaggerated facial expressions. The characteristic spin-and-twirl execution demanded couples stay in tight synchronization. The best jitterbuggers claimed the dance was unteachable, that it was an expression of spontaneity, that the dance was never quite the same song to song. In the years leading up to World War II, the jitterbug became a standard at dance clubs, most notably the legendary Savoy Club in Harlem. Unlike the Cotton Club, the Savoy welcomed white patrons and white-dominated bands (most notably Benny Goodman and Glenn Miller), and hence the jitterbug initially became associated with white audiences.

Young jitterbuggers. (Michael Ochs Archives/Getty Images)

Impact World War II created the international buzz over the dance. American troops stationed initially in Britain but later in France found in the crazy rhythms a welcome antidote to the rigidity and discipline of military life. The perception of the dance as obscene and its frank mimicry of the gyrations of sex made the dance even more popular with the soldiers. In addition, it was the kind of dancing that did not require instruction and worked well with the consumption of excessive alcohol—all of which made it a standard dance among troops on leave. After the war, the dance was frequently the subject of hugely popular ballroom competitions in which determined couples would be pushed to their creative and physical limits.

Even as during the late 1940's popular music moved away from hard-driving rhythms of big band music to the softer sounds of crooners (indeed, cultural historians point to a controversial late-war federal tax on public dance halls as the beginning of the end of dance hall fever), the jitterbug with its improvised movements, its engaging and teasing sexuality,

and its raw athleticism would feed into the earliest rock-and-roll dance tunes. Indeed, the 1940's ballrooms and dance clubs jammed with dancers, spinning and swirling in unchoreographed energy, became the basic model for a variety of rock-and-roll dance shows that would debut in 1950's television, most notably *American Bandstand.*

Joseph Dewey

Further Reading

Erenberg, Lewis. *Swingin' the Dream: Big Band Jazz and the Rebirth of American Culture.* Chicago: University of Chicago Press, 1999.

Miller, Norma, and Evette Jensen. *Swingin' at the Savoy: The Memoir of a Jazz Dancer.* Philadelphia: Temple University Press, 1996.

Szwed, John. *Crossovers: Essays on Race, Music, and American Culture.* Philadelphia: University of Pennsylvania Press, 2005.

See also Dance; Dorsey, Tommy; Goodman, Benny; Miller, Glenn; Music: Jazz; Music: Popular; Radio in the United States; Recording industry; United Service Organizations; Zoot suits.

■ Journey of Reconciliation

The Event　Series of integrated bus rides throughout segregated southern states that peacefully explored the challenging racial climate in the United States after World War II

Date　April 9-23, 1947

Places　Virginia, North Carolina, Tennessee, and Kentucky

The Journey of Reconciliation, a carefully planned two-week event in April, 1947, in which white men rode in the back of segregated southern buses while black men rode in the front, established nonviolent direct action as the primary model for racial protest in the United States in the years immediately following World War II. The swift arrests of many of these pre-Freedom Riders were ultimately overshadowed by their ability to inspire future nonviolent protesters.

It was largely the effect of two events in 1946 that led to Journey of Reconciliation one year later. First, Irene Morgan, nearly a decade before Rosa Parks's famed bus ride, won a Supreme Court case on June 3 that stated that enforcing segregation laws of interstate bus passengers was unconstitutional, as it forced an "undue burden on interstate commerce." Second, African American soldiers were returning home from active duty in World War II and were honorably resisting riding in segregated vehicles upon their arrival.

Sensing an opportunity to make strong headway based on these events, the Congress of Racial Equality (CORE), which had been formed in 1942, decided that it would establish a team of six white men and six black men to take bus rides throughout the upper South over a two-week span in April, 1947. Led by founding CORE members George Houser and Bayard Rustin, the instructions to the riders were simple: The white passengers were to select a seat toward the back of the bus, while the African Americans were to sit in the front. If a passenger was asked to move, he was instructed to remain in his seat and declare that the United States Supreme Court had ruled that they are legally justified to remain where they were. If arrested, the passengers

were to peacefully acquiesce and enter into police custody until assisted by their lawyer or the National Association for the Advancement of Colored People (NAACP).

Passengers on most rides were swiftly arrested, although a few rides saw no arrests at all. While many of the arrested passengers were released on bond, a handful suffered harsher convictions. In North Carolina, Judge Henry Whitfield sentenced two African American riders, Bayard Rustin and Andrew Johnson, to thirty days on a chain gang, only then to hand down a ninety-day sentence to two white riders, Igal Roodenko and Joseph Felmet, whom the judge thought were most to blame for upsetting southern customs.

Impact　The immediate impact of the Journey of Reconciliation yielded mixed results. In select cities, riders were allowed to sit wherever they wished, offering a glimmer of hope regarding racial progress. On other bus trips, the immediate arrest of the passengers and harsh penalties for their nonviolent actions highlighted the reality that segregation was still a rampant force throughout much of the South. Most important, the bus rides inspired peaceful protesters of later decades who would dominate the Civil Rights movement. The Journey of Reconciliation had a direct influence on Rosa Parks, the Montgomery bus boycott, and the Freedom Rides of the 1960's. It set the standard for direct action by reasonably challenging American racial boundaries during the late 1940's.

Eric Novod

Further Reading

Catsam, Derek Charles. *Freedom's Main Line: The Journey of Reconciliation and the Freedom Rides.* Lexington: University Press of Kentucky, 2008.

D'Emilio, John. *Lost Prophet: The Life and Times of Bayard Rustin.* Chicago: University of Chicago Press, 2004.

See also　Civil rights and liberties; Congress of Racial Equality; *Morgan v. Virginia;* National Association for the Advancement of Colored People; Racial discrimination; Travel in the United States.

K

■ Kaiser, Henry J.

Identification   American industrialist
Born   May 9, 1882; Sprout Brook, New York
Died   August 24, 1967; Honolulu, Hawaii

Kaiser played a major role in the production of Liberty ships and cargo vessels during World War II and developed an automobile line after the war.

Henry J. Kaiser got his start with a road-paving company in California in 1914. In 1927, he obtained a $20 million contract to build roads in Cuba, and during the 1930's his company was involved in the building of the Hoover, Grand Coulee, and Bonneville dams. However, he became famous with his shipbuilding company, Kaiser Shipyard, during World War II. His company built Liberty ships faster than any other shipbuilder, and at a time when the nation needed ships quickly. The quality of his ships was better than those of previous manufacturers because they had fewer welds in the hull. He established Kaiser Steel as the first West Coast steel company to provide materials for shipbuilding.

In 1945, Kaiser joined with automobile executive Joseph Frazer to form the Kaiser-Frazer Automobile Company. The company produced cars for the American market until 1955 and then moved operations to Brazil. The postwar cars were initially popular with consumers, and the company remained competitive until the larger companies had fully retooled from defense production. In 1946, Kaiser established Kaiser Aluminum Company.

Impact   Kaiser's founding of the Kaiser Shipyard and his research on better ways of building ships led him to become known as the "father of American shipbuilding." His company built 1,490 Liberty ships during the war. With his wealth, he established the charitable Kaiser Family Foundation, which has supported health-related research.

Dale L. Flesher

Further Reading

Foster, Mark S. *Henry J. Kaiser: Builder in the Modern American West.* Austin: University of Texas Press, 1989.

Heiner, Albert P. *Henry J. Kaiser, Western Colossus: An Insider's View.* San Francisco: Halo Books, 1991.

See also   Automobiles and auto manufacturing; Business and the economy in the United States; Liberty ships; Wartime industries.

■ Kamikaze attacks

The Event   Suicidal attacks by Japanese pilots against the U.S. Navy during World War II
Date   October, 1944-August, 1945
Places   The Philippines and Okinawa, Japan

As U.S. military operations closed in on the Japanese home islands, these desperate air attacks killed 4,900 American sailors. While the actions were seemingly justified by the traditional Japanese warrior code, Americans were shocked by the losses and increasingly convinced that only extreme measures would end the war in the Pacific.

Although earlier in the war individual Japanese pilots had deliberately crashed their planes into U.S. warships, it was not until October, 1944, that an official policy was implemented to destroy Allied ships with suicide attacks. The American landing at Leyte Gulf in the Philippines and the failure of the Japanese navy to disrupt the invasion led to more desperate measures. The Special Attack Corps, or "kamikaze" (divine wind), offered the outnumbered and ill-equipped Japanese military a means to even the conflict, particularly if the main targets were the U.S. aircraft carriers.

The ancient code of the samurai, called Bushido, stressed that a warrior be willing to die with honor as he fought to the bitter end. Vice Admiral Takijiro Onishi, commanding in the Philippines, applied that code to a systematic program of fitting Zeros

Flight deck of the aircraft carrier USS Bunker Hill *shortly after being hit by two kamikaze airplanes off southern Japan on May 11, 1945.* (National Archives)

and other planes with 500-pound bombs and sending them crashing into American ships. In departing this world for a better one, the pilots would demonstrate their loyalty to the emperor and their families. The first missions began on October 21. Within days, an Australian cruiser and three American carriers were damaged and the carrier *St. Lo* sunk. The U.S. Navy was unprepared for the new tactics.

The strategies for kamikaze success and defense evolved following the invasion of Okinawa in April, 1945. Trained Japanese pilots led novices toward their targets. The American ships lofted balloons tethered with strong cables to bring down the attackers. Increased air patrols to intercept the Japanese pilots had considerable success. Still, enough kamikaze pilots slipped through to inflict terrifying losses.

There is some debate about the exact costs on both sides. Approximately 3,900 kamikaze pilots died. One in seven of them hit a ship. Forty-nine ships were sunk outright, and close to 400 were damaged, many irreparably. Total American losses from kamikaze attacks were around 4,900 sailors killed and more than 4,800 wounded. Off the coast of Okinawa alone, 35 ships were lost and 169 damaged during ten major attacks and dozens of smaller ones. Destroyers suffered the most, but important aircraft carriers were put out of action. The carrier *Bunker Hill* was hit May 11, 1945, with 396 killed and 264 wounded. Ultimately, the kamikaze strategy would not prevent the capture of Okinawa nor stop the decline of Japan's fortunes.

Impact Admiral Onishi argued that the kamikaze's sacrifice would preserve Japan's eternal spirit. Following Japan's unconditional surrender on August 15, he disemboweled himself in a traditional seppuku ceremony.

The American response to the kamikazes was one of bewilderment, repulsion, and anger. The kamikaze represented the type of fanatical resistance that Americans could expect when they invaded Japan. Facing Japan's apparent refusal to accept the logic of surrender, American leaders were more willing to use increasingly harsh tactics—firebombing of Japanese cities and atomic bombs—to end the war.

M. Philip Lucas

Further Reading

Axell, Albert, and Hideaki Kase. *Kamikaze: Japan's Suicide Gods.* New York: Pearson Education, 2002.

Hastings, Max. *Retribution: The Battle for Japan, 1944-1945.* New York: Alfred A. Knopf, 2008.

Inoguchi, Rikihei, Tadashi Nakajimi, and Roger Pineau. *The Divine Wind: Japan's Kamikaze Force in World War II.* Annapolis, Md.: Naval Institute Press, 1958.

See also Aircraft carriers; Atomic bomb; Casualties of World War II; Hiroshima and Nagasaki bombings; *History of the United States Naval Operations in World War II*; Navy, U.S.; Okinawa, Battle of; Philippines; Strategic bombing; World War II.

■ Kelly, Gene

Identification American dancer, choreographer, and film actor
Born August 23, 1912; Pittsburgh, Pennsylvania
Died February 2, 1996; Beverly Hills, California

Kelly's sheer athleticism and colorful style invigorated some of the most beloved film musicals of the 1940's, including Anchors Aweigh *(1945) and* On the Town *(1949).*

After a few roles on Broadway, Gene Kelly landed his first leading role in the musical *Pal Joey* (1940), which he then parlayed into a successful film career in Hollywood. He later starred alongside Rita Hayworth in *Cover Girl* (1944), Jerry Mouse (from Tom and Jerry fame) and Frank Sinatra in *Anchors Aweigh* (1945), and Fred Astaire in *Ziegfeld Follies* (1946). After a stint in the Navy, Kelly starred in *The Pirate* (1948), directed by Vincente Minnelli and costarring Judy Garland and the Nicholas Brothers. Other pictures starring Kelly, including *The Three Musketeers* (1948) and *Take Me Out to the Ball Game* (1949), convinced film producer Arthur Freed that

Kelly was ready to choreograph and direct his own musical. Kelly made *On the Town* (1949), based on Jerome Robbins's 1944 ballet *Fancy Free*, which once again paired Kelly and Sinatra as sailors on leave.

In 1946, Kelly received his first and only Academy Award nomination for best actor for his portrayal of Joseph Brady in *Anchors Aweigh*. In 1952, he was awarded an honorary Academy Award highlighting his contribution to choreography on film.

Impact Whether as a performer, choreographer, or director, Kelly forever changed dance on film. His unique dancing style, with its mixture of vigor, athleticism, and grace, imbued the Hollywood musical with a new awareness of dance. His work during the 1940's set the stage for the pinnacle of his career in the early 1950's. Among Kelly's most memorable sequences are the seventeen-minute ballet at the climax of *An American in Paris* (1951) and his buoyant romp through a downpour in *Singin' in the Rain* (1952), arguably the greatest film musical ever made.

Alex Ludwig

Further Reading

Wollen, Peter. *Singin' in the Rain.* London: British Film Institute, 1992.

Yudkoff, Alvin. *Gene Kelly: A Life of Dance and Dreams.* New York: Back Stage Books, 1999.

See also Broadway musicals; Chuck and Chuckles; Coles, Honi; Dance; Film in the United States; Hayworth, Rita; Robbins, Jerome; Sinatra, Frank.

■ Kennan, George F.

Identification American diplomat
Born February 16, 1904; Milwaukee, Wisconsin
Died March 17, 2005; Princeton, New Jersey

Kennan was the foremost expert on the Soviet Union in the U.S. Department of State during the 1940's. His containment policy helped frame the American Cold War debate for decades.

Born in Wisconsin in 1904, George F. Kennan attended New Jersey's Princeton University and then trained as a foreign service officer in the U.S. Department of State. After Russian language training in Latvia, he joined the staff of the U.S. embassy in Moscow when the Soviet Union was recognized by the United States in 1933. His attitude toward the Soviets was based on a deep disdain for Marxism and a consistent belief that firm pressure on the Soviet Union would allow the United States to blunt the impact of Soviet ambitions worldwide.

During the period from 1944 to 1946, Kennan became exasperated by the actions of American officials who were assuming that an era of Soviet-American friendship was possible. He responded with the famous "Long Telegram" of 1946, a blistering eight-thousand-word indictment of Soviet methods and goals. The harsh tone he employed tended to obscure the fact that Kennan maintained that moderate measures were sufficient to deal with the Soviet challenge.

Kennan's telegram ignited a great deal of discussion in Washington, D.C., and he was recalled from Moscow and given the task of leading an entirely new agency within the Department of State, the Policy Planning Staff. Some of the keenest minds in American diplomacy and military affairs were founding members of this agency, and they churned out a steady stream of policy papers examining both long-range strategy and urgent crises.

The "X Article"   In 1947, Kennan had the opportunity to publish an article, "The Sources of Soviet Conduct," in *Foreign Affairs* magazine. Because State Department employees were not allowed to write for external publications, his article appeared under the byline "X"; it has ever since been known as the "X Article."

Kennan's article analyzed the factors that motivated Soviet leaders and examined their views of the world. He believed that the mix of Marxism-Leninism and traditional Russian suspicion and xenophobia guaranteed that U.S.-Soviet relations would remain tense for an extended period of time. Kennan also believed that as long as the major industrial areas of the world were kept out of the Soviets' grasp, the Soviets would be a persistent nuisance but not a dire threat. The industrial zone of Germany was a region that the Soviets coveted, but Japan, Great Britain, and North America were not realistic targets for Soviet power.

Kennan argued that containment of the Soviets could be accomplished by using a multifaceted diplomatic, economic, and military strategy. Once this strategy was in place, the Soviets would be worn down. Their grip on the satellite nations of Eastern Europe would loosen, and after that the Russians would grow weary of the failed promises of communism. The imposing edifice of Soviet communism would either gradually erode or suffer a sudden collapse. Keenan maintained that the United States would prevail amid the Soviet breakdown, but Americans would need a steady resolve and a great deal of patience in order to wait out the decline.

Impact   Kennan's "X Article" was a carefully thought out and extremely subtle appraisal of the state of the world in 1947. However, this subtlety was its undoing. American policy makers were willing to embrace Kennan's grim portrayal of the Soviets, but they ignored his recommendations for dealing with the Soviet Union. Kennan would repeatedly point this out, but his remonstrances fell on deaf ears. His influence on American foreign policy peaked in 1947 and 1948, and he left the State Department in 1953. After that, he continued to work as a diplomatic historian and pundit until his death in 2005.

Michael Polley

Further Reading

Hixson, Walter L. *George F. Kennan: Cold War Iconoclast.* New York: Columbia University Press, 1989.

Kennan, George F. *Memoirs.* Boston: Little, Brown, 1967.

Polley, Michael. *A Biography of George F. Kennan: The Education of a Realist.* Lewiston, N.Y.: Edwin Mellen Press, 1990.

See also   Acheson, Dean; Anticommunism; Clifford, Clark; Cold War; Foreign policy of the United States; Forrestal, James; Korea; Marshall, George C.; Point Four Program; Truman, Harry S.

■ Kennedy, John F.

Identification   Future U.S. president who was a naval officer during World War II and entered politics during the late 1940's

Born   May 29, 1917; Brookline, Massachusetts

Died   November 22, 1963; Dallas, Texas

Kennedy became a national political figure during the 1940's, publishing his Harvard senior thesis, Why England Slept *(1940), serving as a PT boat commander during World War II, and then being elected as a representative from the Eleventh Congressional District of Massachusetts in 1946, 1948, and 1950.*

John Fitzgerald Kennedy's final two years at Harvard overlapped with his father's appointment as ambassador to England from 1938 to 1940. His published dissertation, *Why England Slept* (1940), which addresses Great Britain's lack of preparedness for World War II, was reviewed well and sold well on both sides of the Atlantic. Failing the physical examinations for entry into both Army and Navy officer candidate schools, Kennedy used his father's diplomatic contacts to gain admission into the Office of Naval Intelligence. After breaking off an affair with Danish journalist Inga Arvad, Kennedy requested sea duty, attending midshipman school for junior naval officers and then PT (patrol torpedo) boat training.

Assigned to the Solomon Islands in March, 1943, Kennedy assumed leadership for *PT-109*. The PT boats, though they could travel at a speed of 40 knots and possessed four torpedoes and fixed machine guns, were dangerous and unreliable. Equipped with World War I-era torpedoes, defective engines, problematic VHF radios, and no armor plating, they could easily become floating infernos. On the night of August 1-2, 1943, *PT-109* was sliced in half by a Japanese destroyer and caught fire. Two crewmen died immediately, and the eleven others were set adrift. Over the next four days, Kennedy's heroics—including swimming badly burned Pappy McMahon to a nearby atoll by the straps of a life preserver in his teeth—became the stuff of legend for a country in need of heroes.

The death of older brother Joseph P. Kennedy, Jr., in an exploding plane over England in 1944 indirectly thrust John F. Kennedy into the politics of postwar Massachusetts. The fact of his being a returning war hero with an older brother who died in combat mitigated the fact that he was a millionaire's son and essentially a "carpetbagger": Although he was born in Brookline, Massachusetts, he had spent most of his life at the family residences in Hyannis Port, Massachusetts, and Palm Beach, Florida. He

Lieutenant John F. Kennedy on his PT boat in the Pacific in 1943. (AP/Wide World Photos)

leased a room at Boston's Bellevue Hotel as his legal residence during the 1946 congressional campaign and soon thereafter rented a small apartment on Bowdoin Street on Beacon Hill, his legal and voting residence for the remainder of his life.

Kennedy succeeded James Michael Curley as representative from Massachusetts' Eleventh Congressional District, having successfully deflected criticisms of family, wealth, and residency to win a plurality in the June Democratic primary, then 73 percent in the general election in November, 1946. He won reelection in 1948 and 1950 by similar margins.

Impact Kennedy's experiences during the 1940's, both personal and professional, presaged his later personal life and political career. His affair with the dramatically beautiful, intelligent, and headstrong Inga Arvad, who was trailed by the Federal Bureau of Investigation and rumored by some to be a Nazi spy, foreshadowed some of the asserted escapades during his ten-year marriage to Jacqueline Bouvier.

However, his abilities to gain the votes and the allegiance of citizens in the socially and economically variegated Eleventh Congressional District of Massachusetts portended his continuing success to attract constituencies from across the voting public.

Richard Sax

Further Reading

Dallek, Robert. *An Unfinished Life: John F. Kennedy, 1917-1963*. Boston: Little, Brown, 2003.

O'Brien, Michael. *John F. Kennedy: A Biography*. New York: Thomas Dunne Books/St. Martin's Press, 2005.

O'Donnell, Kenneth P., and David F. Powers. *"Johnny, We Hardly Knew Ye": Memories of John Fitzgerald Kennedy*. Boston: Little, Brown, 1972.

See also Acheson, Dean; Cold War; Elections in the United States: 1948; *History of the United States Naval Operations in World War II*; Navy, U.S.; World War II.

■ Keynesian economics

Definition Macroeconomic theory based on the ideas of John Maynard Keynes that advocates government intervention in the economy to increase employment and spending

Keynes's book The General Theory of Employment, Interest, and Money *(1936) ultimately produced a radical reorientation of economic theory and created modern macroeconomics, stressing aggregate demand. Keynes focused attention on the causes and possible cures for economic depression and unemployment. His ideas were important in shaping U.S. tax policy and in developing "demand management" policies, and influenced the Employment Act of 1946.*

Writing during the middle of the Great Depression, John Maynard Keynes argued that labor markets did not automatically adjust to produce full employment and could be in equilibrium even with substantial unemployment. Under such conditions, output and employment would be determined by expenditures to buy goods and services ("aggregate demand"). All output could be classified as consumption or investment spending for currently produced capital goods such as machinery and buildings. Consumption was, in his view, determined by total in-

come, reflecting the "marginal propensity to consume." Business decisions might involve a lot of emotion ("animal spirits"), and investment would probably be unstable. Fluctuations in investment would be transmitted to consumption through the "multiplier effect." Spending on capital goods would create income for the people who produced them, and they in turn would spend more on consumption, raising incomes still further. Keynes argued that expanding the money supply would lower interest rates. However, in a depression, that lowering might be small, and business investment might not increase much.

To combat unemployment, Keynes much preferred fiscal policy. Increasing government spending would raise aggregate demand directly and also produce multiplier effects. Reducing tax rates could stimulate more spending by business and households. Government deficits would be appropriate in a depression.

The spread of Keynesian ideas was slow and controversial. The first major American economics textbook to give full attention to Keynesian ideas was Paul Samuelson's *Economics*, originally published in 1948. The spread of Keynesian ideas was aided by the rise of national-income accounting and by the increased statistical modeling of economic variables.

Keynes's qualified endorsement of deficit spending contradicted the moralistic devotion to balanced budgets shared by Presidents Herbert Hoover, Franklin D. Roosevelt, and Harry S. Truman. World War II broke down resistance to deficit finance and ultimately convinced people that fiscal policy could produce full employment, as it did (in combination with the military draft) by 1944. Taxation came to be seen as a means to curb inflation and not simply to raise revenue.

Keynesian ideas figured significantly in debates over the Full Employment bill introduced into Congress in January, 1945. Some supporters expected government forecasters would estimate whether aggregate demand would be sufficient for full employment. Fiscal policy would then be shaped to fill any gap. In the end, however, Congress adopted the milder Employment Act of 1946. This committed the federal government to pursue "maximum employment, production, and purchasing power," and created the Council of Economic Advisers and a joint congressional committee to advise on how to do this. The earliest council members were definitely not Keynesians. Keynesian principles were not an important element in the major tax reduction in 1948, but it turned out to be an appropriate factor in moderating recession. Keynesian thinking contributed to the neglect of monetary policy, as the Federal Reserve continued to support the low yields of Treasury bonds until the Accord of 1950, which gave the Federal Reserve greater independence.

Impact Keynesian economics helped convince people that government could and should take action to remedy economic depressions and unemployment. The topic became prominent in academic study of economics and in political discourse. Countercyclical fiscal policy was legitimized, and the size of the national debt was de-emphasized.

Paul B. Trescott

Further Reading

Backhouse, Roger E., and Bradley W. Bateman, eds. *The Cambridge Companion to Keynes.* New York: Cambridge University Press, 2006.

Lekachman, Robert, ed. *Keynes' General Theory: Reports of Three Decades.* New York: Macmillan, 1964.

Stein, Herbert. *The Fiscal Revolution in America.* Chicago: University of Chicago Press, 1969.

See also Business and the economy in the United States; Credit and debt; Fair Deal; Gross national product of the United States; Inflation; National debt; Social sciences; Unemployment in the United States.

■ Kidney dialysis

Definition Medical procedure designed to treat kidney failure

Patients who have lost kidney function can no longer maintain the body's internal amounts of water and minerals. Kidney dialysis can temporarily treat, though not cure, this bodily imbalance. Because of this, the invention of kidney dialysis saved the lives of thousands of patients with renal failure.

In 1939, at University of Groningen Hospital, in the Netherlands, a young, Dutch doctor named Willem Johan Kolff, watched helplessly as a twenty-two-year-old farmer's son named Jan Bruning died slowly from kidney failure. This inspired him to search for a way to remove toxins and metabolic wastes from the body. In the university library, he found a 1913 study describing a procedure used by Johns Hopkins pharmacologist John Abel, in which he used hemodialysis in rabbits to purge the blood of the metabolic waste product urea. This convinced Kolff that such a procedure was possible in human patients.

World War II started shortly after Kolff began his research on dialysis, and the Germans sent him to an obscure hospital in Kampen, a city in eastern Netherlands. There, he actively participated in resistance to the German occupation, at considerable risk to himself, and continued to work on his dialysis machine. Materials were tight, but Kolff improvised and, in 1943, constructed the first rotating-drum kidney dialysis machine with a washing machine, orange juice cans, and sausage skins. In this process, once a needle was placed in a patient's vein, the rotation of the drum pulled blood through the tubing attached to the needle and into a container filled with purified saline. All bodily toxins soaked through the tubing into the saline, but because the concentration of the minerals in the saline was the same as those in the blood, the blood-based concentration of those vital minerals remained unchanged.

Kolff began treating patients with the kidney dialysis machine in 1943, but his first sixteen patients died. Continued adjustments and improvements to his machine resulted in his first major success in 1945, when he treated a sixty-seven-year-old woman who was in a uremic coma. After eleven hours of treatment with the dialysis machine, she regained consciousness and lived another seven years. By the end of World War II, Kolff had made five kidney dialysis machines, all of which he donated to hospitals around the world.

In 1950, Kolff left the Netherlands for the United States, where he continued to work on improving his dialysis machine. Opposition to dialysis was widespread; some called it "an abomination." Nevertheless, the success Kolff had treating patients with renal failure was difficult to confute. Kolff gave the blueprints of his machine to George Thorn at the Peter Bent Brigham Hospital in Boston, who designed the next generation of dialysis machines, the Kolff-Brigham artificial kidney.

Impact Kolff's invention represented a genuine case of innovative thinking. More important, kidney dialysis treated patients for whom, before Kolff's invention, nothing could be done. Kolff-Brigham dialyzers were instrumental in the treatment of American soldiers during the Korean War. This dialyzer also paved the way for the first kidney transplant, because patients with renal failure could be kept alive for a time before a suitable tissue match was found.

Michael A. Buratovich

Further Reading

Blagg, Christopher R. "The Early History of Dialysis for Chronic Renal Failure in the United States: A View from Seattle." *American Journal of Kidney Diseases* 46 (2007): 482-496.

Broers, Herman. *Inventor for Life: The Story of W. J. Kolff, Father of Artificial Organs.* Kampen, Netherlands: B&V Media, 2007.

Twardowski, Zbylut J. "History of Hemodialyzers' Designs." *Hemodialysis International* 12 (2008): 173-208.

See also Cancer; Fluoridation; Health care; Inventions; Medicine; Science and technology.

■ King, William Lyon Mackenzie

Identification Prime minister of Canada, 1921-1926, 1926-1930, and 1935-1948
Born December 17, 1874; Berlin (now Kitchener), Ontario, Canada
Died July 22, 1950; Kingsmere, Quebec, Canada

King used his skill at compromise to keep Canada united during World War II. After the war, he presided over a welcome period of prosperity as well as the beginnings of the Cold War.

When he became prime minister on December 29, 1921, forty-seven-year-old William Lyon Mackenzie King was well prepared. He had studied political science and economics at the University of Toronto and received a doctorate from Harvard University, as well as a degree in law from Osgoode Hall, which later became part of the University of Toronto. Hired by the newly created Department of Labor in 1900, he became deputy minister of labor and proved an excellent conciliator, successfully resolving three-quarters of the strikes in which he intervened. Elected to Parliament in 1908, he loyally served Sir Wilfred Laurier as minister of labor until the Liberal Party lost the election of 1911.

When Laurier died in 1919, Canada was convulsed by a series of bitter post-World War I labor strikes. King's reputation as a labor expert and his proven loyalty to the revered Laurier helped him become leader of the Liberals. King won the 1921 and 1926 elections, serving as prime minister until defeated in 1930. King regained his position as prime minister in the election of 1935. The worst of the Great Depression was over, but Europe seemed to be edging toward a new war.

War King did not expect war. He met Adolf Hitler in 1937 and concluded that Hitler would not undertake a general war. He nevertheless quadrupled Canada's defense budget between 1937 and 1939 to $64 million, which supported 10,000 full-time military personnel. For King, Britain was the first line of defense for Canada, in particular Britain's navy. When Britain entered the war on September 3, 1939, King loyally called on the Canadian parliament to declare war. Aware of sensitivities in Quebec, where heavy-handed coercion during World War I had embittered many, he promised that this time there would be no conscription. His conciliatory approach brought a united Canada into the war.

The cabinet King assembled proved adept at organizing the war effort. Canada contributed billions of dollars of food and munitions to the Allied cause. The navy escorted convoys, becoming increasingly effective as more ships were built. A major Canadian contribution to the war was the British Commonwealth Air Training Plan established in December, 1939, through which the overwhelming majority of British, Canadian, and other Commonwealth airmen were trained.

By 1943, the Canadian army in Britain had three infantry divisions, two armored divisions, and two armored brigades totaling more than 250,000 men and women. Including air force and naval personnel, there were 494,000 Canadian forces in Britain, all volunteers. Canada ranked third after Britain and the United States in supporting the Allied cause.

King's friendly personal relationship with U.S. president Franklin D. Roosevelt permitted him to act as an intermediary in 1940 between British prime minister Winston Churchill and Roosevelt, and he helped convince Churchill to trade British bases in the Caribbean for American destroyers.

King and Roosevelt formalized a joint defense of the American continent in the August, 1940, Ogdensburg Agreement. In 1941, a personal appeal to Roosevelt led to the Hyde Park Agreement, solving Canada's dollar shortage and facilitating joint production of weapons.

When King's leadership was challenged by claims that he was not doing enough, he called an election for March, 1940, that resulted in a resounding victory. The Liberal Party won a majority of the popular vote and three-quarters of the seats in Parliament.

Conscription   King's major political problem during the war was the issue of conscription. Fearing disruption of Canadian unity, with Quebec remaining vehemently opposed to a military draft, he resisted imposition of conscription. Many felt that this was

Britain's war and little concern of theirs, and few volunteered for military service. The fall of France had little effect on this sentiment. In fervently Roman Catholic Quebec, France's Marshal Henri Philippe Pétain was more admired than General Charles de Gaulle. English-speaking Canadians accused French Canadians of lack of patriotism, claiming they were not contributing their fair share to the national effort.

After the June, 1940, defeat of the British army in France, King reluctantly agreed to compulsory enlistment for home defense, with service limited to North America. This proved acceptable in Quebec. Pressure for conscription intensified again after the December, 1941, attack on Pearl Harbor that brought the United States into the war. King temporized, calling a national referendum that relieved him of his pledge never to conscript for overseas

Canadian prime minister William Lyon Mackenzie King (center right) and British prime minister Winston Churchill acknowledging the crowd as they tour Quebec together in September, 1943. (AP/Wide World Photos)

service while assuring the public that he would not call for a draft unless absolutely necessary.

The issue surfaced with greater vehemence in late 1944, as the Canadian army suffered heavy casualties during the Normandy invasion and the drive to open the port of Antwerp. Commanders in the field complained that there were no available replacement soldiers. King resisted from September to December before yielding and agreeing that 16,000 men already drafted for domestic service could be sent overseas. Several French Canadian cabinet members resigned over the decision, but King's change of position did not hurt him in Quebec, where the electorate apparently credited him for holding out as long as possible. The Liberal Party carried Quebec in the June, 1945, election, helping King continue as prime minister.

Peace   King began to plan for peace during the war. To prevent a return to the conditions of the 1930's, he pushed through a wide range of reforms. In 1940, Parliament passed an unemployment insurance program. Between 1943 and 1945, Parliament created a Department of Health and Welfare, enacted family allowances, allocated substantial sums for a housing program, and planned large-scale public works programs to provide jobs when war production ceased. A generous package of veteran's benefits aided transition to civilian life.

The feared postwar economic downturn never occurred. Pent-up demand fueled by forced savings during the war, even more than welfare programs based on Keynesian economics, powered the Canadian economy into an unprecedented level of prosperity. King's Liberal Party happily took credit for the unexpected affluence.

King helped found the United Nations at the April-June, 1945, San Francisco Conference, but he was disturbed by the Soviet delegation's tactics. His dislike of communism intensified in September, 1945, when a code clerk in the Soviet embassy defected and provided convincing evidence that a spy ring had operated in Canada, seeking secrets of the atomic energy program in which Canada participated with the United States and Britain. King helped negotiate a formal alliance between Western Europe and North America, but he retired before the North Atlantic Treaty Organization (NATO) was formalized in 1949. On January 20, 1948, he had called on the Liberal Party to choose a leader, with

Louis St. Laurent emerging as the choice of the convention in August. Suffering from heart problems, King retired as prime minister on November 15, having served six terms; he died less than two years later.

Impact   The 1940's were the most challenging, and the most successful, of King's twenty-one years as prime minister of Canada, guiding the country in war and planning a successful postwar reconstruction. His ministers deserve great credit for Canada's vigorous prosecution of the war, but it was King who led them and made the final decisions.

King was primarily a party leader, always seeking a middle ground that would hold together the diverse groups within the Liberal Party. He used his skills as a negotiator to arrive at a consensus when a divisive issue arose, striving for an agreement all could accept, even if it did not fully satisfy anyone. His success made the Liberals the dominant political party in Canada during the twentieth century. Nowhere were his skills as a conciliator more evident than in his maneuvers that kept a reluctant Quebec unified with the rest of the country during the war.

King's reputation plunged after his death, especially when publication of his diary revealed bizarre personal habits, including a lifelong need to consult his dead mother through spiritualists. His search for a middle ground came under attack by historians who thought he should have been more positive. The delays caused by his searches for consensus were condemned as mindless temporizing—one wit remarked that King never did things by halves if he could do them by quarters.

The more problems Canada faced regarding Quebec as the years passed, the more King's reputation rose. Respect for the political skills that kept Canada unified during the war grew. A 1997 poll of historians and political scientists ranked him the greatest Canadian prime minister.

Milton Berman

Further Reading

Bothwell, Robert. *The Penguin History of Canada.* Toronto: Penguin Group, 2006. General history of Canada provides context for King's career.

Douglas, W. A. B., and Brereton Greenhous. *Out of the Shadows: Canada in the Second World War.* Toronto: Oxford University Press, 1977. Patriotic history of Canada's participation in World War II.

Farhmi, Magda, and Robert Rutherdale, eds. *Creating Postwar Canada: Community, Diversity, and Dis-*

sent, 1945-1975. Vancouver: University of British Columbia Press, 2008. Essays discuss the social, political, and cultural history of postwar Canada.

Hutchison, Bruce. *The Incredible Canadian: A Candid Portrait of Mackenzie King—His Works, His Times, and His Nation.* Toronto: Longmans, Green, 1953. Colorful account of King's political career by a journalist who personally observed much of it. Argues that King possessed his country's confidence but never its affection.

Keshen, Jeffrey A. *Saints, Sinners and Soldiers: Canada's Second World War.* Vancouver: University of British Columbia Press, 2004. Excellent treatment of the Canadian home front during the war.

Nolan, Brian. *King's War: Mackenzie King and the Politics of War, 1939-1945.* Toronto: Random House, 1988. Examination of King's conduct of the war.

Pickersgill, J. W., and D. F. Forster. *The Mackenzie King Record.* 4 vols. Toronto: University of Toronto Press, 1960-1970. Edited version of King's voluminous wartime and postwar diary covering the years 1939 to 1948.

See also Atlantic Charter; Canada and Great Britain; Canadian nationalism; Canadian participation in World War II; Canadian regionalism; Churchill, Winston; Elections in Canada; Foreign policy of Canada; Ogdensburg Agreement of 1940; Quebec nationalism; Roosevelt, Franklin D.; St. Laurent, Louis.

■ Knute Rockne: All American

Identification Film biography of University of Notre Dame football coach Knute Rockne
Director Lloyd Bacon (1889-1955)
Date Released in 1940

Knute Rockne: All American depicts the qualities that Rockne instilled in football players during his tenure as coach at the University of Notre Dame, as well as emphasizing the importance of college football programs. The phrase used by actor Ronald Reagan in his role as George "Gipper" Gipp, portraying the dying athlete requesting Rockne to tell the boys to "win just one for the Gipper" became linked with the actor.

Generations after his death in a plane crash in 1931, Knute Rockne remains the epitome of the college football coach. The film *Knute Rockne: All American*

begins by re-creating his early life in Norway and his immigration to the United States during the 1890's. Echoing a theme that was common in American films of the 1940's, the film shows how opportunity and education propelled Rockne, played by actor Pat O'Brien, to success at the University of Notre Dame.

As football players, Rockne and teammate Gus Dorais (actor Owen Davis, Jr.) were among the first to apply the forward pass as an offensive weapon. Much of the film depicts Rockne's courting of and subsequent home life with his wife Bonnie (Gale Page). While the Rockne biography is largely accurate, Ronald Reagan's portrayal of Notre Dame football star George Gipp was highly idealized. The real Gipp rarely allowed school to interfere with his love of sports, gambling, and drinking, behaviors generally overlooked by Rockne.

Impact The film's emphasis on an idealized America proved inspirational before and during World War II. Future president Reagan's portrayal of Gipp played a significant role in advancing both his acting career and his later career in politics. In 1997, the film was placed in the National Film Registry of the United States Library of Congress.

Richard Adler

Further Reading
Chelland, Patrick. *One for the Gipper: George Gipp, Knute Rockne, and Notre Dame.* North Hollywood, Calif.: Panoply Publications, 2008.

Maggio, Frank. *Notre Dame and the Game That Changed Football.* New York: Da Capo Press, 2007.

Robinson, Ray. *Rockne of Notre Dame: The Making of a Football Legend.* New York: Oxford University Press, 1999.

See also *All the King's Men*; Film in the United States; Football; Sports in the United States.

■ Korea

At the end of World War II, the United States and Soviet Union agreed to partition the Korean peninsula but did not consult the region's people. While occupying Korea, the two countries imposed their conflicting economic and political systems. As a result, the two Koreas became antagonists in the developing Cold War.

When World War II began, Korea was under Japanese rule. At the Potsdam Conference in 1945, the United States agreed to partition Korea at the thirty-eighth parallel. The American aim was to prevent an imminent Soviet military takeover of the entire country. According to the agreement, the Soviet Union would occupy the north sector, and the United States would occupy the south sector. In 1948, the the two occupying powers returned sovereignty to two rival Koreas—North Korea, supported by the Soviet Union, and South Korea, supported by the United States.

In 1948, the United Nations offered to hold elections for a reunited Korea. The Soviet Union refused to cooperate and withdrew its troops, and North Korea declared independence. The United States then allowed the south to hold elections, and Syngman Rhee was elected president of the independent South Korea. Afterward, the United States supplied economic and military aid to Rhee's government in order to compete with Soviet aid to the north. While in office, Rhee cracked down on many legitimate political opponents, labeling them communist sympathizers, with the approval of the United States.

Impact Bitter antagonism resulted from Korea's division. Troops of the two Koreas began to clash in mid-1950. Although the two sides agreed to an armistice in 1953, the peninsula remained divided.

Michael Haas

Further Reading

Cumings, Bruce. *The Origins of the Korean War: Liberation and the Emergence of Separate Regimes, 1945-1947*. Princeton, N.J.: Princeton University Press, 1981.

Lee, Jongsoo James. *The Partition of Korea After World War II: A Global History*. New York: Palgrave Macmillan, 2006.

Oberdorfer, Don. *The Two Koreas: A Contemporary History*. Upper Saddle River, N.J.: Addison-Wesley, 1997.

See also Acheson, Dean; Asian Americans; Cold War; Foreign policy of the United States; Japan, occupation of; MacArthur, Douglas; Potsdam Conference; World War II.

■ *Korematsu v. United States*

The Case U.S. Supreme Court ruling upholding the constitutionality of the forced relocation of Japanese Americans during World War II

Date Decided on December 18, 1944

The Supreme Court held that the compulsory exclusion of Japanese Americans from West Coast "military areas" was justified by the exigencies of war and the threat to national security.

In February, 1942, following the Japanese attack on the U.S. naval base at Pearl Harbor and amid growing fears that the West Coast might be invaded, President Franklin D. Roosevelt issued Executive Order 9066, which authorized the secretary of war and military commanders to prescribe "military areas" from which civilians may be excluded. Congress subsequently passed legislation implementing the order and imposing criminal penalties for violations. The military placed an immediate curfew on ethnic Japanese, many of whom were U.S. citizens, in West Coast military areas and prohibited them from remaining in such areas after May 9, 1942. These areas included all of California and much of Washington, Oregon, and Arizona. All ethnic Japanese were also required to report to relocation centers to be removed to internment camps. In *Hirabayashi v. United States* (1943), a unanimous Supreme Court upheld the curfew order as necessary to prevent espionage and sabotage, but the Court avoided ruling on the exclusion and relocation orders.

Fred Korematsu, an American citizen of Japanese ancestry, was convicted in federal court of remaining in a military area in violation of the exclusion order. On review by the Supreme Court, the justices ruled 6-3 that the exclusion order was not beyond the war power of the president and Congress. Justice Hugo L. Black began the majority opinion by noting that legal restrictions that curtailed the civil rights of a single racial group were immediately suspect. This designation, however, did not mean that the restrictions were unconstitutional, but rather that courts had to subject them to the "strictest scrutiny." Under this standard, only a pressing public necessity might justify the restriction. As in *Hirabayashi*, the justices concluded that the twin dangers of espionage and sabotage were sufficiently compelling to warrant the exclusion. While excluding large groups of citizens from their homes was inconsistent with basic governmental institutions, the government's power to protect had to be commensurate with the threatened danger. The opinion concluded by reiterating that the exclusion order was not based upon racial prejudice but upon military necessity: a war was at hand, military leaders feared an invasion of the West Coast, and it was not possible to segregate disloyal Japanese Americans from loyal ones. The Court did not rule on the constitutionality of the relocation or internment.

Impact In constitutional doctrine, *Korematsu* is best known for establishing the precedent that all racial classifications are inherently suspect and subject to the strictest scrutiny. This precedent would be cited in later decades in the contexts of racial discrimination in public education and affirmative action programs. *Korematsu* also stands for the proposition that during times of emergency, courts will often defer to presidential and congressional assessments of threats to national security.

In 1980, Congress established the Commission on Wartime Relocation and Internment of Civilians, which later concluded that the exclusion of Japanese Americans during World War II was not justified by any military necessity. In 1984, a federal court vacated the conviction of Korematsu. In 1988, Congress acknowledged the injustices imposed by the exclusion and relocation and awarded reparations to those directly affected.

Richard A. Glenn

Further Reading

Gotanda, Neil. "The Story of *Korematsu*: The Japanese-American Cases." In *Constitutional Law Stories*, edited by Michael C. Dorf. New York: Foundation Press, 2004.

Irons, Peter. *Justice at War: The Story of the Japanese American Internment Cases*. Berkeley: University of California Press, 1993.

After losing his test case in the Supreme Court in 1944, Fred Korematsu continued to challenge the ruling until 1983, when the Court finally vacated its earlier decision because the government had suppressed evidence. (Asia Week)

Rehnquist, William H. *All the Laws but One: Civil Liberties in Wartime*. New York: Alfred A. Knopf, 1988.

See also Asian Americans; Civil rights and liberties; Executive orders; Japanese American internment; Pearl Harbor attack; Roosevelt, Franklin D.; Wartime espionage in North America; World War II.

■ *Kukla, Fran, and Ollie*

Identification Children's television show
Date Aired from October 13, 1947, to August 30, 1957

This early children's television, consisting of performances by puppeteer Burr Tillstrom's ensemble of childlike puppets in playful conversation with their loving companion, actor Fran Allison, was one of the first children's shows to become

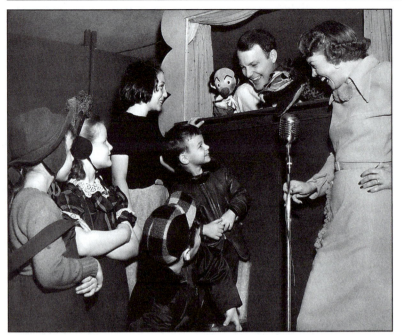

Puppeteer Burr Tillstrom looks over the puppet stage, holding his Kukla puppet in his right hand and Ollie in his left hand, as Fran Allison (right) looks on. (Getty Images)

successful with adult audiences and paved the way for future puppet-based shows.

Beginning broadcast on local Chicago television WBKB, *Kukla, Fran, and Ollie* soon became a national phenomenon. The first NBC network broadcast of the show was on January 12, 1949, and the half-hour show aired each weekday. The show changed time slots, broadcast days, and networks (shifting to ABC in 1954), and viewers protested when it was cut to fifteen minutes in November, 1951. It later returned to the half-hour format but was cut back again when ABC picked up the show.

The two title puppets, created and exclusively manned by Burr Tillstrom, were Kukla, who looked like a clown, and Ollie, a rambunctious dragon. A diverse ensemble cast of puppets included such supporting players as lonely mailman Fletcher Rabbit, diva Madame Oglepuss, spry Beulah witch, and baf-

fling stagehand Cecil Bill. Each puppet developed a personal relationship with comedian and singer Fran Allison, who acted as a normalizing intermediary between the magical world of the puppets and the viewers watching at home.

Although the show featured musical numbers, much of the interplay was spontaneous and unrehearsed, dependent on the mood of the day and the natural chemistry between the inventive puppeteer and his quick-witted costar. Both simple and sophisticated, the show became a favorite of both children and adults.

Impact   *Kukla, Fran, and Ollie* was among the most popular shows of its day and won numerous awards, including a Peabody as the outstanding children's program of 1949. Burr Tillstrom was inducted posthumously into the Hall of Fame of the Academy of Television Arts and Sciences in 1986. He had paved the way for future puppeteers on television, including Shari Lewis, with costar Lamb Chop, and Jim Henson and his Muppets.

Margaret Boe Birns

Further Reading

Baughman, James L. *Same Time, Same Station: Creating American Television, 1948-1961.* Baltimore, Md.: Johns Hopkins University Press, 2007.

Davis, Michael. *Street Gang: The Complete History of "Sesame Street."* New York: Viking, 2008.

Okuda, Ted, and Jack Mulqueen. *The Golden Age of Chicago Children's Television.* Chicago: Lake Claremont Press, 2004.

See also   Animated films; Curious George books; Fads; *Howdy Doody Show*; Television.

L

■ Labor strikes

Definition   Organized work stoppages by laborers, usually planned by labor unions

The numerous labor strikes in the United States and Canada during the 1940's won many of the financial gains that helped move working people in those countries into the middle class. They also helped precipitate the end of communist and other leftist influence in organized U.S. labor.

Most historians consider the 1940's to be the zenith of the American labor movement. In 1941, the two major confederations of labor unions, the American Federation of Labor (AFL) and Congress of Industrial Organizations (CIO), pledged that no strikes would be called for the duration of World War II. There were at least five major strikes in 1941 alone, however. Also, in a victory for labor in 1941, Henry Ford recognized the United Auto Workers.

In 1942, the federal government established the National War Labor Board to mediate labor problems and prevent any further strikes. In 1943, Congress passed the Smith-Connally Act (also called the War Labor Disputes Act), which forbade strikes by labor and limited union activity, especially in war-related industries. Nonetheless, the United Mine Workers (UMW) struck bituminous coal mines, and in response the U.S. government took over operation of the mines. The coal strike eventually ended with a contract that gave the workers what is known as portal-to-portal pay, for time spent in going to work locations, along with other benefits. Although the massive employment in the industrial sector during the war helped improve the lot of American workers, the war was manipulated by some industrial leaders to diminish the power that organized labor had acquired during the turbulent 1930's. Despite this, there were 3,800 strikes in 1943, 4,750 in 1944, and 5,000 in 1945. It is estimated that in 1946 more than 4.6 million workers went on strike for a total of 116 million work days.

Postwar Labor Actions   The fundamentally cooperative nature of labor-management relations during the war changed rapidly once peace was declared in 1945. The Communist Party of the United States and other labor radicals rejected the so-called Charter of Industrial Peace that the AFL and CIO had signed with the U.S. Chamber of Commerce and began pushing unions to organize workers and the unemployed (many of whom were returning soldiers). The efforts of the radicals and the economic situation immediately following the end of the war resulted in what many historians consider to be the most concentrated period of labor strikes in the history of the United States. The renewed vigor on the part of labor was also related to a desire to reap benefits from the New Deal legislation passed by Congress during Franklin D. Roosevelt's presidency.

Strikes took place among oil workers, and coal miners declared a nationwide strike. Workers also went on strike in the electrical manufacturing industry and in the packing house industry, and they

Major Labor Strikes of the 1940's

1940	Ford Motor Corporation
1941	Captive coal miners
	Disney animators
	International Harvester
	New York City busses
1944	Philadelphia transit
1945	Kelsey-Hayes
	Montgomery Ward
	New York City longshoreman
	Oil workers
1946	General Motors
1947	R. J. Reynolds tobacco company

Coal miners in Bellaire, Ohio, reading about their union's refusal of the industry's wage offer in May, 1943. (AP/Wide World Photos)

struck against major companies such as General Motors, the railroads, Pittsburgh Power, and U.S. Steel. The labor actions grew increasingly militant, with government and industry reacting by calling in the U.S. military. In April, 1946, troops seized control of the coal mines. Troops were also called in to take over the railroads, and in October of that year, the U.S. Navy seized control of several oil refineries in an attempt to break the oil workers' strike that had spread to twenty states. The primary demands of the strikes were for cost-of-living wage adjustments to compensate for inflation, health benefits, and better working conditions. Most of the strikes ended either in defeat for the workers or contracts that benefited management much more than labor.

In 1947, Congress passed the Taft-Hartley Act (Labor-Management Relations Act), which severely restricted the political power of labor unions in the United States. In addition, a drive to expel leftists from organized labor was under way. Up to this point, the left wing of the labor movement had been instrumental in organizing workers and encouraging strike actions as a tool to promote union demands. The combination of the new legislation and removing radical labor leaders from power ensured that the power of labor unions in the United States would be diminished.

Labor Unions and African American Workers The rapid expansion in the American job market resulting from the nation's involvement in World War II opened employment opportunities to African Americans and women. In 1941, President Franklin D. Roosevelt signed Executive Order 8802, which created the Fair Employment Practices Commission (FEPC). The order banned racial discrimination in any defense industry receiving federal contracts by declaring "there shall be no discrimination in the employment of workers in defense industries or government because of race, creed, color, or national origin." This order was the result of intense pressure led by African American labor leader and activist A. Philip Randolph, the president of the Brotherhood of Sleeping Car Porters. His calls for more racial equality were echoed by other African American leaders, including Walter White, executive secretary of the National Association for the Advancement of Colored People, and Mary McLeod Bethune, director of the National Youth Administration, a federal agency. Randolph organized a massive march on Washington, D.C., that was called off only after Roosevelt signed the executive order.

Changing racial relations in American industry caused tensions among workers, notably in the auto industry. Many white autoworkers were transplants from the southern United States, where racism not only was part of the white culture but also was codified into law. When African Americans began working side by side with these transplants and other white workers, tensions simmered, sometimes erupting into strikes and other actions by white workers. Generally speaking, these strikes were protests against the hiring and promotion of African American workers. Some estimates of the loss of work time during these strikes exceed 100,000 hours. In 1943, one of the worst race riots in the history of the United States took place in Detroit, the heart of the auto industry, resulting in thirty-four deaths. These actions represented a relatively small minority of American workers but reflected major tensions among workers.

After the end of the war in 1945, the brief era of integrated labor unions in the American South that had begun during the 1930's came to a virtual end. In 1946, in Forsyth County, North Carolina, the Food, Tobacco, Agricultural, and Allied Workers engaged in a concerted effort to organize seasonal tobacco workers not covered by previous contracts with the R.J. Reynolds Tobacco Company. A strike by the tobacco workers eventually put in place a minimum wage of 60 cents per hour and three annual paid holidays for seasonal workers. By the end of the decade, however, the right wing of the national CIO, jumping on the anticommunist bandwagon, destroyed the racially integrated Food, Tobacco, Agricultural, and Allied Workers Local 22 in Winston-Salem, North Carolina, in a national race-baiting campaign. Meanwhile, the steelworkers union took the lead in destroying the interracial Mine Mill locals in Alabama by openly appealing to the racism of white workers.

Roosevelt's FEPC, which had successfully promoted integration in the North, never challenged segregation in southern workplaces. A call by President Harry. S. Truman in 1948 for a permanent FEPC failed, and legislation passed in 1950 by the House of Representatives to create a permanent FEPC died in a Senate filibuster.

Labor Strikes in Canada during the 1940's   As in the United States, Canadian labor reached its historical peak of power during the 1940's. Most Canadian unions adhered to the no-strike pledge made when Canada joined World War II in 1939. In 1940, workers in parts of the rapidly growing aircraft industry went on strike for two months demanding a wage increase. The strike failed. In 1941, workers at a plant owned by the Aluminum Company of Canada occupied the plant and turned off the furnaces, allowing the molten aluminum to solidify. The government labeled the action "enemy sabotage" and sent in troops. A 1941 strike by gold miners in Kirkland Lake was met by newspaper portrayals of the strikers as traitors. Many of the newspaper owners also had financial interests in the gold mines. The strike lasted two months and ended in failure.

In 1943, one in three Canadian workers spent some time on strike. Many of these strikes were to gain recognition for labor unions, and many failed in this goal. When the war ended in 1945, many businesses began revisiting wartime labor-management contracts, and Canadian workers launched a wave of strikes in protest. In the months of June and July, 1946, rubber workers went on strike against Firestone, United Electrical Workers went on strike against management at Westinghouse, and United Steelworkers of America Local 1005 went on strike against the Stelco steel company. The latter strike was resolved in March, 1947, with the union gaining recognition and a contract generally favorable to the workers.

In 1949, Canadian asbestos workers went on strike at four mines in eastern Canada. The majority of the workers were Québécois, and many spoke French, whereas the owners were primarily American or English-speaking Canadians. The divisive strike was violent on both sides, lasting four months and ending after a series of mass arrests. Although the workers gained little in terms of wage increases and many workers were blacklisted from the industry, the strike is seen as a turning point in the history of Quebec and its relations to the Ontario government.

Impact   The wave of labor strikes during the 1940's in the United States and Canada made the power of organized labor abundantly clear in both countries. The strikes, however, did not fully achieve the organizers' goals of improving the lot of workers in terms of wages, working conditions, and job security. In Canada, the strikes were slightly more successful.

In terms of their long-term effects, a notable backlash occurred against labor unions in the wake of the strike wave of 1946. Industrial management and the U.S. Congress worked together to enact laws restricting the right to strike and controlling union involvement in electoral politics. The 1947 Taft-Hartley Act sharply curtailed the limits of unions' political activities. Such laws, when combined with the anticommunist hysteria sweeping across the United States, gave industry and union management a reason to purge leftists from the union rank and file and from union management. With elimination of the most radical elements within the unions, labor-management relations became less confrontational. In Canada, the establishment of government labor relations boards, combined with a similar purging of leftist members from unions, also led to less confrontational relations between workers and management.

Ron Jacobs

Further Reading

Miller, Calvin Craig. *A. Philip Randolph and the African-American Labor Movement.* Greensboro, N.C.: Morgan Reynolds, 2005. A biography of Randolph written for middle school and high school readers. The overview of Randolph's life portrays him as a man of principle. Several photographs enhance the text.

Morton, Desmond. *Working People: An Illustrated History of the Canadian Labour Movement.* Montreal: McGill-Queen's University Press, 1998. Comprehensive illustrated history of the Canadian labor movement. Morton writes in an engaging style that incorporates Canadian social and political history.

Nicholson, Philip. *Labor's Story in the United States.* Philadelphia: Temple University Press, 2004. Nicholson's survey of the labor movement in the United States stands out because of its readability and his thesis connecting the growth of the labor movement to the expansion of America's democratic ideals to more of its citizenry.

Smith, Sharon. *Subterranean Fire: A History of Working-Class Radicalism in the United States.* Chicago: Haymarket Books, 2006. Concise and highly readable history of the history of labor activism in the United States. Told from a leftist perspective, this history emphasizes the grassroots nature of the labor movement.

Zieger, Robert H., and Gilbert J. Gall. *American Workers, American Unions: The Twentieth Century.* Baltimore, Md.: Johns Hopkins University Press, 2002. An understandable and reasonably complete survey of American labor in the twentieth century. The two chapters dealing with the 1940's provide a wealth of information regarding the political situation of the labor movement during the decade.

See also   American Federation of Labor; Anticommunism; Communist Party USA; Congress of Industrial Organizations; Fair Employment Practices Commission; National War Labor Board; Railroad seizure; Randolph, A. Philip; Roosevelt, Franklin D.; Smith-Connally Act; Taft-Hartley Act.

■ La Guardia, Fiorello H.

Identification   Mayor of New York City, 1934-1945
Born   December 11, 1882; New York, New York
Died   September 20, 1947; New York, New York

La Guardia, the first Italian and first Jewish mayor of New York City, had boundless energy in his career in public service. A national figure as mayor, he worked to enact reforms in New York City government.

Fiorello Henry La Guardia, a Republican, was elected mayor of New York City in 1933 with the assistance of influential members of the "brain trust" of President Franklin D. Roosevelt. His platform included various proposals to end corruption in city government and to establish a more rational, nonpartisan administration of the city. He attacked the challenges facing New York City with his characteristic energy. He was an active mayor at a time when the city needed active leadership. His overriding goal was to help the residents of his city. La Guardia was a "hands-on" manager: Residents were not surprised to see the mayor responding to a fire call with the fire department, and the mayor also found an obscure provision in the city charter that allowed him to serve as a municipal court judge.

In 1940, La Guardia considered running for president of the United States. President Roosevelt decided to seek a third term, and La Guardia did not want to run against an ally. He requested an appointed office in the Roosevelt administration, but the president's aides believed that La Guardia lacked the temperament to serve in the cabinet. Roosevelt eventually appointed La Guardia as director of the new Office of Civilian Defense (OCD) in May, 1941. The OCD was responsible for preparing for the protection of the civilian population in case of an attack, maintaining public morale, promoting volunteer service, and coordinating federal departments to meet the needs of a potential war effort.

La Guardia used the radio extensively to publicize his work as mayor. During a newspaper strike in 1945, he read the comics on WNYC radio to an appreciative citywide audience.

With the mayor focusing on national offices during his third term, his administration began to deteriorate. Petty corruption seeped into his administration, and La Guardia was criticized by civil libertarians for his apparent heavy-handed tactics in rooting out racketeers operating in the city. He realized that his political career was ending, so he did not seek reelection in 1945. He was appointed director general of the United Nations Relief and Rehabilitation Administration. He resigned from the position after the United States withdrew its support of the agency at the end of 1946. La Guardia died in September, 1947, in New York City.

Impact   Unlike his immediate predecessors, La Guardia did not become wealthy by serving as mayor of New York City. In fact, when he died, his second wife inherited a relatively meager estate of eight thousand dollars and a house. La Guardia's ambition was to improve New Yorkers' lives and to build the city's infrastructure. As mayor, he worked to have a commercial airport built inside the city limits. This airport, in the Queens borough on Long Island, was later named LaGuardia Airport in his honor.

John David Rausch, Jr.

Further Reading

Brodsky, Alyn. *The Great Mayor: Fiorello La Guardia and the Making of the City of New York.* New York: St. Martin's Press, 2003.

Jeffers, H. Paul. *The Napoleon of New York: Mayor Fiorello La Guardia.* New York: John Wiley & Sons, 2002.

Kessner, Thomas. *Fiorello H. La Guardia and the Making of Modern New York.* New York: McGraw-Hill, 1989.

See also   Civil defense programs; Elections in the United States: 1940; Jews in the United States; Radio in the United States; Roosevelt, Franklin D.; United Nations.

■ LaMotta, Jake

Identification   World middleweight boxing champion, 1949-1951

Born   July 10, 1921; New York, New York

LaMotta is best known for his rivalry with Sugar Ray Robinson during the 1940's. LaMotta defeated Marcel Cerdan for the middleweight title in 1949.

Jake LaMotta was a tough street kid who turned professional boxer in 1941. His loss to Sugar Ray Robinson by decision in 1942 was the beginning of a legendary rivalry. On February 5, 1943, LaMotta handed Robinson his first professional defeat by unanimous decision. Three weeks later, LaMotta lost the rematch. In 1945, LaMotta lost two more close decisions to Robinson.

Known for his aggressive style, LaMotta was a top contender for the middleweight crown but was denied a title fight by the Mafia until he agreed to throw a fight. On November 14, 1947, he was defeated by Billy Fox. LaMotta was immediately investigated by the New York State Boxing Commission and was suspended for seven months.

On June 16, 1949, LaMotta challenged the world middleweight champion, French fighter Marcel Cerdan. When Cerdan failed to answer the bell for the tenth round, LaMotta was declared middleweight champion of the world. Cerdan was killed in an airplane crash on the way to the scheduled rematch. LaMotta successfully defended the title twice but lost it to Robinson on February 14, 1951, in a fight known as the St. Valentine's Day Massacre.

Impact LaMotta's autobiography, *Raging Bull*, was published in 1970. The dramatic story of the colorful boxer was made into a significant eponymous film directed by Martin Scorsese, with Robert DeNiro playing LaMotta.

Susan Butterworth

Further Reading

Brunt, Stephen. *The Italian Stallions: Heroes of Boxing's Glory Days*. Wilmington, Del.: Sport Classic Books, 2003.

LaMotta, Jake, with Joseph Carter and Peter Savage. *Raging Bull: My Story*. Englewood Cliffs, N.J.: Prentice-Hall, 1970.

See also Boxing; Louis, Joe; Robinson, Sugar Ray; Sports in the United States.

■ Landing craft, amphibious

Definition Military vehicles used to transport troops directly from oceans to beaches

Amphibious landing craft provided the means to assault enemy-held beaches directly from the sea without access to a port or harbor. As World War II spread across the globe, amphibious warfare became a means of surprising the enemy and seizing vital territories to gain a military advantage.

Although there were several ad hoc attempts at amphibious warfare by the British during World War I and the Japanese during the 1930's, the first large-scale seaborne invasions occurred during World War II. Both the United States and Great Britain needed amphibious forces. They required the capability to invade Europe to defeat the Germans, and the United States needed specialized landing craft on its island-hopping campaign against the Japanese in the Pacific. Both tasks demanded large numbers of specialized landing craft capable of moving men and material from large oceangoing ships to the beaches to be in-vaded. Some craft were ships designed to run themselves onto the shore, while others remained in deeper water to accomplish their tasks.

Landing craft ranged from the small and simple to the large and complex. At the small end of the range was the DUKW, a 2.5-ton truck fitted with a boat hull that enabled it to float. DUKWs could float out to ships to take on a load, carry it to the beach, and then drive inland to deliver it. Slightly larger was the Landing Craft, Vehicle, Personnel (LCVP), or Higgins boat. Thirty-six feet long, weighing eight tons, and made mostly of plywood, the LCVP drew only twelve inches of water. Its designer, Andrew Higgins, created the boat for use in Louisiana bayous, but the military found it ideal for bringing either 30 men or 4 tons of cargo directly onto a beach. Higgins and other subcontractors built more than twenty thousand of the utilitarian LCVPs during the war.

The Landing Craft, Mechanized (LCM) was an upsized LCVP capable of carrying 120 men or a 30-ton tank. Larger still was the Landing Craft, Tank (LCT), which, in its later versions, could carry four tanks over a distance of 700 miles. The personnel equivalent of the LCT was the Landing Craft, Infan-

The Pacific theater of the war was dominated by naval combat, and most land operations were dependent on naval assistance. Of particular importance in coordinating land and sea operations were amphibious landing craft such as these, which permitted large numbers of troops to go ashore as quickly as possible. (National Archives)

try (LCI). Originally designed as a "large raiding craft" for commando operations, the LCI was a 300-ton ship capable of carrying 200 soldiers or 75 tons of cargo for a longer distance and at higher speed than an LCMP or LCM. The largest craft that landed on the beach, however, was the Landing Ship, Tank (LST). Displacing nearly 5,000 tons but drawing only 8 feet of water, the LST (or "Large Slow Target," as crews grimly called it) could carry 18 tanks or equivalent cargo in a single delivery.

Other craft stayed offshore because of their size or task. Landing Craft, Control (LCC) were direction ships used to guide landing craft onto their designated beaches. Reinforcements arrived in Amphibious Assault Transports (APA), while their supplies were carried in Amphibious Cargo Ships (AKA). Because neither APAs nor AKAs carried sufficient landing craft to move everything in one trip, Landing Ship, Dock (LSD) craft carried only extra landing craft, for use by other ships.

Impact   Without landing craft, Allied victory in World War II seemed unlikely. Considering the density of enemy fortifications and numbers in some areas, amphibious assaults were the only means of success. Because amphibious warfare proved so vital to victory, most modern major navies possess the ability, albeit limited in some cases, to conduct amphibious warfare. After the 1950's, however, the helicopter, with its greater speed and flexibility, became the primary means of amphibious assault, with traditional landing craft used mostly for moving supplies.

Steven J. Ramold

Further Reading

Friedman, Norman. *U.S. Amphibious Ships and Craft: An Illustrated Design History.* Annapolis, Md.: Naval Institute Press, 2002. An exhaustive study that describes the technical development of every amphibious warfare ship employed by the United States.

Lovering, Tristan T. *Amphibious Assault: Manoeuvre from the Sea.* Woodbridge, England: Seafarer Books, 2007. An excellent history of amphibious warfare from its origins to its modern practice, with an emphasis on the strategic value of amphibious warfare's ability to shock and surprise.

Strahan, Jerry E. *Andrew Jackson Higgins and the Boats That Won World War II.* Baton Rouge: Louisiana State University Press, 1994. A thorough biography of the colorful character who conceived, de-

signed, and built the most important landing craft of all.

See also   Iwo Jima, Battle of; Marines, U.S.; Navy, U.S.; Wartime technological advances; World War II.

■ Latin America

Latin America was vital for the United States during both World War II and the early stages of the Cold War because of its abundance of natural resources and political connections. U.S.-Latin American relations during the 1940's featured both close collaboration and confrontation with a growing Latin American nationalism.

Ever since the promulgation of the Monroe Doctrine in 1823, as a statement of North American influence over Latin America, American statesmen had looked upon Latin America as America's "backyard," to be protected from the interference of outside powers. In practice, this policy meant both limited sovereignty for the nations of Latin America and the right of the United States to interfere in their internal affairs to protect American lives, property, and strategic interests.

During the 1940's, the doctrine was formally invoked only once, in 1940, when President Franklin D. Roosevelt's secretary of state, Cordell Hull, warned the Axis Powers—Germany, Italy, and Japan—not to extend their naval power into the Caribbean. The principle behind the doctrine, that Latin America was an American protectorate, was enforced throughout the decade—first against the Axis Powers during World War II, and later in reference to the Soviet Union during the early years of the Cold War.

Hemispheric Security   When President Roosevelt assumed office in 1933, he promised the Latin American nations a new era of cooperation, the Good Neighbor Policy, rather than the perennial U.S. interference that had marred relations in the past. The last U.S. Marines stationed in Nicaragua were withdrawn shortly after his inauguration, and the Platt Amendment to the Cuban constitution—which allowed American military intervention in Cuba—was repealed by the Treaty of Relations in 1934, with the exception that the United States was allowed to keep a naval base at Guantánamo Bay.

Newly inaugurated Argentine president Juan Perón riding to government house to take up his executive duties, on April 6, 1946. (AP/Wide World Photos)

In principle, the Monroe Doctrine was replaced by the concept of collective defense against foreign powers with designs on the Western Hemisphere. At the Havana Conference of 1940, however, the American delegation pressed delegates to declare that any republic could take unilateral action against a foreign threat to the hemisphere. Although Roosevelt claimed to champion democracy in Latin America, he stood firmly behind some reliable but undemocratic American allies, dictators such as Anastasio Somoza of Nicaragua and Rafael Trujillo of the Dominican Republic, on the grounds of American national security.

The Good Neighbor Policy was also a way for the United States to exploit much of the vast natural resources and economic infrastructure of Latin America. American and Canadian firms took over petroleum reserves in Peru and oil exports from Venezuela. Mineral wealth deemed vital to the war effort by the War Department, including tin, manganese, chromium, and mercury, was traded exclusively with the United States, while Brazil supplied rubber for American military vehicles. Governments in Central America seized cotton and coffee

plantations owned by Germans and Japanese and sold them to American firms, particularly the powerful United Fruit Company, while in Bolivia and Colombia, a large share of stock in the national airlines was assumed by American companies with the approval of the State Department, squeezing out German investors. The Office of the Coordinator of Inter-American Affairs, founded in 1940 and headed by Nelson Rockefeller, pressured the Latin American subsidiaries of American companies to stop trade with the Axis Powers while promoting the virtues of the "American way of life" through radio broadcasts, film, and newspaper articles favorable to the United States.

World War II   The Latin American countries followed the United States in declaring war on the Axis during World War II, with the exception of Uruguay. Mexico contributed several air squadrons to the Pacific theater, and Brazil sent an expeditionary force to fight in Italy and provided the United States with a valuable air base in the city of Natal to transport troops and material to North Africa. This wartime alliance for hemispheric defense war formalized after the war in 1947 with the signing of the Inter-American Treaty of Reciprocal Assistance, also known as the Rio Pact, which reasserted the doctrine that an attack on any signatory nation, including Canada, was an aggression against all. Issued at the start of the Cold War, the Rio Pact clearly was aimed at the Soviet Union.

Latin American Nationalism   The idea of a pan-American alliance under the sway of the United States was severely tested with the election of Juan Perón as president of Argentina in 1946. The American ambassador threatened to go public with documentation of Peron's pro-Axis sympathies during the war, but Perón used that to his advantage to charge that the United States wanted to install its own man in the presidency. The Argentine president declared his country neutral in the Cold War, and he sponsored Latin American labor and student organizations free from American control. Elsewhere in Latin America during the late 1940's, the United States faced the threat of strong communist parties, particularly in Brazil, Guatemala, and Cuba, whose prestige had grown on account of Soviet success in fighting fascism in Europe, along with strong efforts at organizing labor.

Impact The United States held a much stronger diplomatic, military, and economic position in Latin America by the end of the 1940's, yet winds of change were blowing. Latin American nationalists and populists gained votes and popularity precisely on account of the heavy hand their northern neighbor wielded in the region.

Julio César Pino

Further Reading

Brewer, Stewart. *Borders and Bridges: A History of U.S.-Latin American Relations.* Westport, Conn.: Praeger Security International, 2006. Incisive look at how the United States has employed the concept of national security to impinge on Latin American sovereignty.

Colby, Gerard, and Charlotte Dennett. *Thy Will Be Done: The Conquest of the Amazon—Nelson Rockefeller and Evangelism in the Age of Oil.* New York: HarperCollins, 1995. History of the crucial role played by Nelson Rockefeller in opening Latin America to U.S. investment.

LaRosa, Michael, and Frank O. Mora, eds. *Neighborly Adversaries: Readings in U.S.-Latin American Relations.* Lanham, Md.: Rowman & Littlefield, 2007. Collection of primary sources documenting the confrontation-collaboration dynamic of the relations of the United States with its southern neighbors.

Schmitz, David F. *Thank God They're on Our Side: The United States and Right-Wing Dictatorships, 1921-1965.* Chapel Hill: University of North Carolina Press, 1999. Critical look at American sponsorship of dictators in Latin American and the Caribbean.

Schoultz, Lars. *Beneath the United States: A History of U.S. Policy Toward Latin America.* Cambridge, Mass.: Harvard University Press, 1998. Dissects the ideological underpinnings of U.S. intervention in Latin America.

Smith, Peter H. *Talons of the Eagle: Dynamics of U.S.-Latin American Relations.* New York: Oxford University Press, 2000. Traces the history of U.S.-Latin American relations by exploring the motivations for imperialism.

See also Cold War; Foreign policy of the United States; Hull, Cordell; Inter-American Treaty of Reciprocal Assistance; Latinos; Mexico; Organization of American States; Roosevelt, Franklin D.; Truman, Harry S.; United Fruit Company.

■ Latinos

Identification People of Spanish American descent or heritage living in the United States

Wartime opportunities, the G.I. Bill, and expanded employment following World War II allowed many Latinos to expand their participation in American life and explore opportunities hitherto not available to them, and they expanded their roles in civic and political life.

At the time the United States took possession of Mexican territories in the Southwest following the 1846-1848 Mexican War, fewer than than 100,000 Latinos were living in the acquired territories of the Southwest. The years following the war saw a slow but continuous flow of Mexicans into the lands that had been settled by the Spanish beginning in the late seventeenth century. The new immigrants settled primarily in the states of Texas, California, Arizona, Colorado, and New Mexico. By 1909, fewer than 5,000 Mexican immigrants were entering the United States annually, but as a result of the Mexican Revolution that lasted from 1910 to 1920, with repercussions afterward, the number grew to approximately 90,000.

By 1920, nearly two million Mexican Americans lived in the United States, with a majority of them being native born. The influx of Latinos from other countries of Latin America was insignificant, although after Puerto Ricans were granted American citizenship in 1917, 70,000 had come to the mainland. During the Great Depression of the 1930's, immigration of Latinos slowed to a trickle. In fact, because of the severe unemployment during this period, the U.S. government began a program of repatriation, forcibly sending to Mexico as many as 458,000 people of Mexican descent, many of whom actually were U.S. citizens. Census data indicate that by 1940 there were only 1,861,400 Mexican Americans in the United States.

Latinos and World War II   World War II had a significant impact on the Latino population of the United States. The war greatly stimulated both industry and agriculture. Hundreds of thousands of Latinos were thrust into the industrial labor force and formed a significant part of the "war machine." Leaving their traditional barrios and communities, primarily in the Southwest, thousands moved to industrial areas in the Midwest to build planes, tanks, and other war supplies.

Nearly one-half million young Latinos enlisted or were drafted into the U.S. armed forces. A high percentage of Mexican Americans volunteered for the more hazardous branches, such as the paratroopers and Marines. Their valor earned them proportionately more military honors than any other ethnic group, and by the end of the war, seventeen Mexican Americans had earned the Congressional Medal of Honor. Puerto Ricans also played a major role in combat units of the armed forces, distinguishing themselves in the major battles in Europe and the Pacific. Latinos fought in every major battle of the European theater and in the Pacific.

Latinas, who traditionally served in the role of homemakers, also found themselves in new roles because of the war effort. Not only did they take on industrial "Rosie the Riveter" roles in the nation's industrial effort to support the war, but many also were involved in branches of the military.

World War II brought into focus much of the discrimination that Latinos had experienced prior to the war. In the zoot-suit riots on the West Coast in 1943, U.S. servicemen attacked Latino youths, identified by the distinctive zoot suits they wore, accusing them of being unpatriotic. Some African Americans were integrated into white military units during the war, but the role of Latinos remained ambiguous. Although they were integrated with white units, they often found themselves in de facto segregated situations.

With respect to employment on the home front, Latinos experienced new opportunities in the war industries. President Franklin D. Roosevelt in 1941 created the federal Fair Employment Practices Commission, which banned discrimination in defense industries and government employment on the basis of race, creed, color, or national origin. This enabled more Latinos to find employment commensurate with their abilities. By the end of the war, the economic status of Latinos in the country had improved, partly as the result of lessened discrimination and partly as a result of the increased power of labor unions. Latinos also found more opportunities in small businesses, and Latino children had better educational opportunities.

Compared to the Anglo mainstream, Latinos remained far behind in educational opportunities and social progress, but gains were made. Latinos mustering out of the military possessed a newfound sense of self-esteem and confidence. The G.I. Bill afforded them educational opportunities, job training, and home and business loans, all of which had been more limited prior to the war.

Many veterans used these new opportunities to improve conditions in their communities. They also defended Latino civil rights more aggressively and formed Latino organizations to improve Latinos' social condition in the United States. Veterans were a core group of the emerging political, educational, and civic leaders of their respective communities.

Latino Labor and the Bracero Program   The decade of the 1930's had been bleak for Latinos with respect to immigration to the United States from Mexico and other Latin American countries. Severe unemployment in the United States had slowed immigration to a trickle. Entry of the United States into World War II following the Pearl Harbor attack in December of 1941 changed conditions dramatically. Employment opportunities expanded with the need to produce materials and food for the war effort. In the Midwest, automobile assembly lines shifted to production of tanks and airplanes. Shipyards on both coasts rushed to produce war vessels, far outpacing both German and Japanese production. Workers and their families migrated from rural areas to the industrial centers, with California adding nearly two million new residents. Union membership grew significantly. In 1935, the Roosevelt administration had successfully passed the Wagner Act, which granted organizing rights to unions under the protection of the newly created National Labor Relations Board. Although union membership did not increase dramatically during the last half of the 1930's, because of the Depression, the war effort resulted in dramatic increases in union membership. Latinos shared in many of these new labor opportunities.

Because so many workers were now serving in the military and in the war industries, agricultural laborers were in short supply. In an effort to find agricultural workers, the U.S. government in 1942 introduced the bracero program; at its height, it brought as many as half a million workers from Mexico per year under contract to work in agriculture and on the railroads. This arrangement with the Mexican government was intended to be a temporary guest-worker program to support the war effort, but it lasted formally until 1964. Many of the bracero guest workers ultimately remained in the United States illegally or gained legal residency status through such means as marriage to U.S. citizens.

California and the agricultural areas of the Southwest received most of these workers. As many as 80,000 Mexican workers were employed by two railroad companies in the West, the Southern Pacific and the Santa Fe. In addition to workers coming into the country legally under the bracero program, thousands came in illegally. Work was plentiful during the war years, and little effort was made by government to stop the flow of illegal immigrants.

Latino Political Participation During the 1940's, Latino participation in American political life was particularly prominent in New Mexico. Because of the area's history during the Spanish-Mexican period, New Mexico Latinos were a majority of the state's population. This afforded Latinos opportunities to win election to local offices. In 1940, Denisio (Dennis) Chávez was elected to a full term in the U.S. Senate; he was the only Latino member of the Senate until his death in 1962. He played a major role in improving Latino political participation during his life, not only in his own state but also in California, where he helped Edward R. Roybal, who was born in New Mexico, to become, in 1949, the first Latino Los Angeles city councilman since 1881. In 1962, Roybal became the first Latino congressman from the state since 1879.

In Texas, the political fortunes of Latinos during the 1940's were bleak. Because of the state's southern connection, Mexican Americans, who had been classified as "Caucasian" for the 1940 census, were still subjected to Jim Crow laws. Poll taxes and other restrictions curtailed Latino political participation in the state. Arnold J. Vale was the sole Latino member of the Texas legislature from 1937 to 1947. Although political opportunities were limited for Latinos, even in the Southwestern states in which they were concentrated, the Latino community did expand its civic involvement through the creation of civic organizations. The League of United Latin American Citizens had been formed in Corpus Christi in 1929, and the G.I. Forum was formed after World War II by returning Latino veterans. The Community Service organization, formed by Roybal and Fred Ross in 1947, had tremendous influence in California, as did another group headed by Roybal, the Mexican American Political Association, formed in 1960.

Although political victories for Latinos were limited during the 1940's, a new sense of citizenship and acculturation resulted from the Latino experience in the war and the new job opportunities that were a part of the war effort. The G.I. Bill and renewed educational opportunities gave Latinos a new sense of citizenship and a desire for political participation.

During the 1940's, Operation Bootstrap attempted to alleviate poor economic conditions on the island of Puerto Rico, and the war effort brought new opportunities for employment on the mainland. In response, nearly 400,000 Puerto Ricans came to the mainland, settling primarily in New Jersey, Connecticut, Chicago, and New York.

Impact World War II gave Latinos the opportunity to distinguish themselves in military service and to participate in the agricultural and industrial activity that supported the war effort. Both military service and new job opportunities allowed Latinos to expand their participation far beyond their local barrios and communities. The bracero program also increased the flow of both legal and illegal workers into the United States from Mexico, and Puerto Ricans moved to the mainland in significant numbers. After the war, Latinos increased their participation in multiple activities of American life in commerce, education, and politics.

Raymond J. Gonzales

Further Reading

Burt, Kenneth C. *The Search for a Civic Voice: California Latino Politics.* Claremont, Calif.: Regina Books, 2007. Discusses the origin and growth of the California Latino civic voice, providing a history of major players and organizations.

Divine, Robert A., H. H. Breen, George M. Fredrickson, and R. Hal Williams. *America, Past and Present.* Glenview, Ill.: Scott, Foresman, 1984. Textbook appropriate for a college survey course. Although the content is broad, there is good information on Latino social movements.

Meier, Matt, S., and Feliciano Ribera. *Mexican Americans/American Mexicans: From Conquistadors to Chicanos.* New York: Hill & Wang, 1993. A broad-ranging history of Mexican Americans, identifying their role in various social movements. More favorable to Mexican Americans than many other histories.

See also African Americans; Asian Americans; Bracero program; Civil rights and liberties; Latin America; Mexico; Native Americans; Zoot-suit riots.

■ *Laura*

Identification Crime drama about a beautiful woman, believed dead, who inspires obsession and loyalty
Director Otto Preminger (1906-1986)
Date Released in 1944

This major film noir, based on a 1943 novel by Vera Caspary, was a top picture directed by Otto Preminger that earned an Academy Award for cinematography by Joseph La Shelle.

The film's opening words come from a voice-over by Waldo Lydecker (played by Clifton Webb), who says he shall never forget the weekend Laura died. However, she actually is not dead. Misdirection continues throughout the film, leaving viewers unsure until the final scene who killed the woman found in Laura Hunt's apartment. The plot unfolds as a mystery, with detective Mark McPherson (Dana Andrews) leading the search to find Laura's killer. Played by Gene Tierney, Laura is the center of the film, although the audience believes her to be murdered until forty minutes into the film. When she returns, she finds Detective McPherson, presumably on duty, in a drunken sleep at her apartment. It is a glorious shock for him to see Laura

alive, but he wonders whether envy drove Laura to murder. Eventually he ferrets out the real murderer, who makes another attempt on Laura's life and is killed.

Impact Depicting the power women can wield in romance and work, *Laura* is a well-crafted mystery and tale of obsession, for which the film is much more important than the novel on which it is based. When Laura returns detective McPherson's love, the movie rewards the masculine type considered most heroic during the 1940's. The film remains notable for its cast and its style, contrived and artificial but somehow balanced and an exemplar of film noir.

Amy Cummins

Further Reading
Meyer, David. *A Girl and a Gun: The Complete Guide to Film Noir on Video.* New York: Avon, 1998.
Selby, Spencer. *Dark City: The Film Noir.* Jefferson, N.C.: McFarland, 1984.
Tibbetts, John, and James Welsh. *The Encyclopedia of Novels into Film.* 2d ed. New York: Facts On File, 2005.

See also Academy Awards; *Double Indemnity*; Film in the United States; Film noir; *The Maltese Falcon*.

Gene Tierney (left) as the title character in Laura, *returning to her apartment after a long absence to find a police detective (Dana Andrews) investigating her murder. Her portrait hangs over the fireplace.* (Getty Images)

■ Lend-Lease

Identification   Program through which the United
   States supplied Great Britain with war materials
Date   March 11, 1941-September 2, 1945

*The Lend-Lease Act of 1941 provided more than $50 bil-
lion to Great Britain, the Soviet Union, China, and other
allies of the United States during World War II, enabling
them to defeat Nazi Germany and Imperial Japan. The program began before the United States entered the war and
was structured so that the United States would technically
not violate its own neutrality.*

By the summer of 1940, Great Britain was the major European opponent of Nazi Germany's conquest of
Europe. The Soviet Union was allied
to Germany by the August, 1939,
nonaggression pact between the two
totalitarian states. The United States
was officially neutral, bound by several neutrality acts that forbade the
export of arms and ammunition
to foreign nations engaged in war.
That prohibition had been modified
in 1939, after the Nazi blitzkrieg
against Poland, to allow the sale of
war materials on a "cash and carry"
basis, but with the stipulation that
such items could not be carried on
American ships.

   After the fall of France in June,
1940, and subsequent Battle of Britain, the economic resources of the
United Kingdom were essentially exhausted. President Franklin D. Roosevelt received a letter from Prime
Minister Winston Churchill on December 9, 1940, noting the heavy
losses of British shipping from German submarine attacks and stating
that Britain would soon run out of
cash to buy American war material.

Suggestions of American Aid A
canny but often cautious politician,
Roosevelt held a news conference
ten days later in which he played
down the cash requirement, using
the analogy that one would be willing to loan a neighbor a garden hose if his house was on fire, and the
neighbor would return the hose once the fire was ex-
tinguished. During a December 29, 1940, "fireside
chat" broadcast on the radio, Roosevelt claimed that
if Britain and its empire fell, the Western Hemisphere
might be next to succumb to Nazi tyranny. The
United States must become "the great arsenal of democracy," although, he emphasized, not a combatant. In an address on January 6, 1941, he announced
that he was sending the Lend-Lease bill to Congress,
thus launching a vigorous national debate.

Lend-Lease Act

*The following text is from the Lend-Lease Act of 1941, "an act, further
to promote the defense of the United States, and for other purposes":*

Sec. 3. (a) Notwithstanding the provisions of any other law, the
President may, from time to time, when he deems it in the interest of national defense, authorize the Secretary of War, the
Secretary of the Navy, or the head of any other department or
agency of the Government,

(1) To manufacture in arsenals, factories, and shipyards under their jurisdiction, or otherwise procure, to the extent
to which funds are made available therefore, or contracts
are authorized from time to time by the Congress, or
both, any defense article for the government of any country whose defense the President deems vital to the defense of the United States.

(2) To sell, transfer title to, exchange, lease, lend, or otherwise dispose of, to any such government any defense article, but no defense article not manufactured or procured
under paragraph (1) shall in any way be disposed of under this paragraph, except after consultation with the
Chief of Staff of the Army or the Chief of Naval Operations of the Navy, or both. The value of defense articles
disposed of in any way under authority of this paragraph,
and procured from funds heretofore appropriated, shall
not exceed $1,300,000,000. . . .

(3) To test, inspect, prove, repair, outfit, recondition, or otherwise to place in good working order, to the extent to
which funds are made available therefore, or contracts
are authorized from time to time by the Congress, or
both, any defense article for any such government, or to
procure any or all such services by private contract.

British destroyer HMS Wells—*formerly the USS* Tillman—*one of fifty destroyers given to Britain's Royal Navy by the United States in exchange for a long lease on Caribbean military bases.* (AP/Wide World Photos)

Congressional hearings began a few days later, with the House of Representatives' bill cleverly given the number of H.R. 1776. Public opinion was strongly supportive, in part because Britain had successfully repelled the German attack in the Battle of Britain. Wendell Willkie, the recently defeated Republican presidential candidate, was chosen by Roosevelt to be the major advocate for Lend-Lease, while in London, Churchill somewhat disingenuously claimed that with Lend-Lease aid he foresaw no need for eventual American troops.

Opponents of the bill, many from the isolationist America First Committee, which included such iconic figures as aviator Charles A. Lindbergh, claimed the opposite and argued that Lend-Lease would inevitably lead to American participation in the war. Some argued that by sending war materials to Britain, the American rearmament program would be slowed. The pro-Nazi German American Bund and the American Communist Party were united in opposition, reflecting the alliance be-

tween Germany and the Soviet Union. The Chicago *Tribune*, the New York *Daily News*, and the Washington *Times-Herald* all opposed the bill. One of the most inflammatory statements against the Lend-Lease bill came from Montana's liberal senator Burton Wheeler. Referring to the New Deal's Agricultural Adjustment Administration (AAA) program, he called Lend-Lease the "triple-A foreign policy; it will plough under every fourth American boy."

To gain support for the Lend-Lease bill, to counter anti-British criticism from many traditional and Midwestern isolationists, and to establish the truth of the claim that Britain was at the end of its financial resources, the Roosevelt administration seized British assets in the United States, much to the private consternation of Churchill. The isolationist opposition was successful in amending the bill as it was debated in Congress, most notably in explicitly stating that United States naval vessels were prohibited from engaging in convoying ships carrying Lend-Lease items to Britain. The administration later got around that restriction by a semantic sleight-of-hand, stating that American ships were merely "escorting," not "convoying," the merchant ships.

Passage and Initial Operation The Lend-Lease bill easily passed both Houses of Congress in early March, 1941, by a margin of 60-31 in the Senate and 317-71 in the House of Representatives. On March 11, Roosevelt signed the bill (Public Law 77-11), and Congress quickly passed legislation providing for an initial $7 billion in aid to Britain. *The New York Times* saw passage of the bill as a reversal of the isolationist position that the United States had taken at the conclusion of World War I, when it had not ratified the Treaty of Versailles and thus not become a founding member state of the League of Nations.

Harry Hopkins, a close confidant of Roosevelt, was appointed the first head of the Office of Lend-Lease Administration. Several months later, he was replaced by Edward Stettinius, Jr., who held the position until 1943, when he was appointed undersecretary of state.

Because of the prohibition against convoying, initial shipments of Lend-Lease materials across the Atlantic to Britain went by British ships. In a speech to the House of Commons, Churchill said that Lend-Lease was the "most unsordid act in the history of any nation." Privately, however, Churchill remained incensed about the forced sale of British assets in the United States. Both sides—the British and the American—remained wary about the aims and actions of the other: whether the United States would continue to send the promised war materials to Britain and, from the American side, whether Britain would continue to fight against Nazi Germany or whether it might revert to the appeasement policies of its former prime minister, Neville Chamberlain. Despite suspicions, both sides were faithful to their commitments.

Extension of Aid By early 1941, the Battle of Britain had been won, but the Battle of the Atlantic had not. German U-boats were rapidly demolishing British shipping and, thus, Lend-Lease materials. To get around the prohibition against convoying, in April Roosevelt extended the American security zone to include Greenland, then later Iceland. Both were proclaimed to be in the Western Hemisphere, greatly increasing the area that legally could be defended by United States naval ships.

After the Nazi German invasion of the Soviet Union on June 22, 1941, in violation of the Soviet-German nonaggression pact of 1939, Lend-Lease aid was extended to the Soviet Union. Neither Roosevelt nor Churchill had any illusions about the Soviet Union and its totalitarian dictatorship, but they regarded Adolf Hitler and Nazi Germany as much worse. Lend-Lease was also extended to other states of the British Empire, including Australia and New Zealand. The United States extended the program to the Republic of China in the summer of 1941; the country had been engaged in war against Imperial Japan since 1937. After Japan's attack on Pearl Harbor on December 7, 1941, Hitler declared war against the United States, bringing to an end the prohibitions against convoying on the Atlantic.

By the end of World War II in 1945, United States Lend-Lease aid to about fifty allied states totaled more than $50 billion, with Great Britain and its empire receiving $31 billion and the Soviet Union more than $11 billion. Aid to Great Britain alone included everything from aircraft to prefabricated housing to cigarettes.

Impact In passing the Lend-Lease Act in March, 1941, the United States moved from its previous policy of providing aid to other democracies, short of war, to assisting the democracies even at the risk of war. Once that threshold had been crossed, Lend-Lease was a crucial element in aiding America's allies, which ultimately led to victory over Nazi Germany and Imperial Japan. The United States also engaged in so-called Reverse Lend-Lease, paying for supplies including food and for sites for military bases in Britain, Australia, and elsewhere; such payments amounted to more than $7 billion, most of that going to Britain.

After World War II was over, Europe was economically exhausted. The Lend-Lease program formally ended on September 2, 1945, but to assist Great Britain, the United States agreed to cancel much of Britain's Lend-Lease debt, allow equipment to stay in place, and sell Lend-Lease materials at drastically reduced prices. Lend-Lease to the Soviet Union ended formally in May, 1945, in a reflection of the increasing Cold War divisions, but shipments of material continued until September 20. The debt with the Soviet Union was not settled even provisionally until 1972, as part of the détente that led to the Strategic Arms Limitation Treaty of the same year.

Eugene Larson

Further Reading

Gilbert, Martin. *Road to Victory, 1941-1945*. Vol. 7 in *Winston S. Churchill*. London: Heinemann, 1986. In this definitive biography of Churchill, the author discusses Lend-Lease from the British perspective.

Herring, George C. *From Colony to Superpower*. New York: Oxford University Press, 2008. In this survey of American diplomacy, the author, a specialist on Lend-Lease, discusses the program.

Kennedy, David M. *Freedom from Fear*. New York: Oxford University Press, 1999. Extensive discussion of Lend-Lease by a major historian.

Kimball, Warren F. *The Most Unsordid Act: Lend-Lease, 1939-1941*. Baltimore, Md.: Johns Hopkins University Press, 1969. A major study of the Lend-Lease program.

Parish, Thomas. *To Keep the British Isles Afloat*. New York: HarperCollins, 2009. Claims that Harry Hopkins and Averell Harriman, a special envoy to Europe, were the key figures in implementing Lend-Lease.

Stettinius, Edward R., Jr. *Lend-Lease: Weapon for Victory*. New York: Macmillan, 1944. Stettinius was the second administrator of the Lend-Lease program.

See also   America First Committee; "Arsenal of Democracy" speech; Atlantic, Battle of the; Churchill, Winston; Destroyers-for-bases deal; Isolationism; Roosevelt, Franklin D.; Submarine warfare; Willkie, Wendell.

■ Levittown

Identification   Mass-produced suburban community

Date   First Levittown built between 1947 and 1951

Place   Long Island, New York

Levittown addressed the need for housing in the postwar period and was part of adjustments to the emerging baby boom and suburban lifestyle.

Located on Long Island in New York, the first Levittown community was the brainchild of William Levitt. Levitt, with his father, Abraham, and brother Alfred, was part of the successful real estate development firm of Levitt and Sons. Before the war, the firm had specialized in building upscale housing on Long Island. In 1941, the firm won a wartime government contract to build sixteen hundred houses for workers at the Norfolk shipyard. The Levitts figured out how to streamline the building process to make it more similar to mass production. Instead of building one house at a time, they divided the building process into twenty-seven steps and trained twenty-seven teams of workers, one to carry out each step.

William Levitt then joined the Seabees, the construction unit of the U.S. Navy, and spent the remainder of World War II building airstrips in the Pacific islands and talking to builders and craftsmen in his unit about how to perfect his building process. When he came back from the war, he saw the need for housing for military veterans. He had a vision not only of building middle-class houses cheaply and quickly, but also of stocking them with modern conveniences and creating neighborhoods around them.

On May 7, 1947, Levitt and Sons announced their plan to build a neighborhood called Island Trees on a stretch of old potato farms in Nassau County, Long Island. The community would contain two thousand brand-new homes, each of which would cost less than seven thousand dollars and would be available to veterans with no down payment.

The company was immediately besieged with offers, and more than half the homes had been rented within two days of the Levitts' announcement. By then, most G.I.'s had come home from Europe and the Pacific, and the post-World War II baby boom was just beginning. People were getting married and starting families at younger ages, and they were having larger families. This expansion in the young population, combined with a lack of available housing, meant that many young families were living either in cramped quarters with their parents or in makeshift housing such as garages and even in villages of Quonset huts.

Understanding that they were addressing a critical need, the Levitts worked with an eye toward precision, speed, and cost-effectiveness. They perfected their technique to the point where they could build up to thirty houses a day by July, 1948. They used concrete slab foundations, which had been forbidden before the housing shortage became acute, and used precut wood and nails from a factory the company created specifically for that purpose. A finished house measured 32 by 25 feet. The demand was so high for these homes that the firm immediately expanded the project to include four thousand more units.

Impact Although the Levitts originally named the community Island Trees, it quickly became known as Levittown. Between 1947 and 1951, the Levitts continually expanded the community until it eventually had 17,447 homes. Levitt and Sons went on to build three other Levittowns, in Pennsylvania, New Jersey, and Puerto Rico. Although Levittown was and is still often criticized for being overly conformist, sanitized, and racially homogeneous, it provided much-needed housing for young middle-class families and returning war veterans. In the long term, it provided a prototype for postwar suburbia.

Sara K. Eskridge

Aerial view of the first Levittown, on Long Island farmland in New York, during the late 1940's. (AP/Wide World Photos)

Further Reading

Matarrese, Lynne. *The History of Levittown, New York.* Levittown, N.Y.: Levittown Historical Society, 1997.

Nicolaides, Becky, and Andrew Wiese, eds. *The Suburb Reader.* London: Routledge, 2006.

See also Architecture; Business and the economy in the United States; G.I. Bill; Home appliances; Home furnishings; Urbanization in the United States.

■ Lewis, John L.

Identification Labor leader
Born February 12, 1880; Lucas, Iowa
Died June 11, 1969; Alexandria, Virginia

As head of the United Mine Workers of America and a founder of the Congress of Industrial Organizations, Lewis is one of the most important labor leaders of the twentieth century. During the 1940's, he led controversial strikes during World War II and challenged the policies of the Roosevelt administration.

John Llewellyn Lewis began life in poverty as the son of Welsh-born parents. He nearly completed high

school, an unusual achievement for a boy of his era and circumstances. After leaving school, Lewis followed his father into the coal mines. In 1901, he became a charter member and secretary of the United Mine Workers of America (UMWA). Lewis then left Lucas County, Iowa, to roam throughout the West as a miner and construction worker. He would later use the experience to bolster his claims of speaking for the working class. Lewis moved up the ranks of the UMWA and became a field representative for the American Federation of Labor (AFL). In 1920, Lewis became president of the UMWA, a position that he would hold until 1960. In 1935, he helped form the Committee for Industrial Organization (CIO), known as the Congress of Industrial Organizations after its 1938 break with the AFL.

By 1940, Lewis had a reputation for using armed force, red-baiting, and ballot-box stuffing to maintain his hold on power. Once a supporter of Franklin D. Roosevelt, Lewis became increasingly critical of the president's preparations for a possible U.S. entry into World War II. He charged that the United States risked the danger of being dragged into a war for the benefit of the British Empire. In a November, 1940, radio broadcast just before the presidential election, Lewis urged union members to support Republican candidate Wendell Willkie.

Lewis stepped down as CIO president in December, 1940. While the CIO supported the fight against fascism, Lewis remained highly critical of Roosevelt and the labor leaders who backed him. He charged that the CIO's dependence on the Roosevelt administration for war jobs threatened to destroy its independence as an advocate for workers. By 1942, Lewis and the UMWA had effectively left the CIO.

Lewis halted his opposition to World War II in the wake of the attack on Pearl Harbor. He and the UMWA then supported the war effort by endorsing the December, 1941, no-strike pledge. However, as inflation rose, coal miners were frustrated by their inability to win wage hikes from the National War Labor Board. In 1943, Lewis took the bituminous (soft coal) miners out on strike. The walkouts never damaged the ability of the United States to wage war, but they still earned near-universal condemnation from the general public. Congress responded to the strikes in June, 1943, by passing the Smith-Connally Act that regulated unions.

Following the end of the war, UMWA strikes became a regular occurrence as Lewis maintained a confrontational stance toward mine owners and the federal government. He managed to win both health care and pension benefits for union members. After 1950, as demand for bituminous coal dropped, Lewis became more conciliatory while the UMWA sunk into corruption. Lewis retired from the much-weakened UMWA in 1960.

Impact   Lewis became the face of labor during the 1940's. A confrontational and power-hungry man who took inconsistent public positions, Lewis benefited coal miners in the short run but cost the labor movement allies in the long run.

Caryn E. Neumann

Further Reading

Dubofsky, Melvyn, and Warren Van Tine. *John L. Lewis: A Biography.* New York: Quadrangle, 1977.
Zieger, Robert H. *John L. Lewis: Labor Leader.* Boston: Twayne, 1988.

See also   American Federation of Labor; Congress of Industrial Organizations; Ford Motor Company; Labor strikes; Smith-Connally Act.

■ Liberty ships

Definition   Mass-produced military cargo ships

Tough, mass-produced cargo vessels, Liberty ships played a significant role in the Allied victory in World War II. The 2,700 ships built during the war supplied both U.S. and allied military units around the world, making it possible for the Allies to fight a successful two-ocean war. The ability of the United States to produce the ships in large numbers reflected the strength of the American economy and the versatility of its manufacturing sector. Moreover, the large shipyard workforces on both coasts reflected American diversity, with male and female, young and old, black and white, and immigrant and native-born workers all contributing to the war effort. About 40 percent of the welders who worked on Liberty ships were women.

American-made Liberty ships were the workhorses of the American, Canadian, and British naval fleets. Most ships were 440 feet long with a 3,435-ton steel hull and lumbered along at a mere ten knots. A single ship could carry as many as 300 railroad freight cars, 2,840 jeeps, 440 tanks, or enough C-ration to provide troops with 3.4 million meals. The deck of a ship alone could carry up to ten locomotives. Some were converted into hospital ships, and others were used as troopships.

President Franklin D. Roosevelt, a former Navy secretary, called the Liberty ship an "ugly duckling," but a more fitting description from that era was "Model T of the Seas," referring to the durable and mass-produced automobiles made by Ford Motor Company. The ships were built in a manner similar to that of Ford's Model's, which were built on assembly lines. Parts of the ships were assembled in huge sheds and put in place by enormous cranes. As a time-saving measure, the ships' hulls were welded together, not riveted. This was a controversial practice, particularly after the hulls of some ships broke open in heavy seas.

Manufacturing the Ships   The first Liberty ship was launched in December, 1941, in Baltimore Harbor, which still has a working Liberty ship on display. Initially, it took almost an entire year to produce a single ship. However, within six months, production time was cut to 105 days. By 1943, it was down to 41 days. The driving force behind this increased rate of production was industrialist Henry J. Kaiser, whose shipyards on both coasts eventually turned out new

Liberty ship loaded with trucks departing for Europe in April, 1944. (AP/Wide World Photos)

ships at a rate of about one per day, using revolutionary techniques of shipbuilding. Kaiser had developed techniques of prefabricating large components while working on dam-building projects. In recognition of his contributions to wartime shipbuilding, Kaiser earned the nickname "Sir Launchalot." As a publicity stunt, Kaiser's Richmond, California, shipyard built the *Robert E. Peary* Liberty ship in only four days, fifteen hours, and twenty-six minutes, using a massive workforce around the clock. Nothing like this speed of modern ship production had ever been seen.

Impact Liberty ships made it possible to supply American and Allied forces throughout the war and transport military ordinance worldwide. Convoys of Liberty ships plied the Atlantic and Pacific Oceans and the Mediterranean Sea throughout the war. The most dangerous journeys the ships undertook were to the Arctic Sea to supply the Soviet Union. In the early stages of the war, German U-boats crippled Al-

lied war efforts in the Battle of the Atlantic by sinking an enormous tonnage of ships. In response, the United States determined to build new ships faster than they could be sunk. Liberty ships made strategy work and helped to overwhelm Axis forces with equipment and supplies, especially after the U-boat menace was curtailed.

Henry Weisser

Further Reading

Bunker, John Gorley. *Liberty Ships: The Ugly Ducklings of World War II*. Annapolis, Md.: Naval Institute Press, 1972.

Elphick, Peter. *Liberty: The Ships That Won the War*. Annapolis, Md.: Naval Institute Press, 2001.

King, Ernest. *U.S. Navy at War, 1941-1945*. Washington, D.C.: Government Printing Office, 1946.

See also Atlantic, Battle of the; *History of the United States Naval Operations in World War II*; Kaiser, Henry J.; Navy, U.S.; Wartime industries.

■ *Life*

Identification   Weekly large-format magazine devoted to pictorial journalism
Publisher   Henry R. Luce (1898-1967)
Date   First issue released on November 23, 1936

Life was the first popular American magazine based on the emotional power and journalistic possibilities of the photographic image. The influential weekly pioneered the concept of the picture essay, built on a series of photographic images, and necessitated new printing technologies able to produce a huge volume of magazines on high-quality paper in a short time. Originally sold at American newsstands for a dime, Life *was an immediate hit with readers (and advertisers) and enjoyed great success for two generations.*

In 1936, Henry R. Luce, with colleagues from Time Inc., solidified plans for a new weekly based on pictorial journalism. Luce bought the name and assets of *Life* magazine, a literary and entertainment magazine in its fifty-fourth year of publication, to use its title for his version of *Life.* Already a major force in the media world, with the magazines *Time* (1923) and *Fortune* (1930) and the newsreel *The March of Time* (weekly beginning in 1931; monthly in 1935) under his control, Luce sought to mobilize what he called "picture magic" into a commercially viable, journalistically respectable publishing venture.

Memorable photographs were vital for the new magazine's success, and *Life* assembled a staff of top photographers. The first issue displayed five pages of photographs by Alfred Eisenstaedt. Margaret Bourke-White, previously at *Fortune,* shot the first cover image, a now iconic view of Fort Peck Dam. Inside the issue were candid photographs of the Montana dam community. In what quickly became a signature style, the new magazine presented a strip of photographs in a narrative sequence over eight pages, resulting in a photographic essay. The images were accompanied by short, clear captions, and the series concluded with a single-paragraph summary.

Many of the key figures in the formation and early production of *Life* were men still in their thirties, as was the first managing editor, John Shaw Billings, who held the post for eight years before becoming director of Time Inc. The first issue of *Life* sold out nationwide the first day; within four months, one million copies were circulating, many with a substantial "pass-along" readership. Be-

The tenth anniversary cover of Life *in November, 1946, featured a picture of a young girl reading a copy of the magazine's first issue.* (Time & Life Pictures/Getty Images)

cause of the huge demand, *Life* actually lost money at first, since advertising rates had been sold for a predicted, far smaller readership; however, by 1938 the magazine was profitable.

Introduced during the Depression years, *Life* nevertheless adopted a conservative tone, supporting business and opposing unions, and was decidedly pro-American. In early 1941, Luce appealed directly to readers in a five-page, picture-free essay titled "The American Century" in which he outlined the responsibilities of American leadership in world affairs. Later that year, the United States entered World War II and *Life* became a war magazine with forty war correspondents (six of them women). For more than two hundred issues, war-connected photographs and stories dominated the pages of *Life*, including home-front coverage, typically emphasizing American pluck, good humor, and optimism. Relations between the magazine and military censors became increasing tense as the war continued, yet the War and Navy departments realized that *Life* supported the war effort and commanded the attention of millions. George Strock's striking photograph of three dead G.I.'s on a beach in New Guinea found its way past censors who had forbidden images of American casualties.

Life stationed journalists in all war theaters; remarkable pictures of the war, often shot on battlefields at great risk by photographers—most notably Bourke-White, Robert Capa, David Douglas Duncan, Henri Huet, and W. Eugene Smith—would leave lasting images in the minds of millions. But it was not only photographs that made an impact: The July 5, 1943, issue, in twenty-three pages, listed the name, state, and hometown of the 12,987 Americans who had been killed in the first eighteen months of the war. Victory was also celebrated pictorially, with the photograph by Eisenstaedt of a sailor embracing a nurse in New York's Times Square on V-J Day becoming one of the most reproduced, and beloved, photographs of the war years.

After the war, *Life* turned its attention to the attractions, complexities, and daily dramas of modern living. In 1946, the newsstand price had risen to fifteen cents, with paid circulation over 5 million and estimates of a weekly readership greater than 20 million. Luce's Republican desires embarrassed him when he approved a story about Thomas E. Dewey, described as "the next president" in an issue that closed a few days before Harry S. Truman was

elected president in November, 1948. Although Luce well understood that photographs such as Rita Hayworth posing in a nightgown and animals in surprising postures drew readers, he also urged attention to art. The art features retained popular appeal, however, such as the 1949 Christmas issue that included a twenty-two-page color essay on Michelangelo's frescoes in the Sistine Chapel.

Under the leadership of the managing editor Edward K. Thompson, *Life* prospered. The skilled efforts of Mary Hamman, modern living editor, Mary Letherbee, movie editor, and Sally Kirkland, fashion editor, dispelled the original fear that *Life* would not appeal to women readers. In the postwar years, *Life* carried fiction by admired authors and serialized the memoirs of Sir Winston Churchill, President Harry S. Truman, and General Douglas MacArthur. In the first twenty years of *Life*, advertising revenue exceeded $1 billion.

The ubiquitous stream of images on television and the changing tastes of Americans during the 1960's diminished the conservative appeal of *Life*. The magazine experimented with different emphases, formats, and even magazine size in the next decades, but it never regained its prominence. Between 1972 and 1978, the magazine appeared intermittently, then as a monthly from 1978 to 2000, and finally as a weekly newspaper supplement from 2004 to 2007. A new Internet life for *Life* photographs emerged in the new century. First, in partnership with Google in November, 2008, *Life* made its photographic archives accessible; then, in March, 2009, Life.com, a joint venture between Getty Images and *Life*, was launched, introducing a new audience to memorable photographs from *Life*.

Impact   The tremendous success of *Life* spawned a cluster of general-interest "look-through" magazines, most immediately and directly the biweekly *Look* (1937-1971). *Life* shaped a new style of American print advertising and solidified the narrative possibilities of striking images.

Carolyn Anderson

Further Reading

Angeletti, Norberto, and Alberto Oliva. *Magazines That Make History: Their Origins, Development, and Influence*. Gainesville: University Press of Florida, 2004. Discusses the evolution of eight of the most successful magazines in the West, including *Life*, *Time*, *National Geographic*, *¡Hola!*, and *People*.

Doss, Erika, ed. *Looking at "Life" Magazine.* Washington, D.C.: Smithsonian Institution Press, 2001. Twelve essays examine the magazine from a variety of perspectives, including class, gender, and race.

Wainwright, Loudon. *The Great American Magazine: An Inside History of "Life."* New York: Alfred A. Knopf, 1986. Wainwright, a longtime columnist for *Life*, offers a book that is part history, part memoir.

See also   Bourke-White, Margaret; Censorship in the United States; *Look*; *Maclean's*; Magazines; Photography; Pinup girls; *Saturday Evening Post.*

■ Literature in Canada

During the 1940's, Canadian writers began to develop a literature that reflected their way of life and their unique history.

During the early part of the twentieth century, Canada was still a frontier country. Although it did have three urban centers—Montreal, Toronto, and Vancouver—between them stretched thousands of acres of prairie and wilderness, dotted with small settlements that were miles apart. The pioneers who lived in this vast area were too preoccupied with survival to have time for thought-provoking reading. Their remedy for isolation was a good thriller, a sentimental love story, or a gripping historical romance. Canadians liked books whose heroes and heroines possessed the character traits that were essential for nation-building. Thus, one of the most popular writers of the early twentieth century was Alan Sullivan, who drew upon his experiences as an engineer, explorer, prospector, and successful capitalist to produce dozens of novels that glorified heroic individualism. Sullivan's works were admired as much by critics as they were by the reading public. One of his last books to be published before his death, the historical romance *Three Came to Ville Marie* (1941), won the Governor General's Award for fiction.

One of the newer writers to emerge during the 1940's was Thomas Head Raddall. Raddall won a Governor General's Award for his first collection of short fiction, *The Pied Piper of Dipper Creek, and Other Tales* (1939). However, though he continued to write short stories during the decade, he also published three impressive historical novels. Although he always insisted that his primary purpose was to entertain his readers, Raddall was acclaimed by critics for his accuracy in his depiction of Nova Scotia, where most of his fiction was set, and for his gifts as a historian, which were evident not only in his novels but also in books such as *Halifax: Warden of the North* (1948), which won the Governor General's Award for nonfiction. Raddall's achievements as a writer were further honored in 1949, when he was made a fellow of the Royal Society of Canada.

New Directions in Prose   Though traditional fiction and nonfiction about Canada's early history continued to be popular during the 1940's, the decade was also a period of experimentation with prose genres. For example, Morley Callaghan, who during the 1920's and 1930's had published fiction that won him international acclaim, now tried his hand at writing film scripts and even made appearances on radio shows. He published only two novels during the decade, and one of them was negligible. However, the other took an established genre in a new direction. *Luke Baldwin's Vow* (1948) was very different from the sentimental fare that had traditionally been offered to children; Callaghan's novel about the relationship between a boy and a dog demonstrated that a story written for young readers could be both as realistic and as profound as one intended for adults.

The autobiographical volumes written by Emily Carr were also destined to become Canadian classics. After decades of neglect, Carr had finally been recognized as one of Canada's most talented artists. In her latter years, however, failing health made it impossible for her to continue spending long hours at her painting, and Carr decided to turn her creative talents to writing. Her first volume of memoirs, *Klee Wyck* (1941), which describes her early years among the First Nations people, won the Governor General's Award for nonfiction. It was followed by *The Book of Small* (1942), *The House of All Sorts* (1944), and *Growing Pains* (1946). Writing with a painter's eye for detail, Carr produced prose as unique as her paintings.

Humorous works had long been popular in Canada. Indeed, from the time his first book of humor appeared in 1910, Stephen Leacock could be said to have dominated the genre and even to have defined it. However, in 1947 Paul Gerhardt Hiebert published a mock biography called *Sarah Binks*, in which he satirized academics, literary critics, and local poets, as well as sentimentality and provincialism. *Sarah Binks* won Hiebert the Stephen Leacock Memorial Medal for Humour. Though he later wrote other humorous books, it was *Sarah Binks* that established Hiebert's reputation as one of Canada's outstanding humorists.

Late in the 1920's, Felix Paul Greve, a German writer, who after his arrival in Canada changed his name to Frederick Philip Grove, began publishing realistic novels about the experiences of immigrants in their new country. Though his books were often clumsily written, they were significant in that their theme was the contrast between what Canada could be, a place where freedom and justice prevailed, and what it was becoming, a country as corrupt, materialistic, and spiritually dead as the societies from which immigrants like himself had fled. In one of his later novels, *The Master of the Mill* (1944), Grove experimented with modernist techniques, relying heavily on symbolism and structuring his story psychologically rather than chronologically. Thus, Grove led the way to a new kind of Canadian novel, one that would be sophisticated enough to compete with fiction imported from Great Britain and the United States, which during the 1940's was still the standard fare of educated Canadians.

Hugh MacLennan saw that the only way to attract Canadian readers to novels written by Canadians was to use local settings and to appeal to national pride. The success of his first novel, *Barometer Rising* (1941), which was set in Halifax, Nova Scotia, and culminated with the disastrous explosion of 1917, proved that MacLennan was right. *Barometer Rising* sold well not only in Canada but also in the United States. The author won a Governor General's Award for each of the two novels that followed, *Two Solitudes* (1945) and *The Precipice* (1948). Throughout a long, productive life, MacLennan was credited with establishing literary fiction in Canada and with making it possible for other new writers to acquire an appreciative audience. Among them were Sinclair Ross, whose *As For Me and My House* (1941) has become one of Canada's best-known novels; Ethel Wilson, whose novel *Hetty Dorval* appeared in 1947; and W. O. Mitchell, whose first novel, *Who Has Seen the Wind*, was also published that year. Gwethalyn Graham won the Governor General's Award and international acclaim for her second novel, *Earth and High Heaven*

(1944), while *Bonheur d'occasion* (1945), translated as *The Tin Flute*, which also won the Governor General's Award, marked the beginning of an illustrious career for the francophone author Gabrielle Roy.

New Directions in Poetry   Though Canada lagged behind the rest of the Western world in accepting modernism, traditional poetry of a high literary quality had been published in Canada as early as the late nineteenth century. E. J. Pratt is generally credited with bridging the gap between those early "Confederation poets" and the more experimental poets of the 1940's. Thus, in the long poem *Brébeuf and His Brethren* (1940), Pratt turns to the epic tradition in order to tell a Canadian story. By emphasizing the heroism not only of the Jesuit missionaries but also of the Iroquois who killed them, Pratt introduced a quality of ambivalence into his poem that would be typical of the modernists. Though some critics found it puzzling, *Brébeuf and His Brethren* was generally much admired, winning the Governor General's Award for poetry.

During the 1920's, A. J. M. Smith, a student at McGill University, initiated a crusade whose purpose was to introduce modernism into Canadian poetry. He was soon joined by a law student, F. R. Scott, and what became known as the "McGill Movement" included, among others, A. M. Klein, Leo Kennedy, and Leon Edel. Since all five of these poets were from Montreal, they were later called the "Montreal Group." By the 1940's, they had made considerable progress in their campaign on behalf of modernism. Their poems were being published both in periodicals and in book form, and they were also being selected for Governor General's Awards. Smith's *News of the Phoenix* won the poetry award in 1943, and Klein's *The Rocking Chair, and Other Poems* in 1948. Smith's influence persisted not only through his poetry but also through his work as an editor. One of his edited works, *The Book of Canadian Poetry: A Critical and Historical Anthology* (1943), which leaned heavily toward modernist poems, was particularly important because it was widely adopted for use as a textbook, thus molding the poetic tastes of the new generation.

Another influential figure in developing a Canadian literary tradition was Earle Birney, who had been a journalist and a scholar for some years before he began writing poetry. His preoccupation with life and death issues was evident in his first volume, *Da-*

vid, and Other Poems (1942), which won a Governor General's Award for poetry, and in *Now Is Time* (1945), which reflected his wartime experiences. In 1946, Birney accepted an academic appointment at the University of British Columbia in Vancouver, where he continued to utilize western materials in his poetry and to work toward introducing westerners to works by Canadian writers. Another poet associated with the Canadian west was Dorothy Livesay, who moved to Vancouver in 1936 and made her home there for the next two decades. During the 1940's, Livesay won two Governor General's Awards for poetry, one for *Day and Night* in 1944, and another for *Poems for People* in 1947. Livesay is now considered one of Canada's most important writers.

Impact   During the 1940's, Canadian writers continued working to establish a Canadian literary tradition. Some utilized traditional forms in order to explore the Canadian past and to express what they saw as a uniquely Canadian view of the world and of its heroic people, while others experimented with various prose genres and with new poetic forms. The efforts of these writers would bear fruit in the next decade, which would see the development of new literary communities, the births of new periodicals, the establishment of new awards and prizes, and the beginnings of a new interest in books of high literary quality that were written by Canadians, which would eventually attract new readers not only within the borders of Canada but also throughout the world.

Rosemary M. Canfield Reisman

Further Reading

Atwood, Margaret. *Survival: A Thematic Guide to Canadian Literature.* Toronto: Anansi, 1972. One of Canada's most illustrious writers argues that the various patterns found in Canadian literature can all be related to the theme of survival. Essential reading for any student of the subject.

Hammill, Faye. *Canadian Literature.* Edinburgh: Edinburgh University Press, 2007. Combines historical and thematic approaches to texts by important writers, including E. J. Pratt. Excellent introduction and historical synopsis. Includes chronology, glossary, list of student resources, and bibliography.

Keith, W. J. *Canadian Literature in English.* New York: Longman, 1985. Sections on fiction and on poetry show how these branches of literature developed during the 1940's. Useful chronology, brief notes on individual authors, bibliography, and index.

Meyer, Bruce, and Brian O'Riordan, eds. *In Their Words: Interviews with Fourteen Canadian Writers.* Toronto: Anansi, 1984. In-depth interviews with several of the major writers of the 1940's are included in this volume. Photographs and index.

New, William H. *A History of Canadian Literature.* 2d ed. Montreal: McGill-Queen's University Press, 2003. Traces the development of Canadian literature from First Nations myths through the early years of the twenty-first century. Chronology and bibliography. Indispensable.

Waterston, Elizabeth. *Children's Literature in Canada.* New York: Twayne, 1992. Shows how traditional types of writing for children and young adults were adapted to reflect Canadian tastes and preoccupations. Chronology, notes, bibliography, and index.

See also   Book publishing; Canadian minority communities; Canadian nationalism; Canadian participation in World War II; Film in Canada; Immigration to Canada; Literature in the United States; *Maclean's*; Theater in Canada; Women's roles and rights in Canada.

■ Literature in the United States

American literature of the 1940's reflects the history and the tensions of this volatile decade, while pointing forward to literary issues of the next half century.

The 1940's is divided evenly by World War II: The first half of the decade was consumed by the war, while the second half recovered from it. Viewed from a perspective only slightly higher—as the middle of the three decades from 1930 to 1960—the 1940's can still be seen as split into two halves, for the period of 1930 to 1945 was a time of first economic and then military sacrifice and suffering, while the second fifteen-year period, from 1945 to 1960, was a time of recovery and normalization. The literature of the 1940's reflects this deep division. Its first half carries echoes of the Depression of the 1930's and a commitment to the war effort, a continuous fifteen years in which Americans were joined in a mutual, national effort of survival, while its second half reflects growing prosperity, but with an increasing spiritual emptiness at its center that would deepen in the decade of the 1950's.

Interwar Period   The literary giants of the interwar period continued to write into the 1940's, even as their popularity waned, and the spirit of the 1920's and 1930's continued to inform their work. John Steinbeck won the Pulitzer Prize in fiction in 1940 for *The Grapes of Wrath* (1939), and the film of the novel appeared in 1941, a fresh reminder—as if Americans needed one—of the economic hardships of the 1930's. Steinbeck continued to publish through the 1940's, producing *Cannery Row* (1945) and *The Pearl* (1947), among other works. Ernest Hemingway's *For Whom the Bell Tolls*, a novel told from the Republican side of the Spanish Civil War (1936-1939), was published in 1940 and stayed on the best seller lists for two years, perhaps because it gave readers the war fiction they were beginning to crave.

F. Scott Fitzgerald's final, unfinished novel, *The Last Tycoon*, was published in 1941. William Faulkner—who was out of print in his own country in 1944 but would win the Nobel Prize in Literature in 1949, as Hemingway would in 1954, and Steinbeck in 1962—continued to produce fiction during the 1940's: *The Hamlet* (the first volume of the trilogy that would include *The Town* in 1957 and *The Mansion* in 1959) appeared in 1940, *Go Down, Moses* (a collection of stories containing most notably "The Bear") in 1942, and *Intruder in the Dust* in 1948. Richard Wright's *Native Son*, a powerful indictment of the brutal conditions for African Americans in Chicago, also appeared in 1940, and his autobiography of his struggles growing up, *Black Boy*, was published in 1945.

The radical literary spirit of the Depression continued to inform these literary works of the early 1940's, as in Lillian Hellman's antifascist play *Watch on the Rhine* (pr. 1940), or James Agee and Walker Evans's *Let Us Now Praise Famous Men* (1941), the powerful photojournalistic account of the plight of tenant farmers in Alabama during the late 1930's. That spirit can also be seen in the best sellers of William Saroyan (*My Name Is Aram*, 1940; *The Human Comedy*, 1943), in popular plays (John Van Druten's *I Remember Mama*, pr. 1944) and novels (Betty Smith's *A Tree Grows in Brooklyn*, 1943), and even in the gritty realism of Nelson Algren's *The Man with the Golden Arm* (1949; winner of the first National Book Award), but

it is in the first years of the 1940's that the figures and themes and progressive spirit of the Depression lived on most forcefully, even as the war deepened.

World War II   World War II emerged as a literary focus soon after the 1940's started. William L. Shirer's *Berlin Diary*, an account of the rise of Adolf Hitler and fascism, was a best seller in 1941; the legendary war correspondent Ernie Pyle's *Here Is Your War* and Richard Tregaskis's *Guadalcanal Diary* in 1943; Pyle's *Brave Men* in 1944; and cartoonist Bill Mauldin's *Up Front* in 1945. Perhaps the most important American writer to come out of World War II was John Hersey, who wrote about the fall of the Philippines to the Japanese in *Men on Bataan* (1942); the novel about the Italian campaign, *A Bell for Adano* (which won the Pulitzer Prize in fiction in 1945); and *Hiroshima*, the single most important account of the consequences of the atomic bombs dropped on Japan and a book that first appeared as an entire 1946 issue of *The New Yorker*.

William Faulkner at the October, 1949, premiere of a film adaptation of his 1948 novel Intruder in the Dust. *(Time & Life Pictures/Getty Images)*

In the second half of the 1940's, more fiction about the war began to appear. Earlier nonfiction accounts of the war were often produced by war correspondents, like Pyle and Mauldin, who collected their reportage into books. Fiction about the war, which took longer to gestate and to shape, appeared during the late 1940's into the 1950's. Thomas Heggen wrote *Mister Roberts* (later a successful play and then a movie) in 1946; John Horn Burns's *The Gallery*, a critically acclaimed novel about the occupying American Army in Europe, appeared in 1947; Norman Mailer's *The Naked and the Dead*, Irwin Shaw's *The Young Lions*, James Gould Cozzens's *Guard of Honor* (which won the Pulitzer Prize in fiction) were published in 1948; John Hawkes's *The Cannibal*, a novel about German reconstruction, appeared in 1949.

The Mailer and Shaw novels, along with James Jones's *From Here to Eternity* (1951), are considered the three best novels to come out of World War II, with Mailer's leading the trio in critical acclaim. Only twenty-six when *The Naked and the Dead* was published, Mailer had served in the Pacific theater, and his realistic novel showed his familiarity with the locale and struggles of that phase of the war. The novel focuses on an infantry platoon stationed on a Japanese-held island in the South Pacific, trying to survive and find meaning and dignity in the midst of the horrors of war. The novel became a best seller in part because readers needed to find meaning in that horrific war as well. Like Saul Bellow and Arthur Miller, Mailer was one of the new generation of writers who would emerge right after World War II and go on to a long writing career.

Postwar Era Bellow, Mailer, Miller, and the other younger writers who emerged during the 1940's as forces in American literature did so in part because the themes they confronted in their works were the concerns Americans had in their own lives. In the first half of the 1940's, those themes were survival and community, as Hemingway, Steinbeck, and other Depression-era writers had established. The lessons of the Depression and the war were that people could only survive if they sacrificed the self for others: the Joads create a larger migrant community in order to survive by the end of *The Grapes of Wrath*, as Robert Jordan sacrifices himself to save the other guerrilla fighters at the end of *For Whom the Bell Tolls*. By 1972, some thirty years later, families would be

crowding around their television sets for the weekly episode of *The Waltons* to recapture that feeling of sacrifice and community, because it had been lost. The change began in the second half of the 1940's, when the issues and themes shifted to much more individual concerns, such as the question of identity, the meaning of freedom, and the fear of conformity. The British-born poet W. H. Auden, who became a U.S. citizen just a year before, titled his 1947 book-length poem *The Age of Anxiety*, and the term applies to the second half of the 1940's as well as any other period.

The war, like the Depression, had given Americans focus and solidarity; the postwar world only echoed the loss of those values. The search for meaning in the midst of suffering was one of Mailer's main themes, but it characterized other important works at the end of the decade as well. Bellow's earliest novels—*Dangling Man* (1944) and *The Victim* (1947)—captured that sense of the loss of meaning before any other American novelist. In those novels, protagonists—"dangling victims"—seem to have little power over their own fates, and their existential condition is primarily characterized by isolation and alienation.

Albert Camus's *L'Étranger* (1942; *The Stranger*, 1946) was the foremost fictional reflection of the French philosophy of existentialism that hit America during World War II and would continue to influence American writers for the next twenty years, including Bellow, Mailer, and Paul Bowles (*The Sheltering Sky*, 1949). The new climate of violence and isolation was also reflected in the proliferation of crime novels during the 1940's, not only by established mystery writers such as Raymond Chandler (*Farewell, My Lovely*, 1940; *The Lady in the Lake*, 1943), James M. Cain (*Mildred Pierce*, 1941), and Rex Stout (*Not Quite Dead Enough*, 1944), but by younger writers such as Mickey Spillane (*I, the Jury*, 1947) and Ross Macdonald (*The Moving Target*, 1949), who even more graphically captured the mood of the late 1940's. The beginnings of film noir during the 1940's mirrored this same feeling.

Drama The themes of loss, isolation, and the search for self were prominent in the drama of the 1940's as well. The giant of the American theater, Eugene O'Neill, continued to produce plays during the 1940's, as he had since 1917—*A Long Day's Journey* *into Night* in 1940, and *The Iceman Cometh* in 1946—but, as in fiction, a new generation of playwrights, led by Arthur Miller and Tennessee Williams, was beginning to emerge. Their themes reflected much more the concerns and anxieties of the United States in a postwar world. In Williams's *The Glass Menagerie* (pr. 1945) and *A Streetcar Named Desire* (pr. 1947) and in Miller's *All My Sons* (pr. 1946) and especially *Death of a Salesman* (pr. 1949), the sense of survival in community that had characterized the plays of Lillian Hellman, Clifford Odets (*Waiting for Lefty*, pr. 1935), Marc Blitzstein (*The Cradle Will Rock*, pr. 1937), William Saroyan (*The Time of Your Life*, pr. 1939, which took the Pulitzer Prize in drama), and other playwrights during the 1930's had been replaced by themes of isolation, disillusionment, and meaninglessness. Williams's characters are emotionally crippled, and sexuality and violence have become their language; in Miller, work and family fail to provide the meaning characters search for, and, as in Williams, characters live in dreams.

Regionalism Williams's southern settings are also a reminder of the beginning regionalization of American literature after the war, and in particular the emerging prominence of southern writing. In addition to Faulkner, other southern writers who published during the 1940's included Thomas Wolfe (*You Can't Go Home Again*, 1940), Marjorie Kinnan Rawlings (*Cross Creek*, 1942), Katherine Anne Porter (*The Leaning Tower*, stories, 1944), Robert Penn Warren (*All the King's Men*, the lightly fictionalized story of the life and death of Governor Huey P. Long of Louisiana that won the Pulitzer in 1946), Eudora Welty (*Delta Wedding*, 1947), Erskine Caldwell, Peter Taylor, and Caroline Gordon.

A subgenre of this regional literature is what would come to be known as Southern Gothic. Faulkner's novels again reveal the origins of this movement, in which southern settings are the locales for stories of sex and violence peopled by a gallery of grotesque, often brutal characters. *Intruder in the Dust* (1948), to cite but one example, includes a murder, a near-lynching, a reopened grave, and a suicide, all taking place in Faulkner's fictional Yoknapatawpha County, Mississippi. Faulkner's gothic moods are echoed during the 1940's in Carson McCullers (*The Heart Is a Lonely Hunter*, 1940; *The Member of the Wedding*, 1946) and Truman Capote

Robert Penn Warren. (©Washington Post/Courtesy of the D.C. Public Library)

(*Other Voices, Other Rooms*, 1948), among other writers.

The West also emerged as a distinctive literary region during the 1940's, both in fiction—Saroyan, Walter Van Tilburg Clark (*The Ox-Bow Incident*, 1940; *Track of the Cat*, 1949), Wallace Stegner (*The Big Rock Candy Mountain*, 1943), and A. B. Guthrie (*The Big Sky*, 1947; *The Way West*, 1949, which won a Pulitzer)—and in history: Carey McWilliams (*Brothers Under the Skin*, 1943; *Southern California Country*, 1946), and Bernard DeVoto (who won a Pulitzer in 1947 for *Across the Wide Missouri*). Another example of this beginning fragmentation of American literature was the development of a distinct Jewish American fiction, which would include Mailer, Bellow, Miller, Budd Schulberg (*What Makes Sammy Run?*, 1941), J. D. Salinger (whose stories began to appear in *The New Yorker* at the end of the 1940's), and a widening number of writers into the 1950's. Finally, African American writers emerged to show that the Harlem

Renaissance of the 1920's had only been preview: In addition to Richard Wright, they included Langston Hughes (*The Big Sea*, autobiography, 1940), Zora Neale Hurston (*Dust Tracks on a Road*, autobiography, 1942), Chester Himes *(If He Hollers Let Him Go*, novel, 1945), Gwendolyn Brooks (*A Street in Bronzeville*, verse, 1945), Willard Motley (*Knock on Any Door*, novel, 1945), and Ann Petry (*The Street*, novel, 1946).

What this regionalization or fragmentation represented was the breakdown of any sense of a cohesive national American literature and the recognition that different regions and varied ethnic and cultural groups in the United States had their own unique and vital voices. Gore Vidal's novel *The City and the Pillar* (1948), for example, is an early model for gay American literature. The literary melting pot was giving way to the salad bowl, which, by the end of the twentieth century, would include the literature of every racial and cultural group in America.

Poetry During this same period, other literary genres were narrowing. Poetry, which had exploded in the interwar period, became much more limited in scope and accessibility. The giants of the poetic renaissance of 1915-1940—Wallace Stevens (*Parts of a World*, 1942), T. S. Eliot (*Four Quartets*, 1943), E. E. Cummings (*1 x 1*, 1944), Ezra Pound (*The Cantos of Ezra Pound*, 1948), and William Carlos Williams (*Paterson, Book III*, 1949)—continued to publish, but they seemed less relevant than the newer generation of poets who appeared after 1940, such as Richard Wilbur (*The Beautiful Changes*, 1947), Robert Lowell (*Lord Weary's Castle*, 1947), and John Berryman (*The Dispossessed*, 1948). Poetry became increasingly ironic, allusive, dense, and obscure, and seemed to be written for college audiences rather than for the general reader. Robert Frost published his *Complete Poems* in 1949, and Stephen Vincent Benét (*Western Star* won the Pulitzer Prize in poetry in 1943) and Edna St. Vincent Millay (*Collected Sonnets*, 1941) continued to publish, but the poetry stage was increasingly occupied by writers like Theodore Roethke (*The Lost Son*, 1948) and Muriel Rukeyser (*The Green Wave*, 1948).

The change in American poetry can be traced to a distinct shift in literary values. The loudest literary critics of the 1930's were on the Left, Marxists who demanded that literature be responsible and address social issues. With or without their shouts, literature often contained social realist themes. Toward the end of the 1930's, Robert Penn Warren and Cleanth Brooks published two very influential textbooks, *Understanding Poetry* (1938) and *Understanding Fiction* (1943), which modeled a much more formalist approach, and their views were codified in what came to be known as "New Criticism," an approach that dominated academic discussions of literature for the next thirty years.

The poet-critic John Crowe Ransom confirmed the critical school in his study *The New Criticism* in 1941. Critics should focus on the formal elements of any literary work—for example, the structure, diction, and versification of a poem—the New Critics argued, and ignore historical and even thematic elements. Many of the New Critics were also poets and college teachers (for example, Warren, Kenneth Burke, Allen Tate, Yvor Winters), and their influence seeped into poetry and the teaching of poetry as well. A literary work became a puzzle that the reader had to unlock; poets who were accessible in meaning (like Robert Frost) lost standing.

The public event that came to symbolize these changes was the awarding of the Library of Congress's newly established Bollingen Prize in Poetry to Ezra Pound in 1949 for *The Pisan Cantos*. Pound had lived in Italy during World War II and had made radio broadcasts in support of Benito Mussolini and Italian fascism. After the fall of Mussolini, Pound was captured by U.S. soldiers and charged with treason; while awaiting trial in Pisa, he wrote *The Pisan Cantos*, poetry that displayed, among other qualities, Pound's anti-Semitism and anti-Americanism. The treason charges were dropped when Pound was judged insane, and he was living in a mental institution near Washington, D.C., when the prize was announced. The Bollingen controversy demonstrated that the liberal attitudes toward literature of the 1930's had been abandoned for views that were apolitical at best.

Impact The literature of the 1940's thus confirms the bifurcated history of the decade. The first half continued the mood of the 1930's, and much of its literature reflected the themes of solidarity, sacrifice, and community. In the second half of the decade, however, as the United States shifted into the recovery gear, those progressive social concerns fell away, and literature began to increasingly reflect personal issues, both the individual alone and—as in poetry and criticism—the literary work as an isolated text, freed from its roots in society and history. These individualistic and ahistorical concerns would continue to deepen into the decade of the 1950's.

David Peck

Further Reading

Eisinger, Chester E. *Fiction of the Forties.* Chicago: University of Chicago Press, 1963. The only study devoted to the novels and short stories of the 1940's, broken into seven chapters ("The War Novel," "The New Fiction," etc.) with assessments of dozens of individual works, including the novels of Schulberg, Cozzens, Warren, Capote, and McCullers.

French, Warren, ed. *The Forties: Fiction, Poetry, Drama.* Deland, Fla.: Everett/Edwards, 1969. Essays by nearly two dozen scholars in sections on "The Literature of World War II" and "Highlights of a Decade," with analyses of *Death of a Salesman, All the King's Men,* Capote, the Bollingen controversy, and a dozen other writers and issues in the period.

Graebner, William. *The Age of Doubt: American Thought and Culture in the 1940's.* Boston: Twayne, 1991. A thorough and perceptive analysis of all the elements during the 1940's—film, advertising, art, music, literature—that helped create and define the decade's thought and culture.

Halttunen, Karen, ed. *A Companion to American Cultural History.* Malden, Mass.: Blackwell, 2008. Comprehensive volume includes Julia L. Foulkes's "Politics and Culture During the 1930's and 1940's," which may be the best single discussion of how the radical culture of the 1930's led into the early 1940's, as in the continuation of President Franklin D. Roosevelt's New Deal, 1932-1944.

Salzman, Jack, ed. *The Survival Years: A Collection of American Writings of the 1940's.* New York: Pegasus, 1969. Still the best anthology of the literature of the 1940's, including the literary controversies of the decade, such as those over the Bollingen award and New Criticism.

See also   Auden, W. H.; Benét, Stephen Vincent; Book publishing; Eliot, T. S.; Faulkner, William; Nobel Prizes; Pound, Ezra; Theater in the United States; Williams, Tennessee; Wright, Richard.

■ Lobotomy

Definition   Surgical procedure in which neural connections between the brain's frontal lobes and the thalamus are severed as a therapeutic measure for sufferers of mental illness

Rarely performed before the mid-1930's, lobotomies became increasingly more common after World War II. More than forty thousand lobotomies had been performed in the United States by the late 1950's. By the middle of that decade, with the introduction of antipsychotic medications, the procedure had fallen out of favor.

During the 1940's, an increasing number of lobotomies were performed on the mentally ill worldwide in the absence of any more effective treatment for severe mood and thought disorders. In America, these operations were championed by two doctors, Walter Freeman and J. W. Watts. Freeman was a particular enthusiast, writing books and giving professional demonstrations of his surgical techniques, which were amazingly crude even by the surgical standards of the 1940's. Freeman showed that the procedure was quick, relatively painless, and could be done with local anesthesia. Given Freeman's relentless promotion, lobotomies were performed for an increasing variety of illnesses, including mild depression and obsessive compulsive disorder.

Impact   Although they decreased severe behavioral problems, lobotomies left patients with marked changes to personality structure, apathy, and increased risk of seizures. Sadly, other contemporary treatments for severe mental illness—such as electroshock or insulin coma therapy—took an even greater physical toll on patients. The medications that were available—mainly sedatives and amphetamines—were either contraindicated or of limited use for most illnesses. The first true antipsychotic medication, chlorpromazine, was not even synthesized until the end of 1950.

In the absence of any viable alternative, lobotomies were considered an important contribution to neurology. In fact, the Portuguese neurosurgeon António Egas Moniz won the 1949 Nobel Prize in Physiology or Medicine mainly for his work in psychosurgery.

Michael R. Meyers

Further Reading

Konner, Melvin. "Too Desperate a Cure?" *The Sciences* 28, no. 3 (May/June, 1988): 6-8.

Tierney, Ann Jane. "Egas Moniz and the Origins of Psychosurgery." *Journal of the History of the Neurosciences* 9, no. 1 (2000): 22-36.

See also Farmer, Frances; Health care; Horney, Karen; Psychiatry and psychology.

■ Lombard, Carole

Identification American film star
Born October 6, 1908; Fort Wayne, Indiana
Died January 16, 1942; near Las Vegas, Nevada

A glamorous movie star who personified the "screwball comedy" genre, Lombard died tragically at the height of her fame while flying home from a war bonds rally.

Born Jane Alice Peters, Carole Lombard appeared in films directed by Mack Sennett during the late 1920's, but her career really took off in the next decade, with *Twentieth Century* (1934), recognized as the first "screwball comedy," the genre with which Lombard's name became synonymous. She soon starred in the screwball classics *My Man Godfrey* (1936) and *Nothing Sacred* (1937). She married actor Clark Gable on March 29, 1939, while he was on a break from filming *Gone with the Wind*. Through her own shrewd negotiations, she became one of the first actors to receive a percentage of the profits of her pictures, on top of her salary.

By 1940, Lombard was at the top of her career. Simultaneously recognized as Hollywood's most madcap playgirl and one of the world's most elegant and glamorous women, she was married to the love of her life and had achieved financial independence. She was a supremely happy woman, and almost the only goal that eluded her was having a baby.

In 1941, Lombard made one film, *Mr. and Mrs. Smith*, a romantic comedy with an unlikely director, Alfred Hitchcock. After the bombing of Pearl Harbor in December, 1941, Lombard wrote to President Franklin D. Roosevelt, offering to help however she could. The president assured her that continuing to make films was the best way she and Gable could serve their country.

Lombard threw her energy into the war effort. On January 15, 1942, she flew to Indiana for a war bond rally that was an outstanding success, with more than $2 million in government bonds sold in a single evening. Early the next morning, Lombard and her mother began the long return flight to California. After stopping in Las Vegas, Nevada, Lombard's plane took off around 7:00 P.M. The plane quickly veered off course, crashing into Table Rock (also known as Olcott Mountain) and instantly killing all nineteen passengers and three crew members.

Gable took Lombard and her mother back to California to be buried. Her funeral was held January 21 at Forest Lawn Cemetery in Glendale. Lombard's last film, *To Be or Not to Be*, was released after her death. While not a box-office success, it received good reviews and later came to be regarded as one of her best.

Impact Lombard defined the genre of screwball comedy. The American Film Institute included *My Man Godfrey* and *To Be or Not to*

Actor Carole Lombard two days before she died in a plane crash during a war bonds tour. (AP/Wide World Photos)

Be in its list of the hundred funniest films ever made. Lombard is equally remembered for her generous and compassionate spirit and for her patriotism. President Roosevelt declared Carole Lombard the first woman killed in the line of duty and posthumously awarded her the Presidential Medal of Freedom.

Jennifer Davis-Kay

Further Reading

Gehring, Wes. *Carole Lombard, the Hoosier Tornado.* Indianapolis: Indiana Historical Society Press, 2003.

Harris, Warren. *Gable and Lombard.* New York: Warner Paperback Library, 1975.

Miller, Frank, ed. *Leading Ladies: The 50 Most Unforgettable Actresses of the Studio Era.* San Francisco: Chronicle Books, 2006.

Ott, Frederick. *The Films of Carole Lombard.* Secaucus, N.J.: Citadel Press, 1972.

Swindell, Larry. *Screwball: The Life of Carole Lombard.* New York: William Morrow, 1975.

See also   Film in the United States; Films about World War II; Garland, Judy; Grable, Betty; Hayworth, Rita; Hitchcock, Alfred; Roosevelt, Franklin D.; War bonds; War heroes; Women's roles and rights in the United States.

■ *Look*

Identification   Popular general-interest magazine
Publisher   Gardner Cowles, Jr. (1903-1985)
Date   Published from 1937 to 1971

Look magazine, along with its competitor, Henry R. Luce's Life magazine, documented Hollywood, World War II at home and abroad, fashion, and cuisine in the United States during the 1940's. Within reach of nearly three million subscribers by decade's end, Look sold for ten cents per copy and made its profits through advertisers that bought space in its 11-by-14-inch issues.

Only three years after its founding in 1937, *Look* magazine was featuring beautiful young models, Hollywood stars and starlets, and cute babies on its large color covers. Like the 1940's itself, *Look*'s progress can be measured and evaluated in terms of the war years and the postwar years. Gardner "Mike" Cowles, Jr., and his older brother John inherited the media empire of their father, the holdings of which included the *Des Moines Register* and *Des Moines Tribune* and later the *Minneapolis Star* and *Minneapolis Times.* Along with radio stations and other newspaper holdings around the country, Cowles Communications was a midwestern media giant with big-city aspirations. *Look* magazine, founded by Mike Cowles, propelled his father's company from its midwestern roots and small media markets to its new corporate headquarters at 488 Madison Avenue in New York City, the architecturally distinctive *Look* Building, giving the family business a national audience and a voice for its progressive Republican platform.

Cowles and his family were internationalists as well as supporters and good friends of failed 1940 Republican presidential candidate Wendell Willkie. In 1943, Willkie and Cowles, in the latter's capacity as deputy director of the Office of War Information,

A 1947 issue of Look *magazine.* (Getty Images)

flew around the world on a diplomatic mission sanctioned by Franklin D. Roosevelt. The purpose of the mission, which Cowles called the highlight of his life, was to demonstrate bipartisan support for international cooperation in a postwar world. The experience was the basis for Willkie's best-selling book, *One World* (1943).

Back home, *Look* magazine replaced its cover shots of actors Judy Garland, Rita Hayworth, and June Allyson with portraits of leaders Winston Churchill, Joseph Stalin, and Dwight D. Eisenhower. Pictures of men and women in uniform, from paratroopers to Army nurses, also graced the covers. The Cowles media empire backed a second run in 1944 for Willkie, but a key early primary loss in Wisconsin to Thomas E. Dewey and Willkie's failing health cut short the campaign. With the war's end, *Look* continued to change with the times and mirror the optimism of its readers while shifting its focus more to glamour and style.

Cowles took a stronger hand in the running of *Look*, leaving his Des Moines base for New York City and a residence on Park Avenue. In December of 1946, having divorced his first two wives, Cowles married Fleur Fenton, a New York advertising executive. Fenton became an influential editor at *Look* and introduced sections on fashion and food. Even though the annual average salary in the United States in 1946 was only $2,500, the war's end brought a new optimism and a renewed hope for prosperity. Fenton, Cowles, and *Look* appealed to the nation's mood.

As a photo magazine, *Look* relied on a staff of talented photographers, including, in its early years, Arthur Rothstein and John Vachon, who had both worked with the New Deal's Farm Security Administration. In addition, *Look* assigned work to freelance photographers. One freelancer, who began working for the magazine in 1946 and accepted more than three hundred assignments, was future film director Stanley Kubrick.

Impact In an age before the domination of television, *Look* brought the world of high fashion, Hollywood, and international politics to the American reader. *Look*'s run lasted thirty-five years, and like its competitor, *Life*, it was finally squeezed out of the marketplace by television's wider availability and less expensive ad rates, combined with increased postal costs and the economic slump of the early 1970's.

Randy L. Abbott

Further Reading

Albrecht, Donald, and Thomas Mellins. *Only in New York: Photographs from "Look" Magazine.* New York: Museum of the City of New York and the Monacelli Press, 2009.

Cowles, Gardner. *Mike Looks Back: The Memoirs of Gardner Cowles, Founder of "Look" Magazine.* New York: G. Cowles, 1985.

See also Churchill, Winston; Dewey, Thomas E.; Eisenhower, Dwight D.; Garland, Judy; Hayworth, Rita; *Life*; *Saturday Evening Post*; Smith Act trials; Willkie, Wendell.

■ Los Angeles, Battle of

The Event Incident in which sightings of unidentified aircraft, presumed to be part of Japanese attacks, prompted antiaircraft fire

Date February 24-25, 1942

Place Los Angeles, California

After the attack on Pearl Harbor on December 7, 1941, the American public feared that Japan would next attack the mainland United States. Less than three months after the United States entered World War II, residents of Los Angeles awoke one night to air sirens and antiaircraft fire. The cause of the incident remains unexplained.

On February 23, 1942, a Japanese submarine fired on an oil production facility near Santa Barbara, California, and reportedly was heading toward Los Angeles. On the night of February 24 and early morning of February 25, strange objects appeared above Los Angeles. At 2:25 A.M. on February 25, air-raid sirens were sounded, a blackout was ordered, and air-raid wardens were mobilized. From 3:16 to 4:14 A.M., the military fired antiaircraft guns at supposed objects illuminated by nine searchlight beams. Military aircraft were ordered on standby alert but never took off. At 7:21 A.M., an "all clear" was sounded, and the blackout order was lifted.

The identity of the flying objects has never been determined. Speculation has included weather balloons, blimps, Japanese fire balloons, extraterrestrial vessels, sky lanterns, or unauthorized commercial or private airplanes.

Impact The artillery damaged several buildings and killed three civilians. Three others died from heart attacks, reportedly due to stress over the incident.

Soon afterward, Secretary of the Navy Frank Knox announced that the incident was due to anxiety and "war nerves." Conflicting reports were written by Army and Navy officers. The public was not told at the time that up to five unidentified airplanes were sighted and that one of these was later recovered off the coast of California. In 1945, Japan denied any involvement in the incident.

Michael Haas

Further Reading

Bishop, Greg, Joe Oesterle, and Mike Marinacci. *Weird California.* New York: Sterling, 2006.

Sword, Terrenz. *Battle of Los Angeles, 1942: The Silent Invasion Begins.* New Brunswick, N.J.: Inner Light-Global Communications, 2003.

See also Army, U.S.; Civil defense programs; Flying saucers; Japanese American internment; Navy, U.S.; Pearl Harbor attack; World War II.

■ Louis, Joe

Identification American heavyweight boxer, champion of the world, 1937–1949

Born May 13, 1914; near Lafayette, Alabama

Died April 12, 1981; Las Vegas, Nevada

The first black heavyweight boxing champion since Jack Johnson, Louis still holds the record for the longest world championship reign: twelve years. His sportsmanship and contribution to American morale during World War II made him a hero to both black and white Americans.

Young Joe Louis showed a remarkable natural talent for boxing, with an accurate left jab, a powerful right, and unexpected combinations. Louis turned professional in 1934, a time when it was a disadvantage to be a black fighter. The extraordinary fighter won his first twenty-seven bouts, twenty-three of them by knockout. During the mid-1930's, Louis defeated the former world champions Primo Carnera and Max Baer, becoming a hero to African Americans throughout the United States.

In June, 1938, Louis became a hero to all Americans when he defeated German heavyweight Max Schmeling in a politically charged rematch. On June 19, 1936, Louis had lost his first professional bout to Schmeling and then gone on to win the heavyweight championship title from James J. Braddock in 1937. Louis stated that the title was not truly his until he had defeated Schmeling. The scheduled rematch was highly charged. German propaganda portrayed Schmeling as the symbol of white German superiority. Black and white Americans rallied behind Louis and cheered when he knocked out Schmeling in the first round of the fight.

Louis successfully fought in more title defense fights than most champions throughout the 1940's. He joined the U.S. Army as a private in 1942, fighting in boxing exhibitions for the troops and serving as a morale booster. His famous words "We'll win 'cause we're on God's side" were featured on recruiting posters. His title was frozen for the duration of World War II. Louis returned to the ring after his honorable discharge in 1946, successfully defending the title in 1947 and 1948. Growing older and slower, the still undefeated champion retired in 1949.

Heavyweight champion Joe Louis (right) punching challenger Buddy Baer, whom he would knock out before the end of the first round on January 9, 1942. Buddy was the brother of former champion Max Baer. (AP/Wide World Photos)

Louis found himself in debt to the Internal Revenue Service and came out of retirement in 1950. He was not the fighter he had been, and he retired again after a loss to Rocky Marciano in 1951 that was a sad day for many, including Marciano himself. Louis's health deteriorated later in his life, and he died of a heart attack on April 12, 1981.

Impact   Louis has been called a black hero in white America. He captured the imagination of the public and was universally admired even outside the world of sports. Generally regarded as a clean-living, clean fighter exhibiting a powerful and exciting style, Louis was instrumental in reawakening an interest in boxing in America. Louis was responsible for integrating the sport of professional golf in 1952, when he became the first black American to play in a PGA Tour event. He was posthumously awarded the Congressional Gold Medal in 1982 and continues to be a role model.

Susan Butterworth

Further Reading

Barrow, Joe Louis, Jr., and Barbara Munder. *Joe Louis: Fifty Years an American Hero*. New York: McGraw-Hill, 1988.

Louis, Joe, with Edna and Art Rust, Jr. *Joe Louis: My Life*. New York: Harcourt Brace Jovanovich, 1978.

Margolick, David. *Beyond Glory: Joe Louis vs. Max Schmeling, and a World on the Brink*. New York: Alfred A. Knopf, 2005.

See also   African Americans; Boxing; LaMotta, Jake; Sports in the United States.

■ *Louisiana ex rel. Francis v. Resweber*

The Case   U.S. Supreme Court ruling on capital punishment

Date   Decided on January 13, 1947

The Supreme Court ruled that it was constitutional for Willie Francis, who had survived a first execution attempt, to be executed a second time.

In 1945, Willie Francis, an African American teenager, was convicted of murder in Louisiana and sentenced to death by electrocution. Mechanical problems with the electric chair prevented the imposition of the sentence. Francis alleged that forcing him to undergo another execution violated his constitutional rights.

In a 5-4 decision, the Supreme Court rejected each of the legal arguments made by Francis. It characterized Francis's case as an accident that could not have been anticipated. Consequently, repeating the execution did not amount to double jeopardy as prohibited by the Fifth and Fourteenth Amendments, nor did it constitute cruel and unusual punishment as banned by the Eighth Amendment. In addition, the Court rejected Francis's claim that a second execution would violate the equal protection clause contained in the Fourteenth Amendment because it would be a more severe punishment than other condemned offenders received.

Impact   The majority claimed that there was no precedent for this case, though it now serves as a precedent. A modern corollary can be drawn to the recent capital punishment case of *Baze v. Rees* (2008). In this case, the Supreme Court upheld the process for administering the death penalty by lethal injection and rejected the argument that an isolated accident in which the chemicals given during the lethal injection process were administered out of order would make the particular method of execution unconstitutional.

Margaret E. Leigey and Christina Reese

Further Reading

King, Gilbert. *The Execution of Willie Francis: Race, Murder, and the Search for Justice in the American South*. New York: Basic Civitas, 2008.

Miller, Arthur S., and Jeffrey H. Bowman. *Death by Installments: The Ordeal of Willie Francis*. New York: Greenwood Press, 1988.

See also   African Americans; Civil rights and liberties; Crimes and scandals; Science and technology; Supreme Court, U.S.

■ Loyalty Program, Truman's

Identification   President Harry S. Truman's loyalty review system for federal employees in the executive branch of government

Date   Announced March 21, 1947

Truman's Loyalty Program attempted to combat communism at home by guaranteeing the loyalty of federal employees. It represented an alternative to the tactics of the Federal Bureau of Investigation (FBI) and the House Committee on Un-American Activities (HUAC) during the Second Red Scare.

By 1947, the United States had solidified its efforts to combat communism both at home and abroad. On March 12, 1947, President Truman presented to Congress the Truman Doctrine, which aimed to limit the spread of communism abroad through containment. Truman's foreign policy, which would dominate for decades to come, spilled over into domestic affairs and helped launch a new wave of anticommunist rhetoric and investigations.

Fighting the Enemy from Within   After World War II, the threat of communist infiltration of the federal government was a national concern. Republicans, who had gained control of both houses of Congress during the 1946 midterm elections, charged that Truman's "soft" polices on communism had allowed communists to infiltrate the federal government. Truman responded late in 1946 by appointing a committee to study employee loyalty. The committee recommended establishing a federal loyalty program to protect the nation against internal subversive activity.

In January, 1947, leaders of HUAC announced that its primary mission was to identify, expose, and investigate known communists. FBI director J. Edgar Hoover joined the fight against communism, stating in March, 1947, that the Communist Party had a main goal of overthrowing the U.S. government. Hoover declared that because of the highly organized nature of the Communist Party, all members should be barred from government service.

Measuring Loyalty   On March 21, 1947, nine days after announcing the Truman Doctrine, Truman signed Executive Order 9835, which launched the federal Loyalty Program. The order provided for the investigation of applicants for posts in the executive branch and for removal of disloyal employees. The program required a nominal check of more than two million government workers as well as full investigations of those for whom evidence indicated possible disloyalty. In an effort to supersede the efforts

---

Executive Order 9835

Executive Order 9835, commonly referred to as the Loyalty Order, was signed by President Harry S. Truman on March 21, 1947, and intended to root out communism within the U.S. federal government. An excerpt of the order is reproduced below.

Whereas, each employee of the government of the United States is endowed with a measure of trusteeship over the democratic processes which are the heart and sinew of the United States; and whereas, it is of vital importance that persons employed in the federal service be of complete and unswerving loyalty to the United States; and whereas, although the loyalty of by far the overwhelming majority of all government employees is beyond question, the presence within the government service of any disloyal or subversive person constitutes a threat to our democratic processes; and whereas, maximum protection must be afforded the United States against infiltration of disloyal persons into the ranks of its employees, and equal protection from unfounded accusations of disloyalty must be afforded the loyal employees of the government: Now, therefore, by virtue of the authority vested in me by the Constitution and statutes of the United States, including the Civil Service Act of 1883 (22 Stat. 403), as amended, and section 9A of the act approved August 2, 1939 (18 U.S.C. 61i), and as president and chief executive of the United States, it is hereby, in the interest of the internal management of the government, ordered as follows: There shall be a loyalty investigation of every person entering the civilian employment of any department or agency of the executive branch of the federal government.

of HUAC and the FBI, the order specified how government investigations of possible subversives would be conducted. The mandate assigned the Civil Service Commission the responsibility of conducting the investigations of current employees and working with agencies to form loyalty boards. The order gave the investigators full access to FBI files, military and naval intelligence records, criminal files, HUAC materials, academic transcripts, and records from past employers. The loyalty boards assessed loyalty based on any activities (including treason, espionage, and being connected to groups advocating violent revolution) or associations that might breach the security of the interests and secrets of the U.S. government. Truman wanted the program to guard against disloyal employees, defend innocent federal workers from unfounded charges, protect atomic secrets, and establish a hard stance against communism.

Truman's Loyalty Program began during the summer of 1947. Executive department agencies organized loyalty boards, while the Civil Service Commission developed a system of regional loyalty boards to oversee the appeals process. Congress passed laws to remove employees or bar applicants from public positions if they were deemed disloyal to the United States. By March, 1948, loyalty boards had reviewed more than 420,000 government employees, with only 399 cases warranting further investigation; of that small number, only 8 cases of disloyalty emerged.

Despite the findings of only rare cases of disloyalty, the issue of domestic communists became a centerpiece of the 1948 presidential election. Truman announced that HUAC hearings, led by a Republican Congress, had created unnecessary public hysteria about communism. Truman argued that his government employee loyalty program was an effective mechanism to identify and investigate subversives. Such statements helped Truman's political future, but the program itself became infused with anticommunist sentiment. Inadequately trained loyalty investigators confused anticommunist liberal affiliations with Marxist causes, relied on hearsay, and often limited the careers of those they investigated. Truman's Loyalty Program nevertheless remained a fixture of government service throughout the 1940's.

The program did not go unchallenged. In the 1955 case of *Peters v. Hobby*, the Supreme Court ruled

as invalid the removal of one consultant to the Civil Service Commission by the commission's loyalty board. The Court stated that the action was beyond the jurisdiction of Executive Order 9835. Executive-judiciary disputes concerning employee loyalty continued into the administration of Dwight D. Eisenhower.

Impact Truman's Loyalty Program was one of the federal government's approaches to investigating suspected communists during the Second Red Scare. Although it was designed to employ a consistent method of investigations, the Loyalty Program was uneven, as well as somewhat subjective rather than fully objective, and it often forced individuals to prove innocence in the face of assumed guilt. Truman later admitted that the Loyalty Program had been a sound idea that spiraled out of control during the midst of the Second Red Scare.

Aaron D. Purcell

Further Reading

Bontecou, Eleanor. *The Federal Loyalty-Security Program.* Ithaca, N.Y.: Cornell University Press, 1953. Describes the origins of the Loyalty Program and compares it to the British loyalty system.

Brown, Ralph S., Jr. *Loyalty and Security: Employment Tests in the United States.* New Haven, Conn.: Yale University Press, 1958. A detailed study of various state and federal programs designed to measure employee loyalty.

McCullough, David G. *Truman.* New York: Simon & Schuster, 1992. This comprehensive biographical source on Truman includes discussion of the political nature behind the Loyalty Program.

Theoharis, Athan. *Seeds of Repression: Harry S. Truman and the Origins of McCarthyism.* Chicago: Quadrangle Books, 1971. Argues that Truman's Loyalty Program intensified popular anxieties about communist takeover and that the program did little to remove subversives from federal service.

Thompson, Francis H. *The Frustration of Politics: Truman, Congress, and the Loyalty Issue, 1945-1953.* Rutherford, N.J.: Fairleigh Dickinson University Press, 1979. Argues that Truman's Loyalty Program may have contributed to the Second Red Scare, even though the era's increase in anticommunist sentiment preceded the program's creation.

See also Anticommunism; Communist Party USA; Elections in the United States: 1948; Federal Bureau of Investigation; Foreign policy of the United States; Hoover, J. Edgar; House Committee on Un-American Activities; Truman, Harry S.; Truman Doctrine.

■ Lynching and hate crime

Definition Extrajudicial punishment, often by hanging and usually by mobs, that is typically based on the victim's membership in a group easily identifiable in some manner, such as by race or nationality

Lynchings and other hate crimes in the United States declined during the 1940's but did not die out altogether; Efforts to promote racial integration created racial tensions that provoked some of these crimes.

The term "lynching" does not have a clear origin; it may have originated from one of several men named Lynch. James Elbert Cutler, who wrote about lynching in 1905, described it as a criminal practice peculiar to the United States in its frequency among advanced societies. Its history in the territory that became the United States began during the early years of European colonialization as an informal, illegal form of social control. Early lynchings most frequently were executions by a few people or a mob and usually were spontaneous reactions to unacceptable behaviors, from minor infractions to heinous crimes such as murder. As with all hate crimes, these were the results of resentments or fears of the accused or of the group of which the accused was a member.

After the creation of the United States, victims of lynchings often were members of some identifiable group, and the most frequently targeted group was African Americans. Lynch mobs often formed in response to some action (often a murder, a rape, or behavior of a black man toward a white woman that contravened social mores). The mob would seize some evidence of a crime or other undesirable behavior and rush to identify a culprit, who would then be pursued without waiting for the legal system to act. The accused could be set upon at any location, including being removed from jail, whether or not the person had yet been convicted. The accused also were taken from their homes, from their workplaces, or off the street. At times, law enforcement stood aside, not interfering. Often, the victims of lynchings were innocent of the crimes of which they were accused. A lynch mob would hear of a crime committed by someone from an identifiable group and attack someone who loosely fit the description of the accused. Lynchings and other hate crimes also occurred on the basis of fabricated crimes or infractions.

Lynching took many forms, but the one most recognized is hanging. Lynchings also involved other forms of execution or torture, sometimes in combination. These included shooting and burning. Males were the most frequent victims, and African Americans as a group suffered the most lynchings. Racial tensions and fears in the South motivated many lynchings, especially from the end of the Civil War through the 1890's.

No accurate statistics exist concerning the numbers of lynchings. Because they are by definition illegal, they often were kept secret from government authorities. Available evidence indicates that the 1890's had the highest number of lynchings of any decade in U.S. history.

Some estimates put the number of lynchings between 1860 and 1890 at about five thousand. The Ku Klux Klan was thought to be behind several hundred lynchings in the immediate postwar years. The majority of lynchings in this period were committed against African Americans. The Tuskegee Institute has estimated that between 1880 and 1951, more than three thousand African Americans were lynched. The Tuskegee Institute also has estimated that between 1882 and 1968, more than twelve hundred white people were lynched. Many of them were members of ethnic minorities, in particular people of Chinese or Mexican heritage, who suffered from various forms of legal and social discrimination, particularly in the West and Southwest.

Lynching During the 1940's On May 10, 1940, *The New York Times* reported that the South had gone twelve months without a recorded lynching. Throughout the 1940's, lynchings were still practiced, though at a much lower frequency: Thirty-three recorded lynchings occurred during the 1940's, but many lynchings likely went unreported. One recorded lynching was of a returning military veteran, an African American who later was shown to be innocent of the crime of which he was accused. In the 1940's, there were no

Some of the twenty-eight white defendants charged with lynching a black man celebrating their acquittal by an all-white jury in Greenville, North Carolina, in May, 1947. (AP/Wide World Photos)

specific legislated sanctions opposing or identifying a crime as a "hate crime." Such designations would come decades later.

The internment of Japanese American citizens in the United States has been viewed as a hate crime against that group, although the action was sanctioned by law. The zoot-suit riots of 1943 also can be considered a hate crime, as American servicemen and others in Los Angeles attacked Mexican Americans, whom they identified by their appearance and especially by the zoot suits that they wore.

Although various areas of life became racially integrated during the 1940's, including the military and many workplaces, segregation continued in many other areas, including education. Not everyone approved of integration, so it created social tensions that sometimes erupted in various sorts of hate crimes against African Americans. The South was, in general, most resistant to integration and continued to be the site of more lynchings than other areas.

Impact In recognition of the civil rights of all Americans, lynching became a felony in every U.S. state. Most of the state laws define lynching as an intentional crime committed by a group of persons, without the authority of law, against another person that results in bodily harm or death. Despite such laws, the estimated number of lynchings rose in the South in the 1960's in response to civil rights activism. A 1969 federal civil rights law made it a federal crime to injure, intimidate, or interfere with another person by force on the basis of that person's race, color, religion, or national origin.

Richard L. McWhorter

Further Reading

Cahalan, Margaret Werner. *Historical Corrections Statistics in the United States, 1850-1984.* Washington, D.C.: U.S. Department of Justice, 1986.

Cutler, James Elbert. *Lynch-Law: An Investigation into the History of Lynching in the United States.* Whitefish, Mont.: Kessinger, 1905.

Ginzburg, Ralph, ed. *One Hundred Years of Lynchings.* Baltimore: Black Classic Press, 1988.

See also African Americans; Crimes and scandals; German American Bund; Jim Crow laws; Racial discrimination.

M

■ M&M candies

Definition Popular sugar-coated chocolate confection

Resistant to melting, M&M candies were invented in 1941 and first given to American G.I.'s during World War II. The candies became commercially available to the American public in 1945.

Chocolate was a scarce commodity during World War II and rationed in the United States. Almost all chocolate was sent overseas to American G.I.'s. During this time, Forrest Mars, Sr., son of the Mars, Inc., candy maker who became famous for Mars, Milky Way, Three Musketeers, and Snickers bars, invented M&M candies. According to a widely speculated, unconfirmed story, Mars had observed soldiers during the Spanish Civil War eating chocolate covered with a hard sugar coating to keep it from melting in hot climates. Partnering with Bruce Murrie, the son of a Hershey candy executive, Mars formed the company M&M, Ltd., using their last-name initials for the company name. Mars patented his product on March 3, 1941. M&M candies had a hard sugar shell and were originally colored brown, yellow, orange, red, green, or violet.

The Hershey Corporation had a contract with the U.S. military to supply troops with chocolate; M&M's were quickly added to soldiers' C-rations and sold in post exchanges and ships' service stores. They soon became very popular with soldiers because their tubular packaging made them easy to carry and they did not melt in hot climates.

Impact M&M's became an immediate success with American soldiers during World War II. When World War II ended in 1945, M&M's became available to the public. Their popularity established M&M/Mars, Inc., as a multinational company and chocolate candy empire.

Alice C. Richer

Further Reading

Jorgensen, Janice. *Encyclopedia of Consumer Brands.* Detroit: St. James Press, 1994.

Smith, Andrew F. *Encyclopedia of Junk Food and Fast Food.* Westport, Conn.: Greenwood Press, 2006.

See also Fads; Food processing; Inventions; Wartime rationing.

■ MacArthur, Douglas

Identification Supreme commander of Allied forces in the South Pacific, 1942-1945, and of the Allied occupation of Japan, 1945-1951
Born January 26, 1880; Little Rock, Arkansas
Died April 5, 1964; Washington, D.C.

Army general Douglas MacArthur was among the most famous military leaders in American history. He added to his prominence by serving as the supreme commander of Allied forces in the southwest Pacific during World War II and subsequently as the commander of U.S. occupation of Japan.

Early Years Douglas MacArthur was the son of General Arthur MacArthur, the U.S. Army's highest-ranking officer from 1906 to 1909. As a boy, the young MacArthur lived on frontier army posts before entering the U.S. Military Academy at West Point and graduating at the head of his class in 1903. Thereafter, he served as an engineering officer in the United States, the Philippines, Panama, and Japan. From 1913 to 1917, MacArthur served on the U.S. Army general staff. Following the U.S. entry into World War I in April, 1917, he went to France to fight with the Forty-second Division in the Champagne-Marne, St. Mihiel, and Meuse-Argonne operations. From 1919 to 1922, Brigadier General MacArthur enacted reforms as superintendent at West Point before serving two command tours in the Philippines. Promoted to general, he became the U.S. Army chief of staff in 1930. His reputation would suffer in 1932, when he employed force to oust protesting World War I veterans in Washington, D.C.

World War II In 1935, MacArthur agreed to serve as military adviser to the Philippine government, organizing Filipino defense forces over the next six years. After accepting appointment as field marshal of Philippine forces, he retired from the U.S. Army in December, 1937. Escalating tensions with Japan prompted the U.S. Army to recall MacArthur to active service as a major general in July, 1941. He received command of the U.S. forces in the Philippines and was promoted to lieutenant general and then general. Unwisely, MacArthur discarded the plan to withdraw American forces to the Bataan Peninsula if Japan attacked the Philippines because he was confident his forces could defend the islands. When Japan attacked Pearl Harbor on December 7, 1941, his ill-advised refusal to approve an immediate retaliatory air strike against the Japanese on Taiwan allowed warplanes deployed there to attack and destroy on the ground roughly half of the U.S. bomb-

General Douglas MacArthur. (NARA)

ers and one-third of the fighters in the Philippines on December 8.

MacArthur commanded a force that was twice the size of the 57,000 Japanese troops that invaded the Philippines, but many of his men were poorly trained and inadequately equipped. With defenders thinly spread, the Japanese easily seized Manila and much of the island of Luzon. MacArthur then ordered his forces to follow the original plan of withdrawal to the Bataan Peninsula. Retreating troops had to abandon stocks of supplies and ammunition as they moved to bases unprepared for defense. Over the next months, MacArthur would spend most of his time on Corregidor. President Franklin D. Roosevelt did not want MacArthur to become Japan's prisoner and therefore ordered him to Australia in February, 1942. Upon his departure, MacArthur declared, "I shall return!"

From Australia, MacArthur, as commander of Allied forces in the southwest Pacific, implemented a deliberate strategy to recapture the Philippines. Frustrated with the slow pace of his advance, American military officials in 1943 insisted upon a leap-frogging approach that would bypass the Japanese fortified islands. Still, it was not until spring of 1944 that MacArthur's troops invaded New Guinea. Seeking agreement on a strategy to hasten the defeat of Japan, Roosevelt traveled to Hawaii in July, 1944, to confer with MacArthur and Admiral Chester W. Nimitz, the commander of forces in the central Pacific. There, Nimitz argued for an assault on Taiwan, while MacArthur insisted on retaking the Philippines. Both operations sought to deny Japanese forces access to key resources in Southeast Asia, but MacArthur's plan would move Allied forces farther away from Japan's home islands. Roosevelt nevertheless relented, approving MacArthur's plan to retake the Philippines, while ordering Nimitz to shift his resources toward the seizure of Okinawa.

Domestic politics undoubtedly played a role in Roosevelt's decision to allow MacArthur to run military operations in the Pacific as MacArthur saw fit. Among the most politically ambitious generals in American history, MacArthur had admirers among influential conservative Republicans. MacArthur made clear his interest in becoming the Republican nominee for president in the 1944 election. Instead, Thomas E. Dewey won the nomination, intensifying MacArthur's efforts to boost his reputation as he looked to the 1948 elections. In October, 1944, U.S. forces under his command invaded Leyte and secured Luzon during the first three months of 1945. The invasion of Japan proved to be unnecessary after the United States staged atomic attacks early in August. In response, Japan asked for surrender terms. Having been promoted to the new rank of general of the army in December, 1944, MacArthur presided at the Japanese surrender ceremony on September 2, 1945, on the battleship *Missouri* in Tokyo Bay.

U.S. Occupation of Japan   Harry S. Truman, who became president when Roosevelt suddenly died in April, 1945, appointed MacArthur to be Supreme Commander for the Allied Powers (SCAP) in August in order to accept the Japanese surrender and then supervise the occupation of Japan. In this position, MacArthur in effect governed the defeated Axis nation as a benevolent despot, presiding over a process aimed at achieving demilitarization and democratization in order to prevent a resumption of Japanese imperialism. Though at times autocratic, MacArthur efficiently implemented a series of political, economic, and social reforms corresponding with plans that U.S. officials had developed during World War II. Working with Japanese leaders and through existing bureaucracy, he achieved the elimination of militarist, ultranationalist, and feudal habits.

In 1946, MacArthur's general headquarters staff drafted a new Japanese constitution, outlawing war and reducing the emperor to a "symbol of the state," that became effective in 1947. In his capacity as SCAP, MacArthur also presided nominally over the U.S. occupation of southern Korea. Preoccupied with affairs in Japan, he rarely played a direct role in determining policy there, but he was a consistent advocate of early U.S. military withdrawal.

By late 1947, the U.S. Defense and State Departments, rather than MacArthur, were setting occupation policy, following a "reverse course" that halted further reforms and sought to transform Japan into a Cold War bulwark against the spread of communism in Asia. MacArthur transferred power to a new Japanese government in 1949, but Washington ignored his recommendation for prompt restoration of Japanese sovereignty. U.S. military leaders re-

fused to risk losing bases in Japan, especially after the communists gained power in China in 1949. Ironically, MacArthur's Far East command was at that time in no shape to fight a war. Drastic cutbacks in the U.S. defense budget had significantly reduced American troops and equipment. The four divisions of the U.S. Eighth Army deployed in Japan were all severely understrength. MacArthur must bear some responsibility for allowing readiness and training in his command to deteriorate until, after five years of soft occupation duty, his forces were unfit to engage a determined foe in combat.

War in Korea   When North Korea attacked South Korea in June, 1950, Truman, acting on a request from the United Nations (U.N.), appointed MacArthur commander of the U.N. forces sent to halt the invasion. Stopping the offensive required the commitment of three divisions of the U.S. Eighth Army. MacArthur then used his remaining forces in Japan, plus a U.S. Marine division, to stage an amphibious landing at Inchon behind enemy lines that pushed the enemy back into North Korea. At the pinnacle of his celebrity, he then acted on orders from Washington that coincided with his recommendations to cross the thirty-eighth parallel and seek forcible reunification of Korea. This action provoked a massive Chinese military intervention, sending U.N. forces into a helter-skelter retreat and inflicting a humiliating defeat on MacArthur. His public criticism of Truman's refusal to extend the war to mainland China compelled the president to relieve the general of command in April, 1951. During U.S. Senate hearings on the recall, the Joint Chiefs of Staff denied MacArthur's claim that they supported his proposals and defended limiting the war. MacArthur spent his remaining years quietly, living with his wife in New York City's Waldorf Hotel and writing his memoirs.

Impact   Many defenders of Bataan and Corregidor thought that the praise MacArthur received in World War II was undeserved. His decisive leadership, however, may have been the vital factor in helping a devastated Japan rebuild itself and establish the foundation for becoming a global economic power. MacArthur was certainly among the most controversial military leaders in American history, not least because of his hubris and political ambition.

James I. Matray

Further Reading

James, D. Clayton. *The Years of MacArthur.* 3 vols. Boston: Houghton-Mifflin, 1970-1985. This three-volume study is the definitive biography of MacArthur. James provides thorough, detailed, and critical coverage of the general's entire career.

Manchester, William. *American Caesar: Douglas MacArthur, 1880-1964.* Boston: Little, Brown, 1978. This highly readable biography is generally favorable toward MacArthur. Manchester is particularly successful in capturing some of the complexity and contradictions of MacArthur's personality

Perrett, Geoffrey. *Old Soldiers Never Die: The Life of Douglas MacArthur.* New York: Random House, 1996. This thorough biography describes how MacArthur learned early in his career to manipulate reporters with great effect. Parrett does not allow what he considers MacArthur's character flaws to overshadow his admiration for the man's military mind or his patriotism.

Schaller, Michael. *Douglas MacArthur: The Far Eastern General.* New York: Oxford University Press, 1989. A damning critique of MacArthur. Schaller provides evidence that exposes the general's numerous personal flaws and exaggeration of his military abilities.

See also Army, U.S.; Bataan Death March; Eisenhower, Dwight D.; Elections in the United States: 1944; Groves, Leslie Richard; Guadalcanal, Battle of; Japan, occupation of; Nimitz, Chester W.; Philippines; *They Were Expendable.*

■ McCormick, Robert R.

Identification American newspaper publisher
Born July 30, 1880; Chicago, Illinois
Died April 1, 1955; Wheaton, Illinois

McCormick, the publisher of the Chicago Tribune, *exemplified an outspoken, personal style of journalism that thrived on controversy. As a spokesman for conservative America during the 1940's, he espoused both a free market economy and an isolationist foreign policy.*

Robert R. McCormick built up the *Chicago Tribune* into one of the most widely circulated and influential newspapers in the United States. Eschewing objectivity, he ran his paper to support his political ideals of limited government. Long an opponent of New Deal economic policies, McCormick found in World War II an issue on which he spoke for many isolationist Americans. Though he favored a strong military, he regarded the war in Europe as potentially destructive for the United States. He opposed American involvement in the war and supported organizations such as the America First Committee until the Japanese bombing of Pearl Harbor in December, 1941. After World War II, McCormick continued his attacks on Washington, criticizing the Harry S. Truman administration's economic regulations and its role in the Cold War.

Impact McCormick's personal and combative journalistic style seems out of fashion with modern newspapers, but it flourishes in media such as talk radio and the Internet. His attacks on big government, which enraged sophisticates in his time, would reflect the disillusionment felt by many Americans after the Vietnam War and Watergate scandal.

Anthony Bernardo, Jr.

Further Reading

Gies, Joseph. *The Colonel of Chicago.* New York: E. P. Dutton, 1979.

Smith, Richard Norton. *The Colonel: The Life and Legend of Robert R. McCormick, 1880-1955.* Boston: Houghton Mifflin, 1997.

See also America First Committee; Conservatism in U.S. politics; Isolationism; Newspapers; Taft, Robert A.; Truman, Harry S.

Mackenzie King, William Lyon. *See* **King, William Lyon Mackenzie**

■ Maclean's

Identification Canadian news and national affairs magazine
Date Founded in 1905

Under editor in chief rArthur Irwin, Maclean's reclaimed its pre-Depression popularity and achieved critical acclaim during the 1940's, promoting a unique and distinctly modern Canadian identity that reflected the social and economic development of Canada during the postwar era.

Established as a business digest in 1905, *Maclean's* developed into one of the most popular magazines in Canada during the early twentieth century. Although the Great Depression diminished its readership and derailed its financial success, the magazine continued to feature some of the country's finest journalists, authors, and essayists during the post-Depression years and to enhance its journalistic reputation with political commentary, critical essays, photographs, and stories relevant to Canada and its citizens. Arthur Irwin, who served as associate editor and editor in chief from 1925 through 1950, had by the 1940's amassed a pool of young talent that would compose the writing and editorial staff of the magazine during the postwar era, and had transformed *Maclean's* from a politically conservative periodical into a voice of moderation, as characterized by its promotion of bilingualism and greater understanding between the nation's French and British cultures.

Impact   For Irwin and *Maclean's*, the 1940's represented a culmination of decades of development of the magazine into a force for Canadian modernism and national identity. Although Irwin retired at the end of the decade, his influence would be felt at *Maclean's* for decades to come as the magazine remained a popular manifestation of the sophistication and diversity of modern Canada.

Michael H. Burchett

Further Reading

Mackenzie, David Clark. *Arthur Irwin: A Biography.* Toronto: University of Toronto Press, 1993.

Mollins, Carl, ed. *Maclean's Canada's Century: An Illustrated History of the People and Events That Shaped Our Identity.* Toronto: Key Porter Books, 1999.

See also   Canadian nationalism; Canadian regionalism; *Life*; Literature in Canada; *Look*; Magazines; Quebec nationalism; *Saturday Evening Post*.

■ Magazines

During the 1940's, magazines furnished timely information, ranging from current events and celebrity gossip to serious technical and scholarly discourses. Their information was usually inexpensive, useful, and readily obtainable in different venues, including via the postal service.

Early magazines were filled with miscellaneous entertainment, such as amusing stories and didactic, uplifting maxims or proverbs promoting personal improvement. New technology providing more illustrations and occasional color enhanced the look and appeal of magazines. By the twentieth century, advertising revenues made magazines more profitable, while larger, more professional staffs and talented freelancers improved the content, all of which kept readers interested.

News and General-Interest Magazines   General-interest magazines were commercially successful at the beginning of the 1940's. Weeklies such as *The Saturday Evening Post* and *Collier's* contained articles, fiction, illustrations, and cartoons by freelance contributors, many of whom later became noted authors and artists. For example, the illustrator Norman Rockwell painted more than two hundred *Saturday Evening Post* covers, and artist Grant Wood contributed several. Frederic Remington painted Collier's Weekly covers. Writers such as Ernest Hemingway, William Faulkner, Will Rogers, and Ring Lardner had pieces published in these magazines. *Collier's Weekly* readership reached 2.5 million during World War II and in 1944, carried one of the first articles published in the United States about concentration camps. After the war, however, it gradually lost readers and finally folded in 1956.

The top-selling 1940 news or current-events magazines were *Look, Life, Time,* and *Newsweek*. *Time*'s Canadian edition, *Time Canada*, appeared in 1943. These magazines used photojournalism and perceptive news stories to report world and national events. As the fighting in Europe and Asia escalated, Americans relied on such magazines for war news.

Though *The New Yorker*, one of the more influential magazines of the decade, focused on New York City, Americans nationwide read it for its sophisticated view of national and world affairs, its famous and important people, and its serious journalism and superior fiction. In 1946, it devoted one entire issue to John Hersey's *Hiroshima*, his firsthand account of one of the Japanese cities devastated by the atom bomb in the last days of World War II.

Digest magazines flourished with the ongoing success of *Reader's Digest*, founded in 1922. Other digest magazines in the 1940's were *Negro Digest, Children's Digest, Editorial Digest, Column Digest,* a book digest called *Omnibook*, and the Canadian *Magazine*

Time founder Henry R. Luce posing with posters of two of his chief magazines in 1941. (Time & Life Pictures/Getty Images)

Digest. The competition for material became fierce because these publications condensed other magazines. Because of its ability to outbid most newcomers for the best articles, *Reader's Digest* soon became a target of other publications who accused it of prohibiting the "free flow of ideas." However, the accusation had little affect on its popularity.

Advertising and Specialized Magazines Advertising revenues have always helped fund magazine publication, and by the 1940's, magazine publishers began filling more pages with lucrative ads. While general magazines boasted that their readers were all kinds of people—both sexes, all ages, different ethnic groups, and folks with varying interests—magazine publishers soon found that advertisers were most interested in magazines that appealed to consumers with a special interest in their product. *Reader's Digest* is notable as a general magazine that managed to refrain from putting any advertising in its pages even after almost all other prominent mag-

azines had done so. In 1942 alone, magazine advertisers spent $2.1 billion. After World War II, as the cost of everything rose, even *Reader's Digest* had to use ads.

To get those special-interest dollars from advertisers, publishers began printing magazines that focused on narrower subjects and interests. Such magazines had always existed, but negligible profits made them less appealing to publishers. Trade publications, for example, designed to serve professionals in specialized areas and help them stay current in their careers, had regular readers, but their numbers were not great.

Similar in their limited readership, a few "highbrow" magazines aimed to appeal to what publisher Henry R. Luce called "the aristocracy of our business civilization." These magazines, such as *Harper's* and *Atlantic*, contained erudite, influential articles that probed and analyzed cultural and political issues. Luce's *Fortune*, printed on thick matte paper with expensive inks, was intended to appeal to elitist, successful businesspeople. By the late 1940's, its familiar format became too expensive to maintain and had to be changed to a more conventional one. *The New Republic*, another highbrow, liberal magazine, increased its prestige in 1946 when former U.S. vice president Henry A. Wallace became editor. In 1947, a *Foreign Affairs* article about a policy to "contain" Russia later became the basis of government policy.

The varied specialized magazines ranged from the serious to the frivolous. Some of the more serious publications of the decade were devoted to science and technology for the general, nonprofessional reader; these included *Popular Science* and *Popular Mechanics*. *Field and Stream* and *National Geographic* focused on activities for the outdoorsman and on unusual, exotic places and things and included photographic illustrations. *Scientific American* served readers with a more serious interest and background in the sciences.

Serious literary magazines included *The Saturday Review of Literature* and, in Canada, *First Statement*, *Contemporary Verse*, *Direction*, and *Enterprise*. *The Saturday Review of Literature*, though never profitable, was highly respected and included reviews by respected critics of contemporary writing. The Canadian magazines brought attention to some of Canada's important writers, such as P. K. Page, A. M. Klein, and F. R. Scott.

Less serious were such publications as the fan magazines that reported on Hollywood happenings. More than ten magazines published during the decade, including *Photoplay, Modern Screen, Silver Screen,* and *Motion Picture,* not only carried the latest gossip about the stars but also gave movie reviews, interviews with actors, and full-page color portraits of the stars. "True story" magazines were also popular at the beginning of the decade: *True Romances* and *Confidential* told stories about either ordinary people with unusual occurrences in their lives or scandalous episodes in the lives of celebrities or would-be celebrities. A "true crime" pulp magazine such as Canada's Quebec-based *Mon magazine policier et d'aventures* was similar in format and style to American pulp magazines, with striking color covers and exciting stories by writers such as Ellery Queen and Agatha Christie translated into French.

Gender-Specific Magazines Magazines focused on either male or female interests had always been popular. The top men's magazine, *Esquire,* had a racy reputation when it started in 1932. By 1943, its second-class mailing privileges were prohibited because its contents were judged "lewd and lascivious." The pinup illustrations of leggy, voluptuous, scantily-dressed young women—the Petty girls and later the Varga girls (named for the artists)—probably contributed to the perception. *Esquire* began changing its image by sponsoring the first big-name jazz musicians' concert in New York's Metropolitan Opera House. It also began emphasizing men's fashions and the works of well-respected writers. Consequently, in 1945, a New York court of appeals voided the ban on the magazine's mailing privileges.

The "Seven Sisters" magazines were *Good Housekeeping, Better Homes and Gardens, Ladies Home Journal, McCall's, Redbook, Woman's Day,* and *Family Circle,* which joined the group in 1946. Women's magazines were the most financially successful category because their readers tended to be those who purchased the most consumer goods. Advertisers loved women's magazines and their cheerful outlooks that presented a wholesome environment for advertisements of clothes, household goods, over-the-counter medications, and practically everything on the market. *Cosmopolitan* and *Seventeen,* with different approaches, addressed urban, single women and the

younger, teenage, and college-age women, respectively.

Impact Magazines in the 1940's brought real images and information about important events as well as advice and entertainment to readers at a low cost. After the war, television changed the mission of magazines to some extent, and costs of printing and labor increased so much that many magazines had to stop production. Nonetheless, because of the format and unique capabilities of magazines, the medium continues to be popular in the United States.

Jane L. Ball

Further Reading

Angeletti, Norberto, and Alberto Oliva. *Magazines That Make History: Their Origins, Development and Influence.* Gainesville: University Press of Florida, 2004. Examines role of specific successful magazines in creating visual media culture. *Time, Life, National Geographic,* and *Reader's Digest* are among eight magazines discussed.

Endres, Kathleen L., and Therese L. Lueck, eds. *Women's Periodicals in the United States: Consumer Magazines.* Westport, Conn.: Greenwood Press, 1995. Discusses women's publications and how they reflect and influence American women's concerns.

Janello, Amy, and Brennon Jones. *The American Magazine.* New York: Harry N. Abrams, 1991. An illustrated history of magazine publishing, its influence on American history, and insights into advertising, photojournalism, and graphic design's impact on the industry.

Sharpe, Joanne. *Condensing the Cold War: Reader's Digest and American Identity.* Minneapolis: University of Minnesota Press, 2000. Discusses how *Reader's Digest* shaped American public opinion during the Cold War.

Sutherland, Fraser. *The Monthly Epic: A History of Canadian Magazines, 1789-1989.* Markham, Ont.: Fitzhenry & Whiteside, 1989. Examines Canadian English-language magazines published over a two-hundred-year period. Part two covers 1930's and 1940's and the composition of specific publications.

Tebbel, John, and Mary Ellen Zuckerman. *The Magazine in America, 1741-1990.* New York: Oxford University Press, 1991. Covers the 250 years of the industry, including its pioneers, mergers, takeovers, advertising, circulation, technological innovations, and different genres.

See also Advertising in Canada; Advertising in the United States; *Hiroshima*; *Life*; *Look*; *Maclean's*; Pinup girls; Pulp magazines; *Reader's Digest*; Rockwell, Norman; *Saturday Evening Post*.

■ "Maisie" films

Identification Popular series of ten B-films starring Ann Sothern as a good-hearted entertainer.

Date Released from 1939 to 1947

The upbeat Maisie films—all but one of which were made during the 1940's—were a reflection of two sentiments in the American filmgoing public: the "can do" attitude prevalent in the immediate prewar years during the final recovery from the Great Depression, and the home front's wish to be able to forget the war, if only for a brief time.

The year 1939 saw the release of some of the most memorable films of all time, nearly all of them designed for sheer entertainment value. Among the more modest films produced at Metro-Goldwyn-Mayer (MGM) that year was *Maisie*, starring vivacious blond Ann Sothern. The film had originally been set to star Jean Harlow, but after she died in 1937 it was scaled down to bottom-of-the-bill fare. Nevertheless, the film surprisingly proved to be a major success, earning back many times its cost, and Sothern was given a long-term contract by the studio.

Born Harriette Lake, Sothern had labored among the ranks of female B-film actors for many years before getting her break at one of the premier Hollywood studios. The Maisie films featured her as a rather brassy but spunky and good-hearted chorus girl named Maisie Ravier (also spelled "Revere"). During the ten-film series, she did everything from solving murders and foiling dastardly plots to working at various jobs that included gold mining and stints at a defense plant, as a secretary, and even as the target in a knife-throwing act.

Extensive travel apparently was required of the average chorus girl, because Maisie found herself traveling widely both at home and abroad. Wherever she landed, it was a hallmark of her character that she ultimately succeeded at everything she tried, and of-

ten helped to straighten out other people's lives as well. She frequently performed musical numbers to validate her talents.

Sothern's real-life talent as a singer enabled her to be cast in occasional MGM musicals, including *Lady Be Good* (1941), *Panama Hattie* (1942), *Words and Music* (1948), and *Nancy Goes to Rio* (1950). She stated that getting roles in a few A-films was her reward for continuing as Maisie, although she actually may not have had much choice in the matter. As long as the series remained profitable, MGM would continue it.

Following the original film, the others in the series were *Congo Maisie* (1940), *Gold Rush Maisie* (1940), *Maisie Was a Lady* (1941), *Ringside Maisie* (costarring actor Robert Sterling, whom Sothern later married), *Maisie Gets Her Man* (1942), *Swing Shift Maisie* (1943), *Maisie Goes to Reno* (1944), *Up Goes Maisie* (1946), and finally *Undercover Maisie* (1947).

Impact Portraying Maisie may have been detrimental to Ann Sothern's long-term career. She largely remained typecast as a brassy peroxide blond at MGM. That she was a fine actor as well was revealed in such films as *Cry "Havoc"* (1943), *A Letter to Three Wives* (1949), and *The Blue Gardenia* (1953). In later years, she played supporting roles in *Lady in a Cage* (1964), *The Best Man* (1964), and *The Whales of August* (1987), for which she received her only Oscar nomination. Sothern also successfully transitioned into television, starring in *Private Secretary* from 1953 to 1957 and then in *The Ann Sothern Show* from 1958 to 1961, winning a Golden Globe Award in 1959.

The Maisie series was very much a product of the 1940's. It fulfilled its mission of pure, if unrealistic, entertainment, helping wartime audiences to escape bad news for a bit more than an hour or so. Reflecting the heightened roles of women during World War II, it was one of the rare cinema feature series to star a strong, self-reliant woman.

Roy Liebman

Further Reading

Basinger, Jeanine. "The Lady Who Was Maisie: Ann Sothern." *Film Comment* 35, no. 6 (1999): 24-35.
Schultz, Margie. *Ann Sothern: A Bio-Bibliography*. New York: Scarecrow, 1990.

See also Andy Hardy films; Film in the United States; Film serials; *Sullivan's Travels*; Women's roles and rights in the United States.

■ The Maltese Falcon

Identification   Classic hard-boiled detective film
Director   John Huston (1906-1987)
Date   Premiered on October 3, 1941

The Maltese Falcon *helped establish Humphrey Bogart as a Hollywood leading man, launched the directorial career of John Huston, and would eventually be considered by many to be the first film noir.*

The Maltese Falcon's story centers on the investigation of detective Sam Spade (Humphrey Bogart) into his partner's murder as well as the theft of a valuable exotic object—a jewel-encrusted statue of a falcon—by a group of eccentric international criminals. Spade's methods are those of the "hard-boiled" detective rather than the gentleman sleuth: He trusts no one, has violent confrontations with suspects, and ultimately insinuates himself into the criminal gang, even having a sexual relationship with the woman (played by Mary Astor) whom he later exposes as a murderer.

The Maltese Falcon is the third and most famous film adaptation of the 1929 Dashiell Hammett novel of the same name, and it adheres most closely to its literary source. Director John Huston used allusive techniques in his handling of story elements that were expressly forbidden by the Hollywood Production Code. This use of allusion in place of clear narrative exposition lends the film a somewhat disorienting and morally murky quality that was of particular interest to French film critics viewing the film for the first time after World War II had ended. These critics noted thematic and visual patterns of alienation and ambiguity in *The Maltese Falcon* and other early 1940's American crime films that led them to posit a new category of "dark" American cinema, or "film noir," and to identify *The Maltese Falcon* as the first entry in this cycle of films.

Impact   *The Maltese Falcon* remains one of the most famous and widely referenced American detective movies of all time.

Christine Photinos

Further Reading

Layman, Richard, ed. *Discovering the Maltese Falcon and Sam Spade.* San Francisco, Calif.: Vince Emery Productions, 2005.
Naremore, James. "John Huston and *The Maltese Fal-* con." *Literature/Film Quarterly* 1, no. 3 (1973): 239-249.

See also   Bogart, Humphrey; Censorship in the United States; *Double Indemnity*; Film in the United States; Film noir; *Laura*; Pulp magazines; *The Treasure of the Sierra Madre.*

■ Manhattan Project

Identification   U.S. Army research project, officially named the Manhattan Engineering District, that designed and built the world's first nuclear weapons

The Manhattan Project ushered the world into the nuclear age, demonstrating that the energy released by nuclear fission could be triggered and controlled. It produced the two atomic bombs dropped on Japan at the end of World War II; achieved the first artificial nuclear chain reaction and laid the scientific and engineering foundations for the generation of electricity from nuclear power; and advanced the art of nuclear chemistry, achieving transmutation of the elements and the artificial production of radioactive isotopes on a practical scale.

Otto Hahn and Lise Meitner discovered uranium fission during the late 1930's. The immense amount of energy released in the process opened up the possibility that uranium could be used as an explosive of unprecedented destructive power. In a letter delivered to President Franklin D. Roosevelt on October 11, 1939, physicists Albert Einstein and Leo Szilard alerted the president that Nazi Germany might be researching nuclear fission to develop a nuclear weapon and that the United States should follow suit. At Roosevelt's direction, an aide set up an Advisory Committee on Uranium to keep the president informed as research continued. In June of 1942, the committee reported that the research had advanced to the point that construction of a pilot plant and preliminary design of production plants for fissionable material were possible. It recommended that the U.S. Army Corps of Engineers begin construction. President Roosevelt agreed. An unnamed engineering district under the direction of Colonel James C. Marshall was created on June 18, 1942, to carry out this responsibility.

In September of 1942, Colonel Marshall was promoted, reassigned overseas, and relieved by Brigadier General Leslie R. Groves. The district was now designated the Manhattan Engineering District after the location of Colonel Marshall's headquarters; General Groves made his new headquarters in Washington, D.C.

The greatest challenge facing the Manhattan Project was the accumulation of sufficient quantities of fissionable material. Physicists had identified two very likely candidates: the natural isotope uranium-235 (U-235), and the artificial isotope plutonium-239 (Pu-239). Natural uranium is only seven-tenths of 1 percent U-235; the remainder is overwhelmingly uranium-238 (U-238), which could not be made to fission with any process available during the 1940's. U-235 cannot be chemically separated from U-238; it must be physically separated using processes that rely on the tiny 1.2 percent difference in mass between the two isotopes. Plutonium is an artificial element created by bombarding U-238 with neutrons to form U-239, which then radioactively

decays into Pu-239. Producing either of these two materials in industrial quantities seemed so difficult and uncertain that it was decided to pursue both in parallel. The plutonium effort was assigned to the Hanford Nuclear Reservation, and the uranium effort was assigned to the Clinton Engineering Works at Oakridge, Tennessee. Design and construction of the nuclear weapons themselves was assigned to a new laboratory known only as Los Alamos.

Hanford Nuclear Reservation Natural uranium contains enough U-235 to support a controllable fission chain reaction under the proper circumstances. The copious amounts of neutrons emitted by the reaction bombard U-238 atoms and transmute them into Pu-239. The Pu-239 can then be chemically separated and used as raw material for nuclear weapons. A team of scientists and engineers led by Enrico Fermi created the first sustainable fission chain reaction in uranium on December 2, 1942. Within weeks, the Manhattan Project acquired

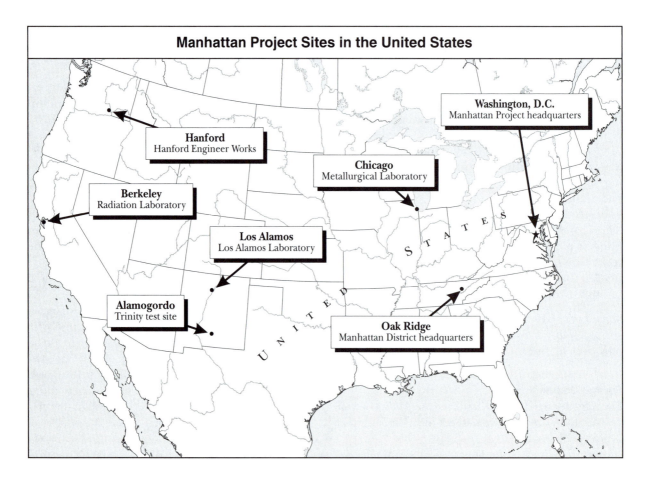

Manhattan Project Sites in the United States

780 square miles of vacant land in south-central Washington State for the Hanford Engineer Works. Construction of three nuclear reactors and four chemical separation plants began in late 1942. In the next three years, this huge facility produced enough Pu-239 for three nuclear devices.

Clinton Engineering Works The Manhattan Project settled on two competing methods to separate U-235 from U-238. In electromagnetic separation, the uranium was rendered into a gas (uranium hexafluoride), the gas ionized and then electrically propelled through a magnetic field. In traveling through the magnetic field, the lighter U-235 followed a more sharply curved path than the U-238. The two isotopes ended their journeys at two different places. In gaseous diffusion, the uranium hexafluoride was pumped through a series of porous barriers with millions of submicroscopic openings per square inch. The gas molecules containing U-235 trickled through the barriers at a slightly higher rate than those with U-238. After passing through several thousand such barriers, the concentration of U-235 was significantly enhanced.

The Manhattan Project acquired 59,000 acres of land along the Clinch River in eastern Tennessee in September, 1942, for the Clinton Engineer Works, anchored by the town of Oak Ridge. The electromagnetic separation complex was known as Y-12; it eventually employed more than 4,800 people. The gaseous diffusion complex was known as K-25, a single four-story building with 43 acres under one roof. In three years, Y-12 and K-25 together separated enough U-235 for a single bomb.

Los Alamos The Manhattan Project acquired the Los Alamos Ranch School outside Santa Fe, New Mexico, to use as the site for the bomb development laboratory. The University of California was contracted to operate the laboratory. J. Robert Oppenheimer was appointed laboratory director. Los Alamos produced two different types of bomb. "Little Boy" used a gun to fire a uranium slug into a subcritical mass of uranium at high velocity. Once the slug and subcritical mass joined, an explosive fission chain reaction was spontaneous. "Fat Man" used chemical explosives to squeeze a subcritical mass of plutonium to a density high enough for explosive fission to occur. The Little Boy design was considered so reliable that no testing was required. The Fat Man design was successfully tested at

5:30 A.M. on July 16, 1945, at a desert site code-named Trinity near Alamogordo, New Mexico.

On August 6, 1945, at 8:15 A.M., Little Boy detonated over the Japanese city of Hiroshima, killing 145,000 people. On August 9, 1945, at 11:02 A.M., Fat Man detonated over the city of Nagasaki, killing 70,000. On August 15, 1945, the Emperor of Japan broadcast a statement to his subjects ordering the acceptance of the Allied surrender terms. The surrender documents were signed aboard the USS *Missouri* on September 2, 1945.

Impact The successful conclusion of the Manhattan Project drastically altered the role of war in international relationships. It put the United States in a place of unprecedented international power and influence. When the Soviet Union joined it in the exclusive club of nuclear powers, the United States had to get used to sharing that power and influence. Deep feelings of mutual distrust and fear kept the two superpowers locked in a subdued conflict known as the Cold War that lasted for decades. Almost all international crises since World War II have been influenced to some degree by the chilling possibility of nuclear war.

Subsequent Events The Atomic Energy Act of 1946 placed all nuclear research and nuclear weapons development under the control of the Atomic Energy Commission, for all intents and purposes bringing the Manhattan Project to an official end. Los Alamos, Oak Ridge, and Hanford continued operations, slowly building up a stockpile of nuclear weapons. Many of the leading scientists working on the project returned to academic posts; some remained with the project to begin work on weapons exploiting thermonuclear fusion rather than fission. The world's first thermonuclear explosion, the work of agencies succeeding the Manhattan Project, took place on November 1, 1952.

On August 29, 1949, the Soviet Union detonated its first atomic explosive device. The Soviet Union detonated its first thermonuclear device on August 12, 1953.

Billy R. Smith, Jr.

Further Reading

Bird, Kai, and Martin J. Sherwin. *American Prometheus: The Triumph and Tragedy of J. Robert Oppenheimer.* New York: Alfred A. Knopf, 2005. Pulitzer Prize-winning biography of the physicist who led the scientific team that developed nuclear weapons.

Groves, Leslie R. *Now It Can Be Told: The Story of the Manhattan Project.* New York: Da Capo Press, 1962. Unabridged republication of the memoirs of the Manhattan Project's military commander.

Howes, Ruth H., and Caroline C. Herzenberg. *Their Day in the Sun: Women of the Manhattan Project.* Philadelphia: Temple University Press, 1999. Documents the frequently overlooked contributions of women to the Manhattan Project.

Joseph, Timothy. *Historic Photos of the Manhattan Project.* Nashville, Tenn.: Turner Publishing, 2009. A stunning visual history of the making of the atomic bomb.

Rhodes, Richard. *The Making of the Atomic Bomb.* New York: Simon & Schuster, 1986. This award-winning book tells the story of the atom bomb from all angles: scientific, political, military, and human.

See also Atomic bomb; Einstein, Albert; *Enola Gay*; Fermi, Enrico; Groves, Leslie Richard; Hanford Nuclear Reservation; Hiroshima and Nagasaki bombings; Oppenheimer, J. Robert; Plutonium discovery; Synchrocyclotron; Wartime industries.

■ Marines, U.S.

Identification Specialized elite branch of the U.S. military trained in coordinated land, sea, and air combat

Also known as United States Marine Corps; USMC

The Marines transformed warfare operations during World War II into an integrated air-land-sea offensive for the first time. Involved in fifteen landings using six divisions across the Pacific, the Marines would become established as amphibious landing specialists and the first to be deployed into hostile territory.

At the start of World War II in 1939, the United States was reluctant to enter into the conflict. However, the surrender of France to Germany on June 17, 1940, made it apparent that the United States would soon become involved. All branches of the U.S. military began preparations, and the Marines were deployed to Iceland on July 7, 1941. A surprise attack by the Japanese on Pearl Harbor, Hawaii, on December 7, 1941, caught the United States off guard, propelling it into war.

The United States Marine Corps is a quick-strike force that conducts amphibious warfare and trains all Marines to be riflemen, including aviators. This comprehensive training distinguishes Marines from all other military forces worldwide. During the 1940's, the Marine Corps contained aviation, fleet marine, and land divisions skilled in amphibious warfare. By mid-1941, the corps had trained 50,000 Marines. Four years later, when World War II ended, the corps comprised almost 460,000 Marines.

During World War II, the Marines were charged with Pacific Fleet war operations, while the Army concentrated on European war operations. Just days after the attack on Pearl Harbor, attacks on Guam, Wake Island, and the Philippines overwhelmed all American military forces stationed there. Marines, along with civilians and Army and Navy specialists, were forced to surrender and taken prisoner. The surrender at Corregidor in the Philippines was a difficult defeat because soldiers had fought valiantly. Prisoners were forced to march sixty miles out of Bataan in intense heat, with no food or water, to a Japanese prison camp. This forced march later became infamously known as the Bataan Death March, in which an estimated 5,000 to 10,000 died.

On August 7, 1942, the first significant Marine Corps battle took place during the Battle of Guadalcanal in the Solomon Islands. The Japanese were building a crucial airstrip at Guadalcanal. The Solomon Islands, along with the British islands and New Guinea, were strategically important to Allied forces because they represented the only supply route open for armed forces and for the defense of Australia. Although the Marines established a secure beachhead quickly, it would not be until February, 1943, when Guadalcanal and the sea-lanes to Australia were firmly in American possession. This victory, and the victory at the Battle of Midway in June, 1942, when Marine aviators intercepted attacking forces of Japanese aircraft, dealt a crucial blow to the Imperial Japanese Navy. Fierce battles also raged on the Russell Islands, New Georgia Islands, and Bougainville (an important staging area and base for the Japanese) because of their proximity to Guadalcanal.

The second pivotal World War II battle proved to be at Tarawa. On Betio Island in the Tarawa Atoll in the central Pacific, the Second Marine Division (with artillery coverage by the U.S. Navy) landed on November 20, 1943. Although the Battle of Tarawa proved to be difficult and deadly, the Marine Corps eventually secured the island four days later. Other strategically important battles for the corps would take place at Cape Gloucester (1943), Saipan (1944), Tinian (1944), and Peleliu (1944). Guam would be retaken in 1944.

The most deadly and historic Marine battle of World War II occurred at Iwo Jima in 1945. Iwo Jima, one of the Volcano Islands south of Japan, was the site of two Japanese airstrips and a strategically important base for Japanese fighter planes. Seventy thousand Marines from the Third, Fourth, and Fifth Marine Divisions landed on February 19, 1945. The Twenty-eighth Marine Regiment fought for Mount Suribachi, raising the American flag in victory on February 23. A photograph of the Marines raising the American flag would later become one of the most famous photographs of the war. The rest of the island was not securely in American possession until March 26, and more than 26,000 Marines, along with almost 3,000 Navy personnel, were killed or wounded during this battle.

Okinawa, the largest island of Japan's Ryukyu chain, was the site of the last battle the Marines would fight during World War II. Combined detachments of Marine and Army soldiers landed on Okinawa on April 1, 1945. Despite Japanese kamikaze pilot attacks, which sank thirty naval ships and killed or wounded almost 10,000 Navy personnel, the Marines were able to secure the island on June 21, 1945.

Besides serving as combat forces, Marines distinguished themselves as couriers, intelligence operatives, occupation troops, and combat correspondents. A total of 19,733 Marines died during World War II. Despite the Marines' distinguished service during the war, ranks were reduced to 92,000 by 1946, and the Army and Air Force argued that amphibious and air operations should become part of their responsibility. The passage of the National Defense Act of 1947 established that the Navy would re-

U.S. Marines on Bougainville in March, 1944. (Digital Stock)

tain air capabilities and the Marine Corps would remain as a separate and distinct branch of the Navy under the command of the secretary of the Navy, capable of fighting on land, at sea, and in the air.

Impact World War II established the Marines as amphibious landing specialists and an elite fighting force throughout the world. Their fighting prowess proved crucial to winning World War II.

Alice C. Richer

Further Reading

Chenoweth, H. Avery, and Brooke Nihart. *Semper Fi: The Definitive Illustrated History of the U.S. Marine Corps.* New York: Sterling, 2005. A lavishly illustrated work that includes more than one thousand photographs.

Isely, Jeter Allen, and Philip A. Crowl. *The U.S. Marines and Amphibious War: Its Theory and Its Practice in the Pacific.* Princeton, N.J.: Princeton University Press, 1951. Addresses many of the questions about operations in the Solomon Islands. A valuable interpretive account of the war in the Pacific.

Rottman, Gordon L. *U.S. Marine Corps World War II Order of Battle: Ground and Air Units in the Pacific War, 1939-1945.* Westport, Conn.: Greenwood Press, 2002. Covers the organizational aspects of the Marine Corps during World War II. Includes twenty-one maps.

See also Army, U.S.; Bataan Death March; Guadalcanal, Battle of; Iwo Jima, Battle of; Midway, Battle of; Navy, U.S.; Okinawa, Battle of; Pearl Harbor attack; War heroes; World War II mobilization.

■ Marshall, George C.

Identification Chief of staff of the U.S. Army, 1939-1945; U.S. secretary of state, 1947-1949

Born December 31, 1880; Uniontown, Pennsylvania

Died October 16, 1959; Washington, D.C.

Marshall has been heralded by scholars as the architect of victory in World War II. He emerged as the key planner in devising and implementing U.S. military strategies during wartime and remained an instrumental figure in the development of foreign policy in the postwar period.

George C. Marshall's father owned a successful coal business, but as a young man Marshall decided that he wanted to become a soldier. In order to achieve his career goal, he graduated from the Virginia Military Institute in 1901 as senior first captain. During World War I, Marshall helped to plan American operations in the Battle of Cantigny and in the offensive of St. Mihiel, working his way to become aide-de-camp to General John J. Pershing. From 1927 until

General George C. Marshall (right) talking to industrialist Henry J. Kaiser in late 1942. (AP/Wide World Photos)

1932, Marshall was in charge of instruction at the military school at Fort Benning, and a few years later he became commandant at the Army War College. These positions enabled him to make contact with figures that would play important roles as war loomed for the United States. In 1939, Marshall accepted a post with the General Staff in Washington, D.C., and one year later President Franklin D. Roosevelt named Marshall as chief of staff with the rank of general.

Mobilization and Planning for War Just prior to the attack on Pearl Harbor in December, 1941, Marshall urged political leaders to plan for the military readiness of American forces. Marshall eventually became responsible for the largest military expansion and mobilization of troops, which numbered more than eight million, and he decided not to promote officers who he thought would not have the physical prowess or mental acuity to be on a battlefield. He drew upon his experience at the Army War College and hand-selected men he knew whose tactical and strategic planning abilities would inspire others. These men included Dwight D. Eisenhower, Leslie McNair, Mark Wayne Clark, and Omar Bradley. Faced with huge increases in forces, Marshall became a strong advocate of universal military training and was instrumental in the passing of the 1941 draft law. He decided to go with McNair's idea of a basic training camp of several weeks so that troops could become proficient in infantry skills, using weapons, and combat techniques.

Despite this training, the inexperience of American commanders on the battlefield was apparent when the Army suffered major losses against German armored combat units at Kasserine Pass in North Africa in early 1943. Despite the implementation of an individual replacement system and refresher training courses by late 1944, the results were still mixed for American combat ability. Marshall began using his powers of persuasion to convince political and military leaders that a cross-channel invasion was a necessary strategy in order to defeat Nazi Germany. He had hoped for the invasion to begin in 1943 but had to wait for another year before Operation Overlord was launched by Allied forces. In December, 1944, Marshall became the first American to be promoted to the rank of five-star general, and *Time* magazine named him man of the year.

After World War II Marshall resigned as chief of staff in 1945, but two years later President Harry S. Truman appointed him as secretary of state. Marshall made his mark on foreign policy in a speech on June 5, 1947, at Harvard University in which he outlined a plan to quickly rebuild and bolster the economic recovery of Europe, known as the Marshall Plan. This plan would provide $13 billion in aid to war-torn countries in Western Europe and initiated the formation of the North Atlantic Treaty Organization (NATO). In 1949, the president sent Marshall to China to mediate a deal between the Nationalists under Chiang Kai-shek and the communists under Mao Zedong, but both sides rejected his proposals.

Impact For his achievements in devising the economic recovery of Europe, Marshall was once again named as *Time*'s man of the year, in 1948. Marshall, although noted as being austere in personality, was recognized as a man of courage, vision, and integrity whose problem-solving skills helped to win World War II and assisted in the pursuit of peace during the postwar period. He was awarded the Nobel Peace Prize in 1953 for these accomplishments.

Gayla Koerting

Further Reading

Husted, Stewart. *George C. Marshall: The Rubrics of Leadership.* Carlisle Barracks, Pa.: U.S. Army War College Foundation, 2006. Examines Marshall's exceptional leadership abilities, especially his talent for managing, negotiating, and building consensus among his peers.

Pogue, Forrest C. *George C. Marshall: Ordeal and Hope, 1939-1942.* New York: Viking Press, 1968. In the second volume of a four-part biographical series, a preeminent military historian emphasizes Marshall's early years as chief of staff.

_____. *George C. Marshall: Organizer of Victory, 1943-1945.* New York: Viking Press, 1973. Addresses how Marshall managed victory for Allied forces in his adept handling of military and political leaders.

_____. *George C. Marshall: Statesman, 1945-1959.* New York: Viking Press, 1987. Analysis of Marshall's political career as a diplomat as Europe struggled to rebuild and as the Cold War escalated.

Stoler, Mark A. *George C. Marshall: Soldier-Statesman of the American Century.* Boston: Twayne, 1989. Intended as reading for undergraduates, Stoler's book combines military and diplomatic history along with the emergence of national security policy in this single-volume biography of Marshall.

Weintraub, Stanley. *Fifteen Stars: Eisenhower, MacArthur, Marshall: Three Generals Who Saved the American Century.* New York: Free Press, 2007. A military historian, Weintraub addresses the complex relationship of three of the most prominent generals during the twentieth century, explaining how they shaped World War II military strategy and Cold War policy.

See also Bradley, Omar N.; D Day; Eisenhower, Dwight D.; Foreign policy of the United States; Marshall Plan; Military conscription in the United States; Patton, George S.; World War II; World War II mobilization.

■ Marshall Plan

Identification American postwar economic aid program for Europe

Also known as European Recovery Program; European Recovery Act of 1948

Date Enabling bill passed on April 3, 1948

Designed to help relieve suffering resulting from World War II's economic devastation and to contain communism by strengthening Western Europe's ability to resist Soviet expansion, the Marshall Plan succeeded in meeting all its basic objectives. In recognition for his contributions toward creating the plan and administering it, U.S. secretary of state George C. Marshall would receive the Nobel Peace Prize in 1953.

At the end of World War II, the United States and the Soviet Union emerged as the world's two greatest powers. Although these nations had been allies during their fight against Nazi Germany, toward the end of the war, it became evident to U.S. policy makers that when the war ended, the West would face a ma-

The Marshall Plan Speech

On June 5, 1947, Secretary of State George Marshall delivered his memorable speech to Harvard University's graduating class. In it he outlined the necessity of assisting in the postwar reconstruction of Europe. An excerpt of his address is reproduced below.

It is logical that the United States should do whatever it is able to do to assist in the return of normal economic health in the world, without which there can be no political stability and no assured peace. Our policy is directed not against any country or doctrine but against hunger, poverty, desperation, and chaos. Its purpose should be the revival of a working economy in the world so as to permit the emergence of political and social conditions in which free institutions can exist.

Such assistance, I am convinced, must not be on a piecemeal basis, as various crises develop. Any assistance that this government may render in the future should provide a cure rather than a mere palliative. Any government that is willing to assist in the task of recovery will find full cooperation, I am sure, on the part of the United States government . . .

It is already evident that before the United States government can proceed much further in its efforts to alleviate the situation and help start the European world on its way to recovery, there must be some agreement among the countries of Europe as to the requirements of the situation and the part those countries themselves will take in order to give a proper effect to whatever actions might be undertaken by this government. It would be neither fitting nor efficacious for our government to undertake to draw up unilaterally a program designed to place Europe on its feet economically. This is the business of the Europeans. The initiative, I think, must come from Europe. The role of this country should consist of friendly aid in the drafting of a European program and of later support of such a program so far as it may be practical for us to do so.

employment, and poverty were widespread. The region seemed a ripe arena for conflict between the United States and the Soviet Union, each of which was concerned with protecting its national security. After both countries had invested heavily in the destruction of the Axis Powers, they found themselves competing for influence in a weakened Western Europe.

U.S. president Harry S. Truman wanted to articulate a doctrine designed to contain communist expansion; one means of doing this was by using foreign aid to help Western Europe rebuild. However, the expansion of Soviet influence into Western Europe was not the only postwar American concern. There was also an even more immediate concern about the postwar American economy. The economy had flourished during World War II, thanks to government spending of huge sums on war-related materials. With the end of heavy wartime spending, the national economy was expected to go into a slump. There was also a concern about what to do with the millions of American service personnel soon to return home. Concerns about the economy tied into recognition that Western Europe's poor economic condition would damage the American economy because Europe would no longer be a strong trading partner. Finally, there was a basic humanitarian concern that Europeans hurt by the war needed to be helped to improve their own lives personally, politically, and economically.

On March 12, 1947, President Truman addressed Congress, appealing for more than $300 million in aid to the European nations. The occasion marked the inauguration of what became known as the Truman Doctrine, which committed the United States to defend governments throughout the world when

jor new adversary in the Soviet Union. This time, however, the conflict—which was to become known as the Cold War—would be fought in a different manner, using different methods, such as economic influence.

The Cold War The Cold War began while much of Western Europe was still in shambles, struggling to recover from physical damage left by World War II and a severe postwar economic slump. Throughout Western Europe, hunger, economic deprivation, un-

they were threatened with communist subversion. In June, Secretary of State George C. Marshall articulated a plan for helping Europe recover economically during his commencement address at Harvard University.

Implementation of the Plan   After hearing Marshall's proposal, British foreign minister Ernest Bevin called a meeting of European ministers to prepare a response. Nothing in what Marshall said excluded the Soviet Union or its satellites, and at the first European planning session in June the Soviets were represented by their foreign minister, Vyacheslav Mikhailovich Molotov. However, the Soviets were reluctant to disclose details of their economic needs and quickly withdrew from the meeting. After long negotiations, the European nations presented a plan to the United States. Following revisions suggested by American officials, the plan became the basis for the European Recovery Act that the U.S. Congress passed in April, 1948.

The names of Truman and Marshall are most frequently cited in discussions of the Marshall Plan but other individuals, such as George F. Kennan and W. Averell Harriman, also played prominent roles in the plan's implementation. In addition, many European leaders also contributed to its success.

The American legislation created what was officially known as the European Recovery Program (ERP) but more popularly known as the Marshall Plan. Over a period of four years, it provided approximately $13.3 billion for European economic relief in seventeen nations. Because the American federal budget at that time was less than $100 billion per year, this sum represented a substantial commitment. Through the nearly four years of the plan's existence, the aid provided to Europe annually amounted to 1.2 percent of the total U.S. gross national product.

After the program had been formulated, the president, the cabinet, and many other officials threw their support behind it. The program provided that most food, raw materials, and machinery would be purchased in America and thus promised a substantial increase in American exports. For this reason, the program also found widespread support among American business and agricultural leaders. Many political leaders viewed it as a means of containing communism through the use of American economic strength. However, polls taken at the time indicated that a majority of Americans supported the Marshall Plan primarily on humanitarian grounds.

Impact   The Marshall Plan has generally been regarded as a success. The European countries that participated in it gained clear economic benefits. Moreover, the United States itself also benefited because the countries receiving aid were able to buy American goods. Although some critics of the plan have suggested that the European nations would have eventually recovered on their own, it is evident that American aid hastened their recovery. In addition, it may be argued that the plan also accelerated European economic and political integration. The Marshall Plan has also been credited with reducing communist influence in Europe and helping to foster the creation of the North Atlantic Treaty Organization (NATO).

William E. Kelly

Further Reading

Bonds, John Bledsoe. *Bipartisan Strategy: Selling the Marshall Plan.* Westport, Conn.: Praeger, 2002. Study of the domestic campaign to urge Congress to pass the Economic Recovery Act.

Gimbel, John. *The Origins of the Marshall Plan.* Stanford, Calif.: Stanford University Press, 1976. Traces the origins of the Marshall Plan to American policy makers and to specific postwar events. Gimbel sees the East-West conflict as a minor influence on development and implementation of the plan.

Hogan, Michael J. *The Marshall Plan: America, Britain, and the Reconstruction of Western Europe, 1947-1952.* New York: Cambridge University Press, 1987. Carefully researched and comprehensive analysis of the Marshall Plan that takes into account the arguments of its critics and concludes that the plan achieved its major economic and political purposes.

Mee, Charles L., Jr. *The Marshall Plan: The Launching of the Pax Americana.* New York: Simon & Schuster, 1984. Clearly written and balanced account of the formulation and adoption of the Marshall Plan, incorporating data and figures into the text. Excellent source for students new to the subject.

Milward, Alan S. *The Reconstruction of Western Europe, 1945-1951.* Berkeley: University of California Press, 1984. Detailed study of all aspects of Europe's postwar economic recovery, with numerous tables documenting progress of the recovery in detail.

Pogue, Forrest C. *George C. Marshall: Statesman, 1945-1959.* New York: Viking Press, 1987. This fourth and final volume of the standard biography of Marshall gives an account of the formulation of the Marshall Plan, clarifying Marshall's own contributions.

Schain, Martin, ed. *The Marshall Plan: Fifty Years Later.* New York: Palgrave, 2001. Collection of essays devoted to revisiting the Marshall Plan to reevaluate its effects during its time and to examine its long-term impact on the Cold War and European economic history.

Wexler, Imanuel. *The Marshall Plan Revisited: The European Recovery Program in Economic Perspective.* Westport, Conn.: Greenwood Press, 1983. Places the Marshall Plan in broad economic context and traces factors other than American aid that promoted or hindered economic recovery.

See also Business and the economy in the United States; Cold War; France and the United States; Germany, occupation of; Kennan, George F.; Lend-Lease; Marshall, George C.; North Atlantic Treaty Organization; Truman, Harry S.; Truman Doctrine.

■ Mathias, Bob

Identification American track and field athlete
Born November 17, 1930; Tulare, California
Died September 2, 2006; Fresno, California

In 1948, Mathias became the youngest individual to win the gold medal in the Olympic decathlon, and he is the only American to win it twice. He was the first person to compete in both the Olympics and the Rose Bowl in the same year.

Due to the suggestion of his high school track and field coach, Bob Mathias began training for the decathlon in early 1948. In June of that year, he won the National Decathlon Championship in Bloomfield, New Jersey, which qualified him for the U.S. Olympic team. His score of 7,224 points was the best in the world for the decathlon since 1940.

On August 5, 1948, the seventeen-year-old Mathias began his competition for a gold medal at the Olympics in London, England. After some difficulties with the broad jump, shot put, and high jump events, he did reasonably well in the 100-meter dash and the 400-meter run. After the end of a long, rainy, exhausting day, Mathias found himself in third place in the Olympic decathlon. On the second day, he experienced difficulties in the 110-meter hurdles and discus events. With good showings in the pole vault, the javelin throw, and the 1,500-meter run, Mathias won the gold medal with 7,139 points.

Impact In winning the Olympic decathlon in 1948, Mathias became the epitome of determination, courage, and perseverance. In 1999, he was named by both the Associated Press and the Entertainment and Sports Programming Network (ESPN) as one of the one hundred greatest athletes of the twentieth century.

Alvin K. Benson

Further Reading

Corrigan, Robert J. *Tracking Heroes: Thirteen Track and Field Champions.* Bloomington, Ind.: iUniverse, 2003.

Mendes, Bob, and Bob Mathias. *A Twentieth Century Odyssey: The Bob Mathias Story.* Champaign: Sports Publishing, 2001.

See also Marines, U.S.; Olympic Games of 1948; Sports in Canada; Sports in the United States; Zaharias, Babe Didrikson.

■ Mauldin, Bill

Identification Cartoonist for *Stars and Stripes* and other American service publications during World War II
Born October 29, 1921; Mountain Park, New Mexico
Died January 22, 2003; Newport Beach, California

Mauldin's satirical illustrations and humorous insights regarding the plight of the average infantry soldier of World War II brought comic relief to soldiers and stateside civilians alike.

Born William Henry Mauldin, Bill Mauldin suffered from rickets during his early childhood as a result of poor diet. Unable to engage in physical activity, he pursued an interest in drawing during his spare time. After high school, he moved to the Midwest, where he studied drawing at the Chicago Academy of Fine Arts. *Arizona Highways* was among his earliest patrons, and his work was prominently displayed in several editions of the magazine.

As the United States began expanding its military capability in anticipation of war in Europe, Mauldin joined the Arizona National Guard as an infantryman. When National Guard units were later federalized, he was transferred to Oklahoma's Forty-fifth Division, where he drew editorial cartoons for the *45th Division Army News,* and later *Stars and Stripes* as a member of that publication's staff. Deployed to North Africa in 1943, Mauldin went on to participate in the invasions of Sicily and Italy. He became best known for Willie and Joe, memorable characters who spent much of World War II fighting the Germans, while doing their best to survive inept commanders and lampoon the absurdity of Army life. Mauldin's cartoons were eventually picked up by newspapers back in the United States, and he developed a huge following across the country. His cartoons were exceptionally popular among enlisted soldiers but were frowned upon by some officers, most notably George S. Patton. General Patton viewed Mauldin's editorial cartoons and commentary as so insubordinate that he pledged to "throw his ass in jail."

Cartoonist Bill Mauldin in late 1944. (Getty Images)

Impact Todd DePastino, Mauldin's biographer, referred to him in his book *Bill Mauldin: A Life Up Front* as "the greatest cartoonist of the greatest generation." Mauldin's popular editorial cartoon featuring Willie and Joe was awarded the Pulitzer Prize in 1945, which resulted in a cover story in *Time* magazine in December of that year.

After the close of the war, Mauldin worked as an editorial cartoonist for the *St. Louis Dispatch,* where he won a second Pulitzer Prize in 1959, before moving on to work for the *Chicago-Sun Times.* Perhaps the most recognizable image ever depicted by Mauldin appeared in the *Chicago-Sun Times* after the assassination of President John F. Kennedy in 1963. The captionless illustration showing President Lincoln's likeness seated at the memorial on the National Mall collapsed in grief and utter disbelief mirrored the mood of the nation.

Mauldin published several books during his career. He tried a brief stint as an actor, appearing in the 1951 film *The Red Badge of Courage* with Audie Murphy, and several other commercial and political endeavors, including a run as a Democratic nominee for New York's Twenty-eighth Congressional District, prior to his retirement.

Donald C. Simmons, Jr.

Further Reading

DePastino, Todd. *Bill Mauldin: A Life Up Front.* New York: W. W. Norton, 2008.

Mauldin, Bill. *Willie and Joe: The WWII Years.* Seattle: Fantagraphics Books, 2008.

Reader's Digest Association. *America in the '40's: A Sentimental Journey.* Foreword by Bill Mauldin. Pleasantville, N.Y.: Author, 1998.

See also Army, U.S.; Comic strips; *Life*; Murphy, Audie; Murrow, Edward R.; Patton, George S.; Pyle, Ernie; *Stars and Stripes.*

■ Medicine

The early 1940's saw a continuation of the medical discoveries that had been made in previous decades, and events of World War II sped these discoveries, notably in the development of antibiotics for the treatment of battlefield wounds, the storage and fractionation of blood plasma, and the creation of vaccines. In addition, the war resulted in increased government funding and involvement in medical research.

The 1930's and 1940's marked the termination of the "Golden Age of Microbiology," a period that had begun at the end of the previous century and was notable for the discovery of the role played by infectious agents in the etiology of disease. The decade that began in 1940 was characterized by a significant application of this knowledge. Even by the end of the 1920's, physicians could provide little beyond psychological support for patients suffering from

Heavyweight boxer Joe Louis with a young, recovering polio patient with whom he is helping publicize a fund-raising appeal in late 1947. (AP/Wide World Photos)

disease. The use of antibiotics would change that, and by 1949 scientists generally believed that with the exception of polio, infectious disease was coming under control. The study of blood chemistry likewise advanced as the instrumentation and methodology developed in earlier decades was more effectively applied.

Polio   Infantile paralysis, usually referred to simply as poliomyelitis or polio, was arguably the most feared of infectious diseases during the 1940's. Though the number of actual polio victims was smaller than the number of patients suffering from influenza, another infectious disease, the seeming randomness of polio and the demographics of its victims, who generally were children and young adults, created waves of fear during the summer months. Polio was a relatively rare disease at the beginning of the twentieth century, but the incidence of polio in the United States doubled to 8 cases per 100,000 people in the first five years of the 1940's, doubled again in the second five years to nearly 30,000 cases, and would double again in the 1950's.

The absence of any preventive measures beyond the isolation of children during "polio season" and the inability to provide any relief for victims added to the fear of the disease. The iron lung had been developed, enabling patients encased in this cylindrical barrel to breathe. Children wore braces or casts to aid in walking or to provide support for muscles undergoing atrophy. In 1940, an Australian nurse, Sister Elizabeth Kenny, and her adopted daughter came to the United States to demonstrate the use of hot compresses and exercises as a means of reviving withered muscles. Kenny had trained as a nurse during World War I (the title "Sister" designated her rank in the Royal Australian Army Nursing Corps), and her rehabilitation work with children had developed from her army service. While the overall usefulness of Kenny's methods remain controversial, her techniques had a far-reaching impact in the growing role of rehabilitation as a means of treating injuries or illnesses.

The development of vaccines to prevent infectious diseases had become well established by the 1940's, and any hope of controlling polio was dependent on such a polio vaccine. The viral agent causing the disease had been isolated by Karl Landsteiner in Vienna some three decades earlier, but earlier attempts at producing such a vaccine had met with disaster; inactivated versions of the virus had actually caused the disease among children during the 1930's. The inability to grow the virus in the laboratory in anything but animals had hindered any progress. The breakthrough for a polio vaccine came in 1948, when Boston researchers John Franklin Enders, Thomas Weller, and Frederick Robbins demonstrated the growth of the virus in nonneural tissues in the laboratory. A method to readily characterize the virus became available. Among the researchers studying the problems in vaccine development was Jonas Salk, who had established his laboratory at the University of Pittsburgh in 1947. Funding for much of the polio research was provided by a private charity, the National Foundation for Infantile Paralysis (NFIP), in its "March of Dimes" program.

Antibiotic Development   The idea of a "magic bullet" that could target infectious agents like bacteria had its origin early in the twentieth century. Salvarsan, an arsenic derivative, had been developed by German scientist Paul Ehrlich, but it was too toxic for general use. German scientist Gerhard Domagk had discovered sulfa drugs during the 1930's, but the rise of the Nazi Party, as well as limitations in the antibiotic itself, had limited its applications. The first highly effective antibiotic, discovered by Sir Alexander Fleming in 1928, was penicillin, derived from the mold *Penicillium*.

While penicillin had been shown to be effective in killing bacteria, particularly deadly strains of *Staphylococcus* and *Streptococcus*, production of the antibiotic in large quantities had been difficult. Knowledge that wound infections had been a significant cause of mortalities in wars provided impetus to develop a technology for the production of penicillin in sufficient quantities for use in treating both soldiers and civilian populations.

Because the survival of Great Britain remained in doubt during the early years of World War II, British scientists Howard Walter Florey (who later became Baron Florey) and Norman George Heatley came to the United States in 1941 in the hope of persuading American scientists to study the effectiveness of penicillin in the treatment of infections. The two scientists also wanted to encourage American laboratories to produce the drug in large quantities. Florey carried spores of the mold in his coat, so if he was captured by the Germans, the enemy would not discover the reason for his trip.

By 1943, the methods for large-scale production of the penicillin had been developed, initially by the Pfizer pharmaceutical firm but eventually by other drug companies, and the drug's effectiveness in treating infections had been demonstrated. By the end of the war, sufficient quantities were available to treat the general population, while the cost of mass producing the drug was significantly reduced.

In 1944, another broad-spectrum antibiotic, streptomycin, was reported by Rutgers University scientist Selman Abraham Waksman. Streptomycin proved effective in treating tuberculosis, one of the world's most common chronic diseases. Before the end of the decade, several additional antibiotics were developed and had begun to be marketed, including chloramphenicol, which was useful for the treatment of typhoid fever, and tetracycline and neomycin.

Blood Chemistry   Advances in the understanding of blood chemistry and genetics produced significant health benefits for persons in the military, as well as members of the civilian population. In 1940, Landsteiner and his associate Alexander S. Wiener reported the discovery of the Rhesus (Rh) factor, a protein on the surface of red blood cells that played a role in both transfusion rejection and in erythroblastosis fetalis, a life-threatening blood disease in fetuses or newborns. Pregnant women lacking the protein Rh^- often produced an immune response against the Rh^+ blood of a fetus that acquired the Rh gene from the father. Landsteiner, who had previously discovered the ABO blood group system, as well as demonstrating the role of a virus as the etiological agent of polio, died in 1943.

The European war generated a need for significant quantities of blood. However, whole blood could not be kept viable during the time necessary to ship fresh blood from the United States to Great Britain. In 1940, African American physician Charles R. Drew developed a storage procedure using plasma, the liquid portion of blood remaining after the cells are removed. The use of plasma played a significant role in treating severely wounded soldiers. Ironically, Drew could not donate his own blood because of the racism of the time.

Improved fractionation techniques for blood allowed the identification and characterization of blood components, such as albumin, which constituted the largest fraction of blood protein, and a series of globular proteins called alpha, beta, and gamma globulins. Antibodies were found primarily in the gamma globulin fraction, enabling their purification as a means of combating infections from the measles virus. Another blood protein isolated with these methods was fibrin, which proved useful in dealing with severe hemorrhaging.

Government Involvement in Research Prior to World War II, the American government's involvement in medical and other forms of scientific research had been minimal, with funding for medical research coming primarily from charitable organizations. The war resulted in a significantly enlarged government presence in the fields of science and medicine. The Manhattan Project, which led to the development of the atomic bomb, was the most notable example of government participation in scientific research. The reorganization and expansion of government agencies, such as the designation of the National Institute of Health (NIH) as a bureau of the U.S. Public Health Service in 1943, also represented a greater government involvement.

Peaceful uses of radioactive materials remained a goal among medical scientists; radiation therapy was one example of the applications of these materials. The increased use of antibiotics to treat infectious diseases resulted in an effective means of controlling battlefield infections and saved untold thousands of lives. In the aftermath of the war, antibiotics, such as penicillin, became readily available to the general public. In addition to its usefulness in treating infections caused by *Staphylococcus* and *Streptococcus*, penicillin was particularly effective in treating syphilis, the most serious of the venereal diseases of the era. The growing availability of penicillin came at an opportune time because there was a significant increase in sexually transmitted diseases during the 1940's, affecting millions of men who enlisted in the military.

In a discovery that would be important for the next generation, chemist Albert Hofmann reported the hallucinogenic effects that followed his accidental ingestion of lysergic acid diethylamide (LSD) in 1943. Hofmann's research had involved the isolation of ergot derivatives, such as LSD, and he tested their effects on postpartum hemorrhaging.

Subsequent Events Although sulfa drugs had been introduced during the 1930's, the development of several generations of penicillin medications in the decades following World War II was the most notable example of a growing arsenal of drugs for the treatment of infectious disease. Penicillin was not the only such example. Antibiotics, such as streptomycin, chloramphenicol, and tetracycline, provided the first effective means to treat chronic infections, such as tuberculosis or typhoid fever, resulting in a growing belief among medical scientists that infectious disease could now be controlled. However, problems quickly appeared. Use of chloramphenicol resulted in life-threatening anemia in a few patients. Some persons also developed allergies against penicillin, in some cases resulting in life-threatening responses to the presence of the drug. Widespread and often inappropriate applications of antibacterials, including their inclusion in animal feed or their use for the treatment of viral illnesses, by the 1970's resulted in a significant proportion of infections demonstrating resistance to antibiotics. A prime example were the infections caused by the potentially deadly bacterium *Staphylococcus*. By the 1980's, most of these "Staph" infections would no longer respond to penicillin treatment.

Impact The greater involvement of government in medical research was demonstrated by the changes involving the NIH. In 1948, the National Institute of Health was renamed the National Institutes of Health (NIH), with NIH incorporating a variety of research institutions under the same governing body. A research hospital was added in 1953, the same year NIH and the Public Health Service were incorporated within a new cabinet position, the Department of Health, Education and Welfare. The budget for NIH grew from $29 million during the 1940's to more than $10 billion in the 1990's. By the 1990's, most medical research in the United States was funded through government agencies, such as NIH.

Private foundations still played a role in medical research. For example, NFIP's funding of research to discover a means of preventing polio proved successful with the development of the Salk vaccine during the mid-1950's and the subsequent introduction of an oral polio vaccine devised by Albert Sabin. By the twenty-first century, polio had largely been eradicated from the world.

Richard Adler

Further Reading

Allen, Arthur. *Vaccine: The Controversial Story of Medicine's Greatest Lifesaver.* New York: W. W. Norton, 2007. A history of vaccine development, including discussion of vaccines' controversial links to autism. Of particular relevance to the 1940's is the account of the inadvertent hepatitis infection of troops receiving yellow fever vaccines.

Dubos, Rene. *The Professor, the Institute, and DNA.* New York: Rockefeller University Press, 1976. Biography of Oswald T. Avery, one of the major medical researchers during the first half of the twentieth century. It was Avery who directed the discovery of DNA as genetic material.

Greenwood, David. *Antimicrobial Drugs: Chronicle of a Twentieth Century Medical Triumph.* New York: Oxford University Press, 2008. Recounts the stories behind the discovery and application of antimicrobial agents, particularly in the years prior to, and following, World War II.

Lax, Eric. *The Mold in Dr. Florey's Coat: The Story of the Penicillin Miracle.* New York: Henry Holt, 2005. The story behind the discovery and development of the most famous of the antibiotics. The title refers to the method of penicillin transport from Great Britain to the United States during the war.

Le Fanu, James. *The Rise and Fall of Modern Medicine.* New York: Carroll and Graf, 2002. Describes the application of medical technologies developed during the war years, as well as the subsequent medical and political controversies resulting from these techniques.

Oshinsky, David. *Polio: An American Story.* New York: Oxford University Press, 2006. The story of polio, from its likely origins as an epidemic disease to its ultimate control. The author describes the significance of John Franklin Enders's research during the 1940's.

See also Antibiotics; Birth control; Cancer; DNA discovery; Fluoridation; Health care; Kidney dialysis; Lobotomy; Psychiatry and psychology; Sexually transmitted diseases; UNICEF.

■ *Meet Me in St. Louis*

Identification Musical film about a turn-of-the-century American family
Director Vincente Minnelli (1903-1986)
Date Released on November 22, 1944

This glossy Technicolor movie featuring box-office star Judy Garland offered wartime moviegoers a tuneful and cinematically lavish family story, if an escapist one.

Named one of the top ten pictures of 1944 by the National Board of Review of Motion Pictures and nominated for four Academy Awards, *Meet Me in St. Louis* was an immediate hit with 1940's audiences and remains one of Metro-Goldwyn-Mayer's most popular musical motion pictures.

The film depicts a year in the comfortable life of the Smiths—Grandpa (played by Harry Davenport), father Lon (Leon Ames), mother Anna (Mary Astor), son Alonzo (Henry H. Daniels, Jr.), and daughters Rose (Lucille Bremer), Esther (Judy Garland), Agnes (Joan Carroll), and "Tootie" (Margaret O'Brien), along with maid Katie (Marjorie Main)—in early St. Louis, Missouri, where family mealtimes, home-based recreation, holidays, and the pending arrival of the 1904 World's Fair mark the seasons.

Like Sally Benson's autobiographical series of stories (published in *The New Yorker* magazine from 1941 to 1942) from which it is adapted, the film centers on the daughters' misadventures and lighthearted dilemmas over beaus, dances, and college. The cheerful domestic tale takes a dark detour when Mr. Smith considers uprooting the family to New York, and the Smiths prepare for loss. Ultimately, home and family remain intact—an especially reassuring outcome for wartime audiences.

Impact Amid the real-life uncertainties of World War II, 1940's audiences relished the warm, idyllic vision of family life, as well as the happy ending, of *Meet Me in St. Louis.* Period nostalgia, star performances, and polished technical production have helped sustain the film's appeal.

Wendy Alison Lamb

Further Reading

Agee, James. *Agee on Film: Reviews and Comments.* New York: McDowell, Obolensky, 1958.

Schatz, Thomas. *Boom and Bust: American Cinema in the 1940's*. New York: Scribner, 1997.

See also Academy Awards; Broadway musicals; *Fantasia*; Film in the United States; Garland, Judy; *It's a Wonderful Life*.

■ Merrill's Marauders

Identification Brigadier General Frank Merrill's three thousand U.S. troops plus Chinese soldiers who operated alongside British general Orde Wingate's Chindits in the Burma campaign during World War II

Also known as 5,307th Composite Unit (provisional)

Dates Active from September, 1943, to August, 1944

Merrill's Marauders engaged in long-range penetration warfare behind Japanese enemy lines and helped recover strategically significant northern Burma for the Allies. Because of their great success and the extremely difficult conditions they overcame, the Marauders captured American headlines and hearts as they bolstered Allied confidence at a turning point in World War II. They were also the forerunners of the U.S. Army Rangers.

At the August, 1943, Quebec Conference, the Allies decided to create a U.S. Army unit based on British general Orde Wingate's long-range penetration group, "the Chindits." Eventually, the U.S. Army 5,307th Composite Unit (provisional) was placed in U.S. major general Joseph Warren Stilwell's command; their mission was to recover northern Burma for the Allies and open a supply route into China.

In September, 1943, the U.S. Army called for volunteers. Three thousand men, including veterans of Guadalcanal, answered. From October 31, 1943, through January, 1944, the volunteers underwent intensive jungle training. Divided into six combat teams, each was equipped to operate as an independent, self-contained unit, relying on flexibility and surprise rather than only firepower. Their final training maneuver was a rugged ten-day foray with the Chindits. The American press, watching them on these final maneuvers, christened the unit "Merrill's Marauders," after their commanding officer, Brigadier General Frank Merrill.

Merrill's Marauders were the first U.S. ground combat force to engage Japanese forces on the continent of Asia. They traveled farther and through worse jungle terrain than any other U.S. Army unit during World War II. Joined by both Chinese and native Kachin soldiers, they battled the Japanese Eighteenth Division in five major engagements: Walawbum, Shadzup, Inkangatawng, Nhpum Ga, and Myitkyina.

The Marauders' final objective was Myitkyina Airfield, the only all-weather airfield in northern Burma. They began the operation on April 28, 1944, and seized the airfield on May 17. However, forty-six hundred Japanese troops still held the town of Myitkyina. Ordered to assist the Chindits with the capture, the Marauders began assault-retreat maneuvers, while battling dysentery, malaria, typhus, leeches, and malnutrition. When Myitkyina finally fell, on August 3, only 200 original Marauders remained. They had suffered 80 percent casualties, including General Merrill, who suffered a heart attack plus malaria. Morale plunged due to horrible physical conditions. Finally, Merrill's Marauders were disbanded and evacuated on August 10, 1944.

Impact The Marauders' exploits were splashed through the headlines in newspapers across America, especially *The New York Times*. Outgunned and outnumbered, the Marauders fought through the cruelest jungle terrain any American soldier faced during World War II. They fought one of the strongest divisions of the Imperial Japanese Army without conventional backup or supplies and somehow managed to succeed. Ill, injured, and malnourished, the Marauders accomplished their mission of linking India to China on an Allied-held road and flight path, and in doing so became ragtag heroes for the American press and people. The Marauders earned a distinguished unit citation naming them an outstanding combat force. By August, 1944, they had collectively earned 110 citations, in addition to many Purple Hearts. Eventually, the Bronze Star was awarded to every member of the unit.

Peggy E. Alford

Further Reading

Hopkins, James E. T., with John M. Jones. *Spearhead: A Complete History of Merrill's Marauder Rangers*. Baltimore, Md.: Galahad Press, 1999.

Latimer, Jon. *Burma: The Forgotten War*. London: John Murray, 2004.

See also Air Force, U.S.; Army, U.S.; Army Rangers; China and North America; China-Burma-India theater; Films about World War II; Guadalcanal, Battle of; Literature in the United States; Stilwell, Joseph Warren; World War II.

■ Mexico

The practical needs of both the United States and Mexico during the years of World War II and a shift in Mexican national politics throughout this decade led to closer relations and increased cooperation between these neighboring countries as well as resolution of some longstanding issues.

The 1940's witnessed a dramatic change in U.S.-Mexican relations. During the previous two decades, sporadic efforts of Mexican presidents to advance provisions of the country's revolutionary and nationalistic 1917 constitution antagonized some powerful American interest groups. This situation led to periods of tension and tough negotiating as the U.S. government pressured Mexico for compromise and concessions. After a lull in tensions, U.S.-Mexican disagreements again boiled up when President Lázaro Cárdenas nationalized foreign oil properties in March of 1938. American and British oil firms rejected Mexico's offer of compensation as inadequate, attempted in various ways to sabotage the country's newly nationalized oil industry, and urged intervention on the part of their governments.

Operating under the precept of the "Good Neighbor Policy," President Franklin D. Roosevelt's administration eschewed forceful actions against Mexico, stressed diplomacy, and accepted the offer to provide compensation. Nevertheless, a settlement with Great Britain and the United States over the terms of compensation had not yet transpired by the end of Cárdenas's presidential term in 1940. Due to a continuing U.S.-British boycott of Mexico's oil industry, the Cárdenas government, in spite of its clear antifascist sentiment, was forced to deal with countries such as the Axis Powers for technological help and markets for oil exports. Nevertheless, signs of change were in the air. Cárdenas seemed to feel that the last six years of intensive reform, which fulfilled most of the Mexican Revolution's original goals but left the country divided, now called for a slowdown of this tempo in a period of stability, consolidation, and economic growth to improve the lives of Mexico's masses.

National Interests and Conflict Resolution In the Mexican election of July 1940, Cárdenas's hand-picked successor, Manuel Ávila Camacho, triumphed over the candidate of conservative and right-wing opponents in a disputed election. The new president immediately indicated that he would steer a more moderate course. Also, the November reelection of President Franklin D. Roosevelt in the United States ensured a continuation of the Good Neighbor Policy and an approach favorable to reaching a settlement of outstanding issues between the two countries.

As World War II took a turn for the worse in Europe, the Roosevelt administration sought Mexican cooperation by effecting an agreement on issues that were now deemed secondary in importance to the threat an Axis victory might pose to U.S. interests and security. On the Mexican side, President Camacho was sympathetic to the Allied powers and saw opportunities to advance his agenda of industrialization under wartime conditions. Soon after the Mexican election, the U.S. government made a number of friendly gestures toward the new Mexican regime. U.S. and Mexican representatives agreed in principle to resolve the remaining unsettled issues between the two countries. From around December, 1940, to late 1941, the United States and Mexico entered into a series of accords settling most major disagreements that had arisen during the previous two decades.

The nationalized oil properties remained the greatest impediment to a comprehensive accord. The U.S. State Department, which had heretofore backed oil company compensation claims, finally grew impatient with the multinational firms' intransigence. In November, 1941, U.S. secretary of state Cordell Hull signed an agreement with Mexico without the companies' consent. The eventual compensation, determined by two experts, amounted to a small portion of the companies' inflated claims. Also settled at this time was the issue of compensation for confiscation of foreign-owned agricultural properties during the extensive agrarian reform and land redistribution under Cárdenas.

Steps Toward a Wartime Alliance The notable change in relations between Mexico and the United States that commenced in 1940 paved the way for military, political, and economic cooperation even before a final settlement was reached. President Camacho and Foreign Affairs Secretary Ezequiel Padilla began to move Mexico toward a strong anti-Axis position and alliance with the United States. Several important treaties were signed, beginning in April, 1941. A trade agreement included U.S. purchases of strategic raw materials from Mexico. Mexico's interior ministry under Miguel Alemán and U.S. counter-intelligence operatives began to cooperate effectively on suppressing espionage and subversive activities of Axis agents in Mexico. When Japan attacked Pearl Harbor in December, 1941, and Germany followed with a declaration of war on the United States, Mexico broke diplomatic relations with Germany. Nevertheless, Mexico stopped short of declaring war on the Axis Powers, although nearly all other Latin American states did so. Nationalist public opinion was still wary of this type of alliance with the country's old nemesis, the "Colossus of the North," and most Mexicans felt that the steps taken to date were sufficient.

In May of 1942, torpedo attacks on Mexican oil tankers by German U-boats took twelve lives and provided the Mexican government sufficient popular support to declare war on May 30. Camacho skillfully promoted national unity by assigning responsibilities for national defense efforts to several former presidents and a prominent labor leader representing various political tendencies. The continuing impact of both government and Allied anti-Axis propaganda served to further consolidate public opinion behind the government's action.

Military and Economic Cooperation In January, 1942, a joint U.S.-Mexican Defense Commission was created to coordinate military efforts, train Mexican officers in the United States, and upgrade Mexican military equipment. Mexico and the United States cooperated in strengthening Mexican coastal defenses while a Japanese naval threat continued through the early stages of the war. With American assistance, Mexico also began developing a modern air force. Three U.S.-trained units of Mexican pilots were formed in 1944, and one of these, Squadron 201, served with distinction in combat in the Philippines during the final months of the war. Moreover, the United States and Mexico agreed to permit military conscription of their own nationals residing in the other country. Through this

means, about 250,000 Mexican nationals resident in the United States were drafted into the U.S. armed forces. Some 14,000 saw combat and roughly 1,000 died in action.

Aside from its modest military involvement, Mexico's major contribution to the war effort was economic in nature. With the oil dispute settled, Mexican petroleum flowed to the United States. Other needed raw materials and minerals coming from Mexico included copper, lead, zinc, graphite, and hard fibers. Mexico's raw materials accounted for 40 percent of the U.S. war industry needs. This help was the most important Latin American contribution to the war against the Axis Powers.

One of the most significant and also controversial areas of economic cooperation was an agreement in 1942 that brought Mexican contract laborers known as braceros into the U.S. to fill manpower needs created by the military draft. Under the bracero program, up to 300,000 Mexican laborers entered the United States. At first the emphasis was strictly on agricultural workers concentrated in California. However, Mexican workers eventually also took jobs in other branches of industry and ventured as far north as Minnesota. This program encountered opposition from organized labor in the United States who saw it as a means to suppress American wages and weaken unions.

Although Mexican workers benefited from this employment and were able to support relatives at home with their earnings, some Mexican nationalists felt it reflected badly on the nation's ability to meet basic needs of its own citizens and would subject these contract workers to prejudice and discrimination. The agreement included provisions to regulate working conditions and protect contract workers' rights but these regulations were not always enforced.

Mexico realized substantial economic benefits from the wartime situation. Cancellation of debts in German-occupied Europe allowed the nation to reduce its foreign indebtedness by 90 percent. Seizure of Axis properties in Mexico included ships that were used to deliver goods sold to the United States. Completion of the Pan-American highway and updating of the national railroad system were realized with U.S. assistance. With the settlement of the oil dispute, Mexico's newly nationalized petroleum industry also received U.S. technical help and expertise. Finally, income from sales of raw materials and other products to the United States was directed toward Mexico's infrastructure and public works projects.

The Postwar Relationship   The closer relationship begun under Roosevelt and Camacho continued through the presidencies of Miguel Alemán (1946-1952) and Roosevelt's successor, Harry S. Truman. In 1947, the two heads of state symbolically reaffirmed their commitment to this new era of friendship in an exchange of visits. In Mexico City Truman made a welcomed gesture when he laid a wreath on the Monument to the Ninos Heroes—the teenage Mexican army cadets who had sacrificed their lives fighting against U.S. troops in 1847. Both countries also returned trophies captured in the Mexican War.

Alemán accelerated industrialization efforts with vast infrastructure and spectacular public construction projects. He aggressively courted American capital to help finance this development. In his public pronouncements Alemán reaffirmed Mexican sovereignty and independence and characterized Mexico's new relationship with the United States as an equal partnership. At the same time, his efforts to acquire foreign capital involved relaxing or finding loopholes around regulations that were enacted during the previous administration to protect Mexican producers and industries from unfair foreign competition or domination. Under Alemán, business leaders of the two countries developed a close alliance. Mexico achieved impressive annual rates of economic growth and increased the size of its middle class. At the same time, however, high-level corruption and self-aggrandizement also flourished. Modernization did not eliminate poverty, as the new wealth that economic growth generated was unevenly distributed.

Impact   Mexican-U.S. relations improved dramatically during the 1940's. The cordial wartime atmosphere continued after the war and constituted the longest crisis-free era in the history of U.S.-Mexican relations. The past was not completely erased, however, and many Mexicans continued to harbor mixed feelings of both admiration and wariness toward their larger, much wealthier, and extremely

Farmworkers returning to Mexico from Brownsville, Texas, after picking cotton under the bracero program in 1949. (AP/Wide World Photos)

powerful neighbor. Mexico cooperated with the United States in the newly formed Organization of American States and was a signatory of the U.S.-sponsored Cold War-era hemispheric defense pact known as the Rio Pact (1947). However, in years to come, Mexico would also maintain its distance from the United States on certain Latin American policy issues. Nevertheless, the two countries entered into a relationship featuring closer economic, military, and political cooperation than at any time before or since in history.

The impact on both countries was significant. With U.S. cooperation and help, Mexico advanced its industrialization and modernization. Mexican material assistance definitely made the U.S. war effort more effective. The bracero program had a lasting effect beyond this decade, as it was renewed until 1964. When the United States reverted to earlier restrictive immigration quotas after the program was terminated, Mexican illegal immigration to the U.S. increased considerably. A final noteworthy consequence was the growth of U.S. economic and cultural influence in Mexico. Seventy-five percent of Mexico's foreign trade became linked to the U.S. despite Mexico's efforts to diversify and broaden economic relationships. U.S. capital investment became significant, although Mexico did place some restrictions on the extent of this penetration. The improvement in Mexico's highway and railroad system also contributed to a massive influx of U.S. tourism and Hollywood films gained a strong foothold in the Mexican cinemas.

David A. Crain

Further Reading

Galarza, Ernesto. *Merchants of Labor: The Mexican Bracero Story.* San Jose, Calif.: Rosicrucian Press, 1964. Critical analysis of the bracero program. Notes the exploitation of Mexican contract workers by agro-business interests and views the program as an obstacle to unionizing California farm workers.

Kirk, Betty. *Covering the Mexican Front: The Battle of Europe vs. America.* Norman: University of Oklahoma Press, 1942. On-the-scene journalist's account of Mexico's foreign and domestic policy in the years leading up to World War II. Praises the policies of Presidents Cárdenas and Camacho and Foreign Affairs Secretary Padilla.

Niblo, Stephen R. *War, Diplomacy and Development:* *The United States and Mexico, 1939-1954.* Wilmington, Del.: Scholarly Resources, 1995. Analyzes Mexico's postwar industrial development in the context of the country's diplomatic, military, and economic dealings with the United States under presidents Cárdenas, Camacho, and Alemán.

Paz, Maria Emelia. *Strategy, Security, and Spies: Mexico and the U.S. as Allies in World War II.* University Park: Pennsylvania State University Press, 1997. Covers many aspects of Mexican-U.S. cooperation during the war years and details Mexico's political strategy of balancing nationalism, security needs, and the danger of economic dependency on the United States.

Schmidt, Karl M. *Mexico and the United States, 1821-1973: Conflict and Coexistence.* New York: John Wiley & Sons, 1974. A scholar of Latin American politics, Schmidt provides a comprehensive, reasonably balanced survey of U.S.-Mexican relations aimed at students and teachers.

Schuler, Frederick. "Mexico and the Outside World." In *The Oxford History of Mexico*, edited by Michael C. Meyer and William Beezley. New York: Oxford University Press, 2000. Analyzes Mexico's dealings with foreign powers, especially its love-hate relationship with the United States, from the 1910 revolution to the end of World War II.

See also Bracero program; Foreign policy of the United States; Immigration to the United States; International trade; Latin America; Latinos; Organization of American States; Wartime espionage in North America.

■ Microwave ovens

Definition Household appliances that use microwave radiation to cook food

Although the first microwave oven for commercial use was introduced in 1947, it would not be until 1955 that the household version became available. These devices not only decreased the amount of time devoted to cooking but also led to a new market for food products needing only to be warmed before serving.

Like many discoveries, the microwave oven developed from research undertaken for an entirely different purpose. During World War II, engineer

Percy L. Spencer was working on radar technology for the Raytheon Corporation when he noticed that the magnetron he was working on could melt candy. He then successfully used this microwave technology on other types of food, leading Raytheon to patent the microwave oven in 1945 and begin producing it for commercial use. Dubbed the Radarange, the device was too cumbersome for household use, standing over five feet tall and weighing more than 750 pounds.

In 1955, the Tappan Corporation introduced the first microwave oven for household use, but this model was large and expensive and therefore sold poorly. Raytheon continued to improve the model until it finally gained some popularity in 1967. By the mid-1970's, microwave ovens had become as common as gas stoves, and their popularity continued through the 1980's. When smaller and lighter versions of the microwave oven were produced during the 1990's, they became the most popular cooking apparatuses in the United States.

Impact In the early twenty-first century, it is estimated that more than 90 percent of American households possess a microwave oven. These devices have made cooking more convenient, particularly as many households depend on two incomes. For his role in the creation of the microwave oven, Spencer was inducted into the National Inventors Hall of Fame in 1999.

Brion Sever

Further Reading

Carlisle, Rodney. *Inventions and Discoveries*. Hoboken, N.J.: John Wiley & Sons, 2004.

Decareau, Robert, and Bernard Schweigert, eds. *Microwaves in the Food Processing Industry*. New York: Academic Press, 1985.

See also Food processing; Home appliances; Inventions; Radar; Wartime technological advances; World War II.

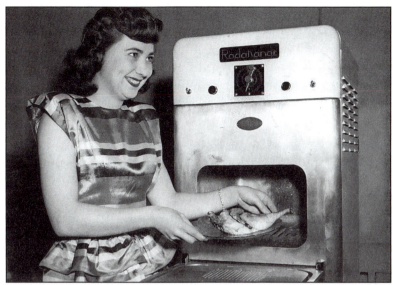

Demonstration of an early microwave oven that has just cooked part of a chicken in less than three minutes. Aptly named the "Radarange," this 1946 model generated heat with the same kind of Raytheon magnetron tube used in radar units. (Popperfoto/Getty Images)

■ Midway, Battle of

The Event U.S. naval victory over a larger Japanese invasion force

Dates June 3-7, 1942

Place Region surrounding Midway Island in the Pacific Ocean

The first strategically significant naval battle since the British defeat of the combined French and Spanish fleets at the Battle of Trafalgar in 1805, the Battle of Midway turned the tide of the war in the Pacific.

From the time that the United States entered World War II after Japan's surprise attack on Pearl Harbor on December 7, 1941, U.S. naval forces in the Pacific had been fighting a defensive action. One after another, U.S. possessions fell to the Japanese, and the Navy could manage only minor hit-and-run raids. Even the history-making Battle of the Coral Sea, the first fought entirely by naval aviation, was strategically inconclusive.

However, U.S. code breakers at Pearl Harbor deciphered Japanese messages indicating plans for a major action aimed at the U.S.-held Midway Island. Pacific Fleet commander Chester W. Nimitz decided to risk all his available forces to stop the Japanese advance. He commanded only three carriers against the six the Japanese had dispatched. Complicating matters, one of the three carriers, the *Yorktown*, was in dry dock after it had been badly damaged and towed home. Repair crews had to work around the clock to make the ship at least marginally seaworthy in time to participate in the battle.

With Admiral William F. "Bull" Halsey ill and unable to lead, Nimitz entrusted command to Raymond A. Spruance, a careful, calculating man. Technically, however, overall command belonged to Admiral Frank Jack Fletcher, who slightly outranked Spruance. However, Fletcher recognized Spruance's acumen and the fragility of his own flagship, which had been hastily repaired after it had been severely damaged at the Battle of the Coral Sea.

At first, the battle went badly for the American ships. The carrier *Yorktown* was torpedoed by a submarine, and many of the first wave of aircraft were destroyed. Then aircraft from the *Enterprise* and *Hornet* found the Japanese carriers just as the Japanese

planes were returning to refuel. Catching them at this vulnerable moment, the U.S. naval aviators were able to destroy almost all the Japanese carriers. Only the *Zuikaku* escaped intact, although it was ultimately destroyed at the Battle of Leyte Gulf.

Realizing that he had lost his air cover and that his invasion force was open to American air attack, Admiral Isoroku Yamamoto initially considered a face-saving attempt of bombarding Midway Island with the guns of his battleships, but he dismissed the idea.

Impact Among naval historians, the Battle of Midway is on the short list of key battles that changed the course of whole wars. From the moment that the battle was fought, the Japanese never regained the naval offensive in the Pacific, and the Americans beat them back slowly and relentlessly to their home islands and into unconditional surrender. For the American people of 1942, however, Midway represented more. After the humiliating defeat at Pearl

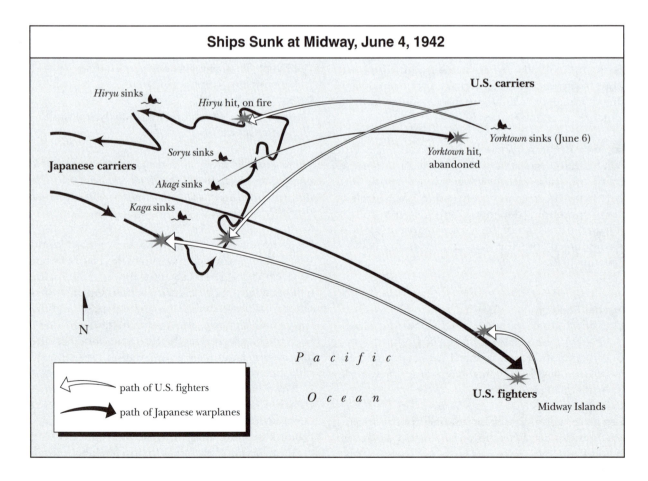

Ships Sunk at Midway, June 4, 1942

Harbor, the battle represented an essential part of the process of rebuilding national self-confidence. The narrowness of the victory gave it mythological stature.

Leigh Husband Kimmel

Further Reading

Nesmith, Jeff. *No Higher Honor: The USS* Yorktown *at the Battle of Midway.* Atlanta, Ga.: Longstreet, 1999.

Parshall, Jonathan, and Anthony Tully. *Shattered Sword: The Untold Story of the Battle of Midway.* Dulles, Va.: Potomac Books, 2007.

Prange, Gordon W. *Miracle at Midway.* New York: McGraw-Hill, 1982.

U.S. Navy fighter planes flying over burning Japanese ships during the Battle of Midway. (National Archives)

See also Aircraft carriers; Aleutian Island occupation; Code breaking; Ford, John; Guadalcanal, Battle of; Halsey, William F. "Bull"; *History of the United States Naval Operations in World War II*; Iwo Jima, Battle of; Nimitz, Chester W.; Pearl Harbor attack; World War II.

■ Military conscription in Canada

Definition   Compulsory military service

During World War II, a majority of English-speaking Canadians wanted to make military service compulsory, but a strong majority of French Canadians were adamantly opposed to the idea. The controversy produced a political crisis in 1944, but it proved much less divisive than a similar crisis that had occurred during World War I.

In March, 1939, as a war in Europe appeared increasingly likely, Canada's Prime Minister William Lyon Mackenzie King pledged to his nation's Parliament that no Canadians would be forced to participate in the war unless Canada itself were directly threatened. His pledge was based on painful memories of the country's 1917 crisis, when French Canadian opposition to compulsory military service had polarized the country and almost destroyed his Liberal Party. Not only were the Liberals dependent on Quebec's support, but King also feared that conscription could destroy the confederation. When Parliament approved a declaration of war against Germany on September 10, 1939, he repeated his no-conscription pledge and declared that Canada's participation in the war would be limited.

Onset of World War II Prime Minister King's cautious policies of limited engagement were popular during the early period of the war. In the national elections of March, 1940, the Liberal Party won a clear majority of parliamentary seats. The Liberals also prevailed in an election in the predominantly French-speaking province of Quebec, demonstrating that the majority of French-speaking Canadians approved of entering the war against Nazi Germany even though they opposed the notion of compulsory military service. However, a significant minority of people in Quebec viewed the war as primarily a struggle to preserve the British Empire.

After Germany defeated France and other countries of Western Europe during mid-1940, a majority of Canada's English-speaking citizens became convinced that conscription was necessary, but most residents of Quebec remained firmly opposed to the notion. The Liberal Party compromised by enacting the National Resources Mobilization Act (NRMA), which authorized registration to compile a list of available men in case that conscription might become necessary for national defense. The act further specified that no Canadian who was conscripted would be required to serve outside the country. Most Quebecers reluctantly accepted the measure, which they perceived as an option that would prevent full conscription. After the Japanese attack on the U.S. naval base at Pearl Harbor in December, 1941, Canada formally declared war on Japan, thereby creating a new demand for soldiers and convincing most military leaders that conscription was necessary.

For two and a half years, King kept his "no conscription" pledge, in large part because he did not want to provoke the kind of national crisis that had erupted in 1917. As pressure from public opinion and within his cabinet increased, he finally announced a plebiscite for April 27, 1942, asking citizens to vote either "yes" or "no" on whether the government should be released from its no-conscription pledge. As anticipated, 72.9 percent of francophone Quebecers voted against the measure, while citizens in the rest of the country voted 80 percent in favor. The outcome of the plebiscite infuriated Quebecers. Although conscription was not immediately proclaimed, its threat resulted in a new anticonscription party in Quebec, the Bloc Populaire Canadien, and it also allowed the Union Nationale party to defeat the Liberal Party in a Quebec election.

Conscription Crisis of 1944 Faced with the demand for additional troops, King responded by introducing Bill 80 on June 10, 1942. It amended the NRMA by repealing the section that forbade it from sending conscripts overseas. In an effort to preserve Canadian unity, however, King assured Quebecers that the amendment was "not necessarily conscription but conscription if necessary." The minister of public works, Pierre-Joseph Cardin, a Quebecer, resigned in protest. When the government finally began conscription on a small scale, King promised to assign conscripts to home defense and to make every effort to continue overseas service on a voluntary basis. In 1943, the military deployed a small number of conscripted soldiers to fight in Alaska's Aleutian Islands, which had been occupied by the Japanese, but because these islands were physically part of North America, King argued that the soldiers had not been sent overseas.

Following the Allied invasion of Normandy in

June, 1944, the number of Canadian volunteers had become insufficient to replace the casualties, particularly in Canadian infantry units. Many of the troops fighting in Europe resented King's refusal to send conscripts as replacements; they commonly referred to "home service only" soldiers as "zombies." When James L. Ralston, the minister of national defense, returned from a tour of Europe, he insisted that it was imperative to begin deploying conscripts abroad. The former commander of the Canadian Army, General Andrew McNaughton disagreed, arguing that conscripts could instead be persuaded to volunteer for oversees service, making compulsion unnecessary. Endorsing McNaughton's position, King asked for Ralston's resignation as defense minister and replaced him with McNaughton. In Quebec, the cabinet change revived the popularity of King and the Liberals.

After McNaughton's optimistic prediction about volunteers failed to materialize, several members of King's cabinet threatened to resign unless conscripts were assigned to overseas service. By this time, King had little choice but to agree. On November 22, 1944, he announced that a one-time levy of 17,000 NRMA conscripts would be sent to France. The decision widened the rift between French and English Canadians. Minister of Air C. G. Powers, who was from Quebec City, resigned in protest to fulfill his pledge to his constituents. When word of the deployment reached the West Coast, soldiers on the army base in Terrace, British Columbia, mutinied on November 25-29. The so-called "Terrace Mutiny" is considered the most serious breach of military discipline in Canadian history.

When deployments of conscripts abroad began in December, Quebecers grumbled. However, few soldiers were actually deployed abroad against their will. Contrary to expectations, no massive protests or incidents of violence occurred. Fortunately for the Liberal Party, the war did not last much longer. Following Germany's surrender in May, 1945, the issue of compulsory service lost most of its force relatively quickly.

Impact Conscripted soldiers made up only about 10 percent of the 1.1 million persons in Canada's military forces. By the war's end, a total of 12,908 conscripted troops were deployed abroad, but only 2,463 actually saw service with units on the front lines. Of the total of 42,000 Canadians who died in combat during the war, only 79 had been conscripted.

From a political perspective, King's cautious approach of gradualism and compromise turned out to be quite successful. This became clear in the national elections of June 11, 1945, when the Liberal Party gained a clear majority of votes in the province of Quebec as well as in the rest of the country. Quebec's anticonscription party, the Bloc Populaire, attracted few votes and ceased to exist within a few years.

Thomas Tandy Lewis

Further Reading

Bercuson, David J. *Maple Leaf Against the Axis: Canada's Second World War.* Toronto: Stoddart, 1995. Written by one of Canada's preeminent military historians, this volume provides an excellent overview of Canada's role in the war.

Dawson, R. MacGregor. *The Conscription Crisis of 1944.* Toronto: University of Toronto Press, 1961. Detailed account of the political and military leaders involved in the controversy; highly favorable toward King's strategies and timing.

Granatstein, Jack L. *Canada's War: The Politics of the Mackenzie King Government, 1939-1945.* Toronto: Oxford University Press, 1975. Balanced account of King's attempt to maintain national unity while also continuing Canada's contribution to the war effort.

Granatstein, Jack L., and J. M. Hitsman. *Broken Promises: A History of Conscription in Canada.* Toronto: Oxford University Press, 1977. Scholarly account of the controversies over compulsory military service during the twentieth century's two world wars.

Stacey, Charles P. *Arms, Men, and Governments: The War Policies of Canada, 1939-1945.* Ottawa: Minister of National Defense, 1970. Useful account with an interesting summary of the conscription issue.

See also Canadian nationalism; Canadian participation in World War II; Conscientious objectors; Duplessis, Maurice Le Noblet; Elections in Canada; King, William Lyon Mackenzie; Military conscription in the United States; Quebec nationalism; St. Laurent, Louis; World War II mobilization.

■ Military conscription in the United States

Definition Procedures and policies used to recruit a massive number of men for military service during World War II and the subsequent changes in conscription regulations during the Cold War and Korean War

The massive need for manpower to meet the challenge of World War II required revisions in existing military recruitment laws and unprecedented attention to issues related to conscription, such as conscientious objection.

The Selective Training and Service Act of 1940 (STSA) was designed to remain in effect for seven years, after which it would be reviewed by Congress for possible renewal or cancellation. The act was administered by an independent agency within the executive branch of the U.S. government. The act stipulated that all men between the ages of twenty-one and thirty should register with locally appointed draft boards responsible for the implementation of all procedures leading to recruitment. These boards were to be composed of panels of three or more civilian members nominated by the governors of each state and appointed by the president. The law also contained a provision to create a National Selective Service Appeals Board, with its members to be appointed by the president.

Initially, the number of people to be recruited for the military was limited to 900,000 men, who would be drafted and trained for active service. More conscripts could be recruited after these initial draftees completed their period of required service. Originally, the period of active military duty was set at one year. In addition, a specific provision of the act stipulated that draftees would serve only in the Western Hemisphere or in territories or possessions of the United States in other areas of the world.

However, only a short time after the STSA was enacted in September, 1940, conditions in other parts of the world were moving the United States closer to entry into World War II. After the United States entered the war in December, 1941, President Franklin D. Roosevelt called for changes in the STSA. He obtained congressional approval to send draftees to any area of the world, not merely the places specified in the original law. All males between the ages of eighteen and sixty-five were now required to register for the draft, although men past the age of forty-five

Military and civilian officials preparing for a new draft lottery, using a goldfish bowl, in Philadelphia in July, 1941. In the background is the famed Liberty Bell. (AP/Wide World Photos)

were barred from active military service. The length of required active duty was expanded from one year to eighteen months. As wartime needs increased, the length of service was futher extended. The method for selection of draftees was also shifted from the more than four thousand local draft boards to a nationwide lottery system under which older registrants would be chosen first.

The number of persons drafted between November, 1940, and October, 1946, was more than 10 million. By comparison, the number of persons drafted between September, 1917, and November, 1918, for service in World War I was slightly more than 2.8 million.

Conscientious Objectors Based on the negative experiences associated with conscription procedures during World War I, Section 5(g) of the STSA spelled out conditions for conscientious objection to service in combatant units of the military. Local draft boards were to review petitions from individuals who, "by reason of religious training and belief . . . opposed participation in war in any form." If draft boards accepted the legitimacy of individual claims of conscientious objection, two possibilities existed. Conscientious objectors could be posted to non-combatant functions, such as medical relief teams or transportation units. However, if individuals were opposed to any service directly related to wartime military operations, they could be assigned to "work of national importance under civilian direction." Church-sponsored organizations were to assume responsibility for determining the type of work that would fit this definition. In October, 1940, an organization called the National Service Board for Conscientious Objectors was established by three religious groups. Its goal was to assist in the possible assignment of conscientious objectors to one of more than 150 Civilian Public Service Camps that were set up in December, 1940.

Postwar Changes   A critical point in the American conscription system came in January, 1947, less than two years after the end of World War II. As the scheduled expiration date of the STSA approached, President Harry S. Truman moved to let the draft system expire. He suggested that American military preparedness in times of peace could be met by means of voluntary recruitment. By 1948, however, the onset of the Cold War, including the possibility of a military confrontation with the Soviet Union, changed public attitudes about defense. The Selective Service Act of 1948 was adopted to reintroduce conscription. The new act required all men between the ages of nineteen and twenty-six to register for military service; registrants who were drafted were required to complete one year of active duty. These provisions were revised with the outbreak of the first major postwar military crisis—the "police action" that became the Korean War of 1950-1953. A selective service draft was quickly put in place that enabled the recruitment of men between the ages of eighteen and twenty-six, who were required to register and could be drafted for two years of active service.

Another development clearly changed the recruitment policies that had evolved during the 1940's. In 1952, Congress passed the Reserve Forces Act, which provided for a total military obligation of eight years—an initial period of active duty, followed by a period of reserve status, during which individuals could be called back to active duty in times of war or national emergency.

Impact   Military conscription during World War II was definitely the largest-scale recruitment challenge faced by the United States during the twentieth century. Although some resistance was registered to draft procedures established in 1940, the obvious need for full-scale mobilization against Nazi Germany and Japan rallied almost universal public support behind the Selective Service System.

The end of World War II created a new challenge, as the United States had to adjust its military recruitment procedures to accommodate the unpredictable circumstances created by the Cold War. The re-turn to peacetime conditions in 1945 presented a possibility to allow the draft to expire and to rely instead on voluntary recruitment. Although the American public initially supported a volunteer military, U.S. commitment to the defense of South Korea against North Korean advances in 1950 necessitated the reintroduction of the Selective Service System that would remain the basis for military recruitment for another twenty-five years.

Byron Cannon

Further Reading

McGill, Kenneth H. "The Development and Operation of a Statistical Program for the Selective Service System." *American Sociological Review* 9, no. 5 (October, 1944): 508-514. Explains the procedures adopted by the Selective Service System to ensure an appropriate balance between geographical regions, ages, and ethnic origins of draftees.

Selective Service System. *The Selective Service Act: Its Legislative History, Amendments, Appropriations, Cognates, and Prior Instruments of Security.* New York: Government Printing Office, 1954. Complete review of all official decisions and documents relating to military conscription through the era of the Korean War.

Senate Committee on Military Affairs. *Deferment of Registrants in Essential Occupations.* New York: Government Printing Office, 1944. Firsthand record of congressional hearings on adjustments to the STSA that were deemed necessary to respond to national workforce requirements, as well as dependent family issues.

Watson, Cynthia Ann. *U.S. Military Service: A Reference Handbook.* Santa Barbara, Calif.: ABC-CLIO, 2007. Deals with a variety of changes in the organization of the U.S. military as concerns about national security shifted from post-World War II conventional military preparedness to the conditions generated by the Cold War. Considers the even more drastic changes that began to be put in place after the terrorist attacks of September 11, 2001.

Wilson, Charles H. "The Selective Service System: An Administrative Obstacle Course." *California Law Review* 54, no. 5 (December, 1966): 2123-2179. Examines the system's operations, based in part on a limited field study of draft registrants and system officials.

See also Army, U.S.; Casualties of World War II; Conscientious objectors; Marines, U.S.; Military conscription in Canada; Navy, U.S.; Office of War Mobilization; *Studies in Social Psychology in World War II*; World War II mobilization.

■ Miller, Glenn

Identification American trombonist and bandleader
Born March 1, 1904; Clarinda, Iowa
Died December 15, 1944; English Channel, en route from London to Paris

Miller was one of the best-known bandleaders of the swing era. His civilian and military swing bands were arguably the most popular of the time, producing such hits as "Chattanooga Choo Choo" and "In the Mood."

After working with various groups around the country (including the Dorsey brothers, Tommy and Jimmy), in 1937 Glenn Miller formed his own group, the Glenn Miller Orchestra, through which he was to achieve lasting fame. The group's performances at various resorts were broadcast over the radio in 1939, leading to regular performances for Chesterfield cigarettes, also broadcast on the radio. These broadcasts provided a nationwide audience for the orchestra, helping to ensure its fame. The orchestra's tight sound as well as its arrangements (using the clarinet to double the saxophone, for example) earned it a special place in the swing era. The orchestra had numerous hits, including "Pennsylvania 65000," "Tuxedo Junction," and "Chattanooga Choo Choo," which earned a gold record. The Glenn Miller Orchestra's popularity continued, and the group was disbanded in 1942, when Miller volunteered for the Army Air Forces. There he formed another swing band, performing over the radio and in person for the troops. In 1944, the orchestra moved to England. On December 15, 1944, on a London-to-Paris flight, his plane disappeared, his body never to be found.

Impact Miller's civilian band was perhaps the most popular swing band during its existence in the United States, producing the country's first gold record. In addition, his wartime band set the standard for wartime entertainment, influencing the United Service Organizations (USO) and other similar groups for years to come. His death in the service of his country confirmed his place as a war hero and further reinforced his place in the annals of swing music.

Lisa Scoggin

Further Reading
Polic, Edward F. *The Glenn Miller Army Air Force Band: Sustineo Alas/I Sustain the Wings*. Metchuen, N.J.: Scarecrow Press, 1989.
Simon, George T. *Glenn Miller and His Orchestra*. New York: Da Capo Press, 1986.

See also Andrews Sisters; Dorsey, Tommy; Goodman, Benny; Jitterbug; Music: Jazz; Music: Popular; Radio in the United States; United Service Organizations.

■ *Miracle on 34th Street*

Identification Classic Christmas film
Date Released on May 2, 1947

This film focuses on the charm of holiday legends. Designed to appeal to all ages, it is a perennial favorite aired during the Christmas season.

Miracle on 34th Street combines fantasy, romance, and a good story. Doris Walker (Maureen O'Hara) plays a single mother and dedicated career woman who has raised her daughter, Susan (Natalie Wood), without childhood myths such as Santa Claus. In an era when women are encouraged to leave the job market to be full-time homemakers, Doris is a successful retail executive.

The film also focuses on the rivalry between Macy's and Gimbels in New York during the Christmas season. As the story opens, Doris hires an elderly man, Kris Kringle (Edmund Gwenn), as Macy's new Santa Claus. Kris believes that he actually is Santa Claus, which leads to his being fired. Attorney Fred Gailey (John Payne) is Doris's neighbor and suitor, who befriends Kris and defends him in a trial to decide whether he is Santa.

The film won three Oscars: Gwenn for best supporting actor, George Seaton for best screenplay, and Valentine Davies for best original story. It lost out as best film to *Gentleman's Agreement*.

Impact *Miracle on 34th Street* emphasizes the need to keep a childlike faith in traditions like Santa

Claus. The film established Wood as a child star. Although seldom noted, it is one of the last post-World War II films to feature a successful career woman. Several remakes of this classic film for television (1955) and feature film (1994) have not been as successful. The 1947 film has been honored by the American Film Institute as one of the top ten films in the category of fantasy. Like *It's a Wonderful Life, Miracle on 34th Street* is a holiday favorite.

Norma C. Noonan

Further Reading

Danielson, Sarah Parker. *Miracle on 34th Street: A Holiday Classic.* New York: Smithmark, 1993.

Davies, Valentine. *Miracle on 34th Street.* New York: Pocket Books, 1952.

Dixon, Wheeler Winston. *American Cinema of the 1940's: Themes and Variations.* New Brunswick, N.J.: Rutgers University Press, 2005.

See also Andy Hardy films; Film in the United States; *It's a Wonderful Life*; Women's roles and rights in the United States.

■ Miranda, Carmen

Identification Portuguese-born Brazilian singer, dancer, and actor
Born February 9, 1909; Marco de Canaveses, Portugal
Died August 5, 1955; Beverly Hills, California

Miranda's signature headdresses, gigantic platform shoes, and exaggerated accent featured in wartime musicals helped to popularize her but also served to mock, malign, and marginalize not only her but also future female actors of Latin American heritage.

As an infant, Carmen Miranda immigrated from her native Portugal to Río de Janeiro with her family. As a teenager, she worked as a hatmaker and model, and she eventually found her way into nightclub appearances as well as radio and motion-picture performances. After catching the eye of American theater impressario Lee Shubert, Miranda was summoned to New York at the age of thirty and was contracted to perform in the summer Broadway musical *The Streets of Paris*. After a handful of performances in New York, she made her American film debut in the Twentieth Century-Fox feature *Down Argentine Way* (1940), which starred Betty Grable in her first leading role.

By April, 1945, more than eighty escapist films featuring Latin American stars and locales had been produced, with Miranda featured in more than a dozen. Miranda portrayed an identical persona in nearly all of her roles: a highly agitated Latina, gyrating her hips, rolling her eyes, and maneuvering her hands, attired in extravagant costumes, wearing hats that were typically piled with arrays of tropical fruits. Eventually, Miranda became disillusioned with her lack of meaningful roles. This, coupled with an unhappy personal life, began to take its toll on her health. She collapsed onstage during a live Jimmy Durante show, not realizing that she had experienced a mild heart attack. A second heart attack hours later, during the early morning of August 5, 1955, caused her death at the age of forty-six.

Impact An able singer, dancer, and light comedian, Miranda became extremely popular, though she

Carmen Miranda wearing one of her trademark headdresses, around 1945. (Getty Images)

never became a superstar on the scale of fellow Latina actors Dolores del Río and Rita Hayworth. Miranda's public persona established a stereotype that lingered for decades in modified ways—a vulgar, flashy, hyperkinetic, language-mangling Latina relegated merely to entertaining others.

Darius V. Echeverría

Further Reading

Gil-Montero, Martha. *Brazilian Bombshell: The Biography of Carmen Miranda.* New York: E. P. Dutton, 1989.

Ruiz, Vicki L., and Virginia Sánchez Korrol. *Latina Legacies: Identity, Biography, and Community.* New York: Oxford University Press, 2005.

Woll, Allen L. *The Latin Image in American Film.* Los Angeles: UCLA Latin American Center Publications, 1980.

See also Dance; Grable, Betty; Hayworth, Rita; Holiday, Billie; Horne, Lena; Latin America; Latinos; World War II.

■ Miss America pageants

Identification Annual female beauty contests and provider of academic scholarships

The Miss America beauty pageant began in Atlantic City, New Jersey, in 1921, evolving from bathing-beauty contest to an event that emphasized wholesomeness. Three dramatic innovations of the 1940's made the decade one of the most important in the pageant's history. These were the creation of the pageant's scholarship program, the inclusion of a talent competition, and the decision to crown Miss America while she was wearing an evening gown rather than a swimsuit. The changes indicated that the pageant wanted to stress more than mere outward beauty, hoping that Miss America would come to represent the ideal, well-rounded, young American woman.

The Miss America Pageant began as an effort to keep tourists in Atlantic City after Labor Day. In 1935, Lenora Slaughter, who would serve as pageant director until 1967, was hired to polish the event's image. It gained respectability throughout the 1930's and by 1940, was an established American tradition.

During the 1940's, contestants were judged in three categories: talent, evening gowns and swimsuits, and personality; a final ballot determined the winner. The 1940 Miss America, Frances Burke, was chosen in a close vote that reportedly took hours. Miss America 1941, Rosemary LaPlanche, had been a runner-up the previous year. This led to a rule stating that no woman could compete for the title more than once.

In 1942, the Air Force took over Boardwalk Hall, so the pageant moved to the Warner Theater. Jo-Carroll Dennison was crowned the winner that year. The 1943 Miss America, Jean Bartel, went on to sell $2.5 million in war bonds, a U.S. record for that year. Her University of Minnesota sorority sisters were the first to suggest the scholarship program to Slaughter.

The first redheaded Miss America, Venus Ramey, who won in 1944, was also the first to participate in political activism, assisting with a bill to secure the District of Columbia's voting rights. In 1945, Bess Myerson received the pageant's first five-thousand-dollar college scholarship. Notably, during a time when anti-Semitism was not uncommon, she was also the first Jewish winner. Many saw her victory as a sign that the United States wanted no part of the bigotry that had almost destroyed Europe.

The pageant returned to Boardwalk Hall in 1946. The scholarship fund of twenty-five thousand dollars was shared among winner Marilyn Buferd and the fifteen finalists. In 1947, Barbara Jo Walker was the last Miss America crowned in a swimsuit. Miss America 1948, BeBe Shopp, was crowned in an evening gown. That year the pageant featured its first Puerto Rican and Asian American contestants. In 1949, Jacque Mercer became the decade's final Miss America.

Impact Since 1921, Miss America has reflected the nation's changing attitudes toward the feminine ideal. Unlike the delicate-flower image ascribed to women of the Victorian era, women of the 1940's were healthy and active. During the war, Miss America was an icon of national pride; the pageant's winners sold more war bonds than any other public figures. The addition of the talent contest and scholarship program further improved the pageant's image. Postwar winners were more likely to attend college than to seek a Hollywood career. The pageant positioned itself as an organization that promoted and supported women, advocating for their higher education and professional achievement. Nonetheless, over the years, the pageant continued to draw

Barbara Jo Walker, the winner of the 1947 Miss America pageant, being crowned by the previous year's winner, Marilyn Buferd, as the runners-up look on. Walker was the last Miss America to be crowned while wearing a bathing suit. (Getty Images)

criticism for its emphasis on physical appearance. Social activists debated whether the pageant was primarily a beauty pageant or a scholarship pageant and whether its female contestants were being exploited or promoted.

Jennifer Davis-Kay

Further Reading

Bivans, Ann-Marie. *Miss America: In Pursuit of the Crown.* New York: MasterMedia Limited, 1991.

Deford, Frank. *There She Is: The Life and Times of Miss America.* New York: The Viking Press, 1971.

Dworkin, Susan. *Miss America, 1945: Bess Myerson's Own Story.* New York: Newmarket Press, 1987.

Watson, Elwood, and Darcy Martin. *There She Is, Miss America: The Politics of Sex, Beauty, and Race in America's Most Famous Pageant.* New York: Palgrave Macmillan, 2004.

See also Fashions and clothing; Hairstyles; Jews in the United States; Pinup girls; "Rosie the Riveter"; War bonds; Women's roles and rights in the United States; Wonder Woman.

■ Morgan v. Virginia

The Case U.S. Supreme Court ruling striking down segregation in interstate public transportation because it created a "burden on commerce"

Date Decided on June 3, 1946

The Morgan *decision partially overturned* Plessy v. Ferguson *(1896), which legalized racial segregation. By weakening segregation, the Supreme Court set the stage for the eventual legal end to this discriminatory practice.*

Irene Morgan, a defense worker, boarded a Greyhound bus in Gloucester County, Virginia, bound for Baltimore, Maryland, in July, 1944. When all the seats in the bus filled with passengers, the bus driver asked Morgan to give up her seat. As an African American woman, Morgan was required by law to defer to a white person by surrendering her seat. Morgan refused to move. A sheriff's deputy, called by the bus driver, put his hand on Morgan to intimidate her to move. Morgan responded to this attempt at bullying by kicking, clawing, and trying to tear the deputy's clothes.

Morgan accepted responsibility for resisting arrest. However, she refused to pay a ten-dollar fine for violating a Virginia law that required segregated seating in public transportation. The National Association for the Advancement of Colored People (NAACP) represented Morgan as she appealed.

On June 3, 1946, by a vote of 6 to 1, the Supreme Court ruled that the Virginia law violated the commerce clause of the Constitution. Justice Stanley F. Reed, writing for the majority, stated that seating arrangements in interstate transportation required a uniform rule to promote and protect national travel. The Court declared that Morgans's right of equal protection under the law had been violated.

Impact Though the *Morgan* decision is barely remembered today, it represented the first legal victory against segregation. With *Morgan*, the Court undermined the *Plessy v. Ferguson* (1896) ruling that had stood for half a century.

Caryn E. Neumann

Further Reading

Dierenfield, Bruce J. *The Civil Rights Movement.* New York: Pearson Longman, 2004.

Tsesis, Alexander. *We Shall Overcome: A History of Civil Rights and the Law.* New Haven, Conn.: Yale University Press, 2008.

See also African Americans; Civil rights and liberties; Jim Crow laws; Journey of Reconciliation; National Association for the Advancement of Colored People; Racial discrimination.

■ Mount Rushmore National Memorial

Identification Mountain monument honoring four American presidents
Date October 31, 1941
Place Black Hills, South Dakota

The carving of the four presidential heads into South Dakota's Mount Rushmore ended in October, 1941, in part because of the death of sculptor Gutzon Borglum, a lack of funding, and the advent of U.S. entry into World War II. The monument remains the largest work of art in the world.

Time Line of Mount Rushmore National Memorial

1923	Black Hills sculpture is suggested by South Dakota state historian Doane Robinson
Mar. 3 and 5, 1925	U.S. government and state of South Dakota authorize carving in the Harney National Forest
Oct. 1, 1925	Dedication of Mount Rushmore as a national memorial
Aug. 10, 1927	President Calvin Coolidge presides at a second dedication ceremony
Oct. 4, 1927	Carving begins on Mount Rushmore
July 4, 1930	Dedication of the George Washington sculpture
Aug. 30, 1936	Dedication of the Thomas Jefferson sculpture
Sept. 17, 1937	Dedication of the Abraham Lincoln sculpture
July 2, 1939	Dedication of the Theodore Roosevelt sculpture
Mar. 6, 1941	Project director Gutzon Borglum dies in Chicago
1941	Gutzon's son, Lincoln Borglum, begins directing project
Oct. 31, 1941	Mount Rushmore National Memorial completed

In 1927, Gutzon Borglum began working on Mount Rushmore's monument to four American presidents—George Washington, Thomas Jefferson, Theodore Roosevelt, and Abraham Lincoln. The challenges were immense: not only the actual engineering and the carving of the presidential faces but also raising money to fund the project, particularly after the onset of the Great Depression. The first face, Washington's, was unveiled on July 4, 1930, and the last, Roosevelt's, on July 2, 1939. Of the twelve years from the initial drilling to Roosevelt's unveiling, seven years saw no activity because of the financial impact of the Depression.

Borglum, not a young man when the project began, died on March 6, 1941, at the age of seventy-three. His original plan was to sculpt the presidents down to their waists, including period clothing, but in part because of the lack of funds and the looming threat of World War II, the monument was left unfinished, portraying only the sixty-foot-high heads. Gutzon Borglum's son, Lincoln, who had already been involved in the project, finished the details; the final drilling ended on October 31, 1941, with the cracks and fissures sealed with white lead and granite dust. In less than two months, the United States was at war. The total cost of the project was approximately $1 million, 90 percent of which was provided by the federal government.

Impact Borglum's Mount Rushmore sculpture became one of the iconic monuments in the United States. It is visited by more than two million people annually.

Eugene Larson

Further Reading

Borglum, Lincoln. *Mount Rushmore: The Story Behind the Scenery.* Reprint. Las Vegas, Nev.: KC Publications, 2006.

Fite, Gilbert C. *Mount Rushmore.* Norman: University of Oklahoma Press, 1952.

See also Art movements; Jackson Hole National Monument; Jefferson Memorial; National parks; Roosevelt, Franklin D.

■ *Murdock v. Pennsylvania*

The Case U.S. Supreme Court decision formalizing the preferred freedoms doctrine

Date Decided on May 3, 1943

The Supreme Court's narrow ruling in this case established the concept that the First Amendment guarantees of freedom of religion, press, and speech occupied a preferred position in U.S. constitutional law.

Murdock v. Pennsylvania was one of several cases involving the Jehovah's Witnesses cases that came before the U.S. Supreme Court during the late 1930's and 1940's. In this case, plaintiffs from the religious sect argued that their constitutional right to free exercise of religion was being denied by a local tax on their door-to-door pamphleteering. They were being charged a flat tax, despite the fact that their pamphleteering included requests for donations and was therefore classified as soliciting, not selling, under local ordinances.

The Court agreed with the plaintiffs, striking down the ordinance as applied to their activities in a 5-4 decision. Justice William O. Douglas stated in his majority opinion that because First Amendment rights such as the free exercise of religion are foundational to other constitutional rights, they must be placed in a "preferred position." The Jehovah's Witnesses' pamphleteering in this case, he said, was a predominantly religious activity, not a commercial one, and government must not place a financial "condition" on the exercise of this First Amendment right.

Only one year earlier, the Court had denied a similar constitutional challenge to another government ordinance by a 5-4 vote; a change in Court personnel allowed for a reversal in the Court's *Murdock* ruling. When President Franklin D. Roosevelt appointed fellow liberal Wiley B. Rutledge to fill the seat of the retiring James F. Byrnes, a new majority had been born.

Impact *Murdock* signaled the Supreme Court's transition toward becoming a champion of individual rights. Since this ruling, the preferred freedoms doctrine has been used to protect many forms of expression and has remained part of the complex and sometimes contradictory realm of constitutional jurisprudence.

W. Jesse Weins

Further Reading

Ahlstrom, Sydney E. *A Religious History of the American People.* New Haven: Yale University Press, 1972.

Butler, Jon, Grant Wacker, and Randall Balmer. *Religion in American Life: A Short History.* Rev. ed. New York: Oxford University Press, 2007.

Lewis, Thomas Tandy, ed. *U.S. Court Cases.* Rev. ed. 3 vols. Pasadena, Calif.: Salem Press, 2011.

_____. *U.S. Supreme Court.* 3 vols. Pasadena, Calif.: Salem Press, 2007.

See also Civil rights and liberties; Religion in the United States; Supreme Court, U.S.

■ Murphy, Audie

Identification Highly decorated World War II hero who would become a film star
Born June 20, 1924; near Kingston, Texas
Died May 28, 1971; near Roanoke, Virginia

Earning thirty-three awards and decorations, Murphy became the most-decorated soldier in U.S. Army history. He exemplified grace under pressure, saving many of his fellow soldiers. After the war, his humility, simplicity, dignity, and patriotism made him an icon, World War II's version of Sergeant York.

With spectacular reflexes and coordination, as a young child Audie Leon Murphy became an excellent marksman, hunting game for his often-hungry sharecropping family. Too scrawny for the Marines or the paratroops, he was finally accepted by the Army, Fifteenth Infantry Regiment, Third Infantry Division. Fighting in Italy and France, he rose from private to first lieutenant, was wounded three times, and killed 240 Axis soldiers.

Murphy's audacity threw the enemy off balance. For example, on January 26, 1945, his small company was attacked by six Nazi tanks and 250 infantry near Holtzwihr, France. Murphy leapt onto a burning tank destroyer, grabbed its machine gun, and drove back the Germans.

Life magazine put Murphy on its July 16, 1945, cover. In 1948, he appeared in the first of several dozen films, most of them Westerns. His 1949 autobiography, *To Hell and Back*, imaginatively ghostwritten by his friend David McClure, was a best seller for fourteen weeks. Murphy died in a small plane crash in 1971 and was buried in Arlington National Cemetery.

U.S. Army lieutenant Audie Murphy in Austria in June, 1945, shortly after he received the Congressional Medal of Honor and the Legion of Merit—both of which he can be seen wearing. (AP/Wide World Photos)

Impact The personification of heroism, Murphy fought in campaigns in North Africa, Sicily, Italy, France, and Germany. He inspired patriotism and promoted Army recruitment. As a film star, he was best known for his roles in *The Red Badge of Courage* (1951) and *To Hell and Back* (1955).

David B. Kopel

Further Reading

Joiner, Ann Levington. *A Myth in Action: The Heroic Life of Audie Murphy.* Baltimore, Md.: PublishAmerica, 2006.

Murphy, Audie. *To Hell and Back.* 1949. Reprint. New York: Henry Holt, 2002.

See also Army, U.S.; Cowboy films; Films about World War II; Italian campaign; *Life*; Mauldin, Bill; Patton, George S.; War heroes.

■ Murrow, Edward R.

Identification American radio journalist
Born April 25, 1908; Greensboro, North Carolina
Died April 27, 1965; Pawling, New York

Through his frequent radio broadcasts, Murrow presented Americans with a gripping account of the wartime sufferings of Great Britain and Europe from 1939 until 1945 and thereby played a role in engaging American interest in the European war.

Born in North Carolina in 1908, Edward R. Murrow grew up in a lumber town in the state of Washington and attended Washington State University, where he participated in student activist campaigns. After he graduated, his activist contacts landed him a job relocating refugee scholars from Nazi Germany. In 1935 he went to work for Columbia Broadcasting System (CBS) radio, and in 1937 that job took him to London, where he worked until after the end of World War II.

As a journalist, Murrow attempted to focus on international politics despite the network preference for lighthearted features and stories about British royalty. His finest reporting took place during Germany's bombing of London in 1940 and 1941. He battled British authorities for permission to broadcast from a rooftop during bombing raids. His descriptions of the raids were vivid and brought a distant war into American homes. He portrayed a nation steadfastly resolute to do whatever was needed to defeat the Nazis. His work was credited with contributing to the erosion of isolationist sentiment across America and with creating strong sympathy for the nations targeted by the Nazis.

Murrow was a talent scout as well as a crack journalist. He hired Eric Sevareid, Howard K. Smith, and William L. Shirer to work for CBS. Smith and Sevareid went on to long careers in radio and television, and Shirer became a best-selling author of renown. Murrow and his colleagues faced constant danger in wartime London. On three different occasions, direct bomb hits destroyed the CBS studio in London. On other occasions Murrow was inside buildings when bombs struck them. He escaped certain death one time when he cancelled plans to attend a party at a hotel that was obliterated by bombs, resulting in extensive loss of life.

In 1943, Murrow disobeyed orders and flew along on a Royal Air Force bombing raid over Berlin. Two of the four journalists accompanying that raid were shot down. Nevertheless, Murrow flew twenty-four more times before the war was over. His postraid broadcast vividly captured the mood of the crew, the mad dodging of flak and fighters, and the somber

Edward R. Murrow broadcasting a report for CBS News in September, 1947. (Getty Images)

postraid atmosphere, with the realization that many of the crews would never return. Murrow was also in London for the Nazi V-1 and V-2 attacks. Just as he had earlier in the war, Murrow did a masterful job of letting Americans know what it was like to live under relentless aerial attack.

Murrow asked CBS to allow him to accompany the June, 1944 landings at Normandy, but his superiors staunchly forbade it. In early 1945 he finally received permission to accompany the Third Army of George S. Patton in Germany. Murrow was present when American troops reached the infamous concentration camp at Buchenwald. He was so shaken that he had to wait three days before he felt able to broadcast about the camp. His report was terse, matter-of-fact, yet also heartfelt in a way few reporters could ever hope to be. Finally, the brutal and evil Nazi regime had become familiar to people in every American home.

Murrow would eventually make the transition to television and garner both accolades and harsh criticism before his death in 1965. Despite his later achievements, colleagues and scholars generally agree that his wartime broadcasts were exemplary, and that they set a standard for future generations of reporters that has rarely been matched.

Impact   Murrow explored and enhanced the powerful new medium of radio by his reporting from Europe during World War II. He realized the medium's ability to capture news events with a greater immediacy and realism than was possible through print journalism, and he masterfully used his radio broadcasts to provide his listeners with a greater understanding of the horrors of combat and the evil of the Nazis. For many Americans, Murrow was the most authoritative source of news about the war, which would have remained a remote series of battles had they not been able to hear his reports.

Michael Polley

Further Reading

Edwards, Bob. *Edward R. Murrow and the Birth of Broadcast Journalism.* New York: John Wiley & Sons, 2004.

Murrow, Edward R. *In Search of Light: The Broadcasts of Edward R. Murrow, 1938-1961.* Edited by Edward Bliss, Jr. New York: Alfred A. Knopf, 1967.

Seib, Philip. *Broadcasts from the Blitz: How Edward R. Murrow Helped Lead America into War.* Washington, D.C.: Potomac Books, 2006.

Smith, R. Franklin. *Edward R. Murrow: The War Years.* Kalamazoo, Mich.: New Issues Press, 1978.

See also   Army, U.S.; D Day; Mauldin, Bill; Pyle, Ernie; Radio in the United States; *Stars and Stripes*; V-E Day and V-J Day; World War II.

■ Music: Classical

Definition   Art music—as opposed to popular music—derived principally from European musical traditions, including ballet and opera as well as solo, chamber, and orchestral music

During the early 1940's, American audiences experienced apprehension toward German and Italian art music, embracing instead the music of the allied European nations. Moreover, leading composers and conductors from Europe, fleeing from the Nazi regime, established and promoted European art music within the United States. Notwithstanding the dominant position of European music (ballets, operas, and instrumental music), works composed by American composers managed to flourish during the decade and increasingly after World War II.

The Nazi regime and World War II forced many of the most influential of the European composers to emigrate to the United States, directly impacting art music composed and performed in America. Forced from his teaching position at the prestigious Prussian Academy of Arts in Berlin, the Jewish composer Arnold Schoenberg fled to the United States in 1933. A composer that advanced the composition of atonal music, Schoenberg taught at the University of California, Los Angeles (UCLA), from 1935 to 1944. The Russian neoclassical composer Igor Stravinsky toured the United States during the late 1930's and gave the Charles Eliot Norton lectures at Harvard University in 1939. Settling in Hollywood, he received numerous American commissions during the 1940's. He was granted American citizenship in 1945.

The Nazis labeled the music of the German composer Paul Hindemith as "degenerate," in part for its modernist elements, and in 1938 Hindemith and his Jewish wife moved to Switzerland, eventually emigrating to the United States in 1940. He taught composition and music theory at Yale University from 1940 to 1953. In 1940, the Hungarian composer Béla Bartók escaped the war in Europe. He settled in New York, continuing to compose in addition to transcribing Yugoslavian folk songs at Columbia University. The two primary European influences on American art music during the decade of the 1940's were expressionism and neoclassicism, the former associated with Schoenberg and the latter with Stravinsky. Simultaneously, American mavericks independent of European art movements experimented with music, foreshadowing a growing American influence upon European music in the following decades.

Ballet American ballet flourished during the 1940's, leaving behind many years of Russian domination. Lucia Chase and Richard Pleasant founded the Ballet Theatre (later renamed American Ballet Theatre) in 1939. Importantly, the formation of the Ballet Theatre led to numerous commissions from American composers. Lincoln Kirstein began with the direction of the Concert Ballet in 1943 and Ballet Society in 1946. With the famed ballet choreographer George Balanchine, Kirstein established the New York City Ballet in 1948. Most dancers in the company consisted of American dancers and ultimately developed a distinctive style and identity separate from European ballet.

American choreographer and dancer Agnes de Mille began in 1939 with Ballet Theatre. She choreographed *Rodeo* (1942), a Western-themed ballet for the Ballet Russe de Monte Carlo. (The dance company operated in the United States during World War II.) Composer Aaron Copland employed American folk tunes and harmonies that evoked the expansive landscape of the American West in the ballet score. American choreographer Jerome Robbins also danced with the Ballet Theatre in 1940. He collaborated with composer Leonard Bernstein on *Fancy Free* (1944), a ballet about three sailors on leave in New York City, and later *Facsimile* (1946). The American dancer and choreographer Martha Graham pioneered modern dance, choreographing to the music of notable American works such as Copland's *Appalachian Spring* (1944), Samuel Barber's *Medea* (1946), William Schuman's *Night Journey* (1947), Gian Carlo Menotti's *Errand into the Maze* (1947), and Norman Dello Joio's *Diversion of Angels* (1948).

Opera Based in New York City, the Metropolitan Opera House was the most important opera

house in the United States. Since its foundation, the Metropolitan Opera Company toured the nation, with shortened tours during the Great Depression. Audiences and the institution favored glamorous and virtuosic singers with strong voices. During World War II, the Metropolitan Opera Company benefited from the influx of talented European conductors.

While the Metropolitan Opera Company was the principal opera company in the city as well as in the nation, other opera companies served different audiences. During the 1940's, affordable and popular opera productions took place in New York City in the large auditorium of the City Center. Opera at the City Center preceded and followed the Metropolitan season and served as a platform for young singers to learn opera roles, many eventually singing for the Metropolitan Opera Company. From 1947, Kenneth Hieber and Max Leavitt operated during the summers the Lemonade Opera (named for the lem-

Coloratura Lily Pons singing in Daughter of the Regiment *during the opening night of a new season at New York City's Metropolitan Opera House in 1942.* (Time & Life Pictures/Getty Images)

onade sold outside the performance location) in a small church auditorium in New York City. In place of an orchestra, two pianos accompanied the singers. New York audiences heard performances of Engelbert Humperdinck's *Hansel and Gretel* (1892) and Wolfgang Amadeus Mozart's *Don Giovanni* (1787), and young singers gained valuable experience at the Lemonade Opera.

In addition to the touring Metropolitan Opera Company, the performance of opera took place throughout the nation. In 1878, during the economic peak of the historic Colorado mining town of Central City, citizens of the town constructed the Central City Opera House. However, the use of the building was short-lived and abandoned until its restoration during the 1930's. During the 1940's, it served as the site for outstanding opera productions that were on a par with European opera houses.

During the 1940's, the Italian-born composer and librettist Gian Carlo Menotti wrote a series of successful operas in the United States, becoming one of the most significant living American opera composers of the decade. He gained positive recognition for the radio opera *The Old Maid and the Thief* (1939); however, his next opera, *The Island God* (1942), was not a success. He received international acclaim for the tragic opera *The Medium* (1946), which later appeared in a motion-picture version that he also supervised. After *The Medium*, he composed the one-act comedy *The Telephone* (1946). German-born composer Kurt Weill's American opera *Street Scene* (1946) was based on Elmer Rice's prizewinning play that depicted American life in New York City. Weill's college opera *Down in the Valley* (1948) gained popular success. In Virgil Thomson's *The Mother of Us All* (1947), with libretto by Gertrude Stein, the composer employed nineteenth century popular songs, hymns, and folk songs in an opera that chronicled the life of Susan B. Anthony. In *The Trial of Lucullus* (1947), Roger Sessions used Bertolt Brecht's radio play for a student opera production at the University of California, Berkeley. The African American composer William Grant Still composed *Troubled Island* (1949) with a libretto written by Langston Hughes and Verna Arvey that dealt with the eighteenth century slave revolt in Haiti.

Instrumental Music The most important symphony orchestras in the United States during the 1940's were in the cities of New York, Boston, and Chicago. The principal conductors of all three orchestras during this period were foreign-born. The oldest American symphony orchestra, the New York Philharmonic Orchestra, was founded in 1842. The orchestra was led at different times during the 1940's by John Barbirolli, Artur Rodzinski, Bruno Walter, Leopold Stokowski, and Dimitri Mitropoulos. The Boston Symphony Orchestra, founded in 1881, was conducted during the 1940's by Serge Koussevitzky and Charles Munch. The third-oldest symphony orchestra was the Chicago Symphony Orchestra, founded in 1891. The orchestra was directed during the 1940's by Frederick Stock, Désiré Defauw, and Artur Rodzinski.

Many American composers adopted traditional methods for composing instrumental music, employing a tonal harmonic language and conventional forms. Dedicated primarily to music composition, Samuel Barber contributed numerous significant American works. Eminent orchestral conductors consistently programmed his music during the 1940's. During World War II, he served in the Air Force and composed *Commando March* (1943) and Symphony No. 2 (1944). Walter Piston studied composition—as did many American composers—with the prominent composer and teacher Nadia Boulanger in France. A conservative composer, he primarily composed orchestral music. In 1938, David Diamond studied composition with Boulanger in France. He composed his first four symphonies during the 1940's. While George Antheil was an avant-garde composer in his youth, by the 1940's his music had become conservative, as demonstrated in his Symphony No. 4 (1942). Pianist and composer Vivian Fine studied composition with modernist composer Ruth Crawford Seeger; however, Fine's music during the 1940's shifted to diatonicism.

Roy Harris achieved widespread popularity with audiences for his approachable musical style. He also studied with Boulanger in France. In his music, he employed *divisi* scoring (divided parts) and asymmetrical rhythms. William Schuman, a student of Harris, composed for the symphony orchestra. In his Symphony No. 6 (1948), he employed polytriads. Possibly more than any composer during the period, Aaron Copland affected the direction of American music, creating a characteristically American style of composition. His accessible style appeared in his symphonic works as well as film scores of the 1940's. Copland's *Fanfare for the Common Man* (1942) and

Symphony No. 3 (1946) represent important works of the period. The composer, conductor, and pianist Leonard Bernstein contributed in all areas of American art music. He employed energetic rhythms and elements of jazz in his Symphony No. 1, "Jeremiah" (1942) and Symphony No. 2, "The Age of Anxiety" (1949). The music of Schoenberg and the Second Viennese School influenced American composers—more so during the 1950's; however, the impact of atonal composition appeared in the work duo for violin and piano (1942) by Roger Sessions.

The works by experimental composers such as Harry Partch and John Cage—both natives of California—represent a significant break with European art music. Partch invented new musical instruments and discarded the European system of twelve pitches to an octave. In the creation of an American music, he made use of principles from ancient Greek drama, Chinese theater, and Yaqui Indian rituals. He employed American texts for many of his works, using inscriptions from hitchhikers in *Barstow* (1941) and text from his hobo train journeys in *US Highball* (1943). In 1940, Cage received a request for music to accompany a dance at the Cornish School in Seattle, and the small stage space inspired him to place small objects (screws, bolts, and weather stripping) between the strings of a piano. His experiment resulted in a "prepared piano" (a piano that evoked the sounds of a percussion orchestra), and the work *Bacchanale* (1940). Further innovations by Cage within the music of the postwar twentieth century ultimately influenced both the American and European avant-garde, changing the art music establishment.

Impact For American classical music and musical establishments, the decade of the 1940's was a period of transition. The impact of World War II led to sudden changes in the music programming of ballets, operas, and symphony orchestras. In addition, the atrocities of the war forced many European composers, conductors, and musicians to either temporarily or permanently move to the United States. While nevertheless closely connected to European musical traditions, American composers gradually forged toward the creation of distinctive American varieties of art music.

Mark E. Perry

Further Reading

Burton, Humphrey. *Leonard Bernstein*. New York: Doubleday, 1994. A thorough biography on the life and works of composer, conductor, and pianist Leonard Bernstein.

Chase, Gilbert. *America's Music: From the Pilgrims to the Present*. Urbana: University of Illinois Press, 1992. A comprehensive history of American music.

Crawford, Richard. *America's Musical Life: A History*. New York: W. W. Norton, 2001. A wide-ranging history of American music that includes the examination of traditional, popular, and art music.

Horowitz, Joseph. *Classical Music in America: A History of Its Rise and Fall*. New York: W. W. Norton, 2005. An overview that traces the development of art music in the United States.

Pendle, Karin, ed. *Women and Music: A History*. Bloomington: Indiana University Press, 2001. A general survey of female composers, performers, patrons, and theorists dating from antiquity to the present.

Pollack, Howard. *Aaron Copland: The Life and Work of an Uncommon Man*. New York: Henry Holt, 1999. A meticulous biography on the life and works of the eminent American composer Aaron Copland.

See also *Appalachian Spring*; Ballet Society; Bernstein, Leonard; Dance; *Fantasia*; Music: Jazz; Music: Popular; Recording industry; *Rodeo*.

■ Music: Jazz

Definition American musical style emphasizing syncopated rhythms, improvisation, and swing

During the 1940's, jazz contributed to both the growing body of American popular music and the feelings of unity needed during World War II. The developments in jazz during the decade were pivotal in defining the direction of the music in the latter half of the twentieth century.

The 1940's was a significant transitional period for jazz. The big-band swing of the 1930's, dominated commercially by white musicians, gave way to the small-group bebop bands dominated by African Americans. The decade also represents the tensions that continue to define jazz and polarize audiences: commercial appeal versus art, progressive versus regressive styles.

The Decline of Swing The end of swing's dominance over the musical landscape was brought about by several events. One of these was the entrance of the United States into World War II. The most obvious effect of the war was conscription, by which many musicians were drafted into the military, making it difficult for bandleaders to staff their organizations consistently with quality musicians. Jack Teagarden replaced seventeen musicians in a four-month period, Count Basie lost feature tenor saxophonist Lester Young and drummer Jo Jones on the same day, and Kansas City bandleader Jay McShann was inducted into the Army during a performance. The Glenn Miller Orchestra, one of the most popular bands of the era, was disbanded so Miller could create an all-star armed forces band. At one point during the war, at least sixty-one bandleaders were serving in the military, plus countless rank-and-file musicians. In October, 1942, popular jazz publication *DownBeat* began running "Killed in Action," a regular feature listing musicians who lost their lives in combat.

Economic factors also hurt swing bands. Transportation was affected by the rationing of resources such as petroleum and rubber; this hindered the abilities of bus companies to keep large fleets running. Buses and trains that did run were largely under the supervision of the military and were increasingly filled with soldiers shuttling between their homes and duty stations. As a result, bands had a difficult time touring, which limited their exposure to the public. The recording industry was also hit by a shortage of the shellac used to make records. In 1943, the federal entertainment tax was reinstated,

DownBeat Magazine Readers Polls, 1940-1949

Listed below are winners from major categories. The table lists the favorite swing band from 1940 to 1946 and the favorite band from 1947 to 1949. The categories of male and female vocalist expanded in 1944 to include vocalists with bands.

Year	Swing band/band	Trumpet	Arranger	Male vocalist(s)	Female vocalist(s)
1940	Benny Goodman	Ziggy Elman	Fletcher Henderson	Bing Crosby	Helen O'Connell
1941	Benny Goodman	Ziggy Elman	Sy Oliver	Frank Sinatra	Helen O'Connell
1942	Duke Ellington	Roy Eldridge	Sy Oliver	Frank Sinatra	Helen Forrest
1943	Benny Goodman	Ziggy Elman	Sy Oliver	Frank Sinatra	Jo Stafford
1944	Duke Ellington	Ziggy Elman	Sy Oliver	Bing Crosby; with band: Bob Eberly	Dinah Shore; with band: Anita O'Day
1945	Woody Herman	Ziggy Elman	Sy Oliver	Bing Crosby; with band: Stuart Foster	Jo Stafford; with band: Anita O'Day
1946	Stan Kenton	Roy Eldridge	Billy Strayhorn	Frank Sinatra; with band: Buddy Stewart	Peggy Lee; with band: June Christy
1947	Stan Kenton	Ziggy Elman	Pete Rugolo	Frank Sinatra; with band: Buddy Stewart	Sarah Vaughan; with band: June Christy
1948	Duke Ellington	Charlie Shavers	Billy Eckstine	Billy Eckstine; with band: Al Hibbler	Sarah Vaughan; with band: June Christy
1949	Woody Herman	Howard McGhee	Pete Rugolo	Billy Eckstine; with band: Al Hibbler	Sarah Vaughan; with band: Mary Ann McCall

Source: "The DownBeat Readers Poll Archive." *DownBeat* magazine. www.downbeat.com

which added 20 percent to the cost of going to dances where these bands played. Two recording bans during the early 1940's, one by the American Society of Composers, Authors, and Publishers against radio and the other by the American Federation of Musicians (AFM) against record companies, cut into the income of musicians as well as their exposure to the public.

Another issue affecting jazz during this era was the splintering of the jazz audience. The overt showiness and tendency toward formula and cliché in swing brought about two factions looking for something different. One group, the progressives, sought jazz that was exciting and unpredictable. One of their criticisms of swing was that it diminished the importance of improvisation in jazz, which they believed took a lot of the life out of the music. They were interested less in musicians as entertainers and more in musicians as artists. They found their new style in bebop. The other group, known as the "moldy figs," looked for their alternatives in the past. Rather than seeking a new style of jazz, they looked to the artists of New Orleans and Chicago that laid the foundations of the genre.

A third group of fans began leaving jazz altogether. This audience had come to jazz when swing bands began performing more familiar, radio-friendly songs and hired singers, such as Ella Fitzgerald, Billie Holiday, Frank Sinatra, and Tony Bennett, to front the bands. As the singers began to leave those bands and start their own careers, their fans tended to follow them, leaving many bands to play for mostly empty halls.

The Survivors   Not all big bands perished during the 1940's; some were able to weather the storms and have a great deal of success. Bandleaders such as Stan Kenton and Woody Herman did so by absorbing the new musical character and vitality of bebop into their arrangements. Count Basie dealt with the loss of Young and Jones, two of the most defining elements of his sound, by changing the musical direction of the orchestra.

Perhaps no bandleader came out of the era with as much success as Duke Ellington, who found ways to keep his band afloat during the tumultuous war years, while remaining fairly consistent musically. He managed to retain his tour buses by making a deal to play free concerts at military bases, virtually every day, and playing dances nearby in the eve-

nings. Eventually, he bought his own Pullman car for the band, which allowed them to travel by train. The biggest impact on the popularity of the Ellington band was the additions of tenor saxophonist Ben Webster; bassist Jimmy Blanton; and lyricist, arranger, and composer Billy Strayhorn in 1939. These three men helped lead to a two-year peak in creativity and popularity of the group and led to a broader audience for Ellington's music. Blanton and Webster were only short-term members of the group, but Strayhorn was a part of the organization until his death in 1967.

The Dixieland Revival   The renewed interest in music of the past was sparked in part by the 1939 publication of the book *Jazzmen*, which chronicled the lives and careers of several musicians associated with the formative years of jazz. Another likely factor was the unstable social environment brought about by the war, which often led people to retreat to the safety of nostalgia. During the late 1930's, bands began playing more older music in their performances; Benny Goodman's played Fats Waller's "Honeysuckle Rose," and Jelly Roll Morton's added "King Porter Stomp" to his 1938 concert at Carnegie Hall.

By the end of the 1930's, fan clubs began offering their members reissues of recordings from the 1920's. By the early 1940's, groups of white musicians formed "Dixieland" bands, a name that references a romanticized Old South, to re-create the sounds of earlier groups such as King Oliver's Creole Jazz Band and the Original Dixieland Jazz Band. The revival also rekindled the careers of some of the early jazz musicians, such as trumpeter Bunk Johnson and clarinetist and soprano saxophonist Sidney Bechet. Johnson made his first recordings ever in 1942, and Bechet made some of his best known American recordings during this period, including his classic version of George Gershwin's "Summertime."

The Birth of Bebop   Progressive or modern jazz, later called bebop, seemed to appear fully formed in the nightclubs of uptown Manhattan. In reality, the AFM's recording ban meant that listeners had little chance to hear this new music in its developmental stages, and by the time the ban was lifted in 1942, the bebop style had solidified. The name bebop, or rebop as it was called by some, came from the rhythmic accents drummers played and the syllables scat singers used. Bebop featured virtuoso improvisation, ag-

Five giants of American jazz jamming in early 1948 during the making of the film A Song Is Born. *From left to right: saxophonist Charlie Barnet, trombonist Tommy Dorsey, clarinetist Benny Goodman, trumpeter Louis Armstrong, and Lionel Hampton on the vibraphones.* (Getty Images)

gressive drumming, a sparse piano style known as "comping," and, often, extremely fast tempos. Bebop also represented the first time in jazz when African American musicians did not make conscious attempts to fit in with the expectations of white audiences. Musicians such as alto saxophonist Charlie Parker and pianist Thelonious Monk were more concerned with the music they were playing than with the image they projected, and while trumpeter Dizzy Gillespie danced and joked and sang novelty lyrics to his songs, he was creating a new image for African American entertainers rather than perpetuating old ones.

There is some contention as to whether bebop represents evolution or revolution in jazz. Most of the musicians were trained in big bands and were influenced by the playing of established figures such as Young and guitarist Charlie Christian, both of whom were associated with the Kansas City jazz scene during the 1930's and 1940's. Parker spent some time in Kansas City and played in McShann's band. Gillespie modeled his playing style after swing trumpeter Roy Eldridge. Monk was a great admirer of the stride piano style exemplified by James P. Johnson and Ellington.

On the other hand, bebop bears little resemblance to swing in its execution or sound. Bebop em-

phasized small groups, often five or six players, rather than the big bands of swing. It was more oriented toward improvisation than swing, which tended toward elaborate written arrangements. Performers took the popular songs that were responsible for the commercial success of swing and used them as raw materials to create new songs, often overlaying the chord progression of the popular song with a new melody and using the chords as a framework for improvisation. Bebop was aimed at the nightclub audience rather than at dance-hall crowds. In contrast to swing's broad popularity and commercial successes, bebop was perceived as elitist and decidedly uncommercial music. Bebop only occasionally featured memorable, singable melodies, and its fast tempos made the music difficult for the average listener to understand in one hearing.

By the end of the 1940's, big bands that blended bebop style playing with swinglike arrangements began to appear. The most successful of these were led by Kenton, Herman, and Gillespie. These arrangements tended to allow for more improvisation than swing arrangements and incorporated more rhythmically oriented written parts.

Jazz in Europe Jazz had been popular in Europe since the first performers started visiting in 1919. The most recognizable native European to be associated with jazz was Belgian-born gypsy guitarist Django Reinhardt, who was the leader of the Quintette du Hot Club de France (Quintet of the hot club of France) during the 1930's and 1940's. His compositions blended jazz and blues with hints of Claude Debussy and Maurice Ravel. He actually recorded Debussy's "Nuages" several times during the 1940's under the name "The Bluest Kind of Blue." He is mostly known for his unique guitar technique, developed out of necessity because he had lost the use of two fingers on his left hand when his gypsy caravan caught fire in 1928.

Jazz flourished in Europe through the 1920's and early 1930's, but that changed under Nazism. Officially, Adolf Hitler banned the playing of any American music, and propaganda minister Joseph Goebbels called jazz "the art of the subhuman." This did little to stop jazz musicians from playing their music. When the Germans banned the use of the word jazz, club owners simply renamed their clubs. For example, the Hot Jazz Club of Belgium became the Rhythmic Club. Musicians in Paris responded to the ban on American music by renaming their favorite jazz songs. Glenn Miller's "In the Mood" became "Ambiance" and Count Basie's "Jumpin' at the Woodside" became "Dansant dans la Clairiere." When Goebbels realized he could not do away with jazz, he attempted to turn it to his advantage by creating a radio swing band that played familiar popular tunes with new anti-Semitic lyrics.

Germany's antijazz stand led to the emergence of a group of young fans known as "swing kids." This underground fanbase met in secret to listen to smuggled records and Allied radio broadcasts. After the war ended, many credited jazz with giving them hope, and several went on to careers in jazz performance.

Impact Jazz provides a musical soundtrack for the 1940's. Swing, particularly the music of Miller, Tommy and Jimmy Dorsey, and Goodman, has become synonymous with World War II. It helped to embed the popular songs of the day into the American conscious and served as a unifying force for Americans anxious about the outcome of the war and the fate of the soldiers fighting it. After the war, bebop became the sound of progress, appealing to the new generation of students who were looking for a musical identity distinct from their parents. Jazz was the rock and roll of its time. Both types of jazz popular in the 1940's continue to impact popular music: Swing dancing has seen a revival, and bebop has been a major influence on hip-hop.

Eric S. Strother

Further Reading

DeVeaux, Scott. *The Birth of Bebop: A Social and Musical History*. Berkeley: University of California Press, 1997. Examines the development of bebop in both musical and cultural contexts.

Driggs, Frank, and Chuck Haddix. *Kansas City Jazz: From Ragtime to Bebop, a History*. New York: Oxford University Press, 2005. A history of jazz in Kansas City.

Gitler, Ira. *Swing to Bop*. New York: Oxford University Press, 1985. An oral history of the transition between swing and bebop during the 1940's. Based on interviews with musicians.

McClellan, Lawrence, Jr. *The Later Swing Era: 1942 to 1955*. Westport, Conn.: Greenwood Press, 2004. Documents the significant performers and works. Picks up where most works on the swing era leave off.

See also Coles, Honi; Davis, Miles; Dorsey, Tommy; Ellington, Duke; Garland, Judy; Goodman, Benny; Holiday, Billie; Horne, Lena; Jitterbug; Miller, Glenn; Parker, Charlie.

■ Music: Popular

Definition Nonclassical genres of music, some of which overlapped varieties of jazz

Often categorized as a decade of stylistic stagnation, the 1940's was a time of great musical change and innovation. This decade saw the demise of the swing band era, the rise of the crooner, and the introduction of new African American-influenced styles of music, such as rock 'n' roll. Popular music of this decade was significantly impacted by World War II, and many songs were about the war. In addition, the development of new musical technologies would permanently alter the course of popular music for future generations.

Popular music during the first half of the 1940's was dominated by instrumental swing bands. Swing band music was a visceral experience and an outlet for a society consumed by the economic plight of the Great Depression. The public flocked to dance halls, and fans followed their favorite bandleaders with a devotion similar to their adoration of their favorite sports heroes. World War II cast a huge shadow over all aspects of American life, and swing music helped foster the public's budding optimism, while also expressing a shared adversity, a cautiousness resulting from the economic depression and impending war. As the decade and the war wore on, popular tastes shifted toward a younger generation of singing stars. Both the economic difficulties of maintaining large bands and the exponential growth of the film industry led the entertainment business to invest heavily in multifaceted artists who could sing, act, and dance, creating the concept of the pop star who was well loved by teenage fans. By the end of the decade, gone were the beloved instrumental bandleaders, such as Glenn Miller. In their place was the crooning voice and larger-than-life personality of Frank Sinatra.

Wartime Music   The onset of World War II greatly influenced the course of musical tastes for the entire decade. By the time the Japanese bombed Pearl Harbor in 1941, the popularity of swing bands began to slowly decline from their heyday during the late 1930's. Despite this subtle but inevitable decline in popularity, the first half of 1941 saw the continuing popularity of swing artists, such as Duke Ellington, Benny Goodman, the Dorsey Brothers, and, most popular of all, the Glenn Miller Orchestra. Miller would later die in an airplane accident while entertaining troops in Europe. However, his musical style and legacy as a swing bandleader personifies the music of World War II. Yet it was the music of the Andrews Sisters and crooners, such as Frank Sinatra, that perhaps best encapsulate the mood and musical style of the war.

Formed as a vocal trio by the Minnesota-born sisters LaVerne, Maxene, and Patty Andrews, the group began performing together as the Andrews Sisters in 1932. The trio toured extensively, performing in dance halls and vaudeville houses throughout the Midwest, often with the Larry Rich Orchestra. Despite their upper-midwestern roots, the Andrews Sisters sang in a close, tight-knit harmony that was sprinkled with Dixieland influences. The group was tremendously versatile and seamlessly performed songs in many genres, from jazz to African American blues to Caribbean folk tunes. The Andrews Sisters first achieved national prominence with the hit "Bei mir bist du schoen" in 1937. Following this early success, the trio made frequent radio appearances throughout the late 1930's and 1940's, often with major swing band artists, such as the Glenn Miller Orchestra. The Andrews Sisters' decidedly optimistic style was well received by G.I.'s stationed throughout the world, and their song "Boogie Woogie Bugle Boy" (1941) became a popular hit and an anthem for the wartime effort. Other popular wartime tunes by the trio included "Don't Sit Under the Apple Tree" (1942) and the Caribbean-flavored "Rum and Coca-Cola" (1944).

Country and Western Music   Uprooted by the industrialization of farming, natural disasters in the Dust Bowl, and the economic disaster that was the Great Depression, millions of white southerners migrated to urban centers during the 1940's in search of industrial employment. These migrants brought their music with them, a folk style derived from the Anglo-American tradition called hillbilly. As the audiences for this music increased, listeners in urban and metropolitan areas, as well as music industry representatives, embraced this new style. The hillbilly style featured conservative lyrics, moral stories, multiple string guitars, fiddles, electrified instruments, smooth-sounding pop vocals, and an expansion of accompanying instruments. Proponents began referring to the style as "country and western music," and this music was quickly embraced by a large audience. By mid-decade, more than one hundred country and western radio shows were nationally syndicated. After

Composer Irving Berlin singing his song "God Bless America" for service personnel at New York City's Stage Door Canteen in July, 1942. The song would become an unofficial national anthem. (AP/Wide World Photos)

the end of the war, country and western music escaped its regional roots, and radio shows, such as the *Grand Ole Opry*, enjoyed success in urban and rural areas in both the North and South of the United States.

A major boon to the success of country and western music was the formation of the musical licensing agency Broadcast Music Incorporated (BMI) in 1939. BMI was conceived by radio networks as a rival agency to the American Society of Composers, Authors and Publishers (ASCAP), which had recently launched a campaign to assert control over radio companies in search of larger royalty payments. BMI was an inclusive agency and allowed artists working outside the Tin Pan Alley music publishing area of New York City to claim substantially higher royalties. This was particularly true in the case of country and western music, which by the end of the 1940's found its mecca in Nashville, Tennessee.

As country and western music gained in popularity, traditional stalwarts, such as the Carter Family and Jimmie Rogers, became household names and the genre began to shed its hillbilly persona. To this end, many performing artists, such as Gene Autry, Roy Rogers, Patsy Montana, Tex Ritter, and Hank Williams, sought to broaden their audiences and adopted a cowboy image. Many country artists, regardless of their places of birth, began wearing cowboy hats, boots, and shirts and adopted stage names like Tex and Hank. Perhaps the most important country and western artist of the 1940's was Roy Acuff. Like his contemporaries, Acuff began his career as a hillbilly singer and made his mark performing on the *Grand Ole Opry*, eventually becoming one of its biggest stars. Acuff was a traditionalist. He was devoted to an old-time sound, singing in a Southern twang with string band accompaniment, yet he was also an early pioneer of the slide guitar, which eventually became one of the genre's most identifiable characteristics.

Another seminal figure in the country and western music of the 1940's was Bob Wills. Along with his Texas Playboys, Wills brought country and western music to a broad audience by incorporating swing, Latin, and dance influences into his style. Prior to the war, Wills toured in country and western territory bands, which were similar to territory jazz bands. Following the war, Wills relocated to California and brought his new country and western style to this area. By incorporating African American and Latin American influences in his music, Wills greatly influenced the trajectory of modern country and western music.

Rise of the Crooners From 1942 to 1944, the Musicians Union instituted a ban on its members who were instrumentalists, prohibiting these musicians from releasing recordings while the union and the radio industry sparred over royalties. As a result, swing band singers enjoyed a new-found popularity and thrived in place of swing band instrumental leaders. Leading figures, such as Benny Goodman, Count Basie, and Glenn Miller, witnessed a swift shift of public taste away from instrumental music toward a decidedly younger generation of singers. These crooners built upon the legacy of Bing Crosby and created a new style of singing that was smooth, cheerful, and at times schmaltzy. Artists such as Doris Day, Peggy Lee, Dean Martin, Sammy Davis, Jr., Nat King Cole, and Perry Como specialized in cover versions of country and western songs, sentimental ballads, and dance craze and novelty tunes. Record companies pounced on these young and photogenic talents and relentlessly promoted the crooners, who often simultaneously became film stars, to teenage audiences.

Perhaps the most prominent crooner of the 1940's was Frank Sinatra. Sinatra was the first singer to inspire pop hysteria as his career reached fever pitch in 1942. He had worked in small nightclubs as a waiter throughout the latter half of the 1930's and got his break in 1939, when he joined the Tommy Dorsey Orchestra. The magnitude of Sinatra's appeal was evident while he was performing with the Benny Goodman Orchestra in 1942, when thousands of screaming fans flocked to his concerts. At first blush, Sinatra was similar to any ordinary American of the 1940's—a wholesome boy about to leave for the war—and he sold this image in order to connect with his rapidly expanding fan base. Image aside, Sinatra was supremely talented, and his style of singing, a combination of Bing Crosby crooning with Italian opera bel canto technique, was brilliantly paired with fresh and thoughtful song interpretations. His style and technique for using the microphone earned him monikers like the Sultan of Swoon and The Voice.

Developments in Music Technology The 1940's bore witness to many lasting developments in music technology. Chief among these developments was magnetic tape recording, which was a German wartime technology that was in many ways superior to disc recording. This technology allowed for longer recordings, overdubbing, and multitrack processing, although the impact of these advances would not be evident until future decades. In the 1940's, a number of advancements were made in disc technology. Wartime restrictions on materials affected many industries throughout the United States, including the recording industry, and as recording companies experimented with new materials they also altered the discs' revolutions per minute (rpm). In 1948, Columbia Records introduced the long-playing record, which was made of vinyl, a new material that made these records lighter than previous discs. These long-playing discs could record as much as twenty minutes of music per side and rotated at 33-$\frac{1}{3}$ rpm. These recordings revolutionized the industry and immediately usurped the 78-rpm disc, which had been the industry standard and could record only four minutes of music per side. In 1949, RCA introduced its own vinyl discs, and despite their limited capacity, these 45-rpm records enjoyed instantaneous popularity in juke boxes. Their success was due in large part to mechanical loaders that enabled consumers to load a stack of discs into a phonograph and create a semiautomated playlist.

Impact Musical and technological developments of the 1940's set the stage for many of the stylistic movements of the 1950's. With the advent of multitracking and overdubbing, the 1940's ushered in the music industry's transition from a focus on live music to an emphasis on recorded music. Moreover, the decade was the last time that instrumental music was more popular than vocal music. Perhaps the decade's greatest impact on future generations was the formation of techniques used to promote and create a pop star. This process was honed with the ascension of Sinatra's career and would be mastered in the following decade with the creation of the Elvis Presley hit machine. In addition, the catalog of songs interpreted and popularized by Sinatra, Dean Martin, and the other crooners of the era would remain tremendously influential for songwriters and artists into the twenty-first century.

Andrew R. Martin

Further Reading

Ewen, David. *The Life and Death of Tin Pan Alley: The Golden Age of American Popular Music.* New York: Funk & Wagnalls, 1964. Despite its date of publication, this text is an excellent resource for studying the rise of the American popular music industry.

Sforza, John. *Swing It! The Andrews Sisters Story.* Lexington: University Press of Kentucky, 1998. The official biography of the popular wartime trio.

Townsend, Charles. *San Antonio Rose: The Life and Music of Bob Wills.* Urbana: University of Illinois Press, 1986. A comprehensive study of Wills and early country and western music, this text includes more than two hundred interviews and is an important source of information for American popular culture, as well as music.

Tyler, Don. *Hit Songs, 1900-1955: American Popular Music of the Pre-Rock Era.* Jefferson, N.C.: McFarland Press, 2007. A tidy and comprehensive look at popular music styles and genres that preceded rock 'n' roll, this text also serves as a resource for the cultural and historical events that affected music in this fifty-five-year time period.

See also Andrews Sisters; Broadway musicals; Fender, Leo; Guthrie, Woody; Miller, Glenn; Music: Classical; Music: Jazz; Radio in the United States; Recording industry; Sinatra, Frank; Williams, Hank.

N

■ *The Naked and the Dead*

Identification   World War II novel about Americans fighting in the Pacific
Author   Norman Mailer (1923-2007)
Date   Published in May, 1948

An immediately popular account of the horrors of war, The Naked and the Dead *helped set the pattern for negative depictions of warfare. It also raised issues of power and violence that Mailer was to explore further in later years.*

Norman Mailer burst upon the American literary scene with the May, 1948, publication of his first book, *The Naked and the Dead,* a fictional account of an attack by American troops on a Japanese-held island during World War II. For eleven weeks, Mailer's book held the top position on *The New York Times* best-seller list, and it sold nearly 200,000 copies during its first year.

Mailer, who had sought a combat role in the Pacific precisely in order to write a novel about it, instantly acquired the fame he had been seeking ever since he was an adolescent. Throughout the rest of his career, in increasingly unorthodox ways, he pursued the limelight through both his books and his personal life.

The Naked and the Dead won praise as one of the best books to come out of the war, and it is notable for its focus on the horrors of life in the Army, horrors that stem less from the Japanese adversary than from heat, exhaustion, the soldiers' petty bickering and bigotry, and the sight of dead bodies. Although the novel was praised at the time for its realism, Mailer himself called it a symbolic book, and later critics have seen Mailer's army as a microcosm of American society and as a warning against the dangers of fascism and bureaucracy in American life. The book is also suffused with a pessimistic sense of the futility of human endeavor in the face of external forces and chance. It is also marked by widespread use of profanity, which went beyond what was common at the time, though Mailer was persuaded to use the word "fug" in place of another expletive.

Though technically more conventional than his later books, the novel does use some "time machine" flashbacks reminiscent of the novels of John Dos Passos during the 1930's. Mailer's novel is often said to have been influenced by the social protest novels of that decade, embodying a left-liberal critique of American society focused on such issues as class privilege, racism, poverty, and the threat of fascism. The latter threat is embodied in the

Norman Mailer. (Library of Congress)

characters of General Cummings and Sergeant Croft, who are devotees of power, violence, and hierarchy. Although these two characters ostensibly are the villains of the novel, Mailer later noted that at some level he was drawn to them, and they triumph over the more liberal Lieutenant Hearn. In the end, however, Croft and Cummings are also thwarted, and victory goes to the bureaucratic, conformist Major Dalleson. Mailer's novel is thus sometimes seen as a prophetic warning against the conformism of the subsequent decade, but as he commented at the time, ultimately *The Naked and the Dead* stands or falls as a realistic portrayal of the horrors of war.

Impact   *The Naked and the Dead* continues to be celebrated as a successful war novel and is pointed to as an early portrayal of the grim realities of war. Even though it was written about a popular war that usually was portrayed in positive terms, the novel conveyed the negative aspects of military life in a way that anticipated the later negative portrayals of less popular wars such as the Vietnam conflict. The novel also launched the eccentric career of Norman Mailer and raised the issues of power and violence, issues that Mailer was to explore more fully in such later works as *Advertisements for Myself* (1959) and in his personal life. The book was turned into a 1958 film.

Sheldon Goldfarb

Further Reading

Huebner, Andrew J. *The Warrior Image: Soldiers in American Culture from the Second World War to the Vietnam Era*. Chapel Hill: University of North Carolina Press, 2008.

Merrill, Robert. *Norman Mailer Revisited*. New York: Twayne, 1992.

Mills, Hilary. *Mailer: A Biography*. New York: Empire Books, 1982.

See also   Army, U.S.; Casualties of World War II; Censorship in Canada; Faulkner, William; *For Whom the Bell Tolls*; Hiroshima; *The Human Comedy*; Literature in the United States.

■ Nation of Islam

Identification   Primarily African American religious body
Also known as   Black Muslims
Date   Established around 1930

The Nation of Islam would draw widespread attention during the 1950's and 1960's by advocating black separatism and rejecting integrationist goals of African American civil rights leaders. Meanwhile, one of its most prominent future leaders, Malcolm X, joined the Nation of Islam in the late 1940's. He would eventually rise to international prominence as a critic of white supremacy and colonialism.

As the United States entered World War II, a small religious movement called the Nation of Islam was barely a decade old. Founded in Detroit by Wallace Dodd Fard, the Nation of Islam taught that white people were evil and only darker people could achieve eternal life. Accordingly, black people should constitute a "nation" separate from the white-led United States. Few black people joined the Nation of Islam during the 1930's, but white authorities found its teachings unsettling. Antagonized by police who considered him a troublemaker, Fard vanished from Detroit in 1934.

Elijah Muhammad (born Elijah Poole in Georgia in 1897) then claimed the leadership of the Nation of Islam. Rivals mocked his argument that Fard had been Allah incarnate and had deemed Muhammad his "messenger." Detroit police pursued Muhammad over minor legal infractions, so he took his family and followers to Chicago. Between 1935 and 1942, Muhammad traveled around the Midwest and the East, starting a handful of Nation of Islam temples while wrestling rivals within the group and in other American Islamic organizations.

World War II significantly affected the Nation of Islam. Since it had prophesied the apocalyptic defeat of the white race by darker races, Muhammad argued that Japan would crush the United States. Nation of Islam members also shunned the segregated military. As the war began, Muhammad was in Washington, D.C., leading the Nation of Islam's fourth temple. On May 8, 1942, while investigating alleged Nation of Islam subversion of the war effort, Federal Bureau of Investigation (FBI) agents arrested Muhammad for draft evasion. The FBI simultaneously raided three of the four Nation of Islam temples, in Washington, D.C., Milwaukee, and Detroit. Released on bail, Muhammad traveled to Chicago, but FBI agents there launched raids against Nation of Islam facilities and members. Arrested again, Muhammad faced charges of sedition.

In 1943, after convicting Muhammad and several dozen Nation of Islam members of draft evasion, prosecutors dropped the sedition charges. FBI attacks on the Nation of Islam ultimately enhanced its status because they implied that the tiny movement was a legitimate threat to the United States. During his more than three years in prison, Muhammad took to modern technology and developed a functioning model of disciplined community life.

Freed in 1946, Muhammad took advantage of his new insights. Nation of Islam members started small businesses to build economic self-sufficiency. Within a decade of Muhammad's release from prison, the organization tripled its number of temples to twelve, and membership grew from fewer than an estimated one thousand people in 1946 to more than twenty thousand by 1960. An important postwar convert was Malcolm Little, who wrote to Muhammad from prison after his siblings persuaded him in 1948 to join the Nation of Islam. After leaving prison in 1952 Little, renamed Malcolm X, became a brilliant orator and drew large audiences to Nation of Islam, or "Black Muslim," gatherings.

Impact The Nation of Islam evolved amid twentieth century struggles against white supremacy. Thousands of black Americans responded positively to its teachings on black superiority and joined the group after World War II. Many thousands more, some white, appreciated the sharp social analyses of Malcolm X and rejected white supremacy but disagreed with the Nation of Islam promotion of black separatism. Muhammad led the group until his death in 1975. Led by Louis Farrakhan into the twenty-first century, the Nation of Islam continued to emphasize black empowerment and increasingly forged global links to more orthodox Muslims.

Beth Kraig

Further Reading

Clegg, Claude Andrew, III. *An Original Man: The Life and Times of Elijah Muhammad.* New York: St. Martin's Press, 1997.

Evanzz, Karl. *The Messenger: The Rise and Fall of Elijah Muhammad.* New York: Random House, 1999.

Lincoln, C. Eric. *The Black Muslims in America.* Boston: Beacon Press, 1961.

Walker, Dennis. *Islam and the Search for African-American Nationhood: Elijah Muhammad, Louis Farrakhan, and the Nation of Islam.* Atlanta: Clarity Press, 2005.

See also African Americans; Conscientious objectors; Federal Bureau of Investigation; Racial discrimination; Religion in Canada; Religion in the United States.

■ National Association for the Advancement of Colored People

Identification Civil rights advocacy organization
Also known as NAACP
Date Founded on February 12, 1909

The National Association for the Advancement of Colored People was established to address the violence, discrimination, and segregation that African Americans faced in the United States. The organization used political and social lobbying, as well as litigation, to advance its causes. During the 1940's, progress against racism was made in the areas of federal employment, the armed forces, home ownership, and education.

The National Association for the Advancement of Colored People (NAACP) was formed in 1909 in response to a race riot in Springfield, Illinois, in which a white mob killed African Americans and set their homes on fire. Of the sixty NAACP founders, only seven were African American, one of whom was W. E. B. Du Bois. The nonprofit organization dedicated itself to securing the rights protected by the post-Civil War constitutional amendments, including the right to vote granted to African Americans and equal protection of the laws for all. During this time, African Americans had few actual rights. Furthermore, lynchings were common, especially in the southern states. Over a forty-year period ending in 1930, there were 3,700 reported lynchings. The NAACP lobbied to make participating in a lynch mob a federal crime. While such legislation was never adopted, the organization's campaign led to an increase in public awareness of this mob violence and a substantial decrease in the incidence of lynchings by 1940.

Significant legal victories were won by the NAACP during the 1940's under the leadership of Thurgood

Marshall, chief counsel for the NAACP Legal Defense and Educational Fund (and later the first African American appointed to the U.S. Supreme Court). One such major advance was the case of *Shelley v. Kraemer* (1948), in which the Supreme Court invalidated the racially restrictive real estate covenants that had kept African Americans from purchasing homes in certain neighborhoods. During the 1940's, the NAACP strove to defeat Jim Crow laws (laws that discriminated and segregated based on race). Chief among those were the practices that disenfranchised African American citizens in the South. In 1940, only 3 percent of African Americans living in the South were registered to vote. A wide range of disenfranchisement tactics were used, including poll taxes, literacy tests, and white-only primaries. The white-only primary came to an end in 1944 in *Smith v. Allwright*, when the NAACP successfully argued to the Supreme Court that this practice was unconstitutional.

Progress was also made in the political and economic arenas, due in part to the NAACP's lobbying. President Harry S. Truman issued two executive orders in 1948 aimed at reducing racial discrimination. Executive Order 9980 established regulations that governed fair employment practices in the federal government. Executive Order 9981 ended racial segregation in the armed forces.

Impact   During the 1940's, the NAACP played a crucial role in promoting the political, educational, social, legal, and economic equality of African Americans. The organization made a strategic decision to focus its litigation efforts on school desegregation cases. That work paved the way for the most consequential of NAACP's legal victories, *Brown v. Board of Education* (1954), in which the Supreme Court ruled that public schools could not segregate students by race. The Civil Rights Act of 1964 followed, prohibiting discrimination in public facilities and public accommodations. Today, though de jure discrimination and segregation have been proscribed, Americans continue to struggle with race issues, and the NAACP continues to work toward ending racial prejudice and ensuring equal rights for all.

Kimberlee Candela

Further Reading

Jonas, Gilbert. *Freedom's Sword: The NAACP and the Struggle Against Racism, 1909-1969*. New York: Routledge, 2007.

Tushnet, Mark V. *The NAACP's Legal Strategy Against Segregated Education, 1925-1950*. Chapel Hill: University of North Carolina Press, 2005.

See also   African Americans; Civil rights and liberties; Congress of Racial Equality; Lynching and hate crime; Racial discrimination; *Shelley v. Kraemer*; *Smith v. Allwright*; Voting rights; White, Walter F.

■ National Basketball Association

Identification   Professional sports league
Date   Formed by a merger on August 3, 1949

The National Basketball Association began slowly during the late 1940's but would become a major presence in American sports during the 1950's and eventually become one of the most popular professional sports leagues in the world.

During the late 1940's, American basketball was a sport whose college games and players were followed by fans and covered by the news media far more closely than the professional version of the sport. Basketball fans were most familiar with the top players on regional college teams, particularly in Kentucky, Indiana, and New York City. They were far more likely to know the players on the teams of the two professional leagues—the Basketball Association of America (BAA), which was based in the East, and the National Basketball League (NBL), whose teams were based in the Midwest. The pro teams featured players few fans had read about or seen in college because they were not local. In the shadow of Major League Baseball, pro basketball was a distinctly minor league sport, and it was also far less popular than college football.

Teams of the BAA, which had formed in 1946, were based in Baltimore, Washington, New York, St. Louis, and Boston. Teams in the older NBL were in mostly smaller markets, such as Anderson, Indiana; Denver, Colorado; Sheboygan, Wisconsin; Syracuse, New York; the Tri-Cities bloc of Moline and Rock Island, Illinois, and Davenport, Iowa; and Waterloo, Iowa. Star players such as Bob Davies and the giant center George Mikan had benefited from the rivalry between the leagues to secure generous contracts for themselves on the grounds that they could switch leagues if teams did not compensate them fairly. At that time, their annual salaries of twelve thousand dollars per year were considered exorbitant. Merging the two leagues would make it easier to hold player salaries in check.

Eventually, owners of the NBL teams determined that they would benefit by merging their league with the eastern teams of the BAA. The eastern teams had several advantages over those in the Midwest: The nation's leading newspapers were in the East, as were the premier arenas, such as New York's Madison Square Garden. In a parting shot, the NBL showed signs of life by creating a new team called the Indianapolis Olympians, whose players were almost all from the University of Kentucky's national college champion team, which had just played in the 1948 London Olympic games. In 1949, owners in both leagues agreed to the merger, with the Indianapolis Olympians included.

Birth of the NBA Combining the names of the National Basketball League and the Basketball Association of America, the newly merged league was called the National Basketball Association. Seventeen teams played their first season under this name in 1949-1950, divided among Eastern, Central, and Western divisions. Led by George Mikan, the Minneapolis Lakers, the reigning BAA champions, won the first "NBA" championship.

Although nothing in the league rules forbade African American players, all the players in the league at its start were white. Ironically, one of the most popular attractions of the new league was its ability to stage exhibition games before its own games featuring the most famous basketball team in the United States—the Harlem Globetrotters, whose players were all black. The Globetrotters had all the top black players in the country, and fans flocked to watch their preliminary games. Often, when the lesser-known NBA players took the court for their regular games, many fans would leave. One apparent reason that NBA team owners were reluctant to sign black players was their fear of angering the owner of the Globetrotters, Abe Saperstein, who might retaliate by refusing to schedule the exhibition games that helped draw fans to NBA arenas.

Bijan C. Bayne

Further Reading

Bayne, Bijan C. *Sky Kings: Black Pioneers of Professional Basketball.* Danbury, Conn.: Scholastic, 1997.

Hubbard, Jan. *The Official NBA Encyclopedia.* 3d ed. New York: Doubleday, 2000.

Original NBA Teams

- Boston Celtics
- Chicago Stags*
- Cleveland Rebels*
- Detroit Falcons*
- New York Knickerbockers
- Philadelphia Warriors
- Pittsburgh Ironmen*
- Providence Steamrollers*
- St. Louis Bombers*
- Toronto Huskies*
- Washington Capitols*

*Defunct since the late 1940's or early 1950's. The Philadelphia Warriors later became the Golden State Warriors.

Koppett, Leonard. *Twenty-four Seconds to Shoot: The Birth and Improbable Rise of the NBA.* New York: Sport Media, 1968.

Peterson, Robert W. *Cages to Jump Shots: Pro Basketball's Early Years.* Lincoln: University of Nebraska Press, 2002.

See also All-American Girls Professional Baseball League; Basketball; Negro Leagues; Olympic Games of 1948; Sports in the United States.

■ National debt

Definition Borrowing by the government from individual citizens, domestic corporations, and international entities, both to meet budget shortfalls and to regulate the economy

During the 1940's, an enormous increase in public indebtedness financed the rapid military expansion that made possible winning the war against Germany and Japan. Government indebtedness revived an economy still faltering in the aftermath of the Great Depression, but failure to retire the war debt set the stage for future fiscal instability.

Public debt has always been a feature of American government. Between 1790 and 1932, the debt followed a cyclical pattern, increasing in wartime and declining (briefly to zero in 1835) during times of peace. It stood at $65 million in 1861, $2.7 billion at the end of the Civil War, $961 million in 1893, $1.15 billion in 1914, and $25.5 billion at the end of World War I. During the 1920's, the federal government repaid some of the cost of America's involvement in World War I. The Great Depression, however, erased budgetary surpluses.

The steady rise in federal debt between 1932 and 1941 departed from a long-standing policy of paying down war debts during peacetime. Following the Keynesian economic model, policy makers began to see America's debt as a way of managing and dampening business cycles. While incurring indebtedness during the Depression, the U.S. government counted on a revived economy later generating higher tax revenues that would erase the debt incurred. By 1940, government spending for infrastructure and employment had declined, but aid to America's allies replaced it, and the national debt continued to grow.

Between 1941 and 1945, the federal debt rose from $69 billion to $293 billion dollars. The ratio of

federal debt to gross domestic product went from 40 percent in 1941 to 120 percent in 1946, then declined to 55 percent by 1950. The American public became its government's creditor. Massive campaigns urged individuals and corporations to buy government bonds. To win World War II, the United States borrowed heavily from its own citizens, exacting current sacrifices in exchange for the promise of future cash payment and a current feeling of patriotic support for the country. Wartime wages and corporate profits, which in peacetime would have fueled consumer spending, were instead invested in the war. At the close of the war, individuals held slightly more than half of the federal government's debt, and corporations an additional 21 percent.

Interest rates remained low throughout the 1940's. The Federal Reserve prime rate was 1.8 percent between 1933 and 1946, then increased to 2.0 percent by 1950. Stable interest rates and a low rate of inflation favored investment in bonds with long maturation times. During the late 1940's and 1950's, the federal government was able to balance its bud-

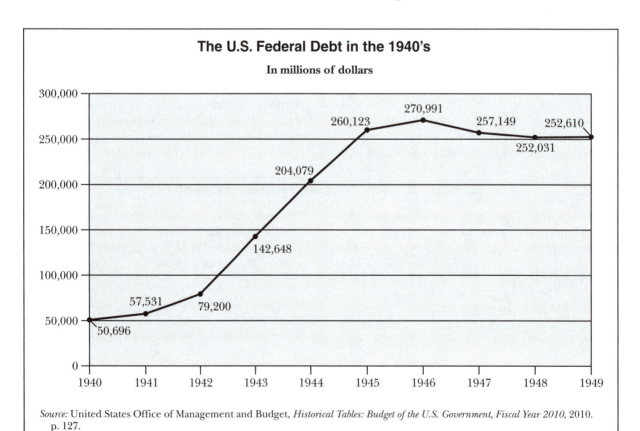

The U.S. Federal Debt in the 1940's

In millions of dollars

Source: United States Office of Management and Budget, *Historical Tables: Budget of the U.S. Government, Fiscal Year 2010,* 2010. p. 127.

get and retire short-term debt obligations as they came due. The long-term war debt, however, remained on the books. Adverse consequences of continued high indebtedness did not become evident until decades later.

Impact The ratio of total indebtedness—federal, local, corporate, and personal—to gross domestic product remained close to 2 from 1941 to 1975, as the economy expanded at roughly the same rate as the debt burden. The ratio was higher during the Depression and has risen since 1975 due to a sluggish economy and increased borrowing in all sectors.

Martha A. Sherwood

Further Reading

Chamber of Commerce of the United States. Committee on Economic Policy. *Debt: Public and Private.* Washington, D.C.: Chamber of Commerce of the United States, 1957.

Gordon, John Steele. *Hamilton's Blessing: The Extraordinary Life and Times of Our National Debt.* New York: Walker, 1997.

Kelley, Robert E. *The National Debt of the United States, 1941-2008.* 2d ed. Jefferson, N.C.: McFarland, 2008.

See also Business and the economy in Canada; Business and the economy in the United States; Credit and debt; Gross national product of Canada; Gross national product of the United States; Keynesian economics; New Deal programs; War bonds; War debt.

■ National parks

Definition Regions of special historic, scenic, or scientific interest that are preserved from commercial development by national governments

During World War II, funds and manpower were directed away from North American national parks, and park grounds were used as resources for the war effort. However, the national parks continued to protect natural scenery and wildlife, and new parks were established in both the United States and Canada during the 1940's, despite budgetary cutbacks. After the war, the number of visitors to the parks greatly increased.

During the 1930's, supplementary funds and manpower had been channeled into the U.S. National Park Service (NPS) through the Civilian Conservation Corps (CCC). The CCC was a popular emergency conservation program that had been established to put unemployed men to work in the national forests. In 1940, the National Park Service still had 310 CCC camps under its supervision. During that same year, Arno B. Cammerer, who had been the director of the NPS since 1933, relinquished his position for health reasons and died a year later. Respected conservationist Newton Drury, who had headed the Save the Redwoods League in California, assumed leadership of the NPS on August 20, 1940, and remained at that post until 1951.

The War Years With America's entry into World War II in December, 1941, Drury drastically curtailed NPS activity. Congress discontinued the CCC program in 1942. Regular appropriations for the NPS shrank from $21 million in 1940 to $5 million in 1943. The number of full-time employees was slashed from 3,500 to fewer than 2,000, and public visits to parks fell from 21 million in 1941 to 6 million in 1942.

World War II had other impacts on the NPS. To free space in Washington, D.C., for the war effort, unrelated government functions were moved to other locations. NPS headquarters was relocated to the Merchandise Mart in Chicago and did not return to Washington, D.C., until October, 1947. Many of the national parklands, including Potomac Park and the Washington Monument grounds, were covered with temporary office buildings and housing to accommodate the influx of war workers. Park hotels, such as the Ahwahnee Hotel in Yosemite National Park, were commandeered for the rest and rehabilitation of servicemen. The armed forces used Mount Rainier National Park for mountain warfare training, Joshua Tree National Monument for desert training, and Mount McKinley for testing equipment under arctic conditions. Some Canadian parks were used as internment camps, particularly for internees of Japanese ancestry.

Other wartime pressures seriously threatened park resources. Timber interests sought to log sitka spruce in Olympic National Park in order to manufacture airplanes. Ranchers pushed to pen many Western areas for grazing. Mining companies wanted to search for copper at the Grand Canyon

American and Canadian National Parks Established in the 1940's		
Year	National Park	State or Province
1940	Isle Royale	Michigan
1940	Kings Canyon	California
1941	Mammoth Cave	Kentucky
1944	Big Bend	Texas
1947	Everglades	Florida
1948	Fundy	New Brunswick

and Mount Rainier, manganese at Shenandoah National Park, and tungsten at Yosemite. Drury successfully fended off most of these demands, yielding only in exceptional circumstances.

After the War After World War II ended in 1945, Americans began enjoying a higher standard of living. More Americans owned cars and had the free time and financial means to travel. Consequently, the number of visitors to the national parks nearly tripled from 11.7 million in 1945 to 31.7 million in 1949.

As America redirected its energies to domestic pursuits after the war, accelerated development of river basins by the U.S. Army Corps of Engineers and the Bureau of Reclamation posed new threats to the park system. A proposed Bridge Canyon Dam on the Colorado River would have impounded water through Grand Canyon National Park into the adjacent national park; Glacier View Dam on the Flathead River in Montana threatened to flood twenty thousand acres of Glacier National Park; City Dam on Kentucky's Green River would have periodically flooded the underground Echo River in Mammoth Cave National Park; and dams on the Potomac River above and below Great Falls would have submerged forty miles of the historic Chesapeake and Ohio Canal.

Although women had been employed as rangers during the 1920's and 1930's, throughout the 1940's women rarely had the opportunity to work in this occupation, unless they were married to rangers. During the 1940's, Drury also waged a campaign against bear feeding and the wildly popular bear feeding shows via park literature and the reevaluation of the

parks' bear management. His campaign proved successful. The final bear feeding show was held at Yellowstone National Park in the fall of 1945.

New Parks Despite the wartime restrictions, new national parks were founded in the United States and Canada throughout the 1940's. For example, Isle Royale National Park in northwest Lake Superior was established in 1940. This park is centered at Isle Royale, the largest island in Lake Superior, and includes many surrounding islets. Kings Canyon National Park in east central California was also established in 1940. Kings Canyon preserves groves of ancient sequoia trees, including some of the largest in the world.

Mammoth Cave National Park in west central Kentucky was established in 1941 and is the site of the world's largest known cave system. Mammoth Cave has at least 330 miles (531 kilometers) of explored passageways with a large variety of limestone formations—stalagmites, stalactites, and columns—and subterranean rivers and lakes. Mount Rushmore National Monument in South Dakota was completed in 1941 after fourteen years of construction. By the end of the 1940's, the number of yearly visitors to Mount Rushmore had risen to 656,717.

Big Bend National Park in southwest Texas was established in 1944. This park includes 801,163 acres where the Rio Grande makes a sharp turn known as the "Big Bend." The Rio Grande forms the international border between Mexico and the United States from El Paso to the Gulf of Mexico, and Big Bend administers approximately 25 percent of this one-thousand-mile boundary.

Buffalo National Park in Alberta, Canada, and Nemiskam National Park in Saskatchewan were founded to protect bison and pronghorn antelope. However, both parks were delisted in 1947. Everglades National Park in southern Florida was established in 1947 in order to protect the Everglades, a freshwater, shallow river of grass, 120 miles long, 50 miles wide, and less than a foot deep, covering much of the southern half of the Florida peninsula. The park contains about 25 percent of the Everglades, or more than 1.5 million acres.

Fundy National Park in New Brunswick, Canada, was established in 1948. The park overlooks the Bay of Fundy, which boasts the highest tides in the world. The height of the tides varies from 11 to 53 feet at various places in the bay.

In 1949, John D. Rockefeller, Jr., deeded 35,000 acres to the federal government for the Jackson Hole National Monument. This monument would later be rededicated as a portion of the Grand Teton National Park.

Impact Despite the demands of war and of domestic development, during the 1940's the national parks continued to protect the nation's natural resources and to provide access to these areas for the public's enjoyment.

Chrissa Shamberger

Further Reading

Kopas, Paul S. *Taking the Air: Ideas and Change in Canada's National Parks.* Vancouver: University of British Columbia Press, 2007.

Mackintosh, Barry. *The National Parks: Shaping the System.* Washington, D.C.: U.S. Department of the Interior, 1991.

Runte, Alfred. *National Parks: The American Experience.* 3d ed. Lincoln: University of Nebraska Press, 1997.

Wondrak, Alice K. "Wrestling with Horace Albright: Edmund Rogers, Visitors, and Bears in Yellowstone National Park. Part 1." *Montana: The Magazine of Western History* 52, no. 3 (2002): 2-15.

See also Automobiles and auto manufacturing; Jackson Hole National Monument; Japanese Canadian internment; Natural resources; Recreation; Women's roles and rights in the United States; World War II.

■ National Security Act of 1947

The Law Federal legislation that established four new federal agencies concerned with security issues

Date Signed July 26, 1947

The National Security Act reorganized the U.S. armed forces, foreign policy, and intelligence community by establishing the National Military Establishment, the National Security Resources Board, the National Security Council, and the Central Intelligence Agency. The act was amended several times between 1947 and 1985, but few significant changes were made after the original act was passed.

The National Security Act of 1947 was signed into law by President Harry S. Truman on July 26, 1947.

The act created four new coordinating agencies: the National Military Establishment, directed by a secretary of defense; a National Security Resources Board to ensure preparedness for a future war; a National Security Council to advise the president on national security policy; and the Central Intelligence Agency (CIA).

Historical Events Leading to the National Security Act After the United States entered World War II in 1941 a number of deficiencies emerged in the ways in which strategic and foreign policies were shaped. After the war ended in 1945, President Truman proposed uniting American military forces under a single Department of Defense and creating the National Security Council to bring together defense, intelligence, and diplomacy. Debate on this proposal continued for two years because of intense opposition to unification of the military services from the Navy and its congressional supporters. Secretary of the Navy James Forrestal also strongly opposed unification. If such legislation were passed, the Army, to the detriment of the Navy, would dominate a unified U.S. armed services. Seeking an alternative to this military plan, Forrestal commissioned a study to recommend a new national security process and became a major architect of the 1947 act.

Although a desire existed to strengthen defenses to counter an emerging threat from the Soviet Union, controversy surrounded the proposal before the act was passed. Interservice rivalry existed, as did clashes of ambitions and alliances with Congress. Dissension also occurred over who would run the CIA. Military intelligence agencies maneuvered to maintain their own autonomy, and the State Department sought to control the proposed intelligence agency. President Truman and his advisers opposed the creation of a statutory National Security Council and worked to weaken what they saw as a threat to the independence of the presidency. The act that finally emerged in 1947 developed from compromises. It realigned and reorganized the armed forces, foreign policy, and the intelligence community. The majority of the act's provisions took effect on September 18, 1947. The press called it a "unification act," although the military was not fully unified.

The National Security Resource Board (NSRB) focused on industrial readiness and military preparedness. In the event of attack on the United

States, the NSRB was to allocate essential resources and oversee the relocation of industries, services, government, and economic activities to protect the nation's security.

National Military Establishment and Department of Defense Before 1947, the Army Air Forces and the Navy had operated as separate entities with no coordinating command structure. Following World War II, political leaders moved to consolidate U.S. armed forces under a unified command. The National Security Act created a unified National Military Establishment that changed the military substantially. The Department of War and the Department of the Navy merged. The Air Force, however, was established as a separate branch of the armed forces. Nevertheless, the secretaries of the Army, the Navy, and the Air Force were placed under the direction of the secretary of defense. The National Military Establishment was renamed the Department of Defense in 1949. The position of secretary of defense was created to govern the new Department of Defense.

Each of the three service secretaries maintained quasi-cabinet status, but the act was amended on August 10, 1949, to assure their subordination to the secretary of defense, who held full Cabinet status. Amendments to the act in 1949 increased the powers of the secretary of defense and created the position of chairman of the U.S. Joint Chiefs of Staff. These changes further centralized the organization of policy among the three branches of the military. The U.S. Joint Chiefs of Staff, consisting of representatives from the three services, assumed responsibility for strategic planning and coordination. The power of the service secretaries was further diminished, and other amendments removed them from the National Security Council.

National Security Council The National Security Council (NSC), chaired by the president, advises the president on domestic, foreign, and military policies related to national security. It facilitates the sharing of information, the formation of strategic foreign policy, and the protection of national security. The council also serves as the president's principal arm for coordinating policies among various government agencies. The NSC is the president's principal forum for considering national security and foreign policy matters with senior national security advisers and cabinet officials. The chairman of the Joint Chiefs of Staff is the military adviser to the council, and the director of national intelligence is the intelligence adviser. They serve in an advisory capacity. The chief of staff to the president, counsel to the president, and assistant to the president for economic policy are also invited to attend NSC meetings. The attorney general and the director of the Office of Management and Budget are invited to attend meetings pertaining to their responsibilities. The heads of other executive departments and agencies, as well as other senior officials, are invited to attend meetings of the NSC when appropriate. The act left the role of the NSC somewhat ambiguous so that each president could use the council in a way that best suited the administration and its foreign-policy agenda.

From left to right: chairman of the Joint Chiefs of Staff General Omar N. Bradley, Secretary of Defense Louis A. Johnson, President Harry S. Truman, and an unidentified official watching an Army Day parade in 1949. (National Archives)

Central Intelligence Agency During the war, the Office of Strategic Services (OSS) was in charge of most intelligence operations and trained a new generation of intelligence personnel. Though the OSS was initially slated for dissolution after the war, advisers persuaded the president that the organization should be reconfigured for peacetime operation. This was necessary because of Cold War tensions with the Soviet Union. The act established the Central Intelligence Agency (CIA), a civilian agency, to succeed the OSS. It is directly responsible to the NSC. The CIA took on the duties of gathering foreign intelligence and conducting strategic surveillance related to national security. The position of director of central intelligence was created to administer the new agency and serve as a liaison between the intelligence community and the executive branch. The act assigned the task of domestic intelligence to the Federal Bureau of Investigation.

Impact In the following decades, both the NSC and the CIA grew into formidable agencies, the National Security Resources Board expired, and the Department of Defense periodically reorganized itself. The National Security Act was one of the most significant pieces of legislation passed in the twentieth century. Amendments to the original 1947 act changed some structural and functional aspects of the military and intelligence communities. However, the basic structure remains in place. The September 11, 2001, terrorist attacks on the United States resulted in the largest reorganization of government security and intelligence agencies since the National Security Act of 1947.

Ski Hunter

Further Reading

Hogan, Michael. *A Cross of Iron: Harry S. Truman and the Origins of the National Security State, 1945-1954.*

National Security Act Declaration of Policy

The National Security Act of 1947, Section 2, which is reproduced below, established the role of the secretary of defense and various military organizations.

In enacting this legislation, it is the intent of Congress to provide a comprehensive program for the future security of the United States; to provide for the establishment of integrated policies and procedures for the departments, agencies, and functions of the government relating to the national security; to provide a Department of Defense, including the three military departments of the Army, the Navy (including naval aviation and the United States Marine Corps), and the Air Force under the direction, authority, and control of the secretary of defense; to provide that each military department shall be separately organized under its own secretary and shall function under the direction, authority, and control of the secretary of defense; to provide for their unified direction under civilian control of the secretary of defense but not to merge these departments or services; to provide for the establishment of unified or specified combatant commands, and a clear and direct line of command to such commands; to eliminate unnecessary duplication in the Department of Defense, and particularly in the field of research and engineering by vesting its overall direction and control in the secretary of defense; to provide more effective, efficient, and economical administration in the Department of Defense; to provide for the unified strategic direction of the combatant forces, for their operation under unified command, and for their integration into an efficient team of land, naval, and air forces but not to establish a single chief of staff over the armed forces nor an overall armed forces general staff.

West Nyack, N.Y.: Cambridge University Press, 1998. Focuses on Forrestal, Truman, and others integral to the consolidation of the departments of the American military. Good overview of the lasting impact the act has had.

Leffler, Melvin. *Preponderance of Power: National Security, the Truman Administration, and the Cold War.* Palo Alto, Calif.: Stanford University Press, 1996. An overview of the policies that emerged after World War II and why Truman felt the consolidation of the military was necessary in the light of emerging political threats from around the world.

Stuart, Douglas T. *Creating the National Security State: A History of the Law That Transformed America.*

Princeton, N.J.: Princeton University Press, 2008. Discusses the formation of the National Security Act and its lasting impact on American society, especially in terms of the increased role of the military.

See also Central Intelligence Agency; Civil defense programs; Clifford, Clark; Congress, U.S.; Department of Defense, U.S.; Executive orders; Federal Bureau of Investigation; Hoover, J. Edgar.

■ *National Velvet*

Identification Hollywood film adaption of the Enid Bagnold book of the same title
Director Clarence Brown (1890-1987)
Date Premiered on December 14, 1944

This film became an almost instant classic upon release, and it is arguably the best-known and most highly acclaimed horse-racing story in film history.

National Velvet, directed by Clarence Brown, made a star of twelve-year-old Elizabeth Taylor in the role of Velvet Brown, a girl determined to enter her horse, Pie, in the Grand National Steeplechase. Mickey Rooney, Taylor's costar, portrays a young trainer who helps Velvet prepare her horse for the big race. Velvet, who would never have been allowed to enter the race because of her gender, rides Pie in the tournament after she cuts her hair to pass as a male jockey. Donald Crisp and Angela Lansbury also appear in the film as members of the Brown family. Anne Revere won an Oscar for best supporting actress, as Velvet's mother, as did Robert J. Kern, for best film editing. *National Velvet* was also nominated for Oscars in several other categories, including best director, best cinematography, and best art direction.

Impact *National Velvet* launched the film and television career of Taylor and several other entertainment professionals. The film subtly addressed issues related to societal limitations of gender at a time when women were taking on new roles as a result of wartime necessity. The National Broadcasting Company (NBC) went on to air a moderately successful television series inspired by the film during the early 1960's, which featured members of the fictional Brown family and a horse named King. Tatum O'Neal and Anthony Hopkins starred in the film sequel of *National Velvet*, titled *International Velvet* (1978).

Donald C. Simmons, Jr.

Further Reading

Bagnold, Enid. *Enid Bagnold's Autobiography.* Boston: Little Brown, 1969.
Marill, Alvin H. *Mickey Rooney: His Films, Television Appearances, Radio Work, Stage Shows, and Recordings.* Jefferson, N.C.: McFarland, 2005.
Walker, Alexander. *Elizabeth: The Life of Elizabeth Taylor.* New York: G. Weidenfeld, 1991.

See also Film in the United States; Horse racing; Rooney, Mickey.

Elizabeth Taylor posing with a horse after making her film debut in National Velvet. *(Time & Life Pictures/Getty Images)*

■ National War Labor Board

Identification   Federal government wartime
   agency
Also known as   War Labor Board
Date   Established on January 12, 1942

The National War Labor Board was a World War II-era
government agency created to maintain industrial produc-
tion during wartime by mediating labor disputes and pre-
venting strikes and lockouts. The NWLB did not always
succeed in its mission, but it helped create lasting advances
in labor-management relations.

The National War Labor Board (NWLB), created in
1942 to address labor-management issues in industry during World War II, was modeled closely on its
World War I predecessor. The first NWLB was intended to maintain industrial production during
the war and to prevent labor unrest. Composed of
ten representatives, evenly divided between labor
and management, the first NWLB pioneered significant advances in labor-management relations, most
of which were lost after the organization's dissolution.

When the United States entered World War II,
President Franklin D. Roosevelt established a new
NWLB by executive order on January 12, 1942. The
new board had twelve members, divided equally
among public officials and representatives of organized labor and business. The organization's purpose was to set wage rates and peacefully negotiate
labor-management disputes. The NWLB also gave
the American labor movement an unprecedented
voice in shaping federal policy.

Impact   The NWLB had a limited impact on wartime industry. Although the board opened regional
offices in 1943, it remained overextended and was
unable to handle all of the labor-related grievances,
which enabled employers, especially those in the
South, to resist unionization. Nonetheless, the
NWLB, which disbanded in 1945, produced more
lasting advances in labor-management relations
than its World War I counterpart.

Susan Roth Breitzer

Further Reading

Atleson, James B. *Labor and the Wartime State: Labor*
   Relations and the Law During World War II. Urbana:
   University of Illinois Press, 1998.
Kersten, Andrew W. *Labor's Home Front: The American*
   Federation of Labor During World War II. New York:
   New York University Press, 2006.

See also   Business and the economy in the United
States; Economic wartime regulations; Executive or-
ders; Income and wages; Labor strikes; Roosevelt,
Franklin D.; Unionism; *United States v. United Mine*
Workers; War Production Board; Wartime industries;
Wartime seizures of businesses.

■ Native Americans

Identification   Members of the aboriginal societies
   of North America and their descendants, who
   are also known as American Indians

The 1940's was a decade of stark contrast for all Ameri-
cans. The decade began in the aftermath of the Depression,
which had changed the nature of American life. American
involvement in World War II, which began in December of
1941, catapulted the country into the most serious, far-
reaching military conflict of its existence. When the war
ended in 1945, Americans settled into a postwar economic
expansion that brought about sustained prosperity for
many in the country. Amid all of this change and turmoil,
U.S. policy regarding Native Americans changed dramati-
cally, but ultimately the lives of Native Americans did not.
Despite the loyal service of 44,000 Native Americans, or
one-third of the able-bodied Native American men, in the
war effort, their economic condition remained abysmal and
their political power virtually nonexistent.

During the first half of the 1940's, government policy toward Native Americans fell under the umbrella
of what was called the "New Deal for Native Americans." Because most Native Americans lived in poverty prior to the Depression, the economic woes of
the 1930's made their lives even more hopeless than
those of most other Americans. Thanks to the tireless work of the persuasive, charismatic John Collier,
commissioner of the Bureau of Indian Affairs from
1933 to 1945, the Franklin D. Roosevelt administration was able to create a series of programs that began to reverse the downward spiral of Native American fortunes.

In contrast to the reformers who had initiated the
Dawes Act in 1887, which promoted the notion of
killing "the Indian" and saving "the man," Collier believed in the restoration of what proponents of the
Dawes Act had called "the Indian." However, given

Native American Populations by State, 1940 and 1950

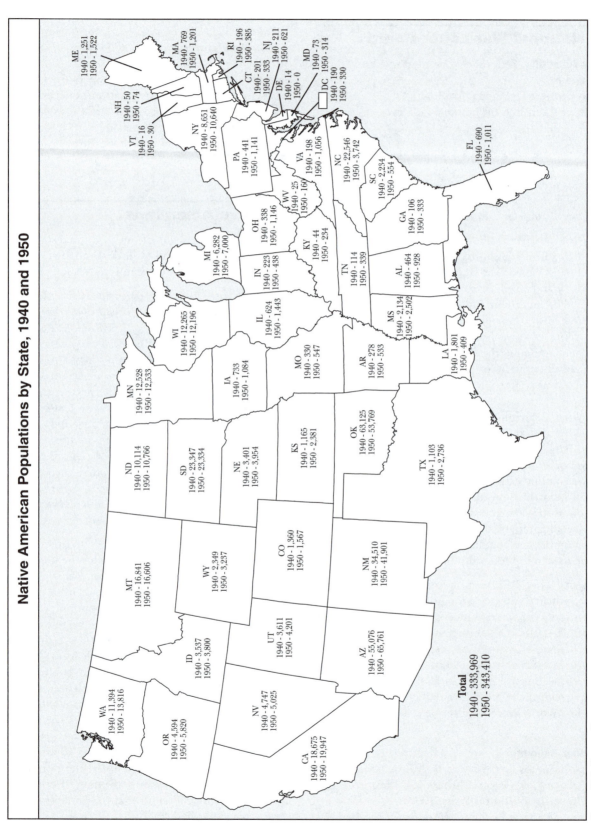

ME
1940 - 1,251
1950 - 1,522

MA
1940 - 769
1950 - 1,201

RI
1940 - 196
1950 - 385

NJ
1940 - 211
1950 - 621

MD
1940 - 73
1950 - 314

NH
1940 - 50
1950 - 74

CT
1940 - 201
1950 - 333

DE
1940 - 14
1950 - 0

DC
1940 - 190
1950 - 330

VT
1940 - 16
1950 - 30

NY
1940 - 8,651
1950 - 10,640

PA
1940 - 441
1950 - 1,141

VA
1940 - 198
1950 - 1,056

NC
1940 - 22,546
1950 - 3,742

FL
1940 - 690
1950 - 1,011

WV
1940 - 25
1950 - 160

SC
1940 - 2,234
1950 - 554

OH
1940 - 338
1950 - 1,146

KY
1940 - 44
1950 - 234

GA
1940 - 106
1950 - 333

MI
1940 - 6,282
1950 - 7,000

IN
1940 - 223
1950 - 438

TN
1940 - 114
1950 - 339

AL
1940 - 464
1950 - 928

WI
1940 - 12,265
1950 - 12,196

IL
1940 - 624
1950 - 1,443

MS
1940 - 2,134
1950 - 2,502

MN
1940 - 12,528
1950 - 12,533

IA
1940 - 733
1950 - 1,084

MO
1940 - 330
1950 - 547

AR
1940 - 278
1950 - 533

LA
1940 - 1,801
1950 - 409

ND
1940 - 10,114
1950 - 10,766

SD
1940 - 23,347
1950 - 23,334

NE
1940 - 3,401
1950 - 3,954

KS
1940 - 1,165
1950 - 2,381

OK
1940 - 63,125
1950 - 53,769

MT
1940 - 16,841
1950 - 16,606

WY
1940 - 2,349
1950 - 3,237

CO
1940 - 1,360
1950 - 1,567

NM
1940 - 34,510
1950 - 41,901

TX
1940 - 1,103
1950 - 2,736

ID
1940 - 3,537
1950 - 3,800

UT
1940 - 3,611
1950 - 4,201

WA
1940 - 11,394
1950 - 13,816

OR
1940 - 4,594
1950 - 5,820

NV
1940 - 4,747
1950 - 5,025

AZ
1940 - 55,076
1950 - 65,761

CA
1940 - 18,675
1950 - 19,947

Total
1940 - 333,969
1950 - 343,410

Source: U.S. Census Bureau

the complex array of tribes and histories that characterized Native American experiences and lives in the United States, one holistic system was unlikely to benefit all tribes. Thus, though Collier sought to reverse the trend started in the nineteenth century of selling off so-called surplus Native American land and reeducating Native Americans to be "real Americans," not all tribes found his policies to be to their advantage. In addition, the war completely changed the point of view of everyone in the country. Causes, such as the plight of Native Americans, faded into the background as the country mobilized to defeat the twin threats of the Nazis and the Japanese.

The Indian New Deal consisted of several important legislative initiatives that carried over into the first half of the 1940's. The Johnson-O'Malley Act of April, 1934, allowed tribes to contract directly with the secretary of the Department of the Interior through their state or territory for medical or educational services that had been provided by the Bureau of Indian Affairs. The Indian Reorganization Act (IRA), passed in June of 1934, was the central component of Collier's policies. It essentially reversed the Dawes Act, bringing an end to the allotment policy and seeking to reverse the damage these policies caused.

The federal government set forth a program to restore tribal lands that had been deemed surplus and to spend up to two million dollars per year to purchase additional land for Indian communities. The federal government also encouraged tribes to develop constitutions and loaned money to them for economic development. This program was actually an attempt to enable tribes to act as corporate entities and thereby manage their own resources and assets. One model for this program was the Klamath Tribes in Oregon, who, after years of seeing the timber on their reservation sold by the Bureau of Indian Affairs for virtually nothing, had sought and won the right to control and thereby profit from their own resources. Finally, in August of 1935, the federal government set up the Indian Arts and Crafts Board in an effort to encourage Native American cultural expressions and art work. The Indian schools of the Dawes Act era had sought to make Native American children forget their heritage and culture so that they could become "Americans."

Despite Collier's good intentions, his policies contained the seeds of their own destruction. Like so many other government solutions to the so-called Indian problem, the Indian New Deal created a one-size-fits-all bureaucratic solution to a complex set of problems and an even more complex array of tribes, each with its own unique history and culture. Thus, though Collier took his proposals to the Native American people whom he sought to help, he did not get the universal support for which he had hoped. Of 258 tribes, 181 voted to support and participate in the new program.

Many of those who opposed the program were simply attempting to protect their way of life, something that Collier thought his program would do. For example, many of the tribes that had been banished from their homeland to Oklahoma had largely assimilated. They had no strong tribal organization left, so they saw little sense in returning to and reforming what they had abandoned. In many respects, Collier was attempting to reconstitute tribes that had been shattered and put on reservations by white expansion into Indian Territory (now Oklahoma). In addition, he wanted to impose democracy on those tribes. Furthermore, though Native American tribes had generally always been democratic, they had also allowed those who disagreed to go their own way, a policy that was partially responsible for the oft-cited failure of Native Americans to mount any sustained effort to curtail white expansion into their territory. Collier's policy demanded that all sign on for his brand of democracy if they participated in the program. Thus, though his policies did become law, they never had the support or participation of all the Native American tribes.

Collier's policies were never fully funded. As the country mobilized for World War II, funding policies that had nothing to do with the war effort became increasingly difficult. By the last year of the war, the IRA had been crippled by funding cuts, and Collier had recognized his own failure. He resigned from his post as commissioner of the Bureau of Indian Affairs in January of 1945. Powerful Collier opponents, such as Senator Burton Kendall Wheeler, chair of the Senate Committee on Indian Affairs, put forward bills that moved U.S. policy toward what would be called "termination and relocation," a complete repudiation of the Indian New Deal. These political operatives did not have the political power to get their programs made into law until the mid-1950's, but, nonetheless, by the mid-1940's, the U.S. government's view of Native Americans had shifted again. Significantly, in 1944, the founding meeting of the National Congress of American Indians occurred in Denver, Colorado. The congress was the first Native American organization that sought to wield political power on a national level for native people.

The Shift to Termination and Relocation   Termination was in many respects a return to the failed policies of the Dawes Act of 1887. Accordingly, the program sought to "make Indians into Americans" by relocating them and terminating federal government protection of Indian sovereign rights to reservation lands. Proponents of this policy argued that moving Native Americans off reservations would enable them to move into mainstream American culture and to become productive, prosperous members of the American family. Much as Collier's policies did, this program presumed that all tribes were the same and that Native American citizens were as ready for urban assimilation as any other American citizen. Its proponents failed to recognize the uneven assimilation of Native Americans into the fabric of American culture and the vast differences among individual Native Americans in their readiness for life off the reservation.

The presumed outcome of the program fit neatly into the evolving idea of a postwar United States where all Americans had equal opportunity and contributed equally to creating a homogeneous country. The ultimate outcome of these and other policies of the postwar period was the United States of the 1950's: picture perfect on the surface but shattered by discord and alienation underneath.

Native Americans as Heroes   For all of the despair of Native American life and the federal government's ineptitude in handling the so-called Indian problem, the image of Native Americans in American culture remained palpable and even seemed at times to have nothing at all to do with the lives of real Native Americans. At least one part of the impetus behind the Indian New Deal was a continuing fascination with Native American culture. In some respects this fascination was demeaning to Native American tribes: In large part, it was a fascination with what might be considered the "primitive." This viewpoint was filled with cultural elitism and illustrated the mainstream American's paradoxical fascination with Native Americans. American policy toward Native American tribes had generally sought to "educate" them out of their primitivism.

World War II produced authentic Native American war heroes. Of the 44,000 Native Americans who served in the war effort, a number of them made important contributions to the "code talking" that enabled U.S. forces to communicate in language that could not be deciphered by enemy eavesdroppers. Native languages were an important part of Army code language. The Navajo code talkers were the most famous of all, contributing to the Marines an entire dictionary of terms used to describe equipment and maneuvers in code.

Ira Hamilton Hayes was arguably the most famous of all Native American war heroes from World War II. Hayes, a Pima Indian, was one of the valiant Marines who was photographed raising the American flag over Iwo Jima, one of the most famous incidents of World War II. In the photograph, Hayes is on the far left and his hands grasp for the flag pole presumably to push it into the ground. Of the six men who were photographed, he was one of only three who survived the war.

The assault on Iwo Jima came at the close of the war and ended with a torturous fight on February 23, 1945. Therefore, the photograph featuring Hays became emblematic the U.S. success in the Pacific theater. Ironically, Hayes himself became a symbol of the unfulfilled government promises to Native Americans. Hayes came home a war hero, celebrated not only for his courage in battle but also for his willing assimilation into American culture demonstrated by his valor in defending his country.

Hayes never understood the adulation he received, and he was always uncomfortable with heroic status. As one of the few survivors of the Battle of Iwo Jima, he felt the title of hero should have been applied to those who died. Nonetheless, the adulation continued; he was celebrated by both presidents and average citizens, who wrote letters to him. Hayes coped with what he felt was his undeserved fame by drinking heavily. Compounding his misery and isolation, he came home to a reservation that was unchanged from the way he left it: arid and incapable of providing his family with any real way to make a living. Like so many Native American veterans, despite his valor in battle, he continued to live in poverty at home. In 1954, when the Marine Corps War Memorial, featuring a monument depicting the famous raising of the flag, was dedicated in Washington, D.C., Hayes was there, thirty-three years old and still

Ira Hamilton Hayes, one of the six U.S. Marines who helped raise the American flag on Iwo Jima, was a Pima Indian. (AP/Wide World Photos)

seeking a way to be comfortable with the many contradictions in his life.

Ten weeks after the dedication of the Marine Corps War Memorial, Hayes froze to death while lying drunk in the single drainage ditch that provided water to his arid reservation. The contradictions of his life and death have inspired a number of works of art, most notably the song "The Ballad of Ira Hayes,"

written by Peter LaFarge and recorded by Johnny Cash, and *House Made of Dawn*, the Pulitzer Prize-winning novel written by Kiowan author N. Scott Momaday.

Impact The 1940's was a decade of change for Native Americans, just as it was for other Americans. However, despite radical changes in U.S. policies toward Native Americans and despite the heroic service of a large segment of the Native American population in World War II, life for Native American citizens changed little during the 1940's. Native Americans remain one of the most impoverished and politically powerless segments of American culture.

H. William Rice

Further Reading

Ballantine, Betty, and Ian Ballantine. *Native Americans: An Illustrated History.* Atlanta: Turner, 1992. Two chapters of this illustrated text explore Native American life during the 1940's. One focuses upon the New Deal for Indians, and the other on the termination policy.

Limerick, Patricia Nelson. *Legacy of Conquest: The Unbroken Past of the American West.* New York: W. W. Norton, 1987. Since its publication in 1987, Limerick's book has become a seminal text for understanding the complex history of westward expansion. Chapter six discusses the contradictory policies of the U.S. government toward the Native American people.

Markowitz, Harvey, and Carole A. Barrett. *American Indian Biographies.* Pasadena, Calif.: Salem Press, 2005. This reference text provides a biographical sketch of Hayes.

Momaday, N. Scott. *House Made of Dawn.* New York: Harper and Row, 1968. Though Momaday's work is fiction, the character of Abel is based in part on the much publicized life and untimely death of Hayes.

Silko, Leslie Marmon. *Ceremony.* New York: Penguin, 1977. Silko's novel explores the post-World War II experience of the fictional character Tayo. Much like Momaday's Abel and the real-life Hayes, Tayo must learn to cope with the memories of World War II while back on the reservation.

Wilson, James. *The Earth Shall Weep: A History of Native America.* New York: Grove, 1999. A complete history of native people in the United States; readable for the nonscholar. The last several chapters explore the political policies of the 1940's.

See also African Americans; Asian Americans; Canadian minority communities; Code talkers; Indian Claims Commission; Iwo Jima, Battle of; Latinos; New Deal programs.

■ Native Son

Identification Novel that graphically depicts a young African American's violence and rage when confronted by white racism

Author Richard Wright (1908-1960)

Date Published on February 28, 1940

Along with Zora Neale Hurston's Their Eyes Were Watching God *(1937) and Ralph Ellison's* Invisible Man *(1952), Richard Wright's groundbreaking, searing, and naturalistic tale of the short, violent life of Bigger Thomas is the hinge between the Harlem Renaissance of the 1920's and the Black Arts movement of the 1960's and 1970's. However, unlike Hurston's and Ellison's novels, which hold out some possibility of individual or communal redemption,* Native Son *provides a far bleaker view of the portrayal of the hopelessness inherent in the lives of African Americans.*

Based in part on a Chicago newspaper account of a murder committed by a young black man, *Native Son* is narrated entirely from the perspective of Bigger Thomas. This narrative device, along with the novel's sections "Fear," "Flight," and "Fate," reinforce the claustrophobic atmosphere of the book. Boxed in by economic deprivation, racism, and his own psychological maladjustments, Bigger lacks the ability to control his life or to exert his power. He is forced by his mother to take a job as a chauffeur and handyman for the Daltons. Mr. Dalton's daughter, Mary, along with her communist boyfriend, Jan, force Bigger to drive them to a secret party meeting. They also force him to drive to his neighborhood and join them in eating "soul" food. Although Bigger gains some power when he plots his escape after accidentally killing Mary, he remains inside a maze without an exit. His capture, trial, and conviction are a fait accompli. The novel's post-Depression sense of individual impotence would be expressed throughout the 1940's, not only in such literary works as *Invisible Man* but also in film noir, a

genre that depicts individuals' hopelessness in confronting their fates.

Impact Wright's unflinching novel paved the way for the so-called protest novel during the Black Arts movement. Although many proponents of this movement rejected protest literature, since it presupposed a white audience as its primary target, *Native Son* was heralded as one of the most important novels written by an African American, and the book continued to maintain this reputation into the twenty-first century.

Tyrone Williams

Further Reading

Butler, Robert. *Native Son: The Emergence of a New Black Hero.* Boston: Twayne, 1991.

Gayle, Addison. *Richard Wright: Ordeal of a Native Son.* Garden City, N.Y.: Anchor Press/Doubleday, 1980.

Wallace, Maurice. "Richard Wright's Black Medusa." *Journal of African American History* 88, no. 1 (2003): 71-77.

See also African Americans; Anticommunism; Communist Party USA; Literature in the United States; Racial discrimination; Smith Act; Socialist Workers Party; Urbanization in the United States; Wright, Richard.

■ Natural disasters

Definition Catastrophic natural and weather-related events resulting in significant impacts on humans

During the 1940's, natural disasters resulted in death, property and agricultural damage, disruptions to mobilization for World War II, and other social and economic ramifications. As a result, developments occurred in the forecasting of potential weather-related disasters and the issuance of timely and accurate public warning systems.

Since the 1930's, natural disasters in the United States and Canada have resulted in fewer deaths but rising property damage because of population growth and urbanization. Weather-related natural disasters that struck the United States and Canada in the 1940's included floods, droughts, blizzards, tornadoes, and hurricanes. Natural occurrences that produced natural disasters during the decade included earthquakes and resulting tsunamis. Major natural disasters of the period revealed the continued need for further developments in timely and accurate forecasting, public warnings for potential natural disasters, and improved state and federal responses in their wake.

Weather-Related Events A powerful low-pressure system caused one of the worst blizzards in U.S. history: the so-called Armistice Day blizzard of 1940. The storm hit the middle part of the country on November 11. Local forecasts gave little warning of the storm's arrival or its severity, which included below-freezing temperatures, winds of up to 75 miles per hour, and snowfalls of up to twenty-seven inches with twenty-foot high drifts. The 154 deaths included stranded hunters, sailors who died on three freighters in Lake Michigan, two casualties of a Minnesota train collision, and people trapped in their cars. Cattle on the open range slowly starved. Disruptions to communications and transportation systems forced the Army to search for survivors and drop supplies by plane. The cold air mass later collided with warm air and set off tornadoes in Arkansas and Louisiana, including one in Warren, Arkansas, that destroyed houses, killed 53 people, and injured more than 400.

In 1948-1949, a series of blizzards, which became known as the Great Blizzard of 1949, struck Nebraska in one of the state's worst winters. From the first storm in November to the last storm in April, parts of the state received up to one hundred inches of snowfall. During Operation Snowbound, relief organizations were once again forced to rescue people and livestock and drop supplies from planes.

On June 22 and 23, 1944, a tornado outbreak struck in the mid-Atlantic region of the United States. Especially hard hit was the town of Shinnston, in the western part of West Virginia, where a tornado more than one thousand feet wide touched down around 8:00 P.M. In addition to the severe winds, there were reports of baseball-sized hail. The outbreak left more than 150 dead and 800 seriously injured and destroyed approximately four hundred homes. On June 17, 1946, the Windsor-Tecumseh tornadoes caused extensive property damage in Ontario, Canada.

On April 9, 1947, the Glazier-Higgins-Woodward tornadoes hit the American Midwest from Texas to Kansas. The tornadoes first hit Texas, then crossed into Woodward, Oklahoma, as a category F5, striking without warning in the early morning. One hundred city blocks lay in ruins, with more than one thousand homes and businesses destroyed. Damages were estimated at $6 million. The tornado and resulting fires killed 181 people and injured approximately 1,000 more in Woodward. A 1948 tornado destroyed thirty-two airplanes at Tinker Air Force Base outside Oklahoma City.

Atlantic hurricane activity occurs historically in a cyclical pattern, and the 1940's was an extremely active period. Twelve hurricanes struck Florida alone from 1941 to 1950, seven of them were major. In October, 1944, a large, category-three hurricane, with wind gusts up to 163 miles per hour, severely damaged Sarasota, Florida, and impacted nearly the entire state, causing property damage, power outages, and devastating citrus-crop losses. A 1945 Florida hurricane struck the city of Richmond, destroying three Navy blimp hangars by wind and fire. Losses included twenty-five blimps, more than two hundred military and civilian planes, and 150 cars.

On the night of September 17-18, 1947, a category-four hurricane hit the southeast Florida coast from Cape Canaveral to Miami. The storm, one of the strongest in this period, knocked out electricity, sank boats, and caused more than $20 million in property damage and fifty-one deaths. A September 18-25, 1948, category-three hurricane entered Florida near Everglades City and moved across the state, exiting around Jupiter on the southeast coast. The storm spawned a tornado in Homestead and left three dead and approximately $18 million in damages. On the night of August 26-27, 1949, a hurricane hit the southeast Florida coast with 120 mile-per-hour winds and heavy rains, causing two drownings and more than $40 million in property damages.

The Great Atlantic Hurricane was one of the period's best known. In mid-September of 1944, a large, fast-moving, category-three hurricane traveled up the coast of the northeastern United States. Although northeastern storms occur with less frequency than those in the southern United States, they tend to be larger and faster moving. Improved knowledge of the effect of air masses on storms as well as the devastating experience of the 1938 New England hurricane gave more advance warning of this storm's arrival. The storm left close to four hundred dead and more than one thousand injured.

Such was the power and reach of the Great Atlantic Hurricane of 1944 that it knocked over a row of trees deep within Manhattan. (AP/ Wide World Photos)

Hurricane-force winds struck the coast from North Carolina to Massachusetts, with some areas recording gusts up to 140 miles per hour. Heavy rains and huge waves also accompanied the storm. Warm air masses and water temperatures and a strong Bermuda high increased the storm's speed and intensity and kept it along the coastline. Some people along the shore were swept out to sea.

High seas affected the numerous ships that were offshore because of wartime surges in shipping. Other impacts included the loss of trees, tree limbs, and electricity and phone services and crop damages. Thousands of buildings suffered major damage, with estimates of more than $100 million. Weather-related events outside North America occasionally disrupted war efforts. On December 17-18,

1944, a series of forecasting errors caused Admiral William F. Halsey's Third Fleet to steam directly into the path of a 1944 typhoon off the Philippine coast. The storm's seventy-foot seas and 115-mile-per-hour winds sank the U.S. destroyers *Hull, Spence*, and *Monahan*, killing almost eight hundred men.

In the spring of 1948, melting winter snows in British Columbia, Washington, and Oregon resulted in severe flooding along the Columbia River, killing at least fifteen people. A 1949-1950 drought in the New York City area resulted in the closing of swimming pools and other restrictions on water use. A cloud-seeding experiment to end the drought led to excessive 1951 rains and numerous complaints from farmers who lost crops as a result. Cloud-seeding experiments also targeted hurricanes. In October of 1947, a hurricane became the first to be seeded as part of Project Cirrus, a classified General Electric cloud-seeding project supported by the U.S. Army Signal Corps, the Office of Naval Research, and the U.S. Air Force. The storm split in two in the Atlantic, with the worst effects hitting Savannah, Georgia.

Seismic Events A number of earthquakes and tsunamis hit the United States and Canada in the 1940's. On May 19, 1940, a magnitude 7.1 earthquake and strong aftershock struck the Imperial Valley in Southern California. Because of the area's small population, the earthquake resulted in only nine deaths, but there was approximately $6 million in damages to buildings and irrigation canals, including the collapse of large water tanks in Holtville and Imperial. Numerous sand boils, which shot water and sand several feet into the air, left behind craters. The area was an extremely important agricultural region, so water restoration became a priority, limiting crop losses.

On June 23, 1946, a magnitude 7.3 earthquake struck Vancouver Island, British Columbia, with impacts felt as far away as Oregon and Washington in the Pacific Northwest. The earthquake caused major damage across the island and resulted in one death when the occupant of a small boat drowned, capsized by a resulting wave.

On April 13, 1949, a magnitude 7.1 earthquake struck Puget Sound in the western region of Washington, causing severe damage to buildings, monuments, and gas lines along the area's coast, with a total cost estimated at approximately $25 million. The epicenter was located between the cities of Olympia and Tacoma, and the quake was felt as far away as Oregon, Idaho, and British Columbia. The earthquake and resulting rock slides also left eight dead and dozens more seriously injured. On August 22, 1949, a magnitude 8.1 earthquake struck the Queen Charlotte Islands, Canada, also affecting the Pacific Northwest. Other earthquakes of the period included two of magnitude 5.5 that struck Ossipee Lake, New Hampshire, in December, 1940; a magnitude 7.4 earthquake that struck Skwenta, Alaska, in November, 1943; a magnitude 6.1 earthquake that struck Sheep Mountain, Idaho, in July, 1944; a magnitude 5.8 earthquake that struck Massena, New York, in September, 1944; and a magnitude 7.2 earthquake that struck Wood River, Alaska, in October, 1947.

On April 1, 1946, a magnitude 8.1 earthquake along the fault system beneath the Aleutian Islands in the North Pacific Ocean triggered one of the decade's biggest natural disasters in the United States. The seafloor disruption produced a tsunami more than one hundred feet high that destroyed a U.S. Coast Guard lighthouse on Unimak Island, Alaska, killing five people. Tsunamis then traveled across the Pacific Ocean, striking Hawaii. Residents of Hilo noticed the water along the shore and harbor basin rapidly receding just before 7:00 A.M., causing some to run inland shouting warnings while others stayed and watched. The narrowing course of Hilo Bay piled the waves higher. Between 7:00 A.M. and 9:00 A.M., a series of waves submerged the city and nearby areas, destroying buildings and railways and causing more than $26 million in damages and more than 160 deaths. Smaller waves were recorded along the West Coast of the United States, resulting in one drowning in Santa Cruz, California.

Impact Several natural disasters had small but significant impacts on U.S. mobilization for World War II. Heavy, war-related shipping along the East Coast increased vulnerability to weather-related disasters. The 1944 Great Atlantic Hurricane caused the loss of two ships, including the Navy destroyer *Warrington*. Local shipyards suffered heavy damages that interfered with wartime production. The 1948 tornado at Tinker Air Force Base in Oklahoma led U.S. Air Force weathermen to conduct pioneering research on the development of tornado watch boxes, for areas likely to be hit within a set time period, and on the usefulness of radar in tracking convective storms. In 1948, the first correct tornado prediction was made in Oklahoma, and by 1951, the Severe Weather Warning Center began operations at Tinker.

The most severe natural disasters of the 1940's were also instrumental in spurring further civilian research into forecasting and for providing timely public warning systems. The work at Tinker spurred the National Weather Service to begin issuing thirty-day weather outlooks and to release tornado alerts to the public. The 1946 Hawaiian tsunamis prompted the founding of the Pacific-wide Tsunami Warning System, based at the Honolulu Observatory, to monitor seismic activity that could result in tsunami formation and to issue warnings to potential impact zones. The inaccurate local forecasts for the Armistice Day blizzard of 1940 spurred the implementation of twenty-four-hour forecasting and the expansion of local weather offices, resulting in more accurate forecasts.

Marcella Bush Trevino

Further Reading

Abbott, Patrick Leon. *Natural Disasters.* 7th ed. New York: McGraw-Hill, 2008. Covers the Earth processes and energy sources that lead to natural disasters and provides case studies.

Burton, I. R., W. Kates, and G. F. White. *The Environment As Hazard.* New York: Guilford Press, 1993. A benchmark reference work covering research and policy issues relating to natural hazards and the human role in natural disasters.

Hyndman, Donald, and David Hyndman. *Natural Hazards and Disasters.* 2d ed. Belmont, Calif.: Brooks Cole, 2008. Details the effects of natural and geological processes underlying natural disasters.

Laskin, David. *Braving the Elements: The Stormy History of American Weather.* New York: Doubleday, 1996. Provides a survey of American weather history.

Steinberg, Theodore. *Acts of God: The Unnatural History of Natural Disaster in America.* New York: Oxford University Press, 2000. Uses case studies to examine American views of natural disasters and man's role in creating them.

See also Armistice Day blizzard; Cloud seeding; Great Blizzard of 1949; Helicopters; Urbanization in Canada; Urbanization in the United States.

■ Natural resources

Definition The productive use in the United States and Canada of deposits of metal ores, nonmetallic minerals, construction stone, and fossil fuels; ground and surface water; wildlife; forests; land; and other naturally occurring commercial or industrial materials or assets

The 1940's marked a time of increased natural resource exploitation for the United States and Canada. As the countries prepared for and waged war and subsequently enjoyed a postwar boom while arming for the Cold War, demand remained high for resources, such as metals and other minerals, building materials, fuel, and hydroelectric power.

The 1939 outbreak of World War II in Europe impacted the demand for natural resources in the United States and Canada. German military successes in Europe in the spring of 1940 spurred the two nations to make rapid defense preparations. The abundance and variety of resources available on the North American continent gave the countries a decided wartime advantage, although not all of their needs for raw materials could be met domestically. Faced with the prospect of volatile prices and unreliable supplies of critical mineral, energy, and agricultural resources in the wartime international market, the Canadian and American governments took a number of precautions. They curtailed exports of critical materials and goods, except where these items provided support to Allied forces. They also researched lower-grade domestic supplies and possible substitutions for some materials traditionally purchased elsewhere; implemented rationing among their citizens; encouraged conservation as a patriotic practice; and conducted salvage and recycling operations to recover usable materials, such as metals, oil, paper, rubber, and cloth fibers from discarded consumer goods.

In both countries, manufacturing efforts increased to meet wartime production needs. When World War II ended in 1945, however, production remained high, as did the demand for natural resources. Both countries had to maintain military vigilance in the face of the Cold War; the United States, aided by research and raw materials from Canada, began to build a nuclear arsenal. Citizens who had gone through the Great Depression of the 1930's and wartime rationing during the 1940's were eager to enjoy new homes, new and abundant consumer goods, and a time of plenty.

Mineral Resources Mobilizing for war after a protracted economic depression abruptly elevated the demand for mineral resources. Production rose sharply and remained high through the war years. Defense preparations created a greater demand for metals, in particular because of their use in munitions. Low- and off-grade domestic deposits of chromium, manganese, and magnesium gained importance as war threatened, and often interrupted, foreign supplies. Other metals critical to the war effort included aluminum, copper, gold, lead, molybdenum, nickel, silver, tin, tungsten, vanadium, and zinc.

Iron ore was especially important for war mobilization, as it is the primary raw material from which steel is produced. (Other key steelmaking materials include limestone and coal, as well as alloying elements, such as chromium, manganese, nickel, and vanadium.) Steel was used to make guns, ammunition, military vehicles, tanks, warships, and airplanes. Steel was also a necessary material for erecting factories, building military bases, constructing shipyards, and producing heavy machinery. During the postwar years, high consumption persisted. Steel was indispensable for automobiles and many other consumer goods, bridges and highways, large urban structures, and missiles and silos. The United States dominated world production of iron ore through the 1940's, with the Lake Superior district deposits in Michigan and Minnesota accounting for most of the nation's production.

Uranium was another metallic element that had a notable influence on Allied success during World War II and would have a profound impact in the postwar years. Before the experimental advances made in nuclear fission during the 1930's, there were few practical applications for uranium. Interest in fission's potential for wartime use led the federal government to begin supporting fission research in 1940. The following year, President Franklin D. Roosevelt gave his approval for the development of an atomic weapon and authorized the creation of the research group that would come to be known as the Manhattan Project (1942-1945). The project's research efforts, and the creation of the world's first nuclear weapons, required uranium.

The United States initially imported uranium ore from the Belgian Congo, but interest in securing reliable wartime sources spurred the project to turn to Canadian and domestic deposits. In 1942, the Port Radium pitchblende deposits in the Northwest Territories of Canada became a major supplier of uranium for the Manhattan Project. Large stocks of uranium had accumulated there as a waste product of radium refining during the 1930's. Within the United States, only lower-grade ores were available. The carnotite-bearing sandstones of the Colorado Plateau in Colorado and Utah, originally mined for their vanadium content and later for their radium, produced a low-grade uranium ore as a by-product. Once World War II ended and the Cold War began, demand for uranium drove increased exploration in the United States and Canada. A flurry of prospect-ing in the late 1940's led to a uranium mining boom for both countries during the 1950's.

Nonmetallic minerals also played an important role during and after the war. Among these were limestone and clay (used in cement production), asphalt, sand, gravel, and building stone, all of which were required in large quantities to satisfy military and civilian construction needs, and potash and phosphate, both components of agricultural fertilizer.

Energy Resources During the war years, petroleum products were critical for fueling military vehicles, aircraft, and warships. Petroleum was also an important raw material for the manufacture of plastics and petrochemicals. At the time, the United States supplied about two-thirds of the world's petroleum. America provided Great Britain with much of its fuel needs, although German submarines took a heavy toll on tankers crossing the Atlantic. To minimize losses closer to home, the United States constructed pipelines that would alleviate the need to ship petroleum products from Texas to the Northeast via tanker. The Big Inch, completed in 1943, was a 24-inch diameter pipeline that carried crude oil. The Little Big Inch, a 20-inch diameter pipeline completed in 1944, transported gasoline and other refined products. During their wartime operation, these pipelines moved more than 350 million barrels of crude oil and refined products. After the war, these pipelines were used to transport natural gas.

Wartime concerns about the vulnerability of tankers also drove pipeline construction in Canada. The Canol pipeline, the first system of its kind to be built in the North American Arctic, moved crude oil from the Norman Wells oilfields in the Northwest Territories to refining facilities in the Yukon capital of Whitehorse; from there, supply lines carried it to other destinations in the Yukon and to Alaska. In operation from 1944 to 1945, the Canol line moved an estimated 975,764 barrels of crude oil. Construction of the Interprovincial Pipeline system, designed to carry crude oil from Alberta to Superior, Wisconsin, began in 1949, two years after massive oilfields were discovered south of Alberta's capital, Edmonton.

Just as the outbreak of World War II increased the need for mineral and fuel resources, the war also expanded the need for electricity to process these resources. Domestic supplies of coal provided both the United States and Canada with electrical energy, as did hydroelectric power plants. The nations' large rivers were ideal for supplying hydroelectricity, and hydropower facilities were well suited to providing plentiful, inexpensive energy for the war effort. Notable 1940's hydropower projects include America's Grand Coulee power plant in Washington State, which generated its first electricity in 1941, and Shasta Dam in California, which came online in 1944. The Grand Coulee facility attracted wartime aluminum smelting operations to the Columbia River basin, as the industry required large amounts of energy for its power-intensive processes.

Smelters sprang up in Vancouver, Canada, and the American Northwest. Similarly, the Manhattan Project established a research facility (later operated under the supervision of the Atomic Energy Commission) at Hanford, Washington, where the Grand Coulee facility could power its energy-intensive nuclear research. In the postwar years, hydropower continued to provide energy for the Canadian and American defense industries, peacetime manufacturing, and the domestic needs of expanding populations of civilian consumers. During and after the war, dams also provided irrigation water for farmland, thereby contributing to food production.

Other Resources The United States and Canada both had a strategic advantage over Europe because they were large and comparatively young nations with vast areas of agricultural and grazing land that were untouched by the war's devastation. They were able to grow enough crops and raise sufficient livestock to feed their own populations, with some help from food-rationing programs and citizens' home gardens, while providing for Allied soldiers at home and abroad. After the war, the two nations exported food to other countries in which production had been interrupted or damaged by combat operations. Farmers took advantage of new petrochemical pesticides developed during the war.

Wartime and peacetime construction during the 1940's consumed large quantities of wood. During the war years, structures for housing and training troops required lumber and plywood, and demand remained high during the postwar construction boom. The military used plywood to make airplanes,

gliders, and boats, and civilian industries manufactured inexpensive, modern furniture from this material. During the 1940's, Canada's forestry management officials began considering the principle of sustained yield—maintaining a balance between growth and harvest. Canadian conscientious objectors were put to work during the war replanting overcut forest lands.

Impact War mobilization during the early 1940's accelerated industrialization and urbanization within the United States and Canada. The race to defeat the Axis Powers resulted in an abrupt increase in the exploitation of natural resources. The end of the war did little to change these nations' industrial expansion and heightened resource consumption. Both countries enjoyed increased world trade in the postwar years. Industrial capacity had been boosted for military purposes; after the war, manufacturing facilities continued to make armaments for the Cold War or turned to civilian production. New technologies that had been developed during the war found applications in the manufacture of consumer goods.

The unfortunate consequences of this rapid industrial expansion would be felt in later decades. In rushing to respond first to military needs, and later to consumer demands, industries devoted little attention to the environmental impact created by their exploitation of natural resources, particularly where there were few or no regulatory constraints on the industries' actions. By the 1960's and 1970's, the Canadian and U.S. governments and their citizens would be familiar with the host of disadvantages that accompanied unregulated or underregulated natural resource exploitation and industrialization: air pollution, groundwater and surface water pollution, soil contamination, pollution-related damage to human health, despoiling of land held by native populations, deforestation, and wildlife habitat and species loss.

Karen N. Kähler

Further Reading

Benke, Arthur C., and Colbert E. Cushing, eds. *Rivers of North America.* Burlington, Mass.: Elsevier Academic Press, 2005. This award-winning reference volume offers a comprehensive view of the continent's river systems, including human impacts. Includes illustrations, maps, bibliographic references, and index.

Hays, Samuel P. "From Conservation to Environment: Environmental Politics in the United States Since World War Two." *Environmental Review* 6, no. 2 (Fall, 1982): 14-41. In this frequently cited article, Hays identifies World War II as the dividing point in the United States between a conservation era focused on efficient resource management and an environmentalist era focused on improving the quality of life.

_____. *A History of Environmental Politics Since 1945.* Pittsburgh, Pa.: University of Pittsburgh Press, 2000. Hays expands on the themes he explored in his 1982 article. Includes a guide to further reading and an index.

Hessing, Melody, Michael Howlett, and Tracy Summerville. *Canadian Natural Resource and Environmental Policy: Political Economy and Public Policy.* 2d ed. Vancouver: University of British Columbia Press, 2005. Multidisciplinary look at how contemporary resource policies in Canada have evolved. Includes figures, tables, notes, bibliography, and index.

Mitchell, Bruce, ed. *Resource and Environmental Management in Canada.* 3d ed. New York: Oxford University Press, 2004. For a historical perspective on Canada's resource management concerns, see part 2, "Enduring Concerns." Includes notes, references, and index.

Pehrson, E. W., and H. D. Keiser, eds. *Minerals Yearbook: Review of 1940.* Washington, D.C.: Government Printing Office, 1941. This and subsequent yearbooks covering the 1940's include front matter describing overall trends in the U.S. mineral industries, world statistics, and chapters that provide a thorough description of how specific minerals and regions fared during the year.

Yergin, Daniel. *The Prize: The Epic Quest for Oil, Money, and Power.* New ed. New York: Free Press, 2008. Chapter 19, "The Allies' War," provides a detailed account of how American oil fueled the Allies' stand against Germany in World War II.

See also Agriculture in Canada; Atomic Energy Commission; Bureau of Land Management; Fish and Wildlife Service, U.S.; Hanford Nuclear Reservation; International trade; Truman proclamations; Wartime industries; Wartime salvage drives.

■ Navy, U.S.

Identification Sea branch of the U.S. armed forces

The United States entered World War II following the attack on Pearl Harbor in December, 1941. The Japanese navy seemed unbeatable to many Americans, but Admiral Chester W. Nimitz, commander of the Pacific Fleet, took the offensive and soon won several decisive battles that led to the surrender of Japan.

At the end of the 1930's, the U.S. Navy began preparing to fight a war in both the Atlantic and the Pacific oceans. The Navy continued to rely heavily on battleships and aircraft carriers, but it also began building a fleet of long-range submarines. Prior to the Japanese attack on Pearl Harbor on December 7, 1941, President Franklin D. Roosevelt moved the Navy from the coast of California to Hawaii as a show of force, hoping to deter the Japanese from attacking. In the Atlantic, American submarines fought German U-boats in an unofficial naval war. When Roosevelt declared a state of emergency on September 8, 1939, the Navy was authorized to increase its number of enlisted personnel by almost sixty thousand, to 191,000. Officers and nurses in the reserves were also called back to active duty. On June 14, 1940, Roosevelt signed a bill authorizing the expansion of the Navy's number of combatant ships by 11 percent as a precautionary measure. As the war in Europe spread, Congress passed a second bill, signed on July 19, increasing the size of the Navy by 1,325,000 tons of combatant ships.

During World War II, Fleet Admiral Ernest King served as the commander in chief of the U.S. Fleet. The fleet was divided into three theaters. As of 1942, the leaders of the Navy were Admiral T. C. Hart, commander in chief of the Asiatic Fleet; Admiral R. E. Ingersoll, commander in chief of the Atlantic Fleet; and Admiral Chester W. Nimitz, commander in chief of the Pacific Fleet. The position of chief of naval operations was a two-year term held by Admiral Harold R. Stark at the beginning of the war. Admiral King became the chief of naval operations in March, 1942, and the duties were combined with those of commander in chief of the U.S. Fleet. Stark then became commander in chief of U.S. naval forces in Europe. The position of fleet admiral (five stars) was created in 1944, making it the top rank in the Navy. Admiral Nimitz was the last surviving fleet admiral when he died in 1966.

Giant Navy landing ships (LSTs) open their jaws in the surf, as soldiers build sandbag piers to facilitate the unloading of the supplies and equipment to be used in the Philippine campaign. (National Archives)

Nimitz defeated the Japanese navy in a number of battles during 1942. His victories at Coral Sea and Midway Island are considered a turning point in the war. Nimitz had proven that the Japanese navy was not unbeatable—a large morale booster for both the Allied forces and the American people. In 1944, the U.S. Navy effectively eliminated Japan as a threat after winning the Battles of the Philippine Sea and Leyte Gulf. In 1945, Allied naval forces took control of Iwo Jima and Okinawa. U.S. Air Force and Navy air strikes inflicted severe damage to Japan before the dropping of the atomic bombs on Hiroshima and Nagasaki in early August. Japan officially surrendered on board the USS *Missouri* in Tokyo Bay on September 2, 1945. Admiral Nimitz signed the surrender papers as the representative of the United States.

Atlantic and Pacific Theaters After the United States officially entered World War II, German U-boats still had control of the Atlantic. The German navy torpedoed Allied ships off the eastern coast of the United States. The U.S. Navy spent most of 1942 relearning lessons from its World War I encounters with U-boats. The German navy remained a threat throughout the war, but by the middle of 1943 the Allies had learned how to diminish that threat using advanced tactics, advances in technology, intelligence, and more efficient shipbuilding.

After the attack on Pearl Harbor, the Japanese navy was perceived to be invincible. Admiral Nimitz, in command of the Pacific Fleet, took the offensive against the enemy as soon as the Navy's resources had recovered from Pearl Harbor. Nimitz relied heavily on intelligence gathered by a joint military agency as well as his previous studies at the Naval War College on the logistics of a possible Pacific war. His strategy, called "island hopping," slowly reclaimed the Pacific with large-scale amphibious assaults that were supported by carrier-borne aircraft. The strategy ended the Japanese occupation of a number of islands throughout the Pacific.

Postwar In December, 1945, Admiral Nimitz began his two-year term as chief of naval operations. One of his main tasks was reducing the Navy to a smaller peacetime fleet. In 1943, the U.S. Navy was larger than all the other combatant navies combined. By the end of the war, the Navy had added several new vessels, including eighteen aircraft carriers and eight battleships. In 1945, the Navy had 1,194 major combatant vessels; three years later, the fleet had been narrowed to just 267. The British navy had suffered significant losses during the war, leaving the U.S. Navy with the responsibility of protecting the world's sea-lanes and oceans. The Navy sent the first postwar expedition to Antarctica during the winter of 1946-1947. The operation was directed by Admiral Richard Byrd, a leading expert on the Arctic region. Into the 1950's, the Navy continued exploration into the Arctic using air, surface, and submarine forces.

However, with the navies of Germany, Italy, and Japan destroyed, many Americans felt that a standing peacetime Navy was unnecessary. Secretary of Defense Louis Johnson called for drastic cuts to the Navy. During the late 1940's, Johnson eliminated the

Navy's plan to build a 65,000-ton aircraft carrier prototype named the *United States*. The carrier was intended to support nuclear-capable aircraft over the next twenty years. Secretary Johnson's severe downsizing of the Navy was still being debated in Congress when the Soviet Union created its first atomic bomb, which was tested in August, 1949. Facing the threat of communism spreading through the world, American leaders increased military funding to all branches, including the Navy. A few months later, in June, 1950, the United States entered the Korean War, in which the Navy played an important role.

Navy Seabees   After the attack on Pearl Harbor, the Navy could no longer use civilian employees to build bases and for other duties internationally. In January, 1942, Rear Admiral Ben Moreell was granted authority to create a militarized naval construction force, and he began recruiting men in the construction trades to form three battalions. Command of the units was given to Civil Engineer Corps officers instead of line officers. The term "construction battalion" was abbreviated as "C.B.," which led to the name "Seabees." The first Seabees were recruits that already had experience working in various construction trades; their average age was thirty-seven. Bases were established on both coasts to train them how to fight and use light arms. The Seabee mottos were "We Build, We Fight" and "Can Do!"—emphasizing their duel role as sailors and construction workers. Most of the work the Seabees did was in the Pacific theater. They landed shortly after the Marines and built airstrips, bridges, warehouses, roads, hospitals, and housing. By the end of World War II, there were more than 325,000 Seabees. By 1950, their number had been reduced to 3,300. The start of the Korean War led to strong Seabee recruitment by the Navy.

Impact   American submarines were responsible for almost one-third of all Japanese ships sunk during the war. The submarines were also responsible for almost two-thirds of the damage caused to Japanese merchant ships and trade. Submarines were also used for reconnaissance, rescues, supply missions, and lifeguarding. The Navy collaborated with the scientific community and manufacturing industry throughout the 1940's in order to improve submarine design, construction, and technology. The United States became a leader in undersea warfare, which was key during the Cold War.

After World War II, the Seabees continued to be a valuable part of the Navy. During the Vietnam War, the Seabees built a number of naval bases, as well as hospitals, roads, bridges, and airstrips. They also conducted a large number of civilian projects for the South Vietnamese people, building schools and churches and repairing roads and villages. In the early twenty-first century, Seabees are stationed throughout the world, including Iraq and Afghanistan, working as carpenters, mechanics, electricians, and large-equipment operators, and in many other related trades.

Jennifer L. Campbell

Further Reading

Howarth, Stephen. *To Shining Sea: A History of the United States Navy, 1775-1991*. New York: Random House, 1991. A political and diplomatic history of the Navy. Includes several maps and photographs.

Kimmel, Jay. *U.S. Navy Seabees: Since Pearl Harbor.* 3d ed. Portland, Oreg.: Corey/Stevens Publishing, 2005. The history of the Seabees, the Navy's construction force, which was formed in 1942. Includes more than two hundred photographs and is based in part on personal accounts.

King, Ernest. *U.S. Navy at War, 1941-1945*. Washington, D.C.: Government Printing Office, 1946. Official reports to the Secretary of the Navy written by Admiral King, chief of naval operations during World War II. Includes appendixes on Japanese naval ships, losses of U.S. naval vessels, and combat vessels added to the U.S. Navy during World War II.

Love, Robert. *History of the U.S. Navy*. 2 vols. Mechanicsburg, Penn.: Stackpole Books, 1992. A detailed strategic history of the Navy. Includes a helpful glossary that explains operations, aircraft types, and acronyms.

Morison, Samuel Eliot. *The Two-Ocean War: A Short History of the United States Navy in the Second World War.* Boston: Little, Brown, 1963. A shorter version of the author's fifteen-volume history of the Navy during World War II. Provides detailed histories of major battles and campaigns throughout the war. Includes several maps and charts.

Weir, Gary E. *Forged in War: The Naval-Industrial Complex and American Submarine Construction, 1940-1961*. Washington, D.C.: Washington Naval Historical Center, 1993. Examines how the joint effort of the Navy, industry, and scientific community led the United States to dominate undersea warfare. Based on extensive research of Navy documents and records of the involved scientific organizations and businesses.

See also Army, U.S.; Department of Defense, U.S.; Halsey, William F. "Bull"; *History of the United States Naval Operations in World War II*; Marines, U.S.; Nimitz, Chester W.; Pearl Harbor attack; Submarine warfare; War heroes; World War II.

■ Negro Leagues

Identification Professional African American baseball federations

The Negro Leagues served as a loose-knit organization in which African Americans could play baseball professionally in a racially segregated country. They brought money to African Americans and were a mostly successful business model for the community.

The Negro Leagues experienced their greatest financial successes during the 1940's, despite the fact that several of their players spent a year or two in the military because of World War II. Although there had been other federations in the Negro Leagues system, by 1940, the two major leagues were the Negro American League and the Negro National League. The latter was the second incarnation of the Negro National League.

In contrast to white Major League Baseball (MLB) teams that had experienced financial setbacks because so many of their big-name players were in the military, the Negro Leagues benefited from the fact that millions of black Americans were newly employed in defense-related industries and had money to spend on entertainment. The popularity and accompanying financial success of the Negro Leagues encouraged the owners to reestablish the Negro League World Series in 1943. When the war ended, returning African American soldiers attended and played in the leagues. However, the end of segregated baseball occurred in 1947, with the debut of Jackie Robinson, despite the efforts of some racist owners and MLB officials who wanted to maintain the status quo. By 1949, the Negro National League had folded, and several African American star players had signed with previously all-white teams.

Prominent Personalities Perhaps no individual was more important to Negro League baseball of the 1930's and 1940's than Gus Greenlee, the founder of the revitalized Negro National League. Greenlee made much of his early money from bootlegging and gambling operations but eventually owned a nightclub and the Pittsburgh Crawfords baseball team. In addition, he built the first black-owned baseball park. The Negro National League featured two of professional baseball's historically best-known and most powerful teams: the Homestead Grays and the Crawfords. The rosters of these teams read like a perennial all-star team: Satchel Paige, Josh Gibson, Cool Papa Bell, Judy Johnson, Oscar Charleston, and Buck Leonard are the best known of these men.

Second baseman Sammy T. Hughes (left) and catcher Roy Campanella of the Negro Leagues' Baltimore Elite Giants in 1942. In 1946, Campanella signed with the major leagues' Brooklyn Dodgers, who called him up two years later. He went on to have a distinguished major league career until it was ended by a crippling automobile accident. (AP/Wide World Photos)

Negro League Players of the 1940's in the National Baseball Hall of Fame

Name	Primary Team	Position	Years Active in Negro Leagues	Year Inducted
Cool Papa Bell	St. Louis Stars	Center field	1922-1938, 1942, 1947-1950	1974
Willard Brown*	Kansas City Monarchs	Center field	1935-1944, 1948-1950	2006
Ray Brown	Homestead Grays	Pitcher	1931-1945	2006
Roy Campanella*	Baltimore Elite Giants	Catcher	1937-1942, 1944-1945	1969
Oscar Charleston	Pittsburgh Crawfords	Center field	1915-1941	1976
Ray Dandridge	Newark Eagles	Third base	1933-1939, 1942, 1944, 1949	1987
Leon Day	Newark Eagles	Pitcher	1934-1939, 1941-1943, 1946, 1949-1950	1995
Larry Doby*	Newark Eagles	Center field	1942-1943, 1946	1998
Josh Gibson	Homestead Grays	Catcher	1930-1946	1972
Monte Irvin*	Newark Eagles	Left field	1938-1942, 1945-1948	1973
Buck Leonard	Homestead Grays	First base	1933-1950	1972
Willie Mays*	Birmingham Black Barons	Center field	1948	1979
Satchel Paige*	Kansas City Monarchs	Pitcher	1927-1947	1971
Jackie Robinson*	Kansas City Monarchs	Second base	1945	1962
Hilton Smith	Kansas City Monarchs	Pitcher	1932-1948	2001
Turkey Stearnes	Detroit Stars	Center field	1920-1942, 1945	2000
Mule Suttles	Newark Eagles	First base	1921, 1923-1944	2006
Willie Wells	St. Louis Stars	Shortstop	1923, 1924-1936, 1942	1997
Jud Wilson	Philadelphia Stars	Third base	1922-1945	2006

Note: Players who also played Major League Baseball are denoted with an asterisk (*).

Greenlee was also responsible for restarting the East-West Negro all-star game.

Effa Manley was another important Negro League team owner. She owned the Newark Eagles and was known for insisting that players be paid well and have better scheduling. She was also active in civil rights causes and donated time and money to the National Association for the Advancement of Colored People. Her 1946 team, which included Negro League and future MLB stars Larry Doby, Monte Irvin, and Don Newcombe, won the 1946 Negro World Series. Manley eventually became the first woman to be elected into the National Baseball Hall of Fame.

Some of the best-known players in Negro League baseball during the 1940's included stalwarts from previous decades, such as pitchers Paige and Raymond Brown, outfielder Bell, sluggers Gibson and Willard Brown, and first baseman Leonard. Some of the better known players who rose to stardom during the 1940's included Bob "The Rope" Boyd, pitcher Joe Black, Doby, Robinson, Ernie Banks, Elston Howard, and Hank Thompson.

The Demise of the Negro Leagues As cries for the desegregation of American life began to crescendo during the late 1940's, and with the introduction of Robinson to the Brooklyn Dodgers' roster by owner Branch Rickey, the financial fortunes of the teams in the Negro Leagues began to flag. Despite the fact that some teams resisted the move toward integration, by 1949 the Negro Leagues were fading fast. The Negro National League folded after the 1948 season, leaving the Negro American League as the only remaining professional African American major league.

Impact The impact of the Negro Leagues continues to be discussed. Its existence disproved racist theories prevalent among white Americans that African Americans could neither play professional sports nor maintain a business entity of its size. Inronically, the leagues' success in highlighting the athletic abilities of so many African American ballplayers in turn helped ensure its demise, once the white major leagues realized the financial possibilities of including African American players on the field and their fans in the seats of MLB ballparks. The business model the Negro Leagues presented remains an example to modern African Americans of the business capabilities of their forefathers.

Ron Jacobs

Further Reading

Holway, John, Lloyd Johnson, and Rachel Borst. *Complete Book of Baseball's Negro Leagues.* New York: Hastings House, 2001. Well-researched and readable encyclopedia of the Negro Leagues.

Lanctot, Neil. *Negro League Baseball: The Rise and Ruin of a Black Institution.* Philadelphia: University of Pennsylvania Press, 2004. A groundbreaking work that de-romanticizes the Negro Leagues. Provides a detailed, objective look at the leagues, focusing on the reality of racial segregation, class antagonisms in the African American community, and the poor pay and working conditions of most of the players.

Nelson, Kadir. *We Are the Ship: The Story of Negro League Baseball.* New York: Hyperion Books, 2008. Beautifully illustrated book geared for middle school readers. Covers essential facts of the league and highlights many of its players.

Paige, Satchel. *Maybe I'll Pitch Forever.* Lincoln, Nebr.: Bison Books, 1993. Paige's witty recollection of his life and times playing baseball in the Negro Leagues and Major League Baseball is an informative and enjoyable narrative.

Peterson, Robert. *Only the Ball Was White: A History of Legendary Black Players and All-Black Professional Teams.* New York: Oxford University Press, 1992. Formative text on the Negro Leagues; covers the players, the owners, and the lives they led.

See also All-American Girls Professional Baseball League; Baseball; Civil rights and liberties; International trade; National Association for the Advancement of Colored People; Paige, Satchel; Racial discrimination; Robinson, Jackie; Sports in the United States.

■ New Deal programs

Definition Laws and regulations enacted under President Franklin D. Roosevelt's administration during the 1930's

Public works programs, business regulations, and agricultural programs were enacted during the 1930's to provide stability to the American economy and increase employment among Americans during the Great Depression. With the onset of the 1940's and World War II, many public works programs were ended, but most business regulations and many agricultural programs remained intact.

Most historians date the onset of the Great Depression as October 29, 1929, the date of the stock market crash. When Roosevelt took office as president in early 1933, the unemployment rate was almost 25 percent. Roosevelt and his advisers immediately began fashioning public works programs to put what Roosevelt termed "the forgotten man" back to work. The Federal Emergency Relief Administration (FERA), one of the first public works programs, began in 1933 and ended in 1935. FERA created the Civil Works Administration in 1933, but it lasted only one year. The National Recovery Administration, which was established in 1933 as a first attempt to regulate business and industry, was struck down by the U.S. Supreme Court in 1935.

Several public works programs continued into the 1940's. For example, the Works Progress Administration, which had been created in 1935, provided more than 8 million jobs to unemployed workers. This program built infrastructure in the form of public buildings and roads, and it operated arts and literacy projects, among other programs. It was suspended by Congress in 1943 because of the low levels of unemployment during World War II. One of the most popular programs, the Civilian Conservation Corps, employed young men conserving natural resources in national and state forests, parks, and other federal public landholdings. The program began in 1933, was extended in 1939, and formally concluded its operations in 1943, although liquidation appropriations did not end until 1948. The Public

Works Administration, created in 1933, also was abolished in 1943. One public works program that survived the Great Depression was the Tennessee Valley Authority, which remained the largest provider of electricity in the United States.

The first Agricultural Adjustment Administration (AAA) was designed to restrict agricultural production and raise the value of crops, but it was declared unconstitutional in 1936. The Soil Conservation and Domestic Allotment Act was passed in 1935, and a second AAA law was passed in 1938.

Most business regulation and agencies survived the Great Depression, including the Federal Deposit Insurance Corporation and the Securities and Exchange Commission, which had been created in the aftermath of the near failure of the American banking system. The Federal Housing Administration, created in 1934, also survived and helped spark the building boom of the World War II era. The Fair Labor Standards Act, which had been enacted in 1938, was amended in 1949 and remained in effect into the twenty-first century. The Social Security Act of 1935 is one of the most far-reaching programs of the New Deal. This social welfare and social insurance program provided unemployment and retirement benefits as well as assistance to needy, aged, and disabled individuals.

Impact By 1940, most of Roosevelt's domestic programs were under attack by congressional conservatives. The bulk of these programs had their budgets slashed during the early 1940's as they were gradually phased out. With the onset of World War II, unemployment virtually disappeared as industry retooled for war and men were drafted into the armed forces. Some of the social programs, notably Social Security, survived the 1940's and expanded. Much of the banking regulation passed in the aftermath of the bank failures of the 1930's remained in effect for decades, with widespread bank deregulation not occurring until the 1980's. The federal government continued various agricultural price support programs.

Yvonne Johnson

Further Reading

Himmelberg, Robert F. *The Great Depression and the New Deal.* Westport, Conn.: Greenwood Press, 2000.
McElvaine, Robert S. *The Great Depression: America, 1929-1941.* New York: Times Books, 1994.
Rosenof, Theodore. *Economics in the Long Run: New Deal Theorists and Their Legacies, 1933-1993.* Chapel Hill: University of North Carolina Press, 1997.
Smith, Jason Scott. *Building New Deal Liberalism: The Political Economy of Public Works, 1933-1956.* New York: Cambridge University Press, 2005.

See also Agriculture in the United States; American Enterprise Institute for Public Policy Research; Business and the economy in the United States; Elections in the United States: 1940; Fair Deal; Fair Employment Practices Commission; Roosevelt, Franklin D.; Unemployment in the United States; Willkie, Wendell.

■ Newfoundland

The Event Admission of Newfoundland as the Canadian confederation's tenth province
Date March 31, 1949

Newfoundland's admission as a province completed the process of Canadian confederation that had begun in 1867 and resolved the territory's constantly evolving political status. The area's union with Canada fostered a newfound closeness between the residents of Newfoundland and other Canadians and granted Newfoundland residents Canadian citizenship, with all of its rights and privileges.

Newfoundland had been governed since 1934 by a commission of six members, three from Newfoundland and three from Great Britain. However, Newfoundland's significant role in World War II as the site of American military forces did much to alter Canadians' image of the area. Even so, strong opposition to confederation was not quickly eliminated. In July, 1941, the Canadian government appointed its first high commissioner for Newfoundland, C. J. Burchell, an expert in maritime affairs and in admiralty and shipping law. Burchell carefully monitored the feelings of Newfoundland residents about confederation, which were generally negative. Despite these attitudes, in June, 1943, British prime minister Clement Attlee dispatched three members of the House of Commons to Newfoundland to explore local conditions and sentiments.

At the same time, Vincent Massey, Canada's high commissioner in London, was corresponding with Norman Robertson, undersecretary of state for external affairs in Ottawa. Robertson eventually wrote to Massey that economic pressures eventually would force Newfoundland to become part of the Canadian confederation, but the initiative for this union would have to come from Newfoundland itself. Robertson realized that British taxpayers did not want to pay for Newfoundland's budgetary deficits. Ottawa, however, was aware that Labrador was rich in iron ore and held out possibilities for much hydroelectric power, although the Canadian government feared that a new province could prove to be a social and political burden.

National Convention   On June 21, 1946, a National Convention was elected, and after considerable study by the nine committees elected to gather information, two delegations were appointed: one to visit London, another to visit Ottawa. A sticking point in the deliberations was the question of Great Britain's financial support of Newfoundland, for if Britain continued to provide these subsidies, the need for confederation would diminish. The delegation from the National Convention left for London on April 24, 1947, and a month later Viscount Addison told the House of Lords that Great Britain would continue to support a commission government in Newfoundland and the area would not become a Canadian province. Before holding another series of meetings on the issue, the Canadian government decided to let Newfoundland residents vote for confederation; if voters approved the union, the new province would be granted all the privileges of other provinces. The Ottawa meetings began on June 25, 1947, with ten subcommittees considering every aspect of confederation. Finally, on October 29, the Canadian government sent Newfoundland officials a *Proposed Arrangement for the Entry of Newfoundland into Confederation*, a document granting Newfoundland seven members in the House of Commons and six senators. The new province would have jurisdiction over its natural resources, and government employees there would receive Canadian civil service jobs.

Three months of heated debate followed the release of the *Proposed Arrangement*, with some nervousness about Newfoundland seeking to join the United States. Newfoundland political leader Joseph R. Smallwood proved an effective advocate for the cause of union. However, in March, 1948, he announced that confederation would be dependent upon the outcome of the referendum on the issue,

with voters deciding if they wanted confederation, the commission-type of government, or the long-standing "responsible government." "Responsible government" meant that the governing body of Newfoundland, which represented the British Commonwealth, was responsible to a local legislature that administered the area. The first referendum, held on June 3, attracted a huge voter turnout, with "responsible government" getting 69,230 votes, confederation receiving 63,110, and a commission of government garnering 21,944. A runoff election on July 22 yielded a final count of 78,323 votes for confederation and 71,334 for responsible government. The next day, Canadian prime minister William Lyon Mackenzie King announced that Ottawa would receive representatives from Newfoundland to hammer out the terms of union. The terms of confederation were signed on December 11, 1948, and Great Britain provided its royal assent to the union on March 23, 1949. A week later, Newfoundland became Canada's tenth province.

Impact   In 1967, writer St. John Chadwick reviewed Newfoundland's progress since becoming a province. He noted the welcome drop in the infant mortality rate of 103 per 1,000 in 1935 and the marked decline in school absences because children no longer lacked adequate clothing. Newfoundland's Fisheries Board had become a model for other provinces, and its financial system had stabilized. Most important, the province enjoyed a well-organized, properly recruited, and permanent staff of civil servants, and its population had grown from 350,000 in 1949 to more than 500,000 in 1967. Despite these benefits, some residents continued to oppose confederation. Chadwick quoted a Canadian senator's bittersweet remark that since Newfoundland became a province, "it is no longer the same. The old character has gone. The people have been Canadianized."

Frank Day

Further Reading

Chadwick, St. John. *Newfoundland: Island into Province.* New York: Cambridge University Press, 1967. Authoritative study of constitutional development in Newfoundland.

Eggleston, Wilfrid. *Newfoundland: The Road to Confederation.* Ottawa, Ont.: Crown Copyrights, n.d. A celebratory history of Newfoundland's struggle to become a province. Well illustrated.

Howe, Frederick W. *The Smallwood Era.* Toronto: McGraw-Hill Ryerson, 1985. Describes the influence of one of Newfoundland's most important founding fathers, Joseph R. Smallwood. Includes historic photographs.

Johnston, Wayne. *The Colony of Unrequited Dreams.* New York: Doubleday, 1999. Excellent novel about Smallwood and his role in Newfoundland history.

Neol, S. J. R. *Politics in Newfoundland.* Toronto: University of Toronto Press, 1971. Describes the area's government and politics, including the battle over confederation.

See also   Atlantic, Battle of the; Business and the economy in Canada; Canada and Great Britain; Canadian nationalism; Canadian participation in World War II; Canadian regionalism; Demographics of Canada; St. Laurent, Louis.

■ Newspapers

Newspaper readership ebbed and flowed throughout the 1940's as a result of the rising popularity and immediacy of alternative media, including radio and television. Though new technologies improved the quality and craft of newspapers, scandals and governmental investigations made consumers wary of the newspaper industry throughout the decade.

The 1940's was a transitional period for all forms of news media, but perhaps the most negative and enduring transition took place in the newspaper industry. Newspapers advanced technologically during this decade; the introduction of offset printing revolutionized the industry. However, the popularity of newspapers was negatively affected by television, which had been introduced during the 1930's; the first radio and television news broadcasts; twenty-four-hour news radio, introduced during the early part of the decade; and the ease and availability of radio. Nonetheless, newspapers did have success throughout this decade because television manufacturing and stations' syndication were unreliable; they were often canceled or limited until 1946.

Another change in this decade was the introduction of interpretative reporting. This quickly led to tabloids such as New York's *PM*, whose policy was to express liberal opinions disguised as news. Apparently Americans appreciated this new style of news reporting, as the first tabloid without advertising lasted until 1949. Some of the most popular newspapers of the decade were owned and operated by the same extended families, the Pattersons and Medills, members of whom owned the *New York Daily News*, the *Chicago Tribune*, and *Newsday*. Other popular newspapers of the decade also hailed from New York, including *The New York Times* and the *New York Herald Tribune*. Several New York daily newspapers reached their all-time circulation peaks during this decade; the *New York Daily News* circulated 2.4 million copies in 1947. The Patterson companies outsold their rivals through the end of the decade. Newspapers during the 1940's cost from two to five cents per copy.

Coverage of World War II   In 1941, the Office of Censorship, an emergency wartime office, banned exposing military plans, presidential trips abroad, intelligence operations, and new weapons, including the atomic bomb—even going as far as to write letters reprimanding Eleanor Roosevelt for publishing articles in newspapers detailing the weather during her husband's presidential trips. From 1942 to 1946, about one-fifth of all newsreel items were war related even in the face of continued and heavy military and government censorship. The Office of Censorship enacted its first voluntary censorship code, which underwent four revisions during the war years. Continuing its efforts to seize control of printed news, the government purchased prowar advertising space in small-town, weekly newspapers for the sale of bonds and notes; this control of newspapers continued six months after the war's end. Because American newsreels were such an effective means of conveying American interests, the government formed and bankrolled the United Newsreel Company, which culled pro-American story segments from the five major American newsreel organizations and sold them worldwide. The government also petitioned newspapers and other media to filter the news propagandistically and push their war agenda, which caused much distrust of newspapers during and after the war. These war-positive newspaper stories were converted to short film segments and played at the beginning of movies in cinemas nationwide.

In the spring of 1946, a survey showed that about 35 percent of Americans listed newspapers as their

New Yorkers eagerly reading newspaper reports of Germany's surrender in May, 1945. (Time & Life Pictures/Getty Images)

war writing, including Hanson W. Baldwin of *The New York Times*, Mark S. Watson of the *Baltimore Sun*, and Homer Bigart of the *New York Herald Tribune*. *Stars and Stripes*, a military daily newspaper, resumed publication during World War II, as it had during previous war periods, but unlike before, the military continued publication after the war effort had ended. Hundreds of weekly newspapers were forced to suspend business throughout the first half of the decade because production and distribution required too much labor to compete with a labor-intensive war. The difficulty of manufacturing newspapers continued after the war when supply, labor, and newsprint costs rose.

The African American Press   Encouraged by the establishment in February, 1940, of the National Negro Publishing Association and with the launching of the *Pittsburgh Courier*'s 1942 "Double V Campaign," black American news writers began pushing for victory in two pressing battles: against the Axis Powers in World War II and against the racial prejudices that tore apart the United States. Because the white press was not reporting issues pertinent to the black American community, black journalists brought much-needed attention to segregation within daily life as well as to the Jim Crow-style segregation rampant in the U.S. military. These journalists used an oft-repeated slogan: "The fight for the right to fight."

By the end of World War II, African American newspapers had a daily readership of more than two million. One significant accomplishment of black newspapers' antiracism campaigns was the part they played in helping desegregate professional sports; one of the reasons Jackie Robinson was signed to the Brooklyn Dodgers in 1947 was because of *Pittsburgh Courier* sports writer Wendell Smith's outspoken efforts. Other popular and influential African American newspapers included Baltimore's *Afro-American*, Norfolk's *Defender*, and the *Norfolk Journal and Guide*.

Beginning in 1942, multiple black newspapers came under review and attack by six U.S. governmental agencies—the U.S. Army, the U.S. Post Office, the Federal Bureau of Investigation, the Office

primary news source, while more than 60 percent listed radio. Sensing the agitation that news censorship might inspire, a group of college professors formed the Commission on Freedom of the Press as an attempt to guard the truthful broadcasting of the news from political, military, and economic influences. Also known as the Hutchins Commission, after one of its founders, Robert M. Hutchins, the group worked from 1942 to 1947 to establish a code of social responsibility by which newsworthy information would be available to all Americans.

Altogether, at least thirty-seven American news persons—both men and women—died in the war. Eleven of them were press-association correspondents, ten were representatives of individual newspapers, nine were magazine correspondents, four were photographers, two were syndicated writers, and one was a radio correspondent. Many newspaper writers were honored with Pulitzer Prizes for their

of Facts and Figures, the Office of War Information, and the Office of Censorship—for what they called "sedition," or unnecessarily inciting the African American population. They blamed the black press for lowering the already abysmal morale of the African American community, often calling their efforts communistic. In 1944, Harry S. Alpin, a writer for the National Negro Press Association and Atlanta's *Daily World*, became the first African American newspaper columnist permitted into White House conferences. In 1947, Louis Lautier, Washington bureau chief of the Negro Newspapers Publishers Association, became the first black American permitted in the Senate and House press galleries.

Newspaper Regulation In 1941, the *Los Angeles Times* was cited by the California Bar Association for publishing dangerous materials in a legal battle known as *Bridges vs. California*. The result was that newspapers could comment on court actions without fear of reprisal so long as the newspaper's action did not threaten the court's ability to function safely. Similar battles were fought by the *Miami Herald* in 1946 and the *Corpus Christi Caller-Times* in 1947. Newspapers strongly endorsed Republican candidates for office during this decade. One major concern in this decade was ownership of the news. Americans feared that if mass media conglomerates were owned by only a small number of owners, the news would be slanted according to individuals' political, social, and personal beliefs. Their fears seem founded, for by 1941, 30 percent of AM radio stations were owned and operated by newspapers. Even twenty-eight of the first sixty television licenses were applied for by newspapers.

As newspaper sales declined as the result of competition from new and more popular forms of media, their publishers quickly learned they could profit more quickly from spreading news via radio than through newspapers. Americans wary of mass media argued that permitting newspaper owners to purchase and operate radio and television stations would prevent a healthy mix of opinions, because one-owner conglomerates could lead to standardization of the news. In 1949, the fairness doctrine was established, giving broadcasters the sole responsibility for the fairness and objectivity of their newscasts and leaving it to the owners to decide how best to present opposing viewpoints fairly. Meanwhile, the government was also busy putting restrictions on

the number of news media outlets any one American could own nationally and city to city. These new regulations caused many Americans to distrust news outlets in general, which in turn encouraged bourgeoning community, local, and independent presses to spring up nationwide.

Famous Journalists Thousands of men and women writers flocked to print, radio, and television journalism throughout the decade, drawn by the exciting lifestyle of war correspondence. Among the most famous newspaper columnists of the time were Ernie Pyle, Bigart, and Marguerite Higgins. Pyle was sent by the Scripps-Howard newspaper chain to North Africa, Italy, and France to report from the front lines. He won a Pulitzer Prize in 1944 for such correspondence shortly before he was killed in 1945 by a sniper while in Ie Shima (also known as Iejima), an island near Okinawa, Japan. Americans liked him because he seemed to understand and convey the plight of ordinary soldiers. Moreover, he was always the first to endanger himself for the scoop.

Bigart won two Pulitzers while writing for the *New York Herald Tribune* and *The New York Times*. He was a member of "The Writing 69th," a group of wartime correspondents known for putting themselves in harm's way to gain eyewitness perspectives on World War II attacks while traveling with military units. Higgins wrote about the wartime experience first as a college correspondent with the *New York Tribune*, but upon initiating a private campaign to be considered an equal to the male news writers, she was eventually recognized as a foreign war correspondent, even receiving prestigious awards for her writing. She went on to write for a number of prestigious newspapers and magazines during the Korean War, where she was killed, and she was the first woman to win a Pulitzer Prize during the 1950's.

Impact Newspapers continued their reign of popularity through the 1960's. In 1950, General Douglas MacArthur imposed full censorship on American reporters concerning the bombings of Hiroshima and Nagasaki, much like he had done with Pearl Harbor a decade earlier. The Korean and Vietnam wars again highlighted the problematic and interconnected natures of racial and gender discrimination as well as the ethical dilemmas intrinsic to regulating and censoring the news. Although offset printing during the 1950's propelled newspapers into a new technological direction, the proliferation of the television throughout American households and the immediacy of radio broadcasts were key reasons for the decline of the newspaper industry.

Ami R. Blue

Further Reading

Davies, David Randall. *The Postwar Decline of American Newspapers, 1945-1965.* New York: Routledge, 2006. Discusses the impact of other media and war on the newspaper industry.

Emery, Edwin, and Michael Emery. *The Press in America: An Interpretive History of the Mass Media.* 5th ed. Englewood Cliffs, N.J.: Prentice-Hall, 1984. Comprehensive history of several American media, including radio, newspapers, and television.

Nord, David Paul. *Communities of Journalism: A History of American Newspapers and Their Readers.* Champaign: University of Illinois Press, 2001. Respected source discusses the role that newspapers play in community formation.

Reporting World War II: Part Two—American Journalism, 1944-1946. New York: Library of America, 1995. An specific history of American wartime journalism; the second of a two-volume set, the first of which covers the earlier part of the decade.

Tebbel, John. *The Compact History of the American Newspaper.* Rev. ed. New York: Hawthorn Books, 1969. Divided into thematic rather than chronological sections, provides a nuanced history of newspapers' social and political ramifications.

See also Advertising in the United States; Censorship in the United States; Civil rights and liberties; Murrow, Edward R.; Racial discrimination; Radio in the United States; *Stars and Stripes*; Television; Wartime propaganda in the United States; World War II.

■ Nimitz, Chester W.

Identification U.S. commander in chief of the Pacific Fleet, 1941-1945; chief of naval operations, 1945-1947
Born February 24, 1885; Fredericksburg, Texas
Died February 20, 1966; Yerba Buena Island, San Francisco, California

Nimitz commanded more than two million personnel, five thousand ships, and twenty thousand planes during World War II. He was the Navy's leading authority on submarines and is credited with winning the war in the Pacific theater. Nimitz also held the position of chief of naval operations, and he was the last surviving fleet admiral in the Navy.

Chester W. Nimitz left high school and entered the United States Naval Academy in 1901. He excelled in mathematics at the academy and graduated seventh in his class of 114. After two years of sea duty, Nimitz was commissioned ensign. He later was court-martialed for grounding the USS *Decatur* in the Philippines, for which he received a letter of reprimand. During World War I, Nimitz served as aide and chief of staff to the commander of the submarine force of the Atlantic Fleet. In 1918, in addition to his regular duties, Nimitz was made a senior member of the Board of Submarine Design. In the years following World War I, he continued to advance in rank. In 1922, Nimitz attended the Naval War College, where he studied logistics of a possible Pacific Ocean war.

World War II After working for three years as assistant chief of the Bureau of Navigation, Nimitz was promoted to rear admiral in 1938. In June, 1939, he was promoted to chief of the Bureau of Navigation, holding that position until the United States entered World War II after the Japanese attack on Pearl Harbor on December 7, 1941. Soon after the attack, Nimitz was promoted to admiral and given command of the Pacific Fleet. He had the difficult task of stopping the Japanese advance while recovering from significant losses suffered during Pearl Harbor. In March, 1942, those in command of the Allied forces gave the United States responsibility for the Pacific theater. The U.S. Joint Chiefs of Staff later divided the theater into three areas: the Pacific Ocean areas, the Southwest Pacific area, and the Southeast Pacific area. Nimitz was named commander in chief of the Pacific Ocean areas, giving him control over all Allied air, land, and sea operations in that region, while he still commanded the Pacific Fleet.

As soon as possible, Nimitz went on the offensive against the Japanese. In early 1942, he had Admiral William F. Halsey's carrier group begin raiding islands under Japanese control. The Battle of Midway in June, 1942, was a turning point in the war. Nimitz relied heavily on the newly formed joint military intelligence agency. Knowing that the Japanese were listening to their radio communications, the Navy sent false messages claiming that two carriers were not near Midway. This false intelligence led the Japanese navy to make several mistakes, including delaying the positioning of its submarines. Nimitz was able to move two carrier groups into the area undetected. His use of intelligence and war tactics led to the first decisive naval victory against the Japanese. Nimitz continued on the offensive, winning battles at Coral Sea and the Solomon Islands.

On December 15, 1944, Nimitz was promoted to the newly created top rank of fleet admiral (five stars). Troops under his command captured several islands in the Philippines and continued defeating Japanese forces. The culmination of his long-range strategy was two amphibious attacks on Iwo Jima and Okinawa. On September 2, 1945, Nimitz signed for the United States when Japan officially surrendered.

Post-World War II On December 15, 1945, Admiral Nimitz became chief of naval operations. He served a single two-year term, during which he scaled down the Navy into a smaller peacetime force. While doing so, Nimitz also needed to make sure that the Navy was organized and prepared to handle issues of national security. After retiring at the end of 1947, he moved to San Francisco. Nimitz still remained on active duty, however, because the rank of fleet admiral is a lifelong appointment. Nimitz continued to hold positions within the Navy, including serving as honorary president of the Naval Historical Foundation. He suffered a stroke, with complications from pneumonia, in late 1965. He died a few months later in February, 1966.

Fleet Admiral Chester W. Nimitz signing documents formalizing Japan's surrender that ended World War II aboard the USS Missouri in Tokyo Bay on September 2, 1945. Standing behind him, from left to right, are General Douglas MacArthur, Admiral William F. Halsey, and Rear Admiral Forrest P. Sherman. (For another view of this occasion, see the title page of this volume.) (Getty Images)

Impact During the early years of World War II, the Japanese navy seemed unbeatable. Admiral Nimitz, however, was able to defeat the enemy using spies, counterintelligence, and superior tactics. His victory at Midway was one of the major turning points of the war. It improved the morale of the entire country. Nimitz also worked as a goodwill ambassador for the United Nations in the years following the war, and he worked to restore relations with Japan. He turned down several high-salaried jobs and business opportunities in the years before his death, not wanting to do anything that might tarnish the image of the U.S. Navy.

Several places have been named after the admiral since his death, including the main library at the United States Naval Academy, the USS *Nimitz* aircraft carrier, a glacier, and several highways, parks, and schools. The Nimitz Foundation was created in 1970, which funds the National Museum of the Pacific War.

Jennifer L. Campbell

Further Reading

Driskill, Frank A., and Dede W. Casad. *Chester W. Nimitz.* Waco, Tex.: Eakin Press, 1983. A biography of Nimitz that includes details of his childhood in Texas through his rise to the top ranks of the Navy.

Hornfischer, James. *The Last Stand of the Tin Can Sailors.* New York: Bantam Books, 2004. Tells the story of the Battle off Samar, part of the effort to liberate the Philippines in October, 1944. A popular history book that reads as easily as a novel.

Hoyt, Edwin. *How They Won the War in the Pacific: Nimitz and His Admirals.* Guilford, Conn.: Lyons Press, 2000. A detailed work about Nimitz and his subordinates. Focuses on how Nimitz was the right man to lead the Navy and win the war in the Pacific.

Moore, Jeffrey. *Spies for Nimitz: Joint Military Intelligence in the Pacific War.* Annapolis, Md.: Naval Institute Press, 2004. A history of the first joint military intelligence agency and how its two thousand operatives supplied Admiral Nimitz with the intelligence he needed to win the war in the Pacific. Based on internal documents and interviews with personnel.

Potter, E. B. *Nimitz.* Annapolis, Md.: Naval Institute Press, 2008. A long, detailed, and inclusive biography of Nimitz, from his poor childhood in Texas through retirement from the Navy and work as a U.N. ambassador.

See also Department of Defense, U.S.; Halsey, William F. "Bull"; Midway, Battle of; Navy, U.S.; Pearl Harbor attack; Submarine warfare; V-E Day and V-J Day; World War II.

■ Nobel Prizes

Identification Annual prizes awarded for significant contributions in the areas of science, economics, literature, and the promotion of peace

The Nobel Prizes are arguably the most prestigious awards in the areas of science, economics, literature, and the promotion of peace. Awards have been made annually since 1901, with the exception of the periods during the world wars, so no awards were made during the first years of the 1940's.

Alfred Nobel, a Swedish chemist and the inventor of dynamite, in 1895 included a provision in his will that his fortune would be used to award prizes for outstanding work in chemistry, literature, physiology or medicine, physics, and the promotion of peace. In the years following Nobel's death in 1896, the Royal Swedish Academy, through the Nobel Academy, established the criteria for the annual awards. The first Nobel Prizes were presented in 1901, with the Peace Prize awarded in Oslo, Norway, then part of Sweden, and the other prizes to be awarded in Stockholm, Sweden. An award in economics was established in 1969. The monetary value of the awards has increased significantly since their origin in 1901.

In the three decades following the establishment of the Nobel Prizes, most of the awards were given to individuals living or working in Europe, reflecting contemporary sites of scientific or political achievement. The Nobel Peace Price was an exception to this European dominance and was awarded to eight Americans in the decades before World War II. The most notable of these American recipients was President Theodore Roosevelt, who received the Nobel Peace Prize in 1906 for his role in ending the Russo-Japanese War the year before, and President Woodrow Wilson, who was given the prize in 1919 for his role in the formation of the League of Nations, although the United States never joined this organization.

War Years, 1940-1945   During the 1920's and 1930's, Americans began to make significant advances in scientific training and research, particularly in the area of medicine, largely because of a marked improvement in the quality of medical schools and hospitals. Though Alexis Carrel had been awarded the Nobel Prize in Physiology or Medicine in 1912, in part for his research at the Rockefeller Institute, he had been born and educated in Europe. Other Americans who were awarded prizes were Theodore William Richards, who received the prize in chemistry in 1914, and Robert Andrews Millikan, who was awarded the prize in physics in 1923. It was during the 1930's, however, that the importance of scientific research in the United States, particularly in the area of medicine, caught the attention of the Nobel committees.

The onset of World War II in 1939 resulted in the suspension of Nobel Prizes during the years from 1940 through 1942. The invasion of Norway by Germany in 1940 also forced the Norwegian committee to flee to neutral Sweden for the duration of the war, and the Peace Prize was not awarded again until 1944.

Presentation of the awards resumed in 1943, and that year the American biochemist Edward Adelbert Doisy received the Nobel Prize in Physiology or Medicine, which he shared with Danish chemist Henrik Dam, for his synthesis of Vitamin K, a necessary molecule for proper blood clotting. This was the first time since 1934 that an American had received this award. Doisy was the first of an increasing number of American Nobel Prize winners who were born or educated in the United States. The 1943 award winner in physics, Otto Stern, was then at the Carnegie Institute of Technology in Pittsburgh, and he represented another type of American winner: a European expatriate who fled the Nazis and immigrated to the United States.

The 1944 Nobel Prize in Physiology or Medicine was shared by two American scientists, Joseph Erlanger and Herbert Spencer Gasser, for their development of methods used to study neuron functions. The Nobel Prize in Physics also went to an American scientist, Isidor Isaac Rabi, for his work on the properties of atomic nuclei. Rabi had been born in Galicia, then part of the Austrian Empire, but he moved to the United States when he was a child and had been educated there. The 1945 Nobel Peace Prize likewise went to an American: Cordell Hull,

former secretary of state, for his work in the establishment of the United Nations. Like Wilson in the previous generation, Hull had recognized the importance of the United States working with its allies to maintain peace.

Postwar Years, 1946-1949   Americans dominated the scientific awards in 1946. Percy Williams Bridgman received the Nobel Prize in Physics for his work in the field of high-pressure physics, applied in the area of electrical conductivity. Three Americans shared the Nobel Prize in Chemistry: James Batcheller Sumner for his work demonstrating the protein makeup of enzymes and their crystallization, and John Howard Northrop and Wendell Meredith Stanley for the purification and crystallization of enzymes and viral proteins. Hermann Joseph Muller completed the American sweep that year, winning the award in physiology or medicine for his demonstration of the role that X-irradiation could play in gene mutation. Muller had begun his scientific career working with Thomas Hunt Morgan, another American Nobel laureate.

Two Americans also shared the Nobel Peace Prize that year: Emily Greene Balch, who founded the Women's International League for Peace and Freedom, and John R. Mott, who established the World Alliance of the Young Men's Christian Association. Both organizations were honored for their work in the promotion of world peace.

Two of the three Nobel Prizes in Physiology or Medicine for 1947 went to the American husband and wife team of Carl F. Cori and Gerty Cori for their work on carbohydrate metabolism (the Cori cycle), the fourth time in five years that Americans had received this honor. The Coris were born in Prague, then part of Austria-Hungary, but like many European scientists they came to the United States during the 1930's. The Nobel Peace Prize that year was awarded to two American organizations: the American Friends Service Council, for its overseas work, primarily in Africa and China, and the Friends Service Committee for its aid to victims of war. Both are Quaker organizations.

No Americans received Nobel awards in 1948. In 1949, William Francis Giauque was given the Nobel Prize in Chemistry for his work in low-temperature chemistry, in which he studied chemical thermodynamics under conditions which approached absolute zero. The Nobel Prize in Literature was also won

Nobel Prizes Awarded in the 1940's

(Prizes were not awarded from 1940 to 1942)

Year	Physics	Chemistry	Physiology or Medicine	Literature	Peace
1943	Otto Stern	Georg von Hevesy	Henrik Dam and Edward Adelbert Doisy	Not awarded	Not awarded
1944	Isidor Isaac Rabi	Otto Hahn	Joseph Erlanger and Herbert Spencer Gasser	Johannes V. Jensen	International Committee of the Red Cross
1945	Wolfgang Pauli	Artturi Ilmari Virtanen	Alexander Fleming, Ernst Boris Chain, and Howard Walter Florey	Gabriela Mistral	Cordell Hull
1946	Percy Williams Bridgman	James Batcheller Sumner, John Howard Northrop, and Wendell Meredith Stanley	Hermann Joseph Muller	Hermann Hesse	Emily Greene Balch and John R. Mott
1947	Edward Victor Appleton	Robert Robinson	Carl F. Cori, Gerty Cori, and Bernardo Alberto Houssay	André Gide	Friends Service Council and American Friends Service Committee
1948	Patrick M. S. Blackett	Arne Tiselius	Paul Hermann Müller	T. S. Eliot	Not awarded
1949	Hideki Yukawa	William Francis Giauque	Walter Rudolf Hess, António Egas Moniz	William Faulkner	John Boyd Orr

by an American, the first time since Pearl S. Buck received the award in 1938. William Faulkner was granted the award for his development of the American short story and novel genres, including *The Sound and the Fury* (1929), *As I Lay Dying* (1930), and *Absalom, Absalom!* (1936). Much of his writing was set in his home state of Mississippi.

Impact The 1940's proved a turning point in the Nobel committees' recognition of the increasingly significant role of the United States in diverse areas of science, in the field of literature, and as a catalyst in the pursuit of peace. The training ground for scientific training and research had undergone a significant shift, moving from centers in nineteenth century Germany, Austria-Hungary, and France to the United States. The reasons for this change are complex. The quality of American medical schools and hospitals significantly improved in the twentieth century, which can be attributed to funding for medical research by the Rockefeller Institute and to improvements in educational facilities, such as Johns Hopkins and Harvard Universities. In addition, political developments in Europe during the 1920's and 1930's caused prominent scientists, the most famous of whom was Albert Einstein, to immigrate to the United States. As a result of these changes, the number of American Nobel laureates began to increase during the 1940's, and American recipients would continue to be the dominant award winners into the twenty-first century.

Richard Adler

Further Reading

Feldman, Burton. *The Nobel Prize.* New York: Arcade, 2001. Describes the history of the prizes and the politics behind the decisions of the Nobel committees.

Friedman, Robert. *The Politics of Excellence: Behind the Nobel Prize in Science.* New York: Henry Holt, 2001. Using archives available from the Nobel Foundation, Friedman explores the cultural history and politics underlying many of the Nobel Prize decisions.

Hargittai, Istvan. *The Road to Stockholm: Nobel Prizes, Science and Scientists.* New York: Oxford University Press, 2003. A history of the establishment of the prizes, as well as the process by which awards are made. Highlights the backgrounds of the scientists who have been awarded the prizes.

Magill, Frank, ed. *The Nobel Prize Winners, Physiology or Medicine.* Pasadena, Calif.: Salem Press, 1991. Biographies of Nobel laureates. Included for each individual is a summary of his or her scientific work, as well as summaries of Nobel lectures and critical reception. Includes brief bibliographies.

Worek, Michael. *Nobel: A Century of Winners.* Westport, Conn.: Firefly Books, 2008. Brief biographies of the most prominent Nobel laureates, as well as entertaining trivia about the awards.

See also   Antibiotics; Big bang theory; Bunche, Ralph; Carbon dating; Eliot, T. S.; Faulkner, William; Fermi, Enrico; Fulbright fellowship program; Hull, Cordell; Marshall, George C.; Science and technology.

■ North African campaign

The Event   Allied military campaign against Axis forces operating in North Africa
Dates   June 10, 1940, to May 16, 1943
Places   Algeria, Egypt, Libya, Morocco, and Tunisia

The first joint American-British invasion of Axis-held territory occurred in November, 1942, and resulted in the first significant victory for American troops against German and Italian forces.

Beginning in the summer of 1940, German and Italian forces and opposing British Commonwealth armies had waged a back-and-forth campaign in northern Africa, from Tunisia to Egypt. Soviet pleas to open a second front against German-led forces and British requests for support against Field Marshall Erwin Rommel's Afrika Korps persuaded President Franklin D. Roosevelt to send American forces to northern Africa. In Operation Torch, which took place from November 8 through 11, 1942, American and British troops invaded Vichy France-held Morocco and Algeria, overcoming French resistance. The Allied objective was to trap and destroy Axis forces between the invasion forces and Lieutenant-General Bernard Law Montgomery's Eighth Army advancing from the east. The German-Italian high command responded to the invasion and the subsequent switch of French forces to the Allied side by initiating a large military buildup in Tunisia. By the end of 1942, Allied and Axis forces were roughly equivalent in strength, and their fight stalemated in the mountainous western Tunisian borders. Rommel was fighting, in a holding action, against the British Eighth Army in Libya.

On January 18, 1943, Axis forces in western Tunisia began an offensive against French-held positions and made significant gains. Meanwhile, Rommel

German field marshal Erwin Rommel (left) in Libya. (National Archives)

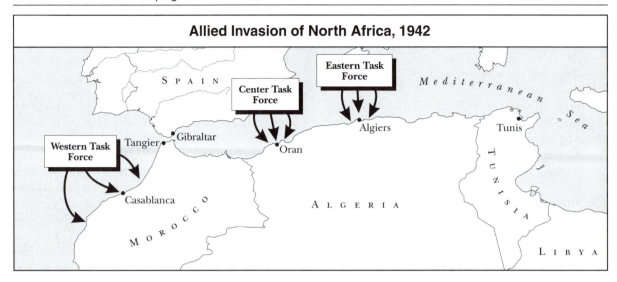

Allied Invasion of North Africa, 1942

was preparing strong defensive positions at the Mareth Line in southeast Tunisia, as the Afrika Korps was withdrawing from Libya. After reaching the Mareth Line, he transferred some units to western Tunisia in order to exploit weaknesses in the Allied defenses. On February 19, Rommel attacked American forces in the western mountains in what become known as the Battle of Kasserine Pass. Inexperienced American forces were routed, and Rommel's troops and armor advanced toward Algeria. However, stiffening American resistance, a surge in Allied reinforcements in the area, and pressure on the Mareth Line by the Eighth Army forced Rommel to end the offensive and withdraw his forces to strengthen the eastern defenses. By February 25, American troops had regained the pass at Kasserine.

In March, the tide of battle began to favor the Allies. Rommel was relieved of command, and Axis offensives in the west and east failed after initial success. The Axis supply line to Sicily was choked by Allied planes and ships; conversely, reinforcements were strengthening Allied forces. The Mareth Line was abandoned in late March, and Allied pressure in northwest Tunisia in early April forced the German-Italian armies to shrink their defensive perimeter to the northeast corner of Tunisia around the ports of Bizerte and Tunis. The final assault by the Allies came on May 6. The next day, the Americans had captured Bizerte, and the British had conquered Tunis. On May 13, 1943, the North African campaign came to an end, as approximately 250,000 Axis troops surrendered.

Impact The initial poor performance of American troops and poor communication among the different Allied commanders prompted improvements in tactics and command structure. These changes resulted in a more effective and efficient Allied military in the European theater. Although the Allies suffered greater casualties than the Axis forces, approximately seventy-five thousand to sixty thousand, the Axis losses in captured men and aircraft destroyed or captured, approximately nine hundred, crippled German-Italian ambitions in the Mediterranean. The capture of the Tunisian ports paved the way to the invasion of Sicily two months later.

Paul J. Chara, Jr.

Further Reading

Atkinson, Rick. *An Army at Dawn: The War in North Africa, 1942-1943.* New York: Holt Paperbacks, 2007.

Hart, Basil Henry Liddell. *The Rommel Papers.* Cambridge, Mass.: Da Capo Press, 1982.

Kitchen, Martin. *Rommel's War: The North African Campaign, 1941-3.* Stroud: Tempus, 2008.

See also Army, U.S.; Bradley, Omar N.; Casualties of World War II; Eisenhower, Dwight D.; Italian campaign; Landing craft, amphibious; Navy, U.S.; Patton, George S.; World War II.

■ North Atlantic Treaty Organization

Identification   Joint military and political organization designed to provide Western Europe with the means to defend itself against Soviet aggression

Date   Founded on April 4, 1949

Also known as   NATO

Because immediate postwar Europe was in a state of chaos and, in many places, almost complete physical destruction, there was a need for a military alliance to ensure the sovereignty of areas that could be menaced by Soviet aggression.

Given the long and complex history of the North Atlantic Treaty Organization (NATO) between its founding in 1949 and the celebration of its sixtieth anniversary in 2009, it is important to consider the wider context of European events during and after World War II that influenced those who signed the treaty creating the organization on April 4, 1949.

British prime minister Winston Churchill included a prophetic statement in a speech he delivered at Harvard University in 1943, predicting that there might soon be a very different need for unity against a potential enemy within the Allies' own ranks. Two years later, bolstered by the advance of victorious Soviet forces deep into eastern Germany and Poland, Soviet leader Joseph Stalin demanded that the Allies honor occupation terms for postwar Germany initially set at the Yalta Conference of February, 1945. These terms included the cession of eastern Poland to the Soviets and recognition of a French zone of occupation in Germany only if it was carved out of areas already occupied by the United States and Britain.

At this early date it was impossible to predict what sort of mediation or military assistance might be provided by the emergent United Nations (UN) should a serious problem result from Stalin's hardline policies. The inexperienced UN Security Council had barely been able to neutralize Soviet territorial claims in Turkey and Iran, countries that had declared war on Germany near the end of World War II. The council could not be expected to force Russia's withdrawal from zones it had "conquered" at Germany's expense. Thus, the question of a postwar military vacuum in Europe became a significant issue between 1945 and 1949.

The presumed military threat of the Soviet Union was compounded dramatically in June, 1948, when Stalin cut off the Western Allies' access to Berlin. A crisis was averted only by an American-orchestrated emergency air delivery of personnel and supplies to the city. A year later, the threat of a potential confrontation increased when the Soviets successfully tested their first atomic bomb.

Awareness of the need to defend Western Europe from Soviet military maneuvers generated serious concerns about the financial condition of this region. Before the creation of NATO, it had become evident that the United States would have to assume a key role in resurrecting the European economy. To this end, the Marshall Plan, a massive injection of American funds to help Europe rebuild its economy, was implemented between 1948 and 1952. Given the disastrous destruction brought on by the war, no one could predict how Europe would respond to the task of reconstruction. It was hoped that the countries that received Marshall Plan aid would be able to avoid complete economic collapse, thereby heading off political chaos that could result in a weakening of democracy or, in the worst case scenario, a communist takeover.

North Atlantic Treaty

The North Atlantic Treaty, signed in 1949, identifies the common goals of the twelve signatory nations as follows:

The Parties to this Treaty reaffirm their faith in the purposes and principles of the Charter of the United Nations and their desire to live in peace with all peoples and all governments.

They are determined to safeguard the freedom, common heritage and civilisation of their peoples, founded on the principles of democracy, individual liberty and the rule of law. They seek to promote stability and well-being in the North Atlantic area.

They are resolved to unite their efforts for collective defence and for the preservation of peace and security. They therefore agree to this North Atlantic Treaty.

The Treaty and Its Goals An important first step toward the creation of NATO was taken in March, 1948. Before then, British foreign secretary Ernest Bevin had been helping to combat postwar communist insurgents in Greece, but he increasingly was counting on the United States to take over this task, a request that President Harry S. Truman rejected. At Bevin's suggestion, five Western European countries—Belgium, France, Luxembourg, the Netherlands, and the United Kingdom—signed the Treaty of Brussels on March 17. This agreement stipulated that if any of the five nations was attacked, the other signatories would defend the victim of aggression. Shortly thereafter, the United States suggested that the treaty be expanded to provide a more effective shield for mutual defense. As a result, the North Atlantic Treaty was signed in Washington, D.C., on April 4, 1949. Twelve countries agreed to the terms of this treaty: the five signatories to the Treaty of Brussels, plus the United States, Canada, Iceland, Norway, Denmark, Italy, and Portugal.

In addition to the treaty's joint military defense provisions, an important aim of the pact was to encourage "the further development of peaceful and friendly international relations by strengthening their [the twelve signatories'] free institutions and bringing about a better understanding of the principles upon which these institutions are founded . . ." Such a goal begged the question of a possible political mandate to accompany the new military alliance. The treaty provided for the creation of the North Atlantic Council, a political decision-making body consisting of representatives of the twelve member nations. However, some critics have maintained that the council's work ran counter to the paramount challenge of achieving a unified military defense.

An early indication of the preeminent role of the United States in NATO could be seen in the provisions of articles 10 and 13 of the treaty. Article 10 stipulated that if an alliance member invited another European country to adhere to the treaty, an "instrument of accession" must be submitted to the United States government, and Americans would subsequently inform the other NATO members. A similar procedure was to apply to any member's decision to leave NATO, an option that was not available until the end of a twenty-year period. However, Charles de Gaulle of France ignored this provision and removed his nation from NATO's military command, basing this decision on the fact that France possessed its own atomic deterrent force.

During the early years of NATO's operations, most Western European members accepted what critics described as an "American predominance" in the organization, especially in military matters. Their acceptance can be attributed to the continuing fear of Soviet aggression and to an awareness that without the assistance of the United States, Western Europe would be unable to defend itself against the Soviet Union.

There were several essential changes to NATO's operations during the first half of the 1950's. The admission of Greece and Turkey as NATO members in 1952 introduced a different perspective to the idea of an "Atlantic community." These two nations were inveterate enemies and, unlike the other signatories, these countries' borders were on Soviet-protected territory. Another key development came in 1955, when Russia replaced bilateral defense agreements with its East European satellites with a unified Warsaw Pact. The effect of this move was to increase concerns on the part of some NATO members that defense of Western Europe could be attained only if the United States increased its commitment to NATO nations in order to match rising Soviet support for Warsaw Pact countries.

Impact At the time of NATO's founding in 1949, it seemed evident that a unified military front would be necessary to meet the threat of further Soviet advances into Western Europe. As one of the two surviving world powers, the United States inevitably would play a dominant role in the organization. As is the case with most major treaties, the changing order of strategic priorities, including the collapse of the Soviet Union four decades later, as well as NATO's involvement in the Serbian-Kosovo crisis and the Afghanistan War, would generate questions about the continuing relevance of the 1949 treaty.

Byron Cannon

Further Reading

Beaufre, General Andre. *NATO and Europe.* New York: Alfred A. Knopf, 1966. Translation of the firsthand account of a French officer who participated in the founding of NATO. Beaufre offers his view of the effectiveness of NATO's structures and policies up to the 1960's.

Heiss, Mary Ann, and S. Victor Papacosma, eds. *NATO and the Warsaw Pact.* Kent, Ohio: Kent State

University Press, 2008. Collection of articles examining a variety of thematic issues as they relate to NATO's policies in response to the Warsaw Pact, as well as internal operations of the Warsaw Pact itself.

Maloney, Sean M. *Securing Command of the Sea: NATO Naval Planning, 1948-1954.* Annapolis, Md.: Naval Institute Press, 1995. Traces the naval command structures and strategies envisaged by NATO members for three key zones: the North Sea, the Atlantic Ocean, and the Mediterranean Sea.

Milloy, John C. *The North Atlantic Treaty Organization, 1948-1957: Community or Alliance?* Montreal: McGill-Queen's University Press, 2006. Examines major issues relating to the internal governance of NATO and its relationship to the Organization for European Economic Cooperation, forerunner to the European Union.

See also   Acheson, Dean; Berlin blockade and airlift; Cold War; Foreign policy of Canada; Foreign policy of the United States; Marshall Plan; Paris Peace Conference of 1946; Vandenberg, Arthur Hendrick; Yalta Conference.

■ Norton County meteorite

The Event   Fall of a large and unusual meteorite in the Midwest
Date   February 18, 1948
Places   Norton County, Kansas; Furnas County, Nebraska

The Norton County meteorite has been classified as an aubrite, an extremely rare type of stone meteorite. The fall of the meteorite provided scientists with important material for research.

At about four in the afternoon on February 18, 1948, a brilliant fireball streaked across the clear skies above Colorado, Kansas, and Nebraska. Hundreds of people observed the event and heard what sounded like loud explosions followed by a roaring sound similar to that of a jet engine. A dark smoke trail clearly marked the flight path of the meteorite. Over the next few months, hundreds of small fragments were collected from a large geographical area straddling the Kansas-Nebraska border.

The largest fragment of the Norton County meteorite was recovered from a wheat field on July 3,

1948. Two ranchers found the one-ton stone in a nearly circular hole six feet across and six feet deep. A recovery team led by Dr. Lincoln La Paz carefully removed it and transported it to the Institute of Meteoritics at the University of New Mexico in Albuquerque, where it is currently on display.

Impact   The Norton County meteorite is one of the largest witnessed falls on record. The meteorite's unusual chemistry and mineralogy strongly suggests that it came from a parent body that formed relatively close to the Sun.

Paul P. Sipiera

Further Reading

Grady, Monica M. *Catalogue of Meteorites.* 5th ed. New York: Cambridge University Press, 2000.

LeMaire, T. R. *Stones from the Stars: The Unsolved Mysteries of Meteorites.* Englewood Cliffs, N.J.: Prentice-Hall, 1980.

Norton, O. Richard. *The Cambridge Encyclopedia of Meteorites.* New York: Cambridge University Press, 2002.

See also   Astronomy; Rocketry; Science and technology.

■ Nuclear reactors

Definition   Devices used to produce controlled nuclear fission, in which a chain reaction occurring in a mass of radioactive material produces new radioactive isotopes and a sustained output of heat and radiation capable of functioning as a power supply

Because the first nuclear chain reaction was produced during World War II, the first application of nuclear reactors in the United States was the production of materials used in the construction of atomic bombs. Following the end of the war, however, research into civil and commercial usage of nuclear reactors was quickly activated and made rapid progress.

Although the phenomenon of radioactivity had been familiar since the turn of the century and Italian American physicist Enrico Fermi had begun experiments bombarding various elements with neutrons during the 1930's, the possibility of sustaining and controlling a nuclear chain reaction emerged from experiments conducted in 1938 by Otto Hahn and Fritz Strassman, which also enhanced the possibility of making atom bombs. The first nuclear reactor was constructed by Fermi and Leo Szilard under the auspices of the University of Chicago Metallurgical Laboratory, commissioned by the Office of Scientific Research and Development. It was assembled from graphite blocks enclosing uranium oxide briquettes and produced the first self-sustaining nuclear chain reaction on December 2, 1942. The reactor was known as Chicago Pile-1 before being rebuilt at Argonne National Laboratory and renamed CP-2.

The Manhattan Project The Manhattan Project, established by Franklin D. Roosevelt in December, 1942, immediately took over the Fermi-Szilard reactor and commissioned the building of several more to manufacture fissionable material for bombs. Fermi and Szilard filed for a patent on December 19, 1944, but the application was delayed for ten years by security issues. Fermi relocated to the Manhattan Project's nuclear facility in Oak Ridge, Tennessee, where he and his colleagues developed the X-10

Graphite Reactor (also known as the Clinton Pile) to produce plutonium-239.

The X-10 continued work on a much larger scale at the Hanford Site on the Columbia River in Washington State, where a series of further reactors were built, including the B reactor, activated in September, 1944, which produced the plutonium used in the Nagasaki bomb (August 9, 1945); the D reactor, activated in December, 1944; and the F reactor, activated in February, 1945.

The Production of Nuclear Power As soon as the war was over, the building of nuclear power stations became an urgent priority for the extrapolation of the Manhattan Project research. In September, 1946, the General Electric Company took over the Hanford Works under the auspices of the Atomic Energy Commission established by Harry S. Truman, whose goal was to promote and control the development of nuclear energy in the United States.

The X-10 was redirected to the production of medical isotopes and isotopes for industrial and agricultural usage. The majority of the Hanford reactors were then redirected to the production of electricity, initially on an experimental basis; they continued to operate for more than twenty years. Although EBR-1, constructed in Arco, Idaho, as the world's first nuclear power plant, did not become operational until 1951, it was the work done in the last few years of the 1940's that established fundamental designs for the building of such plants.

Science Fiction and Nuclear Power The notion of a stabilized atomic power source had been used in fiction long before the first nuclear chain reaction was produced and the notion had become a staple of pulp science fiction by 1940. It was given insistent support by John W. Campbell, Jr., the editor of *Astounding Science Fiction*, in which the most realistic accounts of hypothetical nuclear reactors appeared, including Robert A. Heinlein's "Blowups Happen" (1940), about the psychological and social stresses generated by the establishment of an urban nuclear power plant; Lester del Rey's "Nerves" (1942), in which an accidental spill in a nuclear power station threatens to turn into a major disaster; and Clifford D. Simak's "Lobby" (1944), which anticipates the political problems that might be involved in the introduction of atomic power to

Oak Ridge National Laboratory around 1944. The first nuclear reactor was housed in the large white building. (Courtesy, Martin Marietta)

the United States. The accuracy of these anticipations was, however, overshadowed by a deluge of alarmist fantasies about atomic weaponry and melodramas of radiation-induced mutation, whose legacy haunted the nuclear industry from its inception.

Impact The early nuclear reactors of the 1940's were overtaken by a new generation of so-called breeder reactors. It proved easier to control reactions in which the fission products were washed out with water; when such a system used a pressurized water reactor, the heat generated by the system became adequate to generate electricity of a commercial scale, bringing the promise of the early technology to fulfillment. Commercial reactors made rapid progress during the early 1950's, assisted by the demand for plutonium from the weapons industry.

Brian Stableford

Further Reading

Bernardini, Carlo, and Luisa Bonolis, eds. *Enrico Fermi: His Work and Legacy*. New York: Springer, 2004. An essay collection in which the most relevant items are Carlo Salvetti's "The Birth of Nuclear Energy: Fermi's Pile" and Augusto Gandini's "From the Chicago Pile-1 to the Next-Generation Reactors."

Hughes, Jeff. *The Manhattan Project: Big Science and the Atom Bomb*. New York: Columbia University Press, 2002. A synoptic overview that complements and provides a context for Kelly's more intimate account (below) of the early development of reactors.

Kelly, Cynthia C., ed. *The Manhattan Project: The Birth of the Atomic Bomb in the Words of Its Creators, Eyewitnesses, and Historians*. New York: Black Dog & Leventhal, 2007. Wide-ranging collection of documents; those most relevant to the present topic are the accounts by the people who built and operated the piles at Oak Ridge and Hanford.

Lewis, E. E. *Fundamentals of Nuclear Reactor Physics*. Boston: Elsevier/Academic Press, 2008. A comprehensive account of the physics underlying the practical applications of nuclear fission and the practicalities of its technical application.

Murray, Raymond L. *Nuclear Energy: An Introduction to the Concepts, Systems, and Applications of Nuclear Processes*. 6th ed. Boston: Elsevier/Butterworth-Heinemann, 2009. Standard textbook, first issued in 1993, more easily accessible to the lay reader than Lewis but inevitably less detailed.

See also Atomic bomb; Atomic Energy Commission; Einstein, Albert; Fermi, Enrico; Hanford Nuclear Reservation; Hiroshima and Nagasaki bombings; Manhattan Project; Plutonium discovery; Science and technology.

■ Nuremberg Trials

The Event Series of trials of former Nazi leaders after World War II

Dates November 21, 1945, to October 1, 1946 (International Military Tribunal); December 9, 1946, to April 13, 1949 (American military tribunals)

Place Nuremberg, Bavaria, Germany

The Nuremberg Trials prosecuted political, military, and economic leaders of Germany after World War II. The International Military Tribunal, consisting of the United States, Britain, France, and the Soviet Union, prosecuted high-ranking Nazi officers charged with being war criminals. The later American military tribunals tried lesser-ranked, alleged criminals in the American occupation zone.

As early as 1943, the leaders of the United States, Britain, and the Soviet Union declared their intention to punish German leaders after World War II. The United States was the strongest supporter for a full trial. In April, 1945, U.S. secretary of war Henry L. Stimson, and the War Department in general, created a plan to prosecute the major German war criminals. After the unconditional surrender of Germany, the Allied Powers, which now included France, signed the London Agreement, establishing the ground rules for a major trial. Then, in October, 1945, the Allied Powers established a combined International Military Tribunal to prosecute the surviving, captured German leaders at Nuremberg. Francis Biddle was chosen as the principal and John Parker as the alternate American judges. The chief prosecutor for the United States was Robert H. Jackson, assisted by Telford Taylor and Richard Sonnenfeldt.

Trial of the Major War Criminals In November, 1945, the International Military Tribunal began proceedings against twenty-two leaders of Nazi Germany at the Palace of Justice in Nuremberg. The tribunal charged each of the German leaders with at

German defendants at the Nuremberg Trials included (first row, left to right) Hermann Göring, Rudolf Hess, Joachim von Ribbentrop, Wilhelm Keitel, (second row) Karl Dönitz, Erich Räder, Baldur von Schirach, and Fritz Sauckel. Hess was Adolf Hitler's chief deputy until 1941, when he was captured by the British while on an unauthorized peace mission to Great Britain. Given a life sentence at Nuremberg, he died in 1987 in Berlin's Spandau Prison, where he was the last surviving Nazi prisoner. (NARA)

least two out of four counts, including the conspiracy to wage crimes against peace, the waging of crimes against peace, war crimes, and crimes against humanity. The first two counts included the planning, preparation, initiation, and waging of wars of aggression. This included the wars against Poland, Britain, and France in 1939; Denmark, Norway, Belgium, the Netherlands, and Luxembourg in 1940; and Yugoslavia, Greece, the Soviet Union, and the United States in 1941. The third count of war crimes included murder, ill-treatment, or deportation to slave labor of civilians; murder or ill-treatment of prisoners of war or persons on the seas; killing of hostages; plunder of public or private property; and wanton destruction of cities, towns, and villages. The

last count of crimes against humanity included murder, extermination, enslavement, deportation, and other inhumane acts committed against civilians before and during the war, in addition to persecutions on political, racial, or religious grounds.

The defendants included Hermann Göring, Rudolf Hess, Joachim von Ribbentrop, Wilhelm Keitel, Ernst Kaltenbrunner, Alfred Rosenberg, Hans Michael Frank, Wilhelm Frick, Julius Streicher, Walther Funk, Hjalmar Schacht, Karl Dönitz, Erich Raeder, Baldur von Schirach, Fritz Sauckel, Alfred Jodl, Martin Bormann, Franz von Papen, Arthur Seyss-Inquart, Albert Speer, Konstantin von Neurath, and Hans Fritzsche. Bormann was tried in absentia. The prosecution also indicted six organizations, including the Nazi Party, the Schutzstaffel (SS), the Sicherheitsdienst (SD), the Gestapo, the Sturmabteilung (SA), and the high command of the German armed forces.

During the following ten months, the International Military Tribunal listened to the prosecution present evidence and to the defendants and their counsel. On October 1, 1946, the judges announced their verdicts and sentences concerning the defendants. Eight of the defendants were found guilty of count one, twelve of count two, sixteen of count three, and sixteen of count four. Twelve of the defendants were sentenced to hang. However, just ten were executed by hanging because Bormann was still missing and Göring committed suicide the night before the execution. Three defendants, including Hess, Funk, and Raeder, received life sentences in prison. Schirach and Speer got twenty-year sentences, Neurath a fifteen-year sentence, and Dönitz a ten-year sentence. Schacht, Von Papen, and Fritzsche were acquitted of all charges. The death sentences were carried out on October 16, 1946.

American Military Tribunals at Nuremberg On December 25, 1945, the Allied Powers agreed to Allied Control Council law number 10. The agreement allowed the Allied Powers that occupied Germany to establish military tribunals for the prosecution of less conspicuous German war criminals in their assigned occupation zones. The United States held its tribunals at the Palace of Justice at Nuremberg from December, 1946, to April, 1949. The Americans organized the hearings into twelve different trials, charging and prosecuting a total of 185 Germans. These cases included charges against medical doctors that conducted medical experiments on inmates in concentrations camps; SS officers that administered concentration camps and slave-labor programs; high-ranking military officers that committed offenses against prisoners of war; SS units responsible for mass murder; members of the Foreign Office and

Nuremberg Trials: Statement of the Offense

The Nuremberg court, in its Statement of the Offense in 1945, issued the following "count" against the war criminals on trial:

All the defendants, with divers other persons, during a period of years preceding 8 May 1945, participated as leaders, organizers, instigators, or accomplices in the formulation or execution of a common plan or conspiracy to commit, or which involved the commission of, Crimes against Peace, War Crimes, and Crimes against Humanity, as defined in the Charter of this Tribunal, and, in accordance with the provisions of the Charter, are individually responsible for their own acts and for all acts committed by any persons in the execution of such plan or conspiracy.

The common plan or conspiracy embraced the commission of Crimes against Peace, in that the defendants planned, prepared, initiated, and waged wars of aggression, which were also wars in violation of international treaties, agreements, or assurances. In the development and course of the common plan or conspiracy it came to embrace the commission of War Crimes, in that it contemplated, and the defendants determined upon and carried out, ruthless wars against countries and populations, in violation of the rules and customs of war, including as typical and systematic means by which the wars were prosecuted, murder, ill-treatment, deportation for slave labor and for other purposes of civilian populations of occupied territories, murder and ill-treatment of prisoners of war and of persons on the high seas, the taking and killing of hostages, the plunder of public and private property, the indiscriminate destruction of cities, towns, and villages, and devastation not justified by military necessity.

The common plan or conspiracy contemplated and came to embrace as typical and systematic means, and the defendants determined upon and committed, Crimes against Humanity, both within Germany and within occupied territories, including murder, extermination, enslavement, deportation, and other inhumane acts committed against civilian populations before and during the war, and persecutions on political, racial, or religious grounds, in execution of the plan for preparing and prosecuting aggressive or illegal wars, many of such acts and persecutions being violations of the domestic laws of the countries where perpetrated.

other ministries who assisted in creating Hitler's new order; and industrialists who contributed to the suffering of Jews through the confiscation of property, forced labor, and extermination. In the end, the trials led to the execution of twenty-four defendants, twenty life sentences, eighty-seven shorter prison terms, the release of nineteen individuals for various reasons, and thirty-five acquittals.

Impact At the Nuremberg Trials, the Allied Powers overcame the desire to indiscriminately execute prisoners at the end of the war, instead subjecting them to the rule of law. The Nuremberg Trials had its flaws, but the tribunals had a great influence on the development of international law and served as the model for future war-crime trials.

William Young

Further Reading

Davenport, John. *The Nuremberg Trials.* San Diego, Calif.: Lucent Books, 2006. An introduction for youth to the trials and their aftermath.

Davidson, Eugene. *The Trial of the Germans: An Account of the Defendants Before the International Military Tribunal at Nuremberg.* New York: Macmillian, 1966. Deals with some of the philosophical issues concerning war trials in general and Nuremberg specifically. Discusses the precedent set by the Allies and how these trials served models for similar ones in the future.

Mettraux, Guénaël, ed. *Perspectives on the Nuremberg Trial.* New York: Oxford University Press, 2008. A collection of essays that looks at the implications of the Nuremberg trials. Essays cover philosophical and political issues represented by the trial. Includes historical perspectives on the role of international law.

Washington, Ellis. *The Nuremberg Trials: Last Tragedy of the Holocaust.* Lanham: University Press of America, 2008. A critique of the Nuremberg trials and of the Allied Powers' postwar methodology for bringing war criminals to justice.

See also Biddle, Francis; Convention on the Prevention and Punishment of the Crime of Genocide; Germany, occupation of; Hitler, Adolf; Potsdam Conference; Stimson, Henry L.; Universal Declaration of Human Rights; War crimes and atrocities; World War II.

■ Nylon stockings

Definition Women's hosiery made with a synthetic polymide that had a resilience and elasticity that revolutionized the marketability and production of women's accessories

Nylon became the preferred textile yarn in women's hosiery during the 1940's because it was flexible and could be easily stretched in the knitting process to take on the shapes of women's legs and feet. Nylon was a new product developed in the United States, and as a synthetic it was not subject to easy deterioration either in the manufacturing process or during consumer use.

Traditionally, women's hosiery, particularly full-fashioned stockings, were machine knit from silk, cotton, and wool textile yarns. During the early 1920's, the French began marketing an artificial silk yarn, but it was not until the late 1930's that synthetic yarns became widely available, largely because of the efforts of Du Pont de Nemours & Co. Nylon was almost immediately preferred as a textile yarn because it was cheaper to produce, required no import tariffs, and had greater elasticity when compared to its predecessors, rayon and silk.

Du Pont de Nemours & Co., founded in 1802, established a three-part research agenda that featured new product development. Under the direction of Lammot du Pont, from 1926 to 1940 the company expanded its organic chemical department and reaped discoveries in the manufacture of dyes, rubber, cellophane, and nylon.

Nylon yarn was created in three phases beginning with polymer heat-resistance tests, followed by modifications to the initial compound to enhance tensile strength, and finally by the development of the desired nylon polymer that was melted and stretched into hosiery shapes at du Pont's Seaford, Delaware, nylon production plant.

Charles M. Stine Charles M. Stine was the lead research chemist at du Pont who was primarily responsible for the creation of nylon. He shifted the direction of chemical research from du Pont's hallmark work in explosives to the development of new commercial products, and he was assisted by the Harvard University-trained chemist Wallace Carothers. As a du Pont vice president, Stine opened the company's Seaford, Delaware, plant on October 27, 1938. Because of the demand for and the quality of du Pont's nylon yarn, the firm manufactured nearly eight million pounds of nylon within the first year, and by 1943, du Pont's product dominated the hosiery market.

Impact Nylon, as a malleable yarn, was easily shaped by steam into the body parts needed for hosiery. It did not wrinkle or snag in the knitting process. It resisted decomposition and was inflammable. Socially, nylon, which also came to be used in toothbrushes, sutures, and fishing tackle, improved the everyday lives of many Americans. Women benefited from nylon hosiery, which was a long-lived product, and from a better quality of dresses made from combinations of nylon, rayon, and natural fibers. The development of nylon also reduced American dependency on silk, which was largely imported from Japan. When used for fashions, nylon created less expensive and more durable products that also fulfilled the du Pont company's mission to improve the lives of citizens with its innovative and practical products.

Beverly Schneller

Further Reading

Bolton, E. K. "Development of Nylon." *Industrial and Engineering Chemistry* 34, no. 1 (January, 1942): 53-58. Concentrates on the development of the nylon chemical compound, with special reference to its application in hosiery.

Grew, Henry S., Jr. "Industrial Applications." *Industrial and Engineering Chemistry* 44, no. 9 (September, 1952): 2140-2144. Discusses the history of synthetics and highlights the importance of nylon.

Hoff, G. P. "Nylon as a Textile Fiber." *Industrial and Engineering Chemistry* 32, no. 12 (December, 1940): 1560-1564. Focuses on the use of nylon in full-fashion hosiery.

Hubach, F. F. "Knit Goods." *Industrial and Engineering Chemistry* 44, no. 9 (September, 1952): 2149-2151. Concentrates on nylon as part of the hydrophobic group of synthetics and addresses the value of nylon in everyday life.

See also Fads; Fashions and clothing; Pinup girls; Wartime rationing; Women's roles and rights in the United States.

O

■ Office of Price Administration

Identification Domestic affairs agency within the executive branch of the U.S. government.
Also known as OPA
Date Established on August 28, 1941

The OPA determined prices and rationing of goods and services during World War II. Its power to regulate the market produced much political controversy and affected the outcome of congressional elections.

In late August, 1941, four months before the United States entered World War II, President Franklin D. Roosevelt established, by Executive Order 8875, the Office of Price Administration (OPA). It was seen as an outgrowth of World War I stabilization committees. It became an independent agency in January, 1942, under the Emergency Price Control Act, having the authority to determine ceiling prices of goods (excepting agricultural produce) and to ration scarce commodities. The controversial policies and practices of the first administrator, Leon Henderson, provoked much opposition, and he was blamed for Democratic losses in the congressional elections of 1942. Roosevelt replaced him in December, 1942, with Prentiss Marsh Brown, who served only briefly before returning to private law practice, and then Chester A. Bowles, Connecticut's state director of price administration. Most of the OPA's functions were transferred to the newly created Office of Temporary Controls by President Harry S. Truman's Executive Order 9809 of December 12, 1946. On May 29, 1947, the OPA was abolished, with its remaining functions transferred to the Department of Labor and other government agencies.

Impact The regulation of the free market was a major controversial policy in American politics, although similar methods had been applied in World War I. Conservative critics of Roosevelt and Truman objected strongly, and Republicans used the OPA as a propaganda tool in the congressional elections of 1942 and 1946. The OPA proved largely effective in fighting inflation and making sure that scarce materials were reallocated from civilian to military uses.

Frederick B. Chary

Further Reading
Koistinen, Paul A. C. *Arsenal of World War II: The Political Economy of American Warfare, 1940-1945.* Lawrence: University Press of Kansas, 2004.
Manning, Thomas G. *The Office of Price Administration: A World War II Agency of Control.* New York: Holt, 1960.

See also Agriculture in the United States; Business and the economy in the United States; Gross national product of the United States; Income and wages; Inflation; Keynesian economics; War Production Board; Wartime industries; Wartime rationing; *Yakus v. United States.*

■ Office of Strategic Services

Identification U.S. intelligence organization
Date Established on June 13, 1942
Also known as OSS

The Office of Strategic Services (OSS) conducted numerous sabotage operations behind enemy lines in coordination with local resistance groups. The OSS trained a number of agents who later served in the Central Intelligence Agency and provided a structural framework for the establishment of the CIA.

On July 11, 1941, President Franklin D. Roosevelt created the Office of the Coordinator of Information to handle intelligence matters. He placed Congressional Medal of Honor winner William J. "Wild Bill" Donovan at the head of the organization. Once the United States entered World War II, Roosevelt was persuaded to bring the Office of the Coordinator of Information under the authority of the Joint Chiefs of Staff. He placed Donovan in charge of forming the new intelligence organization that was named the Office of Strategic Services. The OSS combined foreign intelligence gathering and special operations. It was under the tutelage of the British, who split these different missions between two organizations known as the Secret Intelligence Service (commonly called MI6) and Special Operations Executive. The OSS was the first Allied organization to combine the two into one office.

The OSS was divided into sections such as Secret Intelligence, Morale Operations, Research and Analysis, Research and Development, Special Operations, and counterespionage, known as X-2. The Secret Intelligence section was responsible for foreign intelligence collection and operated predominantly in Europe. Morale Operations was responsible for creating propaganda. The Research and Analysis section was designed to evaluate the information gathered by the intelligence section. The Research and Design section was responsible for creating or adapting weapons systems. It also created a number of explosive devices and other weapons for use in sabotage and special operations.

The Special Operations section was the covert-operations wing of the OSS. This section carried out numerous acts of sabotage and worked alongside local resistance groups to disrupt the enemy. X-2 was responsible for counterintelligence, mainly combating foreign intelligence-gathering efforts through information operations. OSS training was often conducted under British instructors, particularly at Camp X on Lake Ontario in Canada. There were also a number of training areas in Maryland and Virginia. The training was meant to be as realistic as possible, with practice operations conducted against domestic targets whose guards were not aware that the operations were training exercises.

Operations   The OSS operated in both the Pacific and European theaters during World War II. In Europe, the OSS aided local resistance groups by supplying weapons and, at times, personnel. It conducted a series of operations during the Italian

---

Creation of the Office of Strategic Services

On July 11, 1941, President Franklin D. Roosevelt announced the creation of the Office of Strategic Services. This excerpt of his memorandum outlines the duties and rights of the organization's Coordinator of Information.

By virtue of the authority vested in me as President of the United States and as Commander in Chief of the Army and Navy of the United States, it is ordered as follows:

There is hereby established the position of Coordinator of Information, with authority to collect and analyze all information and data, which may bear upon national security, to correlate such information and data available to the president and to such departments and officials of the government as the president may determine; and to carry out, when requested by the president, such supplementary activities as may facilitate the securing of information important for national security not now available to the government.

---

campaign. One of the more ambitious, Operation McGregor, was an OSS attempt to get the Italian navy to surrender the Italian fleet to Allied forces. The mission turned out to be a waste because the Italian naval command had already agreed to surrender to the British. Throughout the Italian campaign, OSS agents operated behind German lines to disrupt their communications and supplies. In France, OSS operations were generally used to disrupt the German supply lines and communications through sabotage and coordination with the French resistance forces.

The OSS also stationed an intelligence-gathering unit in Switzerland under the command of Allen Dulles. This unit worked to gather vital intelligence on Nazi Germany and established contact with the German resistance. Instead of sending agents into Germany, Dulles used personal contacts in an effort to gain information.

OSS operations in the Pacific were limited in scope largely because General Douglas MacArthur resented other intelligence organizations operating in his area. The OSS aided the Nationalist troops in China in the effort to fight the Japanese. It also helped train and arm other resistance groups, including the communists under Mao Zedong and the resistance movement in Vietnam. The OSS recruited and provided training focused on sabotage techniques. By the end of World War II, it had carried out many effective operations and gathered vital intelligence for the Allied war effort. In September, 1945, the OSS was effectively disbanded.

Impact The OSS played an instrumental role in World War II. The unit provided substantial aid to resistance fighters and gathered some timely intelligence in Europe. In the Pacific, the OSS was able to establish effective communications with the Chinese resistance movement. After the war, the structure of the OSS was used by President Harry S. Truman as an example to help establish the CIA through the National Security Act of 1947. Many of the original members of the CIA were former OSS officers who learned their trade during World War II.

Michael W. Cheek

Further Reading

Fenn, Charles. *At the Dragon's Gate: With the OSS in the Far East.* Annapolis, Md.: Naval Institute Press, 2004. The story of Charles Fenn, a member of the OSS's Morale Operations section in the Pacific theater.

Ford, Kirk, Jr. *OSS and the Yugoslav Resistance, 1943-1945.* College Station: Texas A&M Press, 1992. Discusses the OSS mission to Yugoslavia and OSS aid to the Partisan forces under Tito.

Lucas, Peter. *The OSS in World War II Albania: Covert Operations and Collaboration with Communist Partisans.* Jefferson, N.C.: McFarland, 2007. Examination of the OSS mission to Albania in which the OSS aided and supported the communist guerillas led by Enver Hoxha.

O'Donnell, Patrick K. *Operatives, Spies, and Saboteurs: The Unknown Story of the Men and Women of World War II's OSS.* New York: Free Press, 2004. Provides a good overview of OSS operations in Europe and is based largely on interviews conducted with former members of the OSS.

Schwab, Gerald. *OSS Agents in Hitler's Heartland: Destination Innsbruck.* Westport, Conn.: Praeger, 1996. Discusses an OSS operation in which three OSS agents infiltrated German territory; based on OSS records and interviews with participants.

Yu, Maochun. *OSS in China: Prelude to Cold War.* New Haven, Conn.: Yale University Press, 1996. Examines the OSS mission in China and argues that the neglect of China by the administration allowed

the OSS to make U.S. foreign policy in the Chinese theater.

See also Bentley, Elizabeth; Bunche, Ralph; Central Intelligence Agency; China-Burma-India theater; D Day; Wartime sabotage; World War II.

■ Office of War Mobilization

Identification Federal agency charged with supervising all war agencies and coordinating economic planning and industrial production during World War II

Date Established on May 27, 1943

Beginning in 1943, the Office of War Mobilization coordinated a uniform program to refocus the American economy on wartime needs. The OWM directed government agencies, including the War Production Board, to make maximum use of natural, industrial, and nonmilitary personnel resources for the war effort.

In May 1943, the Office of War Mobilization (OWM) took control of all domestic mobilization efforts, which included oversight of other government agencies, industrial production, rationing programs, and military procurement. President Franklin D. Roosevelt appointed James Francis Byrnes, a former senator and Supreme Court justice, to lead the agency. Under his leadership, the OWM coordinated overlapping programs, bolstered military production, recalibrated the economy, and improved information sharing on production needs between military and civilian leaders. In 1944, Roosevelt changed the name and scope of the agency to plan for the postwar reconversion process.

Impact The OWM represented a centralized approach to supervising the wartime activities of numerous federal agencies, managing industrial production, and coordinating civilian programs. It was an instrumental agency in the conversion and then reconversion of the American economy during World War II.

Aaron D. Purcell

Further Reading

Dickenson, Matthew J. *Bitter Harvest: FDR, Presidential Power, and the Growth of the Presidential Branch.* New York: Cambridge University Press, 1997.

Kennedy, David M. *Freedom from Fear: The American*

People in Depression and War, 1929-1945. New York: Oxford University Press, 1999.

Somers, Herman Miles. *Presidential Agency: The OWMR, the Office of War Mobilization and Reconversion.* Cambridge, Mass.: Harvard University Press, 1950.

See also Byrnes, James; Dim-out of 1945; Economic wartime regulations; War Production Board; Wartime industries; Wartime rationing; World War II mobilization.

■ Ogdensburg Agreement of 1940

The Treaty Diplomatic accord between the United States and Canada
Date Signed on August 17, 1940
Place Ogdensburg, New York

U.S. president Franklin D. Roosevelt and Canadian prime minister William Lyon Mackenzie King created this agreement for two reasons. The accord defined a cooperative defense strategy for the two countries at a time when Canada was involved militarily in World War II and the United States recognized the possibility of its own eventual involvement. Also, because the negotiation was carried out by King, it represented an early instance of Canadian diplomatic autonomy.

By setting up a Permanent Joint Board on Defense that enabled the United States and Canada to collaborate with each other, the two nations moved closer to common defense planning against an external enemy. The countries had been peaceful neighbors for eighty years; however, their individual military establishments had not kept pace with each other. As historian Jon Latimer pointed out, the U.S. Department of War had a plan for battle against Canada as late as the 1920's, even though such an event would have been highly unlikely at the time. The Ogdensburg Agreement made sure that the two militaries had a coordinated strategy.

King and Roosevelt had different personalities: Roosevelt was a wily improviser; King was an introverted mystic. They did not achieve the rapport that existed between Roosevelt and Great Britain's Winston Churchill, but their working relationship produced some beneficial results. Canada had relinquished the shield of British protection and had to

U.S. president Franklin D. Roosevelt (left) with Canadian prime minister William Lyon Mackenzie King (center) and U.S. secretary of war Henry L. Stimson in Ogdensburg, New York, two days after Roosevelt and King signed the Ogdensburg Agreement. (AP/Wide World Photos)

negotiate with the United States on its own, while the United States illustrated its willingness to permit other nations to have a role in hemispheric defense. The agreement also helped establish U.S.-Canadian cooperation in both World War II and the Cold War.

When the agreement was signed on August 17, 1940, France had fallen to Germany and Britain was suffering under German bombardment. A possibility arose that an exiled British government might move to Canada. Under the Lend-Lease program, American troops were to take over British bases in Newfoundland, which had not yet become a Canadian province. Newfoundland was of particular concern to the United States given its strategic North Atlantic location, which was crucial for refueling aircraft. The amicable military relationship between the United States and Canada helped all parties involved to be comfortable with a U.S. presence in Newfoundland.

Impact   The Ogdensburg Agreement was partially a result of Canada's new-found nationalistic attitude toward foreign policy apart from the influence of England. The United States respected Canada as an equal partner in diplomacy. The agreement helped establish a lengthy and healthy political relationship between the two countries.

Nicholas Birns

Further Reading

Gibson, Frederick W., and Jonathan G. Rossie. *The Road to Ogdensburg: The Queen's/St. Lawrence Conferences on Canadian-American Affairs, 1935-1941.* East Lansing: Michigan State University Press, 1993.

Perras, Galen Roger. *Franklin Roosevelt and the Origins of the Canadian-American Security Alliance, 1933-1945: Necessary but Not Necessary Enough.* Westport, Conn.: Greenwood Press, 1998.

Thompson, John H., and Stephen J. Randall. *Canada and the United States: Ambivalent Allies.* Athens: University of Georgia Press, 2002.

See also   Air pollution; Canada and Great Britain; Canadian nationalism; King, William Lyon Mackenzie; Newfoundland; Plutonium discovery; Roosevelt, Franklin D.

■ Okinawa, Battle of

The Event   Last major military campaign of World War II

Date   April 1-July 2, 1945

Place   Ryukyu Islands, Japan

The largest invasion armada in history met the largest suicide assault in history during the final major battle of World War II. Fierce Japanese resistance in complex fortifications and furious kamikaze attacks failed to stop the Allies, and the desperate Japanese tactics played a role in the decision to drop atomic bombs on Japan.

After the victory at Iwo Jima, the Allies decided to invade the island of Okinawa, which would then be used as the main base for the final assault on the Japanese main islands. The Japanese knew an invasion of Okinawa was coming and hoped to inflict such grievous losses on the Allies that they would settle for a negotiated peace rather than attempt an invasion of the Japanese homeland. To combat American superiority in men and material, the Japanese devised a twofold strategy: *Jikyusen*, a defensive war of attrition fought from an intricate complex of strong fortifications, and *Kikusi*, massive, coordinated suicide attacks, primarily by airplanes.

American troops landed, largely unopposed, near the midpoint of Okinawa on April 1, 1945. The Marines headed east, bisecting the island, and north; the Army headed south. For the first several days, the Americans encountered minimal resistance. The relative calm was broken on April 6, when the Japanese launched the largest suicide assault in history, comprising hundreds of planes and remnants of the Japanese navy that included the largest battleship in the world, the *Yamato*. The Japanese plan to destroy the American invasion fleet failed—the *Yamato* was sunk by planes before it reached Okinawa—but ten American ships were sunk in the two-day battle. Japan was to launch nine more *Kikusi* during the Okinawa campaign.

On April 8, American troops met their first significant ground resistance, as the Marines engaged 2,000 Japanese soldiers dug in on Mount Yaetake on the Motobo Peninsula and Army forces encountered the bulk of Japanese troops entrenched in the outer defenses of a maze of interconnected fortifications known as the Shuri-line. American operations were successful in northern Okinawa as Mount Yaetake was conquered on April 18, and the island of Ie Shima (where noted war correspondent Ernie Pyle died on April 18), a few miles west of Motobo Peninsula, fell a few days later. In southern Okinawa, however, the U.S. offensive was stopped.

Breaking the Shuri-line   From April 8 until early May, a stalemate developed along the Shuri-line defenses. Throughout the month of April, American infantry tried to penetrate the Japanese defenses, with minimal success. On May 3, the Japanese changed strategy and launched a ground attack coordinated with the largest Japanese artillery bombardment of the war and a *Kikusi*—a decision that was to haunt the Japanese commander, Lieutenant General Mitsuru Ushijima. The attack was a colossal failure, and the loss of several thousand troops, numerous artillery pieces, and irreplaceable ammunition weakened the Shuri-line defenses. U.S. Army infantry, reinforced with Marines from northern Okinawa, countered with an offensive of their own, and by mid-May the flanks of the Shuri-line were beginning to crumble. Ushijima began withdrawing his troops during torrential May rains that turned the battlefield into a sea of mud and corpses, for a last stand in the southernmost region of Okinawa. On May 29, Shuri castle, the cornerstone of Japanese defenses, was captured by U.S. Marines, and the Shuri-line was broken.

By the middle of June, the last of the Japanese defenses were disintegrating. Several thousand Japanese naval troops were annihilated on Oroku Peninsula, and Ushijima's army was being divided into isolated pockets of resistance. The Americans declared victory on June 21, but fighting over the next several days resulted in approximately 9,000 more Japanese soldiers being killed. Officially, the Okinawa campaign ended on July 2.

Impact The Japanese exacted a high toll for the Allied victory. American ground casualties were nearly 50,000 men, of whom approximately 12,500 were killed. The American Navy incurred around 10,000 casualties, half of whom died, and lost 36 ships, with another 368 damaged. The naval losses were the highest losses for one campaign in American history. The price Japan paid was steep: an estimated 100,000 dead, approximately 10,000 troops taken prisoner, 16 ships sunk, and the loss of at least 3,000 planes. Okinawans suffered deeply: Thousands of them were conscripted into Japanese forces, and it is estimated that somewhere between 40,000 and 150,000 civilian Okinawans died during the campaign, out of a population of about 450,000.

Memories of Iwo Jima, combined with the death of Franklin

D. Roosevelt early in the Okinawa campaign, seemed to diminish the importance of events on Okinawa on the American home front: It was the sands of Iwo Jima, not the mud of Okinawa, that captivated the American public. In the minds of the American military, however, the high price paid to take the island was influential in the decision to use atomic weapons against Japan. The Japanese hoped that a bloody, prolonged war of attrition, combined with waves of suicide assaults, would convince the Allies to proffer favorable peace terms. Instead, the Japanese strategy prompted the Allies to un-

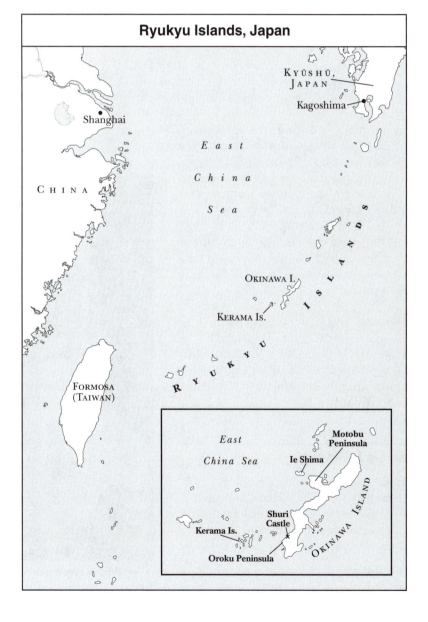

leash a terrifying weapon that ultimately shortened the war by forcing the unconditional surrender of Japan.

Paul J. Chara, Jr.

Further Reading

Appleman, Roy E., James M. Burns, Russell A. Gugelar, and John Stevens. *Okinawa: The Last Battle.* Washington, D.C.: Center for Military History, United States Army, 1948. Comprehensive overview of the Okinawa campaign presented by Army historians.

Reilly, Robin L. *Kamikazes, Corsairs, and Picket Ships: Okinawa, 1945.* Drexel Hill, Pa.: Casemate, 2008. A richly illustrated description of Allied tactics to stave off kamikaze attacks.

Sledge, Eugene B. *With the Old Breed: At Peleliu and Okinawa.* Annapolis, Md.: Naval Institute Press, 1966. A stunning portrait of the battle for Okinawa provided by a former Marine in this highly acclaimed memoir.

Sloan, Bill. *The Ultimate Battle: Okinawa 1945—The Last Epic Struggle of World War II.* New York: Simon & Schuster, 2007. Eyewitness accounts abound in this masterful retelling of the Okinawa campaign.

Yahara, Hiromichi. *The Battle for Okinawa.* New York: John Wiley & Sons, 1995. One of the chief architects of Japanese defenses on Okinawa provides a Japanese perspective on the battle for the island.

See also Aircraft carriers; Army, U.S.; Atomic bomb; Casualties of World War II; *History of the United States Naval Operations in World War II*; Kamikaze attacks; Landing craft, amphibious; Marines, U.S.; Navy, U.S.; World War II.

■ *Oklahoma!*

Identification Broadway musical
Creators Music by Richard Rodgers (1902-1979); book and lyrics by Oscar Hammerstein II (1895-1960)
Date Premiered on March 31, 1943

The first collaboration between composer Richard Rodgers and lyricist Oscar Hammerstein II,

Oklahoma! broke with many of the traditions of Broadway musicals by seamlessly integrating the show's plot, music, and dance into a cohesive whole. The formula proved a success, as the musical ran for 2,212 performances, making it the longest-running musical up to its time.

Oklahoma! is a romantic musical about a cowboy, Curly McClain, and a farm girl, Laurey Williams, in turn-of-the-twentieth-century Oklahoma Territory. This story of a bygone era appealed to the sentimental American public. Its original cast featured Alfred Drake as Curly, Joan Roberts as Laurey, John Da Silva as Jud, Betty Garde as Aunt Eller, Celeste Holm as Ado Annie, Lee Dixon as Will Parker, Ralph Riggs as Andrew Carnes, and Joseph Buloff as Ali Hakim.

The musical was the creation of Richard Rodgers and Oscar Hammerstein II, who brought something new to musicals. Before *Oklahoma!*, the creation of musicals usually began with the composition of original musical selections, to which words were adapted and stories were added. In contrast, Rodgers and

Alfred Drake performing as Curly in the original Broadway production of Oklahoma! (Time & Life Pictures/Getty Images)

Hammerstein began *Oklahoma!* with text—which Hammerstein adapted from the play *Green Grow the Lilacs* (1931) by Oklahoma's Cherokee writer Lynn Riggs. By starting with the text, Rodgers and Hammerstein were able to create a work with a greater sense of musical-dramatic cohesion than was typical of most Broadway musicals. Other innovations included opening the show with an empty stage, instead of the traditional choral number; the use of songs to advance the story, and a willingness to allow characters to die.

They hired ballet choreographer Agnes de Mille to further their aesthetic and dramatic goals. De Mille had no prior experience in musical theater but was known to be talented in using dance as a mode of story telling. Stage-directed by Rouben Mamoulian, *Oklahoma!* opened at Broadway's St. James Theater in New York City on March 31, 1943. The following year, Rodgers and Hammerstein were awarded a Pulitzer Prize for their musical.

Impact   Rodgers and Hammerstein's dramatic and compositional approach in *Oklahoma!* radically altered the path of American musical theater. *Oklahoma!* also initiated a long-standing collaboration between two of the musical genre's greatest artists. In addition, the Decca Records recording of *Oklahoma!* inspired the tradition of creating original-cast recordings of musicals.

Michael Hix

Further Reading

Green, Stanley. *The Rodgers and Hammerstein Story.* Rev. ed. New York: Da Capo Press, 1980.

Kenric, John. *Musical Theater: A History.* New York: Continuum, 2008.

Mordden, Ethan. *Beautiful Mornin': The Broadway Musical in the 1940's.* New York: Oxford University Press, 1999.

Wilk, Max. *OK! The Story of "Oklahoma!": A Celebration of America's Most Beloved Musicals.* New York: Grove Press, 1993.

See also   Broadway musicals; Music: Popular; Rodgers, Richard, and Oscar Hammerstein II; *South Pacific*; Theater in the United States.

■ Olympic Games of 1948

The Event   Only Olympic Games of the 1940's
Date   July 29-August 14, 1948
Place   London, England

Because of cancellations caused by World War II, the 1948 Games were the first Olympiad held in twelve years. They brought together many nations to engage in friendly competition in what had been one of the recent war's most ravaged cities. Although nations such as Germany and Japan were banned from the Games because of their aggressive roles in the war, the Games were successful enough to be regarded as an important symbolic return to peace.

Between 1936 and 1948, the quadrennial Olympic Games that had long symbolized freedom, peace, and world harmony for centuries were cancelled twice because of the disruptions of World War II, which began

Harrison Dillard (center) on the victory stand after winning the 100-meter dash at London. American teammate H. N. Ewell (right) took the silver medal. (AP/Wide World Photos)

in East Asia with Japan's invasion of China in mid-1937 and in Europe two years later with Germany's invasion of Poland. Although many nations that would eventually become involved in the war did not enter the conflict until 1940 or later, the unstable conditions prevailing in Europe and East Asia prompted the cancellation of the 1940 Olympic Games.

Many ironies were involved in the selections of Olympic venues during this period. In 1936, the last city to host the Olympic Games before World War II began was Berlin—the capital of Nazi Germany. The 1940 Games were scheduled for Tokyo, the capital of Japan—which not only started the war in Asia but which would also bring the United States into the war by attacking Pearl Harbor in Hawaii at the end of 1941. The 1944 Games were scheduled for London, which at that time was being heavily bombarded by German planes and rockets. After the war ended in 1945, the 1944 London games were, in effect, moved

to 1948. By then, London was rebuilding, and the city's Olympic Games were an important symbol of its postwar recovery.

Inauspicious Conditions Fifty-nine nations sent athletes to the London Games, including fourteen that had never before participated in the Olympics. Some of these first-time participants were former colonies that had won their independence from European empires after World War II. One such newly independent nation was India, which, appropriately, won its first Olympic gold medal by beating its former colonial master and Olympic host nation, Great Britain, in men's field hockey.

Although the return of the Olympic Games after a twelve-year hiatus was eagerly welcomed around the world, many people had low expectations for the Games themselves. Because many participating nations were still recovering from the devastation they had suffered during the war and postwar economic slumps, they lacked the resources to train their athletes well. Moreover, cancellation of the previous two Olympiads and the distractions of war had taken many of the world's best athletes out of competition and left them with little time to prepare for the 1948 Olympics. Few medal winners from 1936 were expected to defend their Olympic titles. London itself was ill prepared for hosting the Olympics. After having accepted the offer to host the 1948 Games in March, 1946, it had only two and one-half years to prepare for them, and repairing wartime damage was a higher priority. With all these problems, few observers expected to see high levels of competition in London.

Prior to the Games, many Americans had feared that many of the athletes they were sending to England were too raw, too untested, and too new to their sports to compete at the Olympic level. These concerns proved unfounded. Indeed, not only was the American athletes' haul of eighty-four medals the most of any participant nation, it was nearly double that of Sweden, whose forty-four medals were the second-highest totals. Moreover, Americans also won the most gold medals (38), the most silver medals (27), and the most bronze meals (19). The United States was especially strong in the swimming events, in which its athletes won 15 medals. It also won 10 of 12 possible medals in the diving events.

One of the most outstanding American performances was turned in by a track and field athlete

American Gold-Medal Winners in Track and Field, 1948

Event	Name(s)
Field Events	
Decathlon	Bob Mathias
High jump	Alice Coachman
Long jump	Willie Steele
Pole vault	Guinn Smith
Shot put	Wilbur Thompson
Track Events	
100 meters	Harrison Dillard
200 meters	Mel Patton
800 meters	Mal Whitfield
110-meter hurdles	William Porter
400-meter hurdles	Roy Cochran
4×100-meter relay	Barney Ewell, Lorenzo Wright, Harrison Dillard, and Mel Patton
4×400-meter relay	Roy Cochran, Clifford Bourland, Arthur Harnden, and Mal Whitfield

whose youth and lack of experience made him one of the most unlikely Olympic champions of the Games. When seventeen-year-old Bob Mathias won the men's decathlon event, he was the youngest gold-medal winner in Olympic track and field history up to that time. Even more surprising, he had competed in the demanding ten-event competition for only five months before going to London.

Impact After the long hiatus following the 1936 Berlin Games, the 1948 London Games brought together athletes from nations and colonial territories ranging from Afghanistan to Yugoslavia. The London Games have come to be remembered as the game of firsts: They were the first to be held in twelve years, the first to be televised, the first to use starting blocks for runners, the first to use photo-finish judging, and the first to offer such women's events as canoeing singles. They also involved fourteen nations participating for the first time and were the first games to ban nations for having participated in a war. Germany, Japan, and the Soviet Union all were disallowed from competition due to their involvement in World War II.

Keith J. Bell

Further Reading

Hampton, J. *The Austerity Olympics: When the Games Came to London in 1948.* London: Aurum Press, 2009. Explains how the success of the 1948 games provided a model for later Olympiads.

Phillips, Bob. *The 1948 Olympic Games: How London Rescued the Games.* Cheltenham, England: Sportsbooks, 2007. Appreciative examination of what made the 1948 Games important and what London did to save the modern Olympic movement.

Terrence, Chris, and Randall Preister. *Bob Mathias: Across the Fields of Gold.* Lenexa, Kans.: Addax, 2000. Biography of the 1948 Olympic decathlon champion. richly illustrated, telling of Mathias's track-and-field accomplishments and public life.

Wallechinsky, David, and Jaime Loucky. *The Complete Book of the Olympics: 2008 Edition.* London: Aurum Press, 2008. Up-to-date compendium of all the modern Olympiads, with full details on the results of the 1948 Games, along with interesting anecdotal material.

See also Basketball; Boxing; Ice hockey; Soccer; Sports in Canada; Sports in the United States.

Operation Overlord. *See* **D Day**

■ Oppenheimer, J. Robert

Identification American physicist
Born April 22, 1904; New York, New York
Died February 18, 1967; Princeton, New Jersey

During World War II, Oppenheimer led the effort at Los Alamos to develop the atomic bomb. The first atomic bombs used in combat were dropped on Hiroshima and Nagasaki, Japan, and the resulting deaths and destruction shocked Japan into surrendering.

After studying in Europe, J. Robert Oppenheimer returned to the United States as a professor of physics at the University of California, Berkeley. He built a strong school of theoretical physics and brought quantum mechanics to America. In 1942, the Manhattan Project was established, and Oppenheimer was tapped by General Leslie Richard Groves, the head of the project, to build a secret laboratory and develop an atomic bomb that could be used in the war. Nuclear fission had been discovered in Germany in 1939, and there was fear that the Nazis would be able to build an atomic bomb first and use it against the Allies. This fear created intense pressure to develop the bomb quickly. Oppenheimer chose a remote site in New Mexico owned by the Los Alamos Boys School and began recruiting scientists, while the army built housing and laboratories for the people he was hiring.

Oppenheimer brought the best scientists in the country to the new laboratory, and by war's end there were about fifteen hundred people working on the project. He was a hands-on administrator and was active in every aspect of the research. Two types of atomic bombs were developed at Los Alamos, a uranium-235 (U-235) bomb and a plutonium bomb. The first explosion of an atomic bomb was a test of a plutonium bomb on July 16, 1945. The test was completely successful.

As soon as sufficient U-235 and plutonium could be produced, they were used to make bombs. Hiroshima was attacked and destroyed with a U-235 bomb on August 6, 1945, and a plutonium bomb was dropped on Nagasaki on August 9. In each case the city was destroyed and there were approximately

"I Am Become Death, the Destroyer of Worlds"

Years after witnessing the first atomic bomb blast in 1945, Los Alamos Laboratory director J. Robert Oppenheimer remembered the life-changing explosion with words that have become infamous.

We knew the world would not be the same. A few people laughed, a few people cried, most people were silent. I remembered the line from the Hindu scripture, the *Bhagavad-Gita*. Vishnu is trying to persuade the Prince that he should do his duty and to impress him takes on his multi-armed form and says, "Now, I am become Death, the destroyer of worlds." I suppose we all thought that one way or another.

world, and thousands of nuclear weapons were built, creating a situation characterized as mutually assured destruction (MAD). Despite these huge arsenals, the fear of atomic destruction has maintained the peace between major nations since 1945.

Raymond D. Cooper

Further Reading

Bernstein, Jeremy. *Oppenheimer: Portrait of an Enigma.* Chicago: Ivan R. Dee, 2004.

Bird, Kai, and Martin J. Sherwin. *American Prometheus: The Triumph and Tragedy of J. Robert Oppenheimer.* New York: Alfred A. Knopf, 2005.

Herken, Gregg. *Brotherhood of the Bomb.* New York: Henry Holt, 2002.

See also Atomic bomb; Atomic Energy Commission; Groves, Leslie Richard; Hiroshima and Nagasaki bombings; Manhattan Project; Plutonium discovery; Wartime technological advances.

100,000 casualties. The Japanese surrendered on August 14.

The scientists who had worked on the bomb became national heroes. Oppenheimer was appointed to advise the government on science and nuclear weapons policy, and in 1947, he was made director of the Institute for Advanced Study in Princeton, New Jersey. He used his position to lobby for international control of nuclear weapons and against the development of the hydrogen bomb, which he thought was unnecessary and good only for destroying entire cities. His arms control activities and opposition to the hydrogen bomb angered many conservative politicians, who wanted to keep the secrets of the bomb from the Russians. They accused Oppenheimer of communist sympathies and in 1953 held a hearing to remove his security clearance and destroy his reputation. Although many scientists rallied to Oppenheimer's defense, he was found to be a security risk, terminating his role with the government.

By 1963, the political winds had shifted and Oppenheimer was awarded the government's prestigious Enrico Fermi Award. He died in 1967 from throat cancer caused by his many years of chain-smoking.

Impact The development of the atomic bomb led to an arms race among the major nations of the

■ Oregon bombing

The Event Incident in which a small plane piloted by a Japanese naval warrant officer dropped incendiary bombs on pine woods near the Oregon coast

Also known as Lookout air raid

Date September 9, 1942

Place Near Brookings, Oregon

This bombing was among several assaults on American territory carried out by the Japanese early in World War II, but it did not result in the loss of life and caused little damage.

On the morning of September 9, 1942, the Japanese submarine *I-25* surfaced off the coast of Oregon to launch a collapsible Yokosuka E14Y floatplane using a catapult. Up until this time, such planes (which American authorities called "Glens") had been used only for reconnaissance, but Chief Warrant Officer Nobuo Fujita had received approval to carry two 170-pound incendiary bombs on the tiny plane with the objective of starting forest fires.

Fujita flew some fifty miles inland to a point about eight miles south of Brookings. The plane's navigator and gunner, Petty Officer Shoji Okuda, then released the first bomb over Wheeler Ridge. From their vantage point at eight thousand feet, the two were able to determine that the bomb's incendiary pellets had started a fire in the thick forest below them. They then dropped their second bomb a few miles away and returned to their submarine.

Thanks to several witnesses who saw or heard the Glen, the Federal Bureau of Investigation was notified within hours, and the country's Western Defense Command received authorization to strengthen its defenses. Personnel in Forest Service lookout towers pinpointed the blaze and brought it under control easily, as conditions were unseasonably wet. If the second bomb started a fire, it went out quickly.

Fujita and Okuda made a second sortie very early on the morning of September 29 over the Grassy Knob area near Port Orford. Although they dropped two more bombs and believed that they had started another fire, it failed to spread.

Impact   In the wake of the bombing raid led by Lieutenant Colonel Jimmy Doolittle against Japan in April, 1942, Japan undertook several retaliatory operations against United States territory in the hope of damaging American morale while raising that of its own people. Some of these operations, such as the campaign to drop incendiary bombs from balloons over the western United States, were relatively successful. Others, such as the disastrous Battle of Midway in early June, 1942, were failures. Although the Japanese rated the bombing of Oregon a success, it did negligible damage and had no effect on the American war effort.

Grove Koger

Further Reading

Horn, Steve. *The Second Attack on Pearl Harbor: Operation K and Other Japanese Attempts to Bomb America in World War II*. Annapolis, Md.: Naval Institute Press, 2005.

McCash, William. *Bombs over Brookings: The World War II Bombings of Curry County, Oregon, and the Postwar Friendship Between Brookings and the Japanese Pilot, Nobuo Fujita*. Corvallis, Oreg.: William McCash, 2005.

Webber, Bert. *Silent Siege III: Japanese Attacks on North America in World War II—Ships Sunk, Air Raids, Bombs Dropped, Civilians Killed*. Medford, Oreg.: Webb Research Group, 1992.

See also   Balloon bombs, Japanese; Doolittle bombing raid; Midway, Battle of; Submarine warfare; Wartime technological advances; World War II.

■ Organization of American States

Identification   International body made up of the countries of the Western Hemisphere designed to promote inter-American alliance

Also known as   Organización de los Estados Americanos; OAS

Date   Established May 2, 1948

Originally established to confront the pressures of the Cold War through inter-American solidarity, the Organization of American States (OAS) developed into an organization seeking resolution to the shared problems of the Western Hemisphere. The priorities of the OAS include strengthening democracies, reducing poverty, and promoting human rights within the Americas.

The OAS grew out of an inter-American system that began during the 1890's with the creation of the Bureau of American Republics, which became known as the Pan-American Union in 1910. At the beginning, an alliance among the countries of the Americas presented a way to defer European influence and to enhance political and trade relations throughout the hemisphere. However, by 1945, the inter-American system needed an overhaul. World War II had effectively demonstrated the power of inter-American amity. However, Argentina's refusal to rebuff the Axis Powers pointed to weakness in the inter-American system. In 1948, at the Ninth International Conference of American States, held in Bogotá, Colombia, member states of the Pan-American Union voted to reorganize and streamline the inter-American system, creating a stronger organization endowed with a flexibility that could adapt to changes in hemispheric conditions.

Purposes of the Organization   The charter of the OAS outlines five basic purposes of the organization: to strengthen the peace and security of the Americas, to settle hemispheric disputes peacefully, to take common action in the event of aggression upon a member state, to solve political and economic problems through cooperation, and to promote social and cultural development. Above all, the OAS is rooted in the idea of reciprocal assistance, as discussed at the Inter-American Conference on War and Peace (also known as the Conference of Chapultepec) held in Mexico City in 1945. With the Soviet presence extending into Europe, reciprocal assistance mainly meant that member states would give aid or military assistance should another member be attacked. However, the idea of reciprocity soon spread to areas other than defense, such as economic and cultural sectors, where mutual exchange could prove beneficial.

The OAS began with twenty-one member countries and expanded to thirty-five members. The organization conducts its business in its four official languages: English, Spanish, Portuguese, and French. Countries voluntarily participate in the OAS, and admission is open to any sovereign state in the Western Hemisphere, following ratification by the OAS. Unlike the United Nations, the OAS created a charter that includes provisions for a country to withdraw its membership, if it so chooses. Cuba, although an original member of the OAS, has been excluded from participation since 1962 on the grounds that its ties with the Soviet Union violated the purposes of the organization.

Alberto Lleras Camargo of Colombia served as the organization's first secretary-general from its inception in 1948 to 1954. The secretary-general is the head of the governing council of the OAS, which consists of one representative from each member country. The purposes of the OAS were soon tested as Costa Rica accused Nicaragua of violating its borders. The OAS negotiated a pact of amity between the two members, signed February 21, 1948. Another test of the OAS's ability to settle disputes occurred on February 16, 1949, when the Haitian government alleged that the Dominican Republic

frequently broadcast radio programs attacking Haiti. Unlike the situation between Costa Rica and Nicaragua, this disagreement fell outside the original scope of the OAS. Thus, the OAS created the Inter-American Peace Committee within its own organization to deal with less serious conflicts among its members, adding to its power to resolve disputes.

Cultural Exchange To promote cultural development among its member states, the OAS often organized various performances and exhibits, the majority of which were held at its headquarters in Washington, D.C., or at the Hall of the Americas in the Pan-American Union. The OAS began organizing exhibitions of contemporary Latin American visual art as early as 1941. It presented around four exhibitions a year that featured the work of well-known artists, such as Guatemalan Carlos Merida, Uruguayan Pedro Figari, and Venezuelan Alejandro Otero, as well as younger artists hoping to make an impact. Additionally, the OAS presented exhibits showcasing textiles and sculptures from various countries. Music constituted another form of cultural exchange, and the OAS sponsored a monthly concert series that featured the best performers of the Americas: Uruguayan pianist Hugo Balzo; Lillian Evanti, the first African American opera singer in the United States; and the Peruvian folkloric group, the Inka Taki Trio. The OAS also began publishing a monthly magazine *Américas*, a general-interest magazine containing stories about the mem-

---

Organization of American States Members (Year of joining)

Antigua and Barbuda (1981)	Dominica (1979)	Panama (1948)
Argentina (1948)	Dominican Republic (1948)	Paraguay (1948)
Bahamas (1982)	Ecuador (1948)	Peru (1948)
Barbados (1967)	El Salvador (1948)	St. Kitts and Nevis (1984)
Belize (1991)	Grenada (1975)	St. Lucia (1979)
Bolivia (1948)	Guatemala (1948)	St. Vincent and Grenadines
Brazil (1948)	Guyana (1991)	(1981)
Canada (1989)	Haiti (1948)	Suriname (1977)
Chile (1948)	Honduras (1948)	Trinidad and Tobago (1967)
Colombia (1948)	Jamaica (1969)	United States (1948)
Costa Rica (1948)	Mexico (1948)	Uruguay (1948)
Cuba (1948)	Nicaragua (1948)	Venezuela (1948)

ber countries, and another publication, *The Inter-American Music Bulletin*, that focused on musical topics. These magazines were produced in both Spanish and English and distributed widely throughout the United States and Latin America.

Impact The OAS has done much to promote peace and democracy in the Americas. Little by little, it has added more councils and committees—such as the Inter-American Peace Committee, the Inter-American Economic and Social Council, the Inter-American Commission on Human Rights, and the Inter-American Cultural Council—to help fulfill its stated purposes. The OAS has recognized that hemispheric security is intertwined with issues of democracy, economics, and human rights. However, it must maintain a careful balance so its intervention in a country's affairs does not conflict with the country's right to sovereignty. Some critics of the OAS have argued that the United States influences the organization to favor its interests above those of other members. However, the decentralized structure of the OAS safeguards against the concentration of power. Moreover, the OAS has implemented measures so that one member cannot trump the interests of other, less powerful members. Although the OAS has its shortcomings, it continues to work for better conditions in the Western Hemisphere.

Alyson Payne

Further Reading

Cooper, Andrew F., and Thomas Legler. *Intervention Without Intervening? The OAS Defense and Promotion of Democracy in the Americas*. New York: Palgrave MacMillan, 2006. Questions how much the OAS should intervene in their efforts to defend democracy throughout the Americas.

Dreier, John C. *The Organization of American States and the Hemisphere Crisis*. New York: Harper & Row, 1962. Dreier, who was the U.S. representative to the OAS from 1950 to 1960, details the challenges facing the OAS during the 1960's, namely the Cuban Revolution and the spread of communism in Latin America. He reviews tactics employed by OAS and U.S. foreign policies in Latin America.

Sanjurjo, Annick, ed. *Contemporary Latin American Artists: Exhibitions at the Organization of American States, 1941-1964*. Lanham, Md.: Scarecrow Press, 1997. Details the art exhibits presented by the OAS to promote intercultural awareness among the Americas. Includes brief biographies of each artist, a list of the works displayed, and the duration of each exhibition.

Shaw, Carolyn. *Cooperation, Conflict, and Consensus in the Organization of American States*. New York: Palgrave MacMillan, 2004. Discusses how the OAS uses peaceful settlement procedures to resolve hemispheric conflicts. Reviews twenty-six cases of conflict resolution among nations, beginning in 1948, giving the context of these conflicts and whether the outcome resulted in a consensus, a compromise, or unilateral U.S. dominance.

Sheinin, David. *The Organization of American States*. London: Transaction, 1996. Annotated research guide to the OAS. Lists and describes general works and addresses specific countries and issues such as human rights, peacekeeping, refugees, and security.

Thomas, Ann Van Wynen, and A. J. Thomas. *The Organization of American States*. Dallas: Southern Methodist University Press, 1963. One of the most complete histories of the OAS, from its roots in the Monroe Doctrine to the 1960's. Explains its organizational structure, its founding principles, and the scope of its power.

Thomas, Christopher R., and Juliana T. Magloire. *Regionalism Versus Multilateralism: The Organization of American States in a Global Changing Environment*. Boston: Kluwer Academic, 2000. Illustrates how globalization affects the Americas. Details how the OAS has adapted to these changes and suggests how the OAS can continue its relevancy in the twenty-first century.

See also Anticommunism; Cold War; Decolonization of European empires; Foreign policy of the United States; Inter-American Treaty of Reciprocal Assistance; Latin America; Magazines; Mexico.

■ Organized crime

Definition Organizations set up to operate illegal enterprises, or extort money from legal businesses by means of criminal tactics, with profits often being reinvested into legitimate operations

Organized crime, known variously as the Mafia, the Mob, or the Syndicate, had become a fixture in several American cities after the turn of the twentieth century. During the

1940's, organized crime elements operated with virtual impunity in many areas. Leaders managed to increase revenues, consolidate gains made in formalizing and expanding operations, and establish ties with local and state-level politicians that allowed them to obtain protection from criminal investigation and prosecution for their illegal activities.

After surviving two bloody decades of infighting, the rival gangs in New York were brought together in 1931 by Charles "Lucky" Luciano, who guided leaders toward a more businesslike approach to running their operations. Three years later, Luciano formed a syndicate with mob leaders in twenty-four major cities, and these in turn divided the country into spheres of influence where they exercised some control over operations in smaller municipalities. Although Luciano was sent to prison in 1936, he continued to direct his own group's operations from behind bars, while his deputy, Frank Costello, exercised daily control in New York and provided leadership for the national organization. Costello believed that bribery was better than confrontation as a strategy for advancing the interests of organized crime, and under his direction Mafia organizations began systematically courting politicians at all levels to buy protection for their enterprises. The strategy worked surprisingly well throughout the decade. By

1940, organized crime had become a thriving enterprise throughout America.

Organized Crime During World War II In some ways, organized crime was better positioned to convert to the wartime economy than the nation at large. Almost as soon as the United States began gearing up for war with the Axis forces, organized crime mounted highly lucrative black-market operations across the country, offering goods that the government had decided to ration. Bribing legitimate businesses to obtain scarce goods, acquiring them with counterfeit ration coupons, or stealing them when those methods failed, criminal elements amassed quantities of items such as rubber, leather goods, and foodstuffs that they sold at a high profit. At the same time, activities for which the Mafia had become famous—extortion, theft, gambling, racketeering, and prostitution—continued with virtual impunity, especially as the country mobilized for war and law-enforcement agencies saw their ranks depleted due to military call-ups.

One of the more unusual twists occurred shortly after the United States entered the war in December, 1941. Many in the federal government worried that enemy agents might try to sabotage efforts to ship goods overseas to U.S. forces and the Allies. The major ports were controlled by the longshoremen's unions, which had been heavily infiltrated by organized crime decades earlier. In February, 1942, an explosion and fire aboard the SS *Normandie*, a cruise liner being converted to a transport ship at a New York City pier, convinced authorities that help was needed. Although later investigation proved that the fire had been caused accidentally, at the time officials in Naval Intelligence, fearing more of the same activity, launched a secret program dubbed Operation Underworld, aimed at getting leaders of organized crime to assist in preventing sabotage. The real beneficiary of this initiative was Luciano, who was provided better prison accommodations in exchange for assistance in getting his organization and others to

Lucky Luciano relaxing in his Italian exile in 1949. (AP/Wide World Photos)

keep the ports open and goods flowing. Ostensibly, Luciano also arranged for associates in Sicily and Italy to aid the U.S. invasion there in 1943. Ironically, one of the men who ended up as a translator for the Allies was Carlo Gambino, future leader of one of the five principal crime families in New York, who had fled to Italy from the United States in 1937 to escape arrest for murder.

Organized Crime After the War After hostilities ceased, organized crime entities continued operations as if nothing had changed. Although their black-market operation dried up when rationing ceased, they quickly shifted back into traditional activities such as racketeering, extortion, gambling, and prostitution. Additionally, their activities in the drug trade increased, as they were once again able to obtain illegal substances from suppliers in the Far East and Middle East over shipping routes that had been closed during the war.

Perhaps the Mafia's most significant move in the years immediately after the war ended was an expansion into the newly flourishing gambling mecca in Las Vegas. In 1946, Benjamin "Bugsy" Siegel, a mob associate who had been living in California since the mid-1930's to oversee Mafia interests in Hollywood, convinced other mob leaders to invest in construction of the Flamingo casino. Once a base had been established in the city, mobsters were able to infiltrate other gambling houses, often becoming silent partners in these operations. Casinos provided places where mob leaders could "launder" funds—that is, invest illegal profits into legitimate enterprises in order to hide the original source from which the money had been obtained.

The effectiveness of law enforcement in meeting these new challenges was mixed. In 1946, the U.S. Congress passed the Hobbs Act, an amendment to a 1934 law, to help combat the increase in robbery and extortion associated with interstate commerce. In the long run, this act would provide the basis for more effective enforcement, but its immediate impact was negligible. Part of the problem lay in the nature of criminal activity, much of which was confined within state borders. Additionally, some politicians seemed willing to turn a blind eye to the activities of organized crime, especially if it meant they could get support for elections. The case of William O'Dwyer, elected mayor of New York with behind-the-scenes help from Frank Costello in exchange for

O'Dwyer's aid in thwarting investigations of Mafia activities, is the most egregious example of a common practice.

Law-enforcement officials were especially chagrined when New York governor Thomas E. Dewey, who had made his reputation fighting organized crime during the 1930's, granted a pardon to Lucky Luciano in 1946 in recognition of his assistance with the war effort. Although Luciano was deported to Italy as a condition of his pardon, his continued involvement from abroad in drug smuggling and other illegal enterprises demonstrated that the move had done little to curb criminal activity.

Despite the successes organized crime leaders enjoyed during the decade, organized crime in America began its slow demise in the final years of the 1940's. Across America, district attorneys determined to reduce the Mafia's influence empanelled grand juries to investigate its activities. In 1947, journalist Herbert Asbury began a series of articles exposing Costello's involvement with New York politicians. At the start of the next decade, the activities of a congressional committee chaired by Tennessee senator Estes Kefauver, aided by committee counsel Robert F. Kennedy, would shine the national spotlight on organized crime, finally marshalling law-enforcement agencies to begin putting real pressure on the vast illicit empire.

Impact Acting with virtual impunity during the first half of the decade, organized crime groups were able to consolidate gains made during the previous ten years and solidify their hold over a number of key legitimate industries across America. Many businesses were forced to purchase from mob-controlled suppliers or provide substantial portions of their profits for ostensible protection. At the same time, theft, arson, and other violent crimes took a toll on thousands of innocent citizens who were not able to obtain relief from law-enforcement agencies that lacked either the manpower or the political will to deal with organized criminal groups. The positive role organized crime played in helping keep American ports open and goods flowing to the armed forces overseas was outweighed by the enormous negative impact these groups had in operating a black-market system to steal and sell rationed goods at exorbitant prices—goods that would otherwise have been available to the fighting forces or sold on the legitimate market. Additionally, the expansion of organized crime into the Las Vegas gambling industry gave leaders of organized crime a valuable new outlet for laundering illegal funds through a legal enterprise where business was transacted almost exclusively in cash.

Laurence W. Mazzeno

Further Reading

Fox, Stephen. *Blood and Power: Organized Crime in Twentieth-Century America.* New York: William Morrow, 1989. Survey providing a historical perspective on the activities of key leaders of organized crime in cities throughout America.

Lunde, Paul. *Organized Crime: An Inside Guide to the World's Most Successful Industry.* New York: Dorling Kindersley, 2004. Describes operations conducted by American criminal groups during the 1940's. Part of a historical review of organized crime activities worldwide.

Peterson, Virgil. *The Mob: Two Hundred Years of Organized Crime in New York.* Ottawa, Ill.: Green Hill, 1983. Contains a chapter focused on organized crime activities during the 1940's; explains the relationship between leaders of criminal groups and elected officials.

Raab, Selwyn. *Five Families: The Rise, Decline, and Resurgence of America's Most Powerful Mafia Empires.* New York: St. Martin's Press, 2005. Detailed history of organized crime in New York, supplemented by discussions of activities conducted by criminal organizations in other parts of the United States.

Reppetto, Thomas. *American Mafia: A History of Its Rise to Power.* New York: Henry Holt, 2004. Detailed examination of the rise of organized crime in America; provides information on activities by key criminal leaders during World War II and immediately after.

See also Business and the economy in the United States; Crimes and scandals; Dewey, Thomas E.; Hobbs Act; Siegel, Bugsy; Wartime sabotage.

OSS. *See* **Office of Strategic Services**

■ *Our Plundered Planet*

Identification   Book about environmental destruction
Author   Henry Fairfield Osborn, Jr. (1887-1969)
Date   Published in 1948

A landmark in environmental writing, Our Plundered Planet *helped shift the focus of American environmentalists away from Theodore Roosevelt-style conservationism, which emphasized the creation of national parks and forests, toward the enactment of government regulation designed to prevent or reduce ecological damage.*

Henry Fairfield Osborn, Jr., the president of the New York Zoological Society, published *Our Plundered Planet* in 1948, a year before the publication of Aldo Leopold's more measured view of the environment, *A Sand County Almanac.* Osborn's book had a darker tone and a more apocalyptic vision, predicting that humankind's environmental abuse would lead to global disaster.

Foreshadowing later works, such as Paul Ehrlich's

Plundering the "Good Earth"

Our Plundered Planet *opens with the following cautionary words:*

There is beauty in the sounds of the words "good earth." They suggest a picture of the elements and forces of nature working in harmony. The imagination of men through all ages has been fired by the concept of an "earth-symphony." Today we know the concept of poets and philosophers in earlier times is a reality. Nature may be a thing of beauty and is indeed a symphony, but above and below and within its own immutable essences, its distances, its apparent quietness and changelessness it is an active, purposeful, co-ordinated machine. Each part is dependent upon another, all are related to the movement of the whole. Forests, grasslands, soils, water, animal life—without one of these the earth will die—will become dead as the moon. This is provable beyond questioning. Parts of the earth, once living and productive, have thus died at the hand of man. Others are now dying. If we cause more to die, nature will compensate for this in her own way, inexorably, as already she has begun to do.

The Population Bomb (1968), Osborn's book emphasized the environmental impact of the rising population, while decrying humankind's actions throughout history as "plunder." He concluded that the United States was on a "downward spiral" at a time when most Americans were optimistic about the use of new products, such as the pesticide DDT (dichlorodiphenyltrichloroethane), which had been made possible by wartime advances in technology. Like Leopold, Osborn advanced moral arguments for environmental measures. Unlike Leopold, who focused on the need for individuals to develop and follow their own "land ethic," Osborn placed greater faith in government action at the state, national, and international levels.

Impact   As one of the landmarks of environmental writing during the 1940's, *Our Plundered Planet* played an important role in shifting American environmentalism away from conservationism and toward a new reliance on legislation and governmental action as the preferred means of preserving the planet.

Andrew P. Morriss

Further Reading

Buell, Frederick. *From Apocalypse to Way of Life: Environmental Crisis in the American Century.* London: Taylor & Francis, 2003. A thorough survey of the apocalyptic narrative in American environmentalism.

Rothman, Hal K. *Saving the Planet: The American Response to the Environment in the Twentieth Century.* Chicago: Ivan R. Dee, 2000. A thorough evaluation of the evolution of modern environmental thinking.

See also   Air pollution; Natural resources; *A Sand County Almanac;* Water pollution.

P

■ Paige, Satchel

Identification Professional baseball player
Born July 7, 1906; Mobile, Alabama
Died June 8, 1982; Kansas City, Missouri

Paige was a baseball legend in his own time. His pitching prowess, showmanship, and statements to the press helped legitimize Negro League baseball to white Americans.

By the 1940's, Leroy Robert "Satchel" Paige had played more than two decades of semiprofessional and professional baseball in the United States and several Latin American countries. He was already a legend. He began the 1940 season with the Travelers, a roving division of the Kansas City Monarchs. By the end of the season, he was pitching for the Monarchs. The 1941 Monarchs season did not begin until July, so in the meantime Paige traveled with his barnstorming team and pitched for various Negro League teams that needed his drawing power to sell tickets. After the United States entered World War II in December, 1941, Paige pitched several exhibition

Paige's Negro League Statistics for 1940's

Season	GP	GS	CG	IP	HA	BB	SO	W	L	S	ShO
1940	2	2	2	12	10	0	15	1	1	0	1
1941	13	11	3	67	38	6	61	7	1	0	0
1942	20	18	6	100	68	12	78	8	5	0	1
1943	24	20	4	88	80	16	54	5	9	1	0
1944	13	—	—	78	47	8	70	5	5	0	2
1945	13	7	1	68	65	12	48	3	5	0	0
1946	9	9	1	38	22	2	23	5	1	0	0
1947	2	2	2	11	5	—	—	1	1	0	0

Major League Statistics for 1940's

Season	GP	GS	CG	IP	HA	BB	SO	W	L	S	ShO	ERA
1948	21	7	3	72.2	61	25	45	6	1	1	2	2.48
1949	31	5	1	83.0	70	33	54	4	7	5	0	3.04

Combined Negro League and Major League Baseball Statistics for 1940's

	GP	GS	CG	IP	HA	BB	SO	W	L	S	ShO	ERA
Totals	148	81	23	617.2	466	114	448	45	36	7	6	—

Notes: Because of inconsistent record keeping in the Negro Leagues, some data are incomplete or unavailable. GP = games played; GS = games started; CG = complete games; IP = innings pitched; HA = hits allowed; BB = bases on balls (walks); SO = strikeouts; W = wins; L = losses; S = saves; ShO = shutouts; ERA = earned run average

games to help sell war bonds. On May 24, 1943, he became the first African American to play baseball at Wrigley Field in one such game.

In 1947, Jackie Robinson became the first African American to play in major-league baseball when he debuted with the Brooklyn Dodgers. On July 7, 1948, at age forty-two, Paige signed with the Cleveland Indians to become the first black pitcher in the American League and the oldest rookie ever in the major leagues. He ended the 1948 season with a 6-1 record and a 2.48 earned run average. His 1949 season was not as successful, and he left the team at the end of the season. Paige played during the 1951-1953 seasons for the St. Louis Browns, and he pitched his last major-league game in 1965 for the Kansas City Athletics.

Impact   Paige was one of the first African Americans to play major-league baseball, and he is considered one of the greatest pitchers in history. His outspokenness on issues of racism helped to break down the color barrier in the major leagues.

Ron Jacobs

Further Reading

Holway, John, Lloyd Johnson, and Rachel Borst. *The Complete Book of Baseball's Negro Leagues: The Other Half of Baseball History.* Foreword by Buck O'Neil. Fern Park, Fla.: Hastings House, 2001.

Nelson, Kadir. *We Are the Ship: The Story of Negro League Baseball.* New York: Hyperion, 2008.

Paige, Satchel. *Maybe I'll Pitch Forever.* Lincoln, Nebr.: Bison Books, 1993.

See also   Baseball; Civil rights and liberties; Negro Leagues; Racial discrimination; Robinson, Jackie; Sports in the United States.

■ Paris Peace Conference of 1946

The Event   Meeting among Allied Powers to determine postwar sanctions

Dates   July 29 to October 15, 1946

Place   Paris, France

Planned at the Moscow Conference of Foreign Ministers in 1945, the Paris Peace Conference brought together the victorious wartime Allied Powers—principally the United States, the Soviet Union, Great Britain, France, and China—to negotiate peace treaties with the minor defeated nations, such as Italy, Romania, Hungary, Bulgaria, and Finland.

The mission of the Paris Peace Conference, held in the Luxembourg Palace, Paris, France, was to recommend changes in the draft treaties that had been prepared by the Council of Foreign Ministers during its sessions in London and in Paris in 1946. Representatives from twenty-one Allied countries worked together to write treaties that negotiated the payment of war reparations, a commitment to minority rights, and territorial adjustments. The conference started amid rising Cold War tensions, different ideas about the meaning of wartime declarations, and the structure and purposes of the society of states.

Among the substantive issues discussed were the border conflict between Italy and Yugoslavia, control of Trieste, Italian reparations, and Danube River navigation. No penalties were to be imposed on countries that displayed wartime partisanship for the Axis, such as Finland. The conclusion of peace treaties with the minor countries was expected to ease the tensions when the time came to negotiate treaties with the two major Axis states, Germany and Japan. The conference adopted fifty-three recommendations by votes of at least two-thirds and forty-one by majority votes of less than two-thirds. The Council of Foreign Ministers adopted forty-seven of the former recommendations and twenty-four of the latter in its final draft of the treaties in New York later in 1946.

Impact   At the conference, conflicts developed between the Soviet Union and the United States. None of the negotiators were able to resolve these differences, which resulted in a decline in trust between the Soviet Union and the West. In many ways, the conference signaled the beginning of the Cold War.

Martin J. Manning

Further Reading

Byrnes, James F. *Report on the Paris Peace Conference by the Secretary of State.* Washington, D.C.: Government Printing Office, 1946.

Gaddis, John Lewis. *The Cold War: A New History.* New York: Penguin Press, 2005.

See also   Byrnes, James; Cairo Conference; Casablanca Conference; Decolonization of European empires; Foreign policy of the United States; Hull, Cordell; Potsdam Conference; Tehran Conference; Truman, Harry S.; Yalta Conference.

■ Parker, Charlie

Identification   American jazz saxophonist
Also known as   Yardbird; Bird
Born   August 29, 1920; Kansas City, Kansas
Died   March 12, 1955; New York, New York

A self-taught saxophonist, Parker is recognized as the forefather of the bebop era in jazz. His creative improvisations set a new and lasting standard of excellence, influencing generations of musicians.

Charlie Parker endured some embarrassing incidents as a teenager during jam sessions in Kansas City. As a result, he would often practice twelve hours a day or more. From 1938 to 1942, Parker performed in the Jay McShann band, where he earned his nickname "Yardbird," shortened to "Bird," because of his appetite for chicken. By 1939, he had developed an addiction to morphine and then heroin, which plagued him throughout his life.

American saxophonists Charlie Parker (left) and Sidney Bechet riding a train to the 1949 International Paris Jazz Festival. (Getty Images)

Living in New York City, Parker was a colleague of jazz legends Earl Hines, Dizzy Gillespie, Thelonius Monk, and numerous others. The American Federation of Musicians' strike of 1942-1943 effectively shut down the recording industry. Lacking recording opportunities, jazz musicians congregated at Minton's Playhouse and Clark Monroe's Uptown House for frequent jam sessions. A new form of jazz music emerged as a result—bebop. Bebop was a rebellious change of direction from jazz as played by white swing bands. Because of the small combo setting and open space for improvisation, musicians experimented freely, developing creative new approaches to soloing. Parker perceived jazz improvisation differently from others. Rather than adhering to standard chord progressions that utilized roots, thirds, and fifths, Parker included the extensions of ninths, elevenths, and thirteenths. He added chromatic passing tones that resolved to chord tones, creating embellished melodies. Parker also replaced traditional chord progressions with more complex substitutions.

Bebop featured extremely fast tempos, encouraging dazzling displays of technical virtuosity among the performers. The fast tempos were reminiscent of the hot jazz of the 1920's and a direct violation of the swing era's rules of preserving danceable tempos. Bebop was unpopular with dancers because they became listeners instead.

Parker married three times and had a son, yet his addictions to alcohol, heroin, and anything else he could obtain to get high destroyed any pretense of a happy home life. In 1946, he was committed to Camarillo State Hospital for the mentally ill for about six months. It was enough time to recover from his addictions and make a fresh start. He returned to Fifty-second Street in New York, the site of much of his best work, in the hope of resurrecting his career.

In 1947, Parker reunited with Gillespie and his band to perform

<table>
<tr><td colspan="2" align="center">**Parker's 1940's Discography**</td></tr>
<tr><td>1945</td><td>*Bebop's Heartbeat*</td></tr>
<tr><td>1945</td><td>*The Complete "Birth of the Bebop"*</td></tr>
<tr><td>1946</td><td>*Jazz at the Philharmonic, 1946*</td></tr>
<tr><td>1947</td><td>*Diz 'n Bird at Carnegie Hall*</td></tr>
<tr><td>1947</td><td>*In a Soulful Mood*</td></tr>
<tr><td>1947</td><td>*The Legendary Dial Masters*, Volume 1</td></tr>
<tr><td>1948</td><td>*Bird on Fifty-second Street*</td></tr>
<tr><td>1948</td><td>*Charlie Parker Memorial*, Volume 1</td></tr>
<tr><td>1948</td><td>*Charlie Parker Memorial*, Volume 2</td></tr>
</table>

Source: Rolling Stone magazine internet archive, 2009.

at Carnegie Hall, a concert that set new attendance records. In 1949, Parker appeared at the Paris Jazz Festival, where he combined jazz and classical elements, recording three albums with strings. Jazz critics regard the recordings as inspired and historic.

As the 1950's emerged, Parker continued to struggle with his dependencies on alcohol and drugs. He had two more children with a girlfriend, but his personal and professional lives were in shambles. He unsuccessfully tried to commit suicide twice. Parker died in 1955 from the combination of a heart attack and several serious illnesses.

Impact   Parker is a jazz icon, recognized as perhaps the singular most important saxophonist in jazz history. He transformed jazz from the dance-oriented big bands to an art form during the bebop era. His legacy survives with the emergence of each new generation of jazz musicians.

Douglas D. Skinner

Further Reading

Giddens, Gary. *Celebrating Bird: The Triumph of Charlie Parker.* New York: Da Capo Press, 1998.

Woideck, Carl. *The Charlie Parker Companion: Six Decades of Commentary.* New York: Schirmer Books, 1998.

See also   African Americans; Davis, Miles; Ellington, Duke; Holiday, Billie; Music: Jazz.

■ Patton, George S.

Identification   U.S. Army general during World War II
Born   November 11, 1885; San Gabriel, California
Died   December 21, 1945; Heidelberg, Germany

Patton was one of the leading military figures in World War II not only for his success on the battlefield but also for his capabilities in strategic planning and the development of amphibious warfare. The armies commanded by Patton played prominent roles in the conquest of North Africa and Sicily and in the European theater from D-Day, June 6, 1944, through May, 1945.

George S. Patton always believed that he was born to achieve great things and to become an American hero. He came from a family with a long tradition of military service, his ancestors having fought in the Revolutionary War, the Mexican War, and the Civil War. At the age of eighteen, following in the footsteps of his grandfather and father, Patton entered the Virginia Military Institute (VMI). After completing his first year at VMI, Patton accepted an appointment to the United States Military Academy at West Point. During his three years at West Point, he received many academic and athletic honors. Patton graduated in 1909 and received his commission as a second lieutenant with assignment to the Fifteenth Cavalry Regiment.

In 1916, Patton served in Mexico under General John J. Pershing. Patton greatly admired Pershing and modeled himself after him in many ways. When the United States entered World War I in 1917, Pershing was selected to command the American Expeditionary Forces. Pershing valued Patton and asked him to join his staff. It was during this period that Patton became infatuated with tanks and mechanized warfare. Patton's World War I combat role was cut short by a bullet wound to his upper leg, but the lessons he learned from combat would serve him well in later years.

By 1939, Patton was the leading American expert on tank warfare and amphibious landings. In 1942, he was given the assignment of creating the Desert Training Corps in the Mojave Desert. During this time, he developed the tactical skills necessary to achieve victory in North Africa and Europe. Later that year, Patton was also involved in planning the 1942 invasion of French Morocco. Initially, American forces were ill-prepared for combat. Once Patton took command of the II Corps, his high-profile style of command, coupled with his demands for organization and strict discipline, quickly turned the tide of battle from defeat to brilliant victories. In July, 1943, as commander of the Seventh Army, Patton led an amphibious assault on the island of Sicily. After a bloody and hard-fought campaign, his troops liberated the strategic cities of Palermo and Messina.

Following his military successes in Sicily, Patton was given command of the Third Army in England. There he became involved in the preparations for the Normandy invasion of Europe. His expertise in amphibious warfare played an important role in preparing and training the troops for the invasion. Shortly after the Normandy landings, Patton's Third Army arrived and quickly dashed across Europe exploiting weaknesses in the German defenses. Perhaps Patton's finest hour came in December, 1944, when his troops relieved the besieged U.S. forces around Bastogne, Belgium, during the Battle of the Bulge. Patton did not die in battle but from injuries sustained in a car accident in Mannheim, Germany, on December 21, 1945.

Impact General Patton played a significant role in the Allied victory over the Nazis in Europe during World War II. The military expertise and insight that he developed between the two world wars led to the modernization of the U.S. military in both its technological capabilities and its strategic planning. His brilliant military victories pressured the German government to accept defeat and surrender sooner rather than later.

Paul P. Sipiera

Further Reading

Axelrod, Alan. *Patton: A Biography.* New York: Palgrave Macmillan, 2006.

Hymel, Kevin M., and Martin Blumenson. *Patton.* Dulles, Va.: Potomac Books, 2008.

Showalter, Dennis E. *Patton and Rommel: Men of War in the Twentieth Century.* New York: Berkley Caliber, 2005.

See also Army, U.S.; Bulge, Battle of the; D Day; Landing craft, amphibious; Marshall, George C.; North African campaign; War heroes; World War II; World War II mobilization.

Major General George S. Patton (left) talking with British rear admiral Lord Louis Mountbatten at the time of the Casablanca Conference in Morocco in early 1943. (Library of Congress)

■ Pearl Harbor attack

The Event Surprise Japanese air attack on the home base of the United States Pacific Fleet

Date December 7, 1941

Place Pearl Harbor, Island of Oahu, Territory of Hawaii

This attack thrust the United States into World War II, which had begun in Europe in 1939, and the cost and devastation of the war forever changed life in the United States and the world.

The background for the Japanese attack dates back to July 8, 1853, when Commodore Matthew C. Perry sailed a U.S. fleet into Tokyo Bay and forced Japan, after centuries of isolation under the rule of sho- guns (military dictators), to open its doors to trade with the outside world. This development was wel- comed by many Japanese leaders, led to the Meiji (enlightened rule) Restoration of 1868 under Em- peror Mutsuhito, and set Japan on a course of indus- trial, economic, military, and territorial expansion. The island of Formosa (now Taiwan) and the Ko- rean Peninsula were soon under Japanese control. Japan conquered Manchuria in 1931, but its 1937 in- vasion of mainland China soon bogged down, tying up thousands of Japanese soldiers.

Japanese American Relations, 1922-1941 Japan's position as a world power was solidified following World War I with the Washington Naval Treaty in 1922, which allowed Japan to have a navy approxi- mately three-fifths the size of the navies of Great Brit- ain and the United States. The treaty emboldened the Japanese and instilled in them the desire to pur- sue further expansion in the Pacific. Military leaders began to argue that the major hindrances to that ex- pansion were the British in Hong Kong and Singa- pore and the United States in the Philippines and Guam. As early as 1931, there were discussions in Japanese military academies about the best way to attack Pearl Harbor, an American naval base in the Territory of Hawaii, which had been acquired by the United States in 1898 as a result of the Spanish-American War.

In May, 1940, the United States transferred the bulk of its Pacific Fleet from the West Coast to Pearl Harbor, which by then had a dry dock and industrial plant capable of maintaining and repairing the largest vessels in the fleet. Dock- ing locations included berths on the east side of Ford Island, in the center of the harbor, which be- came known as Battleship Row. The island also had a naval air sta- tion. Pearl Harbor was one of the most modern naval bases in the world.

The United States had trade agreements that allowed Japan to buy large amounts of scrap iron,

steel, and aviation fuel. By the late 1930's, Japan had used these resources to build thousands of ships and aircraft. In July, 1940, President Franklin D. Roose- velt, through the new Export Control Act, placed an embargo on this trade. He also froze Japanese assets in the United States and closed all ports to Japanese ships.

Although Admiral Isoroku Yamamoto, com- mander in chief of the Imperial Japanese Navy, had urged Japanese leaders to avoid war with the United States, he was planning an attack on Pearl Harbor in case it became necessary. In September, 1940, when Japan formally joined the Tripartite Pact with Ger- many and Italy, both nations already at war in Eu- rope, that necessity was on the horizon. By January, 1941, Yamamoto was convinced that war was inevita- ble and that the U.S. fleet must be destroyed in a sur- prise attack.

Attack and Devastation "All warfare is based on de- ception. If the enemy leaves a door open, you must rush in." These words of Sunzi (Sun Tzu) in *The Art of War*, a Chinese classic written in about 500 B.C.E, were an accurate description of the events of Decem- ber 7, 1941. The American mind-set before the at-

Japan planned its attack on Pearl Harbor hoping to knock the U.S. Pacific Fleet out of ac- tion. However, although damage done to the fleet was temporarily crippling, its effects were not long lasting. This photo shows the USS West Virginia, *one of the battleships most badly damaged at Pearl Harbor.* (National Archives)

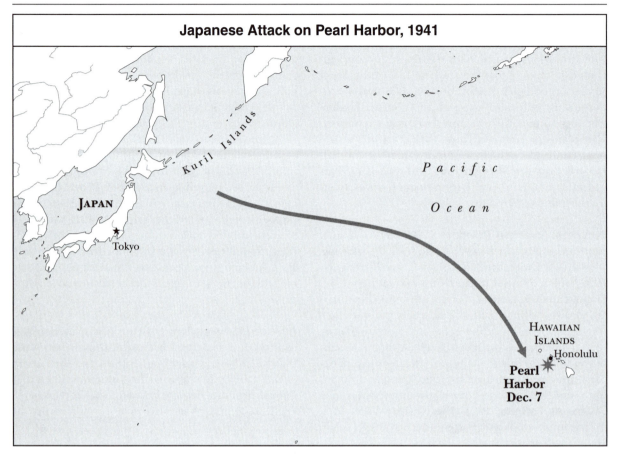

tack was that Japan would never strike supposedly well-protected military installations so far from their own country. Numerous warning signs, including sightings on the new medium of radar, were either ignored or misinterpreted, and the attack was a complete surprise.

On November 26, the Japanese naval task force left Japan and began its journey through the north Pacific. Although the United States had broken the Japanese code, the task force was operating with sealed orders and under radio silence. By the predawn hours of December 7, the task force was 274 miles north of Pearl Harbor, still undetected by American forces, and soon launched the first of the 360 aircraft involved in the attack.

The attack came in two waves, the first beginning at 7:53 A.M. when the first target was hit. This wave, in which the heaviest damage was inflicted, lasted about thirty minutes. The second wave began at 8:55 A.M. and ended one hour later. By 1:00 P.M., the task force was headed back toward Japan.

To prevent American air resistance, among the first targets were aircraft at Hickam Field, Wheeler Field, and several smaller air fields. At Hickam, American planes were lined up in neat rows, some without sufficient fuel, and were easy targets for Japanese dive bombers. A total of 188 aircraft were destroyed, mostly on the ground. Only about a dozen planes got into the air. Schofield Barracks, the major army base in Hawaii, was also attacked. Defensive action there, as elsewhere, was hindered by lack of access to weapons and ammunition.

Of the ninety-seven ships in the harbor at the time, nineteen were damaged or destroyed. The biggest losses were on Battleship Row. The *Arizona*, *Oklahoma*, and *Utah* were sunk. Five other battleships were heavily damaged. The *Arizona* was later sealed with 1,177 men entombed as a memorial. Fortunately, the American aircraft carriers were at sea and were not damaged. Submarines and the all-important fuel storage facilities also escaped damage. All of the damaged ships were repaired in record time and saw service against Japan later in the war, beginning with the Battle of Midway just six months later, when U.S. aircraft carriers proved their superiority.

About 85,000 American military personnel were stationed on the island at the time. More than 2,300 were killed; with the addition of civilians and federal employees, the official death toll reached 2,390 men, women, and children.

The top military commanders at Pearl Harbor at the time of the attack were Admiral Husband Edward Kimmel, the commander in chief of the Pacific Fleet, and Major General Walter C. Short, the army commander. They were to share the responsibility for not being prepared for a surprise attack. Kimmel was replaced by Admiral Chester W. Nimitz on December 31, 1941, and he retired in March, 1942. Ten days after the attack, Short was replaced by Lieutenant General Delos Carlton Emmons, a U.S. Army Air Corps commander.

The Japanese expected to lose about half of their planes. Of the 360 involved in the attack, they lost only 29, as well as 55 men. Another 9 men were killed on midget submarines that tried to penetrate Pearl Harbor, raising the Japanese death toll to 64.

Within twenty-four hours after the attack on Pearl Harbor, the Japanese struck the Philippines, Guam, and Wake Island. They also attacked Hong Kong, Malaysia, and Thailand, and they soon occupied Indochina.

Impact Yamamoto best described the result of the Japanese attack when he declared, "We have awakened a sleeping giant and instilled in him a terrible resolve." That resolve led to Yamamoto's death in 1943, when his plane was shot down in the South Pacific, and ended when Japan surrendered unconditionally to the United States on August 14, 1945.

On December 8, 1941, the day after the attack, President Roosevelt asked Congress for a declaration of war against Japan. Without a single speech, and with only one negative vote, Congress granted his request. Three days later, Germany and Italy, Japan's Axis allies, declared war on the United States. Pearl Harbor thus catapulted the United States into the most deadly and destructive war in the history of

the world. Fought in Asia, North Africa, and Europe, World War II ended with atomic bombs on the Japanese cities of Hiroshima and Nagasaki.

Glenn L. Swygart

Further Reading

Lord, Walter. *Day of Infamy.* New York: Henry Holt, 1957. One of the earliest detailed accounts of the attack, chronicling the reactions of American military personnel at Pearl Harbor, ranging from disbelief to anger to horror.

Prange, Gordon. *At Dawn We Slept: The Untold Story of Pearl Harbor.* New York: McGraw-Hill, 1981. The result of many years of research. A classic account of the planning for the attack by Japan and the lack of preparation by the United States. Most of the more than seven hundred cover the period before December, 1941.

Richardson, K. D. *Reflections of Pearl Harbor: An Oral History of December 7, 1941.* Westport, Conn.: Praeger, 2005. Personal accounts, the result of surveys sent to various organizations seeking eyewitness reports from survivors of the attack.

Rosenberg, Emily S. *A Date Which Will Live: Pearl Harbor in American Memory.* Durham, N.C.: Duke University Press, 2003. Explores how Pearl Harbor and memories thereof have affected American culture since 1941, focusing on the period after the fiftieth anniversary of the attack in 1991.

Smith, Carl. *Pearl Harbor, 1941: The Day of Infamy.* Westport, Conn.: Praeger, 2004. Excellent photos, biographical vignettes, and a detailed chronology from 1936 to January, 1942, especially useful for the events of 1941.

Van Der Vat, Dan. *Pearl Harbor: The Day of Infamy—An Illustrated History.* Toronto: Madison Press, 2001. Excellent illustrated coverage of the prelude, attack, and aftermath of the event. One of the best collections of Pearl Harbor photographs and maps available in print.

See also Arcadia Conference; *Duncan v. Kahanamoku*; Films about World War II; Japanese American internment; Japanese Canadian internment; Navy, U.S.; Nimitz, Chester W.; Radar; War heroes; World War II.

■ Pentagon building

The Event Construction of the headquarters of the U.S. War Department

Dates Groundbreaking on September 11, 1941; dedicated on January 15, 1943

Place Arlington, Virginia

The world's largest office building, the Pentagon was built during World War II to house the entire War Department, which occupied various buildings throughout Washington, D.C., before moving to the Pentagon. Named for its five-sided shape, the Pentagon has become the symbol of the U.S. military and the Department of Defense.

At the onset of the 1940's, the War Department employed more than 26,000 civilian and military personnel. The department occupied seventeen buildings throughout Washington, D.C. The number of employees was projected to reach 30,000 by 1942. The headquarters of the War Department was located in the Munitions Building, a temporary structure built during World War I. Secretary of War Henry L. Stimson told President Franklin D. Roosevelt in May, 1941, that his department needed more space, especially with war raging in Europe.

The head of the War Department's construction division, Brigadier General Brehon B. Somervell, was put in charge of finding a solution. On July 17, 1941, he outlined plans for a permanent fix to Lieutenant Colonel Hugh Casey, who like Somervell was an engineer, and civilian architect George Bergstrom. He told the two men to design an air-conditioned office building with no more than four stories and without elevators, to conserve steel. Somervell wanted the building to include four million square feet of floor space, enough room to hold up to 40,000 employees. Casey and Bergstrom were given until the following Monday morning, four days away, to create the basic layout. The early design was approved by Somervell on that Monday and by Stimson the following day. A supplemental bill was quickly passed by Congress and signed by the president. The amendment gave the War Department $35 million for its new headquarters.

The unique shape of the building was a result of the original proposed location, Arlington Farm. The building would have been between Arlington National Cemetery and Memorial Bridge. There were several objections to this site, concerning the enormous building obstructing the view between the cemetery and the Lincoln Memorial. The building site eventually changed to a location near Washington National Airport, which opened in June, 1941 (renamed Ronald Reagan Washington National Airport in 1998). As the official approval process continued, Somervell selected contractors. The general contractor was John McShain, out of Philadelphia, whose firm had also built the Jefferson Memorial and the Naval Medical Center in Bethesda, Maryland. Bergstrom planned a reinforced concrete building made up of five concentric pentagons connected by spokelike hallways radiating from a central courtyard. The pentagon shape was kept because the planners liked the design, even though it no longer was dictated by location, and there was not time to redesign the entire building.

The Pentagon Building during its early stages of construction. Despite the immense size of the building, it was completed and dedicated only sixteen months after its September 11, 1941, groundbreaking. (AP/Wide World Photos)

Construction   Before construction could begin, the government needed to purchase 287 acres of additional land, costing around $2.2 million. The neighborhood was a slum known as Hell's Bottom and contained factories, pawnshops, and about 150 homes. Unneeded acreage acquired in the deal was divided between Arlington National Cemetery and Fort Myer. Groundbreaking for the Pentagon occurred on September 11, 1941, the same day that the construction contracts were finalized. The project continued to be accelerated. Construction moved so rapidly that the architects had little lead time. Occasionally, construction proceeded faster than planning, resulting in the use of materials different from those intended.

On December 1, 1941, President Roosevelt transferred control of military construction from the Quartermaster Corps to the Army Corps of Engineers. At that time, a combined four thousand men worked three shifts on the construction. The attack on Pearl Harbor a few days later increased the urgency of the project. Somervell wanted one million square feet of office space ready for use by the beginning of April, 1942.

On April 11, David Witmer replaced George Bergstrom as chief architect. The first section was completed by the end of April, and the first employees moved in. The overall frame and roof of the Pentagon building were completed within a year. Construction of the Pentagon was finished on January 15, 1943, just sixteen months after it started. Total costs are estimated to have reached $83 million.

During the early twenty-first century, the Pentagon remained the world's largest office building, as measured by floor space (6.5 million square feet). It covers 28.7 acres, not counting its 5.1-acre center courtyard. It contains 17.5 miles of corridors. Construction on a building of its size would normally take four years. The five concentric pentagons are referred to as "rings," labeled A-E, with the A ring the innermost. Senior officers tend to be given offices in the outermost E ring. Each room is designated by floor, ring, and office number. The building has five floors above ground (1-5) and two subterranean levels (basement and mezzanine).

Impact   The Pentagon is a symbol of the American military. Housing the entirety of the Department of Defense, the Pentagon illustrates the cohesiveness and cooperation between branches of the military

and officials in a way that separate buildings could not. On September 11, 20001, exactly sixty years after the groundbreaking, the Pentagon was the target of a terrorist suicide attack carried out using a commercial airliner. Everyone on board the plane and more than one hundred Pentagon employees were killed when the plane crashed into the building. Even though more than 40 percent of the building sustained damage, the Pentagon was open for business the following day, presenting a strong image of courage, stability, reassurance, and valor to the American public and the rest of the world.

Jennifer L. Campbell

Further Reading

Alexander, David. *The Building: A Biography of the Pentagon.* Minneapolis: Zenith Press, 2008. The history of national security and defense since the Pentagon's construction. Also tells the stories of key players who have worked in the Pentagon, its politics, and its role in American history.

Creed, Patrick. *Firefight.* New York: Presidio Press, 2008. Based on public records and more than 150 personal accounts of the attack on September 11, 2001, this book tells the story of those fighting to rescue their coworkers, protect national security, and save the Pentagon itself. Tells an often overlooked part of 9/11 history.

Goldberg, Alfred. *The Pentagon.* Washington, D.C.: Government Printing Office, 1992. Detailed history of the Pentagon's design, construction, architecture, cost, and environmental impact. Tells the story of the first fifty years of the world's largest office building.

Vogel, Steve. *The Pentagon: A History.* New York: Random House, 2008. Vogel tells what he calls the story of deceit that led to the construction of the Pentagon, citing examples of lies told to Congress, including some concerning the size and cost of the building.

Williams, Paul. *Washington, D.C.: The World War II Years.* Mount Pleasant, S.C.: Arcadia, 2004. A collection of nearly two hundred photographs of the capital taken during World War II. Includes a chapter on the Pentagon building and its construction.

See also   Air Force, U.S.; Architecture; Army, U.S.; Department of Defense, U.S.; Marines, U.S.; Navy, U.S.; World War II.

■ The Philadelphia Story

Identification Romantic film comedy
Director George Cukor (1899-1983)
Date Opened on December 24, 1940

An adult comedy that was less devoted to screwball antics than to acid wit and wordplay, The Philadelphia Story *propelled one of American cinema's most independent female actors, Katharine Hepburn, back into the popular spotlight, while earning another to-be legend, James Stewart, his only Oscar.*

Following a successful yearlong run on stage during 1939, Phillip Barry's play *The Philadelphia Story* was ready to be made into a feature film. However, since the rights were owned by billionaire Howard Hughes and actor Katharine Hepburn (who had starred in the play), the film would be made on their terms. Hepburn, having been labeled "box-office poison" following a number of film failures, insisted that she play the lead role and have some say in casting the other main parts. Warner Bros. offered to pay $225,000 for the rights, but without Hepburn; Hughes lobbied on her behalf before Joseph L. Mankiewicz and Louis B. Mayer of Metro-Goldwyn-Mayer (MGM), who signed on. Hepburn received $75,000, with another $175,000 paid out for the rights. Director George Cukor, who had worked with Hepburn on other films, was attached, as was rising star James Stewart and familiar Hepburn comedy cohort Cary Grant, with whom she had just appeared in 1938's *Holiday*. (Grant agreed to the role on the condition that his salary be donated to the British War Relief Fund.)

The Philadelphia Story focused on Tracy Lord, a wealthy Philadelphia socialite about to be married for the second time. Her first husband, C. K. Dexter Haven (Grant), however, continues to linger around the Lord mansion. Her fiancé, George Kittredge (John Howard), is a social climber and more of a snob than Tracy herself. Into this mix come gossip columnists Macauley "Mike" Connor (Stewart) and Liz Imbrie (Ruth Hussey), who are allowed to photograph the wedding because their editor is blackmailing the Lords. Over the course of twenty-four hours, Tracy learns a few lessons about herself, falls for Mike (and he her), loses Kittredge, and again weds Dexter. The film differed in several aspects from the play, most notably the absence of Tracy's brother. The screenplay was written by Donald Ogden Stewart, with assistance from producer Mankiewicz.

Impact In retrospect, *The Philadelphia Story* is more than just the tale of a rich girl getting comeuppance; it poked gently at the social order in a way that few films of the era did, while creating characters who were finely drawn and full of intelligent dialogue. Although films were often designed to have broad audience appeal, *The Philadelphia Story* was clearly for adults, and adults responded: The film opened to glowing reviews, ultimately grossing about $3 million ($45.6 million in 2009 dollars). It earned six Academy Award nominations and two wins—best actor for James Stewart and best adapted screenplay for Donald Ogden Stewart. The film had a longer-lasting effect, too, having shown audiences that Hepburn could laugh at herself (Tracy Lord was similar to Hepburn) and still entertain. Her acting career was thus revitalized.

Randee Dawn

Further Reading
Berg, A. Scott. *Kate Remembered.* New York.: G. P. Putnam's Sons, 2003.
Dickens, Homer. *The Films of Katharine Hepburn.* Secaucus, N.J.: Citadel Press, 1974.
McGilligan, Patrick. *George Cukor: A Double Life.* New York: St. Martin's Press, 1991.

See also Academy Awards; Film in the United States; Hughes, Howard; Stewart, James; *Sullivan's Travels*; Theater in the United States; Women's roles and rights in the United States.

■ Philippine independence

The Event Release of the Philippines from its Commonwealth status and creation of an independent republic
Date July 4, 1946
Place Philippines

Philippine independence brought to an end the one large-scale formal undertaking in imperialism of the United States and was expedited by American calls for the swift granting of independence to British and other European colonies in Asia. Philippine independence turned the page from an era in which the United States sought formal possessions beyond its borders to one in which it acted as a global superpower through a network of alliances and inter-dependencies with other sovereign states.

When the United States conquered the Philippines in the Spanish-American War of 1898, the islands were not envisioned as a permanent imperial posses-sion of the United States. The islands were largely ruled as a colony for nearly forty years. By the mid-1930's, the United States foresaw eventual independ-ence, as the Tydings-McDuffie Act of 1934 (Philip-pine Independence Act) established a Common-wealth of the Philippines, under U.S. suzerainty but with an elected Filipino president, Manuel Quezón. Some of the pressure for Philippine independence during the 1930's emerged from racist motives, as immigration by Filipinos and economic competi-tion from Philippine products were feared by many white Americans. Before the Japanese invasion of the Philippine islands, Philippine independence was scheduled for 1944; despite the disruptions of war, the process went on nearly as scheduled, though the United States could have chosen to delay it out of war-time exigencies.

Independence possibly was made more urgent by two factors. First, there was considerable American pressure on Britain to decolonize its Asian posses-sions swiftly. This in turn meant the United States needed to exit the Philip-pines for appearance's sake, especially because the West's colonial presence in Asia was a handy propaganda weapon for the Soviet Union to employ in the incipient Cold War. In addition, there was discontent concerning the large numbers of American soldiers sta-tioned in the Philippines, who wished to return home.

Another factor was the Hukbalahap, or "Huk," rebellion. The Hukbalahaps engaged in a guerrilla insurgency with substantial communist ties formed origi-nally to fight the Japanese occupation. The Huks sympathized neither with the Americans and their Philippine allies—they assassinated Quezón's widow, Au-rora, in 1949—nor with the leaders who emerged at the head of the indepen-dent Philippines, considering Manuel

Roxas to have been too friendly with the Japanese. The Huk rebellion both prompted American politi-cal withdrawal from the Philippines—as the United States did not wish a second war against a Philippine insurgency, as had happened when the islands were first occupied—and cemented American aid to the new country, seen as justified by its utility in helping suppress the Huk rebellion.

Osmeña, Roxas, and Public Opinion   Quezón died during World War II, and his deputy, Sergio Os-meña, was the Commonwealth president in 1946. The United States expected Osmeña to win the April 23, 1946, presidential election handily, as he was as-sociated with the successful struggle against Japa-nese occupation. Osmeña was able and well inten-tioned but was seen as too much of an American puppet. Quezón, having died while both men were in exile from Japanese occupation, never had an op-portunity to establish his own power base as presi-

---

U.N. Treaty Establishing Philippine Independence

The 1947 United Nations treaty between the United States and the Republic of the Philippines established the independence of the Asian archipelago and outlined the terms of that independence in relation to the United States. Article 1 is reproduced below.

The United States of America agrees to withdraw and sur-render, and does hereby withdraw and surrender, all right of possession, supervision, jurisdiction, control, or sover-eignty existing and exercised by the United States of Amer-ica in and over the territory and the people of the Philip-pine Islands, except the use of such bases, necessary appurtenances to such bases, and the rights incident thereto, as the United States of America, by agreement with the Republic of the Philippines, may deem necessary to re-tain for the mutual protection of the United States of Amer-ica and of the Republic of the Philippines. The United States of America further agrees to recognize, and does hereby recognize, the independence of the Republic of the Philippines as a separate self-governing nation and to ac-knowledge, and does hereby acknowledge, the authority and control over the same of the Government instituted by the people thereof, under the Constitution of the Republic of the Philippines.

dent. This was exacerbated by Osmeña's refusal to campaign, which many Filipinos saw as arrogant.

The electoral victory of Manuel Roxas was seen as a surprise by observers who underestimated Filipino nationalism. Although most Filipinos had opposed Japanese rule, they nonetheless sensed a kernel of truth in Japanese rhetoric of anticolonialism, and men who had cooperated with the Japanese, such as Roxas and José Laurel, were seen less as collaborationists than as motivated by a laudable nationalism. Roxas's election was also an expression of Philippine national confidence.

The Philippines was a different nation from the one the United States had conquered: English as a universal language of education had given the different nationalities and islands of the Philippines a common medium of communication. Original Filipino literature in English was being produced by internationally recognized writers such as José Garcia Villa. Moreover, the many Filipino émigrés to the United States who had been repatriated under the Tydings-McDuffie Act brought American lifestyles and business practices back home.

Counterinsurgency and Military Ties Roxas was indeed less pliable with regard to the United States than many Filipinos feared Osmeña would have been. Economic and military links remained tight—Clark Air Field and the Subic Bay air base were anchors of the postwar American presence in the Pacific. It soon became clear that independence was a political reality but not necessarily an economic or geopolitical one. The U.S. government invested heavily in counterinsurgency efforts against the Hukbalahaps, who had considerable support among the poor and disenfranchised and were under the dynamic leadership of the young Luis Taruc. The Huks made a tactical mistake, though, in endorsing Osmeña in the hope that he would be the less creditable figure, and then taking to the hills when the more nationalistic Roxas won the race. Roxas died in 1948, but the insurgency was largely quelled under the leadership of Roxas's successor, Elpidio Quirino—albeit with considerable American aid.

Impact July 4, 1946, was chosen as Philippine Independence Day to commemorate the liberty the United States had, with respect for its own traditions, handed to its former possession. July 4 was not retained as Philippine independence day. In 1962, president Diosdado Macapagal switched the date to June 12 in honor of the Philippine independence movement that had been suppressed by the United States from 1899 through 1901. Although Filipinos appreciated the American withdrawal in 1946, for the people of the Philippines the sense of nationhood truly began during the 1890's with the successive insurgencies against Spanish and American occupations. Still, the 1946 granting of independence marked the inception of the modern Philippine state.

Nicholas Birns

Further Reading

Carlson, Keith. *The Twisted Road to Freedom: America's Granting of Independence to the Philippines.* Manila: University of the Philippines Press, 1997. History of the U.S.-Philippines relationship focusing on Philippine independence.

Golay, Frank Hindman. *Face of Empire: United States-Philippine Relations, 1898-1946.* Madison: University of Wisconsin, 1998. Examines the intricate relationship as it developed until Philippine independence, exposing some of the hidden forces at work.

Karnow, Stanley. *In Our Image: America's Empire in the Philippines.* New York: Random House, 1989. One of the most comprehensive studies of the Philippine-United States relationship by an author who has published extensively on Southeast Asia.

Lieurance, Suzanne. *The Philippines.* Berkeley Heights, N.J.: Enslow, 2004. A brief, accurate presentation of the history of the Philippines aimed at juvenile readers. Excellent illustrations, valuable supplementary features.

Nadeau, Kathleen. *The History of the Philippines.* Westport, Conn.: Greenwood Press, 2008. Comprehensive account, with good coverage of the nation's struggle to attain an identity. A good resource for high school and general readers.

Olesky, Walter. *The Philippines.* New York: Children's Press, 2000. A comprehensive view of the Philippines from a historical perspective. This beautifully illustrated book is intended for a young adult audience and contains helpful features such as a time line and a section entitled "Fast Facts." Chapter 4, "The Long Struggle for Independence," is especially relevant.

See also Anticommunism; Asian Americans; Bataan Death March; Cold War; Decolonization of European empires; Philippines.

■ Philippines

While still an American dependency, the Philippines played a central role in the Pacific theater of World War II. The 1941 and 1944 Philippines battles were the first and next-to-last campaigns against the Japanese; each had a vastly different outcome.

Through several centuries leading up to the end of the nineteenth century, the Philippines were a Spanish colony. In 1898, possession of the islands passed to the United States after it won the Spanish-American War (1898). Although a Filipino nationalist movement contested this, the United States acted like it meant to stay during the early twentieth century. It fortified islands in Manila Bay to protect the harbor against possible hostile invasion, built a naval base at Cavite for its Asiatic Fleet, formed the Philippine Scouts, and built Clark Airfield for the Army Air Corps. By the 1930's, however, the U.S. Congress was reluctant to modernize Philippine defenses further because of depressed economic conditions and the imminent likelihood of Philippine independence.

Meanwhile, as the Japanese Empire began expanding throughout the Pacific, the United States formulated a scheme called Plan Orange in preparation for a possible war with Japan. It called for defending only the areas around Manila Bay on Luzon Island. From there, U.S. forces were to retreat to the Bataan Peninsula, where U.S. and Filipino ground forces were to hold out until an American rescue force could arrive—an eventuality that might take months.

General Douglas MacArthur was assigned to command U.S. Army Forces Far East (USAFFE). Confident that the Philippines could defend itself, he insisted that all parts of the archipelago could be defended. He envisioned U.S. and Filipino troops meeting the enemy on the beaches and pushing them back to the sea. Believing that the Japanese could not strike before April, 1942, he garnered American support for his plan. As the Japanese threat strengthened, the United States sent last-minute reinforcements and gave the Philippines its first priority for war materials. The Philippine army was expanded to more than ten divisions, but the U.S. government equipped it with World War I rifles, pre-World War I artillery, and obsolete aircraft. The training of Filipino troops had barely started when

the Japanese invasion came. Many Filipino soldiers had never even fired their weapons before.

The Japanese Invasion Early on December 8, 1941—the day after the Japanese attacked Pearl Harbor in Hawaii—General MacArthur heard about the Pearl Harbor attack and alerted Filipino forces. In anticipation of a surprise attack on the Philippines, the Army Air Corps put planes aloft at dawn. Fog over Taiwan delayed the Japanese attack, but when the Japanese planes arrived over the Philippines, many USAFFE aircraft were on the ground refueling. About half the planes were destroyed on the first day alone.

With most American planes out of action, the Japanese could freely bomb the Cavite base. The old ships of the Asiatic Fleet were no match for the more modern and powerful Japanese vessels and planes. Admiral T. C. Hart, the commander of the Asiatic Fleet, ordered his ships to sail south to join with the British, Australian, and Dutch fleets, leaving only PT boats and submarines behind. Because of the damage done to the Navy's Pacific Fleet at Pearl Harbor, no rescue fleet would reach the Philippines for several years.

Given fifty days to capture Manila, Japanese general Masaharu Homma tried to divide MacArthur's forces by landing his troops at scattered points. The main Japanese landing, on December 22, 1941, was in Lingayen Gulf, where Filipino forces offered limited resistance. Inexperienced, poorly trained, and underequipped, the Filipinos were no match for the experienced Japanese troops supported by modern artillery and aircraft. The U.S. Twenty-sixth Cavalry covered their retreat.

USAFFE withdrew in stages. Manila was abandoned on December 31. The Japanese entered the capital city on January 2, 1942. The Japanese had expected they would need a major battle to take Manila and were surprised when Filipino and American forces retreated to Bataan. The retreat to Bataan had been carefully planned during the 1930's, but its actual implementation proved difficult because of limited resources. MacArthur's scheme for trying to stop the enemy on the beaches meant that military supplies were dispersed throughout the archipelago, with few supplies on Bataan. Unable to stop the Japanese landing in the Lingayen Gulf, USAFFE resumed War Plan Orange. Various factors slowed shifting supplies to Bataan. Although the retreat was ultimately successful, supplies remained tight while the troops awaited help. Short of ammunition, medical supplies, and food, the army went on half-rations.

USAFFE held Bataan till April 9, when General Jonathan Wainwright, the chief allied commander in the Philippines surrendered. MacArthur had already left on March 11. Now only the island of Corregidor and some island forts were not yet in Japanese hands. The Japanese started a continuous artillery bombardment. On May 6, 1942, Corregidor surrendered.

The Japanese Occupation Japanese propaganda touted Japan's creation of a Greater East Asia Coprosperity Sphere, in which both Japan and the occupied territories would benefit. Some Filipinos who were glad to see the Americans leave regarded the Japanese as liberators and collaborated with them. Under Japanese occupation, the Philippines got their own president, legislature, and autonomy in local government. However, most Filipinos viewed the United States favorably and resisted the Japanese occupation. Meanwhile, Japan treated the Philippines as a colony for extracting resources.

After months of struggling, not only against the Japanese, but also against starvation and disease, USAFFE troops were relieved to be able to surrender. However, things soon got worse, not better, for them. During the infamous ten-day Bataan Death March, as many as 10,000 of the 80,000 USAFFE prisoners died. Weakened by starvation and disease, many could not keep up with the march and were summarily executed. The harsh treatment that the Japanese captors gave to their prisoners reflects both cultural and historical factors. Used to a harsh life, the Japanese were impatient with weakness. They were also resentful of the history of Westerners treating Asians poorly. Moreover, the Japanese considered surrender a disgrace and disrespected their prisoners. Moreover, the Japanese had been embarrassed by the fact that the long resistance that USAFFE had staged spoiled their occupation timetable. Finally, Japan was unprepared to look after the huge number of prisoners and lacked the food and materials to care for them properly. After the POWs reached the prison camps, the survivors gradually succumbed to starvation, disease, and mistreatment.

After USAFFE's May surrender, Filipino guerilla units took over fighting against the Japanese. An esti-

mated 200,000 Filipinos were directly involved, and millions more supported their struggle. Wherever the Japanese imposed military control, civil control was undermined. At one point Japan effectively controlled only twelve of forty-eight provinces. Philippine communists, the Hukbalahap, gained control of central Luzon. Agents, radio equipment, and some weapons were delivered by submarine. The guerrillas collected information on Japanese forces and engaged in raids and sabotage.

Japanese restrictions on American civilians still in the Philippines increased over time. First came registration and mandatory weekly reports on their activities. Some Americans were confined to their neighborhoods. Eventually, many American civilians were rounded up and confined to camps, where most slowly starved. Despite the risks, many spied for the United States.

Return of American Forces In June, 1944, a U.S. force landed in the Marianas Islands. Japan responded with aircraft carriers. The Third Fleet, under Admiral William F. Halsey, moved west of the Marianas to protect the landing. Thanks to air cover, U.S. losses were light. During this Battle of the Philippine Sea, Japan lost four aircraft carriers, and its naval air arm was effectively destroyed. Later, U.S. troops landed on Leyte Island (the Battle of Leyte Gulf). Once again, the Third Fleet was present. Halsey's fleet had large aircraft carriers and fast battleships. The landing force had small escort aircraft carriers and slow battleships. Converted merchant ships, escort carriers were slow and lightly armed. They attacked submarines and provided air support for the landing, as Admiral Thomas C. Kincaid's slow battleships bombarded the beaches.

Japan launched a three-pronged counterattack. Admiral Jiraburo Ozawa's remaining aircraft carriers were sent north as bait. Admiral Takeo Kurita attacked with a battleship force through the San Bernardino Strait. Vice Admiral Shoji Nishimura's battleship force went through Surigao Strait. While Kincaid's force demolished Nishimura's ships on October 25, 1944, the plan worked. The Third Fleet pursued Ozawa's force, while Kurita's ships slipped away. At dawn Kurita's ships entered Leyte Gulf. The U.S. invasion fleet was doomed. The puny escort carrier fleets could only distract the enemy. Steaming at top speed, these carriers could not outrun battleships. Japanese aircraft launched ferocious attacks.

General Douglas MacArthur (center) redeeming his pledge to return to the Philippines by leading the U.S. landing at Leyte in October, 1944. (Digital Stock)

Their destroyers made suicidal torpedo attacks and many were lost. Then miraculously, Kurita's force retreated, allowing many U.S. carriers to survive. Kurita thought he had encountered the Third Fleet and believed that Kincaid's ships were coming.

With the Japanese navy subdued, U.S. forces continued the recapture of Leyte, taking several airstrips. During this landing, the famous incident in which General MacArthur waded ashore to redeem his pledge that he would return occurred. After mistaken reports of major U.S. ship loses, Japan changed its defense plan. The main effort was switched from Luzon to Leyte. Because of limited U.S. aircraft in the area, the Japanese quickly reinforced Leyte by sea. However, the Japanese offensive failed. After months of fighting, Ormoc was captured on December 10. Most organized resistance collapsed and the island was declared secure on December 25, but scattered Japanese fought on into 1945.

On January 6, 1945, U.S. forces landed on the main island of Luzon, at Lingayen Gulf. MacArthur landed there for quick access to the central plains, which offered maneuvering room and a good road network. Troops quickly captured Bataan, so the Japanese could not use it. Meanwhile, General Tomoyuki Yamashita prepared three areas of resistance. One was in the mountains controlling Clark Airfield. The mountains controlling Manila's water supply were fortified. The strongest spot was in the mountains of northwest Luzon. The Japanese considered abandoning Manila but instead fortified it.

On February 3, U.S. forces entered Manila against stiff resistance. House-to-house fighting destroyed large portions of the city. It took a full month to clear out all the Japanese. The mountains east of Manila were cleared by mid-June. Paratroopers captured Corregidor in late February. Luzon was declared secure on July 4. The Philippines were finally out of Japanese hands.

Impact In early 1942, the United States learned that it had grossly underestimated the military capabilities of the Japanese. The fighting that American and Filipino forces undertook to defend and later retake the Philippines from Japanese occupation forces was some of the fiercest and most difficult of World War II. American resistance at Bataan and Corregidor has been remembered as an icon of U.S. military history.

Jan Hall

Further Reading

Cannon, M. Hamlin. *Leyte: The Return to the Philippines.* Washington, D.C.: United States Army, Center of Military History, 1993. The Army's official history provides good coverage of the Leyte battle.

Cutler, Thomas J. *The Battle of Leyte Gulf, 23-26 October 1944.* New York: HarperCollins, 1994. Well balanced between Japanese and U.S. accounts of the battle, placing it in its proper context.

Stephens, James R. *Camera Soldiers.* Charleston, S.C.: BookSurge, 2007. Combat photographers record scenes in the Philippine war.

Tarling, Nicholas. *A Sudden Rampage: The Japanese Occupation of Southeast Asia, 1941-1945.* Honolulu: University of Hawaii Press, 2001. Covers Japan's conquest of the Philippines and other parts of Southeast Asia. Includes details of Filipino reactions to the battle.

Vego, Milan. *The Battle for Leyte, 1944: Allied and Japanese Plans, Preparations, and Execution.* Annapolis, Md.: Naval Institute Press, 2006. Comprehensive examination of the background, events, and effects of the Battle for Leyte Gulf. Bibliographic references, index, maps, and eighteen appendixes.

Wise, William. *Secret Mission to the Philippines.* Lincoln, Nebr.: iUniverse.com, 2001. An exciting story, based on actual events, about guerrillas in the Philippines. Suitable for both teenage and adult readers.

See also Aircraft carriers; Army, U.S.; Bataan Death March; Casualties of World War II; Decolonization of European empires; Films about World War II; Great Marianas Turkey Shoot; Kamikaze attacks; MacArthur, Douglas; Philippine independence.

■ Philosophy and philosophers

The 1940's were critical years for internationalizing American philosophy, for its evolution as an academic field, and for expanding the public sphere for intellectual work and critical social analysis.

Global war, cross-national exile, and international politics all had a significant impact on North American philosophy during the 1940's. This international flow of people and ideas sparked dialogue and sharp debate, sometimes reframing the ways various thinkers grappled with perennial questions for Western philosophy, such as which aspects of human experience are unique to particular cultures, times, and places, and which are universal; how human beings acquire knowledge; what the relationship between the objective world and the subjective knower is; what the relationship between thought and action is; how ethical norms are individually and collectively derived; and how societies and individuals can handle conflicts between ethical values. Other questions addressed the relationships between ethics and politics, ethics and science, and science and religion. Still others probed the nature of language, the limits to human knowledge, the limits to human control over nature, and how historical context shapes human consciousness, perception, and action.

In addition to those questions, North American philosophical thinkers during the 1940's confronted difficult questions sparked in historically specific terms by the rise of fascism and anti-Semitism in Europe, the decade-long catastrophes of war across the globe, and the realities of entrenched racial segregation in the United States. They explored the idea of "race" and its function as a category of human thought; the social, political, and humanitarian consequences of race-based thoughts and actions; what philosophy can offer in the face of genocide; whether philosophy can illuminate the sources of human violence; and how geopolitics and war on a global scale (namely, World War II and the Cold War) shape culture and thought in particular national contexts such as the United States and Canada.

North American philosophy during this time also developed further as an academic discipline, where pressures associated with increased professionalism tended to track philosophical inquiry into analytical, linguistic, and science-based projects.

The 1940's include a wide range of philosophers, philosophical orientations, and subtopics, but it is helpful as a starting point to look at two key areas:

- pragmatism and American philosophy
- war, exile, and the influences of world philosophy

Pragmatism Pragmatism is an American movement in philosophy that has its origins in the nineteenth century, but the 1940's saw important publications by a diverse group of philosophers associated with pragmatism. Key philosophical tendencies associated with pragmatism include a strong focus on meaning and truth claims in historical context, and an interest in assessing the consequence of any idea as part of the meaning of the idea. This is not, as is sometimes claimed, a simplistic theory that "whatever works is valid" but rather the argument that observable consequences of an idea are part of its actual meaning. Pragmatism as a philosophy resists "universal" truth claims and rejects the notion that history unfolds in patterns set by necessity. Philosophers instead focus on philosophical and cultural "particulars" and the contingency (or unpredictability) of history. Many of these philosophers, including those active during the 1940's, put high value on philosophy as social thought, arguing that thought itself is a mode of social action.

John Dewey, a leading philosopher in pragmatism, published several of his most important works on the threshold of the 1940's. These texts contributed to subsequent debates during the decade related to education and social theory. *Experience and Education* (1938) and *Freedom and Culture* (1939) exemplify the preoccupation with historical context and social action in Dewey's philosophy, while his text near the end of the decade, *Knowing and the Known* (1949; coauthored with Arthur F. Bentley), focuses on epistemology, the inquiry into how individuals know what they know.

Similarly, philosopher Sidney Hook published two books toward the end of the 1930's that had a strong impact on North American philosophy during the 1940's: *From Hegel to Marx* (1936) and *John Dewey: An Intellectual Portrait* (1939). In the first, which interpreted key nineteenth century German philosophers for English-reading audiences, Hook mediated his own critique of democratic socialist political philosophy through the lens of pragmatism. Hook's political positions began to shift during the 1940's, but he published several books still working via the methods of pragmatism: *Reason, Social Myths, and Democracy* (1940), *The Hero in History* (1943), and *Education for Modern Man* (1946).

W. E. B. Du Bois was a sociologist and political philosopher also strongly inclined toward activist modes of pragmatism, and he shared with Hook an interest in critiquing American history and culture through the pragmatic lens, especially in relation to African American history, race as a philosophical category, and the social philosophy of civil rights. During the 1940's, Du Bois published *Dusk of Dawn: An Essay Toward an Autobiography of a Race Concept* (1940), *Color and Democracy: Colonies and Peace* (1945), and *The World and Africa* (1947). Du Bois was a leading black intellectual in the United States, a key figure in Pan-African theory and international political philosophy, a student of German philosophy during his formative academic years in Berlin, and a contemporary of Dewey and Hook. He used the close study of concrete social and historical events (including, in *Dusk of Dawn*, the details of his own life) to open broader philosophical questions

John Dewey. (Library of Congress)

about identity, consciousness, the nature of social knowledge, and the philosophical relationship between social experience and perception.

Philosopher Morris Raphael Cohen, a well-known teacher for many key figures in pragmatism, also worked with logic. Cohen, a Jewish philosopher from an immigrant family, emphasized the importance of both individual and collective ethical action. He published four books during the 1940's: *A Preface to Logic* (1944), *The Faith of a Liberal* (1946), *The Meaning of Human History* (1947), and *Reason and Law: Studies in Juristic Philosophy* (1950).

A pragmatic social philosopher who worked in an explicitly Christian key was theologian Reinhold Niebuhr. Niebuhr had to some degree embraced a liberal theological optimism about human nature during the early twentieth century, but like many philosophers he began to revise his philosophical stance in the wake of World War I and rise of fascism in Europe in the 1930's. Whereas his earlier works had expressed more optimism about human nature, his philosophy during the 1940's showed more concern about human limits and capacities for violence. Key publications marking these shifts in his thinking included *Christianity and Power Politics* (1940), *The Nature and Destiny of Man* (two volumes, 1941 and 1943), *The Children of Light and the Children of Darkness* (1944), and *Faith and History* (1949).

War, Exile, and World Philosophy   The impact of war on social thought during the 1940's cannot be overstated, with global conflicts bringing a significant internationalization of philosophy, often the result of emigration and forced exile. A number of European philosophers arrived in North America during the 1930's and 1940's, many having been pressed to emigrate under pressure from various forms of European fascism.

Rudolf Carnap, a German philosopher and logical positivist who was also interested in social analysis, arrived in the United States in 1935 after fleeing fascism in Europe. Working in more academic philosophical modes and professionally committed to the analysis of science, language, and logic, Carnap wrote *Introduction to Semantics* in 1942. He published two noted works in 1950 based on research he conducted during the 1940's: *Logical Foundations of Probability* and an essay entitled "Empiricism, Semantics, and Ontology."

German Jewish political philosopher Hannah Arendt arrived in the United States in 1941, after several years of transitory exile from Germany. A sharp critic of Carnap while simultaneously skeptical about many forms of Marxian social theory, Arendt published one of her most enduring philosophical works ten years later, *The Origins of Totalitarianism* (1951), a text deeply grounded in the political conflicts of mid-twentieth century Europe. In fact, the work can be read as philosophical war literature on every level and remains a key text emerging from World War II.

In a strikingly different political key, philosopher Ayn Rand, whose family had fled to the United States from Russia after the 1917 Revolution, published one of her most explicitly philosophical novels, *The Fountainhead*, in 1943. Through fiction, Rand advanced her key philosophical arguments in support of individualism, philosophical objectivism, and atheism, and against any system of ethics grounded in altruism or socialism.

Shifting sharply across the political spectrum, a number of key émigré philosophers associated with the Marxist Frankfurt School found safe haven in the United States during the war years, some of them staying permanently and others returning to Germany after the war. The Frankfurt School included diverse thinkers during the mid-twentieth century who often disagreed among themselves about the forms that a Marxian social philosophy should take. Theodor W. Adorno and Max Horkheimer coauthored in 1947 a key Frankfurt School work of critical theory, *Dialectic of Enlightenment*. Horkheimer also published *The Eclipse of Reason* in 1947. Other philosophers associated with the Frankfurt School who lived and published in the United States during the 1940's included Erich Fromm, who wrote works of psychoanalytic philosophy such as *Escape from Freedom* (1941) and *Man for Himself: An Inquiry into the Psychology of Ethics* (1947), and Herbert Marcuse, who published a key work of political theory, *Reason and Revolution*, in 1941.

Many European philosophers who stayed on the Continent during the war years influenced North American philosophy. For example, key existentialist texts appeared during the 1940's: Jean-Paul Sartre published *Being and Nothingness* (1943), *Anti-Semite and Jew* (1946), and *No Exit* (1944). Maurice Merleau-Ponty published *Phenomenology of Perception* in 1945 and Gabriel Marcel finished *The Mystery of Being* (1950). Simone de Beauvoir published a groundbreaking work of feminist philosophy, *The Second Sex*, in 1949.

Later in the decade, geopolitics emerging from Cold War global maneuvering for political and economic dominance had a significant impact on North American social thought. For example, both Hook and Niebuhr revised key political elements in their political philosophy, moving in differing degrees from former commitments to democratic socialism to liberal anticommunism. Dewey, Arendt, and Du Bois crafted important philosophical positions in relation to the impact of the Cold War on international and domestic politics, as did members of the Frankfurt School who returned to Germany at the end of the 1940's. Later during the 1940's, the opening salvos of the Second Red Scare, grounded in intense anticommunism, had an especially strong influence on political philosophy across the political spectrum.

Anticolonialist political philosophy also significantly affected North American philosophy. To give just one example, the social philosophy of Indian thinkers such as Mohandas K. Gandhi provided philosophical support for African American social philosophers as the Civil Rights movement gained major traction during the late 1940's. The Indian independence movement was just one of many international events that played out on the North American philosophical and political stage.

Impact   The 1940's are especially significant for the degree to which war, international political events, and cross-national philosophical movements influenced North American philosophy. Especially in the realm of social philosophy, the decade's international dynamics was critical for philosophers, who hoped to provide conceptual ground for taking concrete action in response to war, globalization, science, and geopolitics. These challenges persist, and much philosophical work done during the 1940's remains relevant for critical inquiry, ethical deliberation, and political action.

Sharon Carson

Further Reading

King, Richard H. *Race, Culture, and the Intellectuals: 1940-1970.* Washington, D.C.: Woodrow Wilson Center Press, 2004. Excellent study of the impact of World War II on social philosophers as diverse as Du Bois, Arendt, Adorno, Horkheimer, Sartre, and C. L. R. James. King pays close attention to the effects of racism and anti-Semitism on philosophy and social theory of the era.

Kuklick, Bruce. *A History of Philosophy in America: 1720-2000.* New York: Oxford University Press, 2001. Strong discussion of the 1940's in the crosscurrents of American history and international developments in philosophy as an academic field. Helpful and fair-minded treatment of specific philosophical issues and frameworks. Includes analysis of the impact of academic specialization and of dynamic tensions between professionalized philosophy and public intellectuals.

Marsoobian, Armen T., and John Ryder, eds. *The Blackwell Guide to American Philosophy.* Hoboken, N.J.: Wiley-Blackwell, 2004. Good blend of sections on specific philosophers, such as Dewey and Du Bois, placed in the broader context of American philosophical history.

Pells, Richard H. *The Liberal Mind in a Conservative Age: American Intellectuals in the 1940's and 1950's.* 2d ed. Middletown, Conn.: Wesleyan University Press, 1989. Especially illuminating about the impact of war and domestic politics on key thinkers in North America.

West, Cornel. *The American Evasion of Philosophy: A Genealogy of Pragmatism.* Madison: University of Wisconsin Press, 1989. Historically grounded treatment of pragmatism as an American philosophical movement, with strong sections on Dewey, Hook, Du Bois, and Niebuhr. Includes a good analysis of the role of race and religious thought in pragmatism.

See also   African Americans; Education in the United States; Jews in the United States; Literature in the United States; Psychiatry and psychology; Rand, Ayn; Refugees in North America; Religion in the United States; Social sciences; Theology and theologians.

■ Photography

By the 1940's, photography had largely won acceptance as a legitimate artistic medium, signaled by the creation of a Department of Photography at New York's Museum of Modern Art in 1940. Many artistic concerns of the 1930's carried forward into the 1940's, but new directions also emerged. Technical innovations extended photography's possibilities.

While the early years of the 1940's saw America still trying to overcome the social and economic trauma of the Great Depression, the first half of the decade was dominated by World War II. Afterward, America craved a return to normalcy, celebrated its industrial might and consumer comforts, yet had to adjust to a world beset by the onset of the Cold War and decolonization. New literary and artistic movements were in gestation, and the first stirrings of demands for racial justice were in the air. Photography reflected these trends.

Documentary Photography Among the achievements of the previous decade had been the cultivation of documentary photography, notably under the auspices of the Farm Security Administration (FSA) and the New York Photo League, publicizing unpleasant aspects of American life ignored by other media. Photographs of the period were direct, descriptive, often confrontational and accusatory, and intended to convince Americans of the necessity of federal economic policies.

By the 1940's, documentary photography had changed in tandem with changes in popular attitudes. Americans had grown tired of photographic depictions of poor sharecroppers and struggling migrants. Although the FSA would continue into 1943, when it was merged into the Office of War Information in the War Department, the photographers it now hired, Marion Post Wolcott and John Vachon among others, tended to emphasize the pastoral beauty of the land and to celebrate traditional rural values of family, work, and worship. Only Gordon Parks continued with the same level of social conscience, producing images highlighting racial injustice in American cities. In New York, the Photo League still sponsored explorations of the urban scene, but again, social protest was tempered with the search for beauty.

Outside the auspices of the FSA, documentary photography morphed into street photography, as spontaneously produced images began to celebrate the lyricism and fast pace of urban life. Walker Evans resumed an earlier project of making candid portraits of commuters on the New York subway using a concealed 35mm camera. Helen Levitt pursued the lives of children in New York's working-class neighborhoods, capturing their chalk drawings on the sidewalks as well as their games, mischief, and moments of discovery. Louis Faurer found beauty and drama in storefronts and Times Square. Aaron Siskind, who befriended the abstract expressionist painters of New York, turned his lens on the details of signs, buildings, graffiti, and the detritus of urban life to produce abstract images of pure shape, tone, and texture.

Magazines Magazine photography differed from documentary photography in several ways. First, magazine photography illustrated a broader range of themes, including political events, cultural and popular celebrities, and human interest stories, the latter often featuring the odd or humorous. Second, photographers in this medium usually did not print their own negatives but turned their film over to editorial departments that selected the images to use and determined how to crop, sequence, and caption them. Brief essays might also accompany photographs to provide context and a distinct narrative independent from the vision of the photographer. This often led to tension between the photographers and their employers.

Magazines such as *Life* and *Look* had begun publication as weeklies or biweeklies during the middle of the previous decade. They and others continued to field photographers of distinction. Margaret Bourke-White had already built a reputation as a photographer of industry. In 1940, she was the only Western photographer in Moscow as the German armies invaded the Soviet Union, pushing to the outskirts of Moscow and Stalingrad. Later, she accompanied American troops in North Africa, Italy, and Germany, where she documented the liberation of Buchenwald. After the war, she recorded the struggles for independence in India and the secession of Pakistan. Her image of Mohandas K. Gandhi at his spinning wheel, taken shortly before his assassination, remains a classic.

The Pacific campaign was also covered extensively. W. Eugene Smith was twice wounded as he traveled with battle-hardened troops from island to island. Unlike war photographers until then, Smith did not flinch from presenting the costs of war. His soldiers were dirty, exhausted, depressed, and traumatized. His image of two soldiers finding a naked and wounded infant on Saipan remains haunting to this day. After the war, he would master the form of the picture story, notably in "Country Doctor," a photo essay of a young physician confronting the emergency of an injured child, published in *Life* in 1948.

Magazine photography remained a vital form for the decade and well into the next two decades. Advertising also extended the scope of artistic photography as the desire to market fashion and consumer goods became pronounced after the war. Color images began to be preferred and were developed to high accomplishment by Irving Penn and other fashion photographers. Karsh and Arnold Newman pursued portraiture, the latter depicting his subjects in their work environments.

Pictorialism and Straight Photography If photography had to struggle for recognition as a valid artistic medium, photographers struggled among themselves to find the best path to artistic expression. One answer, dominant in the earlier decades of the century, was pictorialism. This movement held that artistic validity depended on emulating existing visual arts, notably painting and etching. Exotic printing processes, toning, soft-focus lenses, and hand manipulation of the images, either on the print or on the negative, were employed to achieve ethereal effects similar to impressionist painting.

Under the leadership of Alfred Stieglitz and Paul Strand in New York, and West Coast photographers of the Group f/64, especially Edward Weston and Ansel Adams, pictorialism had been largely supplanted by the 1940's. Their approach, called straight photography, sought to utilize the unique characteristics of photography, avoiding all attempts to copy other art forms. They emphasized clarity and transparency of the carefully composed image, with all details in sharp focus and avoiding manipulation of the image after development. By the 1940's, Stieglitz had ceased photographing, and arguably Weston's best work was behind him. Nonetheless, Weston was touring the country creating images for a special edition of Walt Whitman's *Leaves of Grass* when Pearl Harbor was attacked. He hurried back to California, where he spent the war years photographing primarily at his home in Carmel, sometimes to satirical effect. His beloved Point Lobos was closed off by the military for several years. As the war emergency lifted, he returned to Point Lobos, but by this time his physical stamina had begun to fail him due to the onset of Parkinson's disease. He made his last elegiac image, of stones on a beach at Point Lobos, in 1948.

Ansel Adams was at the height of his artistic powers throughout the decade. The war disrupted a national parks photographic project commissioned by the Department of the Interior, but it was during the 1940's that Adams created many of the images that have achieved iconic status for their beauty and spirituality.

After the war, younger photographers came to the fore. Some, such as Harry Callahan, Wynn Bullock, and Minor White, continued to practice the techniques and largely the aesthetic of Weston and Adams, but with a more personal vision. Others,

An Associated Press photographer using his "Big Bertha" camera for a closeup shot of a play in a New York Yankee's baseball game in October, 1946. (AP/Wide World Photos)

such as Clarence John Laughlin, Barbara Morgan, and Frederick Sommer, reached back to some of the manipulative techniques of pictorialism, including montage, multiple exposures, moving light sources, odd angles, and abstractions to explore inner realities, under the influence of surrealism and psychoanalytic theory.

Technology Technological advances continued to improve the tools available to photographers. Films offered increased sensitivity and finer grain structures that permitted enlargements of high quality. Improved lens design and coatings created clearer images without color distortion. However, two developments merit special mention.

The first practical color transparency film, Kodachrome, was released in 1937, followed by Ektachrome in 1942. A color negative film, Kodacolor, was released in 1941, followed by Ektacolor in 1947. These films became popular among amateurs and in advertising and magazine work. Artistically, they were considered limited in value at the time, although Eliot Porter explored the colors of nature and Irving Penn produced vivid still lifes in color that would lead to greater acceptance of color photography for artistic purposes in future decades.

The second innovation was instant film, invented by Edwin H. Land. Manufactured by Polaroid Corporation, the earliest such films produced black-and-white positive images within minutes of exposure. This limited their enlargement or reproduction until an instant negative film was subsequently released. Even so, the Polaroid print had attractive qualities. Ansel Adams became an early champion of Polaroid films.

Impact Dominated by war and recovery, the 1940's are better seen as a decade of continuity rather than innovation. Even so, the art of photography continued to develop. If the decade began with a waning interest in social documentation, it ended with a more diverse understanding of the medium's potential, laying the foundation for more radical experimentation that would occur in the next several decades.

John C. Hughes

Further Reading

Enyeart, James, ed. *Decade by Decade: Twentieth-Century American Photography from the Collection of the Center for Creative Photography.* Boston: Bulfinch Press, 1989. Essays on each decade of the century and images by all the photographers discussed here.

Newhall, Beaumont. *The History of Photography.* New York: Museum of Modern Art, 1982. Brief but classic history of photography.

Rosenblum, Naomi. *A World History of Photography.* New York: Abbeville Press, 1984. Comprehensive history of photography.

Szarkowski, John. *Photography Until Now.* New York: Museum of Modern Art, 1989. Emphasizes technological developments as they influenced the history of art photography.

Westerbeck, Colin, and Joel Meyerowitz. *Bystander: A History of Street Photography.* Boston: Little, Brown, 1994. History of street photography.

See also Art movements; Bourke-White, Margaret; *Life; Look*; Magazines; Polaroid instant cameras; Wartime propaganda in the United States.

■ Pinup girls

Definition Photographed or illustrated icons of American female beauty popular during World War II, especially among servicemen

Ubiquitous throughout the 1940's, pinup girl images circulated as Esquire *gatefolds, graced* Life *covers, and appeared in Army publications like* Yank. *Servicemen plastered pinups on their barracks walls and re-created them as bomber nose art. Calendars, playing cards, matchbook covers, and mutoscope cards (small, collectable cards sold in arcade vending machines) featured pinup girls. These images of American female pulchritude encouraged heterosexual fantasy in the sex-segregated military and represented the "girls next door" that servicemen left home to defend.*

The phrase "pinup girl" first appeared in the July 7, 1941, edition of *Life* magazine; the article used the expression to describe actor Dorothy Lamour, hailing her as the U.S. Army's preferred pinup girl. The pinup genre includes both illustrations of scantily clad women, evoking a playful story often accompanied by a cheeky one-liner, and cheesecake photography meant for fixing to a wall. *Esquire* illustrator Alberto Vargas (known for his Varga Girls), Brown & Bigelow's calendar artist Gil Elvgren, as well as female artists Zoë Mozert, Joyce Ballantyne, and Pearl

Frush, among others, created pinup illustrations for the American public and the fighting men overseas.

In addition to these artist-rendered beauties, pinup photography of female film stars proliferated throughout the war. Hollywood disseminated promotional photographs of popular actors, such as Veronica Lake, Lana Turner, and Esther Williams, for pinning up. Commissioned by Twentieth Century-Fox in 1941, photographer Frank Powolny's iconic image of Betty Grable wearing a one-piece white bathing suit and high heels, looking over her shoulder, is perhaps the most iconic pinup of the era. Several periodicals, both civilian and military, published cheesecake photos regularly. *Life* magazine featured photographs of favorite wartime pinups, including Bob Landry's famous image of Rita Hayworth posing on a bed, wearing a revealing black-and-white nightgown, which appeared in the magazine's August, 1941, issue. This image of Hayworth, second in popularity among white servicemen to Powolny's image of Grable, adorned an atomic bomb dropped on Bikini Atoll in 1946. *Yank*, an official War Department publication by and for servicemen, included a weekly "*Yank* Pin-Up Girl." At the same time, images of African American pinup girls—such as Lena Horne, Katherine Dunham, and Hilda Simms—popular among black servicemen, appeared in the black press as part of its campaign against fascism abroad and racism at home.

Impact The popularity of pinup girls inspired Hollywood films, such as the Grable vehicle *Pin Up Girl* (1944), and songs, such as "Peggy, the Pin Up Girl," performed by Glenn Miller and the Army Air Force Band. Women with sweethearts in the service created cheesecake photography featuring themselves as pinup girls, striking poses reminiscent of popular wartime pinup art, and sent them to their loved ones overseas. Servicemen, dreaming of life following the war, looked to images of pinup girls—Hollywood stars, illustrated fantasies, and home-front loves—to remember their motivations for fighting; pinup girls

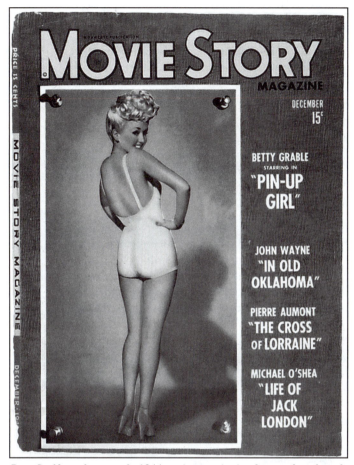

Betty Grable on the cover of a 1944 movie magazine in what may have been the single most-popular pin-up photo of the 1940's. (AP/Wide World Photos)

reminded G.I.'s of the women, and the way of life, they sought to protect.

Megan E. Williams

Further Reading

Buszek, Maria Elena. *Pin-up Grrrls: Feminism, Sexuality, Popular Culture.* Durham, N.C.: Duke University Press, 2006.

Martignette, Charles G., and Louis K. Meisel. *The Great American Pin-Up.* New York: Taschen, 1996.

Westbrook, Robert. *Why We Fought: Forging American Obligations in World War II.* Washington, D.C.: Smithsonian Books, 2004.

See also Fads; Films about World War II; Grable, Betty; Hayworth, Rita; Horne, Lena; *Life*; Magazines; Pornography.

■ Plutonium discovery

The Event   First production of a sample and the first positive recognition of the ninety-fourth element of the periodic table

Dates   December, 1940, to February, 1941

The discovery of plutonium, and, thus the discovery of its high probability of fissioning by neutrons, suggested the possibility of a second type of atomic bomb that differed from the uranium-235 bomb. The first atomic bomb tested and the bomb dropped on Nagasaki, Japan, were both plutonium bombs.

Edwin Mattison McMillan was a young scientist hired by Ernest Orlando Lawrence to work in the University of California, Berkeley, cyclotron lab. McMillan chose to investigate the possible existence of elements with atomic numbers higher than uranium. Together with a recent doctoral graduate,

Glenn Theodore Seaborg, one of the principal discoverers of plutonium. (©The Nobel Foundation)

Philip Abelson, McMillan bombarded uranium with neutrons from the cyclotron and obtained element 93, which they named neptunium. After many studies of the chemistry and radioactive decay of neptunium, they found evidence of another element with a lower decay rate and thus a longer lifetime that could be element 94.

McMillan wanted to become more active in the war effort, so he left Berkeley to work on radar at the Massachusetts Institute of Technology and turned over the search for elements beyond uranium to the chemist Glenn Seaborg. Seaborg made a comprehensive study of element 93, neptunium, hoping that a small amount of element 94 might also have been produced. By allowing the neptunium to decay away over several weeks, a small alpha-particle activity remained with a much longer half-life than the neptunium. On February 25, 1941, Seaborg and his student Arthur C. Wahl proved by chemical means that the alpha activity they saw was from element 94. They named the new element plutonium after the planet Pluto, following in the series that began with uranium (for the planet Uranus) and neptunium (for Neptune).

Because of the small amounts of irradiated uranium that could be made in the cyclotron, Seaborg had to research the separation on a submicroscopic scale, which had never been tried. In March, 1941, after the scientists laboriously separated a tiny sample of the new element, experiments were done to show that the sample would fission when bombarded by neutrons. The fission rate was found to be higher than that of U-235, the fissile isotope of uranium, and its half-life measured at around thirty thousand years, both of which made plutonium a better candidate for an atomic bomb than U-235. At this point, the U.S. military became interested in the discovery, and work began on the atomic bomb. The publication of research on plutonium ceased until after the war.

After plutonium fission was proven, the next step was to separate it from uranium and the by-products of the chain reaction. The plutonium would be present in a concentration of about only 250 parts per million, and the material would be radioactive, so remote handling and other safety measures were required.

Producing Plutonium for the Bomb   Because kilogram masses of plutonium were needed for the atomic bomb, production had to be expanded. Only about one pound of plutonium was contained in two tons of irradiated uranium. Therefore, the laboratory process had to be altered to expand production and separation of plutonium from uranium by a factor of approximately ten billion. This was the largest scale-up of a chemical process ever attempted. The main element of the scale-up was to make use of the chain reaction in specially designed nuclear reactors, which would produce plutonium by neutron bombardment of uranium rather than by cyclotron irradiation of uranium. This was followed by chemical separation of plutonium from uranium by a precipitation method, resulting in plutonium metal. Both the reactors and the separation plants were huge and costly, and it took great effort to produce a few kilograms of plutonium for the first bombs.

Impact After the plutonium bomb was dropped on Nagasaki, the United States began producing plutonium-type atomic bombs as quickly as the plutonium could be made in the production reactors at Hanford, Washington. Besides its use in nuclear weapons, one of the isotopes of plutonium, Pu-238, was found to emit alpha particles over a fairly long half-life, making it useful as a power source in thermal electric generators for research in space.

Raymond D. Cooper

Further Reading

Bernstein, Jeremy. *Plutonium. A History of the World's Most Dangerous Element.* Washington, D.C.: Joseph Henry Press, 2007. Well-written story of the people and science associated with the discovery of plutonium. It tells clearly why plutonium is important and how it works in nuclear weapons and other applications. Includes illustrations and an index.

Kelly, Cynthia C., ed. *The Manhattan Project: The Birth of the Atomic Bomb in the Words of Its Creators, Eyewitnesses, and Historians.* New York: Black Dog and Leventhal, 2007. Anthology of the writings of many people covering the history of the Manhattan Project. Includes illustrations, bibliography, chronology, and index.

Seaborg, Glenn T. *The Plutonium Story. The Journals of Professor Glenn T. Seaborg, 1939-1946.* Columbus, Ohio: Battelle Press, 1994. Seaborg's research journals covering the period of the discovery of the transuranic elements, including plutonium. With illustrations and name and subject indexes.

Seaborg, Glenn T., with Eric Seaborg. *Adventures in the Atomic Age—From Watts to Washington.* New York: Farrar, Straus and Giroux, 2001. An autobiography of Seaborg written with his son. It describes the discovery of plutonium and other transuranic elements. Includes illustrations and an index.

Smyth, Henry. *Atomic Energy for Military Purposes.* Rev. ed. Princeton, N.J.: Princeton University Press, 1946. Includes statements by the British and Canadian governments. The official account by the U.S. government of the development of the atomic bomb. Includes illustrations.

See also Atomic bomb; Atomic Energy Commission; Fermi, Enrico; Groves, Leslie Richard; Hanford Nuclear Reservation; Hiroshima and Nagasaki bombings; Manhattan Project; Nobel Prizes; Nuclear reactors; Wartime technological advances.

■ Point Four Program

Identification Postwar U.S. economic aid program for underdeveloped countries
Date Articulated on January 20, 1949

The Point Four Program established a system of technical assistance designed to improve the social and economic conditions of underdeveloped countries after World War II. As the Marshall Plan sought to rebuild the postwar European economy, the Point Four Program expanded financial support to a wider geographical landscape. The program focused its aid on advancing technology, science, and education abroad as the 1940's ended and the 1950's began.

President Harry S. Truman sealed the legacy of wartime victory with his aggressive and wide-sweeping inaugural address in January, 1949. His first three points—widespread support for the United Nations, economic assistance to war-torn European countries (the Marshall Plan), and aid to all free nations threatened by open aggression (through the soon-to-be-formed North Atlantic Treaty Organization)—represented the landmarks of American foreign policy at the end of the 1940's. His fourth point—embarking on a bold, new program to make the benefits of scientific and industrial progress available to underdeveloped areas—was his newest and most noticeable advancement. Appropriately enough, his proposal soon became known as the Point Four Program.

In a more detailed discussion with Congress on June 24, 1949, Truman urged the United States government, private investors, and volunteer organizations to provide economic aid with the purpose of expanding modernity in the underdeveloped areas of Africa, Asia, and Central and South America. According to the president, supplying these areas with a solid economic base and the latest technological resources would help stabilize the democratic future of these politically vulnerable regions.

Truman separated the types of aid into two closely related categories. The first category stressed "technical, scientific and managerial knowledge" and included specific aid in "medicine, sanitation, communications, road building and government services, but also, and perhaps most important, assistance in the survey of resources and in planning for long-range economic development." The second category encouraged "productive enterprises" and the development of machinery that could be used for local "harbor development, roads and communications, [and] irrigation and drainage projects."

In 1950, Congress approved $35 million (approximately $312 million in 2010 dollars) for the Point Four Program. At its start, the Technical Cooperative Administration was created under the Department of State to assist in the planning, aid dispensation, and evaluation of all aspects of the program. Aside from governmental support, Truman called for a continued increase in capital from private American companies interested in investing abroad.

Due to Truman's tireless advocacy, the program flourished during the final years of his presidency, especially as Cold War tensions grew stronger. During this time, the call to strengthen the social, economic, and political core of unstable countries that could potentially fall into communist hands resonated louder than ever. Upon his 1953 inauguration, President Dwight D. Eisenhower terminated the program and incorporated it into his broader foreign aid program soon thereafter.

Impact Although the Point Four Program only existed under its original name for a few years, Truman laid the groundwork for the modernization of underdeveloped countries with his combination of governmental and private aid to advance technology and education in underdeveloped nations. Although the overall efficiency with which these countries actually absorbed and applied these scientific advancements has been historically debated, the manner in which the United States has assisted developing nations in the last half of the twentieth and the early twenty-first centuries has been greatly influenced by the agenda introduced in Truman's 1949 inaugural address.

Eric Novod

Further Reading

Bass, Paul William. *Point Four: Touching the Dream.* Stillwater, Okla.: New Forums Press, 2009.

Lancaster, Carol. *Foreign Aid: Diplomacy, Development, Domestic Politics.* Chicago: University of Chicago Press, 2006.

See also Elections in the United States: 1948; Foreign policy of the United States; Marshall Plan; North Atlantic Treaty Organization; Truman, Harry S.; United Nations.

■ Polaroid instant cameras

Definition Technology incorporating innovative film and chemical processes to produce photographs within one minute

Polaroid's instant camera, invented during the 1940's, provided North American photographers, both amateur and professional, a tool that allowed for quick visual documentation. Consumer demand for instant cameras benefited Polaroid financially, and the company secured a position as a leading U.S. corporation within years of the instant camera's first appearance.

Since the early nineteenth century, cameras had enabled photographers to preserve images. Early photographic techniques required time, usually several hours, to record and expose images on chemically prepared plates. Many North Americans paid photographers at studios to take photographs of their families, soldiers leaving for war service, or prized belongings. By the late nineteenth century, cameras, notably those made by the Eastman Kodak Company, had become more affordable and available to consumers. Despite delays to develop pictures, photography appealed to many North Americans who bought cameras to document their lives.

Camera Technology In December, 1943, Edwin Herbert Land, a Harvard-educated physicist, experienced an epiphany that inspired him to design the

Polaroid instant camera. As a result of his previous light-polarization research, Land established the Polaroid Corporation in 1937. While vacationing with his family in Santa Fe, New Mexico, six years later, he photographed his three-year-old daughter. She wanted to see her picture soon after Land had taken it and asked why she had to wait. Her question was the catalyst for Land's contemplating the possibility of instant photography.

After returning to his laboratory, Land selected Polaroid colleagues, directed by engineer William J. McCune, to assist him in developing his instant-camera concept. Another engineer, David Grey, focused on optics for the instant camera's lens. Land utilized his chemistry expertise to create film that could be quickly transformed into photographs. By 1944, he began applying for U.S. patents for instant-camera components.

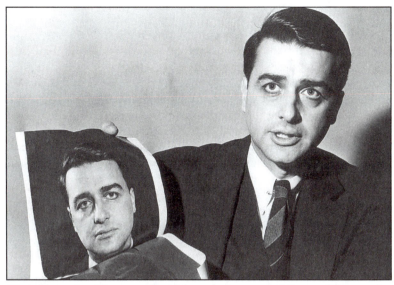

Edwin Herbert Land demonstrating his instant-print process. (Library of Congress)

The first Polaroid instant camera, dubbed 95, could produce photographs in one minute because of Land's unique film system. The instant camera contained rollers and two rolls of photographic materials. One roll held the negative with silver halide. The other roll consisted of paper with pods filled with hydroquinone and sodium thiosulfate, commonly used for developing photographs. The exposed negative and paper pressed together as they moved through rollers which broke the pods, distributing chemicals on the paper and negative, causing the silver halide to develop images on paper before the negative was peeled off to reveal the photograph. At first, only sepia instant film was available.

Promoting Instant Photography Land described the invention of the instant camera in the February, 1947, issue of the *Journal of the Optical Society of America*. On February 21, 1947, he displayed the Model 95 when members of the Optical Society of America met in New York City. Land posed for an instant camera, showing the audience the resulting photograph only one minute later. Newspapers and magazines printed a photograph of Land with his instant pho-

tograph. At that same conference Land met famed photographer Ansel Adams, whom he asked to evaluate the instant camera's artistic possibilities. Adams became a consultant for Polaroid the next year.

Because Land preferred research, he arranged for other companies to manufacture his cameras. The Rochester, New York, business Samson United initially produced instant cameras before Land selected the U.S. Time Corporation in Waterbury, Connecticut, to make them. He later secured additional contractors, including Eastman Kodak, to construct various parts.

Land exhibited the Model 95 in early November, 1948, at the Photographic Society of America meeting in Cincinnati, Ohio—an event that heightened public anticipation of the camera's commercial distribution. On November 26, 1948, Land promoted the Model 95 to customers; it debuted for sale at the Jordan Marsh department store in Boston, Massachusetts. The camera cost $89.75, and film for eight photographs sold for $1.50. Demand soon outstripped supply, and clerks had to sell display cameras. Land selected department stores where managers agreed to pay promotional costs. In May, 1949, consumers bought four thousand instant cameras in one week at Macy's in New York City.

Impact The Polaroid instant camera altered how people perceived photography. Although many professional photographers initially dismissed instant cameras, the camera attracted new amateurs to take up photography. In addition to their convenience and efficiency, instant cameras offered photographers privacy, because they did not require film to be processed by commercial developers. Polaroid expanded sales of instant cameras to foreign countries in September, 1949. The next month, *U.S. Camera* magazine presented Polaroid a U.S. Camera Achievement Award for the instant camera. Land received several honorary doctorates recognizing his instant-photography achievements.

Polaroid became a widely known brand name. Improved camera designs and black-and-white film resulted in one million instant cameras being sold by 1956. Polaroid's stock-market value reached one billion dollars in August, 1960. Color film and reduced development times for such models as the SX-70 helped Polaroid surpass the sales of all other photography corporations except Eastman Kodak. By the early twenty-first century, however, electronic digital photography was taking over the camera market and making most film cameras obsolete. Polaroid eventually stopped selling its instant film and began manufacturing its own digital cameras.

Elizabeth D. Schafer

Further Reading

Blout, Elkan. "Polaroid: Dreams to Reality." *Daedalus* 125, no. 2 (Spring, 1996): 38-53. Blout worked for Polaroid from 1943 to 1962 as a research chemist and administrator and provides memories of Land, colleagues, and instant-camera development.

Crist, Steve, and Barbara Hitchcock. *The Polaroid Book: Selections from the Polaroid Collections of Photography.* Los Angeles: Taschen, 2008. Includes four hundred photos taken with the Polaroid instant camera. Features an introduction outlining the history of the camera and the Polaroid company.

Kao, Deborah Martin. "Edwin Land's Polaroid: 'A New Eye'." In *Innovation/Imagination: Fifty Years of Polaroid Photography,* introductions by Barbara Hitchcock and Deborah Klochko. New York: Harry N. Abrams, 1999. Essay incorporates quotations by Land and Adams regarding photography as an art form and how this perception influenced Land when creating instant cameras.

Kimmelman, Michael. "Imperfect, yet Magical." *The New York Times,* December 28, 2008, p. WK-1. Comments on the cultural impact of instant cameras, noting famous photographers who used them. Describes people's reactions to Polaroid ceasing to produce film for instant cameras.

McElheny, Victor K. *Insisting on the Impossible: The Life of Edwin Land.* Reading, Mass.: Perseus Books, 1998. Biography examines Land's instant camera work during the 1940's and afterward. Chronology includes 1940's section. Illustrations feature instant cameras.

See also   Advertising in the United States; Bourke-White, Margaret; Hobbies; Inventions; Magazines; Newspapers; Photography; Science and technology.

■ Pollock, Jackson

Identification   Abstract expressionist painter
Born   January 28, 1912; Cody, Wyoming
Died   August 11, 1956; East Hampton, Long Island, New York

A leading figure in abstract expressionism and action painting, Pollock is famous for his revolutionary technique of pouring, dripping, and flinging liquid paint onto large unstretched canvases placed on the floor. He abandoned traditional ideas regarding imagery and composition to explore the expressive process of painting. His dynamic technique led to his nickname "Jack the Dripper."

Jackson Pollock's work during the 1940's reflected several influences. Impressions from his childhood in the American Southwest were apparent, as were the rhythmic figural patterns of Thomas Hart Benton, with whom he studied at New York's Art Students League. While working with the Federal Art Project from 1935 to 1942, Pollock encountered Mexican artists who acquainted him with large-scale murals and the use of liquid paint. Undergoing treatment for alcoholism with Jungian analysts, he also became interested in the role of the subconscious in creativity.

Pollock's paintings of the early 1940's featured coarse, semiabstract cubist imagery with spontaneous brushstrokes inspired by surrealist automatism. Representative works included *Male and Female* (1942), *The She-Wolf* (1943), and *Guardians of the Secret* (1943). He had his first solo exhibition at Peggy Guggenheim's Art of This Century gallery in 1943.

Pollock developed his personal iconography and style. He experimented with liquid paint in *Composition with Pouring I* (1943). His work evolved from the cubist-inspired *Water Figure* (1945) to the rhythmic color figuration of *Water Bull* (c. 1946) to the densely veiled imagery of *Shimmering Substance* (c. 1946), with overall composition resembling surrealist automatic writing.

After moving to East Hampton, New York, in 1945 with his wife, fellow painter Lee Krasner, Pollock developed the technique for which he became famous. With a new directness, he laid large pieces of canvas on his studio floor and proceeded to drip, pour, and spatter liquid commercial paint. He gave equal emphasis to all parts of the paintings as he moved around and within the canvas surfaces to apply pigment from every direction. Lines and shapes recorded the momentum of the artist's gestures. He further manipulated the paintings with sticks, trowels, knives, and even basting syringes. Sometimes he trimmed the canvases or added objects for texture. His work was a mixture of controlled and spontaneous factors. By 1947, he had dispensed with easily discernable imagery.

From 1947 through 1950, Pollock created his greatest compositions: large-scale, intricately interwoven labyrinths of fluid lines and shapes with no particular focal points. Works such as *Cathedral* and *Full Fathom Five* (both 1947) exemplified densely layered "all-over" compositions. In works such as *Number 23, 1948* and *Number 2, 1949*, he abandoned dense surfaces for rhythmic linear webs. He explored expressive qualities of the spontaneous painting process itself (though some people discerned figurative elements in his swirling lines and shapes). When his drip paintings were first shown at the Betty Parsons Gallery in 1948, many were shocked by his revolutionary style. In 1949, however, *Life* magazine published a profile suggesting that Pollock was America's greatest living painter.

Impact By the end of the 1940's, Pollock's battle with alcoholism had intensified, and in 1956 he was killed in an alcohol-related single car crash. Since his premature death at the age of forty-four, there have been numerous retrospective exhibitions of his work. He challenged the traditional views about what painting should be and created a visual language unlike anything seen before. His influence is still apparent in avant-garde movements. Recog-

nized as a major figure in American abstract expressionism, many critics list him among the most important artists in Western history.

Cassandra Lee Tellier

Further Reading
Emmerling, Leonhard. *Jackson Pollock*. Los Angeles: Taschen, 2003.
Engelmann, Ines Janet. *Jackson Pollock and Lee Krasner*. New York: Prestel, 2007.

See also Art movements; Art of This Century; De Kooning, Willem; Hopper, Edward; Rockwell, Norman.

■ Pornography

Definition Representations of erotic behavior in various media that is intended to cause sexual excitement

Despite state and local laws that prohibited "obscene" materials that portrayed sexual behavior, sexually charged entertainment gained popularity in American culture during the 1940's. The rigid censorship standards of previous decades began to erode after World War II as a more open attitude toward sex began to prevail among the general populace. As a result, sexually charged media flourished in the publishing and film industries.

Sexually explicit images, films, and prose persisted during the 1940's despite laws that penalized or banned media content that was deemed harmful to society. The U.S. Postal Service was authorized to deny mailing services to materials deemed "obscene." Hollywood's Production Code denied a seal of approval to movies that failed to meet standards of public decency. As men left the workforce to fight in World War II, ideal images of the American woman shifted to emphasize independence and self-reliance. These ideals contributed to more brazen depictions of femininity in popular culture.

Men's magazines such as *Esquire* included "pinup" illustrations of provocatively clad models among their otherwise respectable repertoire of fiction, short essays, and topical articles. These images were intended to sexually excite viewers but were not obviously vulgar or obscene. Pinups became ubiquitous among American servicemen during the war. Girlie pictures on posters, calendars, and playing cards and painted on the noses of airplanes were said to boost morale by reminding American troops of whom they were fighting for and what they could look forward to when the fighting ended.

Not all pinups might be considered pornographic, and they presented a less controversial form of viewing pleasure than more obviously pornographic alternatives. "Tijuana bibles," comic books depicting famous cartoon characters or celebrities having sex, were still bought and sold illegally in some bookstores and newsstands, but they were rare. More popular were the new fetish magazines such as *Bizarre* and *Wink*, which included scantily clad women in bondage poses, along with stories describing humiliation and spanking. These magazines proliferated after the 1946 Supreme Court decision *Hannegan v. Esquire*, in which the Court ruled that the U.S. postmaster general could not deny second-class postage rates to *Esquire* simply because he found its images objectionable.

Nudity in photography and movies was generally considered more tolerable if it claimed to have educational or artistic merit. "Exploitation films" sometimes used this idea as an excuse to present sexually charged images, usually of women in perilous situations. These found circulation among independent theaters and metropolitan art houses. Nude photography gained limited acceptance as legitimate art during this period. Overt sexuality was avoided, but some images sexually excited viewers whether or not they were intended to do so. "Stag films," short films of people engaged in sex (mostly heterosexual couples), were universally illegal but continued to be produced and distributed for small audiences in clandestine "stag parties" across the United States.

Impact The increasing availability and variety of sexually explicit materials after World War II set the stage for the social and legal debates over the concept of "obscenity" and the limits of free expression beginning in the mid-1950's. Hugh Hefner, an employee of *Esquire* during the 1940's, introduced *Playboy* magazine in 1953, with the first issue featuring a nude photo of Marilyn Monroe taken in 1949. *Playboy*'s "playmate" images supplanted the outdated pinups of *Esquire* as the quintessential feminine object of male desire.

Shaun Horton

Further Reading

Buszek, Maria Elena. *Pin-up Grrrls: Feminism, Sexuality, Popular Culture.* Durham, N.C.: Duke University Press, 2006.

Schaefer, Eric. *"Bold! Daring! Shocking! True!": A History of Exploitation Films, 1919-1959.* 2d ed. Durham, N.C.: Duke University Press, 1999.

Slade, Joseph. *Pornography and Sexual Representation: A Reference Guide.* 3 vols. Westport, Conn.: Greenwood Press, 2001.

See also Censorship in the United States; Comic books; Film in Canada; Film in the United States; Magazines; Photography; Pinup girls; Pulp magazines; Sex and sex education; *United States v. Paramount Pictures, et al.*

■ Port Chicago naval magazine explosion

The Event Noncombat military disaster
Date July 17, 1944
Place Port Chicago, Contra Costa County, California

The explosion of two munitions ships at the Port Chicago supply depot in San Francisco Bay is significant because it was the worst disaster of its kind during World War II and because the African American personnel who were its chief victims refused to return to work immediately afterward.

Until after World War II, African Americans in the military were consigned to racially segregated units and usually limited to menial duties. At the United States Navy ammunition depot at Port Chicago, California, African Americans primarily worked as stevedores, loading ammunition onto warships. The men received no specialized training in munitions handling. They were frequently pressured to work faster by white officers who had been encouraged to compete with each other for speed. On June 17, 1944, two ships exploded, and 321 people, most of them African Americans, died.

A few weeks after the blast, 300 men were ordered to return to ammunition loading, but 258 employees refused to obey. Their action was regarded as mutiny and fifty men were eventually court-martialed. Lawyer Thurgood Marshall appealed the men's cases, and in 1946, President Harry S. Truman granted clemency. Only one survivor eventually received a full pardon, which came from President Bill Clinton in 1999.

Impact The Port Chicago naval magazine explosion raised awareness of the need for safer design of munitions and for better training in munitions handling. The deaths of 321 people and the court-martial of the many survivors also exposed the depths of racism in the American military during the 1940's and played a role in the eventual desegregation of the armed forces.

Susan Roth Breitzer

Further Reading

Allen, Robert L. *The Port Chicago Mutiny: The Story of the Largest Mass Mutiny Trial in U.S. Naval History.* Berkeley, Calif.: Heydey Books, 1993.

McLeod, Dean L. *Port Chicago.* Charleston, S.C.: Arcadia, 2007.

See also Desegregation of the U.S. military; Liberty ships; Military conscription in the United States; National Association for the Advancement of Colored People; Navy, U.S.; Racial discrimination; Tuskegee Airmen; Wartime sabotage; World War II.

Workmen searching debris from the carpenter shop on the pier of Port Chicago after the structure was leveled by the munition ship explosions. (AP/Wide World Photos)

■ Post, Emily

Identification: American writer on personal etiquette
Born: October 27, 1872; Baltimore, Maryland
Died: September 25, 1960; New York, New York

Americans followed Post's advice on proper social conduct from her first publication of Etiquette in Society, in Business, in Politics, and at Home *in 1922 into the 1960's, when social mores were becoming more relaxed. Her name became synonymous with etiquette and deportment, and her advice was especially sought during the 1940's, when the special needs of military etiquette prompted her to revise her book.*

Most Americans considered Emily Post an artifact who dispensed advice appropriate to an earlier era.

At the end of 1941, questions about table settings and decorum took a back seat to the American commitment to the war. Post answered questions generated about military protocol and servicemen's interactions with civilians in her newspaper column. She published a revised edition of her book *Etiquette* in 1942, adding a thirteen-page wartime supplement. This new edition became highly recommended reading for military officers and gentlemen in training.

The supplement suggested that in a time of war, it was necessary to ignore certain conventions to permit women to write letters to anonymous soldiers, young women to dance with strangers, and couples to rush their weddings during the grooms' furloughs. Post also warned against subversive activities that endangered the country, while cautioning against unwarranted suspiciousness toward aliens. She easily adapted her advice to fit new, perplexing situations. Military chaplains used her book to help in their counseling work with service personnel.

After the war, Post published another revision of *Etiquette,* from which she removed the chapter on espionage and added a new section on military and postwar etiquette. This new section included advice on how to interact with seriously wounded war veterans.

Impact During the war years, Post's column saw its highest popularity in twelve years. It was printed in ninety-eight newspapers across the United States and reached 5.5 million readers. Post received upward of five thousand letters per week, some of which she answered in her column. The Office of War Information and Army and Navy officials often asked her advice on proper etiquette for service personnel. During 1946, the year after World War II ended, Post's book sold more than five thousand copies per week. Over the next few years, demand for her advice grew even greater as members of all classes and sectors of American society grew more anxious to improve their manners.

Rebecca Tolley-Stokes

Further Reading

Claridge, Laura. *Emily Post: Daughter of the Gilded Age, Mistress of American Manners.* New York: Random House, 2008.

Post, Emily. *Etiquette in Society, in Business, in Politics, and at Home.* New York: Funk & Wagnalls, 1942.

See also: Book publishing; Fads; Fashions and clothing; Sex and sex education; Women's roles and rights in the United States.

■ Postage stamps

Postage stamps interested countless people around the world during the 1940's, and many stamp dealers prospered in this decade. Many people became devoted stamp collectors who learned much about geography, history, famous people, art, and other subjects through their stamp collections.

Postage stamps issued during the 1940's reflected the dramatic changes taking place throughout the world. Some stamps displayed portraits of dictators and other world leaders, while others depicted the military campaigns of World War II. In some cases, bold colors and creative artwork depicted a nation's identity, with these stamps often incorporating elements of propaganda.

In the United States, a series of stamps with portraits of famous authors, poets, educators, scientists, composers, artists, and inventors was issued in 1940. After the nation entered World War II, there were stamps exhorting America to "win the war," featuring the flags of the European nations that had been overrun by Germany, and depicting American troops passing under the Arc de Triomphe as they liberated Paris from Nazi occupation. Stamps issued in Germany during this period similarly featured German soldiers engaged in victorious combat.

The design and diverse content of stamps issued in the 1940's increased the popularity of stamp collecting. Collectors soaked stamps off paper and envelopes and then sorted, arranged, and placed them in albums. Fellow collectors might spend an evening together augmenting their collections by swapping their duplicate stamps for ones they needed.

President Franklin D. Roosevelt was one of the many people who found solace and relaxation by collecting postage stamps. Wealthy individuals spent small fortunes acquiring the rarest of stamps from the nineteenth century. Some of their collections were of such value that they were kept in safes. However, since it took little money to start a collection, individuals of limited means could also enjoy the hobby. All schoolchildren had to do was cut off the portion of the envelope containing a stamp, soak it in water to remove the stamp, dry the stamp off, and put it into an album or on a blank page. The equipment that was needed for stamp collecting was minimal. An album, a pair of tweezers, a magnifying glass, and some lightly gummed hinges to paste stamps in albums were the only essential materials—other than the stamps themselves.

Countless collectors added to their holdings by buying "approvals"—sheets of hinged stamps that dealers mailed to hobbyists. Dealers' advertisements lured customers, particularly children, by promising free packets of attractive stamps for those who would consider their approvals. These advertisements usually would be illustrated with pictures of the most irresistible stamps. In addition to receiving stamps via the mail, many collectors obtained stamps at stores specializing in stamps and stamp collecting equipment.

Many hobbyists specialized. Some collected "first-day covers"—stamps on envelopes that had been mailed on the first day they were issued. Others obtained the stamps of only one country, which was often the collector's native nation. Others focused their collections on airmail stamps, stamps depicting animals, portrait stamps, or the stamps of a specific chronological period.

Governments worldwide continued to issue new stamps at a fast clip during the 1940's. Many stamps, such as those issued by the Soviet Union, were primarily designed for propaganda purposes. Nevertheless, many collectors tried to maintain collections of all of the stamps they could acquire from all of the world's nations.

Impact   Some people have argued that stamp collecting in the 1940's strengthened world democracy. This popular hobby taught countless Americans and people from other nations about culture and society, heightened appreciation of art, and strengthened knowledge of world events, geography, and history.

Henry Weisser

Further Reading

Scott's New Handbook for Philatelists. New York: Simon & Schuster, 1967.

Williams, L., and M. Williams. *Scott's Guidebook to Stamp Collecting.* New York: Simon & Schuster, 1963.

See also   Architecture; Art of This Century; Coinage; Hobbies; Photography; Recreation.

■ Potsdam Conference

The Event   Conference held by the United States, Great Britain, and the Soviet Union to discuss postwar Europe and the unfinished war against Japan

Date   July 17-August 2, 1945

Place   Potsdam, Germany

This was the third, last, and longest of the wartime meetings by the "Big Three" leaders during World War II. Major topics discussed were boundaries and peace terms for Europe, Poland's future borders and government, and the terms of surrender for Japan.

The Grand Alliance forced Nazi Germany to surrender in May, 1945. Two months later, the Big Three leaders—Harry S. Truman, Joseph Stalin, and Winston Churchill—met at the Cecilienhof in Potsdam, near Berlin, to discuss

postwar issues. After the British general election in July, however, a new prime minister, Clement Attlee, replaced Churchill midway through the conference at Potsdam.

The conference was tense from the start. President Truman and Secretary of State James Byrnes sought to settle European problems so that the United States could concentrate on defeating Japan. Truman sought agreements on the Allied occupation of Germany and sought to acquire a Soviet commitment to the conflict in the Far East.

Over the two-week conference, the leaders hammered out the so-called Potsdam Agreement, which established the Council of Foreign Ministers. This council, consisting of the United States, the Soviet Union, Britain, France, and China, was given the task of coming up with peace treaties concerning Germany and its Axis satellites. In respect to Germany, the leaders agreed that the nation should be demilitarized, denazified, and democratized. The Allied Control Council, comprising the United

---

Dismantling Germany's Political and Military Structure

The Potsdam Agreement, signed August 1, 1945, by the leaders of the United States, the United Kingdom, and the Soviet Union, established guidelines for the postwar reconstruction and occupation of Germany by the Allied Powers. Section II of the agreement, partially reproduced below, focuses on the dismantling on the political, military, and philosophical structure of German society.

The purposes of the occupation of Germany by which the Control Council shall be guided are:

(i) The complete disarmament and demilitarization of Germany and the elimination or control of all German industry that could be used for military production. . . .

(iii) To destroy the National Socialist Party and its affiliated and supervised organizations, to dissolve all Nazi institutions, to ensure that they are not revived in any form, and to prevent all Nazi and militarist activity or propaganda.

(iv) To prepare for the eventual reconstruction of German political life on a democratic basis and for eventual peaceful cooperation in international life by Germany.

Source: A Decade of American Foreign Policy: Basic Documents, 1941-1949. Washington, D.C.: Government Printing Office, 1950.

Winston Churchill (left), Harry S. Truman, and Joseph Stalin at the Potsdam Conference. (National Archives)

States, Britain, Soviet Union, and France, would supervise these procedures in their respective military occupation zones. Germany, Austria, and their respective capitals of Berlin and Vienna were divided into four military occupation zones. Furthermore, the Big Three decided that the surviving top Nazi leaders would be prosecuted for crimes committed during the war. As for changes to German borders and reparations, the Big Three had different opinions that made an agreement difficult. In the end, the United States and Britain tentatively agreed to recognize Stalin's adjustment of the German-Polish border westward to the Oder-Neisse line. The Poles would be allowed to occupy and administer former German territory east of the Oder-Neisse line until the conclusion of a peace settlement. The Big Three decided that each power would extract reparations from its respective zone. The Western powers also acceded to Stalin's demands for reparations from Soviet-occupied

Germany along with 10 percent of the industrial output from the military occupation zones in the west.

In regards to the war in the Far East, Stalin confirmed that the Soviet Union would be ready to attack Japan by mid-August. Truman then informed Stalin that the United States had a new weapon of destructive force, alluding to the atomic bomb. Then, on July 26, Truman issued the Potsdam Declaration, calling on Japan to surrender unconditionally to avoid its utter destruction.

Impact   The Potsdam Conference was the last wartime meeting of the Big Three. Some postwar agreements were made, but the end of the war in August, 1945, would see the continuing unraveling of the Grand Alliance. In fact, some historians regard the Potsdam Conference as the beginning of the Cold War.

William Young

Further Reading

Gormly, James L. *From Potsdam to the Cold War: Big Three Diplomacy, 1945-1947.* Wilmington, Del.: Scholarly Resources, 1990.

Mee, Charles L., Jr. *Meeting at Potsdam.* New York: M. Evans, 1975.

Offner, Arnold A. *Another Such Victory: President Truman and the Cold War, 1945-1953.* Stanford, Calif.: Stanford University Press, 2002.

See also   Atomic bomb; Byrnes, James; Churchill, Winston; Cold War; Foreign policy of the United States; Germany, occupation of; Korea; Truman, Harry S.; Unconditional surrender policy; World War II; Yalta Conference.

■ Pound, Ezra

Identification: American-born expatriate poet and critic

Born: October 30, 1885; Hailey, Idaho

Died: November 1, 1972; Venice, Italy

A poet, critic, editor, and prolific supporter of the arts, Pound acted as editor to T. S. Eliot's The Waste Land *(1922) and worked hard on behalf of other poets and writers while also publishing his own significant literary essays and works of poetry. He is considered a leading proponent of Modernism, and one of the creators of Imagism. During World War II, however, he made controversial radio broadcasts from Fascist Italy that led to his arrest and incarceration.*

Ezra Pound grew up in Pennsylvania, and studied Romance languages in college. In 1908, after a brief stint teaching at Wabash College, Pound moved to Europe. In 1914, he married Dorothy Shakespear with whom he later moved from London to Paris before settling permanently in Rapallo, Italy. After 1924, Pound resided full-time in Italy. Pound had a daughter, Mary de Rachewiltz, with his mistress, concert violinist Olga Rudge in 1925. In 1926, Pound's wife, Dorothy, had a son, Omar. During the 1940's, Pound spent most of his time in Rapallo (where his parents had previously retired in order to be near their son) working on various projects, primarily focusing on Confucian translations.

In late 1941, Pound broadcast the first of more than one hundred radio lectures within Italy, which became an ally of Nazi Germany in World War II. After the fall of Benito Mussolini's Fascist regime in 1943, Pound stopped broadcasting his lectures; however, during these Radio Rome broadcasts, he always referred to himself as an American. On May 3, 1945, he was taken by Italian partisans to Zoagli and subsequently arrested by American forces as a possible traitor because of his radio broadcasts and presumed Fascist sympathies.

After his arrest, Pound was moved first to Genoa, then to an outdoor cage at the Disciplinary Training Center in Pisa, where he suffered what was thought to be a mental breakdown. Many colorful poetic images of this incarceration would later appear in his *Pisan Cantos* (1948). While he was incarcerated, Pound continued working on the Confucian translations and writing cantos that would later appear in his most famous collection, *The Cantos of Ezra Pound* (1948). In November, 1945, he was transported by airplane to the United States to stand trial; it was his first time in a plane. After he arrived

Ezra Pound in Italy in early 1941. (AP/Wide World Photos)

in the United States, it was determined that he was unable to stand trial for treason due to his mental state. He was then admitted to St. Elizabeths Hospital, outside Washington, D.C., where he was incarcerated from December 21, 1945, until his release in 1958.

Despite the treason charges made against him, Pound won the newly created Bollingen Prize for his *Pisan Cantos* in 1949. This award came with a cash prize; however, many Americans were upset that an apparent Fascist sympathizer should receive so prestigious an award. Nevertheless, T. S. Eliot—another expatriate American poet—accepted the award on Pound's behalf.

After Pound's release in 1958, he returned to Italy, where he split his time between Rapallo and Venice, alternately living with his wife, Dorothy, and his mistress, Olga Rudge. Shortly after celebrating his eighty-seventh birthday, Pound was hospitalized and died in a Venice hospital, with Olga Rudge holding his hand.

Impact Pound's influence upon twentieth century literature and poetry is evidenced by his contribution to the Modernist movement and the creation of the poetic movements known as Imagism and vorticism. Pound wrote key literary essays and collections of poetry, including his most famous work, *The Cantos of Ezra Pound*. He altered the course of twentieth century literature through his contributions as a writer, editor, and literati.

Andy K. Trevathan

Further Reading

Conover, Anne. *Olga Rudge and Ezra Pound: What Thou Lovest Well*. New Haven, Conn.: Yale University Press, 2001.

Spoo, Robert, and Omar Pound, eds. *Ezra and Dorothy Pound: Letters in Captivity, 1945-1946*. New York: Oxford University Press, 1999.

Stock, Noel. *The Life of Ezra Pound*. San Francisco: North Point, 1982.

See also: Auden, W. H.; Benét, Stephen Vincent; Eliot, T. S.; Italian campaign; Literature in Canada; Literature in the United States; War crimes and atrocities; Wartime propaganda in the United States.

■ President Roosevelt and the Coming of the War

Identification Revisionist interpretation of American entry into World War II
Author Charles A. Beard (1874-1948)
Date Published in 1948

Beard's book provoked a furious protest from his professional colleagues with his claim that President Franklin D. Roosevelt manipulated the United States into entering World War II, and that the president may even have had some foreknowledge of the bombing of Pearl Harbor. In the president's deviousness, Beard maintained, Roosevelt betrayed American trust and violated the U.S. Constitution.

Charles A. Beard frames his indictment of Roosevelt in three parts: appearances, unveiling realities, and realities as described by the Pearl Harbor documents. He stresses Roosevelt's pledge to the American people that troops were not going to be sent into foreign wars, but the United States would provide material aid to nations under attack. Thus, in his State of the Union address on January 6, 1941, Roosevelt announced a plan to send large quantities of munitions and supplies to the Allies. The resulting Lend-Lease program became the subject of great debate in Congress, with remarks by Senator Pat McCarran, a Democrat from Nevada, and Senator Arthur Hendrick Vandenberg, a Michigan Republican, typical of the bipartisan criticism that the program inflated the president's power and would move America toward war.

More controversy followed the unofficial practice of convoying British ships to guard against German submarines. The Atlantic Conference of August, 1941, took place on board the warship *Potomac*, with Roosevelt and British prime minister Winston Churchill. The president's comments were evasive, but it was generally assumed that he agreed with Churchill on the need to defeat Adolf Hitler. In October, Roosevelt urged Congress to repeal section 6 of the Neutrality Act, which prohibited arming American ships engaged in foreign commerce.

Roosevelt described the Japanese attack on Pearl Harbor as a surprise, but Beard's evidence suggests this claim was disingenuous, and both Congress and the press soon began raising questions. On the evening of November 25, Roosevelt met with his war cabinet, and Secretary of War Henry L. Stimson recorded in his diary

> in spite of the risk involved, however, in letting the Japanese fire the first shot, we realized that in order to have the full support of the American people it was desirable to make sure that the Japanese be the ones to do this . . .

In a long, final chapter devoted to this meeting, Beard rests his case. Eventually, in June, 1944, a joint resolution of Congress promised a complete investigation of the circumstances of the Pearl Harbor attack, especially the actions of the commanding officers, Major General Walter C. Short and Admiral Husband Edward Kimmel, who had been found accountable and relieved of their commands. They were never exonerated.

Impact Beard's professional colleagues were almost unanimous in their condemnation of his thesis, and Yale University Press, the publisher of his book, was threatened with a boycott. Writer Campbell Craig argues that Beard's critics are wrong in their attempts to draw a straight line from his opposition to the war before Pearl Harbor to his single-minded determination to convict Roosevelt after it. Craig sees an issue of means and ends in Roosevelt actions—devious means used to justify a worthy end. Writer Robert B. Stinnett, in his excellently documented study. agrees with Craig's view.

Frank Day

Further Reading

Craig, Campbell. Introduction to *President Roosevelt and the Coming of War, 1941: A Study in Appearances and Realities*, by Charles A. Beard. New Brunswick, N.J.: Transaction, 2003.

Sperber, Ann. *Murrow: His Life and Times.* New York: Freundlich, 1986.

Stinnett, Robert B. *Day of Deceit. The Truth About FDR and Pearl Harbor.* New York: Simon & Schuster, 2000.

See also "Arsenal of Democracy" speech; Atlantic, Battle of the; Atlantic Charter; Churchill, Winston; "Four Freedoms" speech; Lend-Lease; Military conscription in the United States; Presidential powers; Roosevelt, Franklin D.; Stimson, Henry L.; World War II mobilization.

■ Presidential powers

Definition Expansion of the powers perceived to be held by the U.S. president

The expansion of presidential powers transformed the nature of the presidency and the relationship between the president and Congress.

By the end of the 1940's, it was recognized that the role of the presidency had grown significantly, if gradually, over the preceding twenty years. Presidential powers expanded with the emergency measures initiated during the Depression of the 1930's, but their consolidation and the president's largely unmonitored foreign policy activity during World War II transformed the nature of the presidency.

President Franklin D. Roosevelt's victory in 1940 gave him an unprecedented third term as president, breaking the unwritten tradition of a two-term limit for any president. The election came as the result of Roosevelt's tremendous popularity as the president who had steered the United States during the Great Depression with his New Deal and confidence in him as fear spread of the war raging in Europe and the Far East.

Roosevelt played a strong role in American participation in World War II, which officially began on December 7, 1941, after the Japanese attacked Pearl Harbor. The United States already was committed to supporting the United Kingdom and the Soviet Union against the Axis Powers (Germany, Italy, and Japan) as part of the Atlantic Charter drafted by the United States and United Kingdom in August, 1941. During the war, Roosevelt virtually unilaterally handled American foreign policy at the "Big Three" conferences in Casablanca with Great Britain and at Yalta, with both Great Britain and the Soviet Union, as well as other conferences. Few outside the presidential circle knew the details of the agreements reached, though they shaped the conduct of the war and postwar arrangements, including formation of the United Nations and decisions about the treatment of the defeated Axis nations.

Roosevelt's popularity resulted in victory for the fourth time in 1944, even though he was ill during much of the campaign. Harry S. Truman, who became president after Roosevelt's death in April, 1945, only gradually learned of Roosevelt's policies. Truman faced difficult years after the war, not only because of domestic and international issues but also because Congress sought to roll back some presidential powers that had expanded in the previous decade. The Twenty-second Amendment to the Constitution, passed by Congress in 1947 and ratified by the states by 1951, formally limited the president to two terms, thus ensuring that no president could run for a third term.

Truman had a stormy relationship with Congress during his presidency. Congress, cognizant of having lost ground during the Roosevelt years, passed the Legislative Reorganization Act of 1946, which gave Congress wide-ranging investigative powers. The investigative powers were notably applied in the investigations of communists and organized crime over the next decade. Congressional backlash against the presidency was not a new phenomenon but was especially sharp in the Truman years, just as it was after Richard Nixon's resignation during the 1970's. Historians nevertheless have rated Truman as one of the most effective of the modern presidents.

Impact The growth in the presidency during the 1940's proved impossible to roll back entirely, despite countermeasures by Congress in the later part of the decade. The presidency continued to expand during the 1960's and 1970's, and historian Arthur Schlesinger, Jr., coined the term "the imperial presidency" in a 1973 book with that title. Despite attempts to reduce the powers of the presidency after Nixon, the office never returned to its pre-Roosevelt status.

Norma C. Noonan

Further Reading

Greenstein, Fred I. *The Presidential Difference: Leadership Style from FDR to George W. Bush.* Princeton, N.J.: Princeton University Press, 2004.

Jones, Charles O. *The Presidency in a Separated System.* 2d ed. Washington, D.C.: Brookings Institution, 2005.

Neustadt, Richard. *Presidential Power: The Politics of Leadership from Roosevelt to Reagan.* Rev. ed. New York: Free Press, 1991.

See also Atlantic Charter; Bretton Woods Conference; Congress, U.S.; Economic wartime regulations; Elections in the United States: 1940; Elections in the United States: 1944; Executive orders; Foreign policy of the United States; Presidential Succession Act of 1947; Roosevelt, Franklin D.; Truman, Harry S.; Truman Doctrine.

■ Presidential Succession Act of 1947

The Law Federal legislation revising the order of succession to the U.S. presidency

Date Signed into law on July 18, 1947

This act changed the line of presidential succession to ensure that elected officials from Congress would fill the position of president before appointed members of the executive branch. It placed the Speaker of the House and the president pro tempore of the Senate before the cabinet in the line of succession.

Article II, section 1 of the United States Constitution specifies that the vice president assumes the role of chief executive should the incumbent president be unable to fulfill his duties. However, the founders did not offer an extensive list of successors should there be a double vacancy in the offices of both the presidency and the vice presidency. Rather, they gave Congress the authority to determine the line of succession. This was particularly important prior to the 1967 ratification of the Twenty-fifth Amendment when a vacancy in the vice presidency went unfilled until the next presidential election.

Historical debate over presidential vacancies has focused on two fundamental controversies: whether executive or legislative officials should take over in the event of a double vacancy, and whether there should be an interim election to replace an acting president. Prior to 1947, potential vacancies were covered by the Presidential Succession Act of 1886, which placed executive cabinet officials first in the succession line in the event of a double vacancy. Additionally, Congress was given the power to determine whether an interim election would be held to name a permanent presidential successor.

The debate over the passage of the Presidential Succession Act of 1947 rehashed the same political and democratic questions as previous acts on presidential vacancies. President Franklin D. Roosevelt's death in April, 1945, at the beginning of his fourth term, meant that Harry S. Truman would serve without a vice president for almost four years until the election of 1948. Given these circumstances, Truman asked Congress to change the order of presidential succession. He argued that placing the

Speaker of the House and then the president pro tempore of the Senate in line behind the vice president was inherently more democratic since both had won election to Congress and then been chosen for leadership positions by their elected peers. Truman also requested that Congress make provisions for an interim election if a president died or resigned during the first two years of his term. The Democratic Congress did not act on Truman's request. However, after Republicans took control of Congress following the 1946 elections, the act was passed, reordering the presidential line of succession after the vice president to the Speaker of the House, the president pro tempore of the Senate, and then the cabinet. Any person serving as the acting president was required to resign his or her existing position. The legislation did not include provisions for a special interim presidential election.

Impact The Presidential Succession Act of 1947 placed congressional leadership ahead of executive cabinet members in the line of succession. This change sought to make the presidential succession more democratic. However, Congress did not make the process even more accountable to citizens by setting up interim elections to replace the acting president. Since there has never been a double vacancy in the presidency and the vice presidency, the provisions of the act have not been invoked.

J. Wesley Leckrone

Further Reading

Crockett, David A. "The Contemporary Presidency: Unity in the Executive and the Presidential Succession Act." *Presidential Studies Quarterly* 34, no. 2 (2004): 394-411.

Feerick, John D. *From Failing Hands: The Story of Presidential Succession.* New York: Fordham University Press, 1965.

Neale, Thomas H. *Presidential Succession: Perspectives, Contemporary Analysis, and 110th Congress Proposed Legislation.* Washington, D.C.: Congressional Research Service, 2008.

See also Congress, U.S.; Elections in the United States: 1940; Elections in the United States: 1944; Elections in the United States: 1948; Roosevelt, Franklin D.; Truman, Harry S.

■ Prisoners of war, North American

Definition American and Canadian service personnel held prisoner by Axis forces in Europe and the Far East

The treatment of prisoners of war (POWs) by the Axis Powers was a subject of grave concern for citizens in the United States and Canada. The governments of both countries were forced to develop strategies to avoid putting Allied POWs in danger as the Allies advanced in Europe and the Pacific, and to negotiate for the release and repatriation of POWs both during and after the conflict.

At the beginning of World War II, international agreements were in place to govern the treatment of captured enemy combatants. The 1929 Geneva Convention Relative to the Treatment of Prisoners of War provided specific guidance for managing prisoners, to include provisions for food and lodging, receipt of mail and Red Cross packages, and conditions under which they could be required to work. The grave concern for the Allies, however, was whether the Axis Powers would abide by the terms of the Geneva Conventions. Germany was a signatory to the 1929 treaty, but Japan was not. Given the large numbers of prisoners held by the Germans and Japanese, it is not surprising that their treatment varied widely or that conditions under which they lived deteriorated as the war progressed and the Axis Powers began to suffer serious shortages of foodstuffs and other supplies. Nevertheless, there were notable systemic differences in the ways the governments of Japan and Germany approached their responsibilities for treating POWS, and policies emanating from Tokyo and Berlin had profound effects on the lives of those unfortunate enough to fall into enemy hands.

Prisoners of War in the Pacific Although Canada had entered the war in September, 1939, its active military operations were centered in Europe until 1942. In the spring of that year the Japanese conducted a Far East version of the German blitzkrieg, striking outposts of American and European powers all along the western edge of the Pacific Rim. When Hong Kong fell to the Japanese, nearly 1,700 Canadians were captured. That number would rise slightly over the next two years, largely as a result of the capture of Canadian airmen. The United States suffered a similar catastrophe. When U.S. military

Allied prisoners of war celebrating the news of Japan's surrender at a prisoner camp in Aomori, Japan. (Digital Stock)

leaders decided to evacuate the bulk of their forces from the Philippines, the rear guard left to defend the main island had to surrender to the Japanese. Similar catastrophes at Wake Island and Guam swelled those numbers. By the summer of 1942, nearly 22,000 American men had been taken prisoner. By the end of the war, in mid-1945, Japan was holding more than 25,000 American POWs.

Living conditions for Allied POWs in the Far East were horrendous. The Japanese had not prepared in advance to handle large numbers of prisoners. Consequently, they had to throw up makeshift facilities, often failing to provide running water, shelter from the sun, and sufficient means for food preparation. Malnutrition, exacerbated by the stark change from Western foods to Japanese cuisine, took a heavy toll. Medical care was scarce, and in some instances nonexistent. Many prisoners were given brutal work assignments, and those who refused—even officers who were not required to work under terms of the Geneva Convention—were often starved or executed. Prisoners worked in factories and mines, on runways, and on projects such as the infamous Burma-Thailand railroad. Prisoners rarely attempted to escape, and most of those tried were unsuccessful. Prisoners were routinely executed for even slight violations of the strict disciplinary code imposed on them. The Japanese treated prisoners cruelly because they thought it a disgrace to be captured; their warrior code made death in battle or suicide preferable to surrender.

After hostilities ended, the repatriation of North American POWs from Japanese camps went fairly smoothly. By the fall of 1945, almost all the survivors had been returned to the custody of their home governments and were back on North American soil. However, the harsh conditions under which they had been held took a heavy toll on them. Seventeen percent of Canadian POWs died in captivity. American POWs fared even worse: 41 percent did not live to return to the United States at the end of the war.

Prisoners of War in Europe   Canadians fighting as part of the forces assembled by Great Britain from its worldwide Commonwealth were the first North Americans captured in Europe. Nearly 2,000 were taken in the disastrous Dieppe raid in 1942. By war's end, nearly 8,000 Canadians were held by the Germans. American soldiers were not captured in significant numbers until 1943, when U.S. military forces participated in the North African campaign. More Americans were captured during battles after the landings in Italy in September, 1943, and at Normandy in June, 1944. A total of approximately 96,000 Americans ended up in German POW camps.

Generally, the Germans evacuated POWs to camps in Germany and surrounding territories in the East. Many of these Stalags, as they were known, were built specifically to house prisoners. Large barracks often held as many as 150 or more men and had water, electricity, and other amenities. Until the closing months of the war, Canadians and Americans were allowed to receive Red Cross packages and mail. Work camps that were satellites from the main POW installations were home to smaller groups whom the Germans put to work in ways that the Geneva Convention allowed. The Germans used prisoners on farms, in factories, and occasionally in mines. Officers were not forced to work, and noncommissioned officers were given supervisory positions. Prisoners who attempted to escape and were recaptured suffered some punishment, but the Germans executed relatively few POWs for infractions of camp rules. Individual camp commanders and industrialists employing prison labor occasionally treated their charges harshly and made their lives difficult. However, with a few notable exceptions, the Germans adhered to the spirit of the Geneva Conventions.

Changing Conditions　After the Allies invaded France and began their push toward Berlin from the West, and especially after the Soviet armies launched a westward offensive through Poland toward the German capital in early 1945, widespread resentment developed among Germans who saw their country being devastated. Allied officials worried that both civilians and military forces might seek reprisals against Allied prisoners. Some incidents occurred, but the increasing hardships that most prisoners endured happened because the German government was finding it increasingly difficult to provide even basic foodstuffs to captured soldiers. Meanwhile, camp officials made prisoners go on forced marches to keep them from being liberated by advancing Allied forces. Some American prisoners of the Germans were, in fact, subjected to death-camp conditions. One group was sent to the forced labor camp at Berga, near Germany's border with Czechoslovakia in spring, 1945. Many of these prisoners were Jews whom the Germans hand-picked to go there. Nearly 20 percent of the camp's 350 American prisoners died within two months.

At the war's end, the majority of American prisoners held in areas that came under the control of the United States, Great Britain, and France were repatriated rapidly. Some American POWs, however, found themselves in areas under the control of Soviet occupying forces. The Soviets had no intention of keeping these Americans permanently but saw them as useful bargaining chips in negotiating for additional territorial concessions and especially for the repatriation of Soviet soldiers captured by the Germans who were being held in areas controlled by the three Western powers. Repatriating the Soviet soldiers was a tricky issue, as many of them expressed a desire not to return to the Soviet Union. Eventu-

ally, however, their return was guaranteed as a condition for the release of Allied POWs.

Impact　The imprisonment of American and Canadian military members by the Axis Powers was an expected, if unfortunate, outcome of the war. Both governments did all they could to effect prisoner exchanges during the war and to repatriate these men when hostilities ended. Many POWs were treated as heroes upon their return to North America, but many—especially those held by the Japanese—suffered from what would later be designated as post-traumatic stress syndrome. North Americans had some lingering animosity toward the Germans for harsh handling of some POWs, but their strongest resentment was directed against the Japanese, whose mistreatment of captured soldiers became widely known after the war. One particularly tragic outcome affected not the North American prisoners freed at the end of the war, but the Soviet POWs held by Germany during the war and forcibly repatriated as a condition for releasing Allied POWs in Soviet-controlled zones. Almost all those soldiers were treated as traitors; most were sent to penal camps in Siberia, and some were even executed by their own government.

Laurence W. Mazzeno

Further Reading

Dancocks, Daniel G. *In Enemy Hands: Canadian Prisoners of War, 1939-45.* Edmonton, Alta.: Hurtig, 1983. Describes experiences of Canadians taken prisoner by Axis forces and held in Germany, Italy, Hong Kong, and Japan.

Drooz, Daniel B. *American Prisoners of War in German Death, Concentration, and Slave Labor Camps.* Lewiston, N.Y.: Edwin Mellen Press, 2004. Uses accounts of sixteen former POWs who were sent to German concentration camps; describes the horrific conditions under which these men were forced to live and work.

Kerr, E. Bartlett. *Surrender and Survival: The Experience of American POWs in the Pacific, 1941-1945.* New York: William Morrow, 1985. Detailed account of the experiences of prisoners held by the Japanese; describes daily life, efforts to escape, and dangers faced by prisoners as the Allies advanced on Japan near the end of the war.

Kochavi, Arieh J. *Confronting Captivity: Britain and the United States and Their POWs in Nazi Germany.* Chapel Hill: University of North Carolina Press, 2005.

Comprehensive examination of the plight of Allied POWs in Europe. Describes daily life in prison camps, outlines issues surrounding negotiations relative to prisoner exchange and treatment, and explores difficulties posed during the final months of the conflict. Also discusses the fate of prisoners liberated by the Soviets.

La Forte, Robert, Ronald Marcello, and Richard Himmel, eds. *With Only the Will to Live: Accounts of Americans in Japanese Prison Camps, 1941-1945.* Wilmington, Del.: Scholarly Resources, 1994. Presents first-hand accounts by Americans held in Japanese prison camps, outlining the inhumane treatment these prisoners received and describing some of the subtle ways these men resisted their captors.

See also Bataan Death March; Bulge, Battle of the; Canadian participation in World War II; Casualties of World War II; Geneva Conventions; "Great Escape" from Stalag Luft III; Philippines; Prisoners of war in North America; Red Cross; War crimes and atrocities.

■ Prisoners of war in North America

Definition: Foreign and "enemy alien" prisoners of war captured by U.S. and British armed forces and confined in camps in the United States and Canada

World War II brought German, Italian, and Japanese prisoners to the United States and Canada and exposed them to generally humane incarceration systems. The prisoners of war (POWs) contributed camp and contract labor, which benefited the economies of both nations. Contacts between POWs and civilians improved public attitudes and international understanding, both in the United States and abroad.

At the outset of World War II, most U.S. government leaders did not want to hold foreign POWs on domestic soil. However, because British capacity for holding prisoners had become severely overtaxed, the United States began accepting POWs after Operation Torch, the Allied landing in North Africa in November, 1942. By this time, internment camps built by the War Relocation Authority to house first- and second-generation Japanese Americans were already holding some German "enemy aliens" from Central American countries and some captured German sailors.

By accepting these prisoners, the United States followed the lead of Canada, which had accepted a small group of British-captured German POWs in 1939. In 1940, Canada accepted from Britain approximately 4,000 suspected Nazi sympathizers and three thousand German POWs; another 7,000 German POWs were added in January, 1941. Even though Canada began accepting prisoners earlier than the United States did, its POW population eventually numbered around 38,000 by 1945, far less than the domestic U.S. POW population. Foreign POWs on U.S. soil, mostly Germans, exceeded 425,000 by the end of the war. Italians accounted for fewer than one-eighth of the total, while Japanese prisoners made up an even smaller fraction.

U.S. camps were designated "internment camps" until June, 1943, and "prisoner of war camps" afterward. A majority of the camps, 340 out of 511, were established in southern states, with 120 in Texas alone. The forty Canadian camps were concentrated in Ontario, Quebec, and Alberta.

German Prisoners of War German prisoners on U.S. soil numbered almost 379,000. Arriving in increasing numbers between May, 1943, and May, 1945, they were placed in camps with facilities that included hobby workshops, recreational areas, and post-exchange (PX) stores. They received meals that met high standards of nutrition until Germany's surrender, when the U.S. military began caving to charges it was "coddling" enemy prisoners. At Camp Stark, the only New Hampshire POW camp, for example, the daily food rations were sharply reduced from 5,500 to 1,800 calories per day at that point. The most severe discomforts suffered by prisoners, however, tended to arise from political clashes among the Germans themselves; these sometimes rose to brutal levels.

In the case of both German and Italian prisoners, interaction with local farmers and industry workers began early. The prisoners, on a voluntary basis, initially worked at paid jobs within the camps themselves, then at military bases and outside the camps on a contract-labor basis. In Florida, many became fruit pickers and packers, sugar-cane harvesters, potato diggers, and pulpwood cutters. Logging provided the main source of outside employment at Camp Stark. Similarly in Canada, many German prisoners were put to work in the pulpwood and lumber industry, which had encountered a severe labor shortage at a time of mounting demand. Of all prisoners participating, 58 percent worked on army posts and about 30 percent in contract work. The remainder held jobs in the POW camps.

In the United States, the Prisoner of War Special Projects Division undertook the reeducation of 372,000 German prisoners. Instead of discrediting Nazism, the program was designed to foster respect for the American democratic alternative.

Italian Prisoners of War Italian Canadians in Canada fell under the surveillance of the Royal Canadian Mounted Police soon after Italy declared of war on Canada in June, 1940. Approximately 700 Italian Canadians were interned for the duration of the war. In the United States, the Italian POW population was around 50,000; most of them arrived in spring and summer, 1943, and were distributed among twenty-seven camps in twenty-three states. Virtually all had been taken by British, not American, forces in North Africa and Sicily. The United States also held about 82,000 Italian POWs in North Africa and Sicily. The political status of the Italians in Allied camps was somewhat unclear, because an armistice was signed by Italy and the Allies in September, 1943, shortly before Germany began its brutal Italian occupation.

In Canada, imprisoned Italians endured a less positive popular image than German prisoners did. However, in the United States the public attitude toward Italian POWs was generally positive. At the time, Italians constituted the largest foreign-born fraction of the U.S. population. The U.S. military encouraged congenial portrayals of the Italians as cheerful and sociable to further its plans for organizing them into auxiliary service units, within which three-fifths eventually served.

Japanese POWs Japanese POWs—distinct from interned Japanese Americans—numbered only 5,435.

German prisoners disembarking from a train in Quebec in July, 1940, who were part of the first shipload of POWs sent from Great Britain to camps in Canada. (AP/Wide World Photos)

Compared with the Italians, Japanese prisoners were guarded under high security, mostly in Wisconsin and Iowa. Negative stereotyping of Japanese soldiers by the American public contributed to the situation.

At the end of the war, an unusual situation arose when more than seven hundred Japanese Americans were officially classified as "enemy aliens" and moved from the internment camp at Tule Lake, California, to POW camps at Santa Fe, New Mexico, and Bismarck, North Dakota. A preexisting federal law had provided that American citizens could only renounce citizenship by applying to U.S. consuls abroad, and not while within U.S. borders. However, Congress amended the law in 1944 to make it possible for Japanese Americans to renounce citizenship, which then allowed for the transfer of newly designated "enemy aliens" from internment to POW camps. Ironically, the majority of the citizenship-renunciation requests were sent to the U.S. Department of Justice after the announcement that the mass-exclusion order of 1942 had been rescinded. Most of the internees who made these requests did so out of a sense of family obligation or because of intense group pressure, not nationalist fervor. Of the seven hundred people reclassified as enemy aliens, the seventy judged the most extreme militarists were placed in the Santa Fe camp.

Postwar Repatriation   Although many POWs developed a taste for North American life, they were repatriated or sent to other Allied countries. Canada and the United States turned over roughly 123,000 German POWs to Britain, where they provided labor for postwar rebuilding efforts. Similarly, in a May 26, 1945, agreement, the United States provided France with German POWs for its reconstruction work. Of the 378,000 German POWs held on U.S. soil, only 53 percent were repatriated directly back to Germany.

Closing the camps was a slow process; about 46,000 German POWs still remained in the United States in May, 1946. The last of them departed on July 22, 1946. Canada repatriated most of its POWs in 1946, a treatment that stood in marked contrast to that of its Japanese Canadian internees, whose camps were not closed until three years later.

Impact   The work provided by German and Italian POWs in the United States proved significant economically. It provided in excess of one billion mandays of voluntary paid labor in camps, on army posts, and in contract arrangements during the final two years of the war. Canada also benefited significantly from German POW labor at a time when demand for its wood products was at its highest. The humanely operated POW camps, moreover, helped improve the international image and stature of both countries after the war.

Mark Rich

Further Reading

Billinger, Robert D., Jr. *Hitler's Soldiers in the Sunshine State.* Gainesville: University Press of Florida, 2000. Regional study of prisoner camps, with a history of early enemy-alien internments and a record of POW work in local agriculture and industry.

_____. *Nazi POWs in the Tar Heel State.* Gainesville: University Press of Florida, 2008. Examination of one state's camps within the context of the larger U.S. camp system.

Carter, David J. *POW Behind Canadian Barbed Wire: Alien, Refugee, and Prisoner of War Camps in Canada, 1914-1946.* Elkwater, Alta.: Eagle Butte Press, 1998. Pioneering and authoritative study of the Canadian experience in handling POWs.

Christgau, John. *Enemies: World War II Alien Internment.* Lincoln: University of Nebraska Press, 2009. Collection of stories of individual prisoners at Fort Lincoln, near Bismarck, offering valuable insight into both the German POW and the Japanese "enemy alien" situations.

Gansberg, Judith M. *Stalag: USA.* New York: Thomas Y. Crowell, 1977. History of the U.S. camp system and the German reeducation programs.

Keefer, Louis E. *Italian Prisoners of War in America, 1942-1946: Captives or Allies?* New York: Praeger, 1992. History of Italian POWs, describing their unusual political situation.

Robin, Ron. *The Barbed-Wire College: Reeducating German POWs in the United States During World War II.* Princeton, N.J.: Princeton University Press, 1995. Study of reeducation efforts for German POWs.

Smith, Arthur L., Jr. *The War for the German Mind.* Providence, R.I.: Berghahn Books, 1996. Examines and compares U.S., British, and Russian reeducation efforts.

See also   Agriculture in Canada; Agriculture in the United States; Freezing of Japanese assets; Geneva Conventions; German American Bund; Immigration to Canada; Immigration to the United States; Japanese American internment; Japanese Canadian internment; North African campaign; Prisoners of war, North American.

■ *Prudential Insurance Co. v. Benjamin*

The Case   U.S. Supreme Court ruling on insurance taxation
Date   June 3, 1946

This decision held that the states could tax insurance companies and could specifically tax out-of-state insurance companies more heavily than in-state firms. The ruling favored in-state companies and enabled states to raise money through insurance taxes. Although taxation of interstate commerce was a federal matter, in this case the federal government had previously passed a law allowing each state to set its own policy regarding insurance taxation.

In an opinion written by Associate Justice Wiley Blunt Rutledge, Jr., the U.S. Supreme Court considered the question of whether states could tax insurance companies, as insurance companies were involved in interstate commerce. According to the

U.S. Constitution, interstate commerce is regulated by the federal government. However, the year before the Supreme Court heard this case, the federal government had passed a law allowing states to tax insurance companies. This act stated that "continued regulation and taxation" of the insurance industry by the states was "in the public interest," and the law amended several previously enacted statutes in order to grant states this taxation authority. The court ruling maintained that Congress had delegated this authority to the states (or had at least maintained that the states should be permitted to exert this authority), and therefore the states were allowed to tax insurers.

A second question raised by opponents of the federal law was whether states could favor companies based in their own states over those headquartered elsewhere. The Supreme Court held that it generally would be illegal for a state to favor those companies not involved in interstate commerce, that is, those firms headquartered within their own states. However, the court concluded that the federal law delegating taxation authority allowed states to assess taxes that were favorable to in-state insurance companies.

Those opposing the taxation law brought up many other arguments against it, but the court essentially rejected all of these objections. Opponents maintained that because Congress was not allowed to discriminate against interstate commerce, Congress could not grant states the authority to practice this form of discrimination. However, the court held that there was no specific provision in the Constitution that prohibited discrimination against interstate commerce, so Congress was allowed to discriminate and also to delegate the authority to do so. Opponents also argued that the federal statute violated the Fifth Amendment, which requires uniform taxation, and that it specifically violated the amendment's due process clause. The due process argument was rejected by the court, with a citation of precedents that demonstrated the constitutionality of the federal statute; the uniform tax argument was dismissed by stating that only Congress was forbidden from levying disparate taxes, not the states. The court's decision was unanimous among the seven justices who decided the case. (Associate Justice Robert H. Jackson was in Germany taking part in the Nuremberg war crimes trials, and the position of chief justice was vacant because Harlan Fiske Stone had died and Fred M. Vinson had not yet been appointed.)

Impact   The Court's opinion in *Prudential Insurance Co. v. Benjamin* broadened the power of state governments by allowing states to tax insurance corporations, and, in levying these taxes, to favor insurance companies that were based in their own states. The authority to levy these taxes also provided a new form of revenue for the states. The court's approval of this state taxing authority might have easily evaded public notice, as most people pay their insurance only once a year and often do not look at the taxes and other specific charges included in their payment.

Scott A. Merriman

Further Reading

Cartano, David J. *Federal and State Taxation of Limited Liability Companies.* Riverwoods, Ill.: CCH, 2007.

Ferren, John M. *Salt of the Earth, Conscience of the Court: The Story of Justice Wiley Rutledge.* Chapel Hill: University of North Carolina Press, 2004.

Moss, Rita W., and Diane Wheeler Strauss. *Strauss's Handbook of Business Information: A Guide for Librarians, Students, and Researchers.* Westport, Conn.: Libraries Unlimited, 2004.

See also   Business and the economy in the United States; Gross national product of the United States; Health care; Income and wages; Psychiatry and psychology; Supreme Court, U.S.; Unionism.

■ Psychiatry and psychology

Definition   Study and treatment of the human mind, human behavior, human development, other mental functions, and mental disorders

During the 1940's, the fields of psychiatry, psychology, and psychoanalysis experienced expansive change and growing influence on American society. The decade saw the rise of lobotomies and electroconvulsive shock therapy, federal legislation on mental health, and growing awareness of psychological effects of war. Ideas developed in the mental health fields led to the standardization of psychiatric diagnosis and to publication in 1952 of the first edition of Diagnostic and Statistical Manual of Mental Disorders.

As early as 1938, psychologists, psychiatrists, and psychoanalysts were involved in the war effort, and the experience gleaned from this military service had important impacts on the mental health professions. Psychiatric and psychological professionals aided in developing testing requirements for the Selective Service System, a process by which men underwent psychological screening upon beginning military service. Harry S. Sullivan, an American psychiatrist and social scientist whose work centered on interpersonal relationships, had a large role in establishing psychiatric standards and acted as a consultant to the White House. Sullivan advocated for the merging of psychiatry and the social sciences.

Treatment of Veterans In the years after the war, this shifting emphasis radically altered the nature of the mental health professions, which previously had been more connected with mental institutions, chronic patients, and severe mental illnesses. The psychoanalytical approach, concerned with neuroses rather than severe psychosis, was particularly adept at responding to the psychological needs of sol-

Army veteran undergoing psychological testing in late 1944 as part of a vocational guidance program to help veterans find suitable postwar employment. (Time & Life Pictures/Getty Images)

diers. Roy R. Grinker, John P. Spiegel, and their counterparts helped to train a new generation of physicians in psychoanalytical concepts. By the end of the war, psychiatry was on equal footing with other medical specialties of the Army Medical Corps and boasted 2,400 members. Military need, combined with evidence of psychiatry's usefulness to combat veterans, helped to produce greater visibility and acceptance of mental health professionals. It also helped to solidify the idea that environmental factors were at least partially responsible for some mental illnesses.

During and after World War II, the term "battle fatigue," also known as "combat fatigue" or "combat exhaustion," was developed for conditions that might now be called post-traumatic stress disorder (PTSD). In their 1943 publication *War Neurosis*, Grinker and Spiegel used psychoanalytical concepts to describe the effect of environmental trauma in developing war neurosis. Battle fatigue was a concept distinct from the concept of "shell shock" developed during World War I because it emphasized environmental factors over biological factors. The unprecedented access of psychiatrists to soldiers brought about further observations of battle fatigue. In an effort to provide relief from the traumas of war, various branches of the military began to implement rotation policies by the spring of 1945 in addition to employing greater numbers of psychiatrists to treat fatigued soldiers in noninstitutional settings.

Institutions, Professional Organizations, and Legislation At the beginning of the decade, there were about 560 mental institutions across the United States, about 300 of which were under state, county, and municipal authorities. These institutions housed 469,000 patients and, in 1940 alone, admitted 105,000 new patients. The years during and after World War II saw a substantial increase in patient admittance, culminating in a new patient count of 446,000 in 1946. Institutional treatment peaked in the mid-1950's, at which time the move away from institutional care began to gather serious momentum.

Habitually understaffed, overcrowded, and underfunded, state institutions lost many of their staff members to the war effort. Although standards set by the American Psychiatric Association required a minimum of one attendant for every six patients, one nurse for every forty patients, and one psychiatrist for every two hundred patients, these standards rarely were achieved. In 1949, the Council on State Governments conducted an investigation into the conditions of state institutions. This culminated in a 1950 report, *The Mental Health Programs of the Forty-eight States*, that made clear the failing conditions of American mental hospitals.

The American Psychiatric Association was a strong presence in 1940's American psychiatry beyond the institutional setting, and in 1948 it assigned a small group of members to discuss the regularization and standardization of psychiatric classifications. This effort ultimately resulted in the 1952 publication of the first edition of the *Diagnostic and Statistical Manual of Mental Disorders* (DSM). Although the classification of mental illness had a long tradition, it was not until 1949 that the World Health Organization included mental disorders in its *International Statistical Classification of Diseases and Related Health Problems* (ICD). This sixth edition of the ICD and the first edition of the DSM established for the first time a national and international regularization of shared psychiatric knowledge.

The year 1949 also marked the establishment of the Committee for the Preservation of Medical Standards in Psychiatry (CPMSP). Along with the Group for the Advancement of Psychiatry, which was founded in 1946 with army chief of psychiatry William Menninger at its head, the CPMSP made efforts to promote the authority of psychiatry over psychology. Members of the field of psychology, however, had long been at work organizing and expanding. In 1938, the American Psychological Association formed the Committee on Displaced Foreign Psychologists (CDFP) to represent displaced European scholars. By October, 1940, the American Psychological Association had established the Emergency Committee on Psychology (ECP) to assist federal agencies and address issues of civilian morale during the war. The American Psychological Association began to include a section on "Psychology and War" in its official publication, the *Psychological Bulletin*, and in 1942 formed the Office of Psychological Personnel (OPP). For the American Psychological Association, the war years were important for emphasizing the efficacy of applying psychological theory to social problems, a trend that continued in the postwar years.

During the postwar years, American psychology became increasingly organized and regularized. In 1947, for example, the American Psychological Association established the American Board of Examiners in Professional Psychology. Despite the resistance of some in the psychiatric profession, psychologists increasingly participated in private practice. During the midst of these professional debates and in response to growing demand for federal intervention, President Harry S. Truman signed the National Mental Health Act (NMHA) into law on July 3, 1946. The act called for the formation of a National Advisory Mental Health Council (NAMHC) and a National Institute of Mental Health (NIMH), and it was designed to help prevent, treat, and research mental illnesses. On April 15, 1949, the NIMH was formally established and replaced the Division of Mental Hygiene, with Robert Felix as its director.

Debates Concerning Treatment and Practice During the 1940's, particularly in the postwar years, the professions of psychology and psychiatry experienced increased external influence as well as decreased professional solidarity. A large proportion of internal debates centered on increased interest in biological treatment methods, therapeutic approaches, and the social role of psychiatry and psychology.

One of the most controversial methods of the 1940's was the treatment of severe psychosis with a neurological surgery known as lobotomy. Walter Freeman, an American neurologist convinced of the somatic, or bodily, origins of mental illness, introduced the surgery to American neurologists and psychiatrists in 1936. In this procedure, the nerves that connect the patient's frontal lobe to the thalamus are cut. In January, 1946, ten years after he and neurosurgeon James W. Watts performed the first lobotomy in the United States, Freeman performed the first transorbital lobotomy. This procedure was much quicker than the prefrontal procedure, allowing the frontal lobe to be detached by a sharp instrument that could be inserted into the brain through the patient's eye cavities. By 1949, the number of lobotomies performed annually in the United States had reached five thousand, despite bitter conflicts within the profession.

At nearly the same time that Freeman was introducing American practitioners to the lobotomy procedure, electroconvulsive shock therapy was on the rise. The *American Journal of Psychiatry* first covered the procedure in 1937, and by 1940 it was widely in use. Over the course of the 1940's, practitioners attempted various modifications in an effort to reduce the procedural side effects. Modifications included the introduction of muscle relaxants and short-term anesthetics that were thought to make the patient's experience less frightening. The introduction in 1954 of Thorazine (chlorpromazine), nicknamed the "chemical lobotomy," ushered in a new era of psychotropic drugs that in many ways replaced earlier and more invasive procedures.

In sharp contrast to the biological emphasis of practitioners such as Freeman and Watts, Karen Horney, a German psychoanalyst, argued that therapeutic approaches should emphasize the workings of the conscious mind and the isolating effects of a highly competitive, modern society. Her early writings on female sexuality successfully destabilized Freudian assessments of female psychology. Horney moved to New York City in 1934 and published her first of five books, *The Neurotic Personality of Our Time*, in 1937. During the 1940's, Horney's work focused on revitalizing psychoanalysis through an emphasis on the ego, or conscious mental awareness, and on developing theories of what came to be known as narcissism. Horney came to be perceived as a radical within the profession, and in 1941 she started the Horney Institute in New York City to promote her ideas.

Like Horney, B. F. Skinner sought to expand the uses and functions of psychiatry beyond the institution. Skinner was an American psychologist who emphasized the interplay between humans and external forces and was most widely known for *The Behavior of Organisms* (1938) and *Walden Two* (1948). In the first of those books, he laid out the fundamentals for a behaviorist theory of human nature that emphasized the role of punishment and reinforcement and the interaction between humans and their environment. *Walden Two* was a utopian novel that conceived of a type of human community that would be governed by the basic principles put forth in *The Behavior of Organisms*.

Skinner's ideas on "behavioral technology" represented a greater shift during the 1940's that sought not only to emphasize environmental factors but also to expand the influence of psychiatry into the realm of the social sciences. The growing emphasis on environmental factors and the widespread acceptance by psychiatrists also opened a space for the increased influence of psychoanalytic and psychodynamic methods of treatment. The emphasis of psychodynamic methods dovetailed with psychiatry's growing interest in the late 1940's in psychological life beyond the mental institution. During the last years of the 1940's, the Group for the Advancement of Psychiatry helped to further the ideas of psychoanalysis by reorienting psychiatry toward a psychosocial model emphasizing community care and social outreach.

Impact The expansion of psychiatry, psychology, and psychoanalysis during the 1940's had great import for the direction of these professions over succeeding decades. Psychoanalytic and psychodynamic methods of therapy dominated the psychiatric profession for decades to come. The late 1950's and 1960's saw the widespread use of psychological and psychiatric drugs such as Thorazine and lithium to treat severe psychosis. With the introduction of psychotropic drugs, lobotomies and electroconvulsive shock therapy largely fell out of favor. Large mental institutions came to be viewed as an unnecessary social evil, and professional emphasis continued to shift toward noninstitutional, community-based mental health care. The antipsychiatry movement gained momentum during the late 1950's and the 1960's, bolstered by such works as Erving Goffman's *Asylums* (1961), Thomas Szasz's *The Myth of Mental Illness* (1961), and Ken Kesey's novel *One Flew over the Cuckoo's Nest* (1962), which negatively dramatized inpatient psychiatric treatment. Many social movements of the 1960's, particularly the feminist and collectivist movements, drew heavily on the works of such notable theorists as Skinner and Horney in their critiques of American society.

Kathleen M. Brian

Further Reading

El-Hei, Jack. *The Lobotomist: A Maverick Medical Genius and His Tragic Quest to Rid the World of Mental Illness.* New York: John Wiley & Sons, 2007. A judicious biography of Walter Freeman that details the rise and fall of the use of lobotomy procedures in mid-century medical thought and practice.

Grob, Gerald. *From Asylum to Community: Mental Health Policy in Modern America.* Princeton, N.J.: Princeton University Press, 1991. A concise yet thorough overview of twentieth century changes and developments in mental health policy.

Hilgard, E. R. *Psychology in America: A Historical Survey*. New York: Harcourt Brace Jovanovich, 1987. A comprehensive overview of the rise of American psychology.

Jones, Edgar. *Shell Shock to PTSD: Military Psychiatry from 1900 to the Gulf War*. New York: Psychology Press, 2005. A comprehensive analysis of twentieth century developments in the treatment of soldiers and war veterans.

Mitchell, Stephen A., and Margaret J. Black. *Freud and Beyond: A History of Modern Psychoanalytic Thought*. New York: Basic Books, 1996. An overview of major conceptual developments in twentieth century psychoanalytic thought and practice.

Shorter, Edward. *A History of Psychiatry: From the Era of the Asylum to the Age of Prozac*. New York: John Wiley & Sons, 1997. A concise yet thorough introduction to the history of psychiatry in the United States.

Wallace, Edwin R., and John Gach, eds. *Encyclopedic Handbook of the History of Psychiatry and Medical Psychology*. New York: Springer, 2007. A highly recommended, wonderfully diverse collection of articles covering the history of psychiatry and psychology.

See also   G.I. Bill; Health care; Horney, Karen; Lobotomy; Medicine; *Studies in Social Psychology in World War II*; World Health Organization.

■ Pulp magazines

Definition   Popular serial publications known for the cheap paper on which they were printed

Pulp magazines met the desires of general readers for vivid, stirring, fast-paced, fanciful stories narrated in straightforward, linear, serial fashion and reflecting popular values in a decade of global war and its aftermath.

So called because of the rough, inexpensive, woodpulp paper on which they were printed, pulp magazines had acquired a loyal readership of millions by the early 1940's. They appealed largely, though not exclusively, to working-class readers who sought entertainment through stories of action, adventure, suspense, romance, and mystery. Major publishers included Munsey, Clayton, Street and Smith, Popular, and Dell. Pulp magazine titles, usually priced between ten and twenty-five cents, numbered more than one hundred at the start of the 1940's.

The stories in the magazines immersed readers in intense worlds of unconstrained imagination, as reflected in their fantastic, bright covers, in bold colors—reds, yellows, blacks, blues, and greens—that American and Canadian authorities occasionally deemed to be pornographic. The magazine titles promised excitement, danger, surprise, or the incredible, as with *The Shadow, Western Story, Thrilling Wonder Stories, Weird Tales, Fighting Aces, Love Book, Ace G-Man Stories, The Spider, Popular Love, Doc Savage,* and *Amazing Stories.*

America's entry into World War II had severe consequences for the pulp magazines. Paper and ink rationing and rising production costs led to lowered production runs and the gradual demise of some titles. The economy forced some pulp magazines to appear bimonthly or quarterly instead of monthly. Some magazines, seeking to maintain a monthly schedule, made such changes as reducing the page size from the standard seven by eleven inches to the digest size of five and one-half by eight inches, reducing the number of pages, and reducing print size to fit more text on a page. At the same time, pulp publishers lost writers and artists to military service or to the war effort at home. For highbrow readers, the war, as the ultimate drama of life and death, demonstrated that the pulp magazines were providing no more than emotional, sensational, escapist stories—daydreams for those who never grew up. They therefore condemned the pulps.

Role in World War II   Pulp magazines underwent a transformation in their content from that of the 1930's and before. During the 1940's, they included more stories that, though offering diversion from the reader's personal circumstances or distress, tended to rivet attention on immediate and tangible facts—an escape, for the sake of a story, into the exceptional within the actual, rather than escape into unreality. Pulp fiction, often working for the propagation of the war effort, brought encouragement, inspiration, some useful facts, and resolve to keep heart.

Pulp magazine publishers and editors, constantly alert to the desires of readers, encouraged writers and artists to learn actualities of wartime life on both the home front and the battle front, to make stories more true to life. Factual accuracy, especially first-hand combat experience, kept magazines credible and potent. In addition, the United States government created the Office of War Information (OWI); it made available to print and radio media the latest, most detailed information that wartime censorship permitted, concerning the war on land, sea, and air, in every part of the world.

In addition, the OWI included a Magazine Bureau that recognized the importance of magazines in the war effort. Consequently, the pulp magazines, often contacted directly by the OWI, offered authentic frameworks for fiction. Those frameworks involved military personnel who, in combat, entered a world of destruction and won their way back, turning survival to success, often remaining gallantly anonymous. They also involved the first line of defense, those on the home front who in varying ways battled Axis Powers, even spies and saboteurs. The OWI declared the primary subject for 1943 to be the power of women and how heroically, in or out of uniform, they contributed to the war effort. Pulp magazines demonstrated that patriotism, honor, and love were as certain as other facts of life.

Impact   As World War II ended, the pulp magazines had been fighting a losing battle, despite publishing what arguably were artistically better stories of men and women reunited in the wake of war, or of life variables in new contexts. Comic books, paperback books, and, by the end of the 1940's, television transformed American popular culture, leaving the pulp magazines outdated. Many of the magazines disappeared between 1949 and 1953, though the genres of Westerns, detective stories, and science fiction retained loyal followings. The magazines expressed enduring aspects of American character—notably independence, ingenuity, inquisitiveness, imagination, and initiative—that subsequently found expression in later forms of mass entertainment. The superheroic character types from the magazines, prominent during the 1940's, continued to permeate American culture in the form of such characters as Superman and the heroes of Western films.

Many writers who learned their craft in pulp magazines turned to new media such as paperback novels, film, and television. Among them were Dashiell Hammett, Erle Stanley Gardner, Edgar Rice Burroughs, and Ray Bradbury. Indirectly, they also carried on the spirit of pulp magazines, which looms large in the history of popular culture. Pulp artists did not fare as well, finding outlets for their work vastly diminished. Artists such as Frank R. Paul, Virgil Finlay, J. Allen St. John, George and Jerome Rozen, Hannes Bok, and Rudolf Belarski, who produced spectacular cover art for the pulps, remain largely unknown, their work dismissed as pulp art.

Science fiction, which entered the

Staged scene illustrating violations of various Office of Wartime Information censorship rules for pulp magazines. (Time & Life Pictures/Getty Images)

pulp market as a major force in 1926 with Hugo Gernsback's *Amazing Stories*, continued to have a relatively small market share during the early 1940's, but experienced its golden age during the decade and the next. Its futuristic war technology, which was a staple of "space opera" for nearly two decades; its long-predicted atomic bomb; and its grand theme of space exploration, hinted at in 1940's rocket technology, made a deep impression on American life. Perhaps of all 1940's pulp magazines, those publishing science fiction, involving vast, staggering, ever-increasing changes brought about by science and technology, epitomize the energy, action, and excitement of the entire category.

Timothy C. Miller

Further Reading

Goodstone, Tony, ed. *The Pulps: Fifty Years of American Pop Culture.* New York: Bonanza, 1970. A survey and anthology of pulp magazine fiction and art.

Goulart, Ron. *An Informal History of the Pulp Magazine.* New York: Ace Books, 1973. An essential account of the life and context of the magazines.

Hersey, Harold, John L. Locke, and John Gunnison. *The New Pulpwood Editor.* Silver Spring, Md.: Adventure House, 2007. An updated history of pulp magazines. Pulp editor and publisher Hersey published his original *Pulpwood Editor* in 1937, observing how the pulp publishing industry worked, offering personal anecdotes of his experiences, and relating stories of some of the personalities and publications of the pulp magazine industry. Although he died in 1956, the book has been republished and updated several times.

Locke, John, ed. *Pulp Fictioneers: Adventures in the Storytelling Business.* Silver Spring, Md.: Adventure House, 2004. Documentary history featuring articles and letters by editors, writers, and publishers of pulp magazines.

Server, Lee. *Danger Is My Business: An Illustrated History of the Fabulous Pulp Magazines/1896-1953.* San Francisco: Chronicle Books, 1993. A comprehensive, interpretative, evaluative account of pulp magazines.

See also   Censorship in the United States; Comic books; Comic strips; Film noir; Flying saucers; Literature in the United States; Magazines; Pornography; Wartime rationing.

■ Pyle, Ernie

Identification   American journalist and war correspondent
Born   August 3, 1900; near Dana, Indiana
Died   April 18, 1945; Ie Shima, Japan

A veteran columnist when World War II started, Pyle became America's best-read eyewitness to the conflict, offering what he called his "worm's-eye view" of war because he spent most of his time alongside regular troops. He won the 1944 Pulitzer Prize for his folksy stories about common soldiers.

As a youngster, Ernest Taylor Pyle helped his tenant-farmer father and attended school until he enlisted in the Naval Reserve during World War I. The war ended before he shipped out, and he enrolled at Indiana University, where he studied journalism. He left in 1923 before graduating to work as a reporter for the *La Porte Herald* in Indiana. He then moved to Washington to work as a reporter, then copy editor, for the *Washington Daily News.*

In 1925, Pyle wed Geraldine "Jerry" Siebolds to start what would be a rocky twenty-year marriage. He worked at both the *New York World* and the *New York Post* before returning in 1928 to the *Washington Daily News.* There Pyle was a wire editor, aviation columnist, and managing editor until 1935, when he became a roving reporter, writing six columns per week for Scripps-Howard Newspapers. His columns were eventually published in about two hundred newspapers.

After World War II broke out, Pyle went to England in 1940 and covered the Battle of Britain and Europe for about six months. He returned to the United States in mid-1941, but returned to Europe in June, 1942, as a correspondent for United Features. Accompanying troops through North Africa, Italy, the D-Day invasion, and the liberation of Paris, Pyle wrote columns featuring everyday soldiers and their hometowns, and the routine of life and death.

Producing about 2.5 million words of simple and effective journalistic writing over a decade, Pyle became a craftsman of short nonfiction that took readers to people and places they had not known or thought about. Pyle's coverage in more than two hundred daily and four hundred weekly newspapers for three years largely avoided stories about generals or armies, instead featuring the perspective of the common G.I. He was so loyal to the troops that he

War correspondent Ernie Pyle (center) talking to a Marine on Okinawa a few days before Pyle was killed by a Japanese sniper. (Courtesy, U.S. Army Center for Military History)

lobbied Congress to enact extra "combat pay" for soldiers, just as pilots received "flight pay."

Pyle briefly returned home in 1944. In January, 1945, he joined the Allied forces in the Pacific, where he was killed by a Japanese sniper on the island of Ie Shima.

Impact The most widely read and probably the most revered war correspondent of World War II, Pyle became a national celebrity for his down-to-earth style of reporting that connected Americans to the war through soldiers' stories.

The aftermath of Pyle's death included posthumous honors, including a Medal of Merit from the Army, Navy, and federal government, given to his wife at a July screening of the film based on Pyle and his reporting, *The Story of G.I. Joe* (1945). Her health deteriorated, and she died of complications from influenza on November 23, 1945. Eventually, Pyle's re-

mains were moved to Hawaii, where they were buried alongside Army and Navy dead in the National Memorial Cemetery of the Pacific in Punchbowl Crater on the island of Oahu. In 1947, Pyle's Albuquerque house was deeded to the city, and in 1948 it was opened as a library. Indiana established an Ernie Pyle State Historic Site.

Bill Knight

Further Reading

Miller, Lee G. *The Story of Ernie Pyle.* New York: Viking Press, 1950.

Tobin, James. *Ernie Pyle's War: America's Eyewitness to World War II.* New York: Free Press, 1997.

See also Bradley, Omar N.; Casualties of World War II; "Greatest Generation"; Iwo Jima, Battle of; Literature in the United States; Mauldin, Bill; Murrow, Edward R.; Newspapers; Okinawa, Battle of.

Q

■ Quebec Conferences

The Events: Two international conference meetings among Allied leaders planning the next stages of World War II

Dates: August 17-24, 1943; September 12-14, 1944

Place: Quebec City, Quebec, Canada

The Quebec Conferences built on earlier meetings between Winston Churchill and Franklin D. Roosevelt that defined the goals of Allied leaders in the campaign to launch a full-scale invasion of Normandy in northern France and included a discussion on the feasibility of opening a second European front against the Axis Powers.

British prime minister Winston Churchill and U.S. president Roosevelt developed a personal and professional rapport through a series of meetings that began in Newfoundland; Washington, D.C.; and Casablanca, Morocco, as they formulated plans to defeat Adolf Hitler's Germany and Benito Mussolini's Italy. The Quebec meetings were held at the Citadelle and Château Frontenac from August 17 to 24, 1943. The prime minister of Canada, William Lyon Mackenzie King, attended the meetings along with Roosevelt and Churchill. Selected communications from the meetings were extended to the Soviet leader Joseph Stalin and Chinese Nationalist leader Chiang Kai-shek. Codenamed Quadrant, the first conference increased the unity among the Allies on military strategies but reflected increasing political divisions. Churchill wanted to continue Britain's full participation in the Manhattan Project, the U.S. effort to develop the atomic bomb, while Roosevelt wanted to restrict British access. They agreed to share nuclear technology but not to share the information with Stalin.

Churchill agreed to coordinate a central Pacific strategy, code-named Overlord, which would include British naval power. The discussion of a military strategy in Burma was temporarily postponed. The target date to defeat Japan was set at one full year after the defeat of Germany, which was projected to occur in October, 1945. The decision to invade Italy was approved based on Allied successes in Sicily. An additional 600,000 Allied troops and 150,000 airmen were to be sent to the Mediterranean theater.

Churchill and Roosevelt notified Stalin about the military operations to be undertaken during the remainder of 1943 and 1944. A bomber offensive

U.S. President Franklin D. Roosevelt (center), Canadian prime minister William Lyon Mackenzie King (left), and British prime minister Winston Churchill at the first Quebec Conference in August, 1943. (AP/Wide World Photos)

against Germany would continue from bases in both the United Kingdom and Italy. The strategy was to destroy German air-combat capability; to dislocate German military, industrial, and economic bases; and to prepare for the invasion of Normandy. The communique noted the plan for an additional buildup of American forces in Great Britain to assist the existing British and American forces preparing for the channel invasion of France. The Allies informed Stalin that the war in the Mediterranean would be pressed vigorously to knock Italy out of the Axis alliance, occupy the country, and establish bases on the nearby islands of Sardinia and Corsica. There would be no support of an Allied invasion of the Balkans, but the Allies would supply existing Balkan guerrillas. Both Britain and the United States agreed to find opportunities to bring Turkey into the war on the Allied side.

More vaguely stated actions dealt with military operations against Japan in the Pacific and Southeast Asia. The Allied plan was to exhaust Japan's military and shipping resources, cut its lines of communication, and secure future bases of operation against Japan. Zionist actions in British-controlled Palestine were discussed at the first Quebec Conference, but the topic was deferred based on the need to address the war in both Europe and the Pacific. The leaders agreed to a general statement to ease the increasing tensions in Palestine between Palestinians and Jews and both groups toward the British. The Allies at Quebec condemned German atrocities in Poland.

King, Churchill, and Roosevelt attended the second Quebec Conference from September 12 to 14, 1944. The leaders reaffirmed the Allied decision to divide Germany into Soviet, British, and American zones of occupation based on the earlier Moscow Conference. This decision permitted possible allocation of German regions to France after the war. No decision was reached on whether or not the Allies should destroy Germany's industrial zones in the Saar and Ruhr regions based on the proposed Morgenthau Plan. The United States agreed to continue military aid to Great Britain, and Great Britain agreed to the use of British naval forces in the war against Japan.

Impact The discussions and agreements reached at the Quebec Conferences led to future meetings of Allied leaders in Moscow, Cairo, Tehran, and Yalta.

These meetings ultimately led to the successful defeat of the Axis Powers and the Yalta agreements, which shaped postwar Europe and Asia.

William A. Paquette

Further Reading

The Conferences at Washington and Quebec, 1943. Washington, D.C.: Government Printing Office, 1970.

Woolner, David B., ed. *The Second Quebec Conference Revisited: Waging War, Formulating Peace: Canada, Great Britain, and the United States in 1944-1945.* New York: St. Martin's Press, 1998.

See also Atlantic Charter; Atomic bomb; Cairo Conference; Casablanca Conference; Churchill, Winston; D Day; Germany, occupation of; King, William Lyon Mackenzie; Manhattan Project; Roosevelt, Franklin D.; Tehran Conference; *Yakus v. United States.*

■ Quebec nationalism

Definition: French Canadian movement calling for greater autonomy within the Canadian confederation or independence from Canada

The goal of Quebec's French-speaking residents to preserve their language, religion, and culture in order to avoid assimilation into English-speaking Canada during World War II and its aftermath was achieved through increased political action.

Creation of the Canadian federation in 1867 motivated French-speaking Canadians in Quebec, the Québécois, to protect their language, religion, and culture and to resist assimilation into the English-speaking culture. The Québécois renewed ties to France, accepted their clergy's ultraconservative and isolationist worldview, and enabled the Roman Catholic Church to serve as their protector and benefactor. The Church in Quebec opposed industrialization and urbanization and actively promoted rural life and passive reliance on the Church. The Church became the temporal mediator and spiritual protector for the Québécois. The Church maintained that Quebec's salvation would come only through its isolation from the Anglo-Protestant culture of North America. French Canadians viewed government not as an extension of the people but as an external force above the people that made laws that the people must obey and levied taxes that the people must pay. The persecution of French Canadians in New Brunswick, Manitoba, and Ontario and their forced assimilation into Anglo-Canadian culture convinced the Québécois that only their province could preserve their unique identity.

Traditionally, French Canadians lacked democratic convictions and adequate knowledge of parliamentary government as a means to promote Quebec autonomy. The leadership of Henri Bourassa and Lionel Groulx defined Quebec nationalism for the first half of the twentieth century. Bourassa opposed French Canadian participation in World War I and the 1917 Conscription Act. In 1944, he opposed conscripting French Canadians for World War II service and resisted Jewish immigration into Canada. Groulx's writings espoused the idea of ethnic superiority, presenting French Canadians as a heroic pure-blooded race degraded by conquest and foreign influences. The actions and publications of both Bourassa and Groulx encouraged Quebec nationalism from an ultraright perspective more in sympathy with European fascist movements.

Quebec politician Maurice Duplessis was not as extreme in his nationalism as Bourassa and Groulx, but he was determined to preserve Quebec's unique place within a Canadian confederation. Duplessis served as Quebec's premier from 1936 until 1939 and again from 1944 until 1959, shaping policies and public opinion in the province. He championed rural areas and provincial rights and was anticommunist and antiunion. He approved the Padlock Law, which eliminated communist propaganda within unions, but he unsuccessfully sought Quebec's own version of the 1947 Taft-Hartley Act in order to reduce union rights. As premier, Duplessis favored nationalist provincial parties within Quebec, including his own Union Nationale party, over Canadian national parties, such as the Liberal Party. The 1943 Compulsory Education Act requiring all children between the ages of six and fourteen to attend school, which was approved by Quebec's Liberal Party during World War II, was never enforced by Duplessis because he viewed the law as an intrusion of the state into the educational sphere reserved for the family and the Church. Duplessis's most enduring legacy was having the French fleur-de-lis placed on the provincial flag of Quebec on January 21, 1948. This was the first time a provincial flag was officially adopted in Canada. January 21 has remained Quebec's Flag Day and a potent symbol of Quebec nationalism into the twenty-first century.

Duplessis's skillful use of patronage helped keep the Liberal Party in the minority in Quebec elections. Liberals in the Quebec parliament saw roads go unpaved and bridges unbuilt in their districts. This changed when Duplessis's Union Nationale party won the same electoral districts.

World War II slowly changed French Canadian public opinion through increased contact with the rest of Canada and the world. French Canadians recognized that the family and the Church did not have to compete with the state. The realization that French Canadians could use the state to prevent cultural assimilation would redefine Quebec politics in future decades.

Impact   Quebec leaders Bourassa, Groulx, and Duplessis inserted Quebec nationalism into the Canadian national debate during World War I and World War II. Collectively, they encouraged French Canadians to maintain their cultural identity and preserve their language and commitment to Roman Catholicism. They did not advocate outright independence from Canada but instead supported increased provincial autonomy. Dreams of independence would be left for the next generation to consider.

William A. Paquette

Further Reading

Behiels, Michael D. *Prelude to Quebec's Quiet Revolution: Liberalism Versus Neo-Nationalism, 1945-1960.* Kingston, Ont.: McGill-Queen's University Press, 1985.

Coleman, William D. *The Independence Movement in Quebec, 1945-1980.* Toronto: University of Toronto Press, 1984.

Wade, Mason. *The French-Canadians, 1760-1967.* Toronto: MacMillan of Canada, 1968.

See also   Canadian minority communities; Canadian nationalism; Canadian participation in World War II; Canadian regionalism; Duplessis, Maurice Le Noblet; France and the United States; King, William Lyon Mackenzie.

R

■ Race riots

Definition Violent interracial confrontations in cities throughout the United States

The breadth and depth of racism in the United States was exposed by a spate of race riots that erupted in cites across the country during the 1940's. Increased interracial contact engendered by the demographic and employment shifts of World War II combined with increased demands by members of minorities for rights to foster white reprisals and violence. While few significant positive changes came out of the resulting violence, many civil rights leaders of the 1950's and 1960's were shaped by their experiences during the 1940's.

During the 1940's, numerous racial conflicts and riots occurred, with the worst happening in 1943. The industrial buildup to World War II accelerated the Great Migration, as many African Americans in search of work moved from the rural South to urban areas in the North. What has been called a "great compression" in income distribution narrowed the wage gap between skilled and unskilled workers, benefiting more minority workers than white workers, who felt threatened by the change.

Economic and Social Factors Population increases in urban areas, particularly of minority groups, created housing shortages and increased contact and job competition between whites and minorities. Minorities in cities also began frequenting previously all-white recreational areas, such as amusement parks, pools, and skating rinks. Many white people were highly resistant to minorities' economic advancement and intrusion into white enclaves.

By the mid-1940's, the desire of members of minorities for full participation in American society was strengthened by their military participation in World War II. They fought for freedom abroad even as they were denied freedom in their own country. Two important movements grew out of their frustration. The March on Washington Movement called for a mass march demanding an end to discrimina-

tion in the defense industry. This threat was a factor in President Franklin D. Roosevelt's decision to issue Executive Order 8802 in June of 1942. The order established the Fair Employment Practices Commission, which prohibited discrimination based on race, creed, or color in employment in the defense industry.

The "Double V" campaign added a second "V" for victory, over racial discrimination, to the Allied forces single "V" for victory over the Axis Powers. For its symbol, the campaign used two V's over an eagle with the words "Democracy at Home and Abroad." The slogan and emblem quickly spread around the country, inspiring black Americans to demand full rights and respect, while angering white racists. Tension escalated as the war progressed, leading to hundreds of violent racial incidents in cities, at defense plants, and on military bases in 1942 and 1943. Most of the incidents that were sufficiently large-scale to be considered true "race riots" occurred in 1943.

Mobile, Alabama, and Beaumont, Texas, Riots During World War II the promise of jobs led many African Americans and white people to move to Mobile, Alabama. This influx created a local housing shortage, job competition, and increased contact among black and white people. At the Atlanta Dry Dock and Shipbuilding Company of Mobile, some African Americans were promoted to skilled positions. On May 24, 1943, resentful white workers responded by assaulting black dockworkers with fists, bricks, and pieces of metal, driving them from the shipyard. The National Guard was summoned to restore order. At least fifty African Americans suffered injuries, as almost all the violence was white on black. Only one white worker is known to have been injured.

Meanwhile, Texas was experiencing its own wartime shipbuilding and oil-producing boom. As in Alabama, a great influx of black and white job-seekers created housing shortages, strained social services, and increased integration in housing, public transportation, and recreation areas in the port city of

Beaumont. Many white people felt angry and threatened by the erosion of rigid racial boundaries. By mid-1943, tension between the races was reaching a high level. On June 5, a young white woman reported that she had been beaten and stabbed by a black man, who was later arrested. On June 15, another white woman said she had been raped by a black man. That evening, white workers at Beaumont's Pennsylvania Shipyards headed for police headquarters after work. A crowd of three thousand people demanded the police hand over the rape suspect to them for lynching. When told he was not there, the mob descended on the city's two black districts, burning, looting, and attacking people. Three African Americans and one white person died, and about fifty people were injured. On June 16, the governor declared martial law and called in the Texas State Guard. No material evidence was found that the rape occurred.

Detroit Riot   Because its local automobile industry had converted to military production, Detroit was the largest defense center in the United States during World War II. The massive influx of job seekers raised the city's population by 350,000 people, of whom 50,000 were African Americans. A severe housing shortage combined with white resistance to integration to force the city's 200,000 black residents into a crowded, squalid ghetto called Paradise Valley. Although the city's black and white residents did not live in the same neighborhoods, they often came into contact at work and in recreational settings. On the evening of June 20, 1943, black and white youths clashed in the Belle Isle amusement park. Rumors that a black man had raped and killed a white woman—and that a group of white people had thrown a black woman and her baby into a river—resulted in fights, assaults, and vandalism that spread far into the city. The scale of the rioting raised such a high level that President Franklin D. Roosevelt sent in federal troops to restore order.

About twenty-four hours after the Detroit riot had started, one of the bloodiest urban racial incidents in American history was over. Of the thirty-four people who died in the rioting, twenty-five were African Americans. Seventeen rioters were killed by police. About 75 percent of the six to seven hundred people who were injured were African Americans. Despite the evident one-sidedness of the violence, a fact-finding committee appointed by Michigan governor Harry F. Kelly blamed the city's black population for the riot.

Harlem Riot   The race riot that occurred in Harlem in 1943 stemmed from high unemployment, price gouging by local merchants, a lack of recreational areas, inadequate housing, and routine police abuse. On August 1, 1943, a policeman shot and wounded an African American soldier who was believed to be interfering with the arrest of an African American woman. Immediately afterward, rumors that a black soldier had been killed defending his mother from the police spread rapidly and ignited rioting and looting. Many Harlem businesses were under Jewish or other white ownership and thus were prime targets for looters. The response of the police was often excessively brutal.

The rioting lasted two days and resulted in the deaths of six African Americans, about 175 injuries, and 500 arrests. In contrast to the earlier riots in

Suspected rioter arrested by New York police during the August, 1943, Harlem riot. (AP/Wide World Photos)

1943, in which white people were the instigators, this riot was restricted to the nearly all-black Harlem. Cooperation between Mayor Fiorello La Guardia and African American leaders prevented the riot from reaching the size and intensity of the Detroit riot.

Columbia, Tennessee, Riot After World War II, many African Americans, particularly veterans, were no longer willing to accept inferior social and economic status. On February 15, 1946, a nineteen-year-old black veteran and his mother got into an argument with a white repairman in a Columbia, Tennessee, store. The repairman struck the veteran as he left the store. The veteran was arrested and placed in jail, which a mob of white people soon surrounded. People in the African American section of town feared the mob might attack their neighborhood and prepared to defend their homes. Four police who entered the black neighborhood were shot and wounded by frightened residents.

Tennessee's state highway patrol was summoned and, accompanied by local police, ransacked the black neighborhood, destroying property, beating people, and firing guns into homes. Two African Americans were killed, eighteen were wounded, and more than one hundred were arrested. Two days later, the police killed two of the men in jail, saying the men had taken guns from the police in an attempted escape.

The National Association for the Advancement of Colored People sent in a legal team, headed by future Supreme Court justice Thurgood Marshall, that successfully defended twenty-four of the twenty-five men facing charges for the shootings of the white officers. An all-white federal grand jury was convened and absolved the police officers and highway patrolmen of any wrongdoing.

Impact The social, demographic, and economic shifts brought about by World War II increased contact between blacks and whites and exposed the racism of most white people in the United States. Participation in the war also led to an increased desire by minorities for dignity and respect. Rather than trying to accept and adapt to changing racial realities, most white people fought to keep minorities "in their place." The violent riots, mostly initiated and perpetrated by white people, were only the most visible part of the discrimination regularly suffered by minorities.

Most media and political leaders placed the blame for the riots on minority-group hoodlums and outside radical elements rather than on white racism and the deplorable living conditions of minorities. The young people who began their fight for dignity and acceptance during the 1940's became the adults who created the Civil Rights movement of the 1950's and 1960's.

Jerome Neapolitan

Further Reading

Capeci, Dominic, and Martha Wilkerson. *Layered Violence: The Detroit Rioters of 1943.* Jackson: University Press of Mississippi, 1991. Explores the diverse factors that caused one of the most violent race riots in U.S. history.

Johnson, Marilynn. "Gender, Race, and Rumors: Reexamining the 1943 Race Riots." *Gender and History* 10, no. 2 (1998): 252-277. Analyzes the role rumors played, particularly how they are linked to race and gender ideologies, in three of the 1943 riots: Beaumont, Detroit, and Harlem.

McClung, Lee, and Alfred Norman. *Race Riot: Detroit, 1941.* New York: Octagon Books, 1963. Short book that covers all aspects of the worst of the race riots of the 1940's.

Rucker, Walter, and James Upton, eds. *Encyclopedia of American Race Riots.* 2 vols. Santa Barbara, Calif.: Greenwood Press, 2007. A thorough coverage of race riots in the United States with 260 entries and eighty contributors.

See also African Americans; *An American Dilemma: The Negro Problem and American Democracy;* Congress of Racial Equality; Desegregation of the U.S. military; Jim Crow laws; Ku Klux Klan; Racial discrimination; Tuskegee Airmen; Zoot-suit riots; Zoot suits.

■ Racial discrimination

Definition Societal bias based upon an individual's or a group's race or ethnicity

Racial discrimination impedes national unity and increases societal conflict. These negative consequences of racial discrimination are especially pernicious during a time of war, such as World War II, the defining event of the 1940's.

Carried over from previous decades, racial discrimination against many racial and ethnic groups was rampant in the United States and Canada in 1940. Racial segregation in housing, employment, and education was the norm not only in the South but throughout the United States, as documented in the monumental study by Gunnar Myrdal, *An American Dilemma: The Negro Problem and Modern Democracy* (1944). This work is a useful time capsule by which to measure the progress made against racial discrimination during the 1940's and subsequent decades.

Racial discrimination exists in two tightly interrelated forms—direct and indirect. Direct discrimination is blatant; it is explicitly based on race and is usually intentional. The police use of racial profiling to stop selective minority automobile drivers more often than white drivers is an example of direct discrimination. Indirect discrimination is more subtle and often considered less unfair than direct discrimination; it is the perpetuation or expansion of previous acts of direct discrimination. For example, when African Americans are paid lower wages than whites for the same work based upon their race, such discrimination is clearly direct. However, if the ostensible reason for the wage differential is based on the effects of prior direct discrimination, then this discrimination is indirect. Previous discrimination in education, employment, and other areas serves to disadvantage the poorer-paid black workers with inferior qualifications, and is a form of indirect discrimination. During the 1940's, most discrimination was direct and intentional.

During the 1940's, the United States was slowly emerging from the impact of the Great Depression of the 1930's, and there was little prospect for improvement in racial relations until World War II began and initiated widespread change. This global war exposed the nation's racial segregation and discrimination. This racism was evident in the illegal internment of 120,000 Japanese Americans at the start of the war. In addition, African Americans continued to endure discrimination in the armed forces and in the burgeoning war factories, even though they played an integral part in the war effort. One of the worst race riots in United States history erupted in Detroit in 1943. Over the course of three days, thirty-four people were killed, six hundred were injured, and eighteen hundred were arrested, most of them African Americans. In the same year, in downtown Los Angeles, a group of young Latinos wearing zoot suits got into a brawl with white sailors on leave. One sailor was stabbed during this altercation, set-

ting off the so-called Zoot Suit Riot that involved thousands of servicemen clashing with young Latinos. In both the Detroit and Los Angeles riots, the actions of the white police officers were often biased against the minority participants.

However, black Americans and members of other minorities astutely sensed that the nation's need for their participation in the war effort opened new possibilities for an end to racism. White Americans also perceived the changes slowly unfolding and often were threatened by the new minority militancy. The idea started to take hold among Americans that what was unashamedly termed "white supremacy" was not permanent and was being seriously undermined.

Japanese American Internment, 1942-1945 Together with slavery of African Americans and the treatment of Native Americans, the massive internment of Japanese Americans, a majority of whom were U.S. citizens, in World War II remains one of the most shameful acts in United States history. Canada similarly interned Japanese Canadians.

Four aspects of the internment of Japanese Americans in 1942 prove that there was clearly a racial motivation behind this action. First, not one mainland Japanese American was ever convicted of spying or sabotage. Second, the U.S. government interned only selected German Americans and Italian Americans with specific cause, while it imprisoned all Japanese Americans. Third, there was no mass internment of Japanese Americans in Hawaii—a location that was militarily more dangerous than the mainland United States—because Japanese American labor was needed on the islands. Finally, the federal government later asked and finally required young Japanese American men in the internment camps to serve in the U.S. Army, which many did with distinction. However, this was an extraordinary request to make of people who were considered to be disloyal to the nation.

Initial Efforts to Combat Prejudice, 1945-1949 The war's effects carried over into the late 1940's. Adolf Hitler had given American bigotry a bad name, and a postwar human relations movement developed to exploit this sentiment. Such organizations as the American Jewish Committee, the Commission for Interracial Cooperation, and the National Conference of Christians and Jews (now the National Conference for Community and Justice) began educational efforts to "cure" prejudiced individuals.

After becoming the first African American student admitted to the University of Oklahoma in 1948, George W. McLaurin had to listen to lectures from anterooms, sit at a special desk in the library, and eat his meals in a separate room in the student union building. A middle-aged schoolteacher, McLaurin would later win a Supreme Court case that would force the University of Oklahoma to admit him to its law school. (AP/Wide World Photos)

Prejudice was defined broadly as negative attitudes toward Roman Catholics, Jews, Native Americans, Asians, and African Americans. Brotherhood Week, featuring brotherhood dinners and awards, became a common event each February. These well-meaning efforts, however, avoided tackling racism as a societal problem and ignored such politically explosive structural issues as racial segregation. The most serious problems of racial discrimination are systemic; they are less rooted in individual unfairness than in discriminatory laws, regulations, and other structural barriers.

However, some postwar efforts did address the deep, structural underpinnings of racial discrimination. As a way to thank Native Americans for their outstanding service in World War II, the U.S. Congress in 1946 established the Indian Claims Commission. This agency, which operated for more than thirty years, provided a means for tribes to address their grievances and receive monetary compensation for land lost as a result of numerous broken federal treaties. Connecticut, Massachusetts, New Jersey, New York, and Washington enacted and enforced fair employment practices laws to combat widespread job discrimination. However, southern senators filibustered to prevent the federal government from enacting a similar law during the 1940's. Similarly, laws concerning First Canadians slowly began to change, although the rights of Status Indians and Inuits to vote in federal elections was not attained until 1960.

In 1948, two significant events occurred that aimed to combat discrimination in housing and the armed forces. In *Shelley v. Kraemer* (1948), the U.S. Supreme Court ruled that racially based, restrictive covenants could not be enforced by American courts. These covenants were agreements signed by white homeowners that they would not later sell their homes to African Americans. Such discriminatory agreements were one of the major means by which strict racial segregation in housing had been maintained throughout the urban United States. The court ruling was important because racial segregation in housing was the lynchpin of racial discrimination. Racially separate housing results in widespread racial segregation in public schools, especially in neighborhood schools. Housing segregation also enables black neighborhoods to receive inferior mass transit, trash collection, and other municipal services and can result in higher-priced and inferior-quality goods sold in black neighborhood stores.

On July 26, 1948, President Harry S. Truman issued Executive Order 9981, mandating equality of opportunity for all members of the armed services "without regard to race, color, religion or national origin." The order established a seven-person committee to oversee the changes that would be necessary to desegregate the military. The order not only applied to military units but also extended to neighborhoods and schools in which military members lived and educated their children. It took time for the order's broad sweep to be implemented, but by the close of the Korean War five years later the U.S. Army was largely desegregated. However, there was strong opposition to the order. When the Democratic Party at its presidential nominating convention in 1948 adopted a surprisingly strong civil rights plank, many delegates from the South walked out of the convention in protest. These "Dixiecrats" formed the States' Rights Democratic Party. The Dixiecrats nominated Governor Strom Thurmond of South Carolina for president. Thurmond received less than 3 percent of the popular vote, but he later represented South Carolina in the U.S. Senate from 1954 through 2003. At the other end of the social-class ladder, members of the various Ku Klux Klan bodies in the South continued to employ threats and bombs to intimidate African Americans from moving into all-white neighborhoods or seeking the best-paid jobs.

Slow racial improvement was apparent in popular culture and professional sports. During the 1940's, big band swing, jazz, and bebop were popular forms of music and were primarily performed by either all-black or all-white groups. However, some desegregation began to emerge. For example, Benny Goodman's orchestra featured three African American musicians: Teddy Wilson, Lionel Hampton, and Fletcher Henderson.

The 1940's also witnessed the entry of African American athletes in formerly all-white professional sports. After Albert Benjamin "Happy" Chandler became the commissioner of Major League Baseball in 1945, the president of the Brooklyn Dodgers, Branch Rickey, saw his chance to desegregate professional baseball. In 1947, he made Jackie Robinson the first African American player in the modern major leagues. Soon afterward, catcher Roy Campanella and pitcher Don Newcombe joined the Dodgers. At first, these players faced racist resistance from many white players and fans, but in time racial discrimination in Major League Baseball subsided.

In professional basketball, Wataru Misaka, a Japanese American, broke the National Basketball Association's color barrier in 1947. However, it was not until 1950 that numerous African American players were hired by professional basketball teams. Black players had been involved at the start of professional football in 1920, but direct racial discrimination

ended their participation during the 1930's. The color line began to break in 1946, when the Los Angeles Rams were required to recruit black players as a condition for using the Los Angeles Coliseum.

Impact   The 1940's served as a critical transition decade in North American race relations. The decade began with the highly discriminatory practices of previous years. World War II, however, sparked numerous social processes that led to slow but important changes during the late 1940's. These changes, although initially modest, led directly to the sweeping reductions of discrimination that unfolded in later decades: The U.S. Supreme Court's decision in *Brown v. Board of Education*, which would declare racial segregation of public schools unconstitutional in 1954; Canada's Citizenship Act of 1956; the election of America's first Roman Catholic president in 1960 and its first African American president in 2008; and many other critical events marked the erosion of traditional discrimination.

Thomas F. Pettigrew

Further Reading

Feagin, Joe R., and Melvin B. Sikes. *Living with Racism: The Black Middle-Class Experience.* 2d ed. Malabar, Fla.: Krieger, 1994. Provides firsthand accounts of what it is like to be the target of racial discrimination.

Murray, Alice Y. *The Historical Memories of the Japanese American Internment and the Struggle for Redress.* Stanford, Calif.: Stanford University Press, 2007. Presents an excellent account of the effects of the World War II internment of Japanese Americans and their later organized actions for redress.

Myrdal, Gunnar. *An American Dilemma: The Negro Problem and Modern Democracy.* 1944. Reprint. New Brunswick, N.J. : Transaction, 1996. Classic volume on American discrimination against African Americans from 1938 through 1943 by the Nobel Prize-winning Swedish economist.

Pettigrew, Thomas F., and M. C. Taylor. "Discrimination." In *Encyclopedia of Sociology.* 2d ed. Vol. 1, edited by Edgar F. Borgatta and Rhonda J. V. Montgomery. New York: Macmillan Reference, 2000. A brief, technical discussion of the complexity of racial discrimination from a sociological perspective.

Tator, Carol, et al. *Racial Profiling in Canada: Challenging the Myth of "a Few Bad Apples."* Toronto:

University of Toronto Press, 2006. Describes how racial profiling is practiced in Canada.

See also Desegregation of the U.S. military; Fair Employment Practices Commission; Indian Claims Commission; Latinos; Music: Jazz; National Association for the Advancement of Colored People; Randolph, A. Philip; Robinson, Jackie; *Shelley v. Kraemer*; Universal Declaration of Human Rights.

■ Radar

Definition Device using radio waves to measure distances and directions to objects

World War II was the first military conflict in which radar was used. Able to detect and track ships. planes, and other objects too far away to be seen by the human eye in all weather conditions, radar often played a determinative role in battles.

Taking its name from an acronym derived from "*ra*dio *de*tection *a*nd *ra*nging," radar is a system for measuring distances and directions of distant objects by bouncing radio waves off them. Radio waves traveling through the atmosphere or space reflect off the objects with which they come into contact and then return to their sources. The effect is particularly strong when radio waves strike metallic objects, such as planes and ships. Near the beginning of the twentieth century, scientists had the idea of using this property to build instruments to detect unseen objects such as ships. However, the early instruments they devised were temperamental and so difficult to use that they required experts to operate them.

After the great passenger liner HMS *Titanic* struck an unseen iceberg and sank in 1912, work began on more reliable and more easily operated radio-detection systems that would make navigation safer. The possible military uses of such systems were also recognized by the major powers of the world. By 1939, the military forces of every major country had some sort of operational radio-wave detection system. However, the term "radar" itself was not coined until about 1941.

The original radar systems were so massive that they were suitable primarily for permanent, land-based installations. They also emitted long wavelengths that made accurate detection and direction finding difficult. During the late 1930's, technological advances allowed for the use of shorter wavelengths and more compact systems, improving accuracy and permitting installation of radar systems on some ships and aircraft. Ongoing technological improvements throughout World War II made radar increasingly easy to use, more versatile, and more accurate.

Radar became an essential part of British air defenses when Germany bombed Great Britain during the war. At the time, the failure of German planes to target British radar installations on their bombing raids was puzzling. After the war, the reason for the German's sparing the radar installations became clear. Because Britain and Germany used different frequencies and different methods of employing radio waves for detection, German efforts to locate British radar emissions were fruitless.

Impact Throughout World War II, radar was a classified military secret. The British radar system, called the Chain Home system, is generally regarded as a deciding factor in the British victory in the Battle of Britain. Radar might also have played a deciding role in the Japanese attack on Pearl Harbor in December, 1941. U.S. Army radar operators detected the incoming flights of Japanese aircraft prior to the attack; however, the officer who received the detection report did not recognize the significance of the finding and missed the opportunity to launch American aircraft to intercept the incoming Japanese attackers. After World War II, radar was used in numerous civilian applications.

Raymond D. Benge, Jr.

Further Reading

Fisher, David E. *A Summer Bright and Terrible: Winston Churchill, Lord Dowding, Radar and the Impossible Triumph of the Battle of Britain*. Washington, D.C.: Shoemaker & Hoard, 2005.

Latham, Colin, and Anne Stobbs. *Pioneers of Radar*. Stroud, Gloucestershire, England: Sutton, 1999.

Wilkinson, Stephan. "What We Learned . . . from the Battle of Britain." *Military History* 25, no. 2 (2008): 17.

See also Aircraft design and development; Bombers; Inventions; Microwave ovens; Pearl Harbor attack; Science and technology; Strategic bombing; Wartime technological advances; World War II.

■ Radio in Canada

Canadian nationalism has been dependent on maintaining a common sense of community within a dispersed populace that diverges not only geographically but also culturally and linguistically. Throughout the twentieth century, technology in Canada has been used to develop a sense of national and cultural unity. Radio has played a pivotal role in building this sense of Canadian identity, for it was the first centralized, publicly owned mass media to ostensibly forge an electrical "commons" across the vast Canadian landscape.

In Canada, radio broadcasting was first regulated by the Radiotelegraph Act of 1913. This act gave the minister of marine and fisheries the power to grant radio licenses and to charge a minimal licensing fee on each radio receiving set. The first radio license was issued in 1919 to Canadian Marconi Company's Montreal-based experimental radio station XWA. In 1920, XWA was responsible for the first musical broadcast, sending a two-hour concert by a soprano soloist from Marconi's Montreal laboratory to an audience at the Royal Society of Canada in Ottawa. In 1923, the Canadian government started licensing radio stations specifically for private commercial broadcast. The next decade fostered a boom of radio stations, as more than eighty disparate stations were licensed across Canada, primarily to newspapers and retailers, most of which where relatively small and low-powered with unreliable signals. Contrary to the situation in the United States, Canada lacked its own large national electrical companies, who were often the developers of primary radio networks. The Canadian electrical industry was a branch-plant operation of American firms, like General Electric and Westinghouse, who had set up factories in Canada to circumvent Canadian tariff regulations. Because Canadian audiences could receive the radio signals from their powerful northern U.S. flagship stations, there was no impetus for these companies to establish new Canadian stations.

Birth of a National Public Broadcasting Network By the 1930's, a third of Canadian households owned radio receivers. By the 1940's, this radio ownership was almost universal. With the saturation of American radio programming and signals, cultural and political nationalists began to pressure the federal government to create a national public radio network. In fact, the 1928 Royal Commission on Broad-

casting, headed by Sir John Aird and commonly referred to as the Aird Commission, called for a monopoly of radio ownership controlled by the Canadian federal government. This monopoly, modeled after British radio, was never realized in Canada. Instead, the government opted for a balance between private and public radio.

In 1932, the Conservative government of Prime Minister R. B. Bennett passed the Radio Broadcasting Act, thereby establishing the federal government-owned Canadian Radio Broadcasting Commission (CRBC), which was to be funded with fees collected from radio receiver licenses (which ranged from $1 in 1932 to $2.50 in 1940). The functions of the CRBC were twofold: first, to provide programming in both French and English and to network connections from coast to coast; and second, to become the regulatory body for all Canadian broadcasting. In 1936, the Liberal Party government of William Lyon Mackenzie King restructured the CRBC in order to create the Canadian Broadcasting Corporation (CBC). Despite the name change, the CBC shared the primary functions as the CRBC and, although the CBC was designated as the only national radio network operational in Canada, private stations were allowed to continue operating on local/regional levels. Just prior to the beginning of World War II, an internal reorganization separated the English and French language services of the CBC, effectively creating the French-based network Société Radio-Canada.

English Canada and the Golden Age of Radio With the protectionist ideals of Canadian nationalism influencing the formation of the CBC, issues of programming remained a central part of radio throughout the 1940's. Largely because of the polished and marketable productions stemming from the early interest in radio from powerhouses such as the Radio Corporation of America (RCA), the National Broadcasting Company (NBC), and the Columbia Broadcasting System (CBS), American content was very popular in Canada. The restrictions on broadcasting did not deter the affiliation between private radio stations and American networks. The CBC built a reputation as the voice of a nation, providing a nationalist perspective while successfully programming hockey, national news, talk shows, and variety shows such as *The Happy Gang*. Smaller, private radio stations focused on local interest stories, talk shows, and imported American programming, including radio dramas and popular music such as *Ma Perkins, Big Sister, Amos 'n' Andy,* and *Fibber McGee and Molly.* Much like the Canadian film industry, Canadian-made dramas were a hard sell to a population accustomed to the high production values of their American counterparts.

With the outbreak of World War II, the CBC became the primary source for national and international news, and an indispensable tool for providing information and propaganda to Canadians on the war efforts. The CBC established its own news information service in 1941, severing its relationship with the Canadian Press agency, which had previously provided free newswire services to all Canadian radio broadcasters. The Canadian Press created the Press News in an attempt to lure broadcasters to purchase adaptations of print newspaper stories, an effort that met with mixed success. The revolutionary news format created by the CBC, including the introduction of hourly newscasts and frontline broadcasts from foreign correspondents, established a pattern that would be imitated by private radio and attracted a loyal listening audience. During the war, the CBC produced thousands of reports from a mobile recording studio designed by Matthew Halton and Art Holmes. Halton and Holmes reconfigured a six-ton van, nicknamed "Big Betsy," to allow for soft-disk recordings that were sent back to Canada from Europe. Halton and Holmes's weekly broadcasts related news from the front, as well as human-interest stories, interviews with service personnel, and live-action recordings from warplanes and tanks. By 1944, in large part because of their successful news operations, the CBC had garnered enough of a following to mandate the development of a second national English-language network.

The postwar period marked the golden age for Canadian radio productions. While American broadcasters turned their efforts to television, Canadian radio boomed. During this period, the CBC and private broadcasters produced many popular programs: *The Wayne and Shuster Show, The Happy Gang, Maggie Muggins, National Sunday Evening Hour, Wednesday Night, The Stage: Canada's National Theatre Company on the Air, Rawhide, John and Judy,* and *Woodhouse and Hawkins.* Despite the fact that there were twice as many CBC-owned and -affiliated stations as there were private stations, by 1948 the operating revenues of private broadcasters in Canada were twice that of the CBC. With this popularity, the private stations aggressively sought increased power and better frequencies, while insistently challenging the dual role of the CBC as their competitor and regulator. Their pleas were not fulfilled until the revised Canadian Broadcasting Act of 1958 took away the regulatory power of the CBC by creating the Canadian Radio-television and Telecommunications Commission (CRTC) as the government regulator for all broadcasting and telecommunication in Canada.

The Bilingual Divide: Radio in Quebec Although the relative high rates of poverty in Quebec negatively affected radio receiver ownership, both private and public French-language radio stations in the province fared well throughout the 1940's. The legislation that deemed the CBC as the only national broadcasting network had less of an effect on private radio in Quebec. French-language stations did not experience the same threat from American radio.

Approximately thirty French-language radio stations served the three million Québécois, the most powerful of which, CKAC, also provided service for the French-speaking populace in New England. French Canadian radio followed a similar format as its English counterpart, programming musical concerts, drama, variety shows, news, and talk shows. With the outbreak of World War II, Radio-Canada (CBC's French-language network) stayed on the air twenty-four hours a day in order to ensure up-to-the-minute coverage of the war efforts for the francophone audience. Like the English-language CBC network, Radio-Canada had a similar impact on reformatting news broadcasts. However, CKAC (owned by the Montreal newspaper *La Presse*) and CHRC (a French-language private radio station located in Quebec City) also relied on their own news information services and provided in-depth, regular news reports.

Rather than recycling theatrical plays, French Canadian radio dramas were often original productions written specifically for radio broadcast. Similar to the imbalance within the Canadian film industry, while English Canadian dramas struggled to find an audience, French radio dramas were highly successful. French radio dramas explored the distinct cultural issues facing French Canadians, using language as a political tool as well as a vehicle for comedy, drama, and satire. Some of the most successful radio dramas of the 1940's were later adapted into film: *Un homme et son péché, La Pension Velder, Le curé de village,* and *Jeunesse dorée.* The satires *Les amours de Ti-Jos* and *Nazaire et Barnabie,* as well as the variety shows *Radio-Carabin* and *Le Pétit Train du matin,* were also quite popular throughout the 1940's.

Impact Canadian radio lost momentum with the introduction of television broadcasting in 1952. However, the model for regulating television broadcasting was heavily influenced by the experience of radio. Nationalist provisions to create and protect Canadian culture have remained central, with Canadian content and ownership regulations placing restrictions on media imports from the United States and abroad. Arguably, however, the greatest impact of Canadian radio during the 1940's—specifically with regard to news broadcasting—can be seen in television and radio formats across North America.

Kelly Egan

Further Reading

Bird, Roger Anthony, ed. *Documents of Canadian Broadcasting.* Ottawa: Carleton University Press, 1988. Useful collection of documents illuminating the history of radio broadcasting in Canada.

Fortner, Robert S. *Radio, Morality, and Culture: Britain, Canada, and the United States, 1919-1945.* Carbondale: Southern Illinois University Press, 2005. Fascinating comparative study of the cultural impact of radio on three different anglophonic countries through the first quarter century of broadcasting.

Peers, Frank W. *The Politics of Canadian Broadcasting, 1920-1951.* Toronto: University of Toronto Press, 1969. Solid study of government control of Canadian broadcasting, which was essentially all radio before the 1950's.

Sterling, Christopher H., ed. *Encyclopedia of Radio.* New York: Fitzroy Dearborn, 2004. General reference work on radio that includes useful entries on aspects of Canadian broadcasting.

Vipond, Mary. *The Mass Media in Canada.* Toronto: James Lorimer, 2000. Comprehensive survey of the broadcasting and print media in Canada through the twentieth century.

See also Advertising in Canada; *Amos 'n' Andy;* Canadian nationalism; Canadian regionalism; Film in Canada; Foreign policy of Canada; Literature in Canada; Quebec nationalism; Radio in the United States; Wartime propaganda in Canada.

■ Radio in the United States

Radio was the dominant source of news, music, and entertainment in American homes during the 1940's—its Golden Age. As the center of American social and political life it helped unify the nation during World War II.

During the early 1940's, almost every home in the United States had at least one radio that provided a family with hours of music, news, and entertainment programming. Many large cities had two or three radio stations, but most communities had only one. However, people who lived in isolated rural areas of the country could often pick up their favorite radio shows from the distant signals of the clear-channel stations with considerable power. The major radio networks that provided these programs included National Broadcasting Company (NBC), Columbia Broadcasting Company (CBS), and the Mutual Broadcasting System (MBS).

Radio Dramas With a twist of the dial, radio's dramatic live dialogue, mood-creating music, and realistic sound effects transported listeners to imaginary places, such as an Art Deco-style ballroom dance floor in New York, or the busy, dusty streets of a nineteenth century Western town, or the eerie quietness of a distant planet two hundred years in the future. Americans adjusted their daily schedules around their favorite programs that included comedy, drama, music, or sports. Regardless of age, taste, wealth, ethnicity, or gender, radio provided programs to please everyone.

Most radio dramas of the 1940's were performed live, sometimes in front of studio audiences, with actors standing behind microphones while reading from scripts. Sound-effects artists added excitement to the shows with realistic noises, such as squeaky doors, menacing footsteps, glass breaking, gunshots, and car horns blaring in traffic. *The Lux Radio Theater* adapted Broadway stage plays and later films into hour-long radio programs that were performed live before studio audiences. Many prominent actors of the era appeared on *The Lux Radio Theater* to recreate popular roles they had recently performed in films or plays. Some of these actors included Lauren Bacall, Lucille Ball, Ingrid Bergman, Humphrey Bogart, James Cagney, Bette Davis, Charlton Heston, James Stewart, John Wayne, and Vincent Price. Sponsored by du Pont de Nemours &

Co., *Cavalcade of America* (1935-1952) was a popular radio series that dramatized factual stories of American heroes, both famous and obscure, from various periods in history.

Listeners also spent their evenings tuned to their favorite detective dramas, trying to unravel the mysteries along with the programs' main characters, such as detectives Sam Spade, Ellery Queen, Sherlock Holmes, and Nero Wolfe. Radio producers took detective dramas to a different level with nighttime thriller programs that blended mystery and detective elements with horror and psychological suspense. The first successful thrillers of this era were NBC's *Inner Sanctum* (1941-1952) and CBS's *Suspense* (1942-1962). In 1941, sixteen thriller drama programs were on radio; by the end of World War II, there were forty-three, making thrillers the fastest-growing radio genre during World War II, rivaled only by the top comedy shows.

Soap operas were the primary form of programming during the day. The "soap" in soap opera referred to soap manufacturers, such as Colgate-Palmolive, Lever Brothers, and Procter and Gamble, that sponsored and produced these programs. Soap operas were aimed at a predominantly female audience and were broadcast during the weekday, when housewives were available to listen. By 1940, soap operas represented 90 percent of all commercially sponsored daytime broadcast hours.

Other Radio Programming Comedy was the most popular radio genre, with its rising stars, such as Bud Abbott and Lou Costello, George Burns and Gracie Allen, Milton Berle, Red Skelton, Danny Kaye, Jack Benny, and Bob Hope. The comedy-variety shows featured big-name hosts, guest stars, skits, orchestras, and fast tempos. Situation comedies, such as *Amos 'n' Andy* (1928-1954), *The Life of Riley* (1941-1951), and *The Adventures of Ozzie and Harriet* (1944-1954), featured continuing casts of characters who faced new humorous situations in each episode. Popular children's radio programs of the 1940's included *The Green Hornet* (1936-1952), *Captain Midnight* (1938-1949), *Jack Armstrong, the All-American Boy* (1933-1951), and *The Adventures of Superman* (1940-1951).

Other radio programs of the 1940's that attracted listeners included quiz shows, such as *Take It or Leave It* (1940-1947), *Truth or Consequences* (1940-1957), *Information Please* (1938-1952), and *Quiz Kids* (1940-1953); Westerns such as *The Lone Ranger* (1933-1954), *The Tom Mix Ralston Straight Shooters* (1933-1950), and *Straight Arrow* (1948-1951); and special sports events, such as the World Series, the Kentucky Derby, and boxing.

The popular swing music of the big bands dominated radio's music programming during this decade, with well-known performers, such as Glenn Miller, Doris Day, Perry Como, Frank Sinatra, and Bing Crosby.

With the exception of news reports during World War II, NBC and CBS banned prerecorded shows completely, out of fear that their audiences would reject "canned" radio programs. Performing on live programs was difficult for the entertainers and musicians, who had to appear on programs that aired at odd hours or had to perform repeat broad-

Edward R. Murrow chairing a CBS Radio round-table discussion of current news with a panel of news correspondents known collectively as "Murrow's Boys." Clockwise from lower left: Murrow, Larry Le Sueur, Bill Costello, Winston Burdett, David Schoenbrun, Bill Downs, Eric Sevareid, and Howard K. Smith. (Getty Images)

casts for listeners in different time zones. Once magnetic tape became available in 1947, the radio industry gradually realized the advantages of using prerecorded shows, and by the end of the decade airing taped, prerecorded shows had become a standard practice.

Listeners could easily recognize each radio program by its theme music, characters, voices of the performers and announcers, or the product of its sponsor. Companies such as General Electric, General Mills, and Quaker Oats sponsored radio programs not only for the entertainment of the listeners but also to advertise their products that ranged from breakfast cereals to appliances. Parents found themselves buying the cereals, toys, or other products that were heavily advertised by the sponsors of their children's favorite radio programs. The children saved the box tops from these products and mailed them in for one of the premiums offered by the sponsors, such as a Lone Ranger blackout safety belt or a Captain Midnight secret decoder ring. As a result of the large number of programs that were sponsored, radio was criticized for being too commercial. Critics believed that the advertisements for soap, laxatives, automobiles, and other products that were sandwiched within and between programs interfered with the artistic aspects of the radio programs, insulted the intelligence of the listeners, and damaged the credibility and integrity of the stations and networks.

Wartime Radio Families and neighbors of U.S. servicemen closely monitored radio war reports. Previous war coverage had primarily consisted of newspaper reports and government-produced newsreels that were shown in film theaters. The first radio war reports featured announcers in the studios doing little more than reading news updates from the wire services. However, radio journalism significantly changed during World War II, when U.S. radio journalists were sent abroad to cover events ranging from the German invasion of Poland in September, 1939, to Japan's surrender ceremony aboard the USS *Missouri* in September, 1945. Americans were able to visualize and experience the war through the vivid descriptions of the journalists who reported from the battlefields. After the United States entered the war in 1941, the networks expanded their news coverage until it accounted for one-fifth of total radio programming. Americans began to rely more on radio than on newspapers for their war news because the radio provided bulletins and updates faster than newspapers, which were also handicapped by a shortage of newsprint.

The U.S. government did not censor radio reports about World War II, except for bans on the forecasting or reporting of weather (even rain-outs of sports events), in addition to the standard ban on reporting on military activities and war production. To avoid government censorship, the radio industry formed a War Broadcasting Council that created industry guidelines, including a ban on the airing of casualty or damage reports.

As radio news departments provided constant updates and commentary on the war, radio's entertainment programming rallied behind the war effort. Messages and themes in support of the war were aired in commercials, public service messages, patriotic series, and radio programs from comedy and drama to music. Radio game shows even awarded war bonds as prizes. Soap opera characters began discussing the American Red Cross or United Service Organizations (USO) voluntarism and reminded each other to donate blood. Through their favorite soap opera heroines, women learned to save used cooking fats needed in the manufacture of ammunition or used cans and other metals needed to build tanks. Storylines for these wartime daily serials also included the wounded or amnesic soldier who returned home or the grief over the death of the son, husband, or father who had died in battle. Radio dramas that included references to World War II, however, had the potential to include violence and other horrors of war because in the real war soldiers were killing and being killed. Therefore, the U.S. government warned radio stations not to include in their programs any graphic dramatizations of violence associated with World War II.

Wartime Propaganda President Franklin D. Roosevelt understood that radio was a powerful tool that could be used to generate public support for U.S. involvement in World War II. In June, 1942, Roosevelt issued an executive order that established the Office of War Information (OWI), and gave this agency the responsibility of using radio, as well as newspapers, films, art exhibits, and other public programs, to promote the nation's war policies throughout the United States and abroad. Although criticized for often slanting the news to conform to the U.S. wartime position, the OWI attracted some of America's most talented writers and actors, who created programs that reflected the nation's involvement in World War II. Radio networks, Hollywood stars, private agencies, and the U.S. government cooperated in creating radio programming that would alert Americans to the threat of fascism, as well as educate listeners on how they could help the United States win the war.

Inspired partly by U.S. troops' makeshift radio stations in Panama and Alaska, radio broadcasters and the U.S. government collaborated to create the most elaborate military entertainment organization in history—the Armed Forces Radio Service (AFRS). Without charging fees, the AFRS recorded and distributed network shows without commercials to more than seven hundred radio stations that served U.S. servicemen worldwide. AFRS also created its own radio programs designed to improve the morale of U.S. soldiers fighting abroad. Hosted by actor Don Ameche, *Command Performance* featured sports and entertainment celebrities who appeared on the show to fulfill G.I. "commands," such as servicemen's requests for an interview with boxing champion Joe Louis or for a "fiddle fight" between the world's greatest violinist, Jascha Heifetz, and the world's worst violinist, comedian Jack Benny.

During the war, radio producers and entertainers often took their programs to the soldiers by broadcasting live from military sites. In 1941, comedian

During World War II, President Franklin D. Roosevelt continued the "fireside chats" he had begun during the 1930's. For his February 23, 1942, broadcast, listeners were advised in advance to have at hand reference maps, to which Roosevelt referred as he outlined the geography of the developing world war. (AP/Wide World Photos)

Bob Hope aired his popular radio series *The Pepsodent Show* from March Army Air Force Field in Riverside, California, in what would become the first of hundreds of radio (and later television) broadcasts he performed to entertain U.S. troops. Hope's opening monologue always focused on subjects of interest to the soldiers, and the listeners who tuned in back home were able to get a glimpse of how the soldiers lived and the sacrifices they were making for their country.

The radio programs created during the 1940's not only improved the morale of the U.S. soldiers and generated public support for the war but also promoted a democratic way of life that included every American regardless of race and ethnicity. After accusations of racial discrimination in the military and the June, 1943, race riots in Detroit, radio was used as a means of increasing racial tolerance. The networks, along with various government agencies, produced radio programming that dramatized the contributions of African Americans to American music, drama, sports, science, industry, education, and national defense. NBC, in cooperation with the U.S. Immigration and Naturalization Service, produced the radio program *I'm an American*, in which listeners were introduced to naturalized U.S. citizens who talked about what it was like to be an American.

Government Regulation   While the average listener during the 1940's was primarily interested in the various programs radio had to offer, these programs were underpinned by complicated federal regulations designed to control programming content and radio ownership. Because the U.S. government regarded the frequencies that transmitted radio programming as natural resources, similar to the nation's parks and waterways, the Federal Communications Commission (FCC) had the responsibility of ensuring that the radio industry operated in the public interest. For example, the FCC's Mayflower Rule (later renamed the Fairness Doctrine) prohibited radio broadcasters from editorializing only one point of view. By the end of the decade, however, the FCC had softened its ban to allow radio editorializing only if other points of view were also aired to balance those of the station.

Regulating radio ownership was another area in which the FCC sought to protect the public interest. Many newspaper-radio combinations were owned by powerful publishers, such as William Randolph Hearst and Robert R. McCormick, and the FCC was concerned about any potential conflicts that could result from newspapers owning broadcast stations. The FCC began hearings in 1941 to determine if allowing newspaper publishers to own radio stations was a good idea. Although the hearings were interrupted by the U.S. entry into World War II, the investigation continued until 1944.

The FCC was also concerned about the possibility of the radio industry turning into a monopoly in which the majority of U.S. radio stations were either owned or controlled by the major radio networks. By the 1940's, NBC and its owned-and-operated stations dominated U.S. radio's audiences, affiliates, and advertising. In May, 1941, the FCC issued a report that described numerous examples of anticompetition practices by the networks. The FCC found that NBC's use of its dual networks, NBC Red and NBC Blue, stifled competition with CBS. The FCC ordered the Radio Corporation of America (RCA), the owner of NBC, to diversify. RCA challenged the FCC's order in court, but in 1943 the U.S. Supreme Court ruled that the FCC had the legal authority to regulate the radio industry. As a result, RCA was forced to sell its Blue network, which later became the American Broadcasting Company (ABC).

Impact   Radio was the communications lifeline for Americans during the 1940's that helped to create national unity with its ability to share important news with listeners across the United States. On November 7, 1944, when President Roosevelt won his fourth term as president, half the nation's homes that had radios listened to the election reports. Six months later, radio reported Roosevelt's death on April 12, 1945. Radio provided listeners with live remote coverage of Roosevelt's funeral train as it traveled from Warm Springs, Georgia, to New York, and an entire nation sat by the radio to attend the funeral of the man who understood and used the power of radio to calm a nation and win a war.

Ironically, the 1940's would also be radio's last decade of uncontested dominance as a supplier of news and entertainment. The networks began shifting their focus away from radio and toward a new medium—television. By the end of the decade, many of the popular shows that had once been the heart of radio programming began to move to televi-

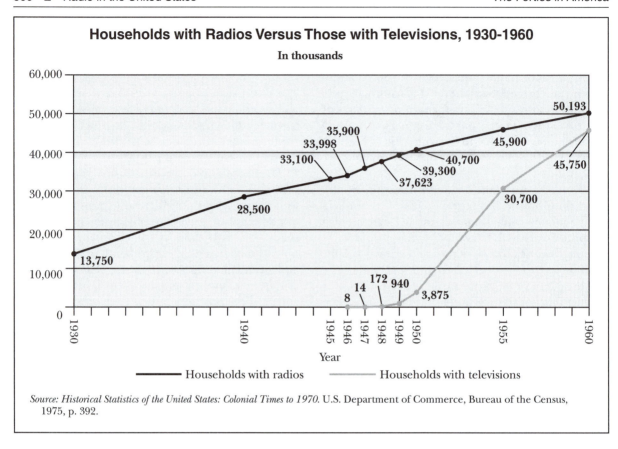

Households with Radios Versus Those with Televisions, 1930-1960

In thousands

Source: Historical Statistics of the United States: Colonial Times to 1970. U.S. Department of Commerce, Bureau of the Census, 1975, p. 392.

sion. With the growing popularity of television, radio was forced to redefine itself during the next decade in order to attract the audiences it needed to survive.

Eddith A. Dashiell

Further Reading

Balk, Alfred. *The Rise of Radio, from Marconi Through the Golden Age.* Jefferson, N.C.: McFarland, 2006. History of radio that analyzes the medium's impact on society, culture, and politics.

Barfield, Ray. *Listening to Radio, 1920-1950.* Westport, Conn.: Praeger, 1996. Cultural history of radio that focuses on the oral histories of ordinary Americans who grew up listening to its programs.

Douglas, Susan J. *Listening In: Radio and American Imagination.* Minneapolis: University of Minnesota Press, 2004. History of radio's development from the early days of wireless to the shock jocks and National Public Radio commentators of the 1990's.

Hilmes, Michelle. *Radio Voices: American Broadcasting,* *1922-1952.* Minneapolis: University of Minnesota Press, 1997. Sociological study of American culture as reflected through radio programming, including racial stereotypes and the portrayal of women.

Hilmes, Michelle, and Jason Loviglio, eds. *Radio Reader: Essays in the Cultural History of Radio.* New York: Routledge, 2001. Collection of essays that provide a broad, interdisciplinary perspective on radio and its effect on all forms of mass media during the twentieth century.

Nachman, Gerald. *Raised on Radio.* Berkeley: University of California Press, 2000. History of radio programming during its Golden Age, including discussion of comedies, quiz shows, soap operas, and ethnic programs.

See also   Abbott and Costello; Advertising in the United States; *Amos 'n' Andy*; Benny, Jack; Goodman, Benny; Guadalcanal, Battle of; Hope, Bob; Murrow, Edward R.; Music: Classical; Music: Jazz; Music: Popular; Radio in Canada; Television.

■ Railroad seizure

The Event Federal government's taking control of U.S. railroads in response to labor strikes

Dates Spring, 1946, and 1948

Place Washington, D.C., and throughout the United States

Truman used the executive powers of the presidency to compel the railroad industry and its workers to act in support of government policies even though these actions were against the industries' own best interests. The railroad seizures set a precedent for later seizure of steel mills, which was ruled unconstitutional.

A Democrat, Harry S. Truman ran for public office on a prolabor platform and acted on those ideas while he was in office as president from 1945 until 1953. His actions included vetoing the Taft-Hartley Act (Labor-Management Relations Act) of 1947, though it passed over his veto. He thought that the act restricted too many labor activities, while giving too much power to management. Despite his objections to this law, Truman invoked it twelve times during his seven-year presidency.

Economic Pressures Truman oversaw the transition of the U.S. economy from military production toward consumer products for the civilian sector. During World War II, U.S. industrial production was under indirect military control to ensure production of suitable products in sufficient quantities to meet U.S. military demands. Prices of many commodities were fixed by the government, as were wages, for the duration of the war. At the conclusion of the war, however, pent-up demand for consumer goods caused severe shortages, thus driving up prices on available goods. Inflation became widespread, so workers began to agitate for higher wages, particularly as expired contracts came up for renegotiation. In response to labor strikes, the U.S. government, under Truman's orders seized operational control of two dozen industries, including steel mills, meatpacking facilities, and Class I railroads.

In the spring of 1946, Truman intervened in a railroad labor dispute when a national railroad workers' strike stopped both passenger and rail freight service for more than a month throughout most of the country. Eighteen railroad unions agreed to federal arbitration that would have resulted in a wage increase of about 18 cents per hour. The two largest railroad unions, however, voted to strike—the Brotherhood of Railway Trainmen and the Brotherhood of Locomotive Engineers. The railroad strike, by severely curtailing transportation, caused shortages of raw materials in manufacturing, forcing factories to idle their workers. The strike also disrupted the distribution of food and fuel throughout the United States. More important, the United States was the largest provider of grain to more than 45 million Europeans struggling to survive in the immediate aftermath of World War II, and the railroad strike disrupted transportation of grain as well. Truman feared large-scale starvation and death in Europe if railroads did not immediately resume grain shipments to American port cities, so that the grain could be sent to Europe.

The strike ended mostly on the government's terms, after one month. Truman intervened again in 1948, when railroad workers serving the Chicago area threatened to strike in order to achieve wage increases. In this instance, the striking workers returned to work while contract negotiations continued.

Truman was under intense pressure to keep the railroads functioning. He argued that the proper functioning of the railroads was essential for national security. By continuing to strike, now against the federal government, railroad employees were engaging in an illegal activity. Truman authorized the immediate firing of any and all railroad employees who called in sick without a doctor's verification. The employee would lose not only his or her job but also all seniority and pension benefits.

Truman ordered the Office of Defense Transportation to form railway battalions of troops who would operate essential routes. Truman further ordered that executive orders be drawn up to draft into immediate military service any railroad employee who refused to report for work. He also informed the leaders of the striking unions that if the Army had to continue operational control of the railroads, the president would permanently deauthorize the railroad unions. All members would lose their jobs, seniority, and benefits. He urged Congress to set up a labor board that would require both management and labor to remain at work and in negotiations, in the railroad industry and other industries that directly affected the American population as a whole.

Impact President Truman proved willing to force organized labor to remain in negotiations with corporate management, even threatening to draft striking workers immediately into the military, claiming "national security interests." The success of this threat led him to believe such threats would work in any large-scale labor dispute, though the action hurt him politically and alienated workers. He tried the same tactics in 1952 against steel mill workers, whose union took the president to court, eventually proving victorious in the Supreme Court case *Youngstown Sheet and Tube Co. v. Sawyer,* decided on June 2, 1952. Seizure of private property for national security reasons, as commander in chief but without congressional approval or even notification, was deemed unconstitutional outside wartime emergencies.

Victoria Erhart

Further Reading

Ayers, Eben A. *Truman in the White House: The Diary of Eben A. Ayers.* Edited by Robert H. Ferrell. Columbia: University of Missouri Press, 1991. Edited by a leading authority on Truman, this is a literate, intelligent, abbreviated account of the flow of events, rail strike included, during the Truman administration. Needs to be supplemented, but useful. Many photos, useful index.

Ely, James. *Railroads and American Law.* Lawrence: University Press of Kansas, 2001. Covers all aspects of railroad law and the impact the growth of railroads had on American economic and labor history. Briefly discusses railroads during the 1940's.

Gosnell, Harold F. *Truman's Crises: A Political Biography of Harry S. Truman.* Westport, Conn.: Greenwood Press, 1980. The author is a noted political scientist. The prose is uninspired but well organized. Chapter notes, useful bibliography, good index. Chapter 22 pertains to the railroad strike and its context.

McCullough, David. *Truman.* New York: Simon & Schuster, 1992. A comprehensive biography of Truman's life and presidency. Covers both domestic issues, such as the post-World War II U.S. economy, and international issues, including Truman's decision to use nuclear weapons against Japan to end World War II.

Miller, Merle. *Plain Speaking: An Oral Biography of Harry S. Truman.* New York: Berkley, 1974. Miller's observations are acute and affectionate.

Much on Truman's special knowledge of railroads. Good index.

Morris, Maeva. *Truman and the Steel Seizure Case: The Limits of Presidential Power.* Durham, N.C.: Duke University Press, 1994. Studies the legal as well as political consequences of the use of presidential power, whether under the guise of national security threat or not, and what constraints the U.S. Constitution and courts put on such power. Truman's prior seizure of railroads is discussed as a precedent to understand the government seizure of steel mills.

Truman, Harry S. *Year of Decisions.* Vol. 1 in *Memoirs.* Garden City, N.Y.: Doubleday, 1955. Inimitable Truman, pithy and deceptively straightforward. Good perspectives on the strike wave, the railroad strike, and presidential reactions. Good index. Refreshing and invaluable.

See also Army, U.S.; Business and the economy in the United States; Department of Defense, U.S.; Economic wartime regulations; Elections in the United States: 1948; Labor strikes; Truman, Harry S.; Unionism; Wartime seizures of businesses.

■ Rand, Ayn

Identification Russian American novelist and screenwriter

Born February 2, 1905; St. Petersburg, Russia

Died March, 6, 1982; New York, New York

Ayn Rand wrote The Fountainhead *(1943), one of the most enduring novels of the 1940's; developed Objectivism, an anticommunist, procapitalist philosophy; and testified as a friendly witness before the House Committee on Un-American Activities. She was a dissenting voice in the United States when the popularity of federal government programs was at its peak.*

Ayn Rand was born Alisa Zinovyevna Rosenbaum, daughter of a pharmacist in St. Petersburg (later renamed Petrograd). In 1917, she personally witnessed the Bolshevik Revolution and became a lifelong anticommunist. Because civil order collapsed in Petrograd, the Rosenbaums fled to Odessa in the Crimea in the fall of 1918, where she finished high school. They returned home in 1921, and Alisa entered the University of Petrograd later that year to study history. After graduating in 1924, she enrolled at the State Institute for Cinema Arts to study screen-writing.

In 1925, Alisa received permission to leave Russia to visit relatives in Chicago. She arrived in February, 1926, and never left. She lived with those relatives for six months before leaving for California to become a screenwriter. It was during this time that she adopted the name Ayn Rand.

Rand began writing *The Fountainhead* in 1935 while working as a clerk in an architect's office to do research. Loosely based on architect Frank Lloyd Wright, the novel's protagonist is Howard Roark. A brilliant man, he never compromises his integrity, unlike the vast majority of the people he meets. Twelve publishers rejected *The Fountainhead* before the Bobbs-Merrill Company published the work in 1943. Despite poor publicity and limited print runs, it became a best seller through word of mouth. Rand also wrote the screenplay for the 1949 film adaptation starring Gary Cooper as Roark.

Rand started writing *Atlas Shrugged* (1957) during the late 1940's. Like *The Fountainhead*, it dramatizes her Objectivist philosophy. The fundamental premise of Objectivism is that reality is independent of human perceptions; the philosophy does not accept sacred texts, such as the Bible, the Book of Mormon, or the Koran, as legitimate. Rand argued that ethical principles must be based on rational self-interest and that the only proper function of government is to protect people's rights, to enforce criminal laws, and to provide a defense against external enemies. Objectivism is probusiness and antigovernment. However, Rand's atheism, a belief she shared with the communists, kept her on the fringe of American politics.

In 1947, Rand testified as a friendly witness before the House Committee on Un-American Activities about the 1944 film *Song of Russia*, which she criticized as procommunist propaganda, and about the overall influence of communism in the film industry.

Impact   Rand's books sell about a quarter of a million copies annually, and both *The Fountainhead* and *Atlas Shrugged* are still in print in the twenty-first century. Her followers include Alan Greenspan, former economic adviser to Presidents Richard M. Nixon, Gerald R. Ford, and Ronald Reagan and former chairman of the Federal Reserve System, and Nathaniel Branden, whose book *The Psychology of*

Self-Esteem (1969) was a best seller in the pop psychology/self-help genre.

Thomas R. Feller

Further Reading

Mayhew, Robert. *Ayn Rand and Song of Russia: Communism and Anti-Communism in 1940's Hollywood.* Lanham, Md.: Scarecrow Press, 2005.

Valliant, James S. *The Passion of Ayn Rand's Critics.* Dallas, Tex.: Durban House, 2005.

Walker, Jeff. *The Ayn Rand Cult.* Chicago: Open Court, 1999.

See also   Anticommunism; Architecture; Film in the United States; Literature in the United States; Wright, Frank Lloyd.

■ Randolph, A. Philip

Identification   American labor and civil rights leader
Born   April 15, 1889; Crescent City, Florida
Died   May 16, 1979; New York, New York

Randolph, sometimes overshadowed by other civil rights activists, stands out as a labor leader and a civil rights leader who attempted to bring the two movements together. He eventually recognized the necessity of focusing on racial issues during the 1940's, when the issue of discrimination in wartime industries and in the U.S. military would come to a head as a result of World War II.

Asa Philip Randolph, the son of the African Methodist Episcopal (AME) minister James Randolph and Elizabeth Robinson Randolph, grew up in Jacksonville, Florida, before migrating to Harlem. While working in various menial jobs and eventually as an elevator operator, he attended classes at New York University and City College and eventually joined the Socialist Party of Eugene V. Debs. His early career included community organizing and publishing the socialist periodical *The Messenger.* As an activist, Randolph was a militant promoter of African American civil and economic rights, while rejecting violence and separatism, and believed that jobs with decent pay and dignity were the key to emancipation. It was in the labor movement, however, that Randolph would first achieve public prominence. In 1925, he founded the Brotherhood of Sleeping Car Porters, the first successful independent African

A. Philip Randolph (left) with John L. Lewis, the president of the United Mine Workers, in early 1940. (Time & Life Pictures/Getty Images)

American labor organization, and twelve years later brought the Pullman Palace Car Company to the table for contract negotiations. In 1936, Randolph became president of the National Negro Congress, but by 1940 he had resigned over the communist domination of the organization. He remained a vocal opponent of the Communist Party for the rest of his career, denouncing it in 1946.

Throughout the 1940's, Randolph also maintained ties with the Socialist Party that had shaped him, accepting an award from the Workers' Defense League in 1944, though declining an offer to run for vice president on the Socialist ticket that same year, claiming union responsibilities. Shifting away from labor issues as the focus of his activism, Randolph then put forth his greatest efforts toward advancing African American civil rights within and without the American labor movement. Most notable, but not unique among them, was the proposed March on Washington. When World War II and the necessary wartime industries finally provided the kind of economic stimulus that pulled the United States out of the Great Depression, most of the newly available jobs went to white people.

At the same time, while the U.S. participation in the war following Pearl Harbor in December, 1941, was promoted as a fight against racist Nazi Germany,

the racial discrimination practiced in American wartime industries and segregation within the U.S. Army became public embarrassments as they were widely reported and became rallying points for the African American civil rights organizations of the period. Randolph, as one of the most prominent civil rights leaders of the period, led the charge, and with the backing of the National Association for the Advancement of Colored People (NAACP), he threatened to bring more than 100,000 African Americans to Washington, D.C., for a protest march. The proposed March on Washington, which was scheduled for July 1, 1941, was also part of the March on Washington movement that Randolph chose to make exclusively black, both to emphasize self-help and to prevent communist infiltration.

Although the later March on Washington of 1963 would be remembered as a beautiful and inspiring event, in 1941 the Franklin D. Roosevelt administration regarded the prospect of this large public protest as a public embarrassment and threat. Therefore, NAACP president Walter White was able to persuade President Roosevelt to address certain demands in exchange for the cancellation of the march. The principal result of the meeting was Roosevelt's issuance of Executive Order 8802, which both outlawed race discrimination in the hiring practices of wartime industries and established a Fair Employment Practices Commission (FEPC) to enforce nondiscrimination in war industries. Although the FEPC was considered a great step forward at the time of its establishment, its effectiveness ended up being limited thanks to weakening measures put in place by southern Democrats, which also stymied the establishment of a permanent commission. Nonetheless, the FEPC was an important step toward federal enforcement on equal opportunity in employment and first illustrated the role the federal government would come to play in advancing and enforcing African American civil rights.

Randolph's struggle to desegregate the military

met with less immediate success, as Roosevelt remained reluctant to push his southern Democratic allies. Moreover, military leadership argued that racial integration would undermine military effectiveness and morale. In response, Randolph pushed for military integration as the best way of breaking down segregation in the rest of American society. In 1943, he also authorized the publication of a pamphlet for the general public that exposed the hypocrisy of fighting against the Nazis with segregated armies.

Although he failed to persuade the federal government during World War II, Randolph continued his campaign against military segregation and discrimination after the war, founding the League for Nonviolent Civil Disobedience Against Military Segregation in response to the Selective Service Act of 1947, which for the first time instituted peacetime registration for the draft. Through this organization, Randolph called for resistance to the draft by both black and white Americans as long as the United States maintained a "Jim Crow military." Randolph's efforts gained enough attention and support to influence President Harry S. Truman, who had been reluctant to push too hard on civil rights. Truman wanted to avoid widespread draft resistance and also recognized the need for the African American vote in the closely contested 1948 presidential election. Therefore, in July, 1948, he ordered the military to desegregate, resulting in an integrated military by the time of the Korean War.

Impact   From these civil rights successes, Randolph secured his place in the American labor movement, and he continued his efforts to bring the two movements together. After the American Federation of Labor (AFL) and the Congress of Industrial Organizations (CIO) merged in 1955, Randolph became one of its vice presidents. In 1959, he also became head of the Negro American Labor Council. However, when the AFL-CIO leadership displayed declining support for organizing African American workers, Randolph increasingly devoted his efforts to the postwar Civil Rights movement. His greatest accomplishment during this era was his role in organizing and participating in the 1963 March on Washington for Jobs and Freedom, a culmination of his earlier March on Washington efforts. In 1964, President

Lyndon B. Johnson awarded Randolph the Presidential Medal of Freedom. In 1966, Randolph founded the A. Philip Randolph Institute in Harlem to provide job skills and training for African American youth.

Susan Roth Breitzer

Further Reading

Anderson, Jervis. *A. Philip Randolph: A Biographical Portrait.* Reprint. Berkeley: University of California Press, 1986. The first complete published biography of Randolph.

Kersten, Andrew E. *A. Philip Randolph: A Life in the Vanguard.* Lanham, Md.: Rowman & Littlefield, 2007. This biography re-places Randolph in the context of the "long Civil Rights movement" throughout all the phases of his career as a labor and civil rights leader.

Pfeffer, Paula. *A. Philip Randolph: Pioneer of the Civil Rights Movement.* Baton Rouge: Louisiana State University Press, 1990. A study of Randolph's shaping role in the American Civil Rights movement and the tension between his roles as civil rights leader and a labor leader.

Taylor, Cynthia. *A. Philip Randolph: The Religious Journey of an African American Labor Leader.* New York: New York University Press, 2006. A revisionist biography that emphasizes the importance of Randolph's religious beliefs, following a brief rejection of religion in favor of socialism, as well as his close ties with religious organizations throughout his career.

Van Horn, Carl E., and Herbert A. Schaffner, eds. *Work in America: An Encyclopedia of History, Policy, and Society.* Santa Barbara, Calif.: ABC-Clio, 2003. A comprehensive encyclopedia of American labor and economic history.

See also   Civil rights and liberties; Congress of Racial Equality; Desegregation of the U.S. military; Executive Order 8802; Fair Employment Practices Commission; National Association for the Advancement of Colored People; Racial discrimination; Roosevelt, Franklin D.; Truman, Harry S.; Unionism; Wartime industries.

Rationing, wartime. *See* **Wartime rationing**

■ Rayburn, Sam

Identification   Speaker of the U.S. House of
Representatives
Born   January 6, 1882; Roane County, Tennessee
Died   November 16, 1961; Bonham, Texas

Rayburn was elected Speaker of the House of Representatives in 1940, a post he held for the next seventeen and a half years. In that position, he proved an effective wartime congressional leader, pushing through essential war measures and advocating postwar financial assistance to European allies.

Prior to his 1912 election to the United States House of Representatives, Democrat Sam Rayburn had spent several years in the Texas state legislature. He was an active supporter of Franklin D. Roosevelt's New Deal during the 1930's, especially programs designed to assist his largely rural constituency. In 1940, he was named Speaker of the House, becoming one of the most powerful men in Washington, D.C.

Rayburn recognized the necessity of preparing America for World War II as the European conflict broadened. With Great Britain standing alone against the Nazi threat, Rayburn and other national leaders orchestrated a multibillion-dollar rearmament campaign and an expansion of the Selective Service System to get American forces combat-ready. Throughout the war, he played a key role in pushing essential war appropriations through Congress, including funding for the top-secret Manhattan Project, the atomic bomb program.

Following Roosevelt's death in the last months of the war, Rayburn's good friend Harry S. Truman assumed the presidency. In his position as Speaker, Rayburn supported Truman's major foreign policy decisions, using his influence and power to encourage congressional support for the Marshall Plan and other foreign assistance programs.

Impact   A forty-eight-year congressional veteran, Rayburn was associated with most of the major domestic and foreign policy decisions embraced by the United States in the first half of the twentieth century.

Keith M. Finley

Further Reading

Hardeman, D. B. *Rayburn: A Biography.* Austin: Texas Monthly Press, 1987.
Remini, Robert V. *The House: The History of the House of Representatives.* New York: HarperCollins, 2006.
Steinberg, Alfred. *Sam Rayburn: A Biography.* New York: Hawthorn Books, 1975.

See also   Manhattan Project; Marshall Plan; Roosevelt, Franklin D.; Truman, Harry S.

■ Reader's Digest

Identification   Monthly general interest magazine
Date   First published in 1922

A success with the American reading public from its first appearance during the early 1920's, Reader's Digest *was one of the most popular magazines in the United States during the 1940's. However, the decade was the last one in which the magazine maintained the innovative features originally envisioned by its creators.*

Reader's Digest was the brainchild of two American midwesterners, a married couple, DeWitt Wallace and Lila Bell Wallace. From an early age, DeWitt Wallace had an obsessive habit of maintaining lists of suggestions for solving everyday problems. An avid reader of popular magazines, he also developed a compulsive drive to synopsize the many books and articles he read. While recovering after suffering an injury in World War I, Wallace thought of publishing a magazine consisting of condensations of articles from other periodicals. Working out of their apartment, the Wallaces sold the first edition of *Reader's Digest* directly to subscribers whom they had attracted through mailed-out publicity. The small, compact magazine was an immediate success. By the end of the 1920's, almost 300,000 Americans had subscriptions, and by 1940, more than four million subscribed.

In 1940, *Reader's Digest* published two articles that presaged the coming U.S. involvement in World War II. One offered a sympathetic account of the sufferings of the United Kingdom during the Battle of Britain, and another warned of the growing militancy and aggression of Japan's leaders. After the attack on Pearl Harbor, however, the Wallaces tended to stress upbeat, encouraging news and to provide how-to articles to help readers further the war effort and endure the tensions and restrictions of the time. Lexicographer Wilfred Funk's columns on vocabulary improvement remained popular, as did humor columns relating humorous real-life anecdotes sent in by readers.

Throughout the 1940's, the Wallaces insisted on maintaining two of their more innovative early practices: sales only through the mail and no advertising within the pages of the periodical. Perhaps the most significant aspect of *Reader's Digest*'s development during the 1940's was its many inroads into the markets of other countries. In 1940, the magazine was published only in the United States and the United Kingdom. During World War II, the Wallaces set up deals with publishers in Sweden and in several Latin American countries to publish foreign-language editions there. From the end of the war until the end of the decade, the magazine appeared in many other countries also, including Australia, Finland, Belgium, Denmark, Canada, Germany, Italy, Switzerland, and others. By 1950, *Reader's Digest* had more than 15 million readers around the world.

Impact   During the 1940's, *Reader's Digest* embodied much of the courage and fortitude of Americans, with its continued growth in sales and its determination to expand into more and more markets in other countries. Within its pages were encoded values such as determination, optimism, and rationality that Americans considered essential. Although the magazine continued to be widely read for many years, much of what had defined it in its earliest decades changed during the 1950's and afterward, as it began to include conventional advertising and to branch out into condensed fiction and elaborate sweepstakes contests.

Thomas Du Bose

Further Reading

Ashby, LeRoy. *With Amusement for All: A History of American Popular Culture Since 1830.* Lexington: University of Kentucky, Press, 2006.

Canning, Peter. *American Dreamers: The Wallaces and Reader's Digest.* New York: Simon & Schuster, 1996.

Sharp, Joanne P. *Condensing the Cold War: "Reader's Digest" and American Identity.* Minneapolis: University of Minnesota Press, 2000.

See also   Book publishing; *Life*; *Look*; *Maclean's*; Magazines; Pulp magazines; *Saturday Evening Post*.

■ Recording industry

Definition   Companies that captured, reproduced, and marketed sound recordings

During the 1940's, the recording industry ushered in such major technological changes as long-playing records, 45-rpm singles, and magnetic tape, that would forever change the ways in which recordings would be made and used.

During the 1920's and 1930's, the recording industry settled on a standard medium for sound recording: flat ten- and twelve-inch diameter discs made primarily of shellac, playing at 78-rpm (revolutions per minute). Each disc could hold about four and one-half minutes of music on each side. Although the recording industry realized that shellac discs were fragile and not suitable for recording longer works, such as classical, Broadway, and jazz music, it was slow to try new materials for its discs. During the 1930's, RCA Victor experimented with Vinylite, a recently invented material developed by Union Carbide, but eventually concluded that its experiments were failures. When shellac supplies dwindled during World War II, the recording industry began trying other materials for its discs.

Long-Playing Vinyl Records   Columbia Records was the first company to create a successful vinyl disc. Its engineers realized that vinyl disc required needed record players with lighter tone arms and lightweight styluses that would not wear down the vinyl upon playback. With these changes, they could cut smaller grooves (which they called microgrooves) into the surfaces of discs, thus creating long-playing recordings with higher fidelity and greater durability than shellac 78-rpm recordings. Columbia decided that a disc spinning at 33-$\frac{1}{3}$ rpm could hold approximately twenty-five minutes on each side, thus making it suitable for most classical compositions. Instead of making its own 33-$\frac{1}{3}$ rpm record players, Columbia Records collaborated with Philco to create an adaptor that plugged into household radio sets. On June 20, 1948, at the Waldorf-Astoria in New York City, Columbia unveiled its new vinyl discs, which it called LPs (for long-playing). It dramatized the significance of its new product by presenting two stacks of discs holding the same recordings. The 78-rpm shellac disc stack was eight feet high; next to it was a stack of vinyl LPs only fifteen inches high.

45-RPM Single Records   Columbia's executives approached RCA and offered it the chance to use the new LP format for its recordings, but RCA refused. Instead, RCA set out to create its own functioning version of the vinyl disc, which was not a long-playing record but a better quality recording that could accommodate the short songs that were staples of its music catalog. RCA decided on a seven-inch disc rotating at 45 rpm with a larger spindle hole to accommodate the movements of the automatic changer on its company-produced record player. During the early part of 1949, RCA released its new vinyl format, the 45-rpm single, which would soon become the standard medium for recording and marketing popular music.

The Battle for a Vinyl Format Standard   In 1949, the introduction of the two new vinyl formats required listeners to own two or three different kinds of record players to be able to hear the older 78-rpm discs, Columbia's 33-$\frac{1}{3}$ rpm LPs, and RCA's 45-rpm singles. Throughout the year, RCA and Columbia competed

Phonograph introduced by RCA in January, 1949, to play 45-rpm records. (AP/Wide World Photos)

for shares of the market, with neither side giving in. Instead of propelling the industry forward, Columbia and RCA's battle made customers reluctant to get rid of the 78-rpm discs. In response, some phonograph manufacturers created adjustable machines that could play discs at all three speeds. By the end of 1949, Columbia finally joined the other major record companies in the United States by agreeing to use the 45-rpm format for singles. RCA, too, capitulated by consenting to release long-playing 33$\frac{1}{3}$ recordings.

Magnetic Tape Recording   During the mid-1930's, the German company BASF created the Magnetophon, a magnetic tape recording and playback device. The recording material it used consisted of paper or plastic tape coated with iron oxide that could be magnetized to record, playback, and, most important, rerecord sound. At the end of World War II, American soldiers brought the German tape machines they had found in radio stations back to the United States to be studied and reproduced. Although tape machines became available commercially in the United States by 1947, the largest market for the machines was the recording industry itself. With previous acoustic and electro-acoustic recordings, a musician who wanted to correct a mistake would have to rerecord the same work in its entirety from the beginning, repeating the process until satisfied. With magnetic tape, different recordings could be spliced together by physically cutting and taping sections of the magnetic tape together to create an error-free master recording. Because of this improvement in recording technology, the recording industry used tape almost exclusively for all master recordings by the end of the 1940's.

Impact   For the recording industry the 1940's ushered in some of the greatest changes in the way it recorded sound. With magnetic tape masters and long-playing vinyl, musicians could record longer, unabridged versions of music without errors. After the 1940's, experiments with vinyl and magnetic tape allowed the recording industry to create stereo and multitrack recordings. The change that had the most influence for decades to come was the 45-rpm single, which became the preferred format for popular music recordings, radio stations, and jukeboxes.

Mark D. Porcaro

Further Reading

Barfe, Louis. *Where Have All the Good Times Gone? The Rise and Fall of the Record Industry.* London: Atlantic Books, 2004. An excellent history of the recording industry, chronicling events, people, and technologies created in the United States, as well as those devised in England and continental Europe.

Coleman, Mark. *Playback: From the Victrola to MP3, One Hundred Years of Music, Machines, and Money.* New York: Da Capo Press, 2003. A concise and easily readable history of the recording industry throughout the twentieth century.

Dawson, Jim, and Steve Propes. *45 RPM: The History, Heroes, and Villains of a Pop Music Revolution.* San Francisco: Backbeat Books, 2003. A detailed history of the events and technology that created the 45-rpm single.

Elborough, Travis. *The Long-Player Goodbye: The Album from Vinyl to iPod and Back Again.* London: Sceptre, 2008. A descriptive but slightly subjective and personalized history of the beginnings of vinyl and magnetic recordings.

Millard, Andre. *America on Record: A History of Recorded Sound.* Cambridge, England: Cambridge University Press, 1995. A comprehensive and thoroughly researched history of recordings from the 1850's to the 1990's.

See also Broadway musicals; Inventions; Music: Classical; Music: Jazz; Music: Popular; Radio in Canada; Radio in the United States; Sarnoff, David.

■ Recreation

Although the 1940's ushered in many changes to American society, the country's recreational activities were restricted because of the war effort. After the war, with a predictable workweek and peacetime prosperity in place, Americans had a wide array of opportunities for organized and informal leisure pursuits.

In his landmark 1940 work *America Learns to Play,* Foster Rhea Dulles noted that two historical trends appeared to explain the nature of Americans' fondness for recreation: the lingering belief that leisure activities should serve some useful purpose and the reduction in the need for extensive manual labor because of industrialization. Thus, leisure in the 1940's was wide ranging. Recreational activities had become defined by whatever a person could imagine doing during nonworking and nonsleeping hours. However, the lingering effects of the Great Depression limited diversions to inexpensive and local options for many. This could include participating in backyard games, watching sports, attending the symphony, playing cards, and joining a club. Dulles observed that people had adapted everyday life to include an expectation of play to counterbalance the intensive effort of rebuilding the economy after the Depression.

Recreation During the War American involvement in World War II overshadowed every aspect of American society during the first half of the 1940's. People adapted their recreational activities to the challenges faced by a wartime society. Domestic recreational programs were geared toward the healthy, active, and young. Many organizations complemented the work of military and community agencies such as the United Service Organizations (USO), which originally comprised six private organizations: the Jewish Welfare Board, the Salvation Army, the National Catholic Community Service, the National Travelers Aid Association, the Young Men's Christian Association (YMCA), and the Young Women's Christian Association (YWCA).

During World War II, the Federal Security Agency's temporary Division of Recreation assisted local communities in providing recreational outlets for service men and women and all of those working in the war effort. This organization, in cooperation with the Federal Works Agency (FWA), expanded recreational facilities and services. In 1944, the U.S. commissioner of education encouraged school-community recreation ventures to better meet the growing need of curricula for training recreation leaders and maximizing community facilities and equipment. During this era, government organizations made unprecedented investments in recreation as a part of the total war effort. Sports and games were the predominant aspects of the expanding concept of comprehensive recreation, but social and entertainment opportunities were also included. The USO became an unparalleled provider of entertainment for soldiers.

The American Red Cross established more than 750 clubs, provided 250 mobile units, and employed more than fifteen hundred hospital and therapeutic recreation specialists. Sports and activities were most extensively incorporated into the Navy Pre-Flight School that required two hours of intramural competition daily. As the war drew to a close in 1945, the Recreation Services division of the Veterans Administration was established.

The National Industrial Recreation Association, advocating recognition and expansion of employee health, recreation, and fitness programming, began annual meetings in 1941, and by the end of the decade, interest had grown in the association's employer-sponsored bowling and softball leagues and other activities for workers and their families. The 1944 Flood Control Act identified recreation among the purposes of reservoirs constructed by the U.S. Army Corps of Engineers. The act authorized the corps to construct, operate, and maintain public-park and recreational facilities in reservoir areas under the Army secretary's jurisdiction.

By 1941, college and university professional preparation programs in recreation existed, and even included an academic major, existed. Recreational facilities operated around the clock as the war effort intensified in 1944, when 40 percent of recreational facilities were geared toward youth programs. Women outnumbered men in recreational leadership positions for the first time since 1930. In addition, local referenda and tax-bond issues provided some funding for public recreation sites after the war. "Recreational therapy," a term first coined by the psychiatrists Karl and Will Menninger, emerged during the 1940's, following the American National Red Cross's inclusion of recreation in its rehabilitation programs.

Post-World War II Recreation   Five professional organizations were responsible for promoting the use of and for the implementation of the standards and expansion of parks and recreation facilities, programs, and services throughout the 1940's. These were the American Institute of Park Executives, the National Recreation Association, the National Conference on State Parks, the American Association of Zoological Parks and Aquariums, and the American Recreation Society. Members of these five organizations realized that opportunities and desires for leisure activities in the United States would surge after the war. In 1948, these organizations looked to consolidate.

Meanwhile, in 1946, the establishment of the Federal Inter-Agency Committee on Recreation spurred a comprehensive national effort to plan for the growing demand for postwar recreational pursuits. The committee represented ten federal agencies: the U.S. Army Corps of Engineers, the National Park Service, the U.S. Fish and Wildlife Service, the Bureau of Reclamation, the Bureau of Land Management, Federal Extension Service, the U.S. Forest Service, the Office of Education, the Public Health Service, and the Public Housing Administration. By the end of the decade, the Federal Inter-Agency Committee on Recreation had been supported by the Bureau of Indian Affairs, the National Capital Park and Planning Commission, the FWA's Public Roads Administration and Bureau of Community Facilities, the Department of Agriculture's Soil Conservation Service, and the Tennessee Valley Authority.

Communities began to organize separate recreation authorities over the course of the decade. Implementing recreation directors and superintendents, who operated under a city, county, or combined policy-making board of directors, became the model for program organization in larger cities. Close coordination with the public schools, the parks and playground supervisors, and the private sector underwent a period of reorganization following the disruption by the war. Eventually, many schools desired that a separate agency organize public recreation during afternoon and evening hours while minimizing the conflicts with school-sponsored sports and activities.

The popularity of Boy Scout and Girl Scout movements resumed. In 1945, the Girls Club began. Local churches and faith-based organizations sustained an ongoing commitment to employing recreational activities as a complement to spiritual growth. YMCAs, YWCAs, Catholic Youth Organizations, Jewish Community Centers, and church camps all promoted the wholesome benefits of recreation as an adjunct to work and a symbolic outcome of a desired, lasting peace.

State Government Programs   Ultimately, no governmental entity had more influence on recreation than the state governments. State-supported parks, forests, camping sites, and recreational areas flourished in part because of the ability to fund and support these through tax assessments rather than through local, county, or municipality initiatives. During the late 1940's, states emerged as the leading providers of services and funds for planning and implementing recreational and leisure activities. Pennsylvania and Alabama were noted for providing inservice training; state colleges and universities in Indiana and Minnesota supported community recreation initiatives through extension services. The emergence of state recreation commissions in North Carolina, Vermont, and California and statewide, interagency committees facilitated coordination within states and with their federal counterparts.

As the rural population declined and the country's workweek shrunk to a standard forty hours by 1950, per capita income increased 35 percent. These trends, along with increased educational opportunities, resulted in an expansion of leisure opportunities and diversity of interests. Newer recreational activities during the late 1940's included boating, fishing, day camping and winter sports; activities such as square dancing and Golden Age Clubs helped to meet the recreational and social needs of the elderly population. Recreational opportunities for wounded veterans, such as wheelchair sports, enabled recreation leaders to provide services more broadly than ever before.

There was a marked increase in outdoor recreation after World War II, as measured by visits to parks and forests, increased sale of hunting and fishing licenses, and increased sales of outdoor equipment. The Bureau of Land Management (BLM) was established in 1946 through the consolidation of the General Land Office, created in 1812, and the U.S. Grazing Service, formed in 1934. Aldo Leopold's *A Sand County Almanac*, published posthumously in 1949, sounded a call for conservation and stewardship of the country's natural resources for recreation and enjoyment. Later that year, the BLM had

Father playing ball with his sons during the mid-1940's. (Getty Images)

two thousand camps and four thousand individual members and had helped set standards for camp administration. This was significant; estimates indicated that in 1949, 10 million youths spent at least one weekend at a camp. Families enjoyed parks and forests for daily trips and short vacations. By the end of the decade, total personal consumption of recreational goods and services exceeded $11 billion, as determined by the U.S. Bureau of Economic Analysis.

In 1946, more than 1,750 communities spent more than $50 million annually and employed thirty thousand people nationwide, with five thousand of those in full-time recreation leadership positions. By 1949, there were more than six thousand full-time professional recreation leaders and a total of fifty thousand employed in recreation fields nationwide. A subsequent amendment to the 1944 Surplus Property Act provided for transfer of surplus athletic

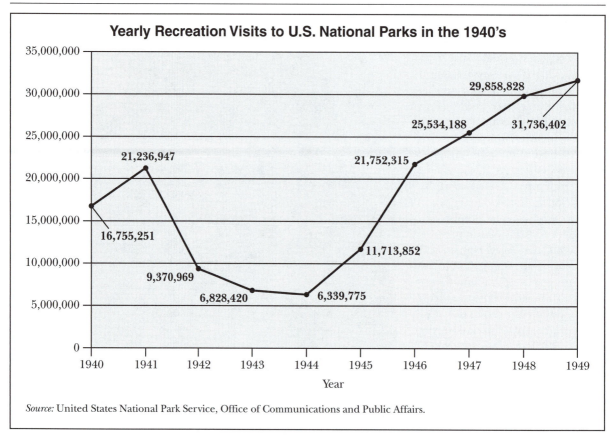

Yearly Recreation Visits to U.S. National Parks in the 1940's

Source: United States National Park Service, Office of Communications and Public Affairs.

equipment to public, private, and charitable entities to promote youth recreation. While the overwhelming majority (75 percent) of all recreational facilities was still connected to public schools, the number of local parks and recreation departments had doubled throughout the decade to more than eighteen hundred nationwide. By 1949, approximately forty colleges and universities offered a recreation major and a year earlier, the College Recreation Association was established.

Public recreation mirrored societal trends. In the southern United States, where racial segregation was commonplace, separate programs and facilities existed for whites and African Americans. After World War II some reversal of that trend occurred. By 1948, the National Recreation Association noted that community recreation encompassed roughly seventy-five interest areas and activities among categories such as arts and crafts, athletics and games, drama, music, outdoor activities, and water and winter sports. Many recreational activities defied categorization.

Impact The pursuit of leisure has often been seen as the goal of humanity. American society was committed to this ideal following World War II. Throughout the 1940's, recreation was viewed simultaneously as a means to an end and as an end in itself. The demand for and quality of recreational activities expanded just as the postwar baby boom signaled the start of a significant growth in American population. Legacies of this time period include the prominent place of leisure pursuits in everyday life, the preservation of the natural environment, and the significant economic industry associated with recreational activities.

P. Graham Hatcher

Further Reading

Dulles, Foster Rhea. *America Learns to Play: A History of Popular Recreation, 1607-1940.* New York: Appleton, 1940. Detailed overview of American recreation and leisure; sets the stage for understanding the decade of the 1940's.

Jensen, Clayne R., and Steven Guthrie. *Outdoor Recre-*

ation in America. 6th ed. Champaign, Ill.: Human Kinetics, 2006. Seminal textbook on the forms of recreation in the United States, stressing the importance of preserving recreational spaces.

Leopold, Aldo. *A Sand County Almanac.* New York: Oxford University Press, 1949. In addition to observation about flora and fauna, this work details a "Land Ethic" promoting environmental stewardship and energizing the conservation movement.

Mitchell, Elmer D., and Bernard S. Mason. *The Theory of Play.* New York: A. S. Barnes, 1941. Examines play as an social movement and offers theoretical interpretations of play in American society.

Sessoms, H. Douglas, Harold D. Meyer, and Charles K. Brightbill. *Leisure Services: The Organized Recreation and Park System.* Englewood Cliffs, N.J.: Prentice-Hall, 1975. Revision of an earlier work on community recreation, emphasizing outdoor recreation and the government's role.

See also   Dance; Education in the United States; Fads; Film in Canada; Film in the United States; Hobbies; National parks; Sports in Canada; Sports in the United States; Travel in the United States.

■ Red Cross

Identification   International relief organization
Also known as   American Red Cross
Date   Established on May 21, 1881

World War I was a turning point in the development of new technology with which to wage war. As a result, the American Red Cross saw a need for advanced medical preparedness to save as many lives as possible in wartime. The Red Cross established a national nursing program that trained volunteers to handle basic health care needs, accident prevention, and disease control. This preparedness would be put to the test during World War II.

Founded in 1881, the American Red Cross began with one woman's ability to envision the need to help people during times of war or disaster. What began as a simple source of supplies for soldiers who desperately needed food, clothing, bedding, and the most basic sanitary items became an intense relief effort on the deadliest battlefields during the Civil War. Nurse Clara Barton risked her life on the frontlines to bring supplies, first aid, comfort, and hope to soldiers on both sides of the conflict. These experiences, coupled with a European trip to view the International Committee of the Red Cross, which had been founded in 1863 by the Swiss Jean-Henri Dunant, prompted Barton to devote the rest of her life to founding and building the American Red Cross. Since its inception, the organization has focused on providing voluntary humanitarian aid during both wartime and peacetime to citizens in the United States and abroad.

Background Information   During its initial years, the Red Cross aided citizens in a variety of ways in the United States. Devastating floods along the Mississippi River in 1884 and in Johnstown, Pennsylvania, in 1889, as well as the deadly hurricane in Galveston, Texas, in 1900, prompted the organization to not only supply food, clothing, and shelter to displaced citizens but also to assist residents in the rebuilding process, which ranged from physically reconstructing buildings to distributing seeds and starter plants to jumpstart the devastated agricultural economy.

The Red Cross became known as an organization whose volunteers were quick to respond to fires, floods, and famines. This reputation was challenged during the Spanish-American War in 1898, when the organization discovered it was not adequately prepared to assist troops in a conflict fought on foreign soil. Despite criticism from President William McKinley and Rough Rider leader Theodore Roosevelt, the Red Cross still managed to provide nurses, doctors, and food to help soldiers and refugees who would otherwise have been deprived of support. Despite his criticism, McKinley publicly supported the Red Cross, praising its high standards that justified "the confidence and support" of the American people. The lessons learned during the Spanish-American War proved to be invaluable for the organization.

Red Cross Nurses in World War II   Before World War I, the Red Cross focused on providing disaster relief, first aid, water safety instruction, and public health nursing programs throughout the United States. The public health nursing programs, which focused on safety training, accident prevention, home care for the sick, and nutrition education, became a catalyst for Red Cross nursing recruitment on campuses nationwide after World War I. The organization's training in basic health management

ganization's training in basic health management played an integral role in cutting mortality rates in World War II. More sophisticated weapons meant increased casualties of both soldiers and civilians. The Red Cross's understanding of how to manage or prevent communicable diseases and wound infections significantly cut the number of fatalities in hospital wards and on the battlefields.

Coordination and communication became the keys to success for nurses during World War II. Many were cross-trained and served in a variety of capacities with the Red Cross and the Army and Navy Nurse Corps. When the war ended in 1945, 100,000 nurses had volunteered, 76,000 of whom had served in the corps. Nurses were given officer rank, which meant that they carried the respect of these titles but not the pay that their male counterparts received. These

nurses also received illness and accident benefits and protection under the terms of the Soldiers and Sailors Relief Act of 1940.

The experiences of these nurses varied depending on the theater in which they served. Some followed invading troops in Africa, others landed under fire at Anzio, while others rode onto the beachheads of Normandy days after the invasion. Nurses stationed in the Pacific theater often faced the same fates as soldiers when the Japanese overcame American forces or marched prisoners to death camps.

In addition to serving on the frontlines, American Red Cross nurses and volunteers worked tirelessly on the home front directing people of all ages to assist with scrap collections and the preparation and shipment of food packages to approximately

President Franklin D. Roosevelt helping to kick off a $50-million fundraising drive for the American Red Cross on December 12, 1941— five days after Japan bombed Pearl Harbor and drew the United States into World War II. (AP/Wide World Photos)

115,000 American prisoners of war (POWs) and more than 1.3 million Allied POWs in Europe and the Pacific. As a result of these efforts, 1.4 million packages each month were processed and distributed by the International Committee of the Red Cross.

American Red Cross, 1946-1950 Following World War II, the Red Cross struggled with the question of what to do with the tens of thousands of women who volunteered their lives to serve in the Red Cross Nursing Service, as well as the Army and Navy Nurse Corps. With the exception of those who decided to spend the remainder of their career as nurses for the army or navy, the Red Cross decided to form a reserve of nurses to be called upon for the provision of home health education and disaster services. The organization's goal was to "carry on a system of national and international relief in time of peace and apply the same in mitigating the sufferings caused by pestilence, famine, fire, floods, and other great national calamities, and to devise and carry on measures for prevention of the same."

Perhaps the most well-known legacy of the period from the end of World War II to the beginning of the Korean War was the Red Cross's introduction of a nationwide civilian blood program. The Red Cross began organizing and sponsoring blood drives during World War II for the sole purpose of shipping blood to international hospitals for soldiers' use. These blood collection and storage procedures continued after the war, and in the twenty-first century the American Red Cross supplied nearly 50 percent of all blood and blood products in the United States.

Impact The restructuring of nursing by the American Red Cross in the years leading up to World War II helped make its team of doctors, nurses, and surgical assistants a crucial force during combat. Many old prejudices about the need for one nurse for each patient were abandoned, and nurses were given the opportunity to become part of a stratified medical team both at home and abroad during the war. This managerial style of health care would be used again in 1950 to assist soldiers and civilians during the Korean War.

Michele Goostree

Further Reading

Banfield, Gertrude S. "American Nurses: We Are at War!" *American Journal of Nursing* 42, no. 4 (April, 1942): 354-358.
Bullough, Bonnie. "Nurses in American History: The Lasting Impact of World War II on Nursing." *American Journal of Nursing* 76, no. 1 (January, 1976): 118-120.
Dunbar, Virginia, and Gertrude Banfield. "Red Cross Nursing Service Contemplates Changes in Enrolment Plan." *American Journal of Nursing* 46, no. 2 (February, 1946): 82-84.
Gilbo, Patrick. *The American Red Cross: The First Century.* New York: Harper & Row, 1981.
Madison, James H. *Slinging Doughnuts for the Boys: An American Woman in World War II.* Bloomington: Indiana University Press, 2007.
"The Nurses' Contribution to American Victory: Facts and Figures from Pearl Harbor to V-J Day." *American Journal of Nursing* 45 (May, 1945): 683-686.
Turk, Michele. *Blood, Sweat, and Tears: An Oral History of the American Red Cross.* Robbinsville, N.J.: E Street Press, 2006.

See also Health care; Prisoners of war, North American; Recreation.

■ Refugees in North America

Definition Displaced persons who settled in the United States and Canada after fleeing their home countries because of social, religious, racial, political, or economic persecution

Canada and the United Stated refused to admit refugees fleeing Nazism and fascism prior to and during World War II. However, both countries adopted policies in the Cold War era to provide refugees with asylum from the various forms of persecution and the loss of rights they experienced in their home countries.

Canada and the United States shared similar policies toward refugees throughout the 1940's. The immigration policies of both countries reflected a definitive preference for Western Europeans. Eastern and southern Europeans were considered less desirable, and Jews, African Americans, and Asians (including South Asians and Arabs) faced severe restrictions and outright exclusion. The United States enacted restrictive quotas to limit the immigration of "undesirable" peoples. Canadian immigration policy did not set specific quotas but simply limited and excluded applicants based on their race and ethnicity. Neither Canada nor the United States considered assisting refugees, especially in the light of economic hardship from the Depression, as well as the persistent xenophobic and anti-Semitic public opinion within both countries.

World War II Refugees Between 1933 and 1945, Canada accepted 37,972 immigrants, of whom fewer than 5,000 were Jewish refugees. During this same period, the United States accepted 316,000 immigrants, of whom 200,000 were Jewish refugees. In both cases, the vast majority of these immigrants were not refugees but immigrants who had not faced persecution in their home countries. Refugees were selected on the basis of their race, ethnicity, and usefulness to the Canadian economy rather than their need for asylum.

Despite the booming postwar economies of both the United States and Canada, policy makers in both countries retained xenophobic and anti-Semitic immigration policies from 1946 to 1948 that severely restricted Jewish and non-Jewish refugees from entering North America, even in light of the horrendous experience of the Holocaust. Admission was given only to those who could meet the immigration categories of preferred race or ethnicity, or farming and rural work.

In 1947, the International Refugee Organization (IRO) required that both Canada and the United States deny immigration to refugees who had been Nazi sympathizers or who had fought against the Allies. At the same time, however, Canadian and American state officials became preoccupied in keeping out refugees or people posing as refugees who were suspected of being communists. In 1948, the United States passed the Displaced Persons Act, which facilitated the entry of refugees fleeing communism in Europe. By 1950, more than 200,000 displaced persons visas had been issued, with 40,000 going to Jewish refugees. Significant numbers of displaced persons visas were also granted to Nazi war criminals and fascist sympathizers whom American intelligence agencies hoped to turn into Cold War spies. Canadian immigration officials admitted a number of Nazi war criminals and fascists as they focused on denying entrance to communist sympathizers.

A number of antifascist German émigrés, including socialists, communists, Jews, and pacifists who fled Nazi Germany after 1933, were able to settle in the United States as writers, scholars, artists, actors, and filmmakers. Their settlement was based on a studio or university contract that guaranteed them employment. Many of these émigrés became well known and had successful careers in the United States. At the same time, they were homesick for the life and culture they had left in Germany. Some of these refugees tried to return to Germany after World War II to resume their lives. In many cases, however, they found it impossible to do so. There were little, if any, opportunities for work, and some émigrés faced deep-seated anti-Semitism and hatred. Virtually all these émigrés returned to the United States soon afterward. Many found themselves revictimized during the McCarthy-era communist witch hunts.

Impact Although both Canada and the United States were reluctant to admit refugees during and after World War II,

---

"Eligible Displaced Orphan"

The Displaced Persons Act of 1948 allowed refugees from war-torn European countries to immigrate to the United States and granted permanent residence status to those individuals that fit the criteria of the act. An excerpt of the act focusing on "displaced orphans" is reproduced below.

"Eligible displaced orphan" means a displaced person who is under the age of sixteen years, and who is qualified under the immigration laws of the United States for admission into the United States for permanent residence, and who is an orphan because of the death or disappearance of both parents, and who, on or before the effective date of this act, was in Italy or in the American sector, the British sector, or the French sector of either Berlin or Vienna or the American zone, the British zone, or the French zone of either Germany or Austria, and for whom satisfactory assurances in accordance with the regulations of the commission have been given that such person, if admitted into the United States, will be cared for properly.

the growing labor demands of the postwar economic boom eventually created a range of opportunities for refugee settlement. The onset of the Cold War provided further incentive for these countries to accept large numbers of refugees from communist countries. These events laid the groundwork for North American refugee policies of the twenty-first century.

Kelly Amanda Train

Further Reading

Abella, Irving, and Harold Troper. *None Is Too Many: Canada and the Jews of Europe, 1933-1948.* New York: Random House, 1983. Detailed discussion of Canadian government policies toward Jewish refugees prior to, during and after World War II.

Bialystok, Franklin. *Delayed Impact: The Holocaust and the Canadian Jewish Community.* Montreal: McGill-Queen's University Press, 2000. Critical analysis of Canadian anti-Semitism, Canadian immigration policy, Jewish refugees, and Canadian Jewish community responses from the 1930's to the 1990's.

Bon Tempo, Carl J. *Americans at the Gate: The United States and Refugees During the Cold War.* Princeton, N.J.: Princeton University Press, 2008. The author explores the exclusionary immigration policy of the United States and the social, political, and economic context in which American refugee policy was shaped and implemented.

Dirks, Gerald E. *Canada's Refugee Policy: Indifference or Opportunism?* Montreal: McGill-Queen's University Press, 1977. Dirks examines the evolution of refugee policy in Canada and how policy makers failed to address the enormity of the refugee problem prior to, during, and after World War II.

Gibney, Matthew J. *The Ethics and Politics of Asylum: Liberal Democracy and the Response to Refugees.* New York: Cambridge University Press, 2004. The author explores the development of refugee policies throughout the West and examines the policies implemented in the United Kingdom, the

European refugees embarking on the U.S. Army transport General Black *at Bremerhaven, Germany, on October 21, 1948. These 813 people were the first immigrants permitted to enter the United States since passage of the Displaced Persons Act of 1948.* (AP/Wide World Photos)

United States, and Australia.

Marrus, Michael. *The Unwanted: European Refugees in the Twentieth Century.* New York: Oxford University Press, 1985. Analyzes the history of refugee movements in Europe from the nineteenth century to the post-World War II era, with particular emphasis on the political context of fascism, Nazism, the Stalinist purges, and later the Cold War in Europe.

Palmier, Jean Michel, and David Fernbach. *Weimar in Exile: The Antifacist Emigration in Europe and America.* London: Verso, 2006. The authors provide a detailed examination of the experiences of antifacist émigrés of Nazi Germany, including writers, scholars, artists, actors, and filmmakers, who fled to various Western European countries and the United States.

See also Canadian Citizenship Act of 1946; Canadian minority communities; Immigration Act of 1943; Immigration to Canada; Immigration to the United States; Jews in Canada; Jews in the United States; National Security Act of 1947; Racial discrimination.

■ Religion in Canada

During the 1940's, Canadian religion, like that in the United States, responded to a world war and eventual post-war prosperity and analyses of conscience. Even more than its neighbor to the south, Canada had felt its fate tied to that of parent nations in Europe. However, victory in World War II left the country self-reliantly seeking its own identity and vocation. French-speaking, Roman Catholic Quebec had been virtually a nation apart from the rest of Canada, which was predominantly English-speaking and Protestant. After the war, the Church's control of Quebec declined, while the rest of the country also started, though less rapidly, responding to the forces of cosmopolitanism and secularism. Mainline Protestants, following the lead of the United Church of Canada, formed in 1925, became more preoccupied with ecumenism and social welfare than with evangelism, seeking a humane nation and a distinctive Canadian Christianity marked by moderation. At the same time, smaller, sometimes more conservative, religious groups proliferated in the Canadian cultural mosaic.

As an independent nation within Great Britain's Commonwealth, Canada has given lip service to the British monarch as head of state and Defender of the Faith. Although Canadians are not bound by the same kind of religious-establishment arrangements applicable in Britain, they have historically regarded themselves as a Christian nation. The preamble to the Canadian Charter of Rights and Freedoms, as well as both the England and French versions of the national anthem refer to God. Nevertheless, Canadians have rarely expressed the sense of divinely guided destiny and exceptionalism that American clergy and politicians have frequently claimed. While Canada lacked the great national myths that helped Americans through World War II, Canadians nevertheless fought during that conflict with moral conviction. A persistent legend of "the crucified Canadian"—subsequently revealed a product of the British World War I propaganda machine—lingered in the popular mind, making accounts of German brutality believable.

Denominations According to Canada's national census of 1941, Roman Catholics made up slightly more than 43 percent of Canadians. The country's second-largest denomination was the United Church of Canada, a Protestant body that had formed in 1925 from the merger of Methodist, Pres-byterian, and Congregationalist churches; it accounted for slightly more than 19 percent of the population. The Anglican Church was third with 15 percent. Other Christian denominations included Presbyterian churches that did not join the United Church, Baptists, and Lutherans. These denominations maintained a visible presence in the Prairie Provinces, which have often been called Canada's Bible Belt.

The country's various regions had different mixes of denominational affiliations. Newfoundland, for example, was dominated by Anglicans, and New Brunswick had a large concentration of Baptists. Smaller groups of Eastern Orthodox Christians, Mennonites, and Pentecostals were scattered throughout the provinces, with the Salvation Army a tiny but highly active group. Some denominations acted as "branch plants" of corresponding religious bodies in the United States, from which they received instructional materials and ministerial reinforcements.

Personal narratives from the 1940's reveal that immigrants often found religious life in North America more vital and exciting than in their homelands because of the varieties of youth activities, uplifting hymns, and abundant lay participation they experienced in the New World. Members of small sects whose practices others considered eccentric sometimes faced prejudice and legal difficulties. For example, Hutterites and the Russian Doukobors living in Alberta found their rights to establish agricultural colonies limited by the province's 1947 Communal Property Act because they were suspected of disloyalty.

In contrast to the United States, religious affiliation among Canadians was more closely tied to family and ethnic identities. Canadians did not shop religions, in the American manner, but remained overwhelmingly loyal to the denominations into which they were born. Devotional activities for Canadians were similar to those across the border. They read inspirational books by Americans such as Rabbi Joshua Liebman, Norman Vincent Peale, and Bishop Fulton J. Sheen. Station WSM from Nashville, Tennessee spread the Gospel according to country and Western singers throughout the prairies, and people of all persuasions tuned in to hear Paul Maier on *The Lutheran Hour.* Quebec celebrated her saints and made pilgrimages to Ste-Anne-de-Beaupré and St. Joseph's Oratory.

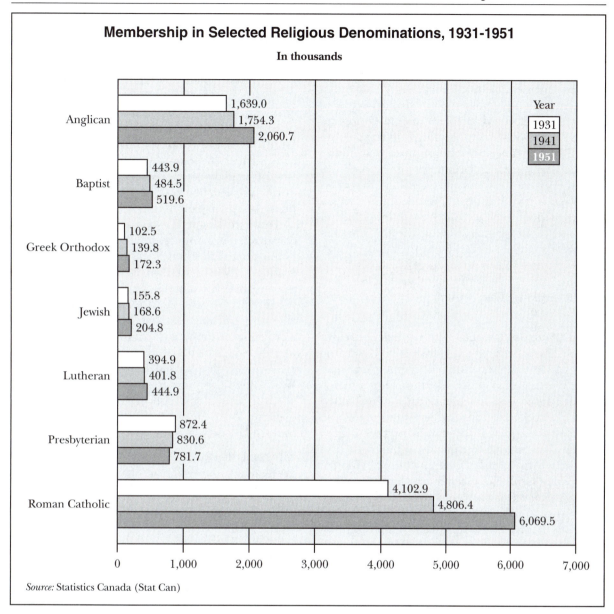

Membership in Selected Religious Denominations, 1931-1951

In thousands

Denomination	Year	Value
Anglican	1931	1,639.0
Anglican	1941	1,754.3
Anglican	1951	2,060.7
Baptist	1931	443.9
Baptist	1941	484.5
Baptist	1951	519.6
Greek Orthodox	1931	102.5
Greek Orthodox	1941	139.8
Greek Orthodox	1951	172.3
Jewish	1931	155.8
Jewish	1941	168.6
Jewish	1951	204.8
Lutheran	1931	394.9
Lutheran	1941	401.8
Lutheran	1951	444.9
Presbyterian	1931	872.4
Presbyterian	1941	830.6
Presbyterian	1951	781.7
Roman Catholic	1931	4,102.9
Roman Catholic	1941	4,806.4
Roman Catholic	1951	6,069.5

Source: Statistics Canada (Stat Can)

Roman Catholicism   The distinguishing fact of Canadian political and religious life during the 1940's remained the Roman Catholic and French-linguistic separation of Quebec from the rest of Canada. Quebec maintained the highest ratio of nuns to the female population of any Catholic country. Along with the male religious orders, they supplied the spiritual, social, and humanitarian services of the region. Outsiders referred to the "priest-ridden province," where villages bore the names of saints and picturesque nuns and priests, in full clerical raiment, were present on every street. The clergy of Quebec were accused of keeping their people isolated, provincial, and poor. They controlled the schools, which were largely undistinguished. Because the province had long ago been abandoned in the ice and snow by France, the mother country, the Catholicism of Quebec was ultramontane, taking its direction from Rome, little influenced by the more free-wheeling Catholicism of France. This Counter-Reformation creed subordinated the State to the Church. Censorship of cinema and reading materials was prevalent, and Catholic newspapers such as *Le Droit, L'Action Catholique,* and *Le Devoir* circulated throughout Quebec.

But there were already intimations of change. Higher education, at least for a growing elite, was a concern. Although women were still expected to rear large families and perform domestic chores, increased attention to their contributions was demonstrated by the movement to canonize Marguerite Bourgeoys, a seventeenth century nun who had ministered to French settlers and raised the first cross over what is now Montreal. Catholicism in Canada was not without internal conflict, with Irish, Italian, and other ethnic groups resenting the long domination of the Quebec hierarchy over their church. Formation of the Canadian Conference of Catholic Bishops in 1943 brought together English- and French-speaking Canadian prelates for the first time.

United Church of Canada The United Church of Canada, the second largest religious body, was the most visible manifestation of ecumenism. The 1940's were a period of consolidation and outreach to other Protestant groups. Although the United Church officially affirmed the Scriptures of the Old and New Testaments, the creeds of the ancient Church, and basic Reformation doctrines, its drift was clearly liberal. It was a leader in the ordination of women and freely embraced social causes. A lack of enthusiasm for missions would eventually culminate in an official apology to Native tribes for earlier attempts to impose white spirituality and culture on them. Conservative elements in the United Church protested what the writer Robertson Davies called a "flabby benevolence" and a "bone-less theology," but church leaders believed their vocation was to foster a commonsense, tolerant Canadian Christianity.

Anglican Church of Canada Known as "the Church of England in Canada" until 1955, the Anglican communion had a presence throughout the country, thriving in Newfoundland and Ontario, with headquarters in Toronto. Anglicans maintained missions to native tribes and valued tradition more than did the United Church. This led to criticisms of complacency, lack of attention to modern issues, and, with their more complicated orders of priesthood, excessive bureaucracy. However, Anglicans still cherished their ties with England, their solid place within world Christianity, and their pride in being one of the founding faiths of the North American continent.

Non-Christian Religions Although Christianity dominated the Canadian religious landscape throughout the 1940's, as it had since Europeans first appeared in North America, Canada already had numerous non-Christian peoples, particularly in the cities of Montreal, Toronto, and Vancouver. Jewish chaplains, such as the beloved Rabbi Julius Berger of the Royal Canadian Air Force, served with distinction during the war, and Jews, though a small minority, flourished in arts and letters.

The first Islamic mosque in Canada had been constructed in Edmonton in 1938. In 1940, only an estimated 700 Muslims lived in the entire country. Loyal members of the British Empire, Sikhs had arrived in British Columbia by the beginning of the twentieth century. World War II gave them an advantage when Japanese citizens and residents of Canada, facing internment, chose to sell their properties to their Sikh neighbors. Sikhs finally mobilized in 1947, demanding full citizenship and voting rights. While the Christianization of native peoples had been an early colonial concern of both Roman Catholics and Protestants, tribal ceremonies would continue to be performed in isolated regions.

Important Religious Personalities Several strong personalities emerged from Canadian religion to influence the culture of the 1940's. Two of them made their careers chiefly in the United States. Aimee Semple McPherson, one of the most dramatic personalities of the age, was born in Ontario, according to her own words "with one foot in the Methodist Church and the other in the Salvation Army." After years as a traveling evangelist, she founded the Church of the Foursquare Gospel in Los Angeles. It is likely that only her untimely death in 1944 prevented her from becoming the first great televangelist.

Serving a very different constituency, Shirley Jackson Case, originally from New Brunswick, became an influential professor of liberal theology at the University of Chicago. Although highly skeptical of the miraculous elements of the New Testament, his writings, countering revisionist historians, still made a strong case for the historical reality of Jesus. Charles Templeton, a Nazarene pastor and journalist, co-founded Youth for Christ International in 1945, calling a generation of young people to Christian service. An early associate of Billy Graham in European evangelistic tours, Templeton later left Christianity for agnosticism.

Two Baptist preachers became provincial prime ministers. William "Bible Bill" Aberhart, whose sermons on prophecy were broadcast across the prairies, served as premier of Alberta from 1935 to 1943. Thomas Clement "Tommy" Douglas became premier of Saskatchewan in 1944. His life has been celebrated in a television miniseries, and the Canadian Broadcasting Corporation designated him "the Greatest Canadian of All Time." He would later be remembered as a father of universal health care and the grandfather of actor Kiefer Sutherland.

Joseph Charbonneau, the Roman Catholic archbishop of Montreal throughout the 1940's, was a graceful, well-spoken man, known as much for his progressive social views as for his piety. His support of labor in the asbestos strike of 1949 was decisive, a turning point in liberalizing Quebec. It was widely believed that, in retaliation, his church later banished him to British Columbia, where he conscientiously served as a hospital chaplain.

Canadian clergymen also made valuable contributions to arts and letters. The most influential was Northrop Frye, who came to prominence in the 1940's with his first book, *Fearful Symmetry*. Born in Sherbrooke, Quebec, he was ordained a minister in the United Church. He was widely acknowledged to be one of the most influential literary critics of his time. His basic insight—derived chiefly from John Milton's *Paradise Lost* (1667) and the Bible—was that the Christian religion had given Western civilization its essential unifying mythology. Despite his international acclaim, Frye remained a Canadian patriot, even while he lamented what he called "the garrison mentality" of his country.

Impact   In retrospect, it is clear that the decade of the 1940's and World War II were turning points in Canadian society and religion. With the opening of Quebec to the rest of North America and the world, the Roman Catholic Church lost its dominance. By the end of the century, Quebec would be the least religiously observant region of Canada. The United Church and other established Protestant denominations would be justly proud of their contributions toward women's rights, better education, and universal health care. As Canada offered greater hospitality to thousands of displaced persons, immigrant reli-

gions naturally proliferated, and Ontario eventually became the world's most religiously diverse region. With Canadian populations concentrated along the United States border, American cultural influences, though often lamented, remained crucial, especially among religious conservatives. Though Canadian churchgoing, which before the war had been higher than in the United States, declined as more and more people pronounced themselves secular and "enlightened," Canadians would still identify with ancestral religions and depend on their churches for the ceremonies marking birth, marriage, and death.

Allene Phy-Olsen

Further Reading

Bibby, Reginald. *Fragmented Gods: The Poverty and Potential of Religion in Canada.* Toronto: Stoddard, 1990. Pessimistic analysis of the modern condition of religious belief in Canada.

Bramadat, Paul, and David Seliak, eds. *Religion and Ethnicity in Canada.* Toronto: University of Toronto Press, 2009. This most comprehensive work on its subject yet published collects scholarly papers on the ethnic dimensions of Canadian religious beliefs. Particular attention is paid to Hindus, Buddhists, Sikhs, Jews, Muslims, followers of Chinese religions.

Murphy, Terrence, and Roberto Perin, eds. *A Concise History of Christianity in Canada.* Ontario: Oxford University Press, 1996. Well-written and authoritative historical survey of Canadian Christian sects.

Noll, Mark A. *A History of Christianity in the United States and Canada.* Grand Rapids, Mich.: William B. Eerdmans, 1992. This standard history of North American Christianity covers all Christian faiths but devotes most of its space to Protestant faiths in the United States. Nevertheless, it has a valuable section on Canadian Christianity.

_____. *The Old Religion in the New World: The History of North American Christianity.* Grand Rapids, Mich.: William B. Eerdmans, 2001. Noll's second and briefer book on North American Christian history is aimed more at students and nonspecialist readers.

Riendeau, Roger. *A Brief History of Canada.* 2d ed. New York: Facts On File, 2007. Survey of Canadian history written for young-adult readers that is useful for placing Canada's religious history in a broader context.

See also Canadian minority communities; Canadian regionalism; Demographics of Canada; Jews in Canada; Religion in the United States; Theology and theologians.

■ Religion in the United States

During the 1940's, American religions responded to a major depression, victory in a world war, and postwar prosperity. The United States emerged from World War II as the world's strongest country, and this strength led to a reexamination of conscience. Church membership grew, and a loosely defined spirituality flourished, even while Americans remained skeptical of systematic theology associated with Europe.

When the United States entered World War II at the end of 1941, its churches were generally supportive. The Roman Catholic Church had deemed the conflict a just war, and the Protestant churches were generally certain that this conflict was a necessary struggle against politically ideologies that despised freedom and religious values. Even Christians from pacifist traditions, such as the Seventh-Day Adventists, felt the urgency of the conflict and frequently served as noncombatants, in medical and other support capacities. Although the full extent of Nazi atrocities in the Holocaust was not known until after the war ended and the death camps were liberated, the American Jewish community was fully aware that Germany sought to destroy its way of life. Americans had feared "godless communism" since it had taken root in Soviet Russia; however, the Soviet Union became an ally in World War II. When British prime minister Winston Churchill was criticized for supporting the Soviet Union, he responded that if Adolf Hitler were to invade Hell he would have a good word for the devil in the House of Commons.

Ecumenism During the war, military chaplains served with dedication. Even though the military at that time classified personnel as either Roman Catholic, Protestant, or Jewish, an informal ecumenical practice developed among clergy of different confessions. Christian chaplains who had learned Hebrew in seminary were sometimes summoned to conduct ad hoc Jewish services when rabbis were not available, and these men ministered to soldiers regardless of their denominational persuasions. A commonplace observance during wartime was that there are "no atheists in foxholes," and another frequent refrain was "praise God, and pass the ammunition." Folk stories emerged from the battlefields of visions of Jesus seen in the clouds or in the smoke from southern Italy's Mount Vesuvius, which did, in fact, erupt during the war. Tales reached home about Bibles in soldiers' pockets that had stopped potentially fatal bullets.

After the armistice, interfaith cooperation continued, as Christians discovered that genuine brotherhood was a matter more of religious temperament than of creedal profession. Conservatives founded the National Association of Evangelicals in 1942. Youth for Christ, an evangelical student movement, flourished on campuses where returning veterans took advantage of the G.I. Bill. Mainline Christian denominations that had participated in the Oxford and Edinburgh conferences in 1937 founded the World Council of Churches, which vowed to combattotalitarianism, in 1948. Although evangelical Protestant groups and Roman Catholics resisted membership in the council, the Eastern Orthodox churches, which were slowly gaining recognition in American life, did choose to take part.

Weapons of Mass Destruction and the Holocaust
Two events of the war had lasting impacts on American religious thought: the atomic bombing of Hiroshima and Nagasaki by the United States and the tragedy of the Holocaust. Under pressure to end the war, bring home American troops, and prevent further loss of life, President Harry S. Truman authorized the deployment of the atomic bomb in Japan in August, 1945, ushering in the age of weapons of mass destruction. Churches debated the ethics of these weapons, even when used as a "deterrent" in the Cold War, which pitted Western democracies against communist powers. Some academic theologians suggested that the atomic bombing of Japan placed Americans on an ethical par with their enemies, but the majority opinion was that President Truman's decision was justified.

When the concentration camps of central and Eastern Europe were liberated by the victorious Allies, the full extent of Nazi genocide was revealed. Six million Jews had been murdered, along with numerous Slavic and Rom peoples. Although several years would pass before the Holocaust was analyzed obsessively in novels, films, and plays, the response to the genocide was immediate. Many liberal Christians who had given little attention to concepts of sin and judgment were left to ponder the reality of evil, while conservative Christians saw a confirmation of their belief that without grace humans were perpetually mired in sin.

The founding of the state of Israel in the Middle East became the most dramatic response by Jews to the Holocaust. Zionism had been discussed during the early 1940's, and for decades it had been a movement of considerable influence in Europe. However, Americans Jews had been less enthusiastic: Liberal Reformed Jews regarded it as anachronistic and romantic, a hindrance to their assimilation into mainstream American life, while Orthodox Jews were skeptical of Zionism as a secularization of traditional messianic hope. Others, both Jewish and Christian, observed that a national homeland in the Middle East would displace Arab populations that had lived on the land for generations and had not committed any of the recent crimes against Jews. However, the war and its displacements, in addition to the Nazi death camps, gave renewed impetus to the Zionist movement. Some evangelical Christians, especially those with strong apocalyptic views, added their support, believing that an "ingathering" of Jewish people to the Holy Land was a precondition for the second coming of Jesus.

Whether Zionist or otherwise, many Jews responded to the Holocaust with a rediscovery of the prophetic values of their faith. An American theologian, Abraham Joshua Heschel, and an Israeli philosopher, Martin Buber, led this movement, which crossed confessional lines and influenced Christian piety as well. Buber's phrase "I-Thou" appeared frequently in religious discourse.

Growth of Religious Diversity In the postwar religious revival a majority of Americans claimed to be religious, and regular church attendance became a part of the American way of life. Church and synagogue affiliation during the 1940's reached 49 percent of the population, according to most polls, which was higher than in earlier decades, yet lower than the 69 percent that pollsters registered during the 1960's, when the revival peaked. As church attendance increased and as wartime restrictions on goods and services ended, church construction became a booming industry. "Brick and mortar Christianity" sometimes took precedence over social programs and missionary endeavor.

Despite continuing efforts toward ecumenism, the United States, more than in any other country in the world except perhaps India, offered a wide range of religious choices. The Eastern Orthodox Christian churches, united in communion though separated by ecclesiastical organization and liturgical languages and not yet fully recognized as distinct by the military, emerged from emigrant status. Initially, these churches—Russian, Serbian, Syrian, Greek, and others—had served in urban settings as centers of social identification for immigrants. However, the Russian Orthodox Church had a long history on the North American continent. Russian missionaries had Christianized much of Alaska and had canonized saints who had toiled on this soil long before the Roman Catholics canonized their first American saint, Mother Frances Xavier Cabrini. During the 1940's, Orthodox churches used the English language more in their ceremonies and sermons, as a new generation appeared for whom the "old country" held less attraction. Roman Catholics also gained status in the postwar period, no longer thought of simply as communities of Irish, Italians, or Poles. Nonetheless, anti-Catholic feeling was not yet dead in a country that had long thought of itself as a Protestant Christian nation. The perception that Catholics really did not understand American institutions was forcefully contended during the 1949 publication of Paul Blanshard's *American Freedom and Catholic Power.* With examples from Europe, especially from Spain, Blanshard outlined the entanglement of the church with foreign powers, its rigid control of the faithful, and its practices that conflicted with Protestant values. The apprehensions Blanshard voiced did not dissipate until the 1960's, with the election of John F. Kennedy to the presidency and the ecumenical generosity of Pope John XXIII.

African American churches were another growing force in American religion. Previously, they had received inadequate attention in the deliberations of religious sociologists and academic theologians. When these churches had been discussed, it was usually to lament the lack of racial integration in American religious institutions. African American Christianity was distinguished by creative vitality, the eloquence of folk preachers, and the dynamism of Gospel music. White liberals who thought black peo-

Membership in Selected Christian Denominations, 1940 and 1949

In thousands

Denomination	1940	1949
Episcopal	2,172	2,512
Methodist	7,360	8,793
Presbyterian	1,971	2,319
Roman Catholic	21,403	26,718
Southern Baptist	5,104	6,761

Source: Historical Statistics of the United States: Colonial Times to 1970. U.S. Department of Commerce, Bureau of the Census, 1975, p. 392.

ple yearned to be part of mainstream Protestantism were wrong. Resisting submersion in the staid denominations ruled by white hierarchies, the distinctive church remained the central institution in black communities. Though basically fundamentalist in theology, the faith proved socially progressive, developing the leaders who emerged two decades later in the Civil Rights movement.

The holiness and charismatic churches, sometimes called "the third force of Christianity," also grew during this period. Once thought of as rural and southern—three Churches of God were headquartered in Cleveland, Tennessee—holiness people moved slowly but surely from the edges of society into the solid middle class that expanded after World War II. They stressed devotion over theology and practiced "signs following," such as speaking in tongues, healing, "slaying in the spirit," and other manifestations of the Holy Spirit, the third person of the Christian trinity, to whom they gave special devotion.

Several groups categorized earlier by the general public as cults or sects came into their own after the war. Because most of these churches had originated

in the New World, they spread a form of Christianity that had a distinct American flavor. The International Church of the Foursquare Gospel, headquartered in Los Angeles, arose from the preaching of Aimee Semple McPherson. The Seventh-Day Adventists, spiritual heirs of Ellen G. White, founded numerous schools and hospitals. Christian Science, which its critics denounced as "neither scientific nor Christian," followed the writings of Mary Baker Eddy; appealed to an educated, prosperous class; and looked for direction to the Mother Church in Boston. However, the most rapidly growing of the native American churches was the Church of Jesus Christ of Latter-day Saints, whose followers are known as Mormons. From its base in Salt Lake City, Utah, the church sent pairs of young men to the ends of the earth, teaching and placing the Book of Mormon in homes.

Popular Religious Personalities Americans have always loved celebrities, who shine as much for personality as for achievement, and religion has provided its share. McPherson may have been the first of the great religious celebrities of the 1940's. Her personal story moved audiences to tears, as she related the death of her first husband, far away on the Chinese mission field, and her sad return to North America with her newborn daughter. Although photographs of McPherson do not suggest a woman of extraordinary beauty, those who heard her preach remember a radiant figure in the pulpit. She dramatized her Christian message by composing and performing biblical operettas and employing dramatic costumes and props to illustrate her sermons. After years as a traveling tent evangelist, she settled in Los Angeles, establishing a temple, a school, a radio station, and a denomination that survives her. Though her later years were touched with sensationalism and scandal, she is best remembered for her effective social programs that helped many people get through the Depression and her willingness to preach anywhere, even in a Utah brothel. Years before women became familiar figures in Protestant pulpits, McPherson was a Gospel star.

Worldwide evangelism was dominated in the twentieth century by Billy Graham, who preached to more people than anyone else in the two-thousand-year history of Christianity. He surfaced first during the 1940's in the Youth for Christ movement. A handsome, vigorous man of scrupulous honesty, Graham had grown up in the southern evangelical tradition of impassioned sermons and emotional altar calls. He was a powerful preacher and stressed the beliefs and values that most Protestants, even most Americans, held in common. He also quickly learned the effective use of music and testimonies by celebrities in his carefully planned and executed "crusades" in major cities throughout the world. His message eventually reached even Roman Catholic audiences and penetrated the Iron Curtain. Newspapers printed pictures of him with popes and presidents. Throughout the 1940's, he prepared for his vocation, but his San Francisco crusade in 1949 made him famous. The newspaper mogul William Randolph Hearst attended one of Graham's services with his mistress, actor Marion Davies, and, pronouncing Graham a national asset, ordered his newspapers to "puff Graham."

Peter Marshall, a Scotsman who became chaplain of the U.S. Senate, preached with an eloquence long associated with the Presbyterian pulpit. His carefully crafted sermons inspired millions when they were posthumously published in 1949 in a book entitled *Mr. Jones, Meet the Master.* Later books by his widow, Catherine Marshall, and a film based on his life perpetuated his name throughout the next decade.

Norman Vincent Peale was an even more influential writer and speaker than Marshall. Called in 1938 as pastor to one of the most venerable churches in the nation, the Marble Collegiate Church in Manhattan, he led his congregation away from its Dutch Calvinist heritage, preaching a popular philosophy called "positive thinking." In the following years his church grew manyfold, even while his critics, especially in divinity schools, complained that he envisioned God as a generous dispenser of unearned blessings, perhaps confusing Him with

Aimee Semple McPherson leading a congregation in song at her Angelus Temple in Los Angeles in June, 1943. (AP/Wide World Photos)

Santa Claus. Nonetheless, Peale's books and magazine were avidly read by people of all denominations.

Not to be outdone, the Roman Catholics produced their own celebrity writer and preacher in Bishop Fulton J. Sheen. Already a popular speaker on *The Catholic Hour*, a Sunday radio program, Sheen became the first person to conduct a religious service on American television in 1940. He was so successful as a television personality that he later was given his own weekly prime-time program. Beginning in 1951 and entitled *Life Is Worth Living*, the program won many awards. An elegant presence for three decades, clad in splendid robes, Sheen was so popular that he aroused the jealousy of other clerics and the permanent animosity of Cardinal Francis Joseph Spellman, the powerful archbishop of New York.

Inspirational Reading Mass circulation periodicals, most notably *The Reader's Digest*, promoted religion as central to the American way of life. Books of an inspirational nature, both novels and nonfiction, were popular during the decade. Rabbi Joshua Liebman's best-selling *Peace of Mind*, published in 1946, incorporated pragmatic spiritual insights from prophetic Judaism and Freudianism. Peale's *Guide to Confident Living*, which summarized his teachings, was published in 1948. Peale's guidelines appealed especially to affluent people living in a relatively peaceful world. Bishop Sheen's *Peace of Soul* followed Peale's guide by a year and was also pragmatic rather than doctrinal in its prescriptions for abundant living.

The writings of Thomas Merton, a convert to Catholicism who had entered the Trappist monastery of Gethsemane in Bardstown, Kentucky, proved in books such as *The Seven Storey Mountain* (1948) that the cloistered life could be interesting as well as spiritually and literarily productive. Merton gained an even larger audience when he later ventured into Eastern mysticism and injected some of its wisdom into his writing.

Religious fiction also found a wide readership. The books of Lloyd C. Douglas, who had given up the ministry for a career as a novelist, presented a simple formula for confident living. *The Big Fisherman* (1948) was one of his novels featuring Bible events and characters. The same audiences read Sholem Asch's *The Nazarene* (1939) and his later novels throughout the 1940's. Though Jewish, Asch

pleased Christian audiences by his reverent portrayals of Jesus, whom he called "Yeshua," and other personalities from the Christian Bible.

Religious Entertainment The line between religious observance and entertainment had frequently been thin in American revivalist tradition. The decade of the 1940's proved again that religion makes for good show business. Gospel music flourished at Nashville's Grand Ole Opry, and African American soul singers such as Mahalia Jackson broke the race barrier to entertain and edify white audiences. Motion pictures also followed the trend. Jewish moguls in Hollywood liked being photographed with Roman Catholic bishops. Louis B. Mayer of Metro-Goldwyn-Mayer cherished his friendship with Cardinal Spellman and decreed that clergy, mothers, and "American values" would always be favorably treated in Metro's pictures. Other studios complied. *Going My Way* (1944) featured two genial Irish Catholic priests played by Bing Crosby and Barry Fitzgerald, while Fredric March donned clerical collar as a Methodist minister in *One Foot in Heaven* (1941). Ingrid Bergman glamorized nuns with her appearance in *The Bells of St. Mary's* (1945). Although the Jewish presence in Hollywood was large, films of the period were hesitant to present either European or American Jewish life. *Gentleman's Agreement* (1947) was considered daring in its examination of anti-Semitism.

Impact Although sociologists and religious historians agree that the United States emerged from World War II a more religious nation, the quality of that spirituality has been debated. Some critics contend that society had become self-satisfied and complacent, vulgarly Americanizing God in their popular culture. Church affiliation, they believed, had become merely another characteristic of good citizenship. Rather than following the creedal faiths inherited from Europe, Americans were accused of settling for a feel-good spirituality, a vague religion-in-general. Public figures exhorted people to attend "the church of your choice" or even worship "the god of your choice."

In *Protestant, Catholic, Jew* (1960), sociologist Will Herbert scrutinized American religion during the postwar period. Highly relevant to the 1940's, his thesis was that religious affiliation had become a way of asserting American identity, with theological differences of minimal importance. He noted that Catholics had commended their priests as holy, Jews their rabbis as learned, and Protestants their pastors as good preachers. However, by midcentury, the clergy of all three major faiths were praised as simply "jolly good fellows." Nevertheless, it was impossible to ignore the many good works of Americans, often inspired by their religious convictions. The Marshall Plan fed millions in war-devastated Europe, and Americans were the most frequent contributors to foreign disaster relief, while their missionaries founded schools and hospitals in many parts of the world.

Allene Phy-Olsen

Further Reading

Ahlstrom, Sydney E. *A Religious History of the American People*. 2d ed. New Haven, Conn.: Yale University Press, 2004. Discusses the way in which worship and theology intermingled with aspects of American culture, forming a unique hybrid.

Butler, Jon, Grant Wacker, and Randall Balmer. *Religion in American Life: A Short History*. Updated ed. New York: Oxford University Press, 2007. A comprehensive and historical look at religion in the United States. Discusses colonialism, economic growth, and industrialization and the influence each has had on American religious life.

Gaustad, Edwin S., and Leigh Schmidt. *The Religious History of America: The Heart of the American Story from Colonial Times to Today*. Rev. ed. New York: HarperSanFrancisco, 2004. A standard text on the history of religion in the United States.

Noll, Mark A. *A History of Christianity in the United States and Canada*. Grand Rapids, Mich.: Wm. B. Eerdmans, 1992. Deals with the evolution of religion, specifically Protestant forms of Christianity, in the United States. Significant discussion of religious revival, a phenomenon present in the 1940's.

Williams, Peter W. *Popular Religion in America: Symbolic Change and the Modernization Process in Historical Perspective*. Urbana: University of Illinois Press, 1998. Looks at the impact of culture, race, and other social factors on the construction of American religion.

See also Chaplains in World War II; Conscientious objectors; Graham, Billy; Jackson, Mahalia; Jews in the United States; *Reader's Digest*; Religion in Canada; Spellman, Francis Joseph; Theology and theologians.

■ Renaldo, Duncan

Identification European-born American film actor
Born April 23, 1904; Romania?
Died September 3, 1980; Santa Barbara, California

Renaldo became one of the most beloved actors of the 1940's after playing numerous film roles alongside some of the biggest names in Hollywood, including the likes of Henry Fonda, John Wayne, and Ingrid Bergman. However, he achieved his greatest fame from his movie and television roles as the Cisco Kid.

Reported to have been orphaned at an early age, Duncan Renaldo grew up in several different European countries and later claimed not to be certain of even what country in which he was born. He worked his way to the United States aboard a steamship during the 1920's. He tried his hand at acting and eventually appeared in and produced a number of short films. After signing a contract with Metro-Goldwyn-Mayer (MGM) in 1928, he appeared in several notable films, such as *The Bridge of San Luis Rey* (1929) and *Trader Horn* (1931). In 1934, while experiencing marital difficulties that included a lawsuit filed by his wife regarding alienation of affection, he was arrested for having entered the United States illegally. He was later pardoned by President Franklin D. Roosevelt at the request of film industry executives, and he returned to acting, this time with Republic Pictures. Most of the films in which he appeared were Westerns, and he frequently played Hispanic roles, although he appears to have had no Hispanic background.

Renaldo's acting career took off during the 1940's. Between 1940 and 1949, he appeared in forty feature films. By this time, he was playing mostly Hispanic roles in films such as *Gaucho Serenade* (1940), *Down Mexico Way* (1941), and *Border Patrol* (1943). A turning point came in 1945, when he played the title role in *The Cisco Kid in Old New Mexico*. This was the first of six feature films about the heroic Mexican caballero that Renaldo made during the 1940's.

Impact The Cisco Kid character had been previously played by César Romero and Warner Baxter and was also played by Gilbert Roland at the same time Renaldo was making his Cisco Kid films. However, it is Renaldo's name that became most indelibly associated with the character because he starred in more than 150 episodes of *The Cisco Kid* television series from 1950 to 1956. At a time when cowboy heroes were embraced by American popular culture, Renaldo, as the Cisco Kid, became the most popular and recognizable Hispanic cowboy hero of film and television.

Donald C. Simmons, Jr.

Further Reading

Nevins, Francis M. *The Films of the Cisco Kid.* Waynesville, N.C.: World of Yesterday Publications, 1998.

Nevins, Francis M., and Gary D. Keller. *Cisco Kid: American Hero, Hispanic Roots.* Tempe, Ariz.: Bilingual Press, 2008.

Tuska, Jon. *The Vanishing Legion: A History of Mascot Pictures, 1927-1935.* Jefferson, N.C.: McFarland, 1999.

See also Cisco Kid; Cowboy films; Film in the United States; Film serials; Latinos; Mexico; Roland, Gilbert; Romero, César; Roosevelt, Franklin D.

■ Rhythm nightclub fire

The Event   Fire that killed more than two hundred African Americans
Date   April 23, 1940
Place   Natchez, Mississippi

Although this fire became the second deadliest nightclub fire in U.S. history—after Boston's Cocoanut Grove fire in December, 1942—and the deadliest up to its own time, the Rhythm Club fire drew little national attention.

The first of several major multiple-fatality fires in the United States during the 1940's took place at the Rhythm Club in Natchez, Mississippi, on April 23, 1940. About 750 African Americans gathered for an evening of dancing to the music of Chicagoan Walter Barnes and his orchestra. The nightclub had only one exit, which had been decorated with Spanish moss. About 11:30 p.m., a discarded match or cigarette, or flames from the hamburger stand near the front door, ignited the moss, which set fire to the structure's wooden floors and wainscoting. Flaming decorations subsequently fell onto the audience. The windows had been boarded up to prevent entry without payment; the doors opened inward, against the direction of exit travel. The fire resulted in the deaths of 209 people, and another 200 were injured.

All but three of the orchestra members perished in the fire, which was later commemorated in several musical tributes, including Gene Gilmore's "The Natchez Fire" (1940). *The Washington Post* reported on April 26 that nearly every African American family in Natchez was affected by the tragedy. There is a fictional account of this event in Leedell W. Neyland's 1994 novel *Unquenchable Black Fires.*

Impact   Although Natchez had a fire code in 1940, it was not enforced in the African American section of town. The Rhythm Club fire prompted calls from the press and from fire safety organizations for enforcement of life safety codes in all areas of American communities.

Rachel Maines

Further Reading

National Fire Protection Association. *NFPA Fire Investigation Report: Dance Hall Fire (Rhythm Club), Natchez, Mi, April 23, 1940.* Quincy, Mass.: Author, 1976.

Neyland, Leedell W. *Unquenchable Black Fires.* Tallahassee, Fla.: Leney Educational and Publishing, 1994.

See also Cocoanut Grove nightclub fire; Natural disasters; Recreation.

■ Richard, Maurice

Identification   Canadian hockey player
Born   August 4, 1921; Montreal, Quebec, Canada
Died   May 27, 2000; Montreal, Quebec, Canada

Richard's goal-scoring prowess cemented his identity as one of the National Hockey League's earliest stars. This physical forward played his entire career in his hometown of Montreal and led the Canadiens to eight Stanley Cup championships.

Maurice "Rocket" Richard's records illustrate his elite status as an offensive powerhouse: He was the first National Hockey League (NHL) player to score fifty goals in a season, in 1944-1945, and the first to score five hundred goals in a career. Alongside Elmer Lach and Toe Blake, Richard led the Montreal Canadiens to Stanley Cup championships in 1944 and 1946. During the 1944-1945 season, Richard, Lach, and Blake—known as the "Punch Line"—finished as the top three point earners in the league and formed the top forward line for the all-star team. Although Richard stood only five feet and ten inches tall and weighed only 180 pounds, he scored almost one point per game in both the regular season and the playoffs.

In addition to his offensive contributions, Richard won the Hart Trophy in 1947, which is awarded to the most valuable player; played in every NHL All-Star Game from 1947 to 1959; and captained five straight Cup wins from 1956 to 1960. His induction into the Hockey Hall of Fame in 1961 bypassed the customary three-year waiting period, and for the remainder of his life Richard was synonymous with the Montreal Canadiens. In 1999, the NHL first awarded the Maurice "Rocket" Richard Trophy to its leading goal scorer. Richard's state funeral in 2000 was the first accorded to any professional athlete in Canada.

Impact   Richard was hockey's first bona fide star. His offensive records, along with his eight Stanley Cup championships, guarantee his place among the pantheon of hockey's elite players.

Alex Ludwig

Further Reading

Carrier, Roch. *Our Life with the Rocket: The Maurice Richard Story.* Translated by Sheila Fischman. New York: Viking Press, 2001.

Jenish, D'Arcy. *The Montreal Canadiens: One Hundred Years of Glory.* Toronto: Doubleday Canada, 2008.

See also   Ice hockey; Quebec nationalism; Sports in Canada; Sports in the United States.

■ Robbins, Jerome

Identification   American dancer and choreographer
Born   October 11, 1918; New York, New York
Died   July 29, 1998; New York, New York

Robbins's achievements in ballet and theatrical dance during the 1940's provided the impetus for change in the performing arts. As a dancer, story developer, choreographer, and director, Robbins cemented an American identity within the dance genre.

Jerome Robbins began the 1940's concluding a four-summer stint as writer, choreographer, and director

Shirley Edd, Jerome Robbins, Michael Kidd, and John Kriza dancing in Fancy Free *in 1946.* (Hulton Archive/Getty Images)

of revues at Tamiment, a resort in Pennsylvania's Pocono Mountains. He then joined New York's Ballet Theatre. While he received favorable reviews for his dancing, his creation of a "three sailors on leave" scenario made a greater career impact. This motif was developed into *Fancy Free*, a ballet choreographed and danced by Robbins with music by Leonard Bernstein; it debuted on April 18, 1944, to rave notices. Eight months later, the *Fancy Free* plot resurfaced in the Broadway musical *On the Town*, which Robbins choreographed to new Bernstein music. *Fancy Free*-inspired *On the Town* enjoyed another incarnation when the film version was released in 1949.

In 1947, Robbins received his first Tony Award for choreographing *High Button Shoes*, a musical featuring ballets inspired by silent film. In 1949, he was appointed associate artistic director of the New York City Ballet.

Impact Robbins's work during the 1940's set the stage for his subsequent contributions to dance. His use of ballet-inspired steps in theater, first glimpsed in *On the Town*, was reprised in two classic 1950's musicals: *The King and I* (1956) and *West Side Story* (1957). Alongside numerous Broadway successes, Robbins continued to serve as a ballet creator, choreographer, and company coordinator through the end of the century.

Cecilia Donohue

Further Reading

Jowitt, Deborah. *Jerome Robbins: His Life, His Theater, His Dance.* New York: Simon & Schuster, 2004.

Vaill, Amanda. *Somewhere: The Life of Jerome Robbins.* New York: Broadway Books, 2006.

See also Bernstein, Leonard; Broadway musicals; Dance; Film in the United States; Jews in the United States; Kelly, Gene; Sinatra, Frank; Theater in the United States.

■ Robinson, Jackie

Identification African American athlete who broke the color barrier in major-league baseball

Born January 31, 1919; Cairo, Georgia

Died October 24, 1972; Stamford, Connecticut

Robinson became the first African American to play major-league baseball in the twentieth century when he debuted

with the Brooklyn Dodgers in 1947. His superb skills and pioneering role paved the way for numerous other African American stars, whose feats profoundly affected major-league baseball, professional basketball, and other team sports.

The son of a Georgia sharecropper who deserted the family, Jackie Robinson grew up in poverty in Pasadena, California. At five feet, eleven inches and weighing two hundred pounds, Robinson starred in football, basketball, track and field, and baseball at the University of California, Los Angeles (UCLA), finishing second in the Pacific Coast Conference (PCC) in total football yardage in 1940 and leading the PCC in basketball scoring for two consecutive seasons. After financial pressures forced him to leave UCLA in 1941, he enlisted in the U.S. Army. Robinson was commissioned a second lieutenant but was discharged after protesting racial discrimination. His professional baseball debut came in 1945 with the Kansas City Monarchs of the Negro Leagues.

Breaking the Racial Barrier Brooklyn Dodgers general manager Branch Rickey hoped to integrate major-league baseball with talented African American and Latino players. He concluded that Robinson was the right man on and off the field to break major-league baseball's racial barrier after Dodger scout Clyde Sukeforth observed some Negro Leaguers. Robinson was very talented, articulate, highly competitive, self-disciplined, and college-educated. He did not drink or smoke, and he had teamed with whites.

On August 29, 1945, Rickey interviewed Robinson for three hours in Brooklyn. He tested how Robinson would respond to racial taunts, hate letters, and threats he might encounter and secured a pledge from him not to retaliate or respond publicly. Robinson promised to contain his own anger when faced with bigotry and hatred so as to win acceptance from teammates, opposing players, the public, and the press.

With the support of his wife, Rachel, Robinson signed with Brooklyn on October 23, 1945, and starred for their Montreal Royals minor-league club in 1946. Amid unprecedented publicity and enormous pressure, he clouted a three-run homer, singled three times, stole two bases, and scored four runs in his April 18 debut against the Jersey City Giants. Besides leading the International League with a .349 batting average, he earned most valuable player (MVP) honors and paced Montreal to the league and Little World Series titles.

Controversial Major-League Debut   Robinson joined the Brooklyn Dodgers in 1947 after signing a $5,000, one-year contract, becoming the first black major leaguer since 1884. In his April 15 debut, he scored the winning run in a 5-3 victory over the Boston Braves at Ebbets Field. The twenty-eight-year-old rookie reacted docilely amid controversy surrounding his presence, concentrating on his batting, base running, and fielding. Robinson endured an ill-fated petition circulated by Brooklyn teammates opposing Rickey's integration, verbal abuse by Philadelphia Phillies manager Ben Chapman, physical intimidation by St. Louis Cardinal Enos Slaughter, constant racial insults from opponents, knock-down pitches, spiking by base runners and fielders, and strike threats by National League (NL) teams. Robinson hit .297, led the NL with 29 stolen bases, was named NL rookie of the year, and sparked the Dodgers to their first NL pennant since 1941. He became the first black participant in the World Series, which Brooklyn lost to the New York Yankees. In 1948, he nearly doubled his run production and paced NL second basemen in fielding.

Brooklyn added black stars Roy Campanella in 1948 and Don Newcombe in 1949, enabling Robinson to end his self-imposed silence. Robinson became a more aggressive team leader, fighting to end the Jim Crow system and advocating racial integration. His sensational 1949 season featured an NL-leading and career-best .342 batting average and 37 stolen bases, 124 runs batted in, and the NL's MVP Award. The Dodgers clinched the NL pennant in the season finale but again lost the World Series to the Yankees.

A line-drive hitter, Robinson batted cleanup, sparked teammates with his clutch hitting and competitive fire, and taunted opposing pitchers with his daring, dancing base running. Although Robinson hit .328 in 1950 and .338 in 1951 and fielded brilliantly, Philadelphia edged out Brooklyn for the 1950 NL pennant on the last day and the New York Giants captured the 1951 NL crown on Bobby Thomson's dramatic ninth-inning playoff home run. Robinson helped Brooklyn win NL pennants in 1952, 1953, 1955, and 1956 and its only World Series in 1955 against the Yankees, stealing home in game 1.

Robinson, who retired following the 1956 season, pursued several business interests and championed civil rights. As vice president of the Chock Full O'Nuts luncheonettes, he hired numerous African Americans, and he chaired the Freedom National Bank of Harlem. Diabetes caused his health to deteriorate. He could barely walk, lost the sight of one eye and most of the other, and suffered several strokes and heart trouble. The Dodgers retired Robinson's uniform number, 42, shortly before his premature death in October, 1972, at the age of fifty-three. In 1997, Major League Baseball officially retired his uniform number on the fiftieth anniversary of his debut.

Jackie Robinson attempting to steal third base in a 1949 Dodgers game at Ebbets Field in Brooklyn. In addition to his strong fielding and batting skills, Robinson was one of the great base runners of his era. (Time & Life Pictures/Getty Images)

Impact During his major-league career with Brooklyn from 1947 to 1956, Robinson batted .311, stole 197 bases, paced the NL in hitting once and stolen bases twice, sparked the Dodgers to six NL pennants and one World Series championship, and made six All-Star teams. In 1962, Robinson was elected as the first African American to the National Baseball Hall of Fame. Robinson made Major League Baseball's All-Century team and ranked fifteenth among ESPN's top century athletes.

Robinson transformed the national pastime, combining speed with power. His charismatic personality and exciting style evoked admiration from whites and African Americans, who flocked to see him play. Robinson inspired Americans as a trailblazer, combining heroics, courage, and persistence and affirming the nation's quest for equitable treatment and social justice. A natural role model for black athletes, he opened the doors for minorities in professional baseball, basketball, and other sports.

David L. Porter

Further Reading

Eig, Jonathan. *Opening Day: The Story of Jackie Robinson's First Season.* New York: Simon & Schuster, 2007. Chronicles Robinson's first major-league season in 1947 from his promotion to the Brooklyn Dodgers to the World Series. Features his outstanding performances; the reaction of teammates, opponents, fans, and the press; and the impact of the season on his family and African Americans.

Frommer, Harvey. *Rickey and Robinson: The Men Who Broke Baseball's Color Barrier.* New York: Macmillan, 1982. Vividly describes how Rickey and Robinson courageously collaborated to overcome adversity to break baseball's racial barrier and how Robinson endured the almost inhuman pressures placed upon him.

Kahn, Roger. *The Boys of Summer.* New York: Harper & Row, 1972. Takes a brilliant nostalgic look at how the 1952-1953 Brooklyn Dodgers brought heartbreak for their fans and how Robinson suffered the tragic personal loss of his oldest son, Jackie, Jr.

Lamb, Chris. *Blackout: The Untold Story of Jackie Robinson's First Spring Training.* Lincoln: University of Nebraska Press, 2006. Examines Robinson's struggles on and off the field during his spring training in segregated Florida in 1946, highlighting his determination and anxiety, the reaction of black and white communities, and the unique, influential role of the press in baseball integration.

Rampersad, Arnold. *Jackie Robinson: A Biography.* New York: Alfred A. Knopf, 1997. Well-researched and comprehensive biography of Robinson as an athlete, husband, father, pioneer, community leader, businessman, and civil rights activist who experienced trauma, humiliation, and loneliness.

Robinson, Jackie, and Alfred Duckett. *I Never Had It Made.* New York: G. P. Putnam's Sons, 1972. The best of Robinson's autobiographies, which candidly assesses how he faced racial intolerance and other challenges as a black man in a white man's world.

Tygiel, Jules. *Baseball's Great Experiment.* New York: Random House, 1983. Still the most comprehensive account of how Rickey and Robinson integrated major-league baseball and paved the way for other black stars. A remarkable story of personal courage, master planning, and heroic achievement.

See also African Americans; All-American Girls Professional Baseball League; Baseball; DiMaggio, Joe; Gehrig, Lou; Negro Leagues; Paige, Satchel; Sports in the United States.

■ Robinson, Sugar Ray

Identification African American boxing champion
Born May 3, 1921; Ailey, Georgia
Died April 12, 1989; Culver City, California

Considered by many to have been the greatest boxer of the twentieth century, Robinson was clearly the most successful and popular professional boxers of the 1940's, during which he suffered only one loss in more than one hundred bouts.

Born Walker Smith, Jr., Sugar Ray Robinson started boxing at a young age. In fact, when he entered his first amateur tournament, he was too young to be eligible, so he borrowed the Amateur Athletic Union membership card of a friend named Ray Robinson and called himself "Sugar Ray Robinson"—a name that he would keep through the rest of his life. After completing an amateur career in which he won eighty-five bouts without a loss, he turned professional in 1940, when he was only nineteen years old.

Robinson's pro career got off to a fabulous start, as he won his first forty professional bouts. In 1942, *Ring Magazine* named him fighter of the year. The following year, he finally lost his first fight to fellow welterweight Jake LaMotta. Only three weeks later, however, he beat LaMotta in a rematch. He did not lose another fight through the next nine years. In 1946, he won the world welterweight title. He held that title until 1951, when he took the world middleweight title from LaMotta.

Impact   After winning the middleweight title in 1951, Robinson went on a boxing tour of Europe, where he was received as a glamorous star, He lived up to the part by traveling first-class with a large entourage. He would go on to win the middleweight title five times during the 1950's, and he continued to fight until he was forty-six years old. His engaging personality and flamboyant style established him as one of the first African Americans to become a celebrity outside the sports world, and he has retained his reputation as one of the greatest boxers of all time.

Susan Butterworth

Further Reading

Boyd, Herb, and Ray Robinson. *Pound for Pound: A Biography of Sugar Ray Robinson.* New York: Amistad, 2006.

Schiffman, Sheldon M. *Sugar Ray Robinson: Beyond the Boxer.* Nashville, Tenn.: Express Media, 2004.

Shropshire, Kenneth L. *Being Sugar Ray: The Life of Sugar Ray Robinson, America's Greatest Boxer and First Celebrity Athlete.* New York: BasicCivitas, 2007.

See also   African Americans; Boxing; LaMotta, Jake; Louis, Joe; Sports in the United States.

■ Rocketry

Definition   Science of rocket design, construction, and flight

Rocketry during the 1940's graduated from the scientific and engineering focus of a small group of spaceflight enthusiasts to a major instrument of war.

North American rocket projects in the wartime 1940's concentrated on small rockets for combat operations. Small, inexpensive, unguided rockets of various types were used extensively in combat. Many of these were so effective that they remained in the operational inventory well into the 1950's. The major challenges were safety and storability. A U.S. Navy group developed self-igniting liquid propellant combinations storable at room temperature. The U.S. Army concentrated on solid-rocket propellants. Both types of propellant saw later application in intercontinental ballistic missiles (ICBMs) and in manned spaceflight.

The major developments in rocketry took place overseas. The Treaty of Versailles, which ended World War I, severely restricted German rearmament. The German army turned to long-range liquid-propelled rockets as an alternative to standard artillery, which was severely restricted by the treaty. By 1942, the German rocket program under the management of General Walter Dornberger, with Dr. Wernher von Braun as the technical director, had developed the V-2 missile, later renamed the V-2, which could carry one ton of explosives over a range of 160 miles. The first combat flight of the V-2 took place on September 8, 1944, with Paris as its target. During the few remaining months of the war, more than 2,000 V-2s were launched in combat, 1,100 targeted in England and the remainder targeted on Allied forces in Europe.

Fearful of falling into the hands of the Soviet army, Dornberger and von Braun arranged a surrender to the U.S. Army, which had made the capture of German rocket technology and personnel a high priority. The U.S. Army brought one hundred scientists and engineers, including Dornberger and von Braun, to the United States after the war to exploit their knowledge for the benefit of domestic rocket projects. The major advances in rocketry during the 1940's were overwhelmingly German. Almost all American rocketry work during the late 1940's consisted of mastering the German state of the art and integrating it into domestic plans and programs.

Civil Applications   More than sixty V-2 rockets were built and flown in the United States using captured parts and equipment. It was discovered that the V-2 flew very poorly without one ton of high explosive in the nose. This mass deficit was corrected with cameras and scientific instruments; one flight included a monkey. The successful flights yielded breakthrough discoveries in high-altitude atmospherics, cosmic rays, and observations of the Sun. The Navy developed the Viking line of sounding rockets to continue this valuable and productive line of research after the limited supply of V-2s was finally exhausted. The last V-2 flight in North America took place on September 15, 1952.

Looking toward the future, scientists and engineers advising the services recommended the development of more powerful propellants, particularly the combination of liquid hydrogen and liquid oxygen, and noted that the high energy content of this combination made an artificial earth satellite a distinct possibility. Project RAND, operated for the Army Air Forces by the Douglas Aircraft Company of Santa Monica, California, issued a report titled "Preliminary Design of an Experimental World-Circling Spaceship" in May 2, 1946, which considered all the important considerations of spaceflight, including orbital motion, attitude control, communications, thermal control, reentry, and landing. It explicitly described the potential of artificial satellites for research on cosmic rays, geophysics, astronomy, meteorology, and upper atmosphere research.

Military Applications   The aerial bombardment of Germany and Japan was based on the theory that "bringing the war home" to the enemy by air and de-

Captured V-2 rocket at White Sands Proving Grounds, in New Mexico. (Library of Congress)

stroying their economies would break their will to fight and starve their armed forces in the field. Nuclear-tipped rockets fit this theory well. First, destruction of entire cities could be achieved with a very small number of warheads. Second, once launched, rockets were virtually unstoppable and could reach targets anywhere in the world in less than two hours without putting aircrews at risk.

After the war, those with strong opinions on the future of rocketry fell into three camps: those convinced that the merger of the long-range rocket and the nuclear warhead would be the weapon of the future, those equally convinced that such a merger was technically unfeasible and would never happen, and those who believed that the highest calling of the rocketeer was use of the rocket for high-altitude research and eventually for spaceflight. The first two were mutually exclusive, but many individuals from those two camps were enthusiastic members of the third.

The challenges were formidable. Postwar nuclear weapons were heavy and low-yield compared to those developed later. Hitting a target as large as a city at a range of 5,000 nautical miles (9,000 kilometers) required significant improvements in guidance and navigation. So little was known of the interior of the Soviet Union in 1945 that the identity and exact location of potential targets were far from certain. The missiles would have to be much larger than the V-2, the largest and most advanced rocket flown at that time. The advances in propellants and flight structures needed for such large missiles were dismaying to many. Dr. Vannevar Bush, head of the National Defense Research Committee, strongly believed that pursuit of the ICBM in 1945 was unwise. Nevertheless, research into advanced rocket and missile technology continued under the sponsorship of the Army, the Navy, and, after its creation as a separate service in 1947, the U.S. Air Force. More than 110 separate rocket research projects were active between 1945 and 1953.

Impact   High-altitude rocket flights were the first to observe the Sun in the ultraviolet and X-ray spectrums. The rocket-powered Bell X-1 airplane with Air Force captain Chuck Yeager as pilot was the first manned aircraft to surpass the speed of sound. Discussions of artificial earth satellites and of manned flight to the Moon were finally taken seriously in scientific and nonscientific circles alike.

Subsequent Events Nuclear weapons were mated to intermediate-range ballistic missiles (IRBMs) during the 1950's and to ICBMs during the 1960's. The Army used experience gained with the V-2 to develop the Jupiter series and later the Redstone IRBMs for the delivery of small tactical nuclear weapons. The rocket that launched Explorer I, the first American artificial satellite, was a modified Jupiter C. Astronauts Alan Shepard and Gus Grissom flew man-rated Redstone rockets in the first two manned flights of the Mercury program. The Air Force developed the Atlas and Titan ICBMs. Man-rated versions of the Atlas were used for the remaining Mercury missions; man-rated versions of the Titan II were used for the Gemini missions. The liquid-fueled Atlas and Titan ICBMs were phased out during the 1960's in favor of the solid-fuel Minuteman and Peacekeeper ICBMs.

A bitter interservice rivalry between the Army, Navy, and Air Force was settled in 1956, with the Air Force given all responsibility for land-based IRBMs and ICBMs. The Navy was awarded responsibility for sea-launched IRBMs and ICBMs. Army missiles were limited to ranges of 200 miles or less. The last American IRBMs were taken out of service during the early 1960's. The Army had intended to follow the Jupiter series with one named Saturn. The Army group led by von Braun throughout the late 1940's and the 1950's transferred to the National Aeronautics and Space Administration (NASA) shortly after its formation in 1958, and NASA took the nascent Saturn series of rockets. The Saturn IB flew the Apollo low-earth orbit equipment checkout missions, and the Saturn V flew the Apollo lunar missions.

Billy R. Smith, Jr.

Further Reading

Friedman, Herbert. *Sun and Earth.* New York: Scientific American Library, 1986. During the 1940's, the author pioneered scientific exploration of the Sun and the upper atmosphere with rockets. His anecdotes illuminate the scientific adventure of rocketry during that decade.

Gruntman, Mike. *Blazing the Trail: The Early History of Spacecraft and Rocketry.* Reston, Va.: American Institute of Aeronautics and Astronautics, 2004. Comprehensive history of rocketry from ancient times to the present. The research is impeccable and impressively thorough.

Launius, Roger D., and Ray A. Williamson. "Rock-

etry and the Origins of Space Flight." In *To Reach the High Frontier: A History of U.S. Launch Vehicles,* edited by Roger D. Launius and Dennis R. Jenkins. Lexington: University Press of Kentucky, 2005. Detailed discussion of the state of scientific rocketry during the 1930's and 1940's.

Neufeld, Michael. *The Rocket and the Reich: Peenemünde and the Coming of the Ballistic Missile Era.* New York: Free Press, 1995. Rocketry during the 1940's cannot be understood without some appreciation of what the Germans accomplished. This book focuses on the technical accomplishments; the following book concentrates on the man who made them happen.

_____. *Von Braun: Dreamer of Space, Engineer of War.* New York: Alfred A. Knopf/Smithsonian Institution, 2007. Werner von Braun is the man most strongly associated with rocketry during the twentieth century. The story of how he became a hero in the United States during the 1950's is fascinating.

See also Air Force, U.S.; Army, U.S.; Arnold, Henry "Hap"; Atomic bomb; Braun, Wernher von; Cold War; Manhattan Project; Navy, U.S.; Science and technology; Strategic bombing.

■ Rockwell, Norman

Identification American painter and illustrator closely associated with the *Saturday Evening Post*

Born February 3, 1894; New York, New York

Died November 8, 1978; Stockbridge, Massachusetts

Rockwell's "Four Freedoms" paintings, his best-known works, are a tribute to American democracy.

Norman Rockwell's inspiration for his paintings *Freedom of Speech, Freedom of Worship, Freedom from Want,* and *Freedom from Fear* was President Franklin D. Roosevelt's speech on January 6, 1941, to the U.S. Congress on the "four essential human freedoms." Using his Vermont neighbors as models for the works, Rockwell depicted the meaning of the speech in scenes that the common person could understand. The paintings were published in the *Saturday Evening Post* in February and March, 1943, and were included in the Four Freedoms War Bond Show, a nationwide tour from April, 1943, through May, 1944.

War bonds worth almost $133 million were sold, and 1.2 million people saw the show.

Shortly after the paintings were finished, Rockwell suffered a sad loss when his studio in Arlington, Vermont, burned down. He continued to work and even made an illustration, *My Studio Burns*, for the July 17, 1943, issue of the *Post*.

One of Rockwell's best-known works is *Rosie the Riveter* (1943), highlighting women's contributions to the war effort and entry into the workforce. Rosie, with part of the Stars and Stripes draped behind her, embodies determination and strength as she eats her lunch sandwich, her foot resting on Adolf Hitler's *Mein Kampf*. Rockwell's *Portrait of a Coal Miner* (1943) represents another worker on the home front. He wears a pin with two Blue Stars indicating his two sons in the Army. A lighter theme was the popular "Willie Gillis" series, depicting a fictitious young soldier in humorous noncombat situations. Willie Gillis appeared on eleven *Post* covers between 1941 and 1946.

After the war, Rockwell painted family scenes such as *Going and Coming* (1947). The painting's upper half shows three generations of a family packed in the car for a day's outing. In the lower half, they are returning home all tired and exhausted—a scene that most people could relate to.

Despite his popularity, Rockwell was not regarded as a "real artist" but merely as an illustrator. Some sixty years would pass before his work would be reevaluated and considered to be on the level of great masters such as Rembrandt and Peter Paul Rubens.

Impact   Rockwell created "great human documents in the form of paint and canvas," in the words of Ben Hibbs, his editor at the *Post*, who added that a "great picture is one that moves and inspires millions of people." The "Four Freedoms" series embodied this definition, and continues to inspire.

Elvy Setterqvist O'Brien

Further Reading

Claridge, Laura. *Norman Rockwell: A Life*. New York: Random House, 2001. Focuses on the artist's life.

Gherman, Beverly. *Norman Rockwell: Storyteller with a Brush*. New York: Simon & Schuster, 1999. An easy-to-read summary of Rockwell's life and work.

Halpern, Richard. *Norman Rockwell: The Underside of Innocence*. Chicago: University of Chicago Press, 2006. Offers a psychoanalytical interpretation of Rockwell's art.

Hennessey, Maureen Hart, and Anne Knutson. *Norman Rockwell: Pictures for the American People*. New York: Harry N. Abrams, 1999. Catalog for a traveling exhibition, November, 1999-February, 2002, with eighty of Rockwell's most appreciated paintings. Essays by artists and prominent art historians advocating reappraisal of Rockwell.

Moffatt, Laurie Norton. *Norman Rockwell: A Definitive Catalogue*. 2 vols. Stockbridge, Mass.: Norman Rockwell Museum, 1986. Presents all of Rockwell's known finished paintings, with preliminary studies. Includes 3,594 illustrations and 96 color plates.

Murray, Stuart, and James McCabe. *Norman Rockwell's Four Freedoms*. New York: Gramercy Books, 1998. Discusses various subjects celebrating American democracy.

Rivoli, Kevin. *In Search of Norman Rockwell's America*. New York: Simon & Schuster, 2008. Foreword by Andrew L. Mendelson. Rivoli juxtaposes his photographs with similar scenes in Rockwell's paintings.

Rockwell, Norman. *My Adventures As an Illustrator*. Garden City, N.Y.: Doubleday, 1960. This seemingly lighthearted autobiography as told to Tom Rockwell with his foreword and afterword gives insight into the complexity of the artist.

See also   Art movements; Comic strips; "Four Freedoms" speech; Roosevelt, Franklin D.; "Rosie the Riveter"; *Saturday Evening Post*.

■ Rodeo

Identification   Ballet about a young girl finding romance in the American West

Creators   Composed by Aaron Copland (1900-1990); choreographed by Agnes de Mille (1905-1993)

Date   Premiered on October 16, 1942

Commissioned by the Ballet Russe de Monte Carlo for a wartime performance in the fall of 1942, Rodeo *represents an American subject by an American dancer and an American composer. This ballet symbolizes the hardworking ethic of the pioneers who lived in the vast spaces of the American West.*

Rodeo (pronounced roh-DAY-oh) emerged from a suite of dances performed by Agnes de Mille in 1938

to cowboy songs arranged by Franklin Guion. De Mille's character was a young girl who sought to find her place on a ranch by riding better than any man. By 1942, de Mille had changed the script to include two men, the Roper and the Wrangler, as love interests for her feisty Cowgirl.

Although a relative unknown in the world of ballet, de Mille accepted a commission from the Ballet Russe de Monte Carlo, one of the premier dance companies in the world, for one of its performances in New York in 1942. The company asked de Mille to create and provide the choreography for a ballet based on an American topic. De Mille did as requested and insisted she dance the lead role while the company was in New York.

De Mille commissioned Aaron Copland to provide music to represent the vast expanses of the West. She knew exactly what she wanted and provided Copland a detailed outline containing the timing, the number of measures, and the mood for each section. Since Copland had only a few months to complete the score for the twenty-five-minute ballet, he incorporated folk tunes including "Sis Joe," "If He'd Be a Buckaroo," "I Ride an Old Paint," and "Bonyparte."

Rodeo is divided into five sections: "Buckaroo Holiday," "Corral Nocturne," "Ranch House Party," "Saturday Night Waltz," and "Hoe-Down." In the opening, "Buckaroo Holiday," a boisterous overture gives way to a quiet interlude as the curtain rises on some young ladies and cowboys walking about on the stage in preparation for the Rodeo. Faster music with static chords and a wood block represent the heroine, the Cowgirl. A group of men from the ranch approach as Copland uses "Sis Joe." The Cowgirl decides to get the men's attention by riding a bronco. Her music is heard again, and then the folk song "If He'd Be a Buckaroo" is played as a three-part round as the Cowgirl is thrown from the bronco. Humiliated, she runs offstage.

"Corral Nocturne" is the quiet movement. De Mille choreographed this as a pas de deux (dance for two) between the Roper and the Cowgirl, yet Copland saw the music as reflecting the Cowgirl's musings in early evening. This section overlaps with the "Ranch House Party." De Mille wanted to contrast the quiet sounds of the outdoor night with the semiraucous sounds of the inside party. The familiar-

sounding music of the "Ranch House Party" is presented faster, with short and detached (staccato) notes in the upper register of an upright piano. The quiet sounds of night return as the Cowgirl realizes that she is alone under the vast western sky.

"Saturday Night Waltz" presents the folk tune "I Ride an Old Paint." Copland used an offbeat (syncopated) rhythm with the slow waltz tempo. In this particular scene, the men are called away in the middle of the waltz, leaving the young ladies to flutter around the stage bored. The men return and the dance resumes.

Perhaps the best-known of all the sections is "Hoe-Down." This music has been used in countless television commercials, primarily by the American Beef Association. The music starts with the brass as all characters come on stage. The Cowgirl enters wearing a dress while the orchestra plays her music from "Buckaroo Holiday." She stuns the assemblage with her beauty and grace, and with her rejection of the Wrangler for the Roper, her friend from "Corral Nocturne." The dancing ends with a joyous abandon.

At its premiere at the Metropolitan Opera House in October, 1942, *Rodeo* received standing ovations. Copland subsequently condensed the music into a well-received orchestral suite for the ages.

Impact This ballet provided war-weary Americans with a much-needed distraction. It represents the American spirit of taming the wild West, the romance of the quiet hours of evening, and the ritual passage of a young girl finding her way in a man's world.

Roberta L. Lindsey

Further Reading

Barker, Barbara. "Agnes de Mille, Liberated Expatriate, and the 'American Suite,' 1938." *Dance Chronicle* 19, no. 2 (1996): 113-150.

Copland, Aaron, and Vivian Perlis. *Copland 1900 Through 1942.* New York: St. Martin's Press/Marek, 1984.

Pollack, Howard. *Aaron Copland: The Life and Work of an Uncommon Man.* New York: Henry Holt, 1999.

See also *Appalachian Spring;* Ballet Society; Bernstein, Leonard; Dance; Music: Classical; Robbins, Jerome.

■ Rodgers, Richard, and Oscar Hammerstein II

Identification   American musical-writing team

Richard Rodgers
Born   June 28, 1902; New York, New York
Died   December 30, 1979; New York, New York

Oscar Hammerstein II
Born   July 12, 1895; New York, New York
Died   August 23, 1960; Doylestown, Pennsylvania

The team of Rodgers and Hammerstein established the standard for successful Broadway musicals. Through the integration of words, music, and dance, they made the musical a reflection of Americana.

Both Richard Rodgers and Oscar Hammerstein II were born in New York City, studied at Columbia University, wrote for Columbia's annual variety show, and had successful careers before they became a team. Rodgers worked with Lorenz Hart during the 1920's and 1930's; he wrote the music and Hart the lyrics. Their successes included *On Your Toes* (1936) and *Pal Joey* (1940). Hammerstein, who authored the words and often the librettos, wrote a number of musicals, including *The Desert Song* (1926) with Sigmund Romberg, and *Showboat* (1927) with Jerome Kern. Following *Showboat*, many believed that Hammerstein's operetta style of musical was dated and, consequently, his career was finished. Rodgers was experiencing problems working with Hart, who had become undependable as he struggled with alcoholism. When Hart turned down the possibility of making a musical version of Lynn Rigg's *Green Grow the Lilacs* (1931), Rodgers turned to Hammerstein.

Many saw the new team as ill-matched. Whereas Hart wrote quickly, Hammerstein's method was slow and deliberate. When working with Hart, Rodgers first wrote the music. However, Hammerstein, whose strength was in developing librettos, almost always provided him with a script and a lyric before Rodgers wrote a note. For Rodgers, fitting his music to the words of the song and actions in the script was a better way of achieving an integrated score. Both Rodgers and Hammerstein were eager to try something new, and the smash hit *Oklahoma!* (1943) was the result. It was followed by another success, *Carousel* (1945). For *Carousel*, Hammerstein took Ferenc Molnár's depressing play *Liliom* (1909) and reworked it into a musical story with well-developed characters. Unlike previous musicals, *Carousel* has no "happy ending," but the song "You'll Never Walk Alone," with its inspirational words and soaring melody, has become a classic, sung at weddings, funerals, graduations, and even by sports teams.

Turning from Broadway to Hollywood, the team wrote the words and music to the film *State Fair* (1945), with the Academy Award-winning "It Might As Well Be Spring." In *Allegro* (1947), they attempted to build a musical reflecting the plight of modern man. However, *Allegro* lacked major songs, and the Greek chorus, narrating the story line, did not wow audiences. Their next musical, *South Pacific* (1949), did, earning the team a Pulitzer Prize in drama. Other hit musicals followed, including *The King and I* (1951), *Flower Drum Song* (1958), and *The Sound of Music* (1959), their final collaboration. Hammerstein died shortly after the opening.

Richard Rodgers (left) and Oscar Hammerstein II in 1949. (AP/Wide World Photos)

Impact   Rodgers and Hammerstein were innovators. They were not reluctant to take a chance on departing from the tradition of what a musical was and, instead, turned the musical comedy into the musical play, supported by the seamless insertion of lyrics, music, and dance. For them, the musical was more than entertainment; it had to have significance. Unafraid to tackle difficult subjects, such as racism, and willing to try new techniques, they crafted timeless musicals that were immensely popular during the 1940's, were translated into film versions, and are periodically re-created on Broadway.

Marcia B. Dinneen

Further Reading

Hischak, Thomas. *The Rodgers and Hammerstein Encyclopedia.* Westport, Conn.: Greenwood Press, 2007.

Mordden, Ethan. *Beautiful Mornin': The Broadway Musical in the 1940's.* New York: Oxford University Press, 1999.

Taylor, Deems. *Some Enchanted Evenings: The Story of Rodgers and Hammerstein.* New York: Harper & Brothers, 1953.

See also   Academy Awards; Broadway musicals; Music: Popular; *Oklahoma!*; *South Pacific*; Theater in the United States.

■ Rogers, Ginger

Identification   American film actor, dancer, and singer
Born   July 16, 1911; Independence, Missouri
Died   April 25, 1995; Rancho Mirage, California

Rogers was an Academy Award-winning actor who was best known for her partnership with dancer Fred Astaire and for helping to revolutionize film genres in the 1930's and 1940's.

Born Virginia Katherine McMath, Ginger Rogers appeared in numerous films during the 1930's, including many in which she danced with Fred Astaire. She enjoyed the height of her success during the early 1940's. She received the Academy Award for best actress for her performance in 1940's *Kitty Foyle.* By 1942, she was said to be the highest-paid film star in Hollywood, and by 1945, she was one of the highest-paid women in America. She made sixteen films during the 1940's. Her last film with Astaire was

The Barkleys of Broadway, released in 1949, for which the two broke from their former affiliation with RKO Studios to work at Metro-Goldwyn-Mayer (MGM).

Meanwhile, Rogers ended her second marriage to actor Lew Ayres in 1941. She married her third husband, Jack Briggs, a former Marine, in 1943, and divorced him six years later. During the 1940's, Rogers often worked with her mother, Lela Owens Rogers, helping to supply military barracks with dairy products from the Oregon ranch Rogers had bought in 1940. She also supported her mother's testimony as a friendly witness before the House Committee on Un-American Activities during the Hollywood blacklisting trials.

Impact   Ginger Rogers exuded class and elegance in films during the height of Hollywood's Golden Age. Her influence was recognized when the American Film Institute placed her at fourteenth on its list of the fifty greatest screen legends. Rogers received an award recognizing her lifetime accomplishments and extraordinary talent at the Kennedy Center Honors in 1992, three years before she died.

Emily Carroll Shearer

Further Reading

Morley, Sheridan. *Shall We Dance: The Life of Ginger Rogers.* New York: St. Martin's, 1995.

Rogers, Ginger. *Ginger: My Story.* 1991. Reprint. New York: Harper, 2008.

See also   Academy Awards; Anticommunism; Crosby, Bing; Dance; Film in the United States; House Committee on Un-American Activities.

■ Roland, Gilbert

Identification   Mexican-born American film star
Born   December 11, 1905; Juárez, Chihuahua, Mexico
Died   May 15, 1994; Beverly Hills, California

One of the few Latinos to play leading film roles during Hollywood's Golden Age, Roland attained his greatest prominence during the 1940's, when he starred in the Cisco Kid film series.

Gilbert Roland helped create the popular image of the Latino for many Americans. Born Luis Antonio Dámaso de Alonso in Mexico, he made his way to

Los Angeles when he was fourteen and renamed himself after silent film stars John Gilbert and Ruth Roland. After landing some extra parts in films, he gradually worked his way up to featured player and finally to leading man. He would eventually appear in more than one hundred films.

Roland began the 1940's with a supporting role opposite Errol Flynn in *The Sea Hawk* (1940). He then alternated between smaller parts in big films and larger parts in low-budget films throughout the decade. Married to actor Constance Bennett from 1941 to 1945, Roland had his greatest impact after serving in the U.S. Army Air Force during World War II. In 1946-1947, he portrayed the Cisco Kid in six Westerns for Monogram Pictures Corporation, beginning with *The Gay Cavalier* (1946). Created in a 1907 O. Henry short story, the character had appeared previously in several films, but Roland's interpretation offered a distinctive masculine elegance. The success of the series helped Roland to return to more significant roles, as in John Huston's Cuban adventure *We Were Strangers* (1949).

Impact During an era when Hollywood films depicted many Latinos as paramours and comic hotheads, Roland overcame these stereotypes by exuding charm, grace, strength, and dignity in a wide variety of roles. He is best remembered for his portrayal of the Cisco Kid in a number of films.

Michael Adams

Further Reading

Castro, Ivan A. *One Hundred Hispanics You Should Know.* Westport, Conn.: Libraries Unlimited, 2007.

Monush, Barry. *The Encyclopedia of Film Actors from the Silent Era to 1965.* New York: Applause Theatre & Cinema Books, 2003.

Pinto, Alfonso. "Gilbert Roland." *Films in Review* 29 (1978): 529-540.

See also Air Force, U.S.; Cisco Kid; Cowboy films; Film in the United States; Flynn, Errol; Latinos; Renaldo, Duncan; Romero, César.

■ Romero, César

Identification American film star
Born February 15, 1907; New York, New York
Died January 1, 1994; Santa Monica, California

Tall, handsome, and graceful, Romero was a cinema veteran before the advent of the 1940's. During World War II, he led by example, serving in the U.S. Coast Guard, and afterward resumed a film career that spanned seven decades.

A former ballroom dancer, Cuban American César Romero, the "Latin from Manhattan," appeared in more than thirty films during the 1930's, playing a variety of ethnic characters before his starring turn as folk hero Cisco Kid in a half-dozen Westerns, including *Viva Cisco Kid* (1940).

After his three-year hiatus for wartime military service, Romero returned to form as a dependable, photogenic lead or supporting actor. His performance as conquistador Hernán Cortéz opposite Tyrone Power in the big-budget Technicolor saga *Captain from Castile* (1947) was particularly well received and energized his career in the following decades. A lifelong bachelor (after his death, it was revealed that he was gay), the charming and sartorially splendid Romero was a popular Hollywood escort

César Romero dancing with Betty Grable in the 1942 musical film Springtime in the Rockies. *(Getty Images)*

during the 1940's and beyond for such actors as Joan Crawford, Ginger Rogers, and Barbara Stanwyck.

Impact Seldom out of work during a film career that lasted from 1933 until 1990, the versatile Romero also performed on television beginning in the 1950's. He was a regular on *Zorro*, *The Man from U.N.C.L.E.*, *Chico and the Man*, and *Falcon Crest*, and he made a long-lasting impact during the mid-1960's playing the Joker on the *Batman* television series, the role for which he is probably best remembered.

Jack Ewing

Further Reading

Benshoff, Harry M., and Sean Griffin. *America on Film: Representing Race, Class, Gender, and Sexuality at the Movies*. Hoboken, N.J.: Wiley-Blackwell, 2009.

Hadleigh, Boze. *Hollywood Gays*. New York: Barricade Books, 1996.

See also Cisco Kid; Cowboy films; Film in the United States; Homosexuality and gay rights; Latinos; Miranda, Carmen; Rogers, Ginger.

■ Rooney, Mickey

Identification American film star and entertainer
Born September 23, 1920; Brooklyn, New York

Rooney's career began in infancy and continued, with alternating highs and lows, into the twenty-first century, but his peak period of popularity occurred at the beginning of the 1940's, when he was one of the top box-office stars in the world.

Born Joe Yule, Jr., into a show business family, Mickey Rooney became part of his family's act when he was seventeen months old. Raised by his mother, he was signed to star as Mickey McGuire in a series of two-reel film shorts that ran from 1926 through 1932. After changing his name to Mickey Rooney in 1932, he performed in several films for various studios and had a stunning role as Puck in Warner Bros.'s *A Midsummer's Night Dream* in 1935. During that same year, he signed a contract with Metro-Goldwyn-Mayer (MGM), with which he would remain for many years. While at MGM, his distinctive, spirited style was evident in the popular Andy Hardy comedy series. He also made several motion pictures with Judy Garland and appeared in occasional dramatic films, such as *Boys Town* (1938).

From 1938 through 1941, Rooney was the top box-office attraction in the world. Before entering the U.S. Army in 1944, he completed fifteen more major films, including *Young Tom Edison* (1940), *Babes on Broadway* (1941), *The Human Comedy* (1943), and *National Velvet* (1944), continuing to perform in his frenetic style. During the twenty-one months he served in the Army, he traveled an estimated 150,000 miles to entertain Allied troops in France and Germany. When he returned to the United States in 1946, he found himself deeply in debt.

Rooney's film career in the late 1940's and early 1950's hit its lowest point. During the late 1940's, he made only five pictures for MGM, the last of which was *Words and Music*, a 1948 biopic about the musical composing team of Richard Rodgers and Lorenz Hart in which he played the brilliant but ill-fated Hart. Following this critical flop and his public and verbal altercations with studio head Dore Schary and director Roy Rowland, Rooney opted out of his MGM contract, a decision that cost him $500,000. Difficult to cast because of his diminutive size, with few prospects for work, and upset by the breakup of his marriage to Martha Vickers, he began to abuse alcohol and drugs. Nevertheless, he continued working in films, radio, television, and on tours.

At times, Rooney managed to overcome his tendency to overact with finely nuanced performances, especially in the film *The Bridges at Toko-Ri* (1954), the made-for-television film *Bill* (1981), and *The Black Stallion* television series (1990-1993). Most of his later films, however, were of poor quality. In 1979, he appeared on Broadway in the wildly successful musical *Sugar Babies* with actor Ann Miller. Despite his advancing age, his film career experienced a resurgence during the early twenty-first century, when he had small parts in as many as two or three films per year.

Impact Mickey Rooney was a consummate actor, singer, dancer, and musician, who also directed and produced films and television programs. His energetic, sometimes over-the-top performance style has influenced all aspects of the entertainment world for almost ninety years. In addition to receiving a juvenile Academy Award in 1938, he earned four Academy Award nominations and many other awards. He had nine children during his eight marriages.

James R. Belpedio

Further Reading

Marill, Alvin H. *Mickey Rooney: His Films, Television Appearances, Radio Work, Stage Shows, and Recordings.* Jefferson, N.C.: McFarland, 2004.

Ray, Robert B. *The Avant-Garde Films of Andy Hardy.* Cambridge, Mass.: Harvard University Press, 1995.

Rooney, Mickey. *Life Is Too Short.* New York: Villard Books, 1991.

See also Andy Hardy films; Bobbysoxers; Cowboy films; *The Human Comedy*; *National Velvet*; *Stars and Stripes*; United Service Organizations.

■ Roosevelt, Eleanor

Identification American First Lady, humanitarian, diplomat, and writer
Born October 11, 1884; New York, New York
Died November 7, 1962; New York, New York

Roosevelt was the figurative eyes and ears of her husband, President Franklin D. Roosevelt, as she traveled throughout the United States. Through her reports, her husband was able to remain knowledgeable about the people of the country. In addition, she was a supporter of human rights and worked tirelessly to upgrade the lives of minorities, the disadvantaged, and the poor.

Eleanor Roosevelt was one of the most admired women of the twentieth century. Her strength of character, abundance of energy, support of her husband as president, and humanitarian efforts were some of her hallmarks. She championed efforts for those people who suffered discrimination, those who were hungry, and those who could not get out of poverty. Her role as First Lady of the United States enabled her to do more and to be more effective in her efforts.

Roosevelt traveled around the country on behalf of her husband. Though President Roosevelt received reports about hardships in the United States, he often had more questions that needed answered. Thus, First Lady Roosevelt investigated the conditions of the populace and wrote reports about her observations. In 1942, Roosevelt toured American military bases around the world at her husband's request. Without her, the president might not have had enough information to make some of his executive decisions.

Roosevelt's Causes As invaluable as Roosevelt was to her husband's presidency, she had her own interests and causes. For example, when news of Japanese American internment camps surfaced in 1942, she spoke out against them. Despite her efforts, however, she was not successful in her fight against such discrimination. Roosevelt was a firm believer in racial justice, and she encouraged her husband to move more quickly on antilynching legislation. In addition, she urged the Works Progress Administration to appoint black educator Mary McLeod Bethune as the director of the Division of Negro Affairs of the National Youth Administration. Not only did Roosevelt make recommendations, she took action. When Marion Anderson was prevented from singing at Constitution Hall by the Daughters of the American Revolution, Roosevelt resigned from the organization, and arrangements were made for Anderson to sing on the steps of the Lincoln Memorial.

Eleanor Roosevelt (right) talking to a woman machinist during her goodwill tour of Great Britain in 1942. (Library of Congress)

Roosevelt also encouraged women to get involved in politics and to work in government positions. President Roosevelt was sympathetic to women in government and employed more women than any previous administration; this was, to a large extent, the result of Eleanor Roosevelt's influence. Roosevelt received a large number of letters each year. Some of them were critical, some were supportive, but many of them were from people who were in need of help. When government offices were available to handle the problems, Roosevelt forwarded the letters to the office. Other problems she often handled herself.

In 1945, the same year as President Roosevelt's death, President Harry S. Truman asked Eleanor Roosevelt to be a part of the U.S. delegation to the United Nations. In 1946, she was elected head of the United Nations Commission on Human Rights and began to draft the Universal Declaration of Human Rights. This document was adopted by the United Nations in 1948.

Words were Roosevelt's tools—both spoken and written. She was a popular speaker and lecturer on radio, on television, and in person. A prolific writer, she wrote articles, books, a syndicated column titled "My Day" from 1935 until shortly before her death, and monthly columns for *Ladies Home Journal* from 1941 to 1949 and *McCall's* from 1949 to 1962. She was paid for much of this work but gave away all her earnings while she was in the White House.

Impact   Eleanor Roosevelt had an immeasurable impact on the United States and on the international community. President Truman referred to her as the "First Lady to the World." Through her travels and her humanitarian work, she affected many and put her words into action.

Linda Adkins

Further Reading

Goodwin, Doris Kearns. *No Ordinary Time: Franklin and Eleanor Roosevelt—The Home Front in World War II.* New York: Simon & Schuster, 1994.

Knepper, Cathy D. *Dear Mrs. Roosevelt: Letters to Eleanor Roosevelt Through Depression and War.* New York: Carroll & Graf, 2004.

Lash, Joseph P. *Eleanor and Franklin: The Story of Their Relationship, Based on Eleanor Roosevelt's Private Papers.* New York: Konecky & Konecky, 1971.

_____. *"Life Was Meant to Be Lived": A Centenary Portrait of Eleanor Roosevelt.* New York: W. W. Norton, 1984.

See also   Executive Order 8802; Japanese American internment; Newspapers; Presidential powers; "Rosie the Riveter"; Spellman, Francis Joseph; United Nations; Universal Declaration of Human Rights; Women's roles and rights in the United States.

■ Roosevelt, Franklin D.

Identification   Thirty-first president of the United States, 1933-1945

Born   January 30, 1882; Hyde Park, New York

Died   April 12, 1945; Warm Springs, Georgia

Roosevelt was a domestic and wartime leader of unparalleled ability and fortitude who fashioned the American response to World War II. He initially supervised efforts to supply aid to the Allies and to safeguard the United States against Nazi aggression. When America entered the war after the Japanese attack on Pearl Harbor, he established numerous agencies and programs aimed at increasing war production, commanded the armed forces, and coordinated war efforts with the Allies.

Before he was elected president for the first time in 1932, Franklin D. Roosevelt had served in the New York State senate, was appointed assistant secretary of the U.S. Navy in 1913, was the vice president of the Fidelity and Deposit Company of Maryland, and was elected governor of New York in 1928 and 1930. He contracted polio in 1921, and the disease instilled in him a deep humanitarian compassion, allowing him to inspire the "forgotten man" and to reinvigorate the economy to restore national confidence.

In 1940, Roosevelt concentrated on international relations, as World War II had broken out in Europe on September 1, 1939, when Adolf Hitler's Germany invaded Poland. America adopted a "cash and carry" policy to provide war materiel to European nations, especially Great Britain and France. Realizing the military dangers abroad, Roosevelt also established the National Defense Advisory Commission and allocated funds to increase the U.S. naval preparedness. In September, 1940, he secured congressional support for the first peacetime universal military service, more commonly known as the draft. After France fell to Germany in June, 1940, Roosevelt was concerned that Great Britain, which was the only country fighting the Axis powers, ur-

Franklin and Eleanor Roosevelt waving from an open car as they return to the White House from the president's third inauguration on January 20, 1941. (Getty Images)

gently needed supplies. He negotiated a deal in which fifty overage American destroyers were exchanged for American naval and air bases to be located on British possessions in the Atlantic, from Newfoundland to British Guiana. These bases were a means of protecting the United States and the rest of the Western Hemisphere.

Election of 1940 Roosevelt's successful New Deal programs and the urgency of overseas threats to national security led him to overcome opposition to serving an unprecedented third term as president. In 1940, he ran for reelection against Republican Wendell Willkie. He received 85 percent of the electoral vote and 55 percent of the popular vote. After his reelection, he proposed the Lend-Lease Act, which was enacted by Congress and enabled the Allies to receive military aid from the United States without monetary payment. Roosevelt sought to assist cash-strapped Great Britain, which was perceived as fighting "America's fight," by allowing supplies to

be lent or leased to that nation and to other Allied forces battling Nazi aggression.

Roosevelt and British prime minister Winston Churchill collaborated on antifascist plans and common war aims. Roosevelt continued to prepare the nation to resist Nazi aggression at home, reminding Americans of the fates of Austria, Czechoslovakia, Poland, Norway, Belgium, the Netherlands, Denmark, and France—nations that had been conquered by the Nazis. He called the Axis powers a "gang of outlaws," and in his fireside chats he told Americans that they must resolve to stand up to dictators and to foreign aggression.

In 1941, the United States established the Good Neighbor Policy to help protect the Western Hemisphere. In March of that year, Roosevelt proclaimed that the United States would be the "arsenal of democracy" for the Allies. He led the ideological fight against the Nazis' ambitions to proclaim a new order in Europe, dominated by an Aryan master race. In a radio address broadcast worldwide on May 27, 1941, he proclaimed that the United States and the Allies would not accept a Hitler-dominated world, pledging to defend the honor, freedom, rights, interests, and well-being of the American people. He advocated the Four Freedoms—freedom of speech and expression, freedom of every person to worship God as he or she pleased, freedom from want, and freedom from terror—maintaining that these freedoms should be the goals for people throughout the world.

Roosevelt and Churchill agreed on common war goals during their Atlantic conference meeting at sea off the coast of Newfoundland on August 9-12, 1941. The two issued the Atlantic Charter, a statement of eight principles that represented an ideological alliance between the United States and Great Britain. During a Navy Day address in October, 1941, Roosevelt called for an increase in American industrial production in order to supply the nation's armed forces. He appointed Averell Harriman to head the American delegation to Moscow and coordinate war strategy with Soviet leader Joseph Stalin, whom Roosevelt praised for his "gallant defense" against the German invasion of the Soviet Union in June, 1941. American warships were granted permission to shoot on sight German submarines that were attacking American convoys of supplies to the Allies.

Entry into the War   The Japanese attack upon the American naval base at Pearl Harbor, Hawaii, on December 7, 1941, led the United States into World War II. Congress responded to Roosevelt's call for a declaration of war against Japan; Germany and Italy then declared war on the United States in support of Japan, their Axis ally. The United States retaliated with war declarations

---

"Day of Infamy"

U.S. president Franklin D. Roosevelt spoke to Congress on December 8, 1941, the day after the bombing of Pearl Harbor by the Japanese. His "Day of Infamy" speech, as it has come to be known, is presented here.

Yesterday, December 7, 1941—a date which will live in infamy—the United States of America was suddenly and deliberately attacked by naval and air forces of the Empire of Japan.

The United States was at peace with that Nation and, at the solicitation of Japan, was still in conversation with its Government and its Emperor looking toward the maintenance of peace in the Pacific. Indeed, one hour after Japanese air squadrons had commenced bombing in the American Island of Oahu, the Japanese Ambassador to the United States and his colleague delivered to our Secretary of State a formal reply to a recent American message. And while this reply stated that it seemed useless to continue the existing diplomatic negotiations, it contained no threat or hint of war or of armed attack.

It will be recorded that the distance of Hawaii from Japan makes it obvious that the attack was deliberately planned many days or even weeks ago. During the intervening time the Japanese Government has deliberately sought to deceive the United States by false statements and expressions of hope for continued peace.

The attack yesterday on the Hawaiian Islands has caused severe damage to American naval and military forces. I regret to tell you that very many American lives have been lost. In addition American ships have been reported torpedoed on the high seas between San Francisco and Honolulu.

Yesterday the Japanese Government also launched an attack against Malaya.

Last night Japanese forces attacked Hong Kong.

Last night Japanese forces attacked Guam.

Last night Japanese forces attacked the Philippine Islands.

Last night the Japanese attacked Wake Island. And this morning the Japanese attacked Midway Island.

Japan has, therefore, undertaken a surprise offensive extending throughout the Pacific area. The facts of yesterday and today speak for themselves. The people of the United States have already formed their opinions and well understand the implications to the very life and safety of our Nation.

As Commander in Chief of the Army and Navy I have directed that all measures be taken for our defense.

But always will our whole Nation remember the character of the onslaught against us.

No matter how long it may take us to overcome this premeditated invasion, the American people in their righteous might will win through to absolute victory. I believe that I interpret the will of the Congress and of the people when I assert that we will not only defend ourselves to the uttermost but will make it very certain that this form of treachery shall never again endanger us.

Hostilities exist. There is no blinking at the fact that our people, our territory, and our interests are in grave danger.

With confidence in our armed forces—with the unbounding determination of our people—we will gain the inevitable triumph—so help us God.

I ask that the Congress declare that since the unprovoked and dastardly attack by Japan on Sunday, December 7, 1941, a state of war has existed between the United States and the Japanese Empire.

against Germany and Italy, and these two nations combined with Japan to form the Tripartite Pact or Axis. Most of the Central American and South American nations declared war in support of the United States against the Axis.

Roosevelt prepared the nation for combat by placing industrial production on a seven-day schedule and building additional factories to manufacture military materiel and equipment. He established the Office of War Mobilization, which unified the various war agencies. The War Production Board allocated raw materials to factories and rationed scarce commodities such as gasoline, and the War Shipping Administration and the Office of Defense Transportation regulated railroads and shipping industries to transport necessities to critical regions. Roosevelt's Fair Employment Practices Commission ended discrimination in the hiring practices of defense industries, and the 1942 bracero program allowed immigrants to work as farm laborers.

The Office of Price Administration established price controls, issued ration coupons, and controlled rents. The National War Labor Board arranged for labor unions to keep their members on the job and not organize strikes; the board also awarded workers a 15 percent salary raise when the cost of living rose 30 percent. The $400 billion needed to fund the massive war effort was borne through taxes, sales of war bonds, and excess profits taxes. The War Manpower Commission coordinated the labor force in the war industries, and the Office of War Information encouraged patriotism and high morale through its broadcasts. Ultimately the battle of production would be won in the war industries and on American farms. Between 1940 and 1945, the United States produced 17.4 million rifles, 296,601 planes, and 2.4 million trucks, and by 1943 the nation launched five new ships every twenty-four hours. Overall production rose 75 percent during the war.

Roosevelt issued Executive Order 8802 and enforced the Smith Act of 1940 in order to ensure loyalty to the nation and prevent the spread of communism. He stepped up the effective New Deal programs and pared down the nonessential government agencies in order to focus on civil defense. Women were encouraged to join the war production effort. Radio was Roosevelt's most effective means of domestic communication, and he established the Voice of America (VOA) in 1942. VOA provided news, information, and entertainment programming to nations throughout the world.

As commander in chief of the armed forces, Roosevelt made major military decisions involving war strategy. He agreed with Churchill that the war in Europe against the Nazis would take precedence over the war in the Pacific against the Japanese. He met with Churchill in December, 1941, and June, 1942, to plan an invasion of North Africa. General Dwight D. Eisenhower's landing in North Africa resulted in Allied victories, and after the Battle of El Alamein the Allies were able to invade Sicily and attack Europe through Italy. The Office of Strategic Services was founded to gather major intelligence, with all of the information submitted to Roosevelt. Construction of the Pentagon was completed in 1943, and military activities were coordinated in this building. The powers of the executive office of the president, which were stipulated in the Reorganization Act of 1939, increased dramatically during World War II.

Global Leadership   Roosevelt told Americans that the price of civilization must be paid in "hard work, sorrow, and blood." His thoughtful words inspired the American people to rise to the challenges of Hitler's tyranny and to make the necessary sacrifices to ensure freedom because "the harder the sacrifice, the more glorious the triumph." His conferences with Churchill at Casablanca in January, 1943, and at Cairo in November, 1943, established the details of the Allies war strategy and set forth the Allies' demand for an unconditional surrender of the Axis powers. Roosevelt met with Stalin at Tehran after the Cairo conference and negotiated an agreement on war strategy. Roosevelt directed that funds be made available for the development of the atomic bomb through the Manhattan Project, believing the bomb would shorten the war and save lives. On January 2, 1942, twenty-six nations representing the Allies signed the Declaration of the United Nations, in which they accepted the goals of the Atlantic Charter and agreed not to conclude a separate peace treaty with the Axis powers. These countries would form the nucleus of the United Nations peacekeeping organization at the war's end.

Election of 1944   By September 23, 1944, the president was able to speak of an ultimate and total military victory and a "victory for democracy." He put plans in motion to begin reconversion to a peacetime economy providing sixty million jobs. He also encouraged the formation of the United Nations to provide international security.

Convinced by his Democratic Party that he was needed for a fourth time, he ran for reelection in 1944, despite his ill health. He defeated Republic challenger Thomas E. Dewey, receiving 82 percent of the electoral vote and 53.3 percent of the popular vote.

Roosevelt encouraged Americans to remain citizens of the world and to support the betterment of all nations in his fourth inaugural address on January 20, 1945. As the war was winding down and an Allied victory was in sight, Roosevelt turned his own sights toward postwar peace arrangements. Roosevelt, Churchill, and Stalin met at Yalta to determine the fate of a postwar occupied Germany, planned for a meeting to form the United Nations organization in San Francisco, and agreed that the Soviet Union would join the war in the Pacific against Japan shortly after the victory against the Axis in Europe. The plans and peace settlements he set in motion were realized after he died from a cerebral hemorrhage at Warm Springs, Georgia, on April 12, 1945. He was buried at his family estate in Hyde Park, New York.

Impact President Franklin D. Roosevelt skillfully guided the United States through the Great Depression and World War II, enabling the nation to attain victory in the war and securing the United States' position as a world leader in the postwar period. His efforts resulted in the liberation of nations conquered by the Axis powers and the creation of the United Nations as a force for international peace and security. He restored America's hope during some of the nation's darkest years, and he earned the admiration and respect not only of Americans but also of people throughout the world.

Barbara Bennett Peterson

Further Reading

Jackson, Robert H. *That Man: An Insider's Portrait of Franklin D. Roosevelt.* New York: Oxford University Press, 2003. Jackson served in Roosevelt's presidential administration before Roosevelt appointed him to the U.S. Supreme Court; after World War II, Jackson was chief counsel for the United States at the Nuremberg war crimes trials. Jackson draws upon his relationship with Roosevelt to provide a portrait of the president.

Jenkins, Roy. *Franklin Delano Roosevelt.* New York: Times Books, 2003. A supportive and sympathetic treatment of Roosevelt, who is described as the most significant politician of his era.

Kennedy, David M. *Freedom from Fear: The American People in Depression and War, 1929-1945.* New York: Oxford University Press, 2001. Focuses on the domestic experiences of American citizens during the Great Depression and World War II.

Leuchtenberg, William E. *The FDR Years: On Roosevelt and His Legacy.* New York: Columbia University Press, 1995. Evaluates the historical impact of Roosevelt on his generation.

Peterson, Barbara Bennett. *Franklin Delano Roosevelt, Preserver of Spirit and Hope.* New York: Nova Science, 2006. Focuses on the inspirational leadership that made Roosevelt an effective president.

See also "Arsenal of Democracy" speech; Churchill, Winston; Elections in the United States: 1940; Elections in the United States: 1944; "Four Freedoms" speech; Japanese American internment; Pearl Harbor attack; *President Roosevelt and the Coming of the War*; Presidential powers; Presidential Succession Act of 1947; World War II.

■ "Rosie the Riveter"

Definition Iconic character representing women working in U.S. wartime industries

As a direct consequence of World War II, women in the United States joined the workforce in unprecedented numbers, often taking jobs that had previously been exclusive to men.

A large number of young men shipped overseas when the United States became involved in World War II in 1941, leaving a gap in the labor force just as the war industries were gearing up. Women soon rose to fill that gap, assuming many traditionally male jobs, including positions in heavy industry. "Rosie the Riveter" was the name given to this new phenomenon and collectively to the thousands of wartime working women, particularly those involved in supporting the U.S. war effort. Rosie was celebrated in popular song and featured in a government propaganda campaign encouraging women to join the workforce. The most iconic image of Rosie is

J. Howard Miller's famous 1942 poster entitled *We Can Do It!*, showing a woman in overalls and kerchief flexing her bicep. Norman Rockwell also painted a "Rosie the Riveter" cover for the *Saturday Evening Post* in 1943.

Impact The visible presence of so many female laborers in American cities helped dispel the prejudice that women were ill-suited for physical work. A large majority of the "Rosies" returned home or to traditionally female jobs after the troops came home, but some historians believe that these women helped pave the way for the feminism of the 1960's by proving that women could succeed in traditionally male jobs.

Janet E. Gardner

Further Reading

Litoff, Judy Barrett, and David C. Smith, eds. *American Women in a World at War: Contemporary Accounts from World War II.* Wilmington, Del.: Scholarly Resources, 1996.

Yellin, Emily. *Our Mothers' War: American Women at Home and at the Front During World War II.* New York: Free Press, 2005.

See also Rockwell, Norman; *Saturday Evening Post*; Wartime industries; Wartime propaganda in the United States; Women's roles and rights in the United States.

One of the most iconic images of World War II is this "Rosie the Riveter" poster calling on women to support the American war effort. (National Archives)